Windows PowerShell Step by Step, Third Edition

Ed Wilson

PUBLISHED BY
Microsoft Press
A division of Microsoft Corporation
One Microsoft Way
Redmond, Washington 98052-6399

Library of Congress Control Number: 2014922916
ISBN: 978-0-7356-7511-7

Printed and bound in the United States of America.

2   17

Microsoft Press books are available through booksellers and distributors worldwide. If you need support related to this book, email Microsoft Press Support at mspinput@microsoft.com. Please tell us what you think of this book at http://aka.ms/tellpress.

Acquisitions and Developmental Editor: Karen Szall
Project Editor: Rosemary Caperton
Editorial Production: Online Training Solutions, Inc. (OTSI)
Technical Reviewer: Brian Wilhite; Technical Review services provided by Content Master, a member of CM Group, Ltd.
Copyeditor: Kathy Krause (OTSI)
Indexer: Susie Carr (OTSI)
Cover: Twist Creative • Seattle

To Teresa: you make life an adventure.

—Ed Wilson

Contents at a glance

Contents

What do you think of this book? We want to hear from you!

Microsoft is interested in hearing your feedback so we can improve our books and learning resources for you. To participate in a brief survey, please visit:

http://aka.ms/tellpress

Chapter 6   Working with functions   179

Chapter 7   Creating advanced functions and modules   217

Chapter 13 Calling WMI methods on WMI classes   361

Chapter 14 Using the CIM cmdlets   375

Chapter 18 Debugging scripts   473

Chapter 19 Handling errors   511

What do you think of this book? We want to hear from you!

Microsoft is interested in hearing your feedback so we can improve our books and learning resources for you. To participate in a brief survey, please visit:

http://aka.ms/tellpress

Introduction

Windows PowerShell is the de facto management standard for Windows administrators. As part of the Microsoft Engineering Common Criteria, Windows PowerShell management hooks are built into all server-based products, including Microsoft SQL Server, Exchange, System Center, and SharePoint. Knowledge of, and even expertise in, this technology is no longer "nice to know"—it is essential, and it often appears as a required skill set in open job notices. *Windows PowerShell Step by Step, Third Edition,* offers a solid footing for the IT pro trying to come up to speed on this essential management technology.

Who should read this book

This book exists to help IT pros come up to speed quickly on the exciting Windows PowerShell 5.0 technology. *Windows PowerShell Step by Step, Third Edition* is specifically aimed at several audiences, including:

- **Windows networking consultants** Anyone who wants to standardize and to automate the installation and configuration of Microsoft .NET networking components.

- **Windows network administrators** Anyone who wants to automate the day-to-day management of Windows or .NET networks.

- **Microsoft Certified Solutions Experts (MCSEs) and Microsoft Certified Trainers (MCTs)** Windows PowerShell is a key component of many Microsoft courses and certification exams.

- **General technical staff** Anyone who wants to collect information or configure settings on Windows machines.

- **Power users** Anyone who wants to obtain maximum power and configurability of their Windows machines, either at home or in an unmanaged desktop workplace environment.

Assumptions

This book expects that you are familiar with the Windows operating system; therefore, basic networking terms are not explained in detail. The book does not expect you to have any background in programming, development, or scripting. All elements related to these topics, as they arise, are fully explained.

This book might not be for you if...

Not every book is aimed at every possible audience. This is not a Windows PowerShell 5.0 reference book; therefore, extremely deep, esoteric topics are not covered. Although some advanced topics are covered, in general the discussion starts with beginner topics and proceeds through an intermediate depth. If you have never seen a computer and have no idea what a keyboard or a mouse is, this book definitely is not for you.

Organization of this book

This book can be divided into three parts. The first part explores the Windows PowerShell command line. The second discusses Windows PowerShell scripting. The third part covers more advanced Windows PowerShell techniques, in addition to the use of Windows PowerShell in various management scenarios. This three-part structure is somewhat artificial and is not actually delimited by "part" pages, but it is a useful way to approach a rather long book.

A better way to approach the book would be to think of it as a big sampler box of chocolates. Each chapter introduces new experiences, techniques, and skills. Though the book is not intended to be an advanced-level book on computer programming, it is intended to provide a foundation that you could use to progress to advanced levels of training if you find an area that you see as especially suited to your needs. So if you fall in love with Windows PowerShell Desired State Configuration, remember that Chapter 21, "Managing Windows PowerShell DSC," is only a sample of what you can do with this technology. Indeed, some Windows PowerShell MVPs are almost completely focused on this one aspect of Windows PowerShell.

Finding your best starting point in this book

The different sections of *Windows PowerShell Step by Step, Third Edition,* cover a wide range of technologies. Depending on your needs and your existing understanding of Microsoft tools, you might want to focus on specific areas of the book. Use the following table to determine how best to proceed through the book.

If you are	Follow these steps
New to Windows PowerShell	Focus on Chapters 1–3 and 5–9, or read through the entire book in order.
An IT pro who knows the basics of Windows PowerShell and only needs to learn how to manage network resources	Briefly skim Chapters 1–3 if you need a refresher on the core concepts. Read up on the new technologies in Chapters 4, 14, and 20–22.
Interested in Active Directory	Read Chapters 15–17.
Interested in Windows PowerShell Scripting	Read Chapters 5–8, 18, and 19.
Familiar with Windows PowerShell 3.0	Read Chapter 1, skim Chapters 8 and 18, and read Chapters 20–22.
Familiar with Windows PowerShell 4.0	Read Chapter 1, skim Chapters 8, 18, and 21, and read Chapter 22.

All of the book's chapters include two hands-on labs that let you try out the concepts just learned.

System requirements

You will need the following hardware and software to complete the practice exercises in this book:

- Windows 10, Windows 7, Windows Server 2012 R2, Windows Server 2012, Windows Server 2008 R2, or Windows Server 2008 with Service Pack 2.

- Computer that has a 1.6 GHz or faster processor (2 GHz recommended)

- 1 GB (32-bit) or 2 GB (64-bit) RAM

- 3.5 GB of available hard disk space

- 5400 RPM hard disk drive

- DirectX 9 capable video card running at 1024 x 768 or higher-resolution display

- Internet connection to download software or chapter examples

Depending on your Windows configuration, you might require Local Administrator rights to run certain commands.

Downloads: Scripts

Most of the chapters in this book include exercises that let you interactively try out new material learned in the main text. All sample scripts can be downloaded from the following page:

> *http://aka.ms/PS3E/files*

Follow the instructions to download the PS3E_675117_Scripts.zip file.

Installing the scripts

Follow these steps to install the scripts on your computer so that you can use them with the exercises in this book.

1. Unzip the PS3E_675117_Scripts.zip file that you downloaded from the book's website.

2. If prompted, review the displayed end user license agreement. If you accept the terms, select the accept option, and then click Next.

Using the scripts

The folders created by unzipping the file are named for each chapter from the book that contains scripts.

Acknowledgments

I'd like to thank the following people: my editors Kathy Krause and Jaime Odell from OTSI, for turning the book into something resembling English and steering me through the numerous Microsoft stylisms; my technical reviewer and good friend Brian Wilhite, Microsoft PFE, whose attention to detail kept me from looking foolish; Jason Walker from Microsoft Consulting Services, and Gary Siepser and Ashley McGlone, both from Microsoft PFE, who reviewed my outline and made numerous suggestions with regard to completeness. Lastly, I want to acknowledge my wife, Teresa Wilson, Windows PowerShell MVP (aka the Scripting Wife), who read every page and made numerous suggestions that will be of great benefit to beginning scripters.

Errata, updates, & book support

We've made every effort to ensure the accuracy of this book and its companion content. You can access updates to this book—in the form of a list of submitted errata and their related corrections—at:

http://aka.ms/PS3E/errata

If you discover an error that is not already listed, please submit it to us at the same page.

If you need additional support, email Microsoft Press Book Support at:

mspinput@microsoft.com

Please note that product support for Microsoft software and hardware is not offered through the previous addresses. For help with Microsoft software or hardware, go to:

http://support.microsoft.com

Free ebooks from Microsoft Press

From technical overviews to in-depth information on special topics, the free ebooks from Microsoft Press cover a wide range of topics. These ebooks are available in PDF, EPUB, and Mobi for Kindle formats, ready for you to download at:

http://aka.ms/mspressfree

Check back often to see what is new!

We want to hear from you

At Microsoft Press, your satisfaction is our top priority, and your feedback our most valuable asset. Please tell us what you think of this book at:

http://aka.ms/tellpress

We know you're busy, so we've kept it short with just a few questions. Your answers go directly to the editors at Microsoft Press. (No personal information will be requested.) Thanks in advance for your input!

Stay in touch

Let's keep the conversation going! We're on Twitter: *http://twitter.com/MicrosoftPress*.

Overview of Windows PowerShell 5.0

After completing this chapter, you will be able to

- Understand the basic use and capabilities of Windows PowerShell.

- Install Windows PowerShell.

- Use basic command-line utilities inside Windows PowerShell.

- Use Windows PowerShell help.

- Run basic Windows PowerShell cmdlets.

- Get help on basic Windows PowerShell cmdlets.

The release of Windows PowerShell 5.0 continues to offer real power to the Windows network administrator. Combining the power of a full-fledged scripting language with access to command-line utilities, Windows Management Instrumentation (WMI), and even Microsoft Visual Basic Scripting Edition (VBScript), Windows PowerShell provides real power and ease. The implementation of hundreds of cmdlets and advanced functions provides a rich ecosystem that makes sophisticated changes as simple as a single line of easy-to-read code. As part of the Microsoft Common Engineering Criteria, Windows PowerShell is the management solution for the Windows platform.

Understanding Windows PowerShell

Perhaps the biggest obstacle for a Windows network administrator in migrating to Windows PowerShell 5.0 is understanding what Windows PowerShell actually is. In some respects, it is a replacement for the venerable CMD (command) shell. In fact, on Windows Server–based computers running Server Core, it is possible to replace the CMD shell with Windows PowerShell so that when the server starts up, it uses Windows PowerShell as the interface.

As shown here, after Windows PowerShell launches, you can use *cd* to change the working directory, and then use *dir* to produce a directory listing in exactly the same way you would perform these tasks from the CMD shell.

```
PS C:\Windows\System32> cd\
PS C:\> dir


    Directory: C:\


Mode                LastWriteTime         Length Name
----                -------------         ------ ----
d-----        7/10/2015     7:07 PM                FSO
d-----         7/9/2015     5:24 AM                PerfLogs
d-r---         7/9/2015     6:59 AM                Program Files
d-r---        7/10/2015     7:27 PM                Program Files (x86)
d-r---        7/10/2015     7:18 PM                Users
d-----        7/10/2015     6:00 PM                Windows


PS C:\>
```

You can also combine traditional CMD interpreter commands with other utilities, such as *fsutil*. This is shown here.

```
PS C:\> md c:\test


    Directory: C:\


Mode                LastWriteTime         Length Name
----                -------------         ------ ----
d-----        7/11/2015    11:14 AM                test


PS C:\> fsutil file createnew c:\test\myfile.txt 1000
File c:\test\myfile.txt is created
PS C:\> cd c:\test
PS C:\test> dir


    Directory: C:\test


Mode                LastWriteTime         Length Name
----                -------------         ------ ----
-a----        7/11/2015    11:14 AM           1000 myfile.txt


PS C:\test>
```

The preceding two examples show Windows PowerShell being used in an interactive manner. Interactivity is one of the primary features of Windows PowerShell, and you can begin to use Windows PowerShell interactively by opening a Windows PowerShell prompt and entering commands. You can enter the commands one at a time, or you can group them together like a batch file. I will discuss this later because you will need more information to understand it.

Using cmdlets

In addition to using Windows console applications and built-in commands, you can also use the *cmdlets* (pronounced *commandlets*) that are built into Windows PowerShell. Cmdlets can be created by anyone. The Windows PowerShell team creates the core cmdlets, but many other teams at Microsoft were involved in creating the hundreds of cmdlets that were included with Windows 10. They are like executable programs, but they take advantage of the facilities built into Windows PowerShell, and therefore are easy to write. They are not scripts, which are uncompiled code, because they are built using the services of a special Microsoft .NET Framework namespace. Windows PowerShell 5.0 comes with about 1,300 cmdlets on Windows 10, and as additional features and roles are added, so are additional cmdlets. These cmdlets are designed to assist the network administrator or consultant to take advantage of the power of Windows PowerShell without having to learn a scripting language. One of the strengths of Windows PowerShell is that cmdlets use a standard naming convention that follows a verb-noun pattern, such as *Get-Help*, *Get-EventLog,* or *Get-Process*. The cmdlets that use the *get* verb display information about the item on the right side of the dash. The cmdlets that use the *set* verb modify or set information about the item on the right side of the dash. An example of a cmdlet that uses the *set* verb is *Set-Service*, which can be used to change the start mode of a service. All cmdlets use one of the standard verbs. To find all of the standard verbs, you can use the *Get-Verb* cmdlet. In Windows PowerShell 5.0, there are nearly 100 approved verbs.

Installing Windows PowerShell

Windows PowerShell 5.0 comes with Windows 10 Client. You can download the Windows Management Framework 5.0 package, which contains updated versions of Windows Remote Management (WinRM), WMI, and Windows PowerShell 5.0, from the Microsoft Download Center. Because Windows 10 comes with Windows PowerShell 5.0, there is no Windows Management Framework 5.0 package available for download—it is not needed. In order to install Windows Management Framework 5.0 on Windows 7, Windows 8.1, Windows Server 2008 R2, Windows Server 2012, and Windows Server 2012 R2, they all must be running the .NET Framework 4.5.

Deploying Windows PowerShell to down-level operating systems

After Windows PowerShell is downloaded from *http://www.microsoft.com/downloads*, you can deploy it to your enterprise by using any of the standard methods.

Here are few of the methods that you can use to accomplish Windows PowerShell deployment:

- Create a Microsoft Systems Center Configuration Manager package and advertise it to the appropriate organizational unit (OU) or collection.

- Create a Group Policy Object (GPO) in Active Directory Domain Services (AD DS) and link it to the appropriate OU.

- Approve the update in Software Update Services (SUS), when available.

- Add the Windows Management Framework 5.0 packages to a central file share or webpage for self-service.

If you are not deploying to an entire enterprise, perhaps the easiest way to install Windows PowerShell is to download the package and step through the wizard.

Note To use a command-line utility in Windows PowerShell, launch Windows PowerShell by choosing Start | Run | PowerShell. At the Windows PowerShell prompt, enter in the command to run.

Using command-line utilities

As mentioned earlier, command-line utilities can be used directly within Windows PowerShell. The advantages of using command-line utilities in Windows PowerShell, as opposed to simply running them in the CMD interpreter, are the Windows PowerShell pipelining and formatting features. Additionally, if you have batch files or CMD files that already use existing command-line utilities, you can easily modify them to run within the Windows PowerShell environment. The following procedure illustrates adding *ipconfig* commands to a text file.

Running *ipconfig* commands

1. Start Windows PowerShell by choosing Start | Run | PowerShell. The Windows PowerShell prompt opens by default at the root of your user folder—for example, C:\Users\Ed.

2. Enter the command **ipconfig /all**. This is shown here.

   ```
   PS C:\> ipconfig /all
   ```

3. Pipeline the result of *ipconfig /all* to a text file. This is illustrated here.

   ```
   PS C:\> ipconfig /all >ipconfig.txt
   ```

4. Open Notepad to view the contents of the text file, as follows.

   ```
   PS C:\> notepad ipconfig.txt
   ```

Entering a single command into Windows PowerShell is useful, but at times you might need more than one command to provide troubleshooting information or configuration details to assist with setup issues or performance problems. This is where Windows PowerShell really shines. In the past, you would have either had to write a batch file or enter the commands manually. This is shown in the TroubleShoot.bat script that follows.

TroubleShoot.bat

```
ipconfig /all >C:\tshoot.txt
route print >>C:\tshoot.txt
hostname >>C:\tshoot.txt
net statistics workstation >>C:\tshoot.txt
```

Of course, if you entered the commands manually, you had to wait for each command to complete before entering the subsequent command. In that case, it was always possible to lose your place in the command sequence, or to have to wait for the result of each command. Windows PowerShell eliminates this problem. You can now enter multiple commands on a single line, and then leave the computer or perform other tasks while the computer produces the output. No batch file needs to be written to achieve this capability.

Tip Use multiple commands on a single Windows PowerShell line. Enter each complete command, and then use a semicolon to separate the commands.

The following exercise describes how to run multiple commands.

Running multiple commands

1. Open Windows PowerShell by choosing Start | Run | PowerShell. The Windows PowerShell prompt opens by default at the root of your user folder.

2. Enter the **ipconfig /all** command. Pipeline the output to a text file called *Tshoot.txt* by using the redirection arrow (>). This is the result.

   ```
   ipconfig /all >tshoot.txt
   ```

3. On the same line, use a semicolon to separate the *ipconfig /all* command from the *route print* command. Append the output from the command to a text file called *Tshoot.txt* by using the redirect-and-append arrow (>>). Here is the command so far.

   ```
   ipconfig /all >tshoot.txt; route print >>tshoot.txt
   ```

4. On the same line, use a semicolon to separate the *route print* command from the *hostname* command. Append the output from the command to a text file called *Tshoot.txt* by using the redirect-and-append arrow. The command up to this point is shown here.

```
ipconfig /all >tshoot.txt; route print >>tshoot.txt; hostname >>tshoot
.txt
```

5. On the same line, use a semicolon to separate the *hostname* command from the *net statistics workstation* command. Append the output from the command to a text file called *Tshoot.txt* by using the redirect-and-append arrow. The completed command looks like the following.

```
ipconfig /all >tshoot.txt; route print >>tshoot.txt; hostname >>tshoot
.txt; net statistics workstation >>tshoot.txt
```

Security issues with Windows PowerShell

As with any tool as versatile as Windows PowerShell, there are bound to be some security concerns. Security, however, was one of the design goals in the development of Windows PowerShell.

When you launch Windows PowerShell, it opens in the root of your user folder; this ensures that you are in a directory where you will have permission to perform certain actions and activities. This is far safer than opening at the root of the drive, or even opening in system root.

The running of scripts is disabled by default and can be easily managed through Group Policy. It can also be managed on a per-user or per-session basis.

Controlling execution of Windows PowerShell cmdlets

Have you ever opened a CMD interpreter prompt, entered a command, and pressed Enter so that you could find out what it does? What if that command happened to be *Format C:*? Are you sure you want to format your C drive? This section covers some parameters that can be supplied to cmdlets that allow you to control the way they execute. Although not all cmdlets support these parameters, most of those included with Windows PowerShell do. The three switch parameters you can use to control execution are -*WhatIf*, -*Confirm*, and suspend. *Suspend* is not really a switch parameter that is supplied to a cmdlet, but rather is an action you can take at a confirmation prompt, and is therefore another method of controlling execution.

Note To use -*WhatIf* at a Windows PowerShell prompt, enter the cmdlet. Type the -*WhatIf* switch parameter after the cmdlet. This only works for cmdlets that change system state. Therefore, there is no -*WhatIf* parameter for cmdlets like *Get-Process* that only display information.

Windows PowerShell cmdlets that change system state (such as *Set-Service*) support a *prototype mode* that you can enter by using the *-WhatIf* switch parameter. The developer decides to implement *-WhatIf* when developing the cmdlet; however, the Windows PowerShell team recommends that developers implement *-WhatIf*. The use of the *-WhatIf* switch parameter is shown in the following procedure.

Using *-WhatIf* to prototype a command

1. Open Windows PowerShell by choosing Start | Run | PowerShell. The Windows PowerShell prompt opens by default at the root of your user folder.

2. Start an instance of Notepad.exe. Do this by entering **notepad** and pressing the Enter key. This is shown here.

    ```
    notepad
    ```

3. Identify the Notepad process you just started by using the *Get-Process* cmdlet. Type enough of the process name to identify it, and then use a wildcard asterisk (*) to avoid typing the entire name of the process, as follows.

    ```
    Get-Process note*
    ```

4. Examine the output from the *Get-Process* cmdlet, and identify the process ID. The output on my machine is shown here. Note that, in all likelihood, the process ID used by your instance of Notepad.exe will be different from the one on my machine.

    ```
    Handles  NPM(K)   PM(K)    WS(K) VM(M)   CPU(s)     Id ProcessName
    -------  ------   -----    ----- -----   ------     -- -----------
       114   8        1544      8712 ...54    0.00    3756 notepad
    ```

5. Use *-WhatIf* to find out what would happen if you used *Stop-Process* to stop the process ID you obtained in step 4. This process ID is found under the Id column in your output. Use the *-Id* parameter to identify the Notepad.exe process. The command is as follows.

    ```
    Stop-Process -id 3756 -whatif
    ```

6. Examine the output from the command. It tells you that the command will stop the Notepad process with the process ID that you used in your command.

    ```
    What if: Performing the operation "Stop-Process" on target "notepad (3756)".
    ```

Confirming actions

As described in the previous section, you can use *-WhatIf* to prototype a cmdlet in Windows PowerShell. This is useful for finding out what a cmdlet would do; however, if you want to be prompted before the execution of the cmdlet, you can use the *-Confirm* parameter.

1. Open Windows PowerShell, start an instance of Notepad.exe, identify the process, and examine the output, just as in steps 1 through 4 in the previous exercise.

2. Use the -*Confirm* parameter to force a prompt when using the *Stop-Process* cmdlet to stop the Notepad process identified by the *Get-Process note** command. This is shown here.

```
Stop-Process -id 3756 -confirm
```

The *Stop-Process* cmdlet, when used with the -*Confirm* parameter, displays the following confirmation prompt.

```
Confirm
Are you sure you want to perform this action?
Performing operation "Stop-Process" on Target "notepad (3756)".
[Y] Yes  [A] Yes to All  [N] No  [L] No to All  [S] Suspend  [?] Help
(default is "Y"):
```

3. Enter **y** and press Enter. The Notepad.exe process ends. The Windows PowerShell prompt returns to the default, ready for new commands, as shown here.

```
PS C:\>
```

Tip To suspend cmdlet confirmation, at the confirmation prompt from the cmdlet, enter **s** and press Enter.

Suspending confirmation of cmdlets

The ability to prompt for confirmation of the execution of a cmdlet is extremely useful and at times might be vital to assisting in maintaining a high level of system uptime. There might be times when you enter a long command and then remember that you need to check on something else first. For example, you might be in the middle of stopping a number of processes, but you need to view details on the processes to ensure that you do not stop the wrong one. For such eventualities, you can tell the confirmation that you would like to suspend execution of the command.

1. Open Windows PowerShell, start an instance of Notepad.exe, identify the process, and examine the output, just as in steps 1 through 4 in the "Using -*WhatIf* to prototype a command" exercise. The output on my machine is shown following. Note that in all likelihood, the process ID used by your instance of Notepad.exe will be different from the one on my machine.

Handles	NPM(K)	PM(K)	WS(K)	VM(M)	CPU(s)	Id	ProcessName
39	2	944	400	29	0.05	3576	notepad

2. Use the *-Confirm* parameter to force a prompt when using the *Stop-Process* cmdlet to stop the Notepad process identified by the *Get-Process note** command. This is illustrated here.

```
Stop-Process -id 3576 -confirm
```

The *Stop-Process* cmdlet, when used with the *-Confirm* parameter, displays the following confirmation prompt.

```
Confirm
Are you sure you want to perform this action?
Performing operation "Stop-Process" on Target "notepad (3576)".
[Y] Yes  [A] Yes to All  [N] No  [L] No to All  [S] Suspend  [?] Help
(default is "Y"):
```

3. To suspend execution of the *Stop-Process* cmdlet, enter **s**. and then a double-arrow prompt appears, as follows.

```
PS C:\>>
```

4. Use the *Get-Process* cmdlet to obtain a list of all the running processes that begin with the letter *n*. The syntax is as follows.

```
Get-Process n*
```

On my machine, two processes appear, the Notepad process I launched earlier and another process. This is shown here.

```
Handles  NPM(K)    PM(K)    WS(K) VM(M)   CPU(s)     Id ProcessName
-------  ------    -----    ----- -----   ------     -- -----------
    269     168     4076     2332 ...98     0.19   1632 NisSrv
    114       8     1536     8732 ...54     0.02   3576 notepad
```

5. Return to the previous confirmation prompt by entering **exit**.

Again, the confirmation prompt appears as follows.

```
Confirm
Are you sure you want to perform this action?
Performing operation "Stop-Process" on Target "notepad (3576)".
[Y] Yes  [A] Yes to All  [N] No  [L] No to All  [S] Suspend  [?] Help
(default is "Y"):
```

6. Enter **y** and press Enter to stop the Notepad process. There is no further confirmation. The prompt now displays the default Windows PowerShell prompt, as shown here.

```
PS C:\>
```

Working with Windows PowerShell

This section goes into detail about how to access Windows PowerShell and configure the Windows PowerShell console.

Accessing Windows PowerShell

After Windows PowerShell is installed on a down-level system, it becomes available for immediate use. However, pressing the Windows logo key on the keyboard and pressing R to bring up a *run* dialog box—or using the mouse to choose Start | Run | PowerShell all the time—will become time-consuming and tedious. (This is not quite as big a problem on Windows 10, where you can just enter **PowerShell** on the Start screen.) On Windows 10, I pin both Windows PowerShell and the Windows PowerShell ISE to both the Start screen and the taskbar. On Windows Server 2012 R2 running Server Core, I replace the CMD prompt with the Windows PowerShell console. For me and the way I work, this is ideal, so I wrote a script to do it. This script can be called through a log-on script to automatically deploy the shortcut on the desktop. On Windows 10, the script adds both the Windows PowerShell ISE and the Windows PowerShell console to both the Start screen and the taskbar. On Windows 7, it adds both to the taskbar and to the Start menu. The script only works for US English–language operating systems. To make it work in other languages, change the value of *$pinToStart* and *$pinToTaskBar* to the equivalent values in the target language.

> **Note** Using Windows PowerShell scripts is covered in Chapter 5, "Using Windows PowerShell scripts." See that chapter for information about how the script works and how to actually run the script.

The script is called PinToStart.ps1, and is as follows.

PinToStart.ps1

```
$pinToStart = "Pin to Start"

$file = @((Join-Path -Path $PSHOME  -childpath "PowerShell.exe"),
          (Join-Path -Path $PSHOME  -childpath "powershell_ise.exe") )
Foreach($f in $file)
 {$path = Split-Path $f
  $shell=New-Object -com "Shell.Application"
  $folder=$shell.Namespace($path)
  $item = $folder.parsename((Split-Path $f -leaf))
  $verbs = $item.verbs()
  foreach($v in $verbs)
    {if($v.Name.Replace("&","") -match $pinToStart){$v.DoIt()}}
```

Configuring the Windows PowerShell console

Many items can be configured for Windows PowerShell. These items can be stored in a PSConsole file. To export the console configuration file, use the *Export-Console* cmdlet, as shown here.

```
PS C:\> Export-Console myconsole
```

The PSConsole file is saved in the current directory by default and has an extension of .psc1. The PSConsole file is saved in XML format. A generic console file is shown here.

```
<?xml version="1.0" encoding="utf-8"?>
<PSConsoleFile ConsoleSchemaVersion="1.0">
  <PSVersion>5.0.10224.0</PSVersion>
  <PSSnapIns />
</PSConsoleFile>
```

Controlling Windows PowerShell launch options

1. Launch Windows PowerShell without the banner by using the *-NoLogo* argument. This is shown here.

   ```
   PowerShell -nologo
   ```

2. Launch a specific version of Windows PowerShell by using the *-Version* argument. This is shown here.

   ```
   PowerShell -version 3
   ```

3. Launch Windows PowerShell using a specific configuration file by specifying the *-PSConsoleFile* argument, as follows.

   ```
   PowerShell -psconsolefile myconsole.psc1
   ```

4. Launch Windows PowerShell, execute a specific command, and then exit by using the *-Command* argument. The command itself must be prefixed by an ampersand (&) and enclosed in braces. This is shown here.

   ```
   Powershell -command "& {Get-Process}"
   ```

Supplying options for cmdlets

One of the useful features of Windows PowerShell is the standardization of the syntax in working with cmdlets. This vastly simplifies the learning of Windows PowerShell and language constructs. Table 1-1 lists the common parameters. Keep in mind that some cmdlets cannot implement some of these parameters. However, if these parameters are used, they will be interpreted in the same manner for all cmdlets, because the Windows PowerShell engine itself interprets the parameters.

TABLE 1-1 Common parameters

Parameter	Meaning
-WhatIf	Tells the cmdlet to not execute, but to tell you what would happen if the cmdlet were to run.
-Confirm	Tells the cmdlet to prompt before executing the command.
-Verbose	Instructs the cmdlet to provide a higher level of detail than a cmdlet not using the verbose parameter.
-Debug	Instructs the cmdlet to provide debugging information.
-ErrorAction	Instructs the cmdlet to perform a certain action when an error occurs. Allowed actions are *Continue, Ignore, Inquire, SilentlyContinue, Stop,* and *Suspend.*
-ErrorVariable	Instructs the cmdlet to use a specific variable to hold error information. This is in addition to the standard *$Error* variable.
-OutVariable	Instructs the cmdlet to use a specific variable to hold the output information.
-OutBuffer	Instructs the cmdlet to hold a certain number of objects before calling the next cmdlet in the pipeline.

Note To get help on any cmdlet, use the *Get-Help <cmdletname>* cmdlet. For example, use *Get-Help Get-Process* to obtain help with using the *Get-Process* cmdlet.

Working with the help options

One of the first commands to run when you are opening Windows PowerShell for the first time is the *Update-Help* cmdlet. This is because Windows PowerShell does not include help files with the product, as of Windows PowerShell version 3. This does not mean that no help presents itself—it does mean that help beyond simple syntax display requires an additional download.

A default installation of Windows PowerShell 5.0 contains numerous modules that vary from installation to installation, depending upon the operating system features and roles selected. In fact, Windows PowerShell 5.0 installed on Windows 7 workstations contains far fewer modules and cmdlets than are available on a similar Windows 10 workstation. This does not mean that all is chaos, however, because the essential Windows PowerShell cmdlets—the *core* cmdlets—remain unchanged from installation to installation. The difference between installations is because additional features and roles often install additional Windows PowerShell modules and cmdlets.

The modular nature of Windows PowerShell requires additional consideration when you are updating help. Simply running *Update-Help* does not update all of the modules loaded on a particular system. In fact, some modules might not support updatable help at all—these generate an error when you attempt to update help. The easiest way to ensure that you update all possible help is to use both the *-Module* parameter and the *-Force* switch parameter. The command to update help for all installed modules (those that support updatable help) is shown here.

```
Update-Help -Module * -Force
```

The result of running the *Update-Help* cmdlet on a typical Windows 10 client system is shown in Figure 1-1.

FIGURE 1-1 Errors appear when you attempt to update help files that do not support updatable help.

One way to update help and not receive a screen full of error messages is to run the *Update-Help* cmdlet and suppress the errors altogether. This technique is shown here.

```
Update-Help -Module * -Force -ea 0
```

The problem with this approach is that you can never be certain that you have actually received updated help for everything you wanted to update. A better approach is to hide the errors during the update process, but also to display errors after the update completes. The advantage to this approach is the ability to display cleaner errors. The UpdateHelpTrackErrors.ps1 script illustrates this technique. The first thing the UpdateHelpTrackErrors.ps1 script does is empty the error stack by calling the *clear* method. Next, it calls the *Update-Help* module with both the *-Module* parameter and the *-Force* switch parameter. In addition, it uses the *-ErrorAction* parameter (*ea* is an alias for this parameter) with a value of 0 (zero). A 0 value means that errors will not be displayed when the command runs. The script concludes by using a *For* loop to walk through the errors and by displaying the error exceptions. The complete UpdateHelpTrackErrors.ps1 script is shown here.

UpdateHelpTrackErrors.ps1

```
$error.Clear()
Update-Help -Module * -Force -ea 0
For ($i = 0 ; $i -lt $error.Count ; $i ++)
  { "`nerror $i" ; $error[$i].exception }
```

Note For information about writing Windows PowerShell scripts and about using the *For* loop, see Chapter 5.

When the UpdateHelpTrackErrors script runs, a progress bar is shown, indicating the progress as the updatable help files update. When the script is finished, any errors appear in order. The script and associated errors are shown in Figure 1-2.

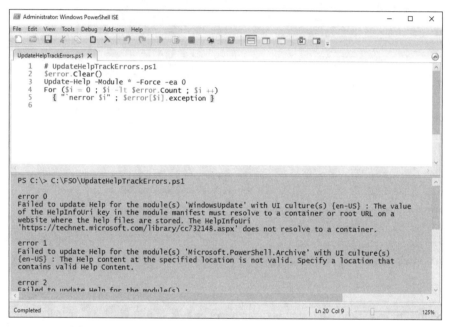

FIGURE 1-2 Cleaner error output from updatable help is generated by the UpdateHelpTrackErrors script.

You can also determine which modules receive updated help by running the *Update-Help* cmdlet with the *-Verbose* switch parameter. Unfortunately, when you do this, the output scrolls by so fast that it is hard to see what has actually updated. To solve this problem, redirect the verbose output to a text file. In the command that follows, all modules attempt to update *help*. The verbose messages redirect to a text file named *updatedhelp.txt* in a folder named fso off the root.

```
Update-Help -module * -force -verbose 4>>c:\fso\updatedhelp.txt
```

Windows PowerShell has a high level of discoverability; that is, to learn how to use Windows PowerShell, you can simply use Windows PowerShell. Online help serves an important role in assisting in this discoverability. The help system in Windows PowerShell can be entered by several methods.

To learn about using Windows PowerShell, use the *Get-Help* cmdlet as follows.

```
Get-Help Get-Help
This command prints out help about the Get-Help cmdlet. The output from this cmdlet is
illustrated here:

NAME
    Get-Help

SYNOPSIS
    Displays information about Windows PowerShell commands and concepts.


SYNTAX
    Get-Help [[-Name] <String>] [-Category <String[]>] [-Component <String[]>]
    [-Full] [-Functionality <String[]>] [-Path <String>] [-Role <String[]>]
    [<CommonParameters>]

    Get-Help [[-Name] <String>] [-Category <String[]>] [-Component <String[]>]
    [-Functionality <String[]>] [-Path <String>] [-Role <String[]>] -Detailed
    [<CommonParameters>]

    Get-Help [[-Name] <String>] [-Category <String[]>] [-Component <String[]>]
    [-Functionality <String[]>] [-Path <String>] [-Role <String[]>] -Examples
    [<CommonParameters>]

    Get-Help [[-Name] <String>] [-Category <String[]>] [-Component <String[]>]
    [-Functionality <String[]>] [-Path <String>] [-Role <String[]>] -Online
    [<CommonParameters>]

    Get-Help [[-Name] <String>] [-Category <String[]>] [-Component <String[]>]
    [-Functionality <String[]>] [-Path <String>] [-Role <String[]>] -Parameter
    <String> [<CommonParameters>]

    Get-Help [[-Name] <String>] [-Category <String[]>] [-Component <String[]>]
    [-Functionality <String[]>] [-Path <String>] [-Role <String[]>] -ShowWindow
    [<CommonParameters>]


DESCRIPTION
    The Get-Help cmdlet displays information about Windows PowerShell concepts and
    commands, including cmdlets, functions, CIM commands, workflows, providers,
    aliases and scripts.

    To get help for a Windows PowerShell command, type "Get-Help" followed by the
    command name, such as: Get-Help Get-Process. To get a list of all help topics
    on your system, type: Get-Help *. You can display the entire help topic or use
    the parameters of the Get-Help cmdlet to get selected parts of the topic, such
    as the syntax, parameters, or examples.

    Conceptual help topics in Windows PowerShell begin with "about_", such as
    "about_Comparison_Operators". To see all "about_" topics, type: Get-Help
    about_*. To see a particular topic, type: Get-Help about_<topic-name>, such as
    Get-Help about_Comparison_Operators.
```

To get help for a Windows PowerShell provider, type "Get-Help" followed by the provider name. For example, to get help for the Certificate provider, type: Get-Help Certificate.

In addition to "Get-Help", you can also type "help" or "man", which displays one screen of text at a time, or "<cmdlet-name> -?", which is identical to Get-Help but works only for commands.

Get-Help gets the help content that it displays from help files on your computer. Without the help files, Get-Help displays only basic information about commands. Some Windows PowerShell modules come with help files. However, beginning in Windows PowerShell 3.0, the modules that come with Windows do not include help files. To download or update the help files for a module in Windows PowerShell 3.0, use the Update-Help cmdlet.

You can also view the help topics for Windows PowerShell online in the TechNet Library. To get the online version of a help topic, use the Online parameter, such as: Get-Help Get-Process -Online. You can read all of the help topics beginning at: http://go.microsoft.com/fwlink/?LinkID=107116.

If you type "Get-Help" followed by the exact name of a help topic, or by a word unique to a help topic, Get-Help displays the topic contents. If you enter a word or word pattern that appears in several help topic titles, Get-Help displays a list of the matching titles. If you enter a word that does not appear in any help topic titles, Get-Help displays a list of topics that include that word in their contents.

Get-Help can get help topics for all supported languages and locales. Get-Help first looks for help files in the locale set for Windows, then in the parent locale (such as "pt" for "pt-BR"), and then in a fallback locale. Beginning in Windows PowerShell 3.0, if Get-Help does not find help in the fallback locale, it looks for help topics in English ("en-US") before returning an error message or displaying auto-generated help.

For information about the symbols that Get-Help displays in the command syntax diagram, see about_Command_Syntax. For information about parameter attributes, such as Required and Position, see about_Parameters.

TROUBLESHOOTING NOTE: In Windows PowerShell 3.0 and 4.0, Get-Help cannot find About topics in modules unless the module is imported into the current session. This is a known issue. To get About topics in a module, import the module, either by using the Import-Module cmdlet or by running a cmdlet in the module.

RELATED LINKS
    Online Version: http://go.microsoft.com/fwlink/p/?linkid=289584
    Updatable Help Status Table (http://go.microsoft.com/fwlink/?LinkID=270007)
    Get-Command
    Get-Member
    Get-PSDrive
    about_Command_Syntax
    about_Comment_Based_Help
    about_Parameters

The good thing about help with Windows PowerShell is that it not only displays help about cmdlets, which you would expect, but it also has three levels of display: normal, detailed, and full. Additionally, you can obtain help about concepts in Windows PowerShell. This last feature is equivalent to having an online instruction manual. To retrieve a listing of all the conceptual help articles, use the *Get-Help about** command, as follows.

```
Get-Help about*
```

Suppose you do not remember the exact name of the cmdlet you want to use, but you remember it was a *get* cmdlet. You can use a wildcard, such as an asterisk (*), to obtain the name of the cmdlet. This is shown here.

```
Get-Help get*
```

This technique of using a wildcard operator can be extended further. If you remember that the cmdlet was a *get* cmdlet, and that it started with the letter *p*, you can use the following syntax to retrieve the cmdlet you're looking for.

```
Get-Help get-p*
```

Suppose, however, that you know the exact name of the cmdlet, but you cannot exactly remember the syntax. For this scenario, you can use the *-Examples* switch parameter. For example, for the *Get-PSDrive* cmdlet, you would use *Get-Help* with the *-Examples* switch parameter, as follows.

```
Get-Help Get-PSDrive -examples
```

To view help displayed one page at a time, you can use the *Help* function. The *Help* function passes your input to the *Get-Help* cmdlet, and pipelines the resulting information to the *more.com* utility. This causes output to display one page at a time in the Windows PowerShell console. This is useful if you want to avoid scrolling up and down to view the help output.

> **Note** Keep in mind that in the Windows PowerShell ISE, the pager does not work, and therefore you will find no difference in output between *Get-Help* and *Help*. In the ISE, both *Get-Help* and *Help* behave the same way. However, it is likely that if you are using the Windows PowerShell ISE, you will use *Show-Command* for your help instead of relying on *Get-Help*.

This formatted output is shown in Figure 1-3.

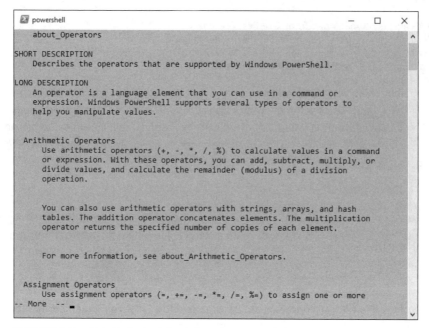

```
powershell                                                    —  □  ✕
    about_Operators                                                    ▲
SHORT DESCRIPTION
    Describes the operators that are supported by Windows PowerShell.

LONG DESCRIPTION
    An operator is a language element that you can use in a command or
    expression. Windows PowerShell supports several types of operators to
    help you manipulate values.


  Arithmetic Operators
        Use arithmetic operators (+, -, *, /, %) to calculate values in a command
        or expression. With these operators, you can add, subtract, multiply, or
        divide values, and calculate the remainder (modulus) of a division
        operation.


        You can also use arithmetic operators with strings, arrays, and hash
        tables. The addition operator concatenates elements. The multiplication
        operator returns the specified number of copies of each element.


        For more information, see about_Arithmetic_Operators.


  Assignment Operators
        Use assignment operators (=, +=, -=, *=, /=, %=) to assign one or more
-- More --  ▪                                                       ▼
```

FIGURE 1-3 Use *Help* to display information one page at a time.

Getting tired of typing *Get-Help* all the time? After all, it is eight characters long. The solution is to create an alias to the *Get-Help* cmdlet. An alias is a shortcut keystroke combination that will launch a program or cmdlet when entered. In the "Creating an alias for the *Get-Help* cmdlet" procedure, you will assign the *Get-Help* cmdlet to the G+H key combination.

Note When creating an alias for a cmdlet, confirm that it does not already have an alias by using *Get-Alias*. Use *New-Alias* to assign the cmdlet to a unique keystroke combination.

Creating an alias for the *Get-Help* cmdlet

1. Open Windows PowerShell by choosing Start | Run | PowerShell. The Windows PowerShell prompt opens by default at the root of your user folder.

2. Retrieve an alphabetic listing of all currently defined aliases, and inspect the list for one assigned to either the *Get-Help* cmdlet or the keystroke combination G+H. The command to do this is as follows.

   ```
   Get-Alias | sort
   ```

3. After you have determined that there is no alias for the *Get-Help* cmdlet and that none is assigned to the G+H keystroke combination, review the syntax for the *New-Alias* cmdlet. Use the *-Full* switch parameter to the *Get-Help* cmdlet. This is shown here.

```
Get-Help New-Alias -full
```

4. Use the *New-Alias* cmdlet to assign the G+H keystroke combination to the *Get-Help* cmdlet. To do this, use the following command.

```
New-Alias gh Get-Help
```

Exploring commands: Step-by-step exercises

In the following exercises, you'll explore the use of command-line utilities in Windows PowerShell. You will find that it is as easy to use command-line utilities in Windows PowerShell as in the CMD interpreter; however, by using such commands in Windows PowerShell, you gain access to new levels of functionality.

Using command-line utilities

1. Open Windows PowerShell by choosing Start | Run | PowerShell. The Windows PowerShell prompt opens by default at the root of your user folder.

2. Change to the root of C:\ by entering **cd c:** inside the Windows PowerShell prompt.

```
cd c:\
```

3. Obtain a listing of all the files in the root of C:\ by using the *dir* command.

```
dir
```

4. Create a directory off the root of C:\ by using the *md* command.

```
md mytest
```

5. Obtain a listing of all files and folders off the root that begin with the letter *m*.

```
dir m*
```

6. Change the working directory to the Windows PowerShell working directory. You can do this by using the *Set-Location* command, as follows.

```
Set-Location $pshome
```

7. Obtain a listing of memory counters related to the available bytes by using the *typeperf.exe* command. This command is shown here.

```
typeperf "\memory\available bytes"
```

8. After a few counters have been displayed in the Windows PowerShell window, press Ctrl+C to break the listing.

9. Display the current startup configuration by using the *bcdedit* command (note that you must run this command with admin rights).

```
bcdedit
```

10. Change the working directory back to the C:\Mytest directory you created earlier.

```
Set-Location c:\mytest
```

11. Create a file named *mytestfile.txt* in the C:\Mytest directory. Use the *fsutil* utility, and make the file 1,000 bytes in size. To do this, use the following command.

```
fsutil file createnew mytestfile.txt 1000
```

12. Obtain a directory listing of all the files in the C:\Mytest directory by using the *Get-ChildItem* cmdlet.

13. Print the current date by using the *Get-Date* cmdlet.

14. Clear the screen by using the *cls* command.

15. Print a listing of all the cmdlets built into Windows PowerShell. To do this, use the *Get-Command* cmdlet.

16. Use the *Get-Command* cmdlet to get the *Get-Alias* cmdlet. To do this, use the *-Name* parameter while supplying *Get-Alias* as the value for the parameter. This is shown here.

```
Get-Command -name Get-Alias
```

This concludes the step-by-step exercise. Exit Windows PowerShell by entering **exit** and pressing Enter.

In the following exercise, you'll use various help options to obtain assistance with various cmdlets.

Obtaining help

1. Open Windows PowerShell by choosing Start | Run | PowerShell. The Windows PowerShell prompt opens by default at the root of your user folder.

2. Use the *Get-Help* cmdlet to obtain help about the *Get-Help* cmdlet. Use the command *Get-Help Get-Help* as follows.

   ```
   Get-Help Get-Help
   ```

3. To obtain detailed help about the *Get-Help* cmdlet, use the *-Detailed* switch parameter, as follows.

   ```
   Get-Help Get-Help -detailed
   ```

4. To retrieve technical information about the *Get-Help* cmdlet, use the *-Full* switch parameter. This is shown here.

   ```
   Get-Help Get-Help -full
   ```

5. If you only want to obtain a listing of examples of command usage, use the *-Examples* switch parameter, as follows.

   ```
   Get-Help Get-Help -examples
   ```

6. Obtain a listing of all the informational help topics by using the *Get-Help* cmdlet and the *about* noun with the asterisk (*) wildcard operator. The code to do this is shown here.

   ```
   Get-Help about*
   ```

7. Obtain a listing of all the help topics related to *get* cmdlets. To do this, use the *Get-Help* cmdlet, and specify the word *get* followed by the wildcard operator, as follows.

   ```
   Get-Help get*
   ```

8. Obtain a listing of all the help topics related to *set* cmdlets. To do this, use the *Get-Help* cmdlet, followed by the *set* verb, followed by the asterisk wildcard. This is shown here.

   ```
   Get-Help set*
   ```

   This concludes this exercise. Exit Windows PowerShell by entering **exit** and pressing Enter.

Chapter 1 quick reference

To	Do this
Use an external command-line utility	Enter the name of the command-line utility while inside Windows PowerShell.
Use multiple external command-line utilities sequentially	Separate each command-line utility with a semicolon on a single Windows PowerShell line.
Obtain a list of running processes	Use the *Get-Process* cmdlet.
Stop a process	Use the *Stop-Process* cmdlet and specify either the name or the process ID parameter.
Model the effect of a cmdlet before actually performing the requested action	Use the *-WhatIf* switch parameter.
Instruct Windows PowerShell to start up, run a cmdlet, and then exit	Use the *PowerShell* command while prefixing the cmdlet with & and enclosing the name of the cmdlet in braces.
Prompt for confirmation before stopping a process	Use the *Stop-Process* cmdlet while specifying the *-Confirm* parameter.

Using Windows PowerShell cmdlets

After completing this chapter, you will be able to

- Understand the basic use of Windows PowerShell cmdlets.

- Use *Get-Command* to retrieve a listing of cmdlets.

- Configure output display.

- Configure cmdlet search options.

- Use *Get-Member*.

- Use *New-Object*.

- Use *Show-Command*.

The inclusion of a large amount of cmdlets in Windows PowerShell makes it immediately useful to network administrators and others who need to perform various maintenance and administrative tasks on their Windows-based servers and desktop systems. In this chapter, you'll review several of the more useful cmdlets as a means of highlighting the power and flexibility of Windows PowerShell. However, the real benefit of this chapter is the methodology you'll use to discover the use of the various cmdlets.

Understanding the basics of cmdlets

In Chapter 1, "Overview of Windows PowerShell 5.0," you learned about using the various help utilities available that demonstrate how to use cmdlets. You looked at a couple of cmdlets that are helpful in finding out what commands are available and how to obtain information about them. In this section, you will learn some additional ways to use cmdlets in Windows PowerShell.

Tip Entering long cmdlet names can be somewhat tedious. To simplify this process, enter enough of the cmdlet name to uniquely distinguish it, and then press the Tab key on the keyboard. What is the result? *Tab completion* completes the cmdlet name for you. This also works with parameter names and other things you are entering (such as .NET objects, directories, and registry keys). Feel free to experiment with this great timesaving technique. You might never have to enter *Get-Command* again! If you do not find the specific cmdlet you are looking for, press the Tab key additional times. You will notice that the cmdlet names cycle through all of the matches.

Because the cmdlets return objects instead of string values, you can obtain additional information about the returned objects. The additional information would not be available if you were working with just string data. To take information from one cmdlet and feed it to another cmdlet, you can use the pipe character (|). This might seem complicated, but it is actually quite simple and, by the end of this chapter, will seem quite natural. At the most basic level, consider obtaining a directory listing; after you have the directory listing, perhaps you would like to format the way it is displayed—as a table or a list. As you can tell, obtaining the directory information and formatting the list are two separate operations. The second task takes place on the right side of the pipe.

Using the *Get-ChildItem* cmdlet

In Chapter 1, you used the *dir* command to obtain a listing of all the files and folders in a directory. This works because there is an alias built into Windows PowerShell that assigns the *Get-ChildItem* cmdlet to the letter combination *dir*.

Obtaining a directory listing

In a Windows PowerShell console, enter the *Get-ChildItem* cmdlet followed by the directory to list. (Remember that you can use tab completion to complete the command. Enter **get-ch** and press Tab to complete the command name.) Here is the command.

```
Get-ChildItem C:\
```

Note Windows PowerShell is not case sensitive; therefore, *get-Childitem*, *Get-childitem*, and *Get-ChildItem* all work the same way, because Windows PowerShell views all three as the same command.

In Windows PowerShell, there actually is no cmdlet called *dir*, nor does Windows PowerShell actually use the *dir* command from the DOS days. The alias *dir* is associated with the *Get-ChildItem* cmdlet. This is why the output from *dir* is different in Windows PowerShell from output appearing in the CMD.exe interpreter. The Windows PowerShell cmdlet *Get-Alias* resolves the association between *dir* and the *Get-ChildItem* cmdlet as follows.

```
PS C:\> Get-Alias dir

CommandType     Name                                              Version    Source
-----------     ----                                              -------    ------
Alias           dir -> Get-ChildItem
```

If you use the *Get-ChildItem* cmdlet to obtain the directory listing, the output appears exactly the same as output produced in Windows PowerShell by using *dir*, because *dir* is an alias for the *Get-ChildItem* cmdlet. This is shown here.

```
PS C:\> dir c:\


    Directory: C:\


Mode                LastWriteTime         Length Name
----                -------------         ------ ----
d-----        7/11/2015  11:55 AM                FSO
d-----         7/9/2015   5:24 AM                PerfLogs
d-r---         7/9/2015   6:59 AM                Program Files
d-r---        7/10/2015   7:27 PM                Program Files (x86)
d-r---        7/10/2015   7:18 PM                Users
d-----        7/10/2015   6:00 PM                Windows


PS C:\> Get-ChildItem c:\


    Directory: C:\


Mode                LastWriteTime         Length Name
----                -------------         ------ ----
d-----        7/11/2015  11:55 AM                FSO
d-----         7/9/2015   5:24 AM                PerfLogs
d-r---         7/9/2015   6:59 AM                Program Files
d-r---        7/10/2015   7:27 PM                Program Files (x86)
d-r---        7/10/2015   7:18 PM                Users
d-----        7/10/2015   6:00 PM  .             Windows


PS C:\>
```

If you were to use *Get-Help* and then *dir*, you would receive the same output as if you were to use *Get-Help Get-ChildItem*. This is shown following, where only the name and the synopsis of the cmdlets are displayed in the output.

```
PS C:\> Get-Help dir | select name, synopsis | Format-Table -AutoSize

Name           Synopsis
----           --------
Get-ChildItem Gets the files and folders in a file system drive.

PS C:\> Get-Help Get-ChildItem | select name, synopsis | Format-Table -AutoSize

Name           Synopsis
----           --------
Get-ChildItem Gets the files and folders in a file system drive.

PS C:\>
```

In Windows PowerShell, an alias and a full cmdlet name perform in exactly the same manner. You do not use an alias to modify the behavior of a cmdlet. (To do that, create a function or a proxy function.)

Formatting a directory listing by using the *Format-List* cmdlet

In a Windows PowerShell console, enter the *Get-ChildItem* cmdlet, followed by the directory to list, followed by the pipe character and the *Format-List* cmdlet. Here's an example.

```
Get-ChildItem C:\ | Format-List
```

Formatting output with the *Format-List* cmdlet

1. Open the Windows PowerShell console.

2. Use the *Get-ChildItem* cmdlet to obtain a directory listing of the C:\ directory.

    ```
    Get-ChildItem C:\
    ```

3. Use the *Format-List* cmdlet to arrange the output of *Get-ChildItem*.

    ```
    Get-ChildItem C:\ | Format-List
    ```

4. Use the *-Property* parameter of the *Format-List* cmdlet to retrieve only a listing of the name of each file in the root.

    ```
    Get-ChildItem C:\ | Format-List -property name
    ```

5. Use the *-Property* parameter of the *Format-List* cmdlet to retrieve only a listing of the name and length of each file in the root. If the *length* property is not displayed, there are no files visible (unhidden) in the root, because folders do not have a value for the *length* property.

    ```
    Get-ChildItem C:\ | Format-List -property name, length
    ```

Using the *Format-Wide* cmdlet

In the same way that you use the *Format-List* cmdlet to produce output in a list, you can use the *Format-Wide* cmdlet to produce output that's more compact. The difference is that *Format-Wide* permits the selection of only a single property; however, you can choose how many columns you will use to display the information. By default, the *Format-Wide* cmdlet uses two columns.

Formatting a directory listing by using *Format-Wide*

1. In a Windows PowerShell prompt, enter the *Get-ChildItem* cmdlet, followed by the directory to list, followed by the pipe character and the *Format-Wide* cmdlet. Here's an example.

    ```
    Get-ChildItem C:\ | Format-Wide
    ```

2. Change to a three-column display and specifically select the *name* property.

    ```
    Get-ChildItem | Format-Wide -Column 3 -Property name
    ```

3. Allow Windows PowerShell to maximize the amount of space between columns and display as many columns as possible. Use the *-AutoSize* switch parameter to do this.

    ```
    Get-ChildItem | Format-Wide -Property name -AutoSize
    ```

4. Force Windows PowerShell to truncate the columns by choosing a number of columns greater than can be displayed on the screen.

    ```
    Get-ChildItem | Format-Wide -Property name -Column 8
    ```

Formatting output by using the *Format-Wide* cmdlet

1. Open the Windows PowerShell console.

2. Use the *Get-ChildItem* cmdlet to obtain a directory listing of the C:\Windows directory.

    ```
    Get-ChildItem C:\Windows
    ```

3. Use the *-Recurse* switch parameter to cause the *Get-ChildItem* cmdlet to walk through a nested directory structure, including only .txt files in the output. Hide errors by using the *-ea* parameter (*ea* is an alias for *ErrorAction*), and assign a value of 0 (which means that errors will be ignored [*SilentlyContinue*]).

    ```
    Get-ChildItem C:\Windows -recurse -include *.txt -ea 0
    ```

Partial output from the command is shown here.

```
PS C:\> Get-ChildItem C:\Windows -recurse -include *.txt -ea 0


    Directory: C:\Windows\InfusedApps\Packages\Microsoft.3DBuilder_10.0.0.0_x64__8we
    kyb3d8bbwe\Common


Mode                LastWriteTime        Length Name
----                -------------        ------ ----
-a---1         7/9/2015     7:01 AM         975 ReadMe.txt


    Directory: C:\Windows\InfusedApps\Packages\Microsoft.BingFinance_4.3.193.0_x86__
    8wekyb3d8bbwe\_Resources


Mode                LastWriteTime        Length Name
----                -------------        ------ ----
-a----         7/9/2015     7:00 AM         163 index.txt
```

4. Use the *Format-Wide* cmdlet to adjust the output from the *Get-ChildItem* cmdlet. Use the *-Columns* parameter, and supply a value of *3* to it. This is shown here.

```
Get-ChildItem C:\Windows -recurse -include *.txt -ea 0 | Format-Wide -column 3
```

When this command is run, you will get output similar to this.

```
PS C:\> Get-ChildItem C:\Windows -recurse -include *.txt -ea 0 | Format-Wide -Column 3


    Directory: C:\Windows\InfusedApps\Packages\Microsoft.3DBuilder_10.0.0.0_x64__8we
    kyb3d8bbwe\Common


ReadMe.txt


    Directory: C:\Windows\InfusedApps\Packages\Microsoft.BingFinance_4.3.193.0_x86__
    8wekyb3d8bbwe\_Resources


index.txt
```

5. Use the *Format-Wide* cmdlet to adjust the output from the *Get-ChildItem* cmdlet. Use the *-Property* parameter to specify the *name* property, and group the outputs by size. The command shown here appears on two lines; however, when entered into Windows PowerShell, it is a single command and can be on one line. In addition, when it is entered

into the Windows PowerShell console, if you continue entering when approaching the end of a line, Windows PowerShell will automatically wrap the command to the next line; therefore, you do not need to press the Enter key.

```
Get-ChildItem C:\Windows -recurse -include *.txt |
Format-Wide -property name -groupby length -column 3
```

Partial output is shown here. Note that although three columns were specified, if there are not three files of the same length, only one column will be used.

```
PS C:\> Get-ChildItem C:\Windows -recurse -include *.txt |
>> Format-Wide -property name -groupby length -column 3
>>
Get-ChildItem : Access to the path 'C:\Windows\CSC' is denied.
At line:1 char:1
+ Get-ChildItem C:\Windows -recurse -include *.txt |
+ ~~~~~~~~~~~~~~~~~~~~~~~~~~~~~~~~~~~~~~~~~~~~~~~~
    + CategoryInfo          : PermissionDenied: (C:\Windows\CSC:String) [Get-ChildI
   tem], UnauthorizedAccessException
    + FullyQualifiedErrorId : DirUnauthorizedAccessError,Microsoft.PowerShell.Comma
   nds.GetChildItemCommand


    Length: 975


ReadMe.txt


    Length: 163


index.txt                     index.txt                     index.txt
index.txt                     index.txt


    Length: 281
```

Formatting a directory listing by using *Format-Table*

In a Windows PowerShell console, enter the *Get-ChildItem* cmdlet, followed by the directory to list, followed by the pipe character and the *Format-Table* cmdlet. Here's an example.

```
Get-ChildItem C:\ | Format-Table
```

Formatting output by using the *Format-Table* cmdlet

1. Open Windows PowerShell by choosing Start | Run | PowerShell. The Windows PowerShell prompt opens by default at the root of your user folder.

2. Use the *Get-ChildItem* cmdlet to obtain a directory listing of the C:\Windows directory.

```
Get-ChildItem C:\Windows -ea 0
```

3. Use the *-Recurse* switch parameter to cause the *Get-ChildItem* cmdlet to walk through a nested directory structure. Include only .txt files in the output.

```
Get-ChildItem C:\Windows -recurse -include *.txt -ea 0
```

4. Use the *Format-Table* cmdlet to adjust the output from the *Get-ChildItem* cmdlet. This is shown here.

```
Get-ChildItem C:\Windows -recurse -include *.txt -ea 0 | Format-Table
```

The command results in the creation of a table, as follows.

```
PS C:\> Get-ChildItem C:\Windows -recurse -include *.txt -ea 0 | Format-Table


    Directory: C:\Windows\InfusedApps\Packages\Microsoft.3DBuilder_10.0.0.0_x64__8we
    kyb3d8bbwe\Common


Mode                LastWriteTime         Length Name
----                -------------         ------ ----
-a---l         7/9/2015     7:01 AM          975 ReadMe.txt


    Directory: C:\Windows\InfusedApps\Packages\Microsoft.BingFinance_4.3.193.0_x86__
    8wekyb3d8bbwe\_Resources


Mode                LastWriteTime         Length Name
----                -------------         ------ ----
-a----         7/9/2015     7:00 AM          163 index.txt


    Directory: C:\Windows\InfusedApps\Packages\Microsoft.BingNews_4.3.193.0_x86__8we
    kyb3d8bbwe\_Resources


Mode                LastWriteTime         Length Name
----                -------------         ------ ----
-a----         7/9/2015     7:00 AM          163 index.txt
```

5. Use the *-Property* parameter of the *Format-Table* cmdlet and choose the *Name*, *Length*, and *LastWriteTime* properties. This is shown here.

```
Get-ChildItem C:\Windows -recurse –include *.txt –ea 0 |Format-Table -property
name, length, lastwritetime
```

This command results in producing a table with the name, length, and last write time as column headers. A sample of this output is shown here.

```
PS C:\> Get-ChildItem C:\Windows -recurse –include *.txt –ea 0 | Format-Table -property
name, length, lastwritetime

Name         Length LastWriteTime
----         ------ -------------
ReadMe.txt      975 7/9/2015 7:01:50 AM
index.txt       163 7/9/2015 7:00:27 AM
index.txt       163 7/9/2015 7:00:18 AM
index.txt       163 7/9/2015 7:00:14 AM
index.txt       163 7/9/2015 7:00:23 AM
index.txt       163 7/9/2015 7:01:27 AM
index.txt       281 7/9/2015 7:00:31 AM
index.txt       163 7/9/2015 7:01:32 AM
index.txt       163 7/9/2015 7:01:44 AM
Configu...     3128 7/9/2015 7:01:39 AM
THIRD P...     1683 7/9/2015 7:02:00 AM
index.txt       163 7/9/2015 7:02:00 AM
index.txt       163 7/9/2015 6:59:55 AM
index.txt      5527 7/9/2015 7:01:21 AM
ThirdPa...    20126 7/9/2015 5:20:48 AM
```

Formatting output with *Out-GridView*

The *Out-GridView* cmdlet is different from the other formatting cmdlets explored thus far in this chapter. *Out-GridView* is an interactive cmdlet—that is, it does not format output for display on the Windows PowerShell console, but it can send content back to the console to use in other forms of output. One of the best things to use *Out-GridView* for, initially, is to facilitate exploration of the pipelined data. This can help you gain familiarity with the data you are working with. It does this by adding the data to a table in a floating window. For example, the following command pipelines the results of the *Get-Process* cmdlet to the *Out-GridView* cmdlet (*gps* is an alias for the *Get-Process* cmdlet).

```
gps | Out-GridView
```

When the *Get-Process* cmdlet completes, a grid appears containing process information arranged in columns and in rows. Figure 2-1 shows the new window displaying the process information in a grid. One useful feature of the *Out-GridView* cmdlet is that the returned control contains the command producing the control in the title bar. Figure 2-1 lists the command *gps | Out-GridView* in the title bar (the command that is run to produce the grid control).

FIGURE 2-1 The *Out-GridView* cmdlet accepts pipelined input and displays a control that permits further exploration.

You can click the column headings to sort the output in descending order. Clicking the same column again changes the sort to ascending order. Figure 2-2 shows the processes sorted by the number of handles used by each process. The sort is ordered from largest number of handles to smallest.

FIGURE 2-2 Clicking the column heading buttons permits sorting in either descending or ascending order.

Out-GridView accepts input from other cmdlets, and from the *Get-Process* cmdlet. For example, you can pipeline the output from the *Get-Service* cmdlet to *Out-GridView* by using the syntax that appears here (*gsv* is an alias for the *Get-Service* cmdlet, and *ogv* is an alias for the *Out-GridView* cmdlet).

```
gsv | ogv
```

Figure 2-3 shows the resulting grid view.

FIGURE 2-3 *Out-GridView* displays service controller information, such as the current status of all defined services.

The *Out-GridView* cmdlet automatically detects the data type of the incoming properties. It uses this data type to determine how to present the filtered and sorted information to you. For example, the data type of the *Status* property is a string. Clicking the Add Criteria button, choosing the *status* property, and selecting Add adds a filter that you can use to choose various ways of interacting with the text stored in the *status* property. The available options include the following: *contains*, *does not contain*, *equals*, *does not equal*, *starts with*, *ends with*, *is empty*, and *is not empty*. The options change depending upon the perceived data type of the incoming property.

To filter only running services, you can change the filter to *equals* and the value to *running*. Keep in mind that if you choose an equality operator, your filtered string must match exactly. Therefore, *equals run* will not return any matches. Only *equals running* works. However, if you choose a *starts with* operator, you will find all the running services with the first letter. For instance, *starts with r* returns every service that begins with the letter *r*. As you continue to type, matches continue to be refined in the output.

Note Keep in the mind the difference in the behavior of the various filters. Depending on the operator you select, the self-updating output is extremely useful. This works especially well when you are attempting to filter out numerical data if you are not very familiar with the data ranges and what a typical value looks like. This technique is shown in Figure 2-4.

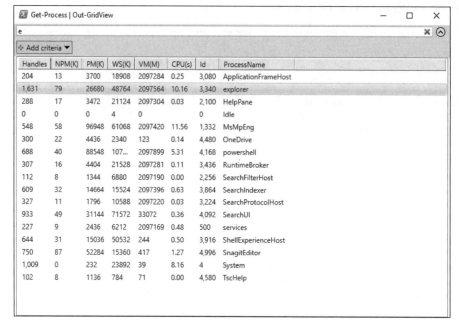

FIGURE 2-4 The *Out-GridView* self-updates when you enter in the filter box.

By the time you enter two letters, *ex,* in the filter box, the resultant process information changes to display a limited collection of processes. The match for *ex* occurs anywhere, including the *Display-Name* or the *ProcessName* fields. The output is shown in Figure 2-5.

FIGURE 2-5 Letters entered into the filter box match any of the available columns.

Filtering processes by using CPU time with a memory working set greater than 20,000

1. Click the blue plus symbol on the Add Criteria button beneath the Filter box.

2. In the Add Criteria menu, place a check box beside CPU(s) and click the Add button.

3. Click Contains, and select Is Not Empty from the menu.

4. Click the blue plus symbol on the Add Criteria button.

5. Select WS(K).

6. Click the Add button to add the working set memory to the criteria.

7. Click Is Less Than Or Equal To to change it to Is Greater Than Or Equal To.

8. Enter **20000** in the box next to Is Greater Than Or Equal To.

Creating a sorted process list

1. Enter the following command into the Windows PowerShell console.

   ```
   Get-Process
   ```

2. Send the output of the *Get-Process* cmdlet to the *Get-Member* cmdlet.

   ```
   Get-Process | Get-Member
   ```

3. Examine the property section. Note that CPU is a *script* property.

4. Pipeline the results from the *Get-Process* cmdlet to the *Sort-Object* cmdlet and use the *cpu* property.

   ```
   Get-Process | Sort-Object cpu
   ```

5. Retrieve the previous command and add the *-Descending* switch parameter.

   ```
   Get-Process | Sort-Object cpu -Descending
   ```

6. Send the whole thing to the *Out-GridView* cmdlet. The command appears here.

   ```
   Get-Process | Sort-Object cpu -Descending | Out-GridView
   ```

7. Next you will remove columns from the grid view. To do this, right-click the column process names and select the columns.

8. When the Select Column prompt appears, click it to open the Select Columns dialog box. Click to add or remove the columns individually.

   The Select Columns dialog box is shown in Figure 2-6.

FIGURE 2-6 Use the Select Columns dialog box to control which columns appear in the gridview control.

 Note Because the process of selecting columns is a bit slow, if you only want to view a few columns, it is best to filter the columns by using the *Select-Object* cmdlet before you send it to the *Out-GridView* cmdlet.

Taking advantage of the power of *Get-Command*

The *Get-Command* cmdlet gets details of every command available to you. These commands include cmdlets, functions, workflows, aliases, and executable commands. By using the *Get-Command* cmdlet, you can obtain a listing of all the cmdlets installed on Windows PowerShell, but there is much more that can be done by using this extremely versatile cmdlet. For example, you can use wildcard characters to search for cmdlets by using *Get-Command*. This is shown in the following procedure.

Searching for cmdlets by using wildcard characters

In a Windows PowerShell prompt, enter the *Get-Command* cmdlet followed by a wildcard character.

```
Get-Command *
```

Finding commands by using the *Get-Command* cmdlet

1. Open Windows PowerShell.

2. Use an alias to refer to the *Get-Command* cmdlet. To find the correct alias, use the *Get-Alias* cmdlet, as follows.

   ```
   Get-Alias g*
   ```

This command produces a listing of all the aliases defined that begin with the letter *g*. An example of the output of this command is shown here.

```
CommandType     Name                                         Version  Source
-----------     ----                                         -------  ------
Alias           gal -> Get-Alias
Alias           gbp -> Get-PSBreakpoint
Alias           gc -> Get-Content
Alias           gcb -> Get-Clipboard                         3.1.0.0  Mic...
Alias           gci -> Get-ChildItem
Alias           gcm -> Get-Command
Alias           gcs -> Get-PSCallStack
Alias           gdr -> Get-PSDrive
Alias           ghy -> Get-History
Alias           gi -> Get-Item
Alias           gjb -> Get-Job
Alias           gl -> Get-Location
Alias           gm -> Get-Member
Alias           gmo -> Get-Module
Alias           gp -> Get-ItemProperty
Alias           gps -> Get-Process
Alias           gpv -> Get-ItemPropertyValue
Alias           group -> Group-Object
Alias           gsn -> Get-PSSession
Alias           gsnp -> Get-PSSnapin
Alias           gsv -> Get-Service
Alias           gu -> Get-Unique
Alias           gv -> Get-Variable
Alias           gwmi -> Get-WmiObject
```

3. By using the *gcm* alias, use the *Get-Command* cmdlet to return the *Get-Command* cmdlet. This is shown here.

```
gcm Get-Command
```

This command returns the *Get-Command* cmdlet. The output is shown here.

```
CommandType     Name                                         ModuleName
-----------     ----                                         ----------
Cmdlet          Get-Command                                  Microsoft.Powe...
```

4. Use the *gcm* alias to get the *Get-Command* cmdlet, and pipeline the output to the *Format-List* cmdlet. Use the wildcard asterisk (*) to obtain a listing of all the properties of the *Get-Command* cmdlet. This is shown here.

```
gcm Get-Command | Format-List *
```

This command will return all the properties from the *Get-Command* cmdlet. The output is shown here.

```
HelpUri          : http://go.microsoft.com/fwlink/?LinkID=113309
DLL              : C:\Windows\Microsoft.Net\assembly\GAC_MSIL\System.Management.A
                   utomation\v4.0_3.0.0.0__31bf3856ad364e35\System.Management.Aut
                   omation.dll
```

```
Verb               : Get
Noun               : Command
HelpFile           : System.Management.Automation.dll-Help.xml
PSSnapIn           : Microsoft.PowerShell.Core
Version            : 3.0.0.0
ImplementingType   : Microsoft.PowerShell.Commands.GetCommandCommand
Definition         :
                     Get-Command [[-ArgumentList] <Object[]>] [-Verb <string[]>]
                     [-Noun <string[]>] [-Module <string[]>]
                     [-FullyQualifiedModule <ModuleSpecification[]>] [-TotalCount
                     <int>] [-Syntax] [-ShowCommandInfo] [-All] [-ListImported]
                     [-ParameterName <string[]>] [-ParameterType <PSTypeName[]>]
                     [<CommonParameters>]

                     Get-Command [[-Name] <string[]>] [[-ArgumentList] <Object[]>]
                     [-Module <string[]>] [-FullyQualifiedModule
                     <ModuleSpecification[]>] [-CommandType <CommandTypes>]
                     [-TotalCount <int>] [-Syntax] [-ShowCommandInfo] [-All]
                     [-ListImported] [-ParameterName <string[]>] [-ParameterType
                     <PSTypeName[]>] [<CommonParameters>]

DefaultParameterSet : CmdletSet
OutputType          : {System.Management.Automation.AliasInfo,
                      System.Management.Automation.ApplicationInfo,
                      System.Management.Automation.FunctionInfo,
                      System.Management.Automation.CmdletInfo...}
Options             : ReadOnly
Name                : Get-Command
CommandType         : Cmdlet
Source              : Microsoft.PowerShell.Core
Visibility          : Public
ModuleName          : Microsoft.PowerShell.Core
Module              :
RemotingCapability  : PowerShell
Parameters          : {[Name, System.Management.Automation.ParameterMetadata],
                      [Verb, System.Management.Automation.ParameterMetadata],
                      [Noun, System.Management.Automation.ParameterMetadata],
                      [Module, System.Management.Automation.ParameterMetadata]...}
ParameterSets       : {[[-ArgumentList] <Object[]>] [-Verb <string[]>] [-Noun
                      <string[]>] [-Module <string[]>] [-FullyQualifiedModule
                      <ModuleSpecification[]>] [-TotalCount <int>] [-Syntax]
                      [-ShowCommandInfo] [-All] [-ListImported] [-ParameterName
                      <string[]>] [-ParameterType <PSTypeName[]>]
                      [<CommonParameters>], [[-Name] <string[]>] [[-ArgumentList]
                      <Object[]>] [-Module <string[]>] [-FullyQualifiedModule
                      <ModuleSpecification[]>] [-CommandType <CommandTypes>]
                      [-TotalCount <int>] [-Syntax] [-ShowCommandInfo] [-All]
                      [-ListImported] [-ParameterName <string[]>] [-ParameterType
                      <PSTypeName[]>] [<CommonParameters>]}
```

5. Using the *gcm* alias and the *Get-Command* cmdlet, pipeline the output to the *Format-List* cmdlet. Use the *-Property* parameter and specify the *definition* property of the *Get-Command* cmdlet. Rather than re-entering the entire command, use the Up Arrow key on your keyboard to retrieve the previous *gcm Get-Command | Format-List* * command. Use the Backspace key to remove the asterisk, and then add *-Property definition* to your command. This is shown here.

```
gcm Get-Command | Format-List -property definition
```

This command returns only the property definition for the *Get-Command* cmdlet. The returned definition is shown here.

```
Definition :
            Get-Command [[-ArgumentList] <Object[]>] [-Verb <string[]>] [-Noun
            <string[]>] [-Module <string[]>] [-FullyQualifiedModule
            <ModuleSpecification[]>] [-TotalCount <int>] [-Syntax]
            [-ShowCommandInfo] [-All] [-ListImported] [-ParameterName <string[]>]
            [-ParameterType <PSTypeName[]>] [<CommonParameters>]

            Get-Command [[-Name] <string[]>] [[-ArgumentList] <Object[]>] [-Module
            <string[]>] [-FullyQualifiedModule <ModuleSpecification[]>]
            [-CommandType <CommandTypes>] [-TotalCount <int>] [-Syntax]
            [-ShowCommandInfo] [-All] [-ListImported] [-ParameterName <string[]>]
            [-ParameterType <PSTypeName[]>] [<CommonParameters>]
```

6. Because objects instead of string data are returned from cmdlets, you can also retrieve the definition of the *Get-Command* cmdlet by directly using the *definition* property. This is done by putting the expression inside parentheses and using *dotted notation*, as shown here.

```
(gcm Get-Command).definition
```

The definition returned from the previous command is virtually identical to the one returned by using the *Format-List* cmdlet.

7. Use the *gcm* alias and specify the *-Verb* parameter. Use *se** for the verb. This is shown here.

```
gcm -verb se*
```

The previous command returns a listing of all the cmdlets that contain a verb beginning with *se*. The result is as follows.

```
CommandType     Name                                    Version     Source
-----------     ----                                    -------     ------
Function        Send-EtwTraceSession                    1.0.0.0     Eve...
Function        Set-AssignedAccess                      1.0.0.0     Ass...
Function        Set-AutologgerConfig                    1.0.0.0     Eve...
Function        Set-BCAuthentication                    1.0.0.0     Bra...
Function        Set-BCCache                             1.0.0.0     Bra...
Function        Set-BCDataCacheEntryMaxAge              1.0.0.0     Bra...
Function        Set-BCMinSMBLatency                     1.0.0.0     Bra...
Function        Set-BCSecretKey                         1.0.0.0     Bra...
Function        Set-ClusteredScheduledTask              1.0.0.0     Sch...
Function        Set-DAClientExperienceConfiguration     1.0.0.0     Dir...
Function        Set-DAEntryPointTableItem               1.0.0.0     Dir...
Function        Set-Disk                                2.0.0.0     Sto...
Function        Set-DnsClient                           1.0.0.0     Dns...
Function        Set-DnsClientGlobalSetting              1.0.0.0     Dns...
Function        Set-DnsClientNrptGlobal                 1.0.0.0     Dns...
Function        Set-DnsClientNrptRule                   1.0.0.0     Dns...
Function        Set-DnsClientServerAddress              1.0.0.0     Dns...
Function        Set-DtcAdvancedHostSetting              1.0.0.0     MsDtc
Function        Set-DtcAdvancedSetting                  1.0.0.0     MsDtc
Function        Set-DtcClusterDefault                   1.0.0.0     MsDtc
Function        Set-DtcClusterTMMapping                 1.0.0.0     MsDtc
```

Function	Set-DtcDefault	1.0.0.0	MsDtc
Function	Set-DtcLog	1.0.0.0	MsDtc
Function	Set-DtcNetworkSetting	1.0.0.0	MsDtc
Function	Set-DtcTransaction	1.0.0.0	MsDtc
Function	Set-DtcTransactionsTraceSession	1.0.0.0	MsDtc
Function	Set-DtcTransactionsTraceSetting	1.0.0.0	MsDtc
Function	Set-DynamicParameterVariables	3.3.5	Pester
Function	Set-EtwTraceProvider	1.0.0.0	Eve...
Function	Set-EtwTraceSession	1.0.0.0	Eve...
Function	Set-FileIntegrity	2.0.0.0	Sto...
Function	Set-FileShare	2.0.0.0	Sto...
Function	Set-FileStorageTier	2.0.0.0	Sto...
Function	Set-InitiatorPort	2.0.0.0	Sto...
Function	Set-IscsiChapSecret	1.0.0.0	iSCSI
Function	Set-LogProperties	1.0.0.0	PSD...
Function	Set-MMAgent	1.0	MMA...
Function	Set-MpPreference	1.0	Def...
Function	Set-NCSIPolicyConfiguration	1.0.0.0	Net...
Function	Set-Net6to4Configuration	1.0.0.0	Net...
Function	Set-NetAdapter	2.0.0.0	Net...
Function	Set-NetAdapterAdvancedProperty	2.0.0.0	Net...
Function	Set-NetAdapterBinding	2.0.0.0	Net...
Function	Set-NetAdapterChecksumOffload	2.0.0.0	Net...
Function	Set-NetAdapterEncapsulatedPacketTaskOffload	2.0.0.0	Net...
Function	Set-NetAdapterIPsecOffload	2.0.0.0	Net...
Function	Set-NetAdapterLso	2.0.0.0	Net...
Function	Set-NetAdapterPacketDirect	2.0.0.0	Net...
Function	Set-NetAdapterPowerManagement	2.0.0.0	Net...
Function	Set-NetAdapterQos	2.0.0.0	Net...
Function	Set-NetAdapterRdma	2.0.0.0	Net...
Function	Set-NetAdapterRsc	2.0.0.0	Net...
Function	Set-NetAdapterRss	2.0.0.0	Net...
Function	Set-NetAdapterSriov	2.0.0.0	Net...
Function	Set-NetAdapterVmq	2.0.0.0	Net...
Function	Set-NetConnectionProfile	1.0.0.0	Net...
Function	Set-NetDnsTransitionConfiguration	1.0.0.0	Net...
Function	Set-NetEventPacketCaptureProvider	1.0.0.0	Net...
Function	Set-NetEventProvider	1.0.0.0	Net...
Function	Set-NetEventSession	1.0.0.0	Net...
Function	Set-NetEventWFPCaptureProvider	1.0.0.0	Net...
Function	Set-NetFirewallAddressFilter	2.0.0.0	Net...
Function	Set-NetFirewallApplicationFilter	2.0.0.0	Net...
Function	Set-NetFirewallInterfaceFilter	2.0.0.0	Net...
Function	Set-NetFirewallInterfaceTypeFilter	2.0.0.0	Net...
Function	Set-NetFirewallPortFilter	2.0.0.0	Net...
Function	Set-NetFirewallProfile	2.0.0.0	Net...
Function	Set-NetFirewallRule	2.0.0.0	Net...
Function	Set-NetFirewallSecurityFilter	2.0.0.0	Net...
Function	Set-NetFirewallServiceFilter	2.0.0.0	Net...
Function	Set-NetFirewallSetting	2.0.0.0	Net...
Function	Set-NetIPAddress	1.0.0.0	Net...
Function	Set-NetIPHttpsConfiguration	1.0.0.0	Net...
Function	Set-NetIPInterface	1.0.0.0	Net...
Function	Set-NetIPsecDospSetting	2.0.0.0	Net...
Function	Set-NetIPsecMainModeCryptoSet	2.0.0.0	Net...
Function	Set-NetIPsecMainModeRule	2.0.0.0	Net...
Function	Set-NetIPsecPhase1AuthSet	2.0.0.0	Net...

Function	Set-NetIPsecPhase2AuthSet	2.0.0.0	Net...
Function	Set-NetIPsecQuickModeCryptoSet	2.0.0.0	Net...
Function	Set-NetIPsecRule	2.0.0.0	Net...
Function	Set-NetIPv4Protocol	1.0.0.0	Net...
Function	Set-NetIPv6Protocol	1.0.0.0	Net...
Function	Set-NetIsatapConfiguration	1.0.0.0	Net...
Function	Set-NetLbfoTeam	2.0.0.0	Net...
Function	Set-NetLbfoTeamMember	2.0.0.0	Net...
Function	Set-NetLbfoTeamNic	2.0.0.0	Net...
Function	Set-NetNat	1.0.0.0	NetNat
Function	Set-NetNatGlobal	1.0.0.0	NetNat
Function	Set-NetNatTransitionConfiguration	1.0.0.0	Net...
Function	Set-NetNeighbor	1.0.0.0	Net...
Function	Set-NetOffloadGlobalSetting	1.0.0.0	Net...
Function	Set-NetQosPolicy	2.0.0.0	NetQos
Function	Set-NetRoute	1.0.0.0	Net...
Function	Set-NetTCPSetting	1.0.0.0	Net...
Function	Set-NetTeredoConfiguration	1.0.0.0	Net...
Function	Set-NetUDPSetting	1.0.0.0	Net...
Function	Set-NetworkSwitchEthernetPortIPAddress	1.0.0.0	Net...
Function	Set-NetworkSwitchPortMode	1.0.0.0	Net...
Function	Set-NetworkSwitchPortProperty	1.0.0.0	Net...
Function	Set-NetworkSwitchVlanProperty	1.0.0.0	Net...
Function	Set-OdbcDriver	1.0.0.0	Wdac
Function	Set-OdbcDsn	1.0.0.0	Wdac
Function	Set-Partition	2.0.0.0	Sto...
Function	Set-PcsvDeviceBootConfiguration	1.0.0.0	Pcs...
Function	Set-PcsvDeviceNetworkConfiguration	1.0.0.0	Pcs...
Function	Set-PcsvDeviceUserPassword	1.0.0.0	Pcs...
Function	Set-PhysicalDisk	2.0.0.0	Sto...
Function	Set-PrintConfiguration	1.1	Pri...
Function	Set-Printer	1.1	Pri...
Function	Set-PrinterProperty	1.1	Pri...
Function	Set-PSRepository	1.0	Pow...
Function	Set-ResiliencySetting	2.0.0.0	Sto...
Function	Set-ScheduledTask	1.0.0.0	Sch...
Function	Set-SmbBandwidthLimit	2.0.0.0	Smb...
Function	Set-SmbClientConfiguration	2.0.0.0	Smb...
Function	Set-SmbPathAcl	2.0.0.0	Smb...
Function	Set-SmbServerConfiguration	2.0.0.0	Smb...
Function	Set-SmbShare	2.0.0.0	Smb...
Function	Set-StorageFileServer	2.0.0.0	Sto...
Function	Set-StoragePool	2.0.0.0	Sto...
Function	Set-StorageProvider	2.0.0.0	Sto...
Function	Set-StorageSetting	2.0.0.0	Sto...
Function	Set-StorageSubSystem	2.0.0.0	Sto...
Function	Set-StorageTier	2.0.0.0	Sto...
Function	Set-VirtualDisk	2.0.0.0	Sto...
Function	Set-Volume	2.0.0.0	Sto...
Function	Set-VolumeScrubPolicy	2.0.0.0	Sto...
Function	Set-VpnConnection	2.0.0.0	Vpn...
Function	Set-VpnConnectionIPsecConfiguration	2.0.0.0	Vpn...
Function	Set-VpnConnectionProxy	2.0.0.0	Vpn...
Function	Set-VpnConnectionTriggerDnsConfiguration	2.0.0.0	Vpn...
Function	Set-VpnConnectionTriggerTrustedNetwork	2.0.0.0	Vpn...
Cmdlet	Select-Object	3.1.0.0	Mic...
Cmdlet	Select-String	3.1.0.0	Mic...

Cmdlet	Select-Xml	3.1.0.0	Mic...
Cmdlet	Send-DtcDiagnosticTransaction	1.0.0.0	MsDtc
Cmdlet	Send-MailMessage	3.1.0.0	Mic...
Cmdlet	Set-Acl	3.0.0.0	Mic...
Cmdlet	Set-Alias	3.1.0.0	Mic...
Cmdlet	Set-AppBackgroundTaskResourcePolicy	1.0.0.0	App...
Cmdlet	Set-AppLockerPolicy	2.0.0.0	App...
Cmdlet	Set-AppxDefaultVolume	2.0.0.0	Appx
Cmdlet	Set-AppXProvisionedDataFile	3.0	Dism
Cmdlet	Set-AuthenticodeSignature	3.0.0.0	Mic...
Cmdlet	Set-BitsTransfer	2.0.0.0	Bit...
Cmdlet	Set-CertificateAutoEnrollmentPolicy	1.0.0.0	PKI
Cmdlet	Set-CimInstance	1.0.0.0	Cim...
Cmdlet	Set-Clipboard	3.1.0.0	Mic...
Cmdlet	Set-Content	3.1.0.0	Mic...
Cmdlet	Set-Culture	2.0.0.0	Int...
Cmdlet	Set-Date	3.1.0.0	Mic...
Cmdlet	Set-DscLocalConfigurationManager	1.1	PSD...
Cmdlet	Set-ExecutionPolicy	3.0.0.0	Mic...
Cmdlet	Set-Item	3.1.0.0	Mic...
Cmdlet	Set-ItemProperty	3.1.0.0	Mic...
Cmdlet	Set-JobTrigger	1.1.0.0	PSS...
Cmdlet	Set-KdsConfiguration	1.0.0.0	Kds
Cmdlet	Set-Location	3.1.0.0	Mic...
Cmdlet	Set-PackageSource	1.0.0.0	Pac...
Cmdlet	Set-PSBreakpoint	3.1.0.0	Mic...
Cmdlet	Set-PSDebug	3.0.0.0	Mic...
Cmdlet	Set-PSReadlineKeyHandler	1.1	PSR...
Cmdlet	Set-PSReadlineOption	1.1	PSR...
Cmdlet	Set-PSSessionConfiguration	3.0.0.0	Mic...
Cmdlet	Set-ScheduledJob	1.1.0.0	PSS...
Cmdlet	Set-ScheduledJobOption	1.1.0.0	PSS...
Cmdlet	Set-SecureBootUEFI	2.0.0.0	Sec...
Cmdlet	Set-Service	3.1.0.0	Mic...
Cmdlet	Set-StrictMode	3.0.0.0	Mic...
Cmdlet	Set-TpmOwnerAuth	2.0.0.0	Tru...
Cmdlet	Set-TraceSource	3.1.0.0	Mic...
Cmdlet	Set-Variable	3.1.0.0	Mic...
Cmdlet	Set-WinAcceptLanguageFromLanguageListOptOut	2.0.0.0	Int...
Cmdlet	Set-WinCultureFromLanguageListOptOut	2.0.0.0	Int...
Cmdlet	Set-WinDefaultInputMethodOverride	2.0.0.0	Int...
Cmdlet	Set-WindowsEdition	3.0	Dism
Cmdlet	Set-WindowsProductKey	3.0	Dism
Cmdlet	Set-WindowsSearchSetting	1.0.0.0	Win...
Cmdlet	Set-WinHomeLocation	2.0.0.0	Int...
Cmdlet	Set-WinLanguageBarOption	2.0.0.0	Int...
Cmdlet	Set-WinSystemLocale	2.0.0.0	Int...
Cmdlet	Set-WinUILanguageOverride	2.0.0.0	Int...
Cmdlet	Set-WinUserLanguageList	2.0.0.0	Int...
Cmdlet	Set-WmiInstance	3.1.0.0	Mic...
Cmdlet	Set-WSManInstance	3.0.0.0	Mic...
Cmdlet	Set-WSManQuickConfig	3.0.0.0	Mic...

8. Use the *gcm* alias and specify the *-Noun* parameter. Use *o** for the noun. This is shown here.

```
gcm -noun o*
```

The previous command returns all the cmdlets that contain a noun that begins with the letter *o*. This result is as follows.

```
CommandType     Name                                              Version   Source
-----------     ----                                              -------   ------
Function        Add-OdbcDsn                                       1.0.0.0   Wdac
Function        Disable-OdbcPerfCounter                           1.0.0.0   Wdac
Function        Enable-OdbcPerfCounter                            1.0.0.0   Wdac
Function        Export-ODataEndpointProxy                         1.0       Mic...
Function        Get-OdbcDriver                                    1.0.0.0   Wdac
Function        Get-OdbcDsn                                       1.0.0.0   Wdac
Function        Get-OdbcPerfCounter                               1.0.0.0   Wdac
Function        Get-OffloadDataTransferSetting                    2.0.0.0   Sto...
Function        Remove-OdbcDsn                                    1.0.0.0   Wdac
Function        Set-OdbcDriver                                    1.0.0.0   Wdac
Function        Set-OdbcDsn                                       1.0.0.0   Wdac
Cmdlet          Compare-Object                                    3.1.0.0   Mic...
Cmdlet          ForEach-Object                                    3.0.0.0   Mic...
Cmdlet          Group-Object                                      3.1.0.0   Mic...
Cmdlet          Measure-Object                                    3.1.0.0   Mic...
Cmdlet          New-Object                                        3.1.0.0   Mic...
Cmdlet          Register-ObjectEvent                              3.1.0.0   Mic...
Cmdlet          Select-Object                                     3.1.0.0   Mic...
Cmdlet          Sort-Object                                       3.1.0.0   Mic...
Cmdlet          Tee-Object                                        3.1.0.0   Mic...
Cmdlet          Where-Object                                      3.0.0.0   Mic...
Cmdlet          Write-Output                                      3.1.0.0   Mic...
```

9. Retrieve only the syntax of the *Get-Command* cmdlet by specifying the *-Syntax* switch parameter. Use the *gcm* alias to do this, as shown here.

```
gcm -syntax Get-Command
```

The syntax of the *Get-Command* cmdlet is returned by the previous command. The output is as follows.

```
Get-Command [[-ArgumentList] <Object[]>] [-Verb <string[]>] [-Noun <string[]>]
[-Module <string[]>] [-FullyQualifiedModule <ModuleSpecification[]>] [-TotalCount
<int>] [-Syntax] [-ShowCommandInfo] [-All] [-ListImported] [-ParameterName
<string[]>] [-ParameterType <PSTypeName[]>] [<CommonParameters>]

Get-Command [[-Name] <string[]>] [[-ArgumentList] <Object[]>] [-Module <string[]>]
[-FullyQualifiedModule <ModuleSpecification[]>] [-CommandType <CommandTypes>]
[-TotalCount <int>] [-Syntax] [-ShowCommandInfo] [-All] [-ListImported]
[-ParameterName <string[]>] [-ParameterType <PSTypeName[]>] [<CommonParameters>]
```

10. Try to use only aliases to repeat the *Get-Command* syntax command to retrieve the syntax of the *Get-Command* cmdlet. This is shown here.

```
gcm -syntax gcm
```

The result of this command is not the nice syntax description of the previous command. The rather disappointing result is as follows.

Get-Command

This concludes the procedure for finding commands by using the *Get-Command* cmdlet.

> ## Quick check
>
> **Q.** To retrieve a definition of the *Get-Command* cmdlet by using dotted notation, what command would you use?
>
> **A.** *(gcm Get-Command).definition*

Using the *Get-Member* cmdlet

The *Get-Member* cmdlet retrieves information about the members of objects. Although this might not seem very exciting, remember that because everything returned from a cmdlet is an object, you can use the *Get-Member* cmdlet to examine the methods and properties of objects. When the *Get-Member* cmdlet is used with *Get-ChildItem* on the file system, it returns a listing of all the methods and properties that are available to work with the *DirectoryInfo* and *FileInfo* objects.

> ## Objects, properties, and methods
>
> One of the fundamental features of Windows PowerShell is that cmdlets return objects. An object gives you the ability to either describe something or do something. If you are not going to describe or do something, there is no reason to create the object. Depending on the circumstances, you might be more interested in the methods or the properties. As an example, let's consider rental cars. I used to travel a great deal when I was a consultant at Microsoft, and I often needed to obtain a rental car.
>
> To put this into programming terms, when I got to the airport, I would go to the rental car counter, and I would use the *New-Object* cmdlet to create a *rentalCAR* object. When I used this cmdlet, I was only interested in the methods available from the *rentalCAR* object. I needed to use the *DriveDowntheRoad* method, the *StopAtaRedLight* method, and perhaps the *PlayNiceMusic* method. I was not, however, interested in the properties of the *rentalCAR* object.
>
> At home, I have a cute little sports car. It has exactly the same methods as the *rentalCAR* object, but I created the *sportsCAR* object primarily because of its properties. It is green and has alloy rims, a convertible top, and a 3.5-liter engine. Interestingly enough, it has exactly the same methods as the *rentalCAR* object. It also has the *DriveDowntheRoad* method, the *StopAtaRedLight* method, and the *PlayNiceMusic* method, but the deciding factor in creating the *sportsCAR* object was the properties, not the methods.

Using the *Get-Member* cmdlet to examine properties and methods

In a Windows PowerShell prompt, enter the *Get-ChildItem* cmdlet followed by the path to a folder, and pipeline it to the *Get-Member* cmdlet. Here's an example.

```
Get-ChildItem C:\ | Get-Member
```

Using the *Get-Member* cmdlet

1. Open Windows PowerShell by choosing Start | Run | PowerShell. The Windows PowerShell prompt opens by default at the root of your user folder.

2. Use an alias to refer to the *Get-Alias* cmdlet. To find the correct alias, use the *Get-Alias* cmdlet as follows.

   ```
   Get-Alias g*
   ```

3. After you have retrieved the alias for the *Get-Alias* cmdlet, use it to find the alias for the *Get-Member* cmdlet. One way to do this is to use the following command, using *gal* in place of the *Get-Alias* name you used in the previous command.

   ```
   gal g*
   ```

   The listing of aliases defined that begin with the letter *g* appears as a result of the previous command. The output is shown here.

```
CommandType     Name                                       Version   Source
-----------     ----                                       -------   ------
Alias           gal -> Get-Alias
Alias           gbp -> Get-PSBreakpoint
Alias           gc -> Get-Content
Alias           gcb -> Get-Clipboard                        3.1.0.0   Mic...
Alias           gci -> Get-ChildItem
Alias           gcm -> Get-Command
Alias           gcs -> Get-PSCallStack
Alias           gdr -> Get-PSDrive
Alias           ghy -> Get-History
Alias           gi -> Get-Item
Alias           gjb -> Get-Job
Alias           gl -> Get-Location
Alias           gm -> Get-Member
Alias           gmo -> Get-Module
Alias           gp -> Get-ItemProperty
Alias           gps -> Get-Process
Alias           gpv -> Get-ItemPropertyValue
Alias           group -> Group-Object
Alias           gsn -> Get-PSSession
Alias           gsnp -> Get-PSSnapin
Alias           gsv -> Get-Service
Alias           gu -> Get-Unique
Alias           gv -> Get-Variable
Alias           gwmi -> Get-WmiObject
```

4. Use the *gal* alias to obtain a listing of all aliases that begin with the letter *g*. Pipeline the results to the *Sort-Object* cmdlet, and sort on the property attribute called *definition*. This is shown here.

```
gal g* | Sort-Object -property definition
```

The listings of cmdlets that begin with the letter *g* are now sorted, and the results of the command are as follows.

CommandType	Name	Version	Source
Alias	gal -> Get-Alias		
Alias	gci -> Get-ChildItem		
Alias	gcb -> Get-Clipboard	3.1.0.0	Mic...
Alias	gcm -> Get-Command		
Alias	gc -> Get-Content		
Alias	ghy -> Get-History		
Alias	gi -> Get-Item		
Alias	gp -> Get-ItemProperty		
Alias	gpv -> Get-ItemPropertyValue		
Alias	gjb -> Get-Job		
Alias	gl -> Get-Location		
Alias	gm -> Get-Member		
Alias	gmo -> Get-Module		
Alias	gps -> Get-Process		
Alias	gbp -> Get-PSBreakpoint		
Alias	gcs -> Get-PSCallStack		
Alias	gdr -> Get-PSDrive		
Alias	gsn -> Get-PSSession		
Alias	gsnp -> Get-PSSnapin		
Alias	gsv -> Get-Service		
Alias	gu -> Get-Unique		
Alias	gv -> Get-Variable		
Alias	gwmi -> Get-WmiObject		
Alias	group -> Group-Object		

5. A more economical procedure for obtaining an alias for a particular cmdlet is to use the *-Definition* parameter of the Get-Alias cmdlet, as shown here.

```
gal -definition Get-ChildItem
```

6. Use the alias for the *Get-ChildItem* cmdlet, and pipeline the output to the alias for the *Get-Member* cmdlet. This is shown here.

```
gci | gm
```

7. To display only the properties that are available for the *Get-ChildItem* cmdlet, using the *-Force* switch parameter to include hidden files and folders, use the *-MemberType* parameter and supply a value of *property*. Use tab completion this time, rather than the *gci | gm* alias. This is shown here.

```
Get-ChildItem -Force | Get-Member -membertype property
```

The output from this command is shown here.

```
    TypeName: System.IO.DirectoryInfo

Name                 MemberType Definition
----                 ---------- ----------
Attributes           Property   System.IO.FileAttributes Attributes {get;set;}
CreationTime         Property   datetime CreationTime {get;set;}
CreationTimeUtc      Property   datetime CreationTimeUtc {get;set;}
Exists               Property   bool Exists {get;}
Extension            Property   string Extension {get;}
FullName             Property   string FullName {get;}
LastAccessTime       Property   datetime LastAccessTime {get;set;}
LastAccessTimeUtc    Property   datetime LastAccessTimeUtc {get;set;}
LastWriteTime        Property   datetime LastWriteTime {get;set;}
LastWriteTimeUtc     Property   datetime LastWriteTimeUtc {get;set;}
Name                 Property   string Name {get;}
Parent               Property   System.IO.DirectoryInfo Parent {get;}
Root                 Property   System.IO.DirectoryInfo Root {get;}


    TypeName: System.IO.FileInfo

Name                 MemberType Definition
----                 ---------- ----------
Attributes           Property   System.IO.FileAttributes Attributes {get;set;}
CreationTime         Property   datetime CreationTime {get;set;}
CreationTimeUtc      Property   datetime CreationTimeUtc {get;set;}
Directory            Property   System.IO.DirectoryInfo Directory {get;}
DirectoryName        Property   string DirectoryName {get;}
Exists               Property   bool Exists {get;}
Extension            Property   string Extension {get;}
FullName             Property   string FullName {get;}
IsReadOnly           Property   bool IsReadOnly {get;set;}
LastAccessTime       Property   datetime LastAccessTime {get;set;}
LastAccessTimeUtc    Property   datetime LastAccessTimeUtc {get;set;}
LastWriteTime        Property   datetime LastWriteTime {get;set;}
LastWriteTimeUtc     Property   datetime LastWriteTimeUtc {get;set;}
Length               Property   long Length {get;}
Name                 Property   string Name {get;}
```

8. Use the *-MemberType* parameter of the *Get-Member* cmdlet to view the methods available from the object returned by the *Get-ChildItem* cmdlet. To do this, supply a value of *method* to the *-MemberType* parameter, as follows.

```
Get-ChildItem | Get-Member -membertype method
```

9. The output from the previous list returns all the methods defined for the *Get-ChildItem* cmdlet. This output is shown here.

```
TypeName: System.IO.DirectoryInfo

Name                        MemberType  Definition
----                        ----------  ----------
Create                      Method      void Create(), void Create(System.Security.A...
CreateObjRef                Method      System.Runtime.Remoting.ObjRef CreateObjRef(...
CreateSubdirectory          Method      System.IO.DirectoryInfo CreateSubdirectory(s...
Delete                      Method      void Delete(), void Delete(bool recursive)
EnumerateDirectories        Method      System.Collections.Generic.IEnumerable[Syste...
EnumerateFiles              Method      System.Collections.Generic.IEnumerable[Syste...
EnumerateFileSystemInfos    Method      System.Collections.Generic.IEnumerable[Syste...
Equals                      Method      bool Equals(System.Object obj)
GetAccessControl            Method      System.Security.AccessControl.DirectorySecur...
GetDirectories              Method      System.IO.DirectoryInfo[] GetDirectories(), ...
GetFiles                    Method      System.IO.FileInfo[] GetFiles(string searchP...
GetFileSystemInfos          Method      System.IO.FileSystemInfo[] GetFileSystemInfo...
GetHashCode                 Method      int GetHashCode()
GetLifetimeService          Method      System.Object GetLifetimeService()
GetObjectData               Method      void GetObjectData(System.Runtime.Serializat...
GetType                     Method      type GetType()
InitializeLifetimeService   Method      System.Object InitializeLifetimeService()
MoveTo                      Method      void MoveTo(string destDirName)
Refresh                     Method      void Refresh()
SetAccessControl            Method      void SetAccessControl(System.Security.Access...
ToString                    Method      string ToString()
```

10. Use the Up Arrow key in the Windows PowerShell console to retrieve the previous *Get-ChildItem | Get-Member -MemberType method* command, and change the value *method* to *m** to use a wildcard to retrieve the methods. The output will be exactly the same as the previous listing of members, because the only member type beginning with the letter *m* on the *Get-ChildItem* cmdlet is the *MemberType* method. The command is as follows.

```
Get-ChildItem | Get-Member -membertype m*
```

11. Use the *-InputObject* parameter to the *Get-Member* cmdlet to retrieve member definitions of each property or method in the list. The command to do this is as follows.

```
Get-Member -inputobject Get-ChildItem
```

The output from the previous command is shown here.

```
TypeName: System.String

Name        MemberType  Definition
----        ----------  ----------
Clone       Method      System.Object Clone(), System.Object IClon...
CompareTo   Method      int CompareTo(System.Object value), int Co...
Contains    Method      bool Contains(string value)
CopyTo      Method      void CopyTo(int sourceIndex, char[] destin...
EndsWith    Method      bool EndsWith(string value), bool EndsWith...
Equals      Method      bool Equals(System.Object obj), bool Equal...
```

```
GetEnumerator        Method                  System.CharEnumerator GetEnumerator(), Sys...
GetHashCode          Method                  int GetHashCode()
GetType              Method                  type GetType()
GetTypeCode          Method                  System.TypeCode GetTypeCode(), System.Type...
IndexOf              Method                  int IndexOf(char value), int IndexOf(char ...
IndexOfAny           Method                  int IndexOfAny(char[] anyOf), int IndexOfA...
Insert               Method                  string Insert(int startIndex, string value)
IsNormalized         Method                  bool IsNormalized(), bool IsNormalized(Sys...
LastIndexOf          Method                  int LastIndexOf(char value), int LastIndex...
LastIndexOfAny       Method                  int LastIndexOfAny(char[] anyOf), int Last...
Normalize            Method                  string Normalize(), string Normalize(Syste...
PadLeft              Method                  string PadLeft(int totalWidth), string Pad...
PadRight             Method                  string PadRight(int totalWidth), string Pa...
Remove               Method                  string Remove(int startIndex, int count), ...
Replace              Method                  string Replace(char oldChar, char newChar)...
Split                Method                  string[] Split(Params char[] separator), s...
StartsWith           Method                  bool StartsWith(string value), bool Starts...
Substring            Method                  string Substring(int startIndex), string S...
ToBoolean            Method                  bool IConvertible.ToBoolean(System.IFormat...
ToByte               Method                  byte IConvertible.ToByte(System.IFormatPro...
ToChar               Method                  char IConvertible.ToChar(System.IFormatPro...
ToCharArray          Method                  char[] ToCharArray(), char[] ToCharArray(i...
ToDateTime           Method                  datetime IConvertible.ToDateTime(System.IF...
ToDecimal            Method                  decimal IConvertible.ToDecimal(System.IFor...
ToDouble             Method                  double IConvertible.ToDouble(System.IForma...
ToInt16              Method                  int16 IConvertible.ToInt16(System.IFormatP...
ToInt32              Method                  int IConvertible.ToInt32(System.IFormatPro...
ToInt64              Method                  long IConvertible.ToInt64(System.IFormatPr...
ToLower              Method                  string ToLower(), string ToLower(culturein...
ToLowerInvariant     Method                  string ToLowerInvariant()
ToSByte              Method                  sbyte IConvertible.ToSByte(System.IFormatP...
ToSingle             Method                  float IConvertible.ToSingle(System.IFormat...
ToString             Method                  string ToString(), string ToString(System....
ToType               Method                  System.Object IConvertible.ToType(type con...
ToUInt16             Method                  uint16 IConvertible.ToUInt16(System.IForma...
ToUInt32             Method                  uint32 IConvertible.ToUInt32(System.IForma...
ToUInt64             Method                  uint64 IConvertible.ToUInt64(System.IForma...
ToUpper              Method                  string ToUpper(), string ToUpper(culturein...
ToUpperInvariant     Method                  string ToUpperInvariant()
Trim                 Method                  string Trim(Params char[] trimChars), stri...
TrimEnd              Method                  string TrimEnd(Params char[] trimChars)
TrimStart            Method                  string TrimStart(Params char[] trimChars)
Chars                ParameterizedProperty   char Chars(int index) {get;}
Length               Property                int Length {get;}
```

This concludes the procedure for using the *Get-Member* cmdlet.

Quick check

Q. To retrieve a listing of aliases beginning with the letter *g* that is sorted on the *definition* property, what command would you use?

A. *gal g* | Sort-Object -property definition*

Using the *New-Object* cmdlet

The use of objects in Windows PowerShell provides many exciting opportunities to do things that are not built into Windows PowerShell. You might recall from using Microsoft Visual Basic Scripting Edition (VBScript) that there is an object called the *wshShell* object. If you are not familiar with this object, see Figure 2-7, which shows a drawing of the object model.

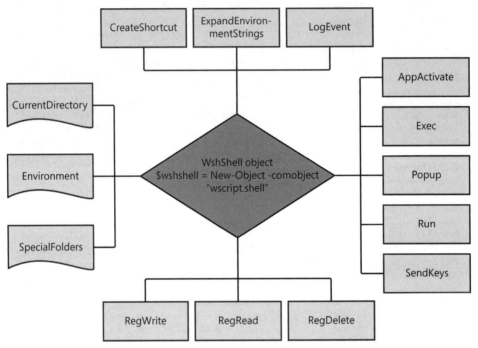

FIGURE 2-7 The VBScript *wshShell* object contributes many easy-to-use methods and properties for the network administrator.

Creating and using the *wshShell* object

To create a new instance of the *wshShell* object, use the *New-Object* cmdlet while specifying the *-ComObject* parameter and supplying the program ID of *wscript.shell*. Hold the object created in a variable. Here's an example.

```
$wshShell = New-Object -comobject "wscript.shell"
```

After the object has been created and stored in a variable, you can directly use any of the methods that are provided by the object. This is shown in the two lines of code that follow.

```
$wshShell = New-Object -comobject "wscript.shell"
$wshShell.run("calc.exe")
```

In this code, you use the *New-Object* cmdlet to create an instance of the *wshShell* object. You then use the *run* method to launch Calculator. After the object is created and stored in the variable, you can use tab completion to suggest the names of the methods contained in the object. This is shown in Figure 2-8.

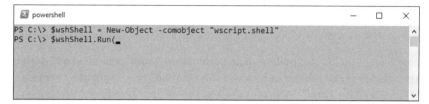

FIGURE 2-8 Tab completion enumerates methods provided by the object.

Creating the *wshShell* object

1. Open Windows PowerShell by choosing Start | Run | PowerShell. The Windows PowerShell prompt opens by default at the root of your user folder.

2. Create an instance of the *wshShell* object by using the *New-Object* cmdlet. Supply the *-ComObject* parameter to the cmdlet, and specify the program ID for the *wshShell* object, which is *wscript.shell*. Assign the result of the *New-Object* cmdlet to the variable *$wshShell*. The code to do this is as follows.

```
$wshShell = New-Object -comobject "wscript.shell"
```

3. Launch an instance of Calculator by using the *run* method from the *wshShell* object. Use tab completion to avoid having to type the entire name of the method. To use the method, begin the line with the variable you used to hold the *wshShell* object, followed by a period and the name of the method. Then supply the name of the program to run inside parentheses and quotes, as shown here.

```
$wshShell.run("Calc.exe")
```

4. Use the *ExpandEnvironmentStrings* method to print out the path to the Windows directory, which is stored in an environment variable called *%windir%*. The tab-completion feature of Windows PowerShell is useful for this method name. The environment variable must be enclosed in quotation marks, as shown here.

```
$wshShell.ExpandEnvironmentStrings("%windir%")
```

This command reveals the full path to the Windows directory on your machine. On my computer, the output looks like the following.

```
C:\WINDOWS
```

Using the *Show-Command* cmdlet

The *Show-Command* cmdlet displays a graphical command picker that you can use to select cmdlets from a list. At first glance, the *Show-Command* cmdlet might appear to be a graphical version of the *Get-Command* cmdlet, but it is actually much more. The first indication of this is that it blocks the Windows PowerShell console—that is, control to the Windows PowerShell console does not return until you have either selected a command from the picker or canceled the operation.

When you run the *Show-Command* cmdlet with no parameters, a window 600 pixels high and 300 pixels wide appears. You can control the size of the window by using the *-Height* and *-Width* parameters. The following command creates a command window 500 pixels high and 350 pixels wide.

```
Show-Command -Height 500 -Width 350
```

The command window created by the this command is shown in Figure 2-9.

FIGURE 2-9 The *Show-Command* cmdlet displays all commands from all modules by default.

To retrieve a specific command, supply the name of a specific cmdlet when calling the *Show-Command* cmdlet. This technique is shown here.

```
Show-Command -Height 500 -Width 350 -Name Get-Process
```

When the command dialog box appears, use the check boxes to enable switch parameters, and the text boxes to supply values for other parameters. This technique is shown in Figure 2-10.

FIGURE 2-10 Use the check boxes to add switch parameters to a command and the text boxes to add values for parameters in the command dialog box.

When you have created the command you want to use, you can either copy the command to the Clipboard or run the command. If, for example, you select the FileVersionInfo check box and enter the name of a process, the appropriate parameters are added to the command being created in the background as you make the changes. If you choose to run the command, the Windows PowerShell console displays both the created command and the output from the command. This is shown in Figure 2-11.

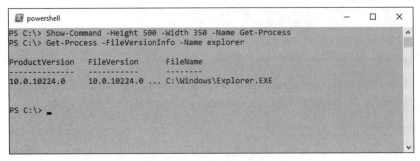

FIGURE 2-11 Both the created command and the output from that command return to the Windows PowerShell console when you are using the *Show-Command* cmdlet.

Windows PowerShell cmdlet naming helps you learn

One of the great things about Windows PowerShell is the verb-noun naming convention. In Windows PowerShell, the verbs indicate an action to perform, such as *set* to make a change or *get* to retrieve a value. The noun indicates the item with which to work, such as a process or a service. By mastering the verb-noun naming convention, you can quickly hypothesize what a prospective command might be called. For example, if you need to obtain information about a process, and you know that Windows PowerShell uses the verb *get* to retrieve information, you can surmise that the command might be called *Get-Process*. To obtain information about services, you could try *Get-Service*, and again you would be correct.

Note When guessing Windows PowerShell cmdlet names, always try the singular form first. Windows PowerShell convention uses the singular form of nouns. It is not a design requirement, but it is a strong preference. For example, the cmdlets are named *Get-Service* and *Get-Process*, not *Get-Service*s and *Get-Process*es.

To view the list of approved verbs, use the *Get-Verb* cmdlet.

```
Get-Verb
```

There are 98 approved verbs in Windows PowerShell 5.0. This number increases the 96 approved verbs from Windows PowerShell 2.0 by only two new verbs. The two additional verbs are *use* and *unprotect* and were introduced in Windows PowerShell 3.0. This means that the number of approved verbs has remained stable for three versions now. This is shown in the command that follows, where the *Measure-Object* cmdlet returns the count of the different verbs.

```
PS C:\> (Get-Verb | Measure-Object).count
98
```

But you do not need to add the *Measure-Object* cmdlet to the previous command, because the *Get-Verb* cmdlet returns an array. Array objects always contain a *count* property. Therefore, an easier form of the command is shown here.

```
PS C:\> (Get-verb).count
98
```

Windows PowerShell verb grouping

Though learning nearly 100 different verbs might be difficult, the Windows PowerShell team grouped the verbs together to make them easier to learn. For example, analyzing the common verbs reveals a pattern. The common verbs appear here.

```
PS C:\> Get-Verb | where group -match 'common' | Format-Wide verb -auto
Add       Clear     Close     Copy      Enter     Exit      Find      Format    Get
Hide      Join      Lock      Move      New       Open      Optimize  Pop       Push
Redo      Remove    Rename    Reset     Resize    Search    Select    Set       Show
Skip      Split     Step      Switch    Undo      Unlock    Watch
```

The pattern to the verbs emerges when you analyze them: *Add/Remove, Enter/Exit, Get/Set, Select/ Skip, Lock/Unlock, Push/Pop,* and so on. By learning the pattern of opposite verbs, you quickly gain a handle on the Windows PowerShell naming convention. Not every verb has an opposite partner, but there are enough that it makes sense to look for them.

By using the Windows PowerShell verb grouping, you can determine where to focus your efforts. The Windows PowerShell team separated the verbs into seven different groups based on common IT tasks, such as working with data and performing diagnostics. The following command lists the Windows PowerShell verb grouping.

```
PS C:\> Get-Verb | select group -Unique
Group
-----
Common
Data
Lifecycle
Diagnostic
Communications
Security
Other
```

Windows PowerShell verb distribution

Another way to get a better handle on the Windows PowerShell cmdlets is to analyze the verb distribution. Though there are nearly 100 different approved verbs (and a variety of unapproved ones), you'll typically use only a fraction of them often in a standard Windows PowerShell installation, and some not at all. If you use the *Group-Object* cmdlet (which has an alias of *group*) and the *Sort-Object* cmdlet (which has an alias of *sort*), the distribution of the cmdlets quickly becomes evident. The following command shows the verb distribution.

```
Get-Command -CommandType cmdlet | group verb | sort count -Descending
```

Note The exact number of Windows PowerShell cmdlets and the exact distribution of Windows PowerShell cmdlet verbs and nouns depend on the version of the operating system used, in addition to which features are enabled on the operating system. In addition, the installation of certain programs and applications adds additional Windows PowerShell cmdlets. Therefore, when you are following along with this section, your numbers probably will not exactly match what appears here. This is fine, and does not indicate a problem with the command or your installation.

Figure 2-12 shows the command and the associated output.

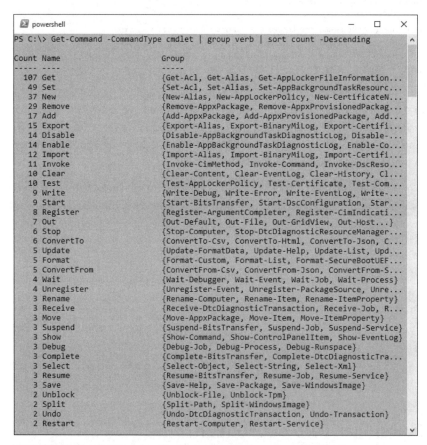

```
powershell                                                    —  □  ×
PS C:\> Get-Command -CommandType cmdlet | group verb | sort count -Descending

Count Name                Group
----- ----                -----
  107 Get                 {Get-Acl, Get-Alias, Get-AppLockerFileInformation...
   49 Set                 {Set-Acl, Set-Alias, Set-AppBackgroundTaskResourc...
   37 New                 {New-Alias, New-AppLockerPolicy, New-CertificateN...
   29 Remove              {Remove-AppxPackage, Remove-AppxProvisionedPackag...
   17 Add                 {Add-AppxPackage, Add-AppxProvisionedPackage, Add...
   15 Export              {Export-Alias, Export-BinaryMiLog, Export-Certifi...
   14 Disable             {Disable-AppBackgroundTaskDiagnosticLog, Disable-...
   14 Enable              {Enable-AppBackgroundTaskDiagnosticLog, Enable-Co...
   12 Import              {Import-Alias, Import-BinaryMiLog, Import-Certifi...
   11 Invoke              {Invoke-CimMethod, Invoke-Command, Invoke-DscReso...
   10 Clear               {Clear-Content, Clear-EventLog, Clear-History, Cl...
   10 Test                {Test-AppLockerPolicy, Test-Certificate, Test-Com...
    9 Write               {Write-Debug, Write-Error, Write-EventLog, Write-...
    9 Start               {Start-BitsTransfer, Start-DscConfiguration, Star...
    8 Register            {Register-ArgumentCompleter, Register-CimIndicati...
    7 Out                 {Out-Default, Out-File, Out-GridView, Out-Host...}
    6 Stop                {Stop-Computer, Stop-DtcDiagnosticResourceManager...
    6 ConvertTo           {ConvertTo-Csv, ConvertTo-Html, ConvertTo-Json, C...
    5 Update              {Update-FormatData, Update-Help, Update-List, Upd...
    5 Format              {Format-Custom, Format-List, Format-SecureBootUEF...
    5 ConvertFrom         {ConvertFrom-Csv, ConvertFrom-Json, ConvertFrom-S...
    4 Wait                {Wait-Debugger, Wait-Event, Wait-Job, Wait-Process}
    4 Unregister          {Unregister-Event, Unregister-PackageSource, Unre...
    3 Rename              {Rename-Computer, Rename-Item, Rename-ItemProperty}
    3 Receive             {Receive-DtcDiagnosticTransaction, Receive-Job, R...
    3 Move                {Move-AppxPackage, Move-Item, Move-ItemProperty}
    3 Suspend             {Suspend-BitsTransfer, Suspend-Job, Suspend-Service}
    3 Show                {Show-Command, Show-ControlPanelItem, Show-EventLog}
    3 Debug               {Debug-Job, Debug-Process, Debug-Runspace}
    3 Complete            {Complete-BitsTransfer, Complete-DtcDiagnosticTra...
    3 Select              {Select-Object, Select-String, Select-Xml}
    3 Resume              {Resume-BitsTransfer, Resume-Job, Resume-Service}
    3 Save                {Save-Help, Save-Package, Save-WindowsImage}
    2 Unblock             {Unblock-File, Unblock-Tpm}
    2 Split               {Split-Path, Split-WindowsImage}
    2 Undo                {Undo-DtcDiagnosticTransaction, Undo-Transaction}
    2 Restart             {Restart-Computer, Restart-Service}
```

FIGURE 2-12 Use *Get-Command* to display the Windows PowerShell verbs.

The output shown in Figure 2-12 makes it clear that most cmdlets only use a few of the verbs. For instance, of 484 cmdlets on my particular machine, 305 of the cmdlets use 1 of only 10 different verbs. This is shown here.

```
PS C:\> (Get-Command -CommandType cmdlet | measure).count
484
PS C:\> $count = 0 ; Get-Command -CommandType Cmdlet | Group verb | sort count -Descending |
select -First 10 | % {$count += $_.count ; $count }
107
156
193
222
239
254
268
282
294
305
```

Therefore, all you need to do is master the 10 different verbs listed earlier and you will have a good handle on more than half of the cmdlets that are included with Windows PowerShell 5.0.

Creating a Windows PowerShell profile

As you create various aliases and functions, you might decide that you like a particular keystroke combination and wish you could use your definition without always having to create it each time you run Windows PowerShell.

> **Tip** I recommend reviewing the listing of all the aliases defined within Windows PowerShell before creating very many new aliases. The reason is that it will be easy, early on, to create duplicate settings (with slight variations).

Of course, you could create your own script that would perform your configuration if you remember to run it; however, what if you want to have a more standardized method of working with your profile? To do this, you need to create a custom profile that will hold your settings. The really useful feature of creating a Windows PowerShell profile is that after the profile is created, it loads automatically when Windows PowerShell is launched.

> **Note** A Windows PowerShell profile is a Windows PowerShell script that runs each time Windows PowerShell starts. Windows PowerShell does not enable script support by default. In a network situation, the Windows PowerShell script execution policy might be determined by your network administrator via Group Policy. In a workgroup, or at home, the execution policy is not determined via Group Policy. For information about enabling Windows PowerShell script execution, see Chapter 5, "Using Windows PowerShell scripts."

The steps for creating a Windows PowerShell profile are listed next.

Creating a personal Windows PowerShell profile

1. In a Windows PowerShell console, check your script execution policy.

   ```
   Get-ExecutionPolicy
   ```

2. If the script execution policy is *restricted*, change it to *remotesigned*, but only for the current user.

   ```
   Set-ExecutionPolicy -Scope currentuser -ExecutionPolicy remotesigned
   ```

3. Review the description about Windows PowerShell execution policies, and enter **Y** to agree to make the change.

4. In a Windows PowerShell prompt, determine whether a profile exists by using the following command. (By default, the Windows PowerShell profile does not exist.)

   ```
   Test-Path $profile
   ```

5. If *Test-Path* returns *false*, create a new profile file by using the following command.

   ```
   New-Item -path $profile -itemtype file -force
   ```

6. Open the profile file in the Windows PowerShell ISE by using the following command.

   ```
   ise $profile
   ```

7. Create an alias in the profile named *gh* that resolves to the *Get-Help* cmdlet. This command appears here.

   ```
   Set-Alias gh Get-Help
   ```

8. Create a function that edits your Windows PowerShell console profile. This function appears here.

   ```
   Function Set-Profile
   {
    Ise $profile
   }
   ```

9. Start the Windows PowerShell *Transcript* command via the Windows PowerShell profile. To do this, add the *Start-Transcript* cmdlet as it appears here. (The *Start-Transcript* cmdlet creates a record of all Windows PowerShell commands, and the output from those commands.)

   ```
   Start-Transcript
   ```

10. Save the modifications to the Windows PowerShell console profile by clicking the Save icon on the toolbar, or by choosing Save from the File menu.

11. Close the Windows PowerShell ISE and close the Windows PowerShell console.

12. Open the Windows PowerShell console. You should now get the output in the console from starting the Windows PowerShell transcript utility.

13. Test the newly created *gh* alias.

14. Open the profile in the Windows PowerShell ISE by using the newly created *Set-Profile* function.

15. Review the Windows PowerShell profile and close the Windows PowerShell ISE.

This concludes the exercise on creating a Windows PowerShell profile.

Working with cmdlets: Step-by-step exercises

In the following exercise, you'll explore the use of the *Get-ChildItem* and *Get-Member* cmdlets in Windows PowerShell. You'll find that it is easy to use these cmdlets to automate routine administrative tasks. You'll also continue to experiment with the pipelining feature of Windows PowerShell.

Working with the *Get-ChildItem* and *Get-Member* cmdlets

1. Open the Windows PowerShell console.

2. Use the *Get-Alias* cmdlet to retrieve a listing of all the aliases defined on the computer for *Get-ChildItem*. As shown here, use the *-Definition* parameter with the value of *Get-ChildItem* to display the aliases for *Get-ChildItem*.

```
gal –definition Get-ChildItem
```

The results from the previous command show three aliases defined for the *Get-ChildItem* cmdlet.

```
CommandType     Name                            Version    Source
-----------     ----                            -------    ------
Alias           dir -> Get-ChildItem
Alias           gci -> Get-ChildItem
Alias           ls -> Get-ChildItem
```

3. Using the *gci* alias for the *Get-ChildItem* cmdlet, obtain a listing of files and folders contained in the root directory. Type **gci** at the prompt.

4. To identify large files more quickly, pipeline the output to a *Where-Object* cmdlet, and specify the *-gt* comparison operator with a value of 1000 to evaluate the *length* property. This is shown here.

```
gci | Where length –gt 1000
```

5. To remove the data cluttering your Windows PowerShell window, use *cls* to clear the screen.

6. Use the *Get-Alias* cmdlet to resolve the cmdlet to which the *cls* alias points. You can use the *gal* alias to avoid typing *Get-Alias* if you want. This is shown here.

```
gal cls
```

7. Use the *Get-Alias* cmdlet to resolve the cmdlet to which the *mred* alias points. This is shown here.

```
gal mred
```

It is likely that no *mred* alias is defined on your machine. In this case, you will get the following error message.

```
gal : This command cannot find a matching alias because an alias with the name
'mred' does not exist.
At line:1 char:1
+ gal mred
+ ~~~~~~~~
    + CategoryInfo          : ObjectNotFound: (mred:String) [Get-Alias],
    ItemNotFoundException
    + FullyQualifiedErrorId :
ItemNotFoundException,Microsoft.PowerShell.Commands.GetAliasCommand
```

8. Use the *Clear-Host* cmdlet to clear the screen. This is shown here.

```
clear-host
```

9. Use the *Get-Member* cmdlet to retrieve a list of properties and methods from the *Get-ChildItem* cmdlet. This is shown here.

```
Get-ChildItem | Get-Member -membertype property
```

10. The output from the preceding command is shown following. Examine the output, and iden-tify a property that could be used with a *Where-Object* cmdlet to find the date when files were modified.

```
   TypeName: System.IO.DirectoryInfo

Name                 MemberType Definition
----                 ---------- ----------
Attributes           Property   System.IO.FileAttributes Attributes {get;set;}
CreationTime         Property   datetime CreationTime {get;set;}
CreationTimeUtc      Property   datetime CreationTimeUtc {get;set;}
Exists               Property   bool Exists {get;}
Extension            Property   string Extension {get;}
FullName             Property   string FullName {get;}
LastAccessTime       Property   datetime LastAccessTime {get;set;}
LastAccessTimeUtc    Property   datetime LastAccessTimeUtc {get;set;}
LastWriteTime        Property   datetime LastWriteTime {get;set;}
LastWriteTimeUtc     Property   datetime LastWriteTimeUtc {get;set;}
Name                 Property   string Name {get;}
Parent               Property   System.IO.DirectoryInfo Parent {get;}
Root                 Property   System.IO.DirectoryInfo Root {get;}
```

11. Use the *Where-Object* cmdlet and include the *LastWriteTime* property, as follows.

```
Get-ChildItem | Where LastWriteTime
```

12. Use the Up Arrow key in the Windows PowerShell console and bring the previous command back up on the command line. Now specify the *-gt* comparison operator, and choose a recent date from your previous list of files, so you can ensure that the query will return a result. My command looks like the following.

```
Get-ChildItem | Where LastWriteTime -gt "12/25/2014"
```

13. Use the Up Arrow key and retrieve the previous command. Now direct the *Get-ChildItem* cmdlet to a specific folder on your hard drive, such as C:\fso, which might have been created in the step-by-step exercise in Chapter 1. You can, of course, use any folder that exists on your machine. This command will look like the following.

```
Get-ChildItem "C:\fso"| Where LastWriteTime -gt "12/25/2014"
```

14. Again, use the Up Arrow key to retrieve the previous command. Add the *-Recurse* switch parameter to the *Get-ChildItem* cmdlet. If your previous folder was not nested, then you might want to change to a different folder. You can, of course, use your Windows folder, which is rather deeply nested. I used the Windows folder, and the command is shown here.

```
Get-ChildItem -Recurse C:\Windows | where lastwritetime -gt "12/12/14"
```

This concludes this step-by-step exercise.

In the following exercise, you'll create a couple of COM-based objects.

One step further: Working with *New-Object*

1. Open the Windows PowerShell console.

2. Create an instance of the *wshNetwork* object by using the *New-Object* cmdlet. Use the *-ComObject* parameter and give it the program ID for the *wshNetwork* object, which is *wscript.network*. Store the results in a variable called *$wshnetwork*. The code looks like the following.

```
$wshnetwork = New-Object -comobject "wscript.network"
```

3. Use the *EnumPrinterConnections* method from the *wshNetwork* object to print a list of printer connections that are defined on your local computer. To do this, use the *wshNetwork* object that is contained in the *$wshnetwork* variable. The command for this is as follows.

```
$wshnetwork.EnumPrinterConnections()
```

4. Use the *EnumNetworkDrives* method from the *wshNetwork* object to print a list of network connections that are defined on your local computer. To do this, use the *wshNetwork* object that is contained in the *$wshnetwork* variable. The command for this is as follows.

```
$wshnetwork.EnumNetworkDrives()
```

5. Press the Up Arrow key twice to retrieve the *$wshnetwork.EnumPrinterConnections()* command. Use the *$colPrinters* variable to hold the collection of printers that is returned by the command. The code looks as follows.

```
$colPrinters = $wshnetwork.EnumPrinterConnections()
```

6. Use the Up Arrow key to retrieve the *$wshnetwork.EnumNetworkDrives()* command. Press the Home key to move the insertion point to the beginning of the line. Modify the command so that it holds the collection of drives returned by the command in a variable called *$colDrives*. This is shown here.

```
$colDrives = $wshnetwork.EnumNetworkDrives()
```

7. Use the *$userName* variable to hold the name that is returned by querying the *username* property from the *wshNetwork* object. This is shown here.

```
$userName = $wshnetwork.UserName
```

8. Use the *$userDomain* variable to hold the name that is returned by querying the *UserDomain* property from the *wshNetwork* object. This is shown here.

```
$userDomain = $wshnetwork.UserDomain
```

9. Use the *$computerName* variable to hold the name that is returned by querying the *Computer-Name* property from the *wshNetwork* object. This is shown here.

```
$computerName = $wshnetwork.ComputerName
```

10. Create an instance of the *wshShell* object by using the *New-Object* cmdlet. Use the *-ComObject* parameter and give it the program ID for the *wshShell* object, which is *wscript.shell*. Store the results in a variable called *$wshShell*. The code for this follows.

```
$wshShell = New-Object -comobject "wscript.shell"
```

11. Use the *Popup* method from the *wshShell* object to produce a pop-up box that displays the domain name, user name, and computer name. The code for this follows.

```
$wshShell.Popup($userDomain+"\$userName on $computerName")
```

12. Use the *Popup* method from the *wshShell* object to produce a pop-up box that displays the collection of printers held in the *$colPrinters* variable. Note that an error arises if there is more than one printer in *$colPrinters*. To fix that error requires adding a loop that is discussed in Chapter 5. The code is as follows.

```
$wshShell.Popup($colPrinters)
```

13. Use the *Popup* method from the *wshShell* object to produce a pop-up box that displays the collection of drives held in the *$colDrives* variable. The code is as follows.

```
$wshShell.Popup($colDrives)
```

This concludes this exercise.

Chapter 2 quick reference

To	Do this
Produce a list of all the files in a folder	Use the *Get-ChildItem* cmdlet and supply a value for the folder.
Produce a list of all the files in a folder and in the subfolders	Use the *Get-ChildItem* cmdlet, supply a value for the folder, and specify the *-Recurse* switch parameter.
Produce a wide output of the results of a previous cmdlet	Use the appropriate cmdlet and pipeline the resulting object to the *Format-Wide* cmdlet.
Produce a listing of all the methods available from the *Get-ChildItem* cmdlet	Use the cmdlet and pipeline the results into the *Get-Member* cmdlet. Use the *-MemberType* parameter and supply *method* as the value.
Produce a pop-up box	Create an instance of the *wshShell* object by using the *New-Object* cmdlet. Use the *Popup* method.
Retrieve the name of the currently logged-on user	Create an instance of the *wshNetwork* object by using the *New-Object* cmdlet. Query the *username* property.
Retrieve a listing of all currently mapped drives	Create an instance of the *wshNetwork* object by using the *New-Object* cmdlet. Use the *EnumNetworkDrives* method.

Understanding and using Windows PowerShell providers

After completing this chapter, you will be able to

- Understand the role of providers in Windows PowerShell.

- Use the *Get-PSProvider* cmdlet.

- Use the *Get-PSDrive* cmdlet.

- Use the *New-PSDrive* cmdlet.

- Use the *Get-Item* cmdlet.

- Use the *Set-Location* cmdlet.

- Use the file system model to access data from each of the built-in providers.

Windows PowerShell provides a consistent way to access information external to the shell environment. To do this, it uses *providers*. These providers are actually Microsoft .NET programs that hide all the ugly details to provide an easy way to access information. The beautiful thing about the way the provider model works is that all the different sources of information are accessed in exactly the same manner by using a common set of cmdlets—*Get-ChildItem*, for example—to work with different types of data. This chapter demonstrates how to take advantage of the Windows PowerShell providers.

Understanding Windows PowerShell providers

By identifying the providers installed with Windows PowerShell, you can begin to understand the capabilities intrinsic to a default installation. Providers expose information contained in different data stores by using a drive-and-file-system analogy. An example of this is obtaining a listing of registry keys—to do this, you would connect to the registry "drive" and use the *Get-ChildItem* cmdlet, which is exactly the same methodology you would use to obtain a listing of files on the hard drive. The only difference is the specific name associated with each drive. Developers familiar with Windows or .NET programming can create new providers, but writing a provider can be complex. (See *msdn.microsoft.com/en-us/library/windows/desktop/ee126192(v=vs.85).aspx* for more information.) When a new provider is created, it might ship in a module or in a snap-in. A *snap-in* is a *dynamic-link library (DLL)* file that must be installed in Windows PowerShell. As such, snap-ins are older technology that require elevated rights to install. After a snap-in has been installed, it cannot be uninstalled unless the developer provides removal logic—however, the snap-in can be removed from the current Windows PowerShell console. The preferred way to ship a provider is via a Windows PowerShell module. Modules are installable via an *xcopy* deployment and therefore do not necessarily require admin rights.

To obtain a listing of the providers, use the *Get-PSProvider* cmdlet. This command produces the following list on a default installation of Windows PowerShell.

Note Windows 10 does not load either the *WSMan* or the *Certificate* provider until their respective drives are accessed.

```
PS C:\> Get-PSProvider

Name            Capabilities                    Drives
----            ------------                    ------
Registry        ShouldProcess, Transactions     {HKLM, HKCU}
Alias           ShouldProcess                   {Alias}
Environment     ShouldProcess                   {Env}
FileSystem      Filter, ShouldProcess, Crede... {C, A, D, H}
Function        ShouldProcess                   {Function}
Variable        ShouldProcess                   {Variable}
WSMan           Credentials                     {WSMan}
Certificate     ShouldProcess                   {Cert}
```

Understanding the alias provider

In Chapter 1, "Overview of Windows PowerShell 5.0," I presented the various help tools that are available that show how to use cmdlets. The alias provider provides easy-to-use access to all aliases defined in Windows PowerShell. To work with the aliases on your computer, use the *Set-Location* cmdlet and specify the Alias:\ drive. You can then use the same cmdlets you would use to work with the file system.

Tip With the alias provider, you can use a *Where-Object* cmdlet and filter to search for an alias by name or description.

Working with the alias provider

1. Open the Windows PowerShell console.

2. Obtain a listing of the providers by using the *Get-PSProvider* cmdlet.

3. The Windows PowerShell drive (PS drive) associated with the alias provider is called *Alias*. This is shown in the listing produced by the *Get-PSProvider* cmdlet. Use the *Set-Location* cmdlet to change to the Alias drive. Use the *sl* alias to reduce typing. This command is shown here.

```
sl alias:\
```

4. Use the *Get-ChildItem* cmdlet to produce a listing of all the aliases that are defined on the system. To reduce typing, use the *gci* alias in place of *Get-ChildItem*. This is shown here.

```
gci
```

5. Use a *Where-Object* cmdlet filter to reduce the amount of information that is returned by using the *Get-ChildItem* cmdlet. Produce a listing of all the aliases that begin with the letter *s*. This is shown here.

```
gci | Where-Object name -like "s*"
```

6. To identify other properties that could be used in the filter, pipeline the results of the *Get-ChildItem* cmdlet into the *Get-Member* cmdlet. This is shown here. (Keep in mind that different providers expose different objects that will have different properties.)

```
Get-ChildItem | Get-Member
```

7. Press the Up Arrow key twice, and edit the previous filter to include only definitions that contain the word *set*. The modified filter is shown here.

```
gci | Where-Object definition -like "set*"
```

8. The results of this command are shown here.

```
PS Alias:\> gci | Where-Object definition -like 'set*'

CommandType     Name                            Version     Source
-----------     ----                            -------     ------
Alias           cd -> Set-Location
Alias           chdir -> Set-Location
Alias           sal -> Set-Alias
Alias           sbp -> Set-PSBreakpoint
Alias           sc -> Set-Content
Alias           scb -> Set-Clipboard            3.1.0.0     Mic...
Alias           set -> Set-Variable
Alias           si -> Set-Item
Alias           sl -> Set-Location
Alias           sp -> Set-ItemProperty
Alias           sv -> Set-Variable
Alias           swmi -> Set-WmiInstance
```

9. Press the Up Arrow key three times, and edit the previous filter to include only names of aliases that contain the letter *w*. This revised command is shown here.

```
gci | Where-Object name -like "*w*"
```

The results from this command will be similar to those shown here.

CommandType	Name	Version	Source
Alias	fw -> Format-Wide		
Alias	gwmi -> Get-WmiObject		
Alias	iwmi -> Invoke-WmiMethod		
Alias	iwr -> Invoke-WebRequest		
Alias	pwd -> Get-Location		
Alias	rwmi -> Remove-WmiObject		
Alias	swmi -> Set-WmiInstance		
Alias	wget -> Invoke-WebRequest		
Alias	where -> Where-Object		
Alias	wjb -> Wait-Job		
Alias	write -> Write-Output		

10. In the preceding list, note that *where* is an alias for the *Where-Object* cmdlet. Press the Up Arrow key one time to retrieve the previous command. Edit it to use the *where* alias instead of spelling out the entire *Where-Object* cmdlet name. This revised command is shown here.

```
gci | where name -like "*w*"
```

Caution When using the *Set-Location* cmdlet to switch to a different PS drive, you must follow the name of the PS drive with a colon. A trailing forward slash or backward slash is optional. An error will be generated if the colon is left out or if the complete drive name is not supplied, as shown in Figure 3-1. I prefer to use the backward slash (\) because it is consistent with normal Windows file system operations.

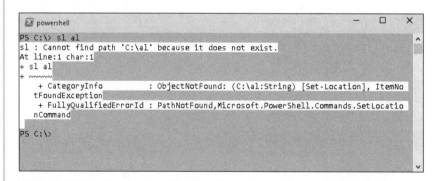

FIGURE 3-1 Using *Set-Location* without a colon or compete name results in an error.

Creating new aliases

One of the useful things about providers is that they enable you to use the same methodology to perform standard activities. For example, to create a new alias, I can use the *New-Item* cmdlet while on the Alias drive. I need to specify only the *Name* and the *Value* parameters. Though this does not directly expose all of the configurable properties of an Alias object, it does expose the main properties: the name of the new alias and the command that the alias resolves to. The following is an example of creating a new alias by using the *New-Item* cmdlet. This example creates a new alias named *listing* that, when called, will run the *Get-ChildItem* cmdlet.

```
PS Alias:\> New-Item -Name listing -Value Get-ChildItem

CommandType     Name                                    Version    Source
-----------     ----                                    -------    ------
Alias           listing -> Get-ChildItem
```

Understanding the certificate provider

The preceding section explored working with the alias provider. Because the file system model applies to the certificate provider in much the same way as it does to the alias provider, many of the same cmdlets can be used. To find information about the certificate provider, use the *Get-Help* cmdlet and search for *about_Providers*. If you are unsure what articles in Help might be related to certificates, you can use the wildcard asterisk (*) parameter. This command is shown here.

```
Get-Help *cer*
```

In addition to allowing you to use the certificate provider, Windows PowerShell gives you the ability to sign scripts; Windows PowerShell can work with both signed and unsigned scripts. The certificate provider gives you the ability search for, copy, move, and delete certificates. By using the certificate provider, you can open the Certificates Microsoft Management Console (MMC). The commands used in the following procedure use the certificate provider to obtain a listing of the certificates installed on the local computer.

Obtaining a listing of certificates

1. Open the Windows PowerShell console.

2. Set your location to the cert PS drive. To do this, use the *Set-Location* cmdlet, as shown here.

   ```
   Set-Location cert:\
   ```

3. Use the *Get-ChildItem* cmdlet, shown here, to produce a list of the certificates.

```
Get-ChildItem
```

The list produced is shown here.

```
Location   : CurrentUser
StoreNames : {SmartCardRoot, Root, Trust, AuthRoot...}

Location   : LocalMachine
StoreNames : {TrustedPublisher, ClientAuthIssuer, Remote Desktop, Root...}
```

4. Use the *-Recurse* parameter to cause the *Get-ChildItem* cmdlet to produce a list of all the certificate stores and the certificates in those stores. To do this, press the Up Arrow key one time and add the *-recurse* argument to the previous command. This is shown here.

```
Get-ChildItem -Recurse
```

5. Use the *-Path* parameter for *Get-ChildItem* to produce a listing of certificates in another store, without using the *Set-Location* cmdlet to change your current location. Use the *gci* alias, as shown here.

```
GCI -Path currentUser
```

Your listing of certificate stores will look similar to the one shown here.

```
Name : SmartCardRoot

Name : Root

Name : Trust

Name : AuthRoot

Name : CA

Name : UserDS

Name : Disallowed

Name : My

Name : TrustedPeople

Name : TrustedPublisher

Name : ClientAuthIssuer
```

6. Change your working location to the currentuser\authroot certificate store. To do this, use the *sl* alias followed by the path to the certificate store (*sl* is an alias for the *Set-Location* cmdlet). This command is shown here.

```
sl currentuser\authroot
```

7. Use the *Get-ChildItem* cmdlet to produce a listing of certificates in the currentuser\authroot certificate store that contain the name *Entrust* in the subject field. Use the *gci* alias to reduce the amount of typing. Use the *where* method instead of pipelining the output to *Where-Object*. The code to do this is shown here.

```
(gci).where({$psitem.subject -match 'entrust'})
```

On my machine, there are three certificates listed; they are shown here.

```
Thumbprint                                Subject
----------                                -------
B31EB1B740E36C8402DADC37D44DF5D4674952F9  CN=Entrust Root Certification Authority...
99A69BE61AFE886B4D2B82007CB854FC317E1539  CN=Entrust.net Secure Server Certificat...
503006091D97D4F5AE39F7CBE7927D7D652D3431  CN=Entrust.net Certification Authority...
```

8. Use the Up Arrow key, and edit the previous command so that it will return only certificates that contain the phrase *2006* in the subject property. The revised command is shown here.

```
(gci).where({$psitem.subject -match '2006'})
```

9. The resulting output on my machine contains three certificates. The results display has been truncated. This is shown here.

```
Thumbprint                                Subject
----------                                -------
B31EB1B740E36C8402DADC37D44DF5D4674952F9  CN=Entrust Root Certification Authority...
...
```

10. Use the Up Arrow key, and edit the previous command. This time, change the *where* method so that it filters on the thumbprint attribute that is equal to B31EB1B740E36C-8402DADC37D44DF5D4674952F9. You do not have to type that, however; to copy the thumbprint, you can highlight it and press Enter in Windows PowerShell, as shown in Figure 3-2. The revised command is shown here.

```
(gci).where({$psitem.thumbprint -eq 'B31EB1B740E36C8402DADC37D44DF5D4674952F9'})
```

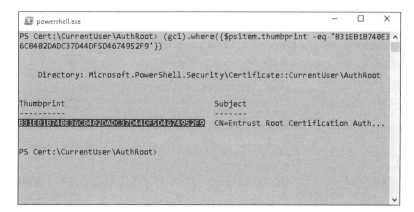

FIGURE 3-2 Highlight items to copy by using a mouse.

Troubleshooting If copying from inside the Windows PowerShell console window does not work, you might need to enable QuickEdit mode. To do this, right-click the Windows PowerShell icon in the upper-left corner of the Windows PowerShell window. Click Properties, click the Options tab, and then select the QuickEdit Mode check box. This is shown in Figure 3-3.

FIGURE 3-3 Select the QuickEdit Mode check box to turn on Clipboard support.

11. To view all the properties of the certificate, pipeline the certificate object to a *Format-List* cmdlet and choose all the properties. The revised command is shown here.

```
(gci).where({$psitem.thumbprint -eq '4EB6D578499B1CCF5F581EAD56BE3D9B6744A5E5'}) |
Format-
List *
```

The output contains all the properties of the certificate object and is shown here.

```
PSPath              : Microsoft.PowerShell.Security\Certificate::CurrentUser\Au
                      thRoot\4EB6D578499B1CCF5F581EAD56BE3D9B6744A5E5
PSParentPath        : Microsoft.PowerShell.Security\Certificate::CurrentUser\Au
                      thRoot
PSChildName         : 4EB6D578499B1CCF5F581EAD56BE3D9B6744A5E5
PSDrive             : Cert
PSProvider          : Microsoft.PowerShell.Security\Certificate
PSIsContainer       : False
EnhancedKeyUsageList : {Server Authentication (1.3.6.1.5.5.7.3.1), Client
```

```
                              Authentication (1.3.6.1.5.5.7.3.2), Secure Email
                              (1.3.6.1.5.5.7.3.4), Code Signing (1.3.6.1.5.5.7.3.3)}
     DnsNameList            : {VeriSign Class 3 Public Primary Certification Authority
                              - G5}
     SendAsTrustedIssuer    : False
     EnrollmentPolicyEndPoint : Microsoft.CertificateServices.Commands.EnrollmentEndPoint
                              Property
     EnrollmentServerEndPoint : Microsoft.CertificateServices.Commands.EnrollmentEndPoint
                              Property
     PolicyId               :
     Archived               : False
     Extensions             : {System.Security.Cryptography.Oid,
                              System.Security.Cryptography.Oid,
                              System.Security.Cryptography.Oid,
                              System.Security.Cryptography.Oid}
     FriendlyName           : VeriSign
     IssuerName             : System.Security.Cryptography.X509Certificates.X500Disting
                              uishedName
     NotAfter               : 7/16/2036 4:59:59 PM
     NotBefore              : 11/7/2006 4:00:00 PM
     HasPrivateKey          : False
     PrivateKey             :
     PublicKey              : System.Security.Cryptography.X509Certificates.PublicKey
     RawData                : {48, 130, 4, 211...}
     SerialNumber           : 18DAD19E267DE8BB4A2158CDCC6B3B4A
     SubjectName            : System.Security.Cryptography.X509Certificates.X500Disting
                              uishedName
     SignatureAlgorithm     : System.Security.Cryptography.Oid
     Thumbprint             : 4EB6D578499B1CCF5F581EAD56BE3D9B6744A5E5
     Version                : 3
     Handle                 : 201509026544
     Issuer                 : CN=VeriSign Class 3 Public Primary Certification
                              Authority - G5, OU="(c) 2006 VeriSign, Inc. - For
                              authorized use only", OU=VeriSign Trust Network,
                              O="VeriSign, Inc.", C=US
     Subject                : CN=VeriSign Class 3 Public Primary Certification
                              Authority - G5, OU="(c) 2006 VeriSign, Inc. - For
                              authorized use only", OU=VeriSign Trust Network,
                              O="VeriSign, Inc.", C=US
```

12. Open the Certificates MMC file. This MMC file is called Certmgr.msc; you can launch it by entering the name inside Windows PowerShell, as shown here.

```
Certmgr.msc
```

13. But it is more fun to use the *Invoke-Item* cmdlet to launch the Certificates MMC. To do this, supply the PS drive name of cert:\ to the *Invoke-Item* cmdlet. This is shown here.

```
Invoke-Item cert:\
```

14. Compare the information obtained from Windows PowerShell with the information displayed in the Certificates MMC. It should be the same. The certificate is shown in Figure 3-4.

FIGURE 3-4 Certmgr.msc can be used to examine certificate properties.

This concludes this procedure.

Searching for specific certificates

To search for specific certificates, you might want to examine the *subject* property. For example, the following code examines the *subject* property of every certificate in the currentuser store beginning at the root level. It does a recursive search and returns only the certificates that contain the word *test* in some form in the *subject* property. This command and associated output are shown here.

```
PS C:\Users\administrator.IAMMRED> dir Cert:\CurrentUser -Recurse | ? subject -match
'test'


    Directory: Microsoft.PowerShell.Security\Certificate::CurrentUser\Root


Thumbprint                                Subject
----------                                -------
8A334AA8052DD244A647306A76B8178FA215F344  CN=Microsoft Testing Root Certificate A...
2BD63D28D7BCD0E251195AEB519243C13142EBC3  CN=Microsoft Test Root Authority, OU=Mi...
```

To delete these *test* certificates, you just pipeline the results of the previous command to the *Remove-Item* cmdlet.

Note When performing any operation that might alter system state, it is a good idea to use the *-WhatIf* parameter to prototype the command prior to actually executing it.

The following command uses the -*WhatIf* parameter from *Remove-Item* to prototype the command to remove all of the certificates from the currentuser store that contain the word *test* in the *subject* property. When this is completed, retrieve the command by using the Up Arrow key and remove the -*WhatIf* switch parameter from the command prior to actual execution. This technique appears here.

```
PS C:\Users\administrator.IAMMRED> dir Cert:\CurrentUser -Recurse | ? subject -match
'test' | Remove-Item -WhatIf
What if: Performing operation "Remove certificate" on Target "Item: CurrentUser\Root\
8A334AA8052DD244A647306A76B8178FA215F344 ".
What if: Performing operation "Remove certificate" on Target "Item: CurrentUser\Root\
2BD63D28D7BCD0E251195AEB519243C13142EBC3 ".
PS C:\Users\administrator.IAMMRED> dir Cert:\CurrentUser -Recurse | ? subject -match
'test' | Remove-Item
```

Finding expiring certificates

A common task for companies that use certificates is to identify certificates that either have expired or that will expire soon. By using the certificate provider, you can easily identify expired certificates. To do this, use the *notafter* property from the certificate objects returned from the certificate drives. One approach is to look for certificates that expire prior to a specific date. This technique is shown here.

```
PS Cert:\CurrentUser> dir -Recurse | where notafter -lt "5/1/2015"
```

A more flexible approach is to use the current date—that way, each time the command runs, it retrieves expired certificates. This technique appears here.

```
PS Cert:\CurrentUser> dir -Recurse | where notafter -lt (Get-Date)
```

One problem with just using the *Get-ChildItem* cmdlet on the currentuser store is that it returns certificate stores in addition to certificates. To obtain only certificates, you must filter out the *psiscontainer* property. Because you will also need to filter based upon date, you can no longer use the simple *Where-Object* syntax. The *$_* character represents the current certificate as it comes across the pipeline. Because you're comparing two properties, you must repeat the *$_* character for each property. The following command retrieves the expiration dates, thumbprints, and subjects of all expired certificates. It also creates a table displaying the information. (The command is a single logical command, but it is broken at the pipe character to permit better display in the book.)

```
PS Cert:\CurrentUser> dir -Recurse |
where { !$_.psiscontainer -AND $_.notafter -lt (Get-Date)}  |
ft notafter, thumbprint, subject -AutoSize -Wrap
```

 Caution All versions of Windows are released with expired certificates to permit verification of old executable files that were signed with those certificates. Do not arbitrarily delete an expired certificate—if you do, you could cause serious damage to your system.

If you want to identify certificates that will expire in the next 30 days, you use the same technique involving a compound *Where-Object* command. The command shown here identifies certificates expiring in the next 30 days.

```
PS Cert:\CurrentUser> dir -Recurse |
where { $_.NotAfter -gt (Get-Date) -AND $_.NotAfter -le (Get-Date).Add(30) }
```

Understanding the environment provider

The environment provider in Windows PowerShell is used to provide access to the system environment variables. If you open a CMD (command) shell and enter **set**, you will obtain a listing of all the environment variables defined on the system. (You can run the old-fashioned command prompt inside Windows PowerShell.)

> **Note** It is easy to forget that you are running the CMD prompt when you are inside of the Windows PowerShell console. Entering **exit** returns you to Windows PowerShell. The best way to determine whether you are running the command shell or Windows PowerShell is to examine the prompt. The default Windows PowerShell prompt is PS C:\>, assuming that you are working on drive C.

If you use the *echo* command in the CMD interpreter to print out the value of *%windir%*, you will obtain the results shown in Figure 3-5.

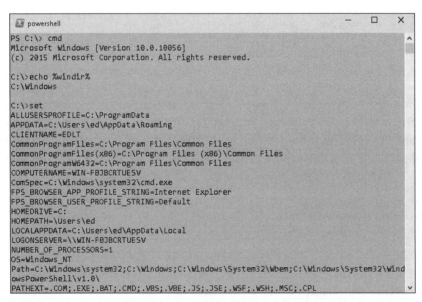

FIGURE 3-5 Use *set* at a CMD prompt to view environment variables.

Various applications and tools use environment variables as a shortcut to provide easy access to specific files, folders, and configuration data. By using the environment provider in Windows PowerShell, you can obtain a listing of the environment variables. You can also add, change, clear, and delete these variables.

Obtaining a listing of environment variables

1. Open the Windows PowerShell console.

2. Obtain a listing of the PS drives by using the *Get-PSDrive* cmdlet. This is shown here.

    ```
    Get-PSDrive
    ```

3. Note that the Environment PS drive is called *Env*. Use the *Env* name with the *Set-Location* cmdlet to change to the Environment PS drive. This is shown here.

    ```
    Set-Location Env:\
    ```

4. Use the *Get-Item* cmdlet to obtain a listing of all the environment variables on the system. This is shown here.

    ```
    Get-Item *
    ```

5. Use the *Sort-Object* cmdlet to produce an alphabetical listing of all the environment variables by name. Use the Up Arrow key to retrieve the previous command, and then pipeline the returned object into the *Sort-Object* cmdlet. Use the *-Property* parameter, and supply *name* as the value. This command is shown here.

    ```
    Get-Item * | Sort-Object -Property name
    ```

6. Use the *Get-Item* cmdlet to retrieve the value associated with the *windir* environment variable. This is shown here.

    ```
    Get-Item windir
    ```

7. Use the Up Arrow key to retrieve the previous command. Pipeline the object returned to the *Format-List* cmdlet and use the wildcard character to print out all the properties of the object. The modified command is shown here.

    ```
    Get-Item windir | Format-List *
    ```

    The properties and their associated values are shown here.

    ```
    PSPath        : Microsoft.PowerShell.Core\Environment::windir
    PSDrive       : Env
    PSProvider    : Microsoft.PowerShell.Core\Environment
    PSIsContainer : False
    Name          : windir
    Key           : windir
    Value         : C:\WINDOWS
    ```

    This concludes this procedure. Do not close Windows PowerShell. Leave it open for the next procedure.

Creating a temporary new environment variable

1. You should still be in the Environment PS drive from the previous procedure. If you are not, use the *Set-Location env:* command.

2. Use the *Get-Item* cmdlet to produce a listing of all the environment variables. Pipeline the returned object to the *Sort-Object* cmdlet by using the *name* property. To reduce typing, use the *gi* alias and the *sort* alias. This is shown here.

```
gi * | sort -Property name
```

3. Use the *New-Item* cmdlet to create a new environment variable. The *-Path* parameter will be dot (.) because you are already on the env:\ PS drive; therefore, it can be omitted in the command. The *-Name* parameter will be *admin*, and the *-Value* parameter will be your given name. The completed command is shown here.

```
New-Item -Name admin -Value mred
```

4. Use the *Get-Item* cmdlet to ensure that the *admin* environment variable was properly created. This command is shown here.

```
Get-Item admin
```

The results of the previous command are shown here.

```
Name                    Value
----                    -----
admin                   mred
```

5. Use the Up Arrow key to retrieve the previous command. Pipeline the results to the *Format-List* cmdlet and choose All Properties. This command is shown here.

```
Get-Item admin | Format-List *
```

The results of the previous command include the PS path, PS drive, and additional information about the newly created environment variable. These results are shown here.

```
PSPath        : Microsoft.PowerShell.Core\Environment::admin
PSDrive       : Env
PSProvider    : Microsoft.PowerShell.Core\Environment
PSIsContainer : False
Name          : admin
Key           : admin
Value         : mred
```

The new environment variable exists until you close the Windows PowerShell console.

This concludes this procedure. Leave Windows PowerShell open for the next procedure.

Renaming an environment variable

1. Use the *Get-ChildItem* cmdlet to obtain a listing of all the environment variables. Pipeline the returned object to the *Sort-Object* cmdlet and sort the list on the *name* property. Use the *gci* and *sort* aliases to reduce typing. The code to do this is shown here.

```
gci | sort -Property name
```

2. The *admin* environment variable should be near the top of the list of system variables. If it is not, create it by using the *New-Item* cmdlet. The *-Name* parameter has the value of *admin*, and the *-Value* parameter should be your given name. If this environment variable was created in the previous exercise, Windows PowerShell will report that it already exists. The command shown here allows you to re-create the *admin* environment variable.

```
New-Item -Name admin -Value mred
```

3. Use the *Rename-Item* cmdlet to rename the *admin* environment variable to *super*. The *-Path* parameter combines the PS drive name with the environment variable name, but it is not necessary if you are working on the Environment PS drive, as in this procedure. The *-NewName* parameter is the new name you want, without the PS drive specification. This command is shown here.

```
Rename-Item admin -NewName super
```

4. To verify that the old *admin* environment variable has been renamed to *super*, use the *Get-Item* cmdlet and specify the name *super*. You will not get the old name of the variable, but you will get the *super* variable with the same value as the previous *admin* variable. This command appears here.

```
Get-Item super
```

This concludes this procedure. Do not close Windows PowerShell. Leave it open for the next procedure.

Removing an environment variable

1. Use the *Get-ChildItem* cmdlet to obtain a listing of all the environment variables. Pipeline the returned object to the *Sort-Object* cmdlet and sort the list on the *name* property. Use the *gci* and *sort* aliases to reduce typing. The code to do this is shown here.

```
gci | sort -Property name
```

2. The *super* environment variable should be in the list of system variables. If it is not, create it by using the *New-Item* cmdlet. The *-Name* parameter has a value of *super*, and the *-Value* parameter should be your given name. If this environment variable was created in the

previous exercise, Windows PowerShell will report that it already exists. If you have deleted the *super* environment variable, the command shown here creates it.

```
New-Item -Name super -Value mred
```

3. Use the *Remove-Item* cmdlet to remove the *super* environment variable. Enter the name of the item to be removed after the name of the cmdlet. If you are still in the Environment PS drive, you will not need to supply a -*Path* parameter value. The command is shown here.

```
Remove-Item super
```

4. Use the *Get-ChildItem* cmdlet to verify that the *super* environment variable has been removed. To do this, press the Up Arrow key two or three times to retrieve the *gci | sort -property name* command. This command is shown here.

```
gci | sort -property name
```

This concludes this procedure.

Understanding the filesystem provider

The filesystem provider is the easiest Windows PowerShell provider to understand—it provides access to the file system. When Windows PowerShell is started, it automatically opens on the user documents folder. By using the Windows PowerShell filesystem provider, you can create both directories and files. You can retrieve properties of files and directories, and you can also delete them. In addition, you can open files and append or overwrite data to the files. This can be done with inline code or by using the pipelining feature of Windows PowerShell.

Working with directory listings

1. Open the Windows PowerShell console.

2. Use the *Get-ChildItem* cmdlet to obtain a directory listing of drive C. Use the *gci* alias to reduce typing. This is shown here.

```
GCI C:\
```

3. Use the Up Arrow key to retrieve the *gci C:* command. Pipeline the object created into a *Where-Object* cmdlet and look for containers. This will reduce the output to only directories. The modified command is shown here.

```
GCI C:\ | where psiscontainer
```

4. Use the Up Arrow key to retrieve the *gci C:\ | where psiscontainer* command, and use the exclamation point (!) (meaning *not*) to retrieve only items in the PS drive that are not directories.

The modified command is shown here. (The simplified *Where-Object* syntax does not support using the *not* operator directly on the input property.)

```
gci | where {!($psitem.psiscontainer)}
```

5. Now use the *-Directory* parameter to display only containers (directories). To do this, use the *Get-ChildItem* cmdlet but specify the *-Directory* parameter. This command is shown here.

```
gci -Directory
```

6. Now look for files. To do this, use the *-File* parameter. Use the Up Arrow key to retrieve the previous command, backspace to remove the *-Directory* parameter, and then add the *-File* parameter. The command appears here.

```
Gci -File
```

This concludes this procedure. Do not close Windows PowerShell. Leave it open for the next procedure.

> **Tip** Aliases in Windows PowerShell are not case sensitive. This makes them easy to type. Therefore, *GCI*, *Gci*, *gci*, and even *GCi* all work as aliases for *Get-ChildItem*.

Identifying properties of directories

1. Use the *Get-ChildItem* cmdlet, and supply a value of C:\ for the *-Path* parameter. Pipeline the resulting object into the *Get-Member* cmdlet. Use the *gci* and *gm* aliases to reduce typing. This command is shown here.

```
gci -Path C:\ | gm
```

2. The resulting output contains methods, properties, and more. Filter the output by pipelining it into a *Where-Object* cmdlet and specifying the *membertype* attribute as equal to *property*. To do this, use the Up Arrow key to retrieve the previous *gci -Path C:\ | gm* command. This time, remove the path parameter, because by default it operates against the current path. Pipeline the resulting object into the *Where-Object* cmdlet, and filter on the *membertype* attribute. The resulting command is shown here.

```
gci | gm | Where {$_.membertype -eq "property"}
```

3. You need to use the *-Force* parameter to view hidden files, and therefore to view both *directory-info* objects and *fileinfo* objects. Also, you do not need to pipeline *Get-Member* to the *Where-Object* cmdlet to filter on *membertype*, because the *Get-Member* cmdlet has a *-MemberType* parameter. Here is the revised command.

```
gci -Force | gm -MemberType Property
```

4. The preceding command returns information about both the *System.IO.DirectoryInfo* and *System.IO.FileInfo* objects. To reduce the output to only the properties associated with the *System.IO.FileInfo* object, you need to use the *-File* parameter. Use the Up Arrow key to retrieve the previous command. Add the *-File* parameter. The modified command is shown here.

```
gci -Force -File | gm -MemberType Property
```

The resulting output contains only the properties for a *System.IO.FileInfo* object. These properties are shown here.

```
    TypeName: System.IO.FileInfo

Name                 MemberType Definition
----                 ---------- ----------
Attributes           Property   System.IO.FileAttributes Attributes {get;set;}
CreationTime         Property   datetime CreationTime {get;set;}
CreationTimeUtc      Property   datetime CreationTimeUtc {get;set;}
Directory            Property   System.IO.DirectoryInfo Directory {get;}
DirectoryName        Property   string DirectoryName {get;}
Exists               Property   bool Exists {get;}
Extension            Property   string Extension {get;}
FullName             Property   string FullName {get;}
IsReadOnly           Property   bool IsReadOnly {get;set;}
LastAccessTime       Property   datetime LastAccessTime {get;set;}
LastAccessTimeUtc    Property   datetime LastAccessTimeUtc {get;set;}
LastWriteTime        Property   datetime LastWriteTime {get;set;}
LastWriteTimeUtc     Property   datetime LastWriteTimeUtc {get;set;}
Length               Property   long Length {get;}
Name                 Property   string Name {get;}
```

This concludes this procedure. Do not close Windows PowerShell. Leave it open for the next procedure.

> **Tip** Spacing in Windows PowerShell commands does not matter. Therefore, *gci|gm* works the same as *gci | gm*, and both commands will retrieve members of objects from whatever provider drive you happen to be working on.

Creating folders and files

1. Set your location to your temp folder. To do this, use the *temp* variable from the Environment PS drive. Use the *Get-Item* cmdlet to obtain a listing of files and folders. Use the *gi* alias and the *sl* alias to reduce typing. The commands and my output appear here.

```
PS C:\> sl $env:TEMP
PS C:\Users\ed\AppData\Local\Temp> gi *
```

2. Use the *New-Item* cmdlet to create a folder named mytempfolder. Use the *-Name* parameter to specify the name of mytempfolder, and use the *-ItemType* parameter to tell Windows PowerShell that the new item will be a directory. This command is shown here.

```
New-Item -Name mytempfolder -ItemType Directory
```

The resulting output, shown here, confirms the operation.

```
    Directory: C:\Users\ed\AppData\Local\Temp


Mode                LastWriteTime         Length Name
----                -------------         ------ ----
d-----        5/2/2015   3:14 PM                 mytempfolder
```

3. Use the *New-Item* cmdlet to create an empty text file. To do this, use the Up Arrow key and retrieve the previous *New-Item -Name mytempfolder -ItemType* Directory command. Edit the *-Name* parameter to specify a text file named *mytempfile*, and specify the *-ItemType* parameter as *file*. The resulting command is shown here.

```
New-Item -Name mytempfile -ItemType File
```

The resulting message, shown here, confirms the creation of the file.

```
    Directory: C:\Users\ed\AppData\Local\Temp


Mode                LastWriteTime         Length Name
----                -------------         ------ ----
-a----        5/2/2015   3:18 PM              0 mytempfile
```

4. Use the *mkdir* function (*md* is an alias) to create a new folder with a temporary name. To do this, use the *GetRandomFileName* method from the *[io.path]* class. Here is the command.

```
md -path ([io.path]::GetRandomFileName())
```

The output from the command will appear similar to the output here.

```
    Directory: C:\Users\ed\AppData\Local\Temp


Mode                LastWriteTime         Length Name
----                -------------         ------ ----
d-----        5/2/2015   3:23 PM                 hdsa2rys.xcs
```

5. Now create a temporary file with a temporary file name. To do this, use the *New-Temporary-File* cmdlet. It is important when using this cmdlet to use a variable to store the name of the returned *fileinfo* object so that you will have access to the name of the file. This command and the output associated with the command are shown here.

```
PS C:\Users\ed\AppData\Local\Temp> $tempfile = New-TemporaryFile
PS C:\Users\ed\AppData\Local\Temp> $tempfile


    Directory: C:\Users\ed\AppData\Local\Temp


Mode                LastWriteTime         Length Name
----                -------------         ------ ----
-a----        5/2/2015     3:26 PM              0 tmpEE3A.tmp
```

Tip Capitalization of variable names does not matter. Therefore, Windows PowerShell interprets *$mytempfile* the same as *$MyTempFile*.

6. Delete the files and folders in the temp folder. To do this, pipeline the results of the *Get-ChildItem* cmdlet (*dir* is an alias) to the *Remove-Item* cmdlet with the *-Recurse* parameter. To prototype the command and view the files and folders that will be deleted, use the *-WhatIf* parameter. This command is shown here.

```
dir | ri -Recurse -WhatIf
dir | ri -Recurse
```

This concludes this procedure. Do not close Windows PowerShell. Leave it open for the next procedure.

Reading and writing for files

1. Use the Up Arrow key to retrieve the *New-Item -Name mytempfile -ItemType File* command. Add the *-Value* parameter to the end of the command line and supply a value of *My file*. This command is shown here.

```
New-Item -Name mytempfile -ItemType File -Value "My file"
```

2. Use the *Get-Content* cmdlet to read the contents of mytempfile. This command is shown here.

```
Get-Content mytempfile
```

3. Use the *Add-Content* cmdlet to add additional information to the *mytempfile* file. This command is shown here.

```
Add-Content mytempfile -Value "ADDITIONAL INFORMATION"
```

4. Press the Up Arrow key twice and retrieve the *Get-Content mytempfile* command, which is shown here.

    ```
    Get-Content mytempfile
    ```

    The output from the *Get-Content mytempfile* command is shown here.

    ```
    My fileADDITIONAL INFORMATION
    ```

5. Press the Up Arrow key twice, and retrieve the *Add-Content mytempfile -Value "ADDITIONAL INFORMATION"* command to add additional information to the file. This command is shown here.

    ```
    Add-Content mytempfile -Value "ADDITIONAL INFORMATION"
    ```

6. Use the Up Arrow key to retrieve the *Get-Content mytempfile* command, which is shown here.

    ```
    Get-Content mytempfile
    ```

    The output produced is shown here. Notice that the second time the command runs, the *"ADDITIONAL INFORMATION"* string is added to a new line in the original file.

    ```
    My fileADDITIONAL INFORMATION
    ADDITIONAL INFORMATION
    ```

7. Use the *Set-Content* cmdlet to overwrite the contents of the *mytempfile* file. Specify the *-Value* parameter as *Setting information*. This command is shown here.

    ```
    Set-Content mytempfile -Value "Setting information"
    ```

8. Use the Up Arrow key to retrieve the *Get-Content mytempfile* command, which is shown here.

    ```
    Get-Content mytempfile
    ```

    The output from the *Get-Content* command is shown here.

    ```
    Setting information
    ```

    This concludes this procedure.

 Tip File names are not case sensitive. Therefore, Windows PowerShell does not distinguish between MyFile.Txt and myfile.txt.

Understanding the function provider

The function provider provides access to the functions defined in Windows PowerShell. By using the function provider, you can obtain a listing of all the functions on your system. You can also add, modify, and delete functions. The function provider uses a file system–based model, and the cmdlets described earlier apply to working with functions.

Listing all functions on the system

1. Open the Windows PowerShell console.

2. Use the *Set-Location* cmdlet to change the working location to the Function PS drive. This command is shown here.

```
Set-Location function:\
```

3. Use the *Get-ChildItem* cmdlet to enumerate all the functions. Do this by using the *gci* alias, as shown here.

```
gci
```

4. The resulting list contains many functions, such as functions that use *Set-Location* to change the current location to different drive letters (for example, *C:*). A partial view of this output is shown here.

```
CommandType      Name                                    Version    Source
-----------      ----                                    -------    ------
Function         A:
Function         B:
Function         C:
Function         cd..
Function         cd\
Function         Clear-Host
<Truncated>
Function         G:
Function         Get-FileHash                            3.1.0.0    Mic...
Function         Get-SerializedCommand                   3.1.0.0    Mic...
Function         Get-Verb
Function         H:
Function         help
Function         I:
Function         ImportSystemModules
<Truncated>
Function         mkdir
Function         more
Function         N:
Function         New-Guid                                3.1.0.0    Mic...
Function         New-TemporaryFile                       3.1.0.0    Mic...
Function         O:
Function         oss
Function         P:
Function         Pause
Function         prompt
Function         Q:
<Truncated>
Function         TabExpansion2
<Truncated>
```

5. To return only the functions that are used for drives, use the *Get-ChildItem* cmdlet and the *Where* method to filter definitions that contain the word *set*. Use the *-match* operator to perform the matching. The resulting command is shown here.

```
(Get-ChildItem).where({$psitem.definition -match 'set'})
```

6. If you are more interested in functions that are not related to drive mappings, you can use the *-notmatch* operator instead of *-match*. The easiest way to make this change is to use the Up Arrow key to retrieve the previous command and change the operator from *–match* to *-notmatch*. The resulting command is shown here.

```
(Get-ChildItem).where({$psitem.definition -notmatch 'set'})
```

The resulting listing of functions is shown here.

```
CommandType     Name                            Version    Source
-----------     ----                            -------    ------
Function        Get-Verb
Function        ImportSystemModules
Function        more
Function        New-Guid                        3.1.0.0    Mic...
Function        New-TemporaryFile               3.1.0.0    Mic...
Function        oss
Function        Pause
Function        prompt
```

7. Use the *Get-Content* cmdlet to retrieve the text of the *pause* function. This is shown here (*gc* is an alias for the *Get-Content* cmdlet).

```
gc pause
```

The content of the *pause* function is shown here.

```
Read-Host 'Press Enter to continue...' | Out-Null
```

This concludes this procedure.

Using the registry provider to manage the Windows registry

In Windows PowerShell 1.0, the registry provider made it easy to work with the registry on the local system. Unfortunately, if you were not using remoting, you were limited to working with the local computer or using some other remoting mechanism (such as a logon script) to make changes on remote systems. Beginning with Windows PowerShell 2.0, the inclusion of remoting makes it possible to make remote registry changes as easily as changing the local registry. In Windows PowerShell 3.0, the registry provider was further improved with the introduction of transactions. In Windows PowerShell 4.0 and Windows PowerShell 5.0, there have been no major increases in functionality.

You can use the registry provider to access the registry in the same manner that the filesystem provider permits access to a local disk drive. The same cmdlets used to access the file system—*New-Item*, *Get-ChildItem*, *Set-Item*, *Remove-Item*, and the rest—also work with the registry.

The two registry drives

By default, the registry provider creates two registry drives. To find all of the drives exposed by the registry provider, use the *Get-PSDrive* cmdlet. These drives are shown here.

```
PS C:\> Get-PSDrive -PSProvider registry | select name, root

Name                            Root
----                            ----
HKCU                            HKEY_CURRENT_USER
HKLM                            HKEY_LOCAL_MACHINE
```

You can create additional registry drives by using the *New-PSDrive* cmdlet. For example, it is common to create a registry drive for the HKEY_CLASSES_ROOT registry hive. The code to do this is shown here.

```
PS C:\> New-PSDrive -PSProvider Registry -Root HKEY_CLASSES_ROOT -Name HKCR


Name        Used (GB)   Free (GB) Provider    Root
----        ---------   --------- --------    ----
HKCR                              Registry    HKEY_CLASSES_ROOT
```

After it is created, the new HKCR drive is accessible in the same way as any other drive. For example, to change the working location to the HKCR drive, use either the *Set-Location* cmdlet or one of its aliases (such as *cd*). This technique is shown here.

```
PS C:\> Set-Location HKCR:
```

To determine the current location, use the *Get-Location* cmdlet. This technique is shown here.

```
PS HKCR:\> Get-Location

Path
----
HKCR:\
```

After you've set the new working location, explore it by using the *Get-ChildItem* cmdlet (or one of the aliases for that cmdlet, such as *dir*). This technique is shown in Figure 3-6.

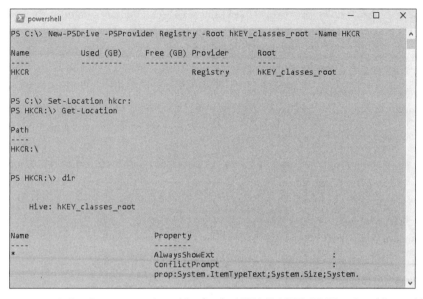

FIGURE 3-6 Creating a new registry drive for the HKEY_CLASSES_ROOT registry hive enables easy access to class registration information.

Retrieving registry values

To view the values stored in a registry key, use either the *Get-Item* or the *Get-ItemProperty* cmdlet. Using the *Get-Item* cmdlet reveals that there is one property (named *default*). This is shown here.

```
PS HKCR:\> Get-Item .\.ps1 | fl *

Property      : {(default)}
PSPath        : Microsoft.PowerShell.Core\Registry::HKEY_CLASSES_ROOT\.ps1
PSParentPath  : Microsoft.PowerShell.Core\Registry::HKEY_CLASSES_ROOT
PSChildName   : .ps1
PSDrive       : HKCR
PSProvider    : Microsoft.PowerShell.Core\Registry
PSIsContainer : True
SubKeyCount   : 1
View          : Default
Handle        : Microsoft.Win32.SafeHandles.SafeRegistryHandle
ValueCount    : 1
Name          : HKEY_CLASSES_ROOT\.ps1
```

To access the value of the *default* property, you must use the *Get-ItemProperty* cmdlet, as shown here.

```
PS HKCR:\> Get-ItemProperty .\.ps1 | fl *

(default)     : Microsoft.PowerShellScript.1
PSPath        : Microsoft.PowerShell.Core\Registry::HKEY_CLASSES_ROOT\.ps1
PSParentPath  : Microsoft.PowerShell.Core\Registry::HKEY_CLASSES_ROOT
PSChildName   : .ps1
PSDrive       : HKCR
PSProvider    : Microsoft.PowerShell.Core\Registry
```

The technique for accessing registry keys and the values associated with them is shown in Figure 3-7.

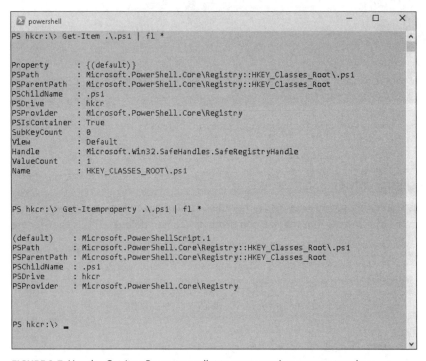

FIGURE 3-7 Use the *Get-ItemProperty* cmdlet to access registry property values.

Returning only the value of the *default* property requires a bit of manipulation. The *default* property requires the use of literal quotation marks to force the evaluation of the parentheses in the name. This is shown here.

```
PS HKCR:\> (Get-ItemProperty .\.ps1 -Name '(default)').'(default)'
Microsoft.PowerShellScript.1
```

The registry provider provides a consistent and easy way to work with the registry from within Windows PowerShell. By using the registry provider, you can search the registry, create new registry keys, delete existing registry keys, and modify values and access control lists (ACLs) from within Windows PowerShell.

Two PS drives are created by default. To identify the PS drives that are supplied by the registry provider, you can use the *Get-PSDrive* cmdlet, pipeline the resulting objects into the *Where-Object* cmdlet, and filter on the *provider* property while supplying a value that matches the word *registry*. This command is shown here.

```
PS C:\> Get-PSDrive | ? provider -match registry

Name            Used (GB)     Free (GB) Provider      Root
----            ---------     --------- --------      ----
HKCR                                    Registry      HKEY_CLASSES_ROOT
HKCU                                    Registry      HKEY_CURRENT_USER
HKLM                                    Registry      HKEY_LOCAL_MACHINE
```

Obtaining a listing of registry keys

1. Open the Windows PowerShell console.

2. Use the *Get-ChildItem* cmdlet and supply *HKLM:\software* as the value for the *-Path* parameter. Specify the software key to retrieve a listing of software applications on the local machine. The resulting command is shown here.

   ```
   GCI -path HKLM:\software
   ```

   The corresponding keys, as displayed in Regedit.exe, are shown in Figure 3-8. A partial listing of example output is shown after the figure.

FIGURE 3-8 The Registry Editor tool shows a Regedit.exe view of HKEY_LOCAL_MACHINE\SOFTWARE.

```
Hive: HKEY_LOCAL_MACHINE\SOFTWARE


Name                          Property
----                          --------
Classes
Clients
Intel
Macromedia
Microsoft
ODBC
OEM
Partner
Policies
RegisteredApplications        Paint                      : SOFTWARE\Microsoft\
                              Windows\CurrentVersion\Applets\Paint\Capabilities
                              Windows Search            :
                              Software\Microsoft\Windows Search\Capabilities
                              Windows Disc Image Burner :
                              Software\Microsoft\IsoBurn\Capabilities
                              Windows File Explorer     : SOFTWARE\Microsoft\
                              Windows\CurrentVersion\Explorer\Capabilities
                              Windows Photo Viewer      :
                              Software\Microsoft\Windows Photo Viewer\Capabilities
                              Wordpad                   : Software\Microsoft\
                              Windows\CurrentVersion\Applets\Wordpad\Capabilities
                              Windows Media Player      :
                              Software\Clients\Media\Windows Media
                              Player\Capabilities
                              Internet Explorer         :
                              SOFTWARE\Microsoft\Internet Explorer\Capabilities
                              Windows Address Book      :
                              Software\Clients\Contacts\Address Book\Capabilities
```

This concludes this procedure. Do not close Windows PowerShell. Leave it open for the next procedure.

Searching for software

1. Use the *Get-ChildItem* cmdlet and supply a value for the *-Path* parameter. Use the HKLM:\ PS drive and supply a path of *SOFTWARE\Microsoft\Windows\CurrentVersion\Uninstall*. To make the command easier to read, use single quotation marks (') to encase the string. You can use tab completion to assist with the typing. The completed command is shown here.

   ```
   gci -Path 'HKLM:SOFTWARE\Microsoft\Windows\CurrentVersion\Uninstall'
   ```

The resulting listing of software is shown in the output here, in abbreviated fashion.

```
Hive: HKEY_LOCAL_MACHINE\SOFTWARE\Microsoft\Windows\CurrentVersion\Uninstall


Name                            Property
----                            --------
AddressBook
CNXT_AUDIO_HDA                  DisplayName     : Conexant 20672 SmartAudio HD
                                DisplayVersion  : 8.32.23.2
                                VersionMajor    : 8
                                VersionMinor    : 0
                                Publisher       : Conexant
                                DisplayIcon     : C:\Program
                                Files\CONEXANT\CNXT_AUDIO_HDA\UIU64a.exe
                                UninstallString : C:\Program
                                Files\CONEXANT\CNXT_AUDIO_HDA\UIU64a.exe -U -G
                                                      -Ichdrt.inf
Connection Manager              SystemComponent : 1
DirectDrawEx
DXM_Runtime
Fontcore
IE40
IE4Data
IE5BAKEX
IEData
MobileOptionPack
MPlayer2
Office15.PROPLUS                Publisher               : Microsoft Corporation
                                CacheLocation           : C:\MSOCache\All Users
                                DisplayIcon             : C:\Program Files\Common
```

2. To retrieve information on a single software package, you will need to add a *Where-Object* cmdlet. You can do this by using the Up Arrow key to retrieve the previous *gci -Path 'HKLM:SOFTWARE\ Microsoft\Windows\CurrentVersion\Uninstall'* command and pipelining the resulting object into the *Where-Object* cmdlet. Supply a value for the *name* property, as shown in the code listed here. Alternatively, supply a name from the previous output.

```
PS C:\> gci -path 'HKLM:SOFTWARE\Microsoft\Windows\CurrentVersion\Uninstall' | where
name -match 'office'
```

This concludes this procedure.

Creating new registry keys

Creating a new registry key by using Windows PowerShell is the same as creating a new file or a new folder—all three processes use the *New-Item* cmdlet. In addition to using the *New-Item* cmdlet, you might use the *Test-Path* cmdlet to determine whether the registry key already exists. You might also want to change your working location to one of the registry drives. If you do this, you might use the *Push-Location*, *Set-Location*, and *Pop-Location* cmdlets. This is, of course, the long way of doing things. These steps appear next.

> **Caution** The registry contains information vital to the operation and configuration of your computer. Serious problems could arise if you edit the registry incorrectly. Therefore, it is important to back up your system prior to attempting to make any changes. For information about backing up your registry, see Microsoft TechNet article KB322756. For general information about working with the registry, see Microsoft TechNet article KB310516.

1. Store the current working location by using the *Push-Location* cmdlet.

2. Change the current working location to the appropriate registry drive by using the *Set-Location* cmdlet.

3. Use the *Test-Path* cmdlet to determine whether the registry key already exists.

4. Use the *New-Item* cmdlet to create the new registry key.

5. Use the *Pop-Location* cmdlet to return to the starting working location.

The following example creates a new registry key named *test* off the HKEY_CURRENT_USERS software registry hive. It illustrates each of the five steps detailed previously.

```
Push-Location
Set-Location HKCU:
Test-Path .\Software\test
New-Item -Path .\Software -Name test
Pop-Location
```

The commands and the associated output from the commands appear in Figure 3-9.

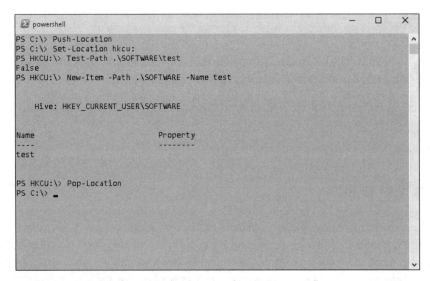

FIGURE 3-9 Create a new registry key by using the *New-Item* cmdlet.

The short way to create a new registry key

It is not always necessary to change the working location to a registry drive when creating a new registry key. In fact, it is not even necessary to use the *Test-Path* cmdlet to determine whether the registry key exists. If the registry key already exists, an error is generated. If you want to overwrite the registry key, use the *-Force* parameter. This technique works for all the Windows PowerShell providers, not just for the registry provider.

> **Note** How to deal with an already existing registry key is one of those *design decisions* that confront IT professionals who venture far into the world of scripting. Software developers are very familiar with these types of decisions and usually deal with them in the analyzing-requirements portion of the development life cycle. IT professionals who open the Windows PowerShell ISE first and think about the design requirements second can easily become stymied, and possibly write in problems. For more information about this, see my book, *Windows PowerShell Best Practices* (Microsoft Press, 2014).

The following example creates a new registry key named *test* in the HKCU:\SOFTWARE location. Because the command includes the full path, it does not need to execute from the HKCU drive. Because the command uses the *-Force* switched parameter, the command overwrites the HKCU:\SOFTWARE\TEST registry key if it already exists.

```
New-Item -Path HKCU:\Software -Name test -Force
```

> **Note** To watch the *New-Item* cmdlet in action when using the *-Force* switched parameter, use the *-Verbose* switched parameter. The command appears here.
>
> ```
> New-Item -Path HKCU:\Software -Name test -Force -Verbose
> ```
>
> The steps for creating a registry key are as follows:
>
> 1. Include the full path to the registry key that you want to create.
>
> 2. Use the *-Force* parameter to overwrite any existing registry key of the same name.

In Figure 3-10, the first attempt to create a test registry key fails because the key already exists. The second command uses the *-Force* parameter, causing the command to overwrite the existing registry key, and therefore it succeeds without creating an error.

```
powershell                                                        —   □   ×
PS C:\> New-Item -Path hkcu:\SOFTWARE -Name test
New-Item : A key in this path already exists.
At line:1 char:1
+ New-Item -Path hkcu:\SOFTWARE -Name test
+ ~~~~~~~~~~~~~~~~~~~~~~~~~~~~~~~~~~~~~~~~~
    + CategoryInfo          : ResourceExists: (Microsoft.Power...RegistryWrapper:Re
   gistryWrapper) [New-Item], IOException
    + FullyQualifiedErrorId : System.IO.IOException,Microsoft.PowerShell.Commands.N
   ewItemCommand

PS C:\> New-Item -Path hkcu:\SOFTWARE -Name test -Force


    Hive: HKEY_CURRENT_USER\SOFTWARE


Name                          Property
----                          --------
test

PS C:\> _
```

FIGURE 3-10 Use the -*Force* parameter when creating a new registry key, to overwrite the key if it already exists.

Setting the default value for the key

The previous examples do not set the default value for the newly created registry key. If the registry key already exists (as it does in this specific case), you can use the *Set-Item* cmdlet to assign a default value to the registry key. The steps to accomplish this are detailed here:

1. Use the *Set-Item* cmdlet, and supply the complete path to the existing registry key.

2. Supply the default value in the -*Value* parameter of the *Set-Item* cmdlet.

    The following command assigns the value *test key* to the default property value of the test registry key contained in the HKCU:\SOFTWARE location.

    ```
    Set-Item -Path HKCU:\Software\test -Value "test key"
    ```

Using *New-Item* to create and assign a value

It is not necessary to use the *New-Item* cmdlet to create a registry key and then use the *Set-Item* cmdlet to assign a default value. You can combine these steps into a single command. The following command creates a new registry key with the name of HSG1 and assigns a default value of *default value* to the registry key.

```
New-Item -Path HKCU:\Software\hsg1 -Value "default value"
```

Modifying the value of a registry property value

Modifying the value of a registry property value requires the use of the *Set-PropertyItem* cmdlet.

1. Use the *Push-Location* cmdlet to save the current working location.

2. Use the *Set-Location* cmdlet to change to the appropriate registry drive.

3. Use the *Set-ItemProperty* cmdlet to assign a new value to the registry property.

4. Use the *Pop-Location* cmdlet to return to the original working location.

When you know that a registry property value exists, the solution is simple: you use the *Set-Item-Property* cmdlet and assign a new value. The code that follows saves the current working location, changes the new working location to the registry key, uses the *Set-ItemProperty* cmdlet to assign a new value, and then uses the *Pop-Location* cmdlet to return to the original working location.

> **Note** The code that follows relies upon positional parameters for the *Set-ItemProperty* cmdlet. The first parameter is *-Path*. Because the *Set-Location* cmdlet sets the working location to the registry key, a period identifies the path as the current directory. The second parameter is the name of the registry property to change—in this example, it is *new-property*. The last parameter is *-Value*, and that defines the value to assign to the *registry* property. In this example, it is *mynewvalue*. The command with complete parameter names would thus be *Set-ItemProperty -Path . -Name newproperty -Value mynewvalue*. The quotation marks in the following code are not required, but do not harm anything either.

```
PS C:\> Push-Location
PS C:\> Set-Location HKCU:\Software\test
PS HKCU:\Software\test> Set-ItemProperty . newproperty "mynewvalue"
PS HKCU:\Software\test> Pop-Location
PS C:\>
```

Of course, all the pushing, popping, and setting of locations is not really required. It is entirely possible to change the registry property value from any location within the Windows PowerShell provider subsystem.

The short way to change a registry property value

To change a registry property value easily, use the *Set-ItemProperty* cmdlet to assign a new value. Ensure that you specify the complete path to the registry key. Here is an example of using the *Set-ItemProperty* cmdlet to change a registry property value without first navigating to the registry drive.

```
PS C:\> Set-ItemProperty -Path HKCU:\Software\test -Name newproperty -Value anewvalue
```

Dealing with a missing registry property

If you need to set a registry property value, you can set the value of that property easily by using the *Set-ItemProperty* cmdlet. But what if the registry property does not exist? How do you set the property value then? You can still use the *Set-ItemProperty* cmdlet to set a registry property value, even if the registry property does not exist, as shown in the following code.

```
Set-ItemProperty -Path HKCU:\Software\test -Name missingproperty -Value avalue
```

To determine whether a registry key exists, you can use the *Test-Path* cmdlet. It returns *true* if the key exists and *false* if it does not exist. This technique is shown here.

```
PS C:\> Test-Path HKCU:\Software\test
True
PS C:\> Test-Path HKCU:\Software\test\newproperty
False
```

Unfortunately, this technique does not work for a registry key property. It always returns *false*—even if the registry property exists. This is shown here.

```
PS C:\> Test-Path HKCU:\Software\test\newproperty
False
PS C:\> Test-Path HKCU:\Software\test\bogus
False
```

Therefore, if you do not want to overwrite a registry key property if it already exists, you need a way to determine whether the registry key property exists—and using the *Test-Path* cmdlet does not work. The following procedure shows how to handle this.

> **Testing for a registry key property prior to writing a new value**
>
> 1. Use the *if* statement and the *Get-ItemProperty* cmdlet to retrieve the value of the registry key property. Specify the *-ErrorAction* (*ea* is an alias) parameter of *SilentlyContinue* (0 is the enumeration value associated with *SilentlyContinue*).
>
> 2. In the script block for the *if* statement, display a message that the registry property exists, or just exit.
>
> 3. In the *else* statement, call *Set-ItemProperty* to create and set the value of the registry key property.
>
>   This technique is shown here.
>
>    ```
>    if((Get-ItemProperty -Path HKCU:\Software\test -Name bogus -ea 0).bogus
>    {'Property already exists'}
>     ELSE { Set-ItemProperty -Path HKCU:\Software\test -Name bogus -Value 'initial value'}
>    ```

Understanding the variable provider

The variable provider provides access to the variables that are defined within Windows PowerShell. These variables include both user-defined variables, such as *$mred*, and system-defined variables, such as *$host*. You can obtain a listing of the cmdlets designed to work specifically with variables by using the *Get-Help* cmdlet and specifying **variable* as a value for the *-Name* parameter. In the following example, the *-Name* parameter is positional, in the first position, and is omitted. To return only cmdlets, you use the *Where-Object* cmdlet and filter on the category that is equal to *cmdlet*. This command is shown here.

```
Get-Help *variable | Where-Object category -eq "cmdlet"
```

The resulting list contains five cmdlets but is a little jumbled and difficult to read. So let's modify the preceding command and specify the properties to return. To do this, use the Up Arrow key and pipeline the returned object into the *Format-List* cmdlet. Add the three properties you are interested in: *name*, *category*, and *synopsis*. The revised command is shown here.

```
Get-Help *variable | Where-Object category -eq "cmdlet"|
Format-List name, category, synopsis
```

> **Note** You will get this output from Windows PowerShell only if you have run the *Update-Help* cmdlet.

The resulting output is much easier to read and understand; it is shown here.

```
Name     : Clear-Variable
Category : Cmdlet
Synopsis : Deletes the value of a variable.

Name     : Get-Variable
Category : Cmdlet
Synopsis : Gets the variables in the current console.

Name     : New-Variable
Category : Cmdlet
Synopsis : Creates a new variable.

Name     : Remove-Variable
Category : Cmdlet
Synopsis : Deletes a variable and its value.

Name     : Set-Variable
Category : Cmdlet
Synopsis : Sets the value of a variable. Creates the variable if one...
```

Working with variables

1. Open the Windows PowerShell console.

2. Use the *Set-Location* cmdlet to set the working location to the Variable PS drive. Use the *sl* alias to reduce the need for typing. This command is shown here.

   ```
   SL variable:\
   ```

3. Produce a complete listing of all the variables currently defined in Windows PowerShell. To do this, use the *Get-ChildItem* cmdlet. You can use the alias *gci* to produce this list. The command is shown here.

   ```
   Get-ChildItem
   ```

4. The resulting list is jumbled. Press the Up Arrow key to retrieve the *Get-ChildItem* command, and pipeline the resulting object into the *Sort-Object* cmdlet. Sort on the *name* property. This command is shown here.

   ```
   Get-ChildItem | Sort-Object Name
   ```

   The output from the previous command is shown here.

   ```
   Name                           Value
   ----                           -----
   $                              name
   ?                              True
   ^                              gci
   alias
   alias:
   alias:\
   args                           {}
   BufferSize                     85,3000
   ConfirmPreference              High
   ConsoleFileName
   DebugPreference                SilentlyContinue
   Error                          {System.Management.Automation.IncompleteParseExcep...
   ErrorActionPreference          Continue
   ErrorView                      NormalView
   ExecutionContext               System.Management.Automation.EngineIntrinsics
   false                          False
   FormatEnumerationLimit         4
   HOME                           C:\Users\ed
   Host                           System.Management.Automation.Internal.Host.Interna...
   InformationPreference          Continue
   input                          System.Collections.ArrayList+ArrayListEnumeratorSi...
   LASTEXITCODE                   0
   Matches                        {0}
   MaximumAliasCount              4096
   MaximumDriveCount              4096
   MaximumErrorCount              256
   MaximumFunctionCount           4096
   MaximumHistoryCount            4096
   ```

```
MaximumVariableCount          4096
MyInvocation                  System.Management.Automation.InvocationInfo
NestedPromptLevel             0
null
OutputEncoding                System.Text.ASCIIEncoding
PID                           3156
PROFILE                       C:\Users\ed\Documents\WindowsPowerShell\Microsoft....
ProgressPreference            Continue
PSBoundParameters             {}
PSCommandPath
PSCulture                     en-US
PSDefaultParameterValues      {}
PSEmailServer
PSHOME                        C:\Windows\System32\WindowsPowerShell\v1.0
PSScriptRoot
PSSessionApplicationName      wsman
PSSessionConfigurationName    http://schemas.microsoft.com/powershell/Microsoft....
PSSessionOption               System.Management.Automation.Remoting.PSSessionOption
PSUICulture                   en-US
PSVersionTable                {PSVersion, WSManStackVersion, SerializationVersio...
PWD                           Variable:\
ShellId                       Microsoft.PowerShell
StackTrace                       at System.Management.Automation.CmdletParameter...
true                          True
VerbosePreference             SilentlyContinue
WarningPreference             Continue
WhatIfPreference              False
WindowSize                    85,27
```

5. Use the *Get-Variable* cmdlet to retrieve a specific variable. Use the *ShellId* variable. You can use tab completion to speed up typing. The command is shown here.

```
Get-Variable ShellId
```

6. Press the Up Arrow key to retrieve the previous *Get-Variable ShellId* command. Pipeline the object returned into a *Format-List* cmdlet and return all properties. This is shown here.

```
Get-Variable ShellId | Format-List *
```

The resulting output includes the description of the variable, the value, and other information, as shown here.

```
PSPath        : Microsoft.PowerShell.Core\Variable::shellid
PSDrive       : Variable
PSProvider    : Microsoft.PowerShell.Core\Variable
PSIsContainer : False
Name          : ShellId
Description   : The ShellID identifies the current shell.  This is used by
                #Requires.
Value         : Microsoft.PowerShell
Visibility    : Public
Module        :
ModuleName    :
Options       : Constant, AllScope
Attributes    : {}
```

7. Create a new variable called *administrator*. To do this, use the *New-Variable* cmdlet. This command is shown here.

```
New-Variable administrator
```

8. Use the *Get-Variable* cmdlet to retrieve the new *administrator* variable. This command is shown here.

```
Get-Variable administrator
```

The resulting output is shown here. Notice that there is no value for the variable.

```
Name                    Value
----                    -----
administrator
```

9. Assign a value to the new administrator variable. To do this, use the *Set-Variable* cmdlet. Specify the *administrator* variable name, and supply your given name as the value for the variable. This command is shown here.

```
Set-Variable administrator -value mred
```

10. Press the Up Arrow key two times to retrieve the previous *Get-Variable administrator* command. This command is shown here.

```
Get-Variable administrator
```

The output displays both the variable name and the value associated with the variable. This is shown here.

```
Name                    Value
----                    -----
administrator           mred
```

11. Use the *Remove-Variable* cmdlet to remove the administrator variable you previously created. This command is shown here.

```
Remove-Variable administrator
```

You could also use the *Del* alias while on the Variable drive, as shown here.

```
del .\administrator
```

12. Press the Up Arrow key two times to retrieve the previous *Get-Variable administrator* command. This command is shown here.

```
Get-Variable administrator
```

The variable has been deleted. The resulting output is shown here.

```
Get-Variable : Cannot find a variable with name 'administrator'.
At line:1 char:13
+ Get-Variable <<<< administrator
```

This concludes this procedure.

Exploring Windows PowerShell providers: Step-by-step exercises

In this exercise, you'll explore the use of the certificate provider in Windows PowerShell. You will navigate the certificate provider by using the same types of commands used with the file system. You will then explore the environment provider by using the same methodology.

Exploring the certificate provider

1. Open the Windows PowerShell console.

2. Obtain a listing of all the properties available for use with the *Get-ChildItem* cmdlet by pipelining the results into the *Get-Member* cmdlet. To filter out only the properties, pipeline the results into a *Where-Object* cmdlet and specify the *membertype* to be equal to *property*. This command is shown here.

   ```
   Get-ChildItem | Get-Member | Where-Object {$_.membertype -eq "property"}
   ```

3. Set your location to the Certificate drive. To identify the Certificate drive, use the *Get-PSDrive* cmdlet. Use the *Where-Object* cmdlet and filter on names that begin with the letter *c*. This is shown here.

   ```
   Get-PSDrive | where name -like "c*"
   ```

   The results of this command are shown here.

   ```
   Name        Used (GB)     Free (GB) Provider       Root
   ----        ---------     --------- --------       ----
   C              110.38         38.33 FileSystem     C:\
   Cert                               Certificate     \
   ```

4. Use the *Set-Location* cmdlet to change to the Certificate drive.

   ```
   Sl cert:\
   ```

5. Use the *Get-ChildItem* cmdlet to produce a listing of all the certificates on the machine.

   ```
   GCI
   ```

The output from the previous command is shown here.

```
Location    : CurrentUser
StoreNames  : {SmartCardRoot, Root, Trust, AuthRoot...}

Location    : LocalMachine
StoreNames  : {TrustedPublisher, ClientAuthIssuer, Remote Desktop, Root...}
```

6. The listing seems somewhat incomplete. To determine whether there are additional certificates installed on the machine, use the *Get-ChildItem* cmdlet again, but this time specify the *-recurse* argument. Modify the previous command by using the Up Arrow key. The command is shown here.

    ```
    GCI -Recurse
    ```

7. The output from the previous command seems to take a long time to run and produces hundreds of lines of output. To make the listing more readable, pipeline the output to a text file, and then open the file in Notepad. The command to do this is shown here.

    ```
    GCI -Recurse > C:\a.txt; notepad.exe a.txt
    ```

    This concludes this step-by-step exercise.

In the following exercise, you'll work with the Windows PowerShell environment provider.

Examining the environment provider

1. Open the Windows PowerShell console.

2. Use the *New-PSDrive* cmdlet to create a drive mapping to the alias provider. The name of the new PS drive will be *al*. The *-PSProvider* parameter is *alias*, and the root will be dot (.). This command is shown here.

    ```
    New-PSDrive -Name al -PSProvider alias -Root .
    ```

3. Change your working location to the new PS drive you called *al*. To do this, use the *sl* alias for the *Set-Location* cmdlet. This is shown here.

    ```
    SL al:\
    ```

4. Use the *gci* alias for the *Get-ChildItem* cmdlet, and pipeline the resulting object into the *Sort-Object* cmdlet by using the *sort* alias. Supply *name* as the property to sort on. This command is shown here.

    ```
    GCI | Sort -Property name
    ```

5. Press the Up Arrow key to retrieve the previous *gci | sort -Property name* command, and modify it to use a *Where-Object* cmdlet to return aliases only when the name begins with a letter after *t* in the alphabet. Use the *where* alias to avoid typing the entire name of the cmdlet.

The resulting command is shown here.

```
GCI | Sort -Property name | Where Name -gt "t"
```

6. Change your location back to drive C. To do this, use the *sl* alias and supply the C:\ argument. This is shown here.

```
SL C:\
```

7. Remove the PS drive mapping for al. To do this, use the *Remove-PSDrive* cmdlet and supply the name of the PS drive to remove. Note that this command does not take a trailing colon (:) or colon with backslash (:\). The command is shown here.

```
Remove-PSDrive al
```

8. Use the *Get-PSDrive* cmdlet to confirm that the al drive has been removed. This is shown here.

```
Get-PSDrive
```

9. Use the *Get-Item* cmdlet to obtain a listing of all the environment variables. Use the *-Path* parameter and supply *env:* as the value. This is shown here.

```
Get-Item -Path env:\
```

10. Press the Up Arrow key to retrieve the previous command, and pipeline the resulting object into the *Get-Member* cmdlet. This is shown here.

```
Get-Item -path env:\ | Get-Member
```

The results from the previous command are shown here.

```
TypeName: System.Collections.Generic.Dictionary'2+ValueCollection[[System.
String, mscorlib, Version=2.0.0.0, Culture=neutral, PublicKeyToken=b77a5c561934e0
89],[System.Collections.DictionaryEntry, mscorlib, Version=2.0.0.0, Culture=
neutral, PublicKeyToken=b77a5c561934e089]]

Name             MemberType   Definition
----             ----------   ----------
CopyTo           Method       System.Void CopyTo(DictionaryEntry[] array, Int32...
Equals           Method       System.Boolean Equals(Object obj)
GetEnumerator    Method       System.Collections.Generic.Dictionary'2+ValueColl...
GetHashCode      Method       System.Int32 GetHashCode()
GetType          Method       System.Type GetType()
get_Count        Method       System.Int32 get_Count()
ToString         Method       System.String ToString()
PSDrive          NoteProperty System.Management.Automation.PSDriveInfo PSDrive=Env
PSIsContainer    NoteProperty System.Boolean PSIsContainer=True
PSPath           NoteProperty System.String PSPath=Microsoft.PowerShell.Core\En...
PSProvider       NoteProperty System.Management.Automation.ProviderInfo PSProvi...
Count            Property     System.Int32 Count {get;}
```

11. Press the Up Arrow key twice to return to the *Get-Item -Path env:* command. Use the Home key to move your cursor to the beginning of the line. Add a variable called *$objEnv* and use it to hold the object returned by the *Get-Item -Path env:* command. The completed command is shown here.

```
$objEnv=Get-Item -Path env:\
```

12. From the listing of members of the environment object, find the *count* property. Use this property to print out the total number of environment variables. As you type **$o**, try to use tab completion to avoid typing. Also try to use tab completion as you type the **c** in *count*. The completed command is shown here.

```
$objEnv.Count
```

13. Examine the methods of the object returned by *Get-Item –Path env:*. Notice that there is a *Get_Count* method. Let's use that method. The code is shown here.

```
$objEnv.Get_count
```

When this code is executed, however, the results define the method rather than execute the *Get_Count* method. These results are shown here.

```
OverloadDefinitions
-------------------
int get_Count()
int ICollection[DictionaryEntry].get_Count()
int ICollection.get_Count()
```

14. To retrieve the actual number of environment variables, you need to use empty parentheses at the end of the method. This is shown here.

```
$objEnv.Get_count()
```

15. If you want to know exactly what type of object is contained in the *$objEnv* variable, you can use the *GetType* method, as shown here.

```
$objEnv.GetType()
```

This command returns the results shown here.

```
IsPublic IsSerial Name                 BaseType
-------- -------- ----                 --------
False    True     ValueCollection      System.Object
```

This concludes this exercise.

Chapter 3 quick reference

To	Do this
Produce a listing of all variables defined in a Windows PowerShell session	Use the cmdlet to change location to the Variable PS drive, and then use the *Get-ChildItem* cmdlet.
Obtain a listing of all the aliases	Use the *Set-Location* cmdlet to change location to the Alias PS drive, and then use the *Get-ChildItem* cmdlet to produce a listing of aliases. Pipeline the resulting object into the *Where-Object* cmdlet and filter on the *name* property for the appropriate value.
Delete a directory that is empty	Use the *Remove-Item* cmdlet and supply the name of the directory.
Delete a directory that contains other items	Use the *Remove-Item* cmdlet, supply the name of the directory, and specify the *-Recurse* switch parameter.
Create a new text file	Use the *New-Item* cmdlet and specify the *-Path* parameter for the directory location. Supply the *-Name* parameter, and specify the *-ItemType* parameter as *file*. Example: *New-Item -Path C:\Mytest -Name Myfile.txt -ItemType file*
Obtain a listing of registry keys from a registry hive	Use the *Get-ChildItem* cmdlet and specify the appropriate PS drive name for the *-Path* parameter. Complete the path with the appropriate registry path. Example: *gci -Path HKLM:\software*
Obtain a listing of all functions on the system	Use the *Get-ChildItem* cmdlet and supply the PS drive name of *function:* to the *-Path* Parameter. Example: *gci -Path function:*

Using Windows PowerShell remoting and jobs

After completing this chapter, you will be able to

- Use Windows PowerShell remoting to connect to a remote system.

- Use Windows PowerShell remoting to run commands on a remote system.

- Use Windows PowerShell jobs to run commands in the background.

- Receive the results of background jobs.

- Keep the results of background jobs.

Understanding Windows PowerShell remoting

The configuration of Windows PowerShell remoting on the server side is easy—it just works. On the client side, it must first be enabled, and then it also just works. When talking about Windows PowerShell remoting, a bit of confusion can arise because there are several different ways of running commands on remote servers. Depending on your particular network configuration and security needs, one or more methods of remoting might not be appropriate.

Classic remoting

Classic remoting in Windows PowerShell relies on protocols such as DCOM and RPC to make connections to remote machines. Traditionally, these protocols require opening many ports in the firewall and starting various services that the different cmdlets use. To find the Windows PowerShell cmdlets that natively support remoting, use the *Get-Help* cmdlet. Specify a value of *computername* for the *-Parameter* parameter of the *Get-Help* cmdlet. This command produces a nice list of all cmdlets that have native support for remoting. The command and associated output are shown on the following page.

```
PS C:\> Get-Help * -Parameter computername | sort name | Format-Table name, synopsis -AutoSize -
Wrap
```

Name	Synopsis
Add-Computer	Add the local computer to a domain or workgroup.
Clear-EventLog	Deletes all entries from specified event logs on the local or remote computers.
Connect-PSSession	Reconnects to disconnected sessions.
Connect-WSMan	Connects to the WinRM service on a remote computer.
Disconnect-WSMan	Disconnects the client from the WinRM service on a remote computer.
Enter-PSSession	Starts an interactive session with a remote computer.
Get-Counter	Gets performance counter data from local and remote computers.
Get-EventLog	Gets the events in an event log, or a list of the event logs, on the local or remote computers.
Get-HotFix	Gets the hotfixes that have been applied to the local and remote computers.
Get-Process	Gets the processes that are running on the local computer or a remote computer.
Get-PSSession	Gets the Windows PowerShell sessions on local and remote computers.
Get-Service	Gets the services on a local or remote computer.
Get-WinEvent	Gets events from event logs and event tracing log files on local and remote computers.
Get-WmiObject	Gets instances of Windows Management Instrumentation (WMI) classes or information about the available classes.
Get-WSManInstance	Displays management information for a resource instance specified by a Resource URI.
Invoke-Command	Runs commands on local and remote computers.
Invoke-WmiMethod	Calls Windows Management Instrumentation (WMI) methods.
Invoke-WSManAction	Invokes an action on the object that is specified by the Resource URI and by the selectors.
Limit-EventLog	Sets the event log properties that limit the size of the event log and the age of its entries.
New-EventLog	Creates a new event log and a new event source on a local or remote computer.
New-PSSession	Creates a persistent connection to a local or remote computer.
New-WSManInstance	Creates a new instance of a management resource.
Receive-Job	Gets the results of the Windows PowerShell background jobs in the current session.
Receive-PSSession	Gets results of commands in disconnected sessions
Register-WmiEvent	Subscribes to a Windows Management Instrumentation (WMI) event.
Remove-Computer	Removes the local computer from its domain.
Remove-EventLog	Deletes an event log or unregisters an event source.
Remove-PSSession	Closes one or more Windows PowerShell sessions (PSSessions).
Remove-WmiObject	Deletes an instance of an existing Windows Management Instrumentation (WMI) class.
Remove-WSManInstance	Deletes a management resource instance.
Rename-Computer	Renames a computer.
Restart-Computer	Restarts ("reboots") the operating system on local and remote computers.
Set-Service	Starts, stops, and suspends a service, and changes its properties.
Set-WmiInstance	Creates or updates an instance of an existing Windows Management Instrumentation (WMI) class.

```
Set-WSManInstance      Modifies the management information that is related to a
                       resource.
Show-EventLog          Displays the event logs of the local or a remote computer in
                       Event Viewer.
Stop-Computer          Stops (shuts down) local and remote computers.
Test-Connection        Sends ICMP echo request packets ("pings") to one or more
                       computers.
Test-WSMan             Tests whether the WinRM service is running on a local or
                       remote computer.
Write-EventLog         Writes an event to an event log.
```

As you can tell, many of the Windows PowerShell cmdlets that have the *-ComputerName* parameter relate to Web Services Management (WSMAN), Common Information Model (CIM), or sessions. To remove these cmdlets from the list, modify the command a bit to use *Where-Object* (*?* is an alias for *Where-Object*). The revised command and associated output are shown here.

```
PS C:\> Get-Help * -Parameter computername -Category Cmdlet | ? modulename -match
'PowerShell.Management' | Sort-Object name | Format-Table name, synopsis -AutoSize -Wrap


Name               Synopsis
----               --------
Add-Computer       Add the local computer to a domain or workgroup.
Clear-EventLog     Deletes all entries from specified event logs on the local or
                   remote computers.
Get-EventLog       Gets the events in an event log, or a list of the event logs, on
                   the local or remote computers.
Get-HotFix         Gets the hotfixes that have been applied to the local and remote
                   computers.
Get-Process        Gets the processes that are running on the local computer or a
                   remote computer.
Get-Service        Gets the services on a local or remote computer.
Get-WmiObject      Gets instances of Windows Management Instrumentation (WMI)
                   classes or information about the available classes.
Invoke-WmiMethod   Calls Windows Management Instrumentation (WMI) methods.
Limit-EventLog     Sets the event log properties that limit the size of the event
                   log and the age of its entries.
New-EventLog       Creates a new event log and a new event source on a local or
                   remote computer.
Register-WmiEvent  Subscribes to a Windows Management Instrumentation (WMI) event.
Remove-Computer    Removes the local computer from its domain.
Remove-EventLog    Deletes an event log or unregisters an event source.
Remove-WmiObject   Deletes an instance of an existing Windows Management
                   Instrumentation (WMI) class.
Rename-Computer    Renames a computer.
Restart-Computer   Restarts ("reboots") the operating system on local and remote
                   computers.
Set-Service        Starts, stops, and suspends a service, and changes its properties.
Set-WmiInstance    Creates or updates an instance of an existing Windows Management
                   Instrumentation (WMI) class.
Show-EventLog      Displays the event logs of the local or a remote computer in
                   Event Viewer.
Stop-Computer      Stops (shuts down) local and remote computers.
Test-Connection    Sends ICMP echo request packets ("pings") to one or more
                   computers.
Write-EventLog     Writes an event to an event log.
```

Some of the cmdlets provide the ability to specify credentials. This allows you to use a different user account to make the connection and to retrieve the data. Figure 4-1 displays the credential dialog box that appears when such a cmdlet runs.

FIGURE 4-1 Cmdlets that support the *–Credential* parameter prompt for credentials when supplied with a user name.

This technique of using the *-ComputerName* and *-Credential* parameters in a cmdlet is shown here.

```
PS C:\> Get-WinEvent -LogName application -MaxEvents 1 -ComputerName ex1 -Credential
nwtraders\administrator

TimeCreated            ProviderName                      Id Message
-----------            ------------                      -- -------
7/1/2015 11:54:14 AM MSExchange ADAccess                 2080 Process MAD.EXE (...
```

However, as mentioned earlier, use of these cmdlets often requires opening holes in the firewall or starting specific services. By default, these types of cmdlets fail when they are run on remote machines that don't have relaxed access rules. An example of this type of error is shown here.

```
PS C:\> Get-WinEvent -LogName application -MaxEvents 1 -ComputerName dc1 -Credential
nwtraders\administrator
Get-WinEvent : The RPC server is unavailable
At line:1 char:1
+ Get-WinEvent -LogName application -MaxEvents 1 -ComputerName dc1 -Cre ...
+ ~~~~~~~~~~~~~~~~~~~~~~~~~~~~~~~~~~~~~~~~~~~~~~~~~~~~~~~~~~~~~~~~~~~~~~~~~
    + CategoryInfo          : NotSpecified: (:) [Get-WinEvent], EventLogException
    + FullyQualifiedErrorId : System.Diagnostics.Eventing.Reader.EventLogException,
    Microsoft.PowerShell.Commands.GetWinEventCommand
```

Other cmdlets, such as *Get-Service* and *Get-Process*, do not have a *-Credential* parameter, and therefore the commands associated with cmdlets such as *Get-Service* or *Get-Process* impersonate the logged-on user. Such a command is shown here.

```
PS C:\> Get-Service -ComputerName hyperv -Name bits

Status    Name             DisplayName
------    ----             -----------
Running   bits             Background Intelligent Transfer Ser...
```

The fact that a cmdlet does not support alternate credentials does not mean that the cmdlet must impersonate the logged-on user. Holding down the Shift key and right-clicking the Windows PowerShell icon on the taskbar brings up a menu from which you can select commands to run the program as a different user. This menu is shown in Figure 4-2.

FIGURE 4-2 You can use commands on the menu from the Windows PowerShell console to run with different security credentials.

The Run As Different User dialog box is shown in Figure 4-3.

FIGURE 4-3 You can use the Run As Different User dialog box to enter a different user context.

Using the Run As Different User dialog box makes alternative credentials available for Windows PowerShell cmdlets that do not support the *-Credential* parameter.

WinRM

Beginning with Windows Server 2012, Windows Server installs with Windows Remote Management (WinRM) configured and running to support remote Windows PowerShell commands. WinRM is the Microsoft implementation of the industry-standard WS-Management protocol. As such, WinRM provides a firewall-friendly method of accessing remote systems in an interoperable manner. It is the remoting mechanism used by the CIM cmdlets. As soon as your Windows Server computer is up and running, you can make a remote connection and run commands, or open an interactive Windows PowerShell console. In Windows 10, on the other hand, WinRM is locked down. Therefore, the first step is to use the *Enable-PSRemoting* cmdlet to configure Windows PowerShell remoting on the client machine. When *Enable-PSRemoting* is run, it performs the following steps:

1. Starts the WinRM service

2. Sets the WinRM service startup type to Automatic

3. Creates a listener to accept requests from any IP address

4. Enables inbound firewall exceptions for WSMAN traffic

5. Sets a target listener named *Microsoft.powershell*

6. Sets a target listener named *Microsoft.powershell.workflow*

7. Sets a target listener named *Microsoft.powershell32* on 64-bit computers

8. Enables all session configurations

9. Changes the security descriptor of all session configurations to allow remote access

10. Restarts the WinRM service to make the changes effective

When *Enable-PSRemoting* is run, the cmdlet prompts you to agree to performing the specified action. If you are familiar with the steps the cmdlet performs and you do not make any changes from the defaults, you can run the command by using the *-Force* switch parameter, and it will not prompt prior to making the changes. The syntax of this command is shown here.

```
Enable-PSRemoting -force
```

The use of the *Enable-PSRemoting* function in interactive mode is shown here, along with all associated output from the command.

```
PS C:\> Enable-PSRemoting

WinRM Quick Configuration
Running command "Set-WSManQuickConfig" to enable remote management of this computer by using the
Windows Remote Management (WinRM) service.
 This includes:
    1. Starting or restarting (if already started) the WinRM service
    2. Setting the WinRM service startup type to Automatic
    3. Creating a listener to accept requests on any IP address
    4. Enabling Windows Firewall inbound rule exceptions for WS-Management traffic
(for http only).

Do you want to continue?
[Y] Yes  [A] Yes to All  [N] No  [L] No to All  [S] Suspend  [?] Help (default is "Y"): y
WinRM is already set up to receive requests on this computer.
WinRM has been updated for remote management.
Created a WinRM listener on HTTP://* to accept WS-Man requests to any IP on this machine.
WinRM firewall exception enabled.

Confirm
Are you sure you want to perform this action?
Performing the operation "Set-PSSessionConfiguration" on target "Name:
microsoft.powershell SDDL:
O:NSG:BAD:P(A;;GA;;;BA)(A;;GA;;;IU)(A;;GA;;;RM)S:P(AU;FA;GA;;;WD)(AU;SA;GXGW;;;WD).
This lets selected users remotely run Windows PowerShell commands on this
computer.".
[Y] Yes  [A] Yes to All  [N] No  [L] No to All  [S] Suspend  [?] Help
(default is "Y"):y
```

```
Confirm
Are you sure you want to perform this action?
Performing the operation "Set-PSSessionConfiguration" on target "Name:
microsoft.powershell.workflow SDDL:
O:NSG:BAD:P(A;;GA;;;BA)(A;;GA;;;RM)S:P(AU;FA;GA;;;WD)(AU;SA;GXGW;;;WD). This lets
selected users remotely run Windows PowerShell commands on this computer.".
[Y] Yes  [A] Yes to All  [N] No  [L] No to All  [S] Suspend  [?] Help
(default is "Y"):y

Confirm
Are you sure you want to perform this action?
Performing the operation "Set-PSSessionConfiguration" on target "Name:
microsoft.powershell32 SDDL:
O:NSG:BAD:P(A;;GA;;;BA)(A;;GA;;;IU)(A;;GA;;;RM)S:P(AU;FA;GA;;;WD)(AU;SA;GXGW;;;WD).
This lets selected users remotely run Windows PowerShell commands on this
computer.".
[Y] Yes  [A] Yes to All  [N] No  [L] No to All  [S] Suspend  [?] Help
(default is "Y"):y
PS C:\>
```

When Windows PowerShell remoting has been configured, use the *Test-WSMan* cmdlet to ensure that the WinRM remoting is properly configured and is accepting requests. A properly configured system replies with the information shown here.

```
PS C:\> Test-WSMan -ComputerName c10


wsmid           : http://schemas.dmtf.org/wbem/wsman/identity/1/wsmanidentity.xsd
ProtocolVersion : http://schemas.dmtf.org/wbem/wsman/1/wsman.xsd
ProductVendor   : Microsoft Corporation
ProductVersion  : OS: 0.0.0 SP: 0.0 Stack: 3.0
```

This cmdlet also works with Windows PowerShell 5.0 remoting. The output shown here is from a domain controller running Windows Server 2012 R2 with Windows PowerShell 5.0 installed and WinRM configured for remote access.

```
PS C:\> Test-WSMan -ComputerName DC1


wsmid           : http://schemas.dmtf.org/wbem/wsman/identity/1/wsmanidentity.xsd
ProtocolVersion : http://schemas.dmtf.org/wbem/wsman/1/wsman.xsd
ProductVendor   : Microsoft Corporation
ProductVersion  : OS: 0.0.0 SP: 0.0 Stack: 3.0
```

If WinRM is not configured, an error returns from the system. Such an error from a Windows 8 client is shown here.

```
PS C:\> Test-WSMan -ComputerName w8c10
Test-WSMan : <f:WSManFault
xmlns:f="http://schemas.microsoft.com/wbem/wsman/1/wsmanfault" Code="2150859046"
Machine="w8c504.nwtraders.net"><f:Message>WinRM cannot complete the operation. Verify
that the specified computer name is valid, that the computer is accessible over the
network, and that a firewall exception for the WinRM service is enabled and allows
access from this computer. By default, the WinRM firewall exception for public
profiles limits access to remote computers within the same local subnet.
</f:Message></f:WSManFault>
At line:1 char:1
+ Test-WSMan -ComputerName w8c10
+ ~~~~~~~~~~~~~~~~~~~~~~~~~~~~~~~
    + CategoryInfo          : InvalidOperation: (w8c10:String) [Test-WSMan], Invalid
    OperationException
    + FullyQualifiedErrorId : WsManError,Microsoft.WSMan.Management.TestWSManCommand
```

Keep in mind that configuring WinRM via the *Enable-PSRemoting* cmdlet does not enable the *Remote Management* firewall exception, and therefore *PING* commands will not work by default when pinging to a Windows 8 client system. This is shown here.

```
PS C:\> ping w8c504

Pinging w8c504.nwtraders.net [192.168.0.56] with 32 bytes of data:
Request timed out.
Request timed out.
Request timed out.
Request timed out.

Ping statistics for 192.168.0.56:
    Packets: Sent = 4, Received = 0, Lost = 4 (100% loss).
```

Pings to a Windows Server 2012 R2 server, however, do work. This is shown here.

```
PS C:\> ping dc1

Pinging dc1.nwtraders.com [192.168.10.1] with 32 bytes of data:
Reply from 192.168.10.1: bytes=32 time<1ms TTL=128
Reply from 192.168.10.1: bytes=32 time<1ms TTL=128
Reply from 192.168.10.1: bytes=32 time<1ms TTL=128
Reply from 192.168.10.1: bytes=32 time<1ms TTL=128

Ping statistics for 192.168.10.1:
    Packets: Sent = 4, Received = 4, Lost = 0 (0% loss),
Approximate round trip times in milli-seconds:
    Minimum = 0ms, Maximum = 0ms, Average = 0ms
PS C:\>
```

Creating a remote Windows PowerShell session

For simple configuration on a single remote machine, entering a remote Windows PowerShell session is the answer. To enter a remote Windows PowerShell session, use the *Enter-PSSession* cmdlet. This creates an interactive remote Windows PowerShell session on a target machine and uses the default remote endpoint. If you do not supply credentials, the remote session impersonates the currently logged-on user. The output shown here illustrates connecting to a remote computer named dc1. After the connection is established, the Windows PowerShell prompt changes to include the name of the remote system. *Set-Location* (which has an alias of *sl*) changes the working directory on the remote system to C:\. Next, the *Get-CimInstance* cmdlet retrieves the BIOS information for the remote system. The *exit* command exits the remote session, and the Windows PowerShell prompt returns to the prompt configured previously.

```
PS C:\> Enter-PSSession -ComputerName dc1
[dc1]: PS C:\Users\Administrator\Documents> sl c:\
[dc1]: PS C:\> gcim win32_bios


SMBIOSBIOSVersion : Hyper-V UEFI Release v1.0
Manufacturer      : Microsoft Corporation
Name              : Hyper-V UEFI Release v1.0
SerialNumber      : 3601-6926-9922-0181-5225-8175-58
Version           : VRTUAL - 1



[dc1]: PS C:\> exit
PS C:\>
```

The good thing is that when you use the Windows PowerShell transcript tool via *Start-Transcript*, the transcript tool captures output from the remote Windows PowerShell session, in addition to output from the local session. Indeed, all commands entered appear in the transcript. The following commands illustrate beginning a transcript, entering a remote Windows PowerShell session, and stopping the transcript.

```
PS C:\> Start-Transcript
Transcript started, output file is C:\Users\administrator\Documents\PowerShell_trans
cript.C10.DyQ6Wy5p.20150711150938.txt
PS C:\> Enter-PSSession -ComputerName dc1
PS C:\> Stop-Transcript
Transcript stopped, output file is C:\Users\administrator\Documents\PowerShell_trans
cript.C10.DyQ6Wy5p.20150711150938.txt
```

Figure 4-4 displays a copy of the transcript from the previous session.

FIGURE 4-4 The Windows PowerShell transcript tool records commands and output received from a remote Windows PowerShell session.

If you anticipate making multiple connections to a remote system, use the *New-PSSession* cmdlet to create a remote Windows PowerShell session. You can use *New-PSSession* to store the remote session in a variable and to enter and leave the remote session as often as required—without the additional overhead of creating and destroying remote sessions. In the commands that follow, a new Windows PowerShell session is created via the *New-PSSession* cmdlet. The newly created session is stored in the *$dc1* variable. Next, the *Enter-PSSession* cmdlet is used to enter the remote session by using the stored session. A command retrieves the remote hostname, and the remote session is exited via the *exit* command. Next, the session is re-entered, and the last process is retrieved. The session is exited again. Finally, the *Get-PSSession* cmdlet retrieves Windows PowerShell sessions on the system, and all sessions are removed via the *Remove-PSSession* cmdlet.

```
PS C:\> $dc1 = New-PSSession -ComputerName dc1 -Credential nwtraders\administrator
PS C:\> Enter-PSSession $dc1
[dc1]: PS C:\Users\Administrator\Documents> hostname
dc1
[dc1]: PS C:\Users\Administrator\Documents> exit
PS C:\> Enter-PSSession $dc1
[dc1]: PS C:\Users\Administrator\Documents> gps | select -Last 1

Handles  NPM(K)    PM(K)      WS(K) VM(M)   CPU(s)     Id ProcessName
-------  ------    -----      ----- -----   ------     -- -----------
    292       9    39536      50412   158     1.97   2332 wsmprovhost
```

```
[dc1]: PS C:\Users\Administrator\Documents> exit
PS C:\> Get-PSSession

Id Name          ComputerName   State      ConfigurationName      Availability
-- ----          ------------   -----      -----------------      ------------
 8 Session8      dc1            Opened     Microsoft.PowerShell      Available


PS C:\> Get-PSSession | Remove-PSSession
PS C:\>
```

Running a single Windows PowerShell command

If you have a single command to run, it does not make sense to go through all the trouble of building and entering an interactive remote Windows PowerShell session. Instead of creating a remote Windows PowerShell console session, you can run a single command by using the *Invoke-Command* cmdlet. If you have a single command to run, use the cmdlet directly and specify the computer name and any credentials required for the connection. You are still creating a remote session, but you are also removing the session. Therefore, if you have a lot of commands to run against the remote machine, a performance problem could arise. But for single commands, this technique works well. The technique is shown here, where the last process running on the Ex1 remote server is shown.

```
PS C:\> Invoke-Command -ComputerName ex1 -ScriptBlock {gps | select -Last 1}

Handles  NPM(K)    PM(K)      WS(K) VM(M)   CPU(s)     Id ProcessName   PSComputerNa
                                                                        me
-------  ------    -----      ----- -----   ------     -- -----------   ------------
    224      34    47164      51080   532     0.58  10164 wsmprovhost   ex1
```

If you have several commands, or if you anticipate making multiple connections, the *Invoke-Command* cmdlet accepts a session name or a session object in the same manner as the *Enter-PSSession* cmdlet. In the output shown here, a new *PSSession* is created to a remote computer named dc1. The remote session is used to retrieve two different pieces of information. When the Windows PowerShell remote session is completed, the session stored in the *$dc1* variable is explicitly removed.

```
PS C:\> $dc1 = New-PSSession -ComputerName dc1 -Credential nwtraders\administrator
PS C:\> Invoke-Command -Session $dc1 -ScriptBlock {hostname}
dc1
PS C:\> Invoke-Command -Session $dc1 -ScriptBlock {Get-EventLog application -Newest 1}

  Index Time          EntryType   Source               InstanceID Message PSCompu
                                                                          terName
  ----- ----          ---------   ------               ---------- ------- -------
  17702 Jul 01 12:59  Information ESENT                       701 DFSR... dc1


PS C:\> Remove-PSSession $dc1
```

By using *Invoke-Command*, you can run the same command against a large number of remote systems. The secret behind this power is that the *-ComputerName* parameter from the *Invoke-Command* cmdlet accepts an array of computer names. In the output shown here, an array of computer names is stored in the variable *$cn*. Next, the *$cred* variable holds the *PSCredential* object for the remote connections. Finally, the *Invoke-Command* cmdlet is used to make connections to all of the remote machines and to return the BIOS information from the systems. The nice thing about this technique is that an additional property, *PSComputerName,* is added to the returning object, so you can easily identify which BIOS is associated with which computer system. The commands and associated output are shown here.

```
PS C:\> $cn = "dc1","dc3","ex1","sql1","wsus1","wds1","hyperv1","hyperv2","hyperv3"
PS C:\> $cred = get-credential nwtraders\administrator
PS C:\> Invoke-Command -cn $cn -cred $cred -ScriptBlock {gwmi win32_bios}


SMBIOSBIOSVersion : BAP6710H.86A.0072.2011.0927.1425
Manufacturer      : Intel Corp.
Name              : BIOS Date: 09/27/11 14:25:42 Ver: 04.06.04
SerialNumber      :
Version           : INTEL  - 1072009
PSComputerName    : hyperv3

SMBIOSBIOSVersion : A11
Manufacturer      : Dell Inc.
Name              : Phoenix ROM BIOS PLUS Version 1.10 A11
SerialNumber      : BDY91L1
Version           : DELL   - 15
PSComputerName    : hyperv2

SMBIOSBIOSVersion : A01
Manufacturer      : Dell Computer Corporation
Name              : Default System BIOS
SerialNumber      : 9HQ1S21
Version           : DELL   - 6
PSComputerName    : dc1

SMBIOSBIOSVersion : 090004
Manufacturer      : American Megatrends Inc.
Name              : BIOS Date: 03/19/09 22:51:32  Ver: 09.00.04
SerialNumber      : 3692-0963-1044-7503-9631-2546-83
Version           : VRTUAL - 3000919
PSComputerName    : wsus1

SMBIOSBIOSVersion : V1.6
Manufacturer      : American Megatrends Inc.
Name              : Default System BIOS
SerialNumber      : To Be Filled By O.E.M.
Version           : 7583MS - 20091228
PSComputerName    : hyperv1
```

```
SMBIOSBIOSVersion : 080015
Manufacturer      : American Megatrends Inc.
Name              : Default System BIOS
SerialNumber      : None
Version           : 091709 - 20090917
PSComputerName    : sql1

SMBIOSBIOSVersion : 080015
Manufacturer      : American Megatrends Inc.
Name              : Default System BIOS
SerialNumber      : None
Version           : 091709 - 20090917
PSComputerName    : wds1

SMBIOSBIOSVersion : 090004
Manufacturer      : American Megatrends Inc.
Name              : BIOS Date: 03/19/09 22:51:32  Ver: 09.00.04
SerialNumber      : 8994-9999-0865-2542-2186-8044-69
Version           : VRTUAL - 3000919
PSComputerName    : dc3

SMBIOSBIOSVersion : 090004
Manufacturer      : American Megatrends Inc.
Name              : BIOS Date: 03/19/09 22:51:32  Ver: 09.00.04
SerialNumber      : 2301-9053-4386-9162-8072-5664-16
Version           : VRTUAL - 3000919
PSComputerName    : ex1


PS C:\>
```

Using Windows PowerShell jobs

Windows PowerShell jobs can be used to run one or more commands in the background. After you start the Windows PowerShell job, the Windows PowerShell console returns immediately for further use, so you can accomplish multiple tasks at the same time. You can begin a new Windows PowerShell job by using the *Start-Job* cmdlet. The command you want to run as a job is placed in a script block, and the jobs are sequentially named *Job1*, *Job2*, and so on. This is shown here.

```
PS C:\> Start-Job -ScriptBlock {get-process}

Id     Name       PSJobTypeName  State     HasMoreData   Location
--     ----       -------------  -----     -----------   --------
10     Job10      BackgroundJob  Running   True          localhost


PS C:\>
```

The jobs receive job IDs that are also sequentially numbered. The first job created in a Windows PowerShell console always has a job ID of 1. You can use either the job ID or the job name to obtain information about the job. This is shown here.

```
PS C:\> Get-Job -Name job10

Id     Name         PSJobTypeName   State       HasMoreData   Location
--     ----         -------------   -----       -----------   --------
10     Job10        BackgroundJob   Completed   True          localhost

PS C:\> Get-Job -Id 10

Id     Name         PSJobTypeName   State       HasMoreData   Location
--     ----         -------------   -----       -----------   --------
10     Job10        BackgroundJob   Completed   True          localhost


PS C:\>
```

When you notice that the job has completed, you can receive the job. The *Receive-Job* cmdlet returns the same information that returns if a job is not used. The Job1 output is shown here (truncated to save space).

```
PS C:\> Receive-Job -Name job10

Handles  NPM(K)    PM(K)      WS(K) VM(M)   CPU(s)     Id ProcessName
-------  ------    -----      ----- -----   ------     -- -----------
     62       9     1672       6032    80     0.00   1408 apdproxy
    132       9     2316       5632    62            1364 atieclxx
    122       7     1716       4232    32             948 atiesrxx
    114       9    14664      15372    48            1492 audiodg
    556      62    53928       5368   616     3.17   3408 CCC
     58       8     2960       7068    70     0.19    928 conhost
     32       5     1468       3468    52     0.00   5068 conhost
    784      14     3284       5092    56             416 csrss
    529      27     2928      17260   145             496 csrss
    182      13     8184      11152    96     0.50   2956 DCPSysMgr
    135      11     2880       7552    56            2056 DCPSysMgrSvc
... (truncated output)
```

After a job has been received, that is it—the data is gone, unless you saved it to a variable or you call the *Receive-Job* cmdlet with the *-Keep* switch parameter. The following code attempts to retrieve the information stored from job10, but as shown here, no data returns.

```
PS C:\> Receive-Job -Name job10
PS C:\>
```

What can be confusing about this is that the job still exists, and the *Get-Job* cmdlet continues to retrieve information about the job. This is shown here.

```
PS C:\> Get-Job -Id 10

Id     Name          PSJobTypeName   State       HasMoreData    Location
--     ----          -------------   -----       -----------    --------
10     Job10         BackgroundJob   Completed   False          localhost
```

As a best practice, use the *Remove-Job* cmdlet to delete remnants of completed jobs when you are finished using the job object. This will avoid confusion regarding active jobs, completed jobs, and jobs waiting to be processed. After a job has been removed, the *Get-Job* cmdlet returns an error if you attempt to retrieve information about the job—because it no longer exists. This is illustrated here.

```
PS C:\> Remove-Job -Name job10
PS C:\> Get-Job -Id 10
Get-Job : The command cannot find a job with the job ID 10. Verify the value of the
Id parameter and then try the command again.
At line:1 char:1
+ Get-Job -Id 10
+ ~~~~~~~~~~~~~~~
    + CategoryInfo          : ObjectNotFound: (10:Int32) [Get-Job], PSArgumentException
    + FullyQualifiedErrorId : JobWithSpecifiedSessionNotFound,Microsoft.PowerShell.
    Commands.GetJobCommand
```

When working with the job cmdlets, I like to give the jobs their own names. A job that returns process objects via the *Get-Process* cmdlet might be called *getProc*. A contextual naming scheme works better than trying to keep track of names such as *Job1* and *Job2*. Do not worry about making your job names too long, because you can use wildcard characters to simplify the typing requirement. When you receive a job, make sure you store the returned objects in a variable. This is shown here.

```
PS C:\> Start-Job -Name getProc -ScriptBlock {get-process}

Id     Name          PSJobTypeName   State       HasMoreData    Location
--     ----          -------------   -----       -----------    --------
12     getProc       BackgroundJob   Running     True           localhost


PS C:\> Get-Job -Name get*

Id     Name          PSJobTypeName   State       HasMoreData    Location
--     ----          -------------   -----       -----------    --------
12     getProc       BackgroundJob   Completed   True           localhost


PS C:\> $procObj = Receive-Job -Name get*
PS C:\>
```

When you have the returned objects in a variable, you can use the objects with other Windows PowerShell cmdlets. One thing to keep in mind is that the object is deserialized. This is shown on the following page, where I use *gm* as an alias for the *Get-Member* cmdlet.

```
PS C:\> $procObj | gm
```

```
    TypeName: Deserialized.System.Diagnostics.Process
```

This means that not all the standard members from the *System.Diagnostics.Process* .NET Framework object are available. The default methods are shown here (*gps* is an alias for the *Get-Process* cmdlet, *gm* is an alias for *Get-Member*, and *-m* is enough of the *-MemberType* parameter to distinguish it on the Windows PowerShell console line).

```
PS C:\> gps | gm -m method
```

```
    TypeName: System.Diagnostics.Process

Name                         MemberType Definition
----                         ---------- ----------
BeginErrorReadLine           Method     System.Void BeginErrorReadLine()
BeginOutputReadLine          Method     System.Void BeginOutputReadLine()
CancelErrorRead              Method     System.Void CancelErrorRead()
CancelOutputRead             Method     System.Void CancelOutputRead()
Close                        Method     System.Void Close()
CloseMainWindow              Method     bool CloseMainWindow()
CreateObjRef                 Method     System.Runtime.Remoting.ObjRef CreateObjRef(type
                                        requestedType)
Dispose                      Method     System.Void Dispose()
Equals                       Method     bool Equals(System.Object obj)
GetHashCode                  Method     int GetHashCode()
GetLifetimeService           Method     System.Object GetLifetimeService()
GetType                      Method     type GetType()
InitializeLifetimeService    Method     System.Object InitializeLifetimeService()
Kill                         Method     System.Void Kill()
Refresh                      Method     System.Void Refresh()
Start                        Method     bool Start()
ToString                     Method     string ToString()
WaitForExit                  Method     bool WaitForExit(int milliseconds), System.Void
                                        WaitForExit()
WaitForInputIdle             Method     bool WaitForInputIdle(int milliseconds), bool
                                        WaitForInputIdle()
```

Methods from the deserialized object are shown here, where I use the same command I used previously.

```
PS C:\> $procObj | gm -m method
```

```
    TypeName: Deserialized.System.Diagnostics.Process

Name     MemberType Definition
----     ---------- ----------
ToString Method     string ToString(), string ToString(string format, System.IFormatProvider
         formatProvider)
```

```
PS C:\>
```

A listing of the cmdlets that use the noun *job* is shown here.

```
PS C:\> Get-Command -Noun job | select name

Name
----
Get-Job
Receive-Job
Remove-Job
Resume-Job
Start-Job
Stop-Job
Suspend-Job
Wait-Job
```

When starting a Windows PowerShell job via the *Start-Job* cmdlet, you can specify a name to hold the returned job object. You can also assign the returned job object in a variable by using a straight-forward value assignment.

```
PS C:\> $rtn = Start-Job -Name net -ScriptBlock {Get-Net6to4Configuration}
PS C:\> Get-Job -Name net

Id    Name    PSJobTypeName    State       HasMoreData    Location
--    ----    -------------    -----       -----------    --------
18    net     BackgroundJob    Completed   True           localhost

PS C:\> $rtn

Id    Name    PSJobTypeName    State       HasMoreData    Location
--    ----    -------------    -----       -----------    --------
18    net     BackgroundJob    Completed   True           localhost
```

Retrieving the job via the *Receive-Job* cmdlet consumes the data. You cannot come back and retrieve the returned data again. The code shown here illustrates this concept.

```
PS C:\> Receive-Job $rtn


RunspaceId         : e8ed4ab6-eb88-478c-b2de-5991b5636ef1
Caption            :
Description        : 6to4 Configuration
ElementName        :
InstanceID         : ActiveStore
AutoSharing        : 0
PolicyStore        : ActiveStore
RelayName          : 6to4.ipv6.microsoft.com.
RelayState         : 0
ResolutionInterval : 1440
State              : 0



PS C:\> Receive-Job $rtn
PS C:\>
```

The next example illustrates examining the command and cleaning up the job. To find additional information about the code, use the job object stored in the *$rtn* variable or the *Get-Net6to4Configuration* job. You might prefer using the job object stored in the *$rtn* variable, as shown here.

```
PS C:\> $rtn.Command
Get-Net6to4Configuration
```

To clean up, first remove the leftover job objects by getting the jobs and removing the jobs. This is shown here.

```
PS C:\> Get-Job | Remove-Job
PS C:\> Get-Job
PS C:\>
```

> **Caution** The following example uses the *Win32_Product* class for illustrative purposes. When the *Win32_Product* class is queried, it will initiate an MSI consistency check, which can have undesirable effects. When working with this class, use caution.

When you create a new Windows PowerShell job, it runs in the background. There is no indication as the job runs whether it ends in an error or it's successful. Indeed, you do not have any way to tell when the job even completes, other than to use the *Get-Job* cmdlet several times to find out when the job state changes from *running* to *completed*. For many jobs, this might be perfectly acceptable. In fact, it might even be preferable, if you want to regain control of the Windows PowerShell console as soon as the job begins executing. On other occasions, you might want to be notified when the Windows PowerShell job completes. To accomplish this, you can use the *Wait-Job* cmdlet. You need to give the *Wait-Job* cmdlet either a job name or a job ID. After you have done this, the Windows PowerShell console will pause until the job completes. The job, with its *completed* status, displays on the console. You can then use the *Receive-Job* cmdlet to receive the deserialized objects and store them in a variable (*cn* is a parameter alias for the *-ComputerName* parameter used in the *Get-WmiObject* command). The command shown here starts a job to receive software products installed on a remote server named hyperv1. It impersonates the currently logged-on user and stores the returned object in a variable named *$rtn*.

```
PS C:\> $rtn = Start-Job -ScriptBlock {gwmi win32_product -cn hyperv1}
PS C:\> $rtn

Id    Name         PSJobTypeName    State    HasMoreData    Location
--    ----         -------------    -----    -----------    --------
22    Job22        BackgroundJob    Running  True           localhost

PS C:\> Wait-Job -id 22

Id    Name         PSJobTypeName    State     HasMoreData    Location
--    ----         -------------    -----     -----------    --------
22    Job22        BackgroundJob    Completed True           localhost

PS C:\> $prod = Receive-Job -id 22
PS C:\> $prod.Count
2
```

In a newly opened Windows PowerShell console, the *Start-Job* cmdlet is used to start a new job. The returned job object is stored in the *$rtn* variable. You can pipeline the job object contained in the *$rtn* variable to the *Stop-Job* cmdlet to stop the execution of the job. If you try to use the job object in the *$rtn* variable directly to get job information, an error will be generated. This is shown here.

```
PS C:\> $rtn = Start-Job -ScriptBlock {gwmi win32_product -cn hyperv1}
PS C:\> $rtn | Stop-Job
PS C:\> Get-Job $rtn
Get-Job : The command cannot find the job because the job name
System.Management.Automation.PSRemotingJob was not found. Verify the value of the
Name parameter, and then try the command again.
At line:1 char:1
+ Get-Job $rtn
+ ~~~~~~~~~~~~
    + CategoryInfo          : ObjectNotFound: (System.Manageme...n.PSRemotingJob:
String) [Get-Job], PSArgumentException
    + FullyQualifiedErrorId : JobWithSpecifiedNameNotFound,Microsoft.PowerShell.
Commands.GetJobCommand
```

You can pipeline the job object to the *Get-Job* cmdlet and find that the job is in a stopped state. Use the *Receive-Job* cmdlet to receive the job information, and the *count* property to determine how many software products are included in the variable, as shown here.

```
PS C:\> $rtn | Get-Job
```

Id	Name	PSJobTypeName	State	HasMoreData	Location
2	Job2	BackgroundJob	Stopped	False	localhost

```
PS C:\> $products = Receive-Job -Id 2
PS C:\> $products.count
0
```

In the preceding list you can tell that no software packages were enumerated. This is because the *Get-WmiObject* command to retrieve information from the *Win32_Product* class did not have time to finish.

If you want to keep the data from your job so that you can use it again later, and you do not want to bother storing it in an intermediate variable, use the *-Keep* switch parameter. In the command that follows, the *Get-NetAdapter* cmdlet is used to return network adapter information.

```
PS C:\> Start-Job -ScriptBlock {Get-NetAdapter}
```

Id	Name	PSJobTypeName	State	HasMoreData	Location
4	Job4	BackgroundJob	Running	True	localhost

When checking on the status of a background job and monitoring a job you just created, use the *-Newest* parameter instead of typing a job number, because it is easier to remember. This technique is shown here.

```
PS C:\> Get-Job -Newest 1

Id    Name      PSJobTypeName   State       HasMoreData   Location
--    ----      -------------   -----       -----------   --------
4     Job4      BackgroundJob   Completed   True          localhost
```

Now, to retrieve the information from the job and keep the information available, use the *-Keep* switch parameter, as illustrated here.

```
PS C:\> Receive-Job -Id 4 -Keep
```

```
ifAlias                      : Ethernet
InterfaceAlias               : Ethernet
ifIndex                      : 4
ifDesc                       : Microsoft Hyper-V Network Adapter
ifName                       : Ethernet_32768
DriverVersion                : 10.0.10224.0
LinkLayerAddress             : 00-15-5D-00-2A-1E
MacAddress                   : 00-15-5D-00-2A-1E
LinkSpeed                    : 10 Gbps
MediaType                    : 802.3
PhysicalMediaType            : Unspecified
AdminStatus                  : Up
MediaConnectionState         : Connected
DriverInformation            : Driver Date 2006-06-21 Version
                               10.0.10224.0 NDIS 6.50
DriverFileName               : netvsc.sys
NdisVersion                  : 6.50
ifOperStatus                 : Up
RunspaceId                   : d5fc4fb6-4db2-46f4-9d38-a79f1c0e0
                               139
Caption                      :
Description                  :
ElementName                  :
InstanceID                   : {A03CCF8C-6D91-49C0-ACBD-B900FC27
                               EAC1}
CommunicationStatus          :
DetailedStatus               :
HealthState                  :
InstallDate                  :
Name                         : Ethernet
OperatingStatus              :
OperationalStatus            :
PrimaryStatus                :
Status                       :
```

```
StatusDescriptions                          :
AvailableRequestedStates                    :
EnabledDefault                              : 2
EnabledState                                : 5
OtherEnabledState                           :
RequestedState                              : 12
TimeOfLastStateChange                       :
TransitioningToState                        : 12
AdditionalAvailability                      :
Availability                                :
CreationClassName                           : MSFT_NetAdapter
DeviceID                                    : {A03CCF8C-6D91-49C0-ACBD-B900FC27
                                              EAC1}

ErrorCleared                                :
ErrorDescription                            :
IdentifyingDescriptions                     :
LastErrorCode                               :
MaxQuiesceTime                              :
OtherIdentifyingInfo                        :
PowerManagementCapabilities                 :
PowerManagementSupported                    :
PowerOnHours                                :
StatusInfo                                  :
SystemCreationClassName                     : CIM_NetworkPort
SystemName                                  : c10.NWTraders.com
TotalPowerOnHours                           :
MaxSpeed                                    :
OtherPortType                               :
PortType                                    :
RequestedSpeed                              :
Speed                                       : 10000000000
UsageRestriction                            :
ActiveMaximumTransmissionUnit               : 1500
AutoSense                                   :
FullDuplex                                  :
LinkTechnology                              :
NetworkAddresses                            : {00155D002A1E}
OtherLinkTechnology                         :
OtherNetworkPortType                        :
PermanentAddress                            : 00155D002A1E
PortNumber                                  : 0
SupportedMaximumTransmissionUnit            :
AdminLocked                                 : False
ComponentID                                 : VMBUS\{f8615163-df3e-46c5-913f-f2
                                              d2f965ed0e}

ConnectorPresent                            : True
DeviceName                                  : \Device\{A03CCF8C-6D91-49C0-ACBD-
                                              B900FC27EAC1}

DeviceWakeUpEnable                          : False
DriverDate                                  : 2006-06-21
DriverDateData                              : 127953216000000000
DriverDescription                           : Microsoft Hyper-V Network Adapter
DriverMajorNdisVersion                      : 6
DriverMinorNdisVersion                      : 50
DriverName                                  : \SystemRoot\System32\drivers\netv
                                              sc.sys

DriverProvider                              : Microsoft
```

```
DriverVersionString                                 : 10.0.10224.0
EndPointInterface                                   : False
HardwareInterface                                   : True
Hidden                                              : False
HigherLayerInterfaceIndices                         : {6}
IMFilter                                            : False
InterfaceAdminStatus                                : 1
InterfaceDescription                                : Microsoft Hyper-V Network Adapter
InterfaceGuid                                       : {A03CCF8C-6D91-49C0-ACBD-B900FC27
                                                      EAC1}
InterfaceIndex                                      : 4
InterfaceName                                       : Ethernet_32768
InterfaceOperationalStatus                          : 1
InterfaceType                                       : 6
iSCSIInterface                                      : False
LowerLayerInterfaceIndices                          :
MajorDriverVersion                                  : 6
MediaConnectState                                   : 1
MediaDuplexState                                    : 0
MinorDriverVersion                                  : 1
MtuSize                                             : 1500
NdisMedium                                          : 0
NdisPhysicalMedium                                  : 0
NetLuid                                             : 1689399616077824
NetLuidIndex                                        : 32768
NotUserRemovable                                    : False
OperationalStatusDownDefaultPortNotAuthenticated    : False
OperationalStatusDownInterfacePaused                : False
OperationalStatusDownLowPowerState                  : False
OperationalStatusDownMediaDisconnected              : False
PnPDeviceID                                         : VMBUS\{F8615163-DF3E-46C5-913F-F2
                                                      D2F965ED0E}\{4933D11F-0119-49D4-9
                                                      6F4-1DF4783FD154}
PromiscuousMode                                     : False
ReceiveLinkSpeed                                    : 10000000000
State                                               : 2
TransmitLinkSpeed                                   : 10000000000
Virtual                                             : False
VlanID                                              :
WdmInterface                                        : False
```

You can continue to work directly with the output in a normal Windows PowerShell fashion, as follows.

```
PS C:\> Receive-Job -Id 4 -Keep | select name

name
----
Ethernet


PS C:\> Receive-Job -Id 4 -Keep | select transmitlinksp*

                                                    TransmitLinkSpeed
                                                    -----------------
                                                         10000000000
```

Using Windows PowerShell remoting and jobs: Step-by-step exercises

In this exercise, you will practice using Windows PowerShell remoting to run remote commands. For the purpose of this exercise, you can use your local computer. First, you will open the Windows PowerShell console, supply alternate credentials, create a Windows PowerShell remote session, and run various commands. Next, you will create and receive Windows PowerShell jobs.

Supplying alternate credentials for remote Windows PowerShell sessions

1. Log on to your computer with a user account that does not have administrator rights.

2. Open the Windows PowerShell console.

3. Notice the Windows PowerShell console prompt. An example of such a prompt is shown here.

    ```
    PS C:\Users\ed.nwtraders>
    ```

4. Use a variable named *$cred* to store the results of using the *Get-Credential* cmdlet. Specify administrator credentials to store in the *$cred* variable. An example of such a command is shown here.

    ```
    $cred = Get-Credential nwtraders\administrator
    ```

5. Use the *Enter-PSSession* cmdlet to open a remote Windows PowerShell console session. Use the credentials stored in the *$cred* variable, and use *localhost* as the name of the remote computer. An example of this command is shown here.

    ```
    Enter-PSSession -ComputerName localhost -Credential $cred
    ```

6. Notice how the Windows PowerShell console prompt changes to include the name of the remote computer and also changes the working directory. An example of a changed prompt is shown here.

    ```
    [localhost]: PS C:\Users\administrator\Documents>
    ```

7. Use the *whoami* command to verify the current context. The results of the command are shown here.

    ```
    [localhost]: PS C:\Users\administrator\Documents> whoami
    nwtraders\administrator
    ```

8. Use the *exit* command to exit the remote session. Use the *whoami* command to verify that the user context has changed.

9. Use WMI to retrieve the BIOS information on the local computer. Use the alternate credentials stored in the *$cred* variable. This command is shown here.

```
gwmi -Class win32_bios -cn localhost -Credential $cred
```

The previous command fails and produces the following error. This error comes from WMI and states that you are not permitted to use alternate credentials for a local WMI connection.

```
gwmi : User credentials cannot be used for local connections
At line:1 char:1
+ gwmi -Class win32_bios -cn localhost -Credential $cred
+ ~~~~~~~~~~~~~~~~~~~~~~~~~~~~~~~~~~~~~~~~~~~~~~~~~~~~~~~
    + CategoryInfo          : InvalidOperation: (:) [Get-WmiObject], ManagementException
    + FullyQualifiedErrorId : GetWMIManagementException,Microsoft.PowerShell.Commands.
  GetWmiObjectCommand
```

10. Put the WMI command into the *-ScriptBlock* parameter for *Invoke-Command*. Specify the local computer as the value for *-ComputerName*, and use the credentials stored in the *$cred* variable. The command is shown here (using *-script* as a shortened version of *-ScriptBlock*).

```
Invoke-Command -cn localhost -script {gwmi -Class win32_bios} -cred $cred
```

11. Press the Up Arrow key to retrieve the previous command, and erase the *credential* parameter. The revised command is shown here.

```
Invoke-Command -cn localhost -script {gwmi -Class win32_bios}
```

When you run the command, it generates the error shown here because a normal user does not have remote access by default (if you have admin rights, the command works).

```
[localhost] Connecting to remote server localhost failed with the following error
message : Access is denied. For more information, see the about_Remote_Troubleshooting
Help topic.
    + CategoryInfo          : OpenError: (localhost:String) [], PSRemotingTransport
  Exception
    + FullyQualifiedErrorId : AccessDenied,PSSessionStateBroken
```

12. Create an array of computer names. Store the computer names in a variable named *$cn*. Use the array shown here.

```
$cn = $env:COMPUTERNAME,"localhost","127.0.0.1"
```

13. Use *Invoke-Command* to run the WMI command on all three computers at the same time. The command is shown here.

```
Invoke-Command -cn $cn -script {gwmi -Class win32_bios} -cred $cred
```

This concludes this step-by-step exercise.

In the following exercise, you will create and receive Windows PowerShell jobs.

Creating and receiving jobs

1. Open the Windows PowerShell console as a non-elevated user.

2. Start a job named *Get-Process* that uses a *-ScriptBlock* parameter that calls the *Get-Process* cmdlet (*gps* is an alias for *Get-Process*). The command is shown here.

   ```
   Start-Job -Name gps -ScriptBlock {gps}
   ```

3. Examine the output from starting the job. It lists the name, state, and other information about the job. Sample output is shown here.

   ```
   Id     Name          PSJobTypeName    State      HasMoreData    Location
   --     ----          -------------    -----      -----------    --------
   9      gps           BackgroundJob    Running    True           localhost
   ```

4. Use the *Get-Process* cmdlet to determine whether the job has completed. The command is shown here.

   ```
   Get-Job gps
   ```

5. Examine the output from the previous command. The *state* reports *completed* when the job has completed. If data is available, the *HasMoreData* property reports *True*. Sample output is shown here.

   ```
   Id     Name          PSJobTypeName    State        HasMoreData    Location
   --     ----          -------------    -----        -----------    --------
   9      gps           BackgroundJob    Completed    True           localhost
   ```

6. Receive the results from the job. To do this, use the *Receive-Job* cmdlet, as shown here.

   ```
   Receive-Job gps
   ```

7. Press the Up Arrow key to retrieve the *Get-Job* command. Run it. Note that the *HasMoreData* property now reports *False*, as shown here.

   ```
   Id     Name          PSJobTypeName    State        HasMoreData    Location
   --     ----          -------------    -----        -----------    --------
   9      gps           BackgroundJob    Completed    False          localhost
   ```

8. Create a new job with the same name as the previous job: *gps*. This time, change the *-ScriptBlock* parameter value to *gsv* (the alias for *Get-Service*). The command is shown here.

   ```
   Start-Job -Name gps -ScriptBlock {gsv}
   ```

9. Now use the *Get-Job* cmdlet to retrieve the job with the name *gps*. Note that the command retrieves both jobs, as shown here.

```
Get-Job -name gps

Id     Name     PSJobTypeName    State        HasMoreData    Location
--     ----     -------------    -----        -----------    --------
9      gps      BackgroundJob    Completed    False          localhost
11     gps      BackgroundJob    Completed    True           localhost
```

10. Use the *Receive-Job* cmdlet to retrieve the job ID associated with your new job. This time, use the *-Keep* switch parameter, as shown here.

```
Receive-Job -Id 11 -keep
```

11. Use the *Get-Job* cmdlet to retrieve your job. Note that the *HasMoreData* property still reports *True* because you're using the *-Keep* switch parameter.

This concludes this exercise.

Chapter 4 quick reference

To	Do this
Work interactively on a remote system	Use the *Enter-PSSession* cmdlet to create a remote session.
Configure Windows PowerShell remoting	Use the *Enable-PSRemoting* cmdlet.
Run a command on a remote system	Use the *Invoke-Command* cmdlet and specify the command by using the *-ScriptBlock* parameter.
Run a command as a job	Use the *Start-Job* cmdlet to execute the command.
Check on the progress of a job	Use the *Get-Job* cmdlet and specify either the job ID or the job name.
Check on the progress of the newest job	Use the *Get-Job* cmdlet and specify the *-Newest* parameter, and supply the number of newest jobs to monitor.
Retrieve the results from a job	Use the *Receive-Job* cmdlet and specify the job ID.

Using Windows PowerShell scripts

After completing this chapter, you will be able to

- Understand the reasons for writing Windows PowerShell scripts.

- Make the configuration changes required to run Windows PowerShell scripts.

- Understand how to run Windows PowerShell scripts.

- Understand how to break lines in a script.

- Understand the use of variables and constants in a script.

- Create objects in a Windows PowerShell script.

- Call methods in a Windows PowerShell script.

Because so many actions can be performed from inside Windows PowerShell in an interactive fashion, you might wonder, "Why do I need to write scripts?" For many network administrators, one-line Windows PowerShell commands will indeed solve many routine problems. This can become extremely powerful when the commands are combined into batch files and called from a login script. However, there are some very good reasons to write Windows PowerShell scripts. You will examine them as you move into this chapter.

Why write Windows PowerShell scripts?

Perhaps the number-one reason to write a Windows PowerShell script is to address recurring needs. As an example, consider the activity of producing a directory listing. The simple *Get-ChildItem* cmdlet does a good job, but after you decide to sort the listing and filter out only files of a certain size, you end up with the command shown here.

```
Get-ChildItem c:\fso | Where-Object Length -gt 1000 | Sort-Object -Property name
```

Even if you use tab completion, the previous command requires a bit of typing. One way to shorten it would be to create a user-defined function (a technique that I'll discuss later in this chapter). For now, the easiest solution is to write a Windows PowerShell script.

The DirectoryListWithArguments.ps1 script is shown here.

DirectoryListWithArguments.ps1

```
foreach ($i in $args)
   {Get-ChildItem $i | Where-Object length -gt 1000 |
   Sort-Object -property name}
```

The DirectoryListWithArguments.ps1 script takes a single, unnamed argument that allows the script to be modified when it is run. This makes the script much easier to work with and adds flexibility. The example that follows assumes that the script is located in the root of C, and the argument given here is the downloads folder in my user profile.

```
PS C:\> .\DirectoryListWithArguments.ps1 C:\Users\iammred\Downloads\
```

An additional reason that network administrators write Windows PowerShell scripts is to run the scripts as scheduled tasks. In the Windows world, there are multiple task-scheduler engines. By using the *Win32_ScheduledJob* Windows Management Instrumentation (WMI) class, you can create, monitor, and delete scheduled jobs. This WMI class has been available since the Windows NT 4 days and indicates jobs created via the AT command.

The ListProcessesSortResults.ps1 script, shown following, is a script that a network administrator might want to schedule to run several times a day. It produces a list of currently running processes and writes the results out to a text file as a formatted and sorted table.

ListProcessesSortResults.ps1

```
$args = "localhost","loopback","127.0.0.1"

foreach ($i in $args)
   {$strFile = "c:\mytest\"+ $i +"Processes.txt"
   Write-Host "Testing" $i "please wait ...";
   Get-WmiObject -computername $i -class win32_process |
   Select-Object name, processID, Priority, ThreadCount, PageFaults, PageFileUsage |
   Where-Object {!$_.processID -eq 0} | Sort-Object -property name |
   Format-Table | Out-File $strFile}
```

One other reason for writing Windows PowerShell scripts is that it makes it easy to store and share both the "secret commands" and the ideas behind the scripts. For example, suppose you develop a script that will connect remotely to workstations on your network and search for user accounts that do not require a password. Obviously, an account without a password is a security risk! After some searching around, you discover the *Win32_UserAccount* WMI class and develop a script that performs to your expectation. Because this is likely a script you would want to use on a regular basis, and perhaps share with other network administrators in your company, it makes sense to save it as a script.

A sample of such a script is AccountsWithNoRequiredPassword.ps1, which is shown here.

AccountsWithNoRequiredPassword.ps1

```
$args = "localhost"

foreach ($i in $args)
   {Write-Host "Connecting to" $i "please wait ...";
    Get-WmiObject -computername $i -class win32_UserAccount |
    Select-Object Name, Disabled, PasswordRequired, SID, SIDType |
    Where-Object {$_.PasswordRequired -eq 0} |
    Sort-Object -property name | Write-Host}
```

The fundamentals of scripting

In its most basic form, a Windows PowerShell script is a collection of Windows PowerShell commands. Here's an example.

```
Get-Process notepad | Stop-Process
```

You can put a command into a Windows PowerShell script and run it directly as written.

To create a Windows PowerShell script, you simply have to copy the command in a text file and save the file by using a .ps1 extension. If you create the file in the Windows PowerShell ISE and save the file, the .ps1 extension will be added automatically. If you double-click the file, it will open in Notepad by default.

Running Windows PowerShell scripts

To run the script, you can open the Windows PowerShell console, drag the file to the console, and press Enter, as long as the script name does not have spaces in the path. Also, if you right-click the script file and select Copy As Path, and later right-click inside the Windows PowerShell console to paste the path of your script there, and press Enter, you will print out a string that represents the path of the script, as shown here. This is because the Copy As Path option will automatically surround the path with quotes.

```
PS C:\> "C:\fso\test.ps1"
C:\fso\test.ps1
```

In Windows PowerShell, when you want to print a string in the console, you put it inside quotation marks. You do not have to use *Wscript.Echo* or similar commands, such as those used in Microsoft Visual Basic Scripting Edition (VBScript). This method is easier and simpler, but it takes some getting used to. For example, assume that you figure out that your previous attempts to run a Windows PowerShell script just displayed a string—the path to the script—instead of running the script. Therefore, you remove the quotation marks and press Enter, and this time, you receive a real error message. "What now?" you might ask. The error message shown in Figure 5-1 relates to the script execution policy that disallows the running of scripts.

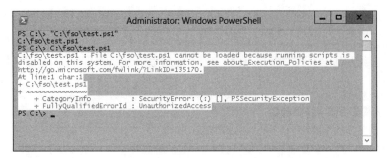

FIGURE 5-1 By default, an attempt to run a Windows PowerShell script generates an error message.

Turning on Windows PowerShell scripting support

By default, Windows PowerShell disallows the execution of scripts. Script support can be controlled by using Group Policy, but if it is not, and if you have administrative rights on your computer, you can use the *Set-ExecutionPolicy* Windows PowerShell cmdlet to turn on script support. There are six levels that can be turned on by using the *Set-ExecutionPolicy* cmdlet. These options are listed here:

- **Restricted**   Does not load configuration files such as the Windows PowerShell profile or run other scripts. *Restricted* is the default.

- **AllSigned**   Requires that all scripts and configuration files be signed by a trusted publisher, including scripts that you write on the local computer.

- **RemoteSigned**   Requires that all scripts and configuration files downloaded from the Internet be signed by a trusted publisher.

- **Unrestricted**   Loads all configuration files and runs all scripts. If you run an unsigned script that was downloaded from the Internet, you are prompted for permission before it runs.

- **Bypass**   Blocks nothing and issues no warnings or prompts.

- **Undefined**   Removes the currently assigned execution policy from the current scope. This parameter will not remove an execution policy that is set in a Group Policy scope.

In addition to six levels of execution policy, there are three different scopes:

- **Process**   The execution policy affects only the current Windows PowerShell process.

- **CurrentUser**   The execution policy affects only the current user.

- **LocalMachine**   The execution policy affects all users of the computer. Setting the *Local-Machine* execution policy requires administrator rights on the local computer. By default, non-elevated users have rights to set the script execution policy for the *CurrentUser* user scope that affects their own execution policies.

With so many choices available to you for script execution policy, you might be wondering which one is appropriate for you. The Windows PowerShell team recommends the *RemoteSigned* setting, stating that it is "appropriate for most circumstances." Remember that even though descriptions of the various policy settings use the term *Internet*, this might not always refer to the World Wide Web, or even to locations outside your own firewall. This is because Windows PowerShell obtains its script origin information by using the Internet Explorer zone settings. This basically means that anything that comes from a computer other than your own is in the Internet zone. You can change the Internet Explorer zone settings by using Internet Explorer, the registry, or Group Policy.

If you do not want to display the confirmation message when you change the script execution policy on Windows PowerShell 5.0, use the *-Force* parameter.

To view the execution policy for all scopes, use the *-List* parameter when calling the *Get-Execution-Policy* cmdlet. This technique is shown here.

```
PS C:\> Get-ExecutionPolicy -List

        Scope                          ExecutionPolicy
        -----                          ---------------
 MachinePolicy                               Undefined
    UserPolicy                               Undefined
       Process                               Undefined
   CurrentUser                            RemoteSigned
  LocalMachine                              Restricted
```

Quick check

Q.   Do Windows PowerShell scripts work by default?

A.   No. Windows PowerShell scripts must be explicitly enabled.

Q.   What cmdlet can be used to retrieve the resultant execution policy?

A.   The *Get-ExecutionPolicy* cmdlet can retrieve the resultant execution policy.

Q.   What cmdlet can be used to set the script execution policy?

A.   The *Set-ExecutionPolicy* cmdlet can be used to set the script execution policy.

Retrieving script execution policy

1. Open Windows PowerShell.

2. Use the *Get-ExecutionPolicy* cmdlet to retrieve the effective script execution policy. This is shown here.

```
Get-ExecutionPolicy
```

This concludes this procedure. Leave Windows PowerShell open for the next procedure.

Setting script execution policy for the entire machine

 Note Setting the script execution policy for the entire machine requires elevated permissions.

1. Use the *Set-ExecutionPolicy* cmdlet to change the script execution policy to *remotesigned*. This command is shown here.

```
Set-ExecutionPolicy remotesigned
```

2. Use the *Get-ExecutionPolicy* cmdlet to retrieve the current effective script execution policy. This command is shown here.

```
Get-ExecutionPolicy
```

The result prints out to the Windows PowerShell console, as shown here.

```
remotesigned
```

This concludes this procedure.

Setting script execution policy for only the current user

 Note Setting the script execution policy for only the current user does not require elevated (Local Administrator) permissions.

1. Use the *Set-ExecutionPolicy* cmdlet to change the script execution policy to *remotesigned*. Specify the *-Scope* parameter and set the value to *CurrentUser*. Use the *-Force* parameter to suppress prompting when making the change. This command is shown here.

```
Set-ExecutionPolicy -Scope CurrentUser -ExecutionPolicy RemoteSigned -Force
```

2. Use the *Get-ExecutionPolicy* cmdlet to retrieve the current effective script execution policy. This command is shown here.

```
Get-ExecutionPolicy
```

The result prints out to the Windows PowerShell console, as shown here.

```
RemoteSigned
```

This concludes this procedure.

> **Tip** If the execution policy on Windows PowerShell is set to *restricted*, how can you use a script to determine the execution policy? One method is to use the *bypass* parameter when calling Windows PowerShell to run the script. The *bypass* parameter bypasses the script execution policy for the duration of the script when it is called.

Transitioning from command line to script

Now that you have everything set up to enable script execution, you can run your StopNotepad.ps1 script. This is shown here.

StopNotepad.ps1

```
Get-Process Notepad | Stop-Process
```

If an instance of the Notepad process is running, everything is successful. However, if there is no instance of Notepad running, the error shown here is generated.

```
Get-Process : Cannot find a process with the name 'Notepad'. Verify the process
 name and call the cmdlet again.
At C:\Documents and Settings\ed\Local Settings\Temp\tmp1DB.tmp.ps1:14 char:12
+ Get-Process  <<<< Notepad | Stop-Process
```

It is important to get into the habit of reading the error messages. The first part of the error message gives a description of the problem. In this example, it could not find a process with the name *Notepad*. The second part of the error message shows the position in the code where the error occurred. This is known as the *position message*. The first line of the position message states that the error occurred on line 14. The second portion has a series of arrows that point to the command that failed. The *Get-Process* cmdlet command is the one that failed. This is shown here.

```
At C:\Documents and Settings\ed\Local Settings\Temp\tmp1DB.tmp.ps1:14 char:12
+ Get-Process  <<<< Notepad | Stop-Process
```

The easiest way to eliminate this error message is to use the *-ErrorAction* parameter and specify the *SilentlyContinue* value. You can also use the *-ea* alias and avoid having to type *-ErrorAction*. This is basically the same as using the *On Error Resume Next* command from VBScript (but not exactly the same, because it only handles nonterminating errors). The really useful feature of the *-ErrorAction* parameter is that it can be specified on a cmdlet-by-cmdlet basis. In addition, there are five enumeration names or values that can be used. The allowed names and values for the *-ErrorAction* parameter are shown in Table 5-1.

TABLE 5-1 Names and values for *-ErrorAction*

Enumeration	Value
Ignore	4
Inquire	3
Continue	2
Stop	1
SilentlyContinue	0

In the StopNotepadSilentlyContinue.ps1 script, you add the *-ErrorAction* parameter to the *Get-Process* cmdlet to skip past any error that might arise if the Notepad process does not exist. To make the script easier to read, you break the code at the pipe character. The pipe character is not the line continuation character. The backtick (`) character, also known as the grave accent character, is used when a line of code is too long and must be broken into two physical lines of code. The key thing to be aware of is that the two physical lines form a single logical line of code. An example of how to use line continuation is shown here.

```
Write-Host -foregroundcolor green "This is a demo " `
        "of the line continuation character"
```

The StopNotepadSilentlyContinue.ps1 script is shown here.

StopNotepadSilentlyContinue.ps1

```
Get-Process -Name Notepad -ErrorAction SilentlyContinue |
Stop-Process
```

Because you are writing a script, you can take advantage of some features of a script. One of the first things you can do is use a variable to hold the name of the process to be stopped. This has the advantage of enabling you to easily change the script to stop processes other than Notepad. All variables begin with the dollar sign. The line that holds the name of the process in a variable is shown here.

```
$process = "notepad"
```

Another improvement you can add to the script is one that provides information about the process that is stopped. The *Stop-Process* cmdlet returns no information when it is used. However, when you use the *-PassThru* parameter of the *Stop-Process* cmdlet, the process object is passed along in the pipeline. You can use this parameter and pipeline the process object to the *ForEach-Object* cmdlet. You can use the *$_* automatic variable to refer to the current object on the pipeline and select the name and the process ID of the process that is stopped. The concatenation operator in Windows PowerShell is the plus sign (+), and you can use it to display the values of the selected properties in addition to the strings that complete your sentence. This line of code is shown here.

```
ForEach-Object { $_.name + ' with process ID: ' +  $_.ID + ' was stopped.'}
```

The complete StopNotepadSilentlyContinuePassThru.ps1 script is shown here.

StopNotepadSilentlyContinuePassThru.ps1

```
$process = "notepad"
Get-Process -Name $Process -ErrorAction SilentlyContinue |
Stop-Process -PassThru |
ForEach-Object { $_.name + ' with process ID: ' +  $_.ID + ' was stopped.'}
```

When you run the script with two instances of Notepad running, output similar to the following is shown.

```
notepad with process ID: 2088 was stopped.
notepad with process ID: 2568 was stopped.
```

An additional advantage of the StopNotepadSilentlyContinuePassThru.ps1 script is that you can use it to stop different processes. You can assign multiple process names (an array) to the *$process* variable, and when you run the script, each process will be stopped. In this example, you assign the Notepad and the Calc processes to the *$process* variable. This is shown here.

```
$process = "notepad", "calc"
```

When you run the script, both processes are stopped. Output similar to the following appears.

```
calc with process ID: 3428 was stopped.
notepad with process ID: 488 was stopped.
```

You could continue changing your script. You could put the code in a function, write command-line help, and change the script so that it accepts command-line input or even reads a list of processes from a text file. As soon as you move from the command line to script, such options suddenly become possible. These topics are covered in Chapter 6, "Working with functions," and Chapter 7, "Creating advanced functions and modules."

Manually running Windows PowerShell scripts

You cannot just double-click a Windows PowerShell script and have it run (unless you change the file association, but that is not supported or recommended). You cannot type the name in the Run dialog box, either. If you are inside Windows PowerShell, you can run scripts if you have enabled the execution policy, but you need to type the entire path to the script you want to run and make sure you include the .ps1 extension.

To run a Windows PowerShell script from inside the Windows PowerShell console, enter the full path to the script. Include the name of the script. Ensure that you include the .ps1 extension.

If you need to run a script from outside Windows PowerShell, you need to enter the full path to the script, but you must feed it as an argument to the PowerShell.exe program. In addition, you probably want to specify the *-NoExit* parameter so that you can read the output from the script. This is shown in Figure 5-2.

FIGURE 5-2 Use the *-NoExit* parameter for the PowerShell.exe program to keep the console open after a script runs.

The RetrieveAndSortServiceState.ps1 script creates a list of all the services that are defined on a machine. It then checks whether they are running, stopped, or disabled, and reports the status of the service. The script also collects the service account that the service is running under.

In this script, the *Sort-Object* cmdlet is used to perform three sorts on the data: it sorts first by the start mode of the service (that is, automatic, manual, or disabled); it sorts next by the state of the service (for example, running or stopped); and it then alphabetizes the list by the name of each service in the two previous categories. After the sorting process, the script uses a *Format-Table* cmdlet and produces table output in the console window. The RetrieveAndSortServiceState.ps1 script is shown following, and the "Running scripts inside the Windows PowerShell console" procedure, which examines the running of this script, follows that.

The script is designed to run against multiple remote machines, and it holds the names of the destination machines in the system variable *$args*. As written, it uses two computer names that always refer to the local machine: *localhost* and *loopback*. By using these two names, you can simulate the behavior of connecting to networked computers.

RetrieveAndSortServiceState.ps1

```
$args = "localhost","loopback"

  foreach ($i in $args)
    {Write-Host "Testing" $i "..."
       Get-WmiObject -computer $args -class win32_service |
       Select-Object -property name, state, startmode, startname |
       Sort-Object -property startmode, state, name |
       Format-Table *}
```

Note For the following procedure, I copied the RetrieveAndSortServiceState.ps1 script to the C:\mytempfolder directory created in Chapter 3, "Understanding and using Windows PowerShell providers." This makes it much easier to type the path and has the additional benefit of making the examples clearer. To follow the procedures, you will need to either modify the path to the script or copy the RetrieveAndSortServiceState.ps1 script to the C:\mytempfolder directory.

Running scripts inside the Windows PowerShell console

1. Open the Windows PowerShell console.

2. Enter the full path to the script you want to run (for example, C:\mytempfolder). You can use tab completion. On my system, I only had to type C:\my and then press Tab. Add a backslash (****), and enter the script name. You can use tab completion for this too. If you copied the Retrieve-AndSortServiceState.ps1 script into the C:\mytempfolder directory, just entering **r** and pressing Tab should retrieve the script name. The completed command is shown here.

```
C:\mytempfolder\RetrieveAndSortServiceState.ps1
```

Partial output from the script is shown here.

```
Testing loopback ...

name            state        startmode     startname
----            -----        ---------     ---------
Alerter         Running      Auto          NT AUTHORITY\Loc...
Alerter         Running      Auto          NT AUTHORITY\Loc...
AudioSrv        Running      Auto          LocalSystem
AudioSrv        Running      Auto          LocalSystem
```

This concludes this procedure. Close the Windows PowerShell console.

 Tip Add a shortcut to Windows PowerShell in your SendTo folder. This folder is located in the Documents and Settings*%username%* folder. When you create the shortcut, make sure you specify the *-NoExit* parameter for PowerShell.exe, or the output will scroll by so fast that you will not be able to read it. You can do this manually.

1. Open the Run dialog box (Choose Start | Run, or press the Windows key + R, or press Ctrl+Esc and then R).

2. Enter **PowerShell** and use the *-NoExit* parameter. Enter the full path to the script. The command for this is shown here.

```
Powershell -noexit C:\mytempfolder\RetrieveAndSortServiceState.ps1
```

This concludes this procedure.

Quick check

Q. Which command can you use to sort a list?

A. The *Sort-Object* cmdlet can be used to sort a list.

Q. How do you use the *Sort-Object* cmdlet to sort a list?

A. To use the *Sort-Object* cmdlet to sort a list, specify the property to sort on in the *-Property* parameter.

Understanding variables and constants

Understanding the use of variables and constants in Windows PowerShell is fundamental to much of the flexibility of the Windows PowerShell scripting language. Variables are used to hold information for use later in the script. Variables can hold any type of data, including text, numbers, and even objects.

Using variables

By default, when working with Windows PowerShell, you do not need to declare variables before use. When you use a variable to hold data, it is declared. All variable names must be preceded with a dollar sign ($) when they are referenced. There are a number of special variables, also known as automatic variables, in Windows PowerShell. These variables are created automatically and have a special meaning. A listing of the commonly used special variables and their associated meanings is shown in Table 5-2.

TABLE 5-2 Use of special variables

Name	Use
$^	This contains the first token of the last line input into the shell.
$$	This contains the last token of the last line input into the shell.
$_	This is the current pipeline object; it is used in script blocks, filters, *Where-Object*, *ForEach-Object*, and *Switch*.
$?	This contains the success/fail status of the last statement.

Name	Use
$Args	This is used with functions or scripts requiring parameters that do not have a *param* block.
$Error	This saves the error object in the $error variable if an error occurs.
$ExecutionContext	This contains the execution objects available to cmdlets.
$foreach	This refers to the enumerator in a *foreach* loop.
$HOME	This is the user's home directory (set to %HOMEDRIVE%\%HOMEPATH%).
$Input	This is input that is pipelined to a function or code block.
$Match	This is a hash table consisting of items found by the -*match* operator.
$MyInvocation	This contains information about the currently executing script or command line.
$PSHome	This is the directory where Windows PowerShell is installed.
$Host	This contains information about the currently executing host.
$LastExitCode	This contains the exit code of the last native application to run.
$True	This is used for Boolean *TRUE*.
$False	This is used for Boolean *FALSE*.
$Null	This represents a null object.
$This	In the Types.ps1xml file and some script block instances, this represents the current object.
$OFS	This is the output field separator used when converting an array to a string.
$ShellID	This is the identifier for the shell; this value is used by the shell to determine the execution policy and what profiles are run at startup.
$StackTrace	This contains detailed stack trace information about the last error.

In the ReadUserInfoFromReg.ps1 script that follows, there are five variables used. These are listed in Table 5-3.

TABLE 5-3 ReadUserInfoFromReg.ps1 variables

Name	Use
$strUserPath	This is for the path to the registry subkey SOFTWARE\MICROSOFT\WINDOWS\CURRENTVERSION\EXPLORER.
$strUserName	This is for the registry value Logon User Name.
$strPath	This is for the path to the registry subkey VOLATILE ENVIRONMENT.
$strName	This contains an array of registry values: LOGONSERVER, HOMEPATH, APPDATA, HOMEDRIVE.
$i	This holds a single registry value name from the $strName array of registry values; $i gets assigned the value by using the *ForEach* alias.

The ReadUserInfoFromReg.ps1 script uses the *Set-Location* cmdlet to change to the HKCU PS drive. This makes it easier to work with the registry. After the location has been set to the HKCU drive, the script uses the *Get-ItemProperty* cmdlet to retrieve the data stored in the specified registry key. The *Get-ItemProperty* cmdlet needs two parameters to be supplied: *-Path* and *-Name*. The *-Path* parameter receives the registry path that is stored in the *$strUserPath* variable, whereas the *-Name* parameter receives the string stored in the *$strUserName* variable.

> **Tip** Because the *$strUserPath* registry subkey was rather long, I used the backtick character (`) to continue the subkey on the next line. In addition, because I had to close out the string with quotation marks, I used the plus symbol (+) to concatenate (glue) the two pieces of the string back together.

After the value is retrieved from the registry, the object is pipelined to the *Format-List* cmdlet, which again uses the string contained in the *$strUserName* variable as the property to display.

> **Note** The *Format-List* cmdlet is required in the ReadUserInfoFromReg.ps1 script because of the way the *Get-ItemProperty* cmdlet displays the results of its operation—it returns information about the object in addition to the value contained in the registry key. The use of *Format-List* mitigates this behavior.

The really powerful aspect of the ReadUserInfoFromReg.ps1 script is that it uses the array of strings contained in the *$strName* variable. To read the values out of the registry, you need to *singularize* the strings contained within the *$strName* variable. To do this, you use the *foreach* construct. After you have an individual value from the *$strName* array, you store the string in a variable called *$i*. The *Get-ItemProperty* cmdlet is used in exactly the same manner as it was used earlier. However, this time, you use the string contained in the *$strPath* variable, and the name of the registry key to read is contained in the *$i* variable, whose value will change four times with the execution of each pass through the array.

When the ReadUserInfoFromReg.ps1 script is run, it reads five pieces of information from the registry: the logon user name, the logon server name, the user's home path location, the user's application data store, and the user's home drive mapping. The ReadUserInfoFromReg.ps1 script is shown here.

ReadUserInfoFromReg.ps1

```
$strUserPath = "\Software\Microsoft\Windows\CurrentVersion\" `
            + "Explorer"
$strUserName = "Logon User Name"
$strPath = "\Volatile Environment"
$strName = "LOGONSERVER","HOMEPATH", "APPDATA","HOMEDRIVE"

Set-Location HKCU:\
    Get-ItemProperty -Path $strUserPath -Name $strUserName |
        Format-List $strUserName
foreach ($i in $strName)
    {Get-ItemProperty -Path $strPath -Name $i |
        Format-List $i}
```

Quick check

Q. Which provider is used to read a value from the registry?

A. The registry provider is used to read from the registry.

Q. Which cmdlet is used to retrieve a registry key value from the registry?

A. The *Get-ItemProperty* cmdlet is used to retrieve a registry key value from the registry.

Q. How do you concatenate two string values?

A. You can use the plus symbol (+) to concatenate two string values.

Exploring strings

1. Open Windows PowerShell.

2. Create a variable called *$a* and assign the value *this is the beginning* to it. The code for this is shown here.

   ```
   $a = "this is the beginning"
   ```

3. Create a variable called *$b* and assign the number 22 to it. The code for this is shown here.

   ```
   $b = 22
   ```

4. Create a variable called *$c* and make it equal to *$a + $b*. The code for this is shown here.

   ```
   $c = $a + $b
   ```

5. Print out the value of *$c*. The code for this is shown here.

   ```
   $c
   ```

6. The results of printing out *c$* are shown here.

   ```
   this is the beginning22
   ```

7. Modify the value of *$a*. Assign the string *this is a string* to the variable *$a*. This is shown here.

   ```
   $a = "this is a string"
   ```

8. Press the Up Arrow key and retrieve the *$c = $a + $b* command.

   ```
   $c = $a + $b
   ```

9. Now print out the value of *$c*. The command to do this is shown here.

   ```
   $c
   ```

10. Assign the string *this is a number* to the variable *$b*. The code to do this is shown here.

```
$b = "this is a number"
```

11. Press the Up Arrow key to retrieve the *$c = $a + $b* command. This will cause Windows PowerShell to reevaluate the value of *$c*. This command is shown here.

```
$c = $a + $b
```

12. Print out the value of *$c*. This command is shown here.

```
$c
```

13. Change the *$b* variable so that it can contain only an integer. (Commonly used data type aliases are shown in Table 5-4.) Use the *$b* variable to hold the number 5. This command is shown here.

```
[int]$b = 5
```

14. Assign the string *this is a string* to the *$b* variable. This command is shown here.

```
$b = "this is a string"
```

Attempting to assign a string to a variable that has an *[int]* constraint placed on it results in the error shown here (these results are wrapped for readability).

```
Cannot convert value "this is a number" to type "System.Int32".
Error: "Input string was not in a correct format."
At line:1 char:3
+ $b  <<<< = "this is a string"
```

This concludes this procedure.

TABLE 5-4 Data type aliases

Alias	Type
[int]	A 32-bit signed integer
[long]	A 64-bit signed integer
[string]	A fixed-length string of Unicode characters
[char]	A Unicode 16-bit character, UTF-16
[bool]	A *true/false* value
[byte]	An 8-bit unsigned integer
[double]	A double-precision 64-bit floating-point number

Alias	Type
[decimal]	A 128-bit decimal value
[single]	A single-precision 32-bit floating-point number
[array]	An array of values
[xml]	An XML document
[hashtable]	A *hashtable* object (similar to a *dictionary* object)

Using constants

Constants in Windows PowerShell are like variables, with two important exceptions: their value never changes, and they cannot be deleted. Constants are created by using the *Set-Variable* cmdlet and specifying the *-Option* parameter to be equal to *constant*.

> **Note** When referring to a constant in the body of the script, you must prefix it with the dollar sign ($), just like any other variable. However, when creating the constant (or variable, for that matter) by using the *Set-Variable* cmdlet, when you specify the *-Name* parameter, you do not use the dollar sign.

In the GetHardDiskDetails.ps1 script that follows, you create a constant called *$intDriveType* and assign the value of 3 to it because the *Win32_LogicalDisk* WMI class uses a value of 3 in the *disktype* property to describe a local hard disk. Because you are not interested in network drives, removable drives, or RAM drives, you use *Where-Object* to return only items that have a drive type of 3.

> ## Quick check
>
> **Q.** How do you create a constant in a script?
>
> **A.** You create a constant in a script by using *Set-Variable* and specifying a value of *constant* for the *-Option* parameter.
>
> **Q.** How do you indicate that a variable will only hold integers?
>
> **A.** To indicate that a variable will only contain integers, use *[int]* in front of the variable name when assigning a value to the variable.

In looking at the GetHardDiskDetails.ps1 script, you can tell that the value of *$intDriveType* is never changed. It is assigned the value of 3 on the *Set-Variable* line. The *$intDriveType* constant is used only with the *Where* filter line. The value of *$strComputer*, however, will change once for each computer name that is specified in the array *$aryComputers*. In this script, it will change twice. The first time through the loop, it will be equal to *loopback*, and the second time through the loop, it will be equal to *localhost*. However, if you added 250 different computer names, the effect would be the same—the value of *$strComputer* would change each time through the loop.

GetHardDiskDetails.ps1

```
$aryComputers = "loopback", "localhost"
Set-Variable -Name intDriveType -Value 3 -Option constant

foreach ($strComputer in $aryComputers)

    {"Hard drives on: " + $strComputer
    Get-WmiObject -Class win32_logicaldisk -ComputerName $strComputer|
        Where {$_.drivetype -eq $intDriveType}}
```

Using the *While* statement

In VBScript, you can use the *While...Wend* loop. An example of using the *While...Wend* loop is the WhileReadLineWend.vbs script that follows. The first thing you do in the script is create an instance of the *FileSystemObject* and store it in the *objFSO* variable. You then use the *OpenTextFile* method to open a test file, and store that object in the *objFile* variable. You then use the *While...Not ...Wend* construction to read one line at a time from the text stream and display it on the screen. You continue to do this until you are at the end of the text stream object. A *While...Wend* loop continues to operate as long as a condition is evaluated as *true*. In this example, as long as you are not at the end of the stream, you will continue to read the line from the text file. The WhileReadLineWend.vbs script is shown here.

WhileReadLineWend.vbs

```
Set objFSO = CreateObject("Scripting.FileSystemObject")
Set objFile = objFSO.OpenTextFile("C:\fso\testfile.txt")

While Not objFile.AtEndOfStream
 WScript.Echo objFile.ReadLine
Wend
```

Constructing the *While* statement in Windows PowerShell

As you probably have already guessed, you have the same kind of construction available to you in Windows PowerShell. The *While* statement in Windows PowerShell is used in the same way that the *While...Wend* statement is used in VBScript. In the DemoWhileLessThan.ps1 script that follows, you first initialize the variable *$i* to be equal to 0. You then use the *while* keyword to begin the *while* loop. In Windows PowerShell, you must include the condition to evaluate inside a set of parentheses. For this example, you determine the value of the *$i* variable with each pass through the loop. If the value of *$i* is less than the number 5, you will perform the action that is specified inside the braces to delimit the script block.

In VBScript, the condition that is evaluated is positioned on the same line with the *While* statement, but no parentheses are required. Although this is convenient from a typing perspective, it actually makes the code a bit confusing to read. In Windows PowerShell, the statement is outside the parentheses and you delimit the condition by using the parentheses.

In VBScript, the action that is performed is added between two words: *While* and *Wend*. In Windows PowerShell, there is no *Wend* statement, and the action to be performed is positioned inside a pair of braces. Although shocking at first to users coming from a VBScript background, the braces are always used to contain code. This is what is called a *script block*, and it is used everywhere. As soon as you are used to seeing script blocks here, you will find them with other language statements also. The good thing is that you do not have to look for items such as the keyword *Wend* or the keyword *Loop* (as in *Do...Loop*).

Understanding expanding strings

In Windows PowerShell, there are two kinds of strings: literal strings and expanding strings. In the DemoWhileLessThan.ps1 script, you use the *expanding string*, which is signified by using a double quotation mark ("). A literal string uses a single quotation mark ('). You want to display the name of the variable, and you want to display the value that is contained in the variable. This is a perfect place to showcase the expanding string. In an expanding string, the value that is contained in a variable is displayed to the screen when a line is evaluated. As an example, consider the following code. You assign the value 12 to the variable $i. You then put $i inside a pair of double quotation marks, making an expanding string. When the line "$i is equal to $i" is evaluated, you obtain "12 is equal to 12," which, while true, is not very illuminating. This is shown here.

```
PS C:\> $i = 12
PS C:\> "$i is equal to $i"
12 is equal to 12
PS C:\>
```

Understanding literal strings

What you probably want to do is display both the name of the variable and the value that is contained inside it. In VBScript, you would have to use concatenation. For this example to work, you have to use the literal string, as shown here.

```
PS C:\> $i = 12
PS C:\> '$i is equal to ' + $i
$i is equal to 12
PS C:\>
```

If you want to use the advantage of the expanding string, you have to suppress the expanding nature of the expanding string for the first variable (*escape* the variable). To do this, you use the escape character, which is the backtick (or grave accent character). This is shown here.

```
PS C:\> $i = 12
PS C:\> "`$i is equal to $i"
$i is equal to 12
PS C:\>
```

In the DemoWhileLessThan.ps1 script, you use the expanding string to print the status message of the value of the $i variable during each trip through the *While* loop. You suppress the expanding nature of the expanding string for the first $i variable so you can tell which variable you are talking about. As soon as you have done this, you increment the value of the $i variable by one. To do this, you use the $i++ syntax. This is identical to saying the following.

```
$i = $i + 1
```

The advantage is that the $i++ syntax requires less typing. The DemoWhileLessThan.ps1 script is shown here.

DemoWhileLessThan.ps1

```
$i = 0
While ($i -lt 5)
 {
  "`$i equals $i. This is less than  5"
  $i++
 } #end while $i lt 5
```

When you run the DemoWhileLessThan.ps1 script, you receive the following output.

```
$i equals 0. This is less than  5
$i equals 1. This is less than  5
$i equals 2. This is less than  5
$i equals 3. This is less than  5
$i equals 4. This is less than  5
PS C:\>
```

A practical example of using the *While* statement

Now that you know how to use the *While* loop, let's examine the WhileReadLine.ps1 script. The first thing you do is initialize the $i variable and set it equal to 0. You then use the *Get-Content* cmdlet to read the contents of testfile.txt and to store the contents into the $fileContents variable.

Use the *While* statement to loop through the contents of the text file. You do this as long as the value of the $i variable is less than or equal to the number of lines in the text file. The number of lines in the text file is represented by the *length* property. Inside the script block, you treat the content of the $fileContents variable like an array (which it is), and you use the $i variable to index into the array to print the value of each line in the $fileContents variable. You then increment the value of the $i variable by one. The WhileReadLine.ps1 script is shown here.

WhileReadLine.ps1

```
$i = 0
$fileContents = Get-Content -path C:\fso\testfile.txt
While ( $i -le $fileContents.length )
 {
  $fileContents[$i]
  $i++
 }
```

Using special features of Windows PowerShell

If you are thinking that the WriteReadLine.ps1 script is a bit difficult, note that it is not really any more difficult than the VBScript version. The difference is that you resorted to using arrays to work with the content you received from the *Get-Content* cmdlet. The VBScript version uses a *FileSystemObject* and a *TextStreamObject* to work with the data. In reality, you would not have to use a script exactly like the WhileReadLine.ps1 script to read the contents of the text file. This is because the *Get-Content* cmdlet does this for you automatically. All you really have to do to display the contents of TestFile.txt is use *Get-Content*. This command is shown here.

```
Get-Content -path c:\fso\TestFile.txt
```

Because the results of the command are not stored in a variable, the contents are automatically emitted to the screen. You can further shorten the *Get-Content* command by using the *gc* alias and by omitting the name of the *-Path* parameter (which is the default parameter). When you do this, you create a command that resembles the following.

```
gc c:\fso\TestFile.txt
```

To find the available aliases for the *Get-Content* cmdlet, you use the *Get-Alias* cmdlet with the *-Definition* parameter. The *Get-Alias* cmdlet searches for aliases that have a definition that matches *Get-Content*. Here is the command, including the output you receive.

```
PS C:\> Get-Alias -Definition Get-Content

CommandType     Name                    Definition
-----------     ----                    ----------
Alias           cat                     Get-Content
Alias           gc                      Get-Content
Alias           type                    Get-Content
```

This section showed that you can use the *While* statement in Windows PowerShell to perform looping. It also showed that activities in VBScript that require looping do not always require you to use the looping behavior in their Windows PowerShell equivalents, because some cmdlets automatically display information. Finally, it discussed how to find aliases for cmdlets you frequently use.

Using the *Do...While* statement

The *Do While...Loop* statement is often used when working with VBScript. This section covers some of the advantages of the similar *Do...While* statement in Windows PowerShell.

The DemoDoWhile.vbs script illustrates using the *Do...While* statement in VBScript. The first thing you do is assign a value of 0 to the variable *i*. You then create an array. To do this, you use the *Array* function, and assign the numbers 1 through 5 to the variable *ary*. You then use the *Do While...Loop* construction to walk through the array of numbers. As long as the value of the variable *i* is less than the number 5, you display the value of the variable *i*. You then increment the value of the variable and loop back around.

The DemoDoWhile.vbs script is shown here.

DemoDoWhile.vbs

```
i = 0
ary = Array(1,2,3,4,5)
Do While i < 5
 WScript.Echo ary(i)
 i = i + 1
Loop
```

When you run the DemoDoWhile.vbs script in Cscript at the command prompt, you get the numbers 1 through 5 displayed at the command prompt.

You can achieve the same thing by using Windows PowerShell. The DemoDoWhile.ps1 and DemoDoWhile.vbs scripts are essentially the same. The differences between the two scripts are due to syntax differences between Windows PowerShell and VBScript. With the Windows PowerShell script, the first thing you do is assign a value of 1 to the variable $i. You then create an array of the numbers 1 through 5 and store that array in the $ary variable. You can use a shortcut in Windows PowerShell to make this a bit easier. Actually, arrays in Windows PowerShell are fairly easy anyway. If you want to create an array, you just have to assign multiple pieces of data to the variable. To do this, you separate each piece of data by a comma. This is shown here.

```
$ary = 1,2,3,4,5
```

Using the range operator

If you needed to create an array with 32,000 numbers in it, it would be impractical to type each number and separate them all with commas. In VBScript, you would have to use a *For...Next* loop to add the numbers to the array. You can also write a loop in Windows PowerShell, but it is easier to use the range operator. To do this, you use a variable to hold the array of numbers that is created, and enter the beginning and the ending number separated by two periods. This is shown here.

```
$ary = 1..5
```

Unfortunately, the range operator does not work for letters. But there is nothing to prevent you from creating a range of numbers that represent the ASCII value of each letter, and then casting it to a string later.

Operating over an array

You are now ready for the *Do...While* loop in Windows PowerShell. You use the *Do* statement and open a set of braces. Inside these braces you have a script block. The first thing you do is index into the array. On your first pass through the array, the value of $i is equal to 0. You therefore display the first element in the $ary array. You next increment the value of the $i variable by one. You are now done with the script block, so you look at the *While* statement. The condition you are examining is the value of the $i variable. As long as it is less than 5, you will continue to loop around. As soon as the value of $i is no longer less than 5, you stop looping.

This is shown here.

DemoDoWhile.ps1

```
$i = 0
$ary = 1..5
do
{
 $ary[$i]
 $i++
} while ($i -lt 5)
```

One thing to be aware of, because it can be a bit confusing, is that you are evaluating the value of *$i*. You initialized *$i* at 0. The first number in your array was 1. But the first element number in the array is always 0 in Windows PowerShell (unlike VBScript, in which arrays can start with 0 or 1). The *While* statement evaluates the value contained in the *$i* variable, not the value that is contained in the array. That is why the number 5 is displayed.

Casting to ASCII values

You can change the DemoDoWhile.ps1 script to display uppercase letters *A* through *Z*. To do this, you first initialize the *$i* variable and set it to 0. You then create a range of numbers from 65 through 91. These are the ASCII values for the capital letter *A* through the capital letter *Z*. Then you begin the *Do* statement and open your script block. To this point, the script is identical to the previous one. To obtain letters from numbers, cast the integer to a char. To do this, you use the *char* data type and put it inside square brackets. You then use this to convert an integer to an uppercase letter. The code to display the uppercase letter *B* from the ASCII value 66 would resemble the following.

```
PS C:\> [char]66
B
```

Because you know that the *$caps* variable contains an array of numbers from 65 through 91, and that the variable *$i* will hold numbers from 0 through 26, you index into the *$caps* array, cast the integer to a char, and display the results, as follows.

```
[char]$caps[$i]
```

You then increment the value of *$i* by one, close the script block, and enter the *While* statement, where you check the value of *$i* to make sure it is less than 26. As long as *$i* is less than 26, you continue to loop around. The complete DisplayCapitalLetters.ps1 script is shown here.

DisplayCapitalLetters.ps1

```
$i = 0
$caps = 65..91
do
{
 [char]$caps[$i]
 $i++
} while ($i -lt 26)
```

This section explored the *Do...While* construction from Windows PowerShell by comparing it to the similar construction from VBScript. In addition, the use of the range operator and casting was also examined.

Using the *Do...Until* statement

Looping technology is something that is essential to master. It occurs everywhere and should be a tool that you can use without thought. When you are confronted with a collection of items, an array, or another bundle of items, you have to know how to easily walk through the mess without resorting to research, panic, or hours searching the Internet. This section examines the *Do...Until* construction. Most of the scripts that do looping at the Microsoft Script Center Script Repository seem to use *Do...While*. The scripts that use *Do...Until...Loop* are typically used to read through a text file (do something until the end of the stream) or to read through an ActiveX Data Objects (ADO) recordset (do something until the end of the file). As you will notice here, these are not required coding conventions and are not meant to be limitations. You can frequently perform the same thing by using any of the different looping constructions.

Comparing the Windows PowerShell *Do...Until* statement with VBScript

Before you get too far into this topic, consider the DemoDoUntil.vbs script. In this script, you first assign a value of 0 to the variable *i*. You then create an array with the numbers 1 through 5 contained in it. You use the *Do...Until* construction to walk through the array until the value of the variable *i* is equal to 5. The script will continue to run until the value of the variable *i* is equal to 5. This is what a *Do...Until* construction does—it runs until a condition is met. The difference between *Do...Until* and *Do...While*, examined in the previous section, is that *Do...While* runs while a condition is true and *Do...Until* runs until a condition becomes true. In VBScript, this means that *Do...Until* will always run at least once, because the condition is evaluated at the bottom of the loop, whereas *Do...While* is evaluated at the top of the loop, and therefore will never run if the condition is not true. This is not true for Windows PowerShell, however, as will be shown later in this section.

Inside the loop, you first display the value that is contained in the array element 0 on the first pass through the loop. This is because you first set the value of the variable *i* equal to 0. You next increment the value of the variable *i* by one and loop around until the value of *i* is equal to 5. The DemoDoUntil.vbs script is shown here.

DemoDoUntil.vbs

```
i = 0
ary = array(1,2,3,4,5)
Do Until i = 5
 wscript.Echo ary(i)
 i = i+1
Loop
```

Using the Windows PowerShell *Do* statement

You can write the same script by using Windows PowerShell. In the DemoDoUntil.ps1 script, you first set the value of the *$i* variable to 0. You then create an array with the numbers 1 through 5 in it. You store that array in the *$ary* variable. You then arrive at the *Do* (do-until) construction. After the *Do* keyword, you open a set of braces. Inside the braces, you use the *$i* variable to index into the *$ary* array and to retrieve the value that is stored in the first element (element 0) of the array. You then increment the value of the *$i* variable by one. You continue to loop through the elements in the array until the value of the *$i* variable is equal to 5. At that time, you end the script. This script resembles the DemoDoWhile.ps1 script examined in the previous section.

DemoDoUntil.ps1

```
$i = 0
$ary = 1..5

Do
{
 $ary[$i]
 $i ++
} Until ($i -eq 5)
```

The *Do...While* and *Do...Until* statements always run once

In VBScript, if a *Do...While...Loop* condition was never true, the code inside the loop would never execute. In Windows PowerShell, the *Do...While* and *Do...Until* constructions always run at least once. This can be unexpected behavior and is something that you should focus on. This is illustrated in the DoWhileAlwaysRuns.ps1 script. The script assigns a value of 1 to the variable *$i*. Inside the script block for the *Do...While* loop, you print out a message that states that you are inside the *Do* loop. The loop condition is "while the variable *$i* is equal to 5." As you can tell, the value of the *$i* variable is 1. Therefore, the value of the *$i* variable will never reach 5, because you are not incrementing it. The DoWhileAlwaysRuns.ps1 script is shown here.

DoWhileAlwaysRuns.ps1

```
$i = 1

Do
{
 "inside the do loop"
} While ($i -eq 5)
```

When you run the script, the text "inside the do loop" is printed out once.

What about a similar script that uses the *Do...Until* construction? The EndlessDoUntil.ps1 script is the same as the DoWhileAlwaysRuns.ps1 script, except for one small detail. Instead of using *Do...While*, you are using *Do...Until*. The rest of the script is the same. The value of the *$i* variable is equal to 1, and in the script block for the *Do...Until* loop, you print the string *inside the do loop*. This line of code should execute once for each *Do* loop until the value of *$i* is equal to 5. Because the value of *$i* is never increased to 5, the script will continue to run.

The EndlessDoUntil.ps1 script is shown here.

EndlessDoUntil.ps1

```
$i = 1

Do
{
 "inside the do loop"
} Until ($i -eq 5)
```

Before you run the EndlessDoUntil.ps1 script, you should know how to interrupt the running of the script. You hold down the Ctrl key and press C (Ctrl+C). This is the same keystroke sequence that would break a runaway VBScript that was run in Cscript.

The *While* statement is used to prevent unwanted execution

If you have a situation where the script block must not execute if the condition is not true, you should use the *While* statement. The use of the *While* statement was examined in an earlier section. Again, you have the same kind of script. You assign the value of 0 to the variable *$i*, and instead of using a *Do...* kind of construction, you use the *While* statement. The condition you are looking at is similar to the condition you used for the other scripts (do something *while* the value of *$i* is equal to 5). Inside the script block, you display a string that states that you are inside the *While* loop. The WhileDoes-NotRun.ps1 script is shown here.

WhileDoesNotRun.ps1

```
$i = 0

While ($i -eq 5)
{
 "Inside the While Loop"
}
```

It is perhaps a bit anticlimactic, but go ahead and run the WhileDoesNotRun.ps1 script. There should be no output displayed to the console.

The *For* statement

In VBScript, a *For...Next* loop is somewhat easy to create. An example of a simple *For...Next* loop is shown in DemoForLoop.vbs. You use the *For* keyword, define a variable to keep track of the count, indicate how far you will go, define your action, and ensure that you specify the *Next* keyword. That is about all there is to it. The DemoForLoop.vbs is shown here.

DemoForLoop.vbs

```
For i = 1 To 5
 WScript.Echo i
Next
```

Using the *For* statement

You can achieve the same thing in Windows PowerShell. The structure of the *For* loop in Windows PowerShell resembles the structure for VBScript; the Windows PowerShell *For* loop construct is *For (<init>; <condition>; <repeat>) {<statement list>}*. They both begin with the keyword *For*, they both initialize the variable, and they both specify how far the loop will progress. One thing that is different is that a *For...Next* loop in VBScript automatically increments the counter variable. In Windows PowerShell, the variable is not automatically incremented; instead, you add *$i++* to increment the *$i* variable by one. Inside the script block (braces), you display the value of the *$i* variable. The DemoForLoop.ps1 script is shown here.

DemoForLoop.ps1

```
For($i = 0; $i -le 5; $i++)
{
 '$i equals ' + $i
}
```

The Windows PowerShell *For* statement is very flexible, and you can leave one or more elements of it out. In the DemoForWithoutInitOrRepeat.ps1 script, you exclude the first and the last sections of the *For* statement. You set the *$i* variable equal to 0 on the first line of the script. You next come to the *For* statement. In the DemoForLoop.ps1 script, the *$i = 0* was inside the *For* statement; here you move it to the first line of the script. The semicolon is still required because it separates the three sections of the statement. The condition portion, *$i -le 5*, is the same as in the previous script. The repeat section, *$i ++*, is not used.

In the script section of the *For* statement, you display the value of the *$i* variable, and you also increment the value of *$i* by one. Remember that there are two kinds of Windows PowerShell strings: expanding and literal. These two types of strings were examined earlier in this chapter. The DemoForLoop.ps1 script demonstrates an example of a literal string—what is entered is what is displayed. This is shown here.

```
'$i equals ' + $i
```

In the DemoForWithoutInitOrRepeat.ps1 script is an example of an expanding string. The value of the variable is displayed—not the variable name itself. To suppress the expanding nature of the expanding string, escape the variable by using the backtick character. When you use the expanding string in this manner, you can avoid concatenating the string and the variable, as you did in the DemoForLoop.ps1 script. This is shown here.

```
"`$i is equal to $i"
```

The value of *$i* must be incremented somewhere. Because it was not incremented in the repeat section of the *For* statement, you have to be able to increment it inside the script block.

The DemoForWithoutInitOrRepeat.ps1 script is shown here.

DemoForWithoutInitOrRepeat.ps1

```
$i = 0
For(;$i -le 5; )
{
 "`$i is equal to $i"
 $i++
}
```

When you run the DemoForWithoutInitOrRepeat.ps1 script, the output that is displayed resembles the output produced by DemoForLoop.ps1. You would never be able to tell that it was missing two-thirds of the parameters.

You can make your *For* statement into an infinite loop by omitting all three sections of the *For* statement. You must leave the semicolons as position holders. When you omit the three parts of the *For* statement, it will resemble the following.

```
for(;;)
```

Although you can create an endless loop with the ForEndlessLoop.ps1 script, you do not have to do this if this is not what you want to do. You could use an *If* statement to evaluate a condition and take action when the condition is met. *If* statements will be covered in the "Using the *If* statement" section, later in this chapter. In the ForEndlessLoop.ps1 script, you display the value of the *$i* variable and increment it by one. The semicolon is used to represent a new line. You could therefore write the *For* statement on three lines if you wanted to. This would be useful if you had a very complex *For* statement, because it would make the code easier to read. The script block for the ForEndlessLoop.ps1 script could be written on different lines and could exclude the semicolon. This is shown here.

ForEndlessLoop.ps1

```
for(;;)
{
 $i ; $i++
}
```

When you run the ForEndlessLoop.ps1 script, you are greeted with a long line of numbers. To break out of the endless loop, press Ctrl+C inside the Windows PowerShell prompt.

You can tell that working with Windows PowerShell is all about choices: how you want to work and the things that you want to try to achieve. The *For* statement in Windows PowerShell is very flexible, and maybe someday you will find just the problem waiting for the solution that you have.

Using the *Foreach* statement

The *Foreach* statement resembles the *For...Each...Next* construction from VBScript. In the Demo-ForEachNext.vbs script, you create an array of five numbers, 1 through 5. You then use the *For...Each...Next* statement to walk your way through the array that is contained in the variable *ary*. The variable *i* is used to iterate through the elements of the array. The *For...Each* block is entered as long as there is at least one item in the collection or array. When the loop is entered, all statements inside the loop are executed for the first element. In the DemoForEachNext.vbs script, this means that the following command is executed for each element in the array.

```
Wscript.Echo i
```

As long as there are more elements in the collection or array, the statements inside the loop continue to execute for each element. When there are no more elements in the collection or array, the loop is exited, and execution continues with the statement following the *Next* statement. This is shown in DemoForEachNext.vbs.

DemoForEachNext.vbs

```
ary = Array(1,2,3,4,5)
For Each i In ary
  WScript.Echo i
Next
Wscript.echo "All done"
```

The DemoForEachNext.vbs script works exactly like the DemoForEach.ps1 script. In the Demo-ForEach.ps1 Windows PowerShell script, you first create an array that contains the numbers 1 through 5, and then you store that array in the *$ary* variable. This is shown here.

```
$ary = 1..5
```

Then you use the *Foreach* statement to walk through the array contained in the *$ary* variable. Use the *$i* variable to keep track of your progress through the array. Inside the script block, you display the value of each variable. The DemoForEach.ps1 script is shown here.

DemoForEach.ps1

```
$ary = 1..5
Foreach ($i in $ary)
{
 $i
}
```

Using the *Foreach* statement from the Windows PowerShell console

The great thing about Windows PowerShell is that you can also use the *Foreach* statement from inside the Windows PowerShell console. This is shown here.

```
PS C:\> $ary = 1..5
PS C:\> foreach($i in $ary) { $i }
1
2
3
4
5
```

The ability to use the *Foreach* statement from inside the Windows PowerShell console can give you excellent flexibility when you are working interactively. However, much of the work done at the Windows PowerShell console consists of using pipelining. When you are working with the pipeline, you can use the *ForEach-Object* cmdlet. This cmdlet behaves in a similar manner to the *Foreach* statement but is designed to handle pipelined input. The difference is that you do not have to use an intermediate variable to hold the contents of the array. You can create the array and send it across the pipeline. The other difference is that you do not have to create a variable to use for the enumerator. You use the *$_* automatic variable (which represents the current item on the pipeline) instead. This is shown here.

```
PS C:\> 1..5 | ForEach-Object { $_ }
1
2
3
4
5
```

Exiting the *Foreach* statement early

Suppose that you do not want to work with all the numbers in the array. In VBScript terms, leaving a *For...Each...Loop* early is done with an *Exit For* statement. You have to use an *If* statement to perform the evaluation of the condition. When the condition is met, you call *Exit For*. In the DemoExitFor.vbs script, you use an inline *If* statement to make this determination. The inline syntax is more efficient for these kinds of things than spreading the statement across three different lines. The key thing to remember about the inline *If* statement is that it does not conclude with the final *End If* statement. The DemoExitFor.vbs script is shown here.

DemoExitFor.vbs

```
ary = Array(1,2,3,4,5)
For Each i In ary
 If i = 3 Then Exit For
 WScript.Echo i
Next
WScript.Echo "Statement following Next"
```

Using the *Break* statement

In Windows PowerShell terms, you use the *Break* statement to leave the loop early. Inside the script block, you use an *If* statement to evaluate the value of the *$i* variable. If it is equal to 3, you call the *Break* statement and leave the loop. This line of code is shown here.

```
if($i -eq 3) { break }
```

The complete DemoBreakFor.ps1 script is shown here.

DemoBreakFor.ps1

```
$ary = 1..5
ForEach($i in $ary)
{
 if($i -eq 3) { break }
 $i
}
"Statement following foreach loop"
```

When the DemoBreakFor.ps1 script runs, it displays the numbers 1 and 2. Then it leaves the *Foreach* loop and runs the line of code following the *Foreach* loop. This is shown here.

```
1
2
Statement following foreach loop
```

Using the *Exit* statement

If you did not want to run the line of code after the loop statement, you would use the *exit* statement instead of the *Break* statement. This is shown in the DemoExitFor.ps1 script.

DemoExitFor.ps1

```
$ary = 1..5
ForEach($i in $ary)
{
 if($i -eq 3) { exit }
 $i
}
"Statement following foreach loop"
```

When the DemoExitFor.ps1 script runs, the line of code following the *Foreach* loop never executes. This is because the *exit* statement ends the script (In the Windows PowerShell ISE, discussed in Chapter 8, "Using the Windows PowerShell ISE," the *exit* command attempts to close the ISE.) The results of running the DemoExitFor.ps1 script are shown here.

```
1
2
```

You could achieve the same thing in VBScript by using the *Wscript.Quit* statement instead of *Exit For*. As with the DemoExitFor.ps1 script, the DemoQuitFor.vbs script never comes to the line of code following the *For...Each* loop. This is shown in DemoQuitFor.vbs here.

DemoQuitFor.vbs

```
ary = Array(1,2,3,4,5)
For Each i In ary
 If i = 3 Then WScript.Quit
 WScript.Echo i
Next
WScript.Echo "Statement following Next"
```

In this section, the use of the *Foreach* statement was examined. It is used when you do not know how many items are contained within a collection. It allows you to walk through the collection and to work with items from that collection on an individual basis. In addition, two techniques for exiting a *Foreach* statement were also examined.

Using the *If* statement

In VBScript, the *If...Then...End If* statement is somewhat straightforward. There are several things to be aware of:

- The *If* and the *Then* statements must be on the same line.

- The *If...Then...End If* statement must conclude with *End If.*

- *End If* is two words, not one.

The VBScript *If...Then...End If* statement is shown in the DemoIf.vbs script.

DemoIf.vbs
```
a = 5
If a = 5 Then
 WScript.Echo "a equals 5"
End If
```

In the Windows PowerShell version of the *If...Then...End If* statement, there is no *Then* keyword, nor is there an *End If* statement. The Windows PowerShell *If* statement is easier to type. This simplicity, however, comes with a bit of complexity. The condition that is evaluated in the *If* statement is positioned between a set of parentheses. In the DemoIf.ps1 script, you are checking whether the variable *$a* is equal to 5. This is shown here.

```
If ($a -eq 5)
```

The code that is executed when the condition is *true* is positioned inside a script block. The script block for the DemoIf.ps1 script is shown here.

```
{
    '$a equals 5'
}
```

The Windows PowerShell version of the DemoIf.vbs script is the DemoIf.ps1 script.

DemoIf.ps1
```
$a = 5
If($a -eq 5)
 {
    '$a equals 5'
 }
```

The one thing that is different about the Windows PowerShell *If* statement is the comparison operators. In VBScript, the equal sign (=) is used as an assignment operator. It is also used as an equality operator for comparison. On the first line of code, the variable *a* is assigned the value 5. This uses the equal sign as an assignment. On the next line of code, the *If* statement is used to find out whether the value of *a* is equal to 5. On this line of code, the equal sign is used as the equality operator.

This is shown here.

```
a = 5
If a = 5 Then
```

In simple examples such as this, it is fairly easy to tell the difference between an equality operator and an assignment operator. In more complex scripts, however, things could be confusing. Windows PowerShell removes that confusion by having special comparison operators. One thing that might help is to realize that the main operators are two letters long. Common comparison operators are shown in Table 5-5.

TABLE 5-5 Common comparison operators in Windows PowerShell

Operator	Description	Example	Result
-eq	Equals	$a = 5 ; $a -eq 4	False
-ne	Does not equal	$a = 5 ; $a -ne 4	True
-gt	Greater than	$a = 5 ; $a -gt 4	True
-ge	Greater than or equal to	$a = 5 ; $a -ge 5	True
-lt	Less than	$a = 5 ; $a -lt 5	False
-le	Less than or equal to	$a = 5 ; $a -le 5	True
-like	Wildcard comparison	$a = "This is Text" ; $a -like "Text"	False
-notlike	Wildcard comparison	$a = "This is Text" ; $a -notlike "Text"	True
-match	Regular expression comparison	$a = "This is Text" ; $a -match "Text"	True
-notmatch	Regular expression comparison	$a = "This is Text" ; $a -notmatch "Text$"	False

Using assignment and comparison operators

Any value assignment in a condition block will evaluate to *true*, and therefore the script block is executed. In this example, you assign the value 1 to the variable *$a*. In the condition for the *If* statement, you assign the value of 12 to the variable *$a*. Any assignment evaluates to *true*, and the script block executes.

```
PS C:\> $a = 1 ; If ($a = 12) { "its true" }
its true
```

Rarely do you test a condition and perform an action. Sometimes you have to perform one action if the condition is *true* and another action if the condition is *false*. In VBScript, you use the *If...Else...End If* construction. The *Else* clause goes immediately after the first action to be performed if the condition is *true*. This is shown in the DemoIfElse.vbs script.

DemoIfElse.vbs

```
a = 4
If a = 5 Then
 WScript.Echo "a equals 5"
```

```
Else
 WScript.Echo "a is not equal to 5"
End If
```

In Windows PowerShell, the syntax is not surprising. Following the closing brace from the *If* statement script block, you add the *Else* keyword and open a new script block to hold the alternative outcome. This is shown here.

DemoIfElse.ps1
```
$a = 4
If ($a -eq 5)
{
 '$a equals 5'
}
Else
{
 '$a is not equal to 5'
}
```

Things become confusing with VBScript when you want to evaluate multiple conditions and have multiple outcomes. The *Else If* clause provides for the second outcome. You have to evaluate the second condition. The *Else If* clause receives its own condition, which is followed by the *Then* keyword. Following the *Then* keyword, you list the code that you want to execute. This is followed by the *Else* keyword and an *End If* statement. This is shown in the DemoIfElseIfElse.vbs script.

DemoIfElseIfElse.vbs
```
a = 4
If a = 5 Then
 WScript.Echo "a equals 5"
ElseIf a = 3 Then
 WScript.Echo "a equals 3"
Else
 WScript.Echo "a does not equal 3 or 5"
End If
```

Evaluating multiple conditions

The Windows PowerShell DemoIfElseIfElse.ps1 script is a bit easier to understand because it avoids the *End If* statement. For each condition that you want to evaluate, you use *ElseIf* (be aware that it is a single word). You put the condition inside a pair of parentheses and open your script block. Here is the DemoIfElseIfElse.ps1 script.

DemoIfElseIfElse.ps1
```
$a = 4
If ($a -eq 5)
{
 '$a equals 5'
}
```

```
ElseIf ($a -eq 3)
{
 '$a is equal to 3'
}
Else
{
 '$a does not equal 3 or 5'
}
```

In this section, the use of the *If* statement was examined. Comparison operators and assignment operators were also covered.

The *Switch* statement

It is a best practice to generally avoid using the *ElseIf* type of construction from either VBScript or Windows PowerShell, because there is a better way to write the same code.

In VBScript, you would use the *Select Case* statement to evaluate a condition and select one outcome from a group of potential statements. In the DemoSelectCase.vbs script, the variable *a* is assigned the value of 2. The *Select Case* statement is used to evaluate the value of the variable *a*. The syntax is shown here.

```
Select Case testexpression
```

The test expression that is evaluated is the variable *a*. Each of the different cases contains potential values for the test expression. If the value of the variable *a* is equal to 1, the code *Wscript.Echo "a = 1"* is executed. This is shown here.

```
Case 1
   WScript.Echo "a = 1"
```

Each of the different cases is evaluated in the same manner. The *Case Else* expression is run if none of the previous expressions evaluate to *true*. The complete DemoSelectCase.vbs script is shown here.

DemoSelectCase.vbs
```
a = 2
Select Case a
 Case 1
   WScript.Echo "a = 1"
 Case 2
   WScript.Echo "a = 2"
 Case 3
   WScript.Echo "a = 3"
 Case Else
   WScript.Echo "unable to determine value of a"
End Select
WScript.Echo "statement after select case"
```

Using the *Switch* statement

In Windows PowerShell, there is no *Select Case* statement. There is, however, the *Switch* statement. The *Switch* statement is the most powerful statement in the Windows PowerShell language. The basic *Switch* statement begins with the *Switch* keyword, followed by the condition to be evaluated positioned inside a pair of parentheses. This is shown here.

```
Switch ($a)
```

Next, a script block is used to mark off the script block for the *Switch* statement. Inside this outer script block, you will find an inner script block to be executed. Each condition to be evaluated begins with a value, followed by the script block to be executed if the value matches the condition. This is shown here.

```
1 { '$a = 1' }
2 { '$a = 2' }
3 { '$a = 3' }
```

Defining the *default* condition

If no match is found in the script block and the *Default* statement is not used, the *Switch* statement exits and the line of code that follows the *Switch* statement is executed. The *Default* statement performs a function similar to the *Case Else* statement from the *Select Case* statement. The *Default* statement is shown here.

```
Default { 'unable to determine value of $a' }
```

The complete DemoSwitchCase.ps1 script is shown here.

DemoSwitchCase.ps1

```
$a = 2
Switch ($a)
{
 1 { '$a = 1' }
 2 { '$a = 2' }
 3 { '$a = 3' }
 Default { 'unable to determine value of $a' }
}
"Statement after switch"
```

Understanding matching with the *Switch* statement

With the *Select Case* statement, the first matching case is the one that is executed. As soon as that code executes, the line following the *Select Case* statement is executed. If the condition matches multiple cases in the *Select Case* statement, only the first match in the list is executed. Matches from lower in the list are not executed. Therefore, make sure that the most important code to execute is positioned highest in the *Select Case* order.

With the *Switch* statement in Windows PowerShell, order is not a major design concern. This is because every match from inside the *Switch* statement will be executed by default. An example of this is shown in the DemoSwitchMultiMatch.ps1 script.

DemoSwitchMultiMatch.ps1

```
$a = 2
Switch ($a)
{
 1 { '$a = 1' }
 2 { '$a = 2' }
 2 { 'Second match of the $a variable' }
 3 { '$a = 3' }
 Default { 'unable to determine value of $a' }
}
"Statement after switch"
```

When the DemoSwitchMultiMatch.ps1 script runs, the second and third conditions will both be matched, and therefore their associated script blocks will be executed. The DemoSwitchMultiMatch.ps1 script produces the output shown here.

```
$a = 2
Second match of the $a variable
Statement after switch
```

Evaluating an array

If an array is stored in the variable *a* in the DemoSelectCase.vbs script, a type-mismatch error will be produced. This error is shown here.

```
Microsoft VBScript runtime error: Type mismatch
```

The Windows PowerShell *Switch* statement can handle an array in the variable *$a* without any modification. The array is shown here.

```
$a = 2,3,5,1,77
```

The complete DemoSwitchArray.ps1 script is shown here.

DemoSwitchArray.ps1

```
$a = 2,3,5,1,77
Switch ($a)
{
 1 { '$a = 1' }
 2 { '$a = 2' }
 3 { '$a = 3' }
 Default { 'unable to determine value of $a' }
}
"Statement after switch"
```

Controlling matching behavior

If you do not want the multimatch behavior of the *Switch* statement, you can use the *Break* statement to change the behavior. In the DemoSwitchArrayBreak.ps1 script, the *Switch* statement will be exited when the first match occurs because each of the match condition script blocks contains the *Break* statement. This is shown here.

```
1 { '$a = 1' ; break }
2 { '$a = 2' ; break }
3 { '$a = 3' ; break }
```

You are not required to include the *Break* statement with each condition; instead, you could use it to exit the switch only after a particular condition is matched. The complete DemoSwitchArrayBreak.ps1 script is shown here.

DemoSwitchArrayBreak.ps1

```
$a = 2,3,5,1,77
Switch ($a)
{
 1 { '$a = 1' ; break }
 2 { '$a = 2' ; break }
 3 { '$a = 3' ; break }
 Default { 'unable to determine value of $a' }
}
"Statement after switch"
```

In this section, the use of Windows PowerShell *Switch* statement was examined. The matching behavior of the *Switch* statement and the use of *Break* was also discussed.

Creating multiple folders: Step-by-step exercises

In the first exercise, you'll explore the use of constants, variables, concatenation, decision-making, and looping as you create 10 folders in the C:\mytempfolder directory. This directory was created earlier. If you do not have this folder on your machine, you can either create it manually or modify the following two exercises to use a folder that exists on your machine. In the second exercise in this section, you will modify the script to delete the 10 folders.

Creating multiple folders by using Windows PowerShell scripting

1. Open the Windows PowerShell ISE.

2. Create a variable called *$intFolders* and have it hold the value 10. The code to do this is shown here.

   ```
   $intFolders = 10
   ```

3. Create a variable called *$intPad*. Do not put anything in the variable yet. This code is shown here.

```
$intPad
```

4. Create a variable called *$i* and put the value 1 in it. The code to do this is shown here.

```
$i = 1
```

5. Use the *New-Variable* cmdlet to create a variable named *strPrefix*. Use the *-Value* parameter of the cmdlet to assign a value of *testFolder* to the variable. Use the *-Option* parameter to make *$strPrefix* into a constant. The code to do this is shown here.

```
New-Variable -Name strPrefix -Value "testFolder" -Option constant
```

6. Begin a *Do...Until* statement. Include the opening brace for the script block. This code is shown here.

```
do {
```

7. Begin an *If...Else* statement. The condition to be evaluated is if the variable *$i* is less than 10. The code that does this is shown here.

```
if ($i -lt 10)
```

8. Open the script block for the *If* statement. Assign the value 0 to the variable *$intPad*. This is shown here.

```
{$intPad=0
```

9. Use the *New-Item* cmdlet to create a new folder. The new folder will be created in the C:\mytempfolder directory. The name of the new folder will be made up of the *$strPrefix* constant *testFolder*, the number 0 from the *$intPad* variable, and the number contained in the *$i* variable. The code that does this is shown here.

```
New-Item -Path c:\mytempfolder -Name $strPrefix$intPad$i -Type directory}
```

10. Add the *Else* clause. This code is shown here.

```
else
```

11. The *Else* script block is the same as the *If* script block, except it does not include the 0 in the name that comes from the *$intPad* variable. Copy the *New-Item* line of code from the *If* statement and delete the *$intPad* variable from the *-Name* parameter. The revised line of code is shown here.

```
{New-Item -Path c:\mytempfolder -Name $strPrefix$i -Type directory}
```

12. Increment the value of the *$i* variable by one. To do this, use the double-plus symbol operator (++) . The code that does this is shown here.

```
$i++
```

13. Close the script block for the *Else* clause and add the *Until* statement. The condition that *Until* will evaluate is whether the *$i* variable is equal to the value contained in the *$intFolders* variable + 1. The reason for adding 1 to *$intFolders* is so the script will actually create the same number of folders as are contained in the *$intFolders* variable. Because this script uses a *Do...Until* loop and the value of *$i* is incremented before entering the *Until* evaluation, the value of *$i* is always 1 more than the number of folders created. This code is shown here.

```
}until ($i -eq $intFolders+1)
```

14. Save your script as *<yourname>*CreateMultipleFolders.ps1. Run your script. You should find 10 folders created in the C:\mytempfolder directory. This concludes this step-by-step exercise.

The next exercise will show you how to delete multiple folders.

Deleting multiple folders

1. Open the *<yourname>*CreateMultipleFolders.ps1 script created in the previous exercise in the Windows PowerShell ISE.

2. In the *If...Else* statement, the *New-Item* cmdlet is used twice to create folders in the C:\mytempfolder directory. You want to delete these folders. To do this, you need to change the *New-Item* cmdlet to the *Remove-Item* cmdlet. The two edited script blocks are shown here.

```
{$intPad=0
      Remove-Item -Path c:\mytempfolder -Name $strPrefix$intPad$i -Type directory}
   else
      {Remove-Item -Path c:\mytempfolder -Name $strPrefix$i -Type directory}
```

3. The *Remove-Item* cmdlet does not have a *-Name* parameter. Therefore, you need to remove this parameter but keep the code that specifies the folder name. You can basically replace *-Name* with a backslash, as shown here.

```
{$intPad=0
      Remove-Item -Path c:\mytempfolder\$strPrefix$intPad$i -Type directory}
   else
      {Remove-Item -Path c:\mytempfolder\$strPrefix$i -Type directory}
```

4. The *Remove-Item* cmdlet does not take a *-Type* parameter. Because this parameter is not needed, it can also be removed from both *Remove-Item* statements. The revised script block is shown here.

```
{$intPad=0
    Remove-Item -Path c:\mytempfolder\$strPrefix$intPad$i}
  else
    {Remove-Item -Path c:\mytempfolder\$strPrefix$i}
```

5. This concludes this exercise. Save your script as *<yourname>*DeleteMultipleFolders.ps1. Run your script. The 10 previously created folders should be deleted.

Chapter 5 quick reference

To	Do this
Retrieve the script execution policy	Use the *Get-ExecutionPolicy* cmdlet.
Set the script execution policy	Use the *Set-ExecutionPolicy* cmdlet.
Create a variable	Use the *New-Variable* cmdlet.
Create a constant	Use the *New-Variable* cmdlet and specify *constant* for the *-Option* parameter.
Loop through a collection when you do not know how many items are in the collection	Use the *ForEach-Object* cmdlet.
Read the contents of a text file	Use the *Get-Content* cmdlet and supply the path to the file as the value for the *-Path* parameter.
Delete a folder	Use the *Remove-Item* cmdlet and supply the path to the folder as the value for the *-Path* parameter.

Working with functions

After completing this chapter, you will be able to

- Understand functions.

- Use functions to provide ease of reuse.

- Use functions to encapsulate logic.

- Use functions to provide ease of modification.

There are clear-cut guidelines that can be used to design functions. These guidelines can be used to ensure that functions are easy to understand, easy to maintain, and easy to troubleshoot. This chapter examines the reasons for the scripting guidelines and provides examples of both good and bad code design.

Understanding functions

In Windows PowerShell, functions have moved to the forefront as the primary programming element used when writing Windows PowerShell scripts. This is not necessarily due to improvements in functions per se, but rather to a combination of factors, including the maturity of Windows PowerShell script writers. In Windows PowerShell 1.0, functions were not well understood, perhaps due to the lack of clear documentation as to their use, purpose, and application.

Microsoft Visual Basic Scripting Edition (VBScript) included both subroutines and functions. According to the classic definitions, a subroutine was used to encapsulate code that would do things like write to a database or create a Microsoft Word document. Functions, on the other hand, were used to return a value. An example of a classic VBScript function is one that converts a temperature from Fahrenheit to Celsius. The function receives a value in Fahrenheit and returns the value in Celsius. The classic function always returns a value—if it does not, a subroutine should be used instead.

> **Note** Needless to say, the concepts of functions and subroutines were a bit confusing for many VBScript writers. A common question I used to receive when teaching VBScript classes was, "When do I use a subroutine and when do I use a function?" After expounding the classic definition, I would then show them that you could actually write a subroutine that would behave like a function. Next, I would write a function that acted like a subroutine. It was great fun, and the class loved it. The Windows PowerShell team has essentially done the same thing. There is no confusion over when to use a subroutine and when to use a function, because there are no subroutines in Windows PowerShell—only functions.

To create a function in Windows PowerShell, you begin with the *Function* keyword, followed by the name of the function. As a best practice, use the Windows PowerShell verb-noun combination when creating functions. Pick the verb from the standard list of Windows PowerShell verbs to make your functions easier to remember. It is a best practice to avoid creating new verbs when there is an existing verb that can easily do the job.

An idea of the verb coverage can be obtained by using the *Get-Command* cmdlet and pipelining the results to the *Group-Object* cmdlet. This is shown here.

```
Get-Command -CommandType cmdlet | Group-Object -Property Verb |
Sort-Object -Property count -Descending
```

When the preceding command is run, the resulting output is as follows. This command was run on Windows 10 and includes cmdlets from the default modules. As shown in the listing, *Get* is used the most by the default cmdlets, followed distantly by *Set*, *New*, and *Remove*.

```
Count Name                Group
----- ----                -----
  107 Get                 {Get-Acl, Get-Alias, Get-AppLockerFileInformation...
   49 Set                 {Set-Acl, Set-Alias, Set-AppBackgroundTaskResourc...
   37 New                 {New-Alias, New-AppLockerPolicy, New-CertificateN...
   29 Remove              {Remove-AppxPackage, Remove-AppxProvisionedPackag...
   17 Add                 {Add-AppxPackage, Add-AppxProvisionedPackage, Add...
   15 Export              {Export-Alias, Export-BinaryMiLog, Export-Certifi...
   14 Disable             {Disable-AppBackgroundTaskDiagnosticLog, Disable-...
   14 Enable              {Enable-AppBackgroundTaskDiagnosticLog, Enable-Co...
   12 Import              {Import-Alias, Import-BinaryMiLog, Import-Certifi...
   11 Invoke              {Invoke-CimMethod, Invoke-Command, Invoke-DscReso...
   10 Clear               {Clear-Content, Clear-EventLog, Clear-History, Cl...
   10 Test                {Test-AppLockerPolicy, Test-Certificate, Test-Com...
    9 Write               {Write-Debug, Write-Error, Write-EventLog, Write-...
    9 Start               {Start-BitsTransfer, Start-DscConfiguration, Star...
    8 Register            {Register-ArgumentCompleter, Register-CimIndicati...
    7 Out                 {Out-Default, Out-File, Out-GridView, Out-Host...}
    6 Stop                {Stop-Computer, Stop-DtcDiagnosticResourceManager...
    6 ConvertTo           {ConvertTo-Csv, ConvertTo-Html, ConvertTo-Json, C...
    5 Update              {Update-FormatData, Update-Help, Update-List, Upd...
    5 Format              {Format-Custom, Format-List, Format-SecureBootUEF...
    5 ConvertFrom         {ConvertFrom-Csv, ConvertFrom-Json, ConvertFrom-S...
```

```
4 Wait              {Wait-Debugger, Wait-Event, Wait-Job, Wait-Process}
4 Unregister        {Unregister-Event, Unregister-PackageSource, Unre...
3 Rename            {Rename-Computer, Rename-Item, Rename-ItemProperty}
3 Receive           {Receive-DtcDiagnosticTransaction, Receive-Job, R...
3 Move              {Move-AppxPackage, Move-Item, Move-ItemProperty}
3 Suspend           {Suspend-BitsTransfer, Suspend-Job, Suspend-Service}
3 Show              {Show-Command, Show-ControlPanelItem, Show-EventLog}
3 Debug             {Debug-Job, Debug-Process, Debug-Runspace}
3 Complete          {Complete-BitsTransfer, Complete-DtcDiagnosticTra...
3 Select            {Select-Object, Select-String, Select-Xml}
3 Resume            {Resume-BitsTransfer, Resume-Job, Resume-Service}
3 Save              {Save-Help, Save-Package, Save-WindowsImage}
2 Unblock           {Unblock-File, Unblock-Tpm}
2 Split             {Split-Path, Split-WindowsImage}
2 Undo              {Undo-DtcDiagnosticTransaction, Undo-Transaction}
2 Restart           {Restart-Computer, Restart-Service}
2 Resolve           {Resolve-DnsName, Resolve-Path}
2 Send              {Send-DtcDiagnosticTransaction, Send-MailMessage}
2 Convert           {Convert-Path, Convert-String}
2 Use               {Use-Transaction, Use-WindowsUnattend}
2 Disconnect        {Disconnect-PSSession, Disconnect-WSMan}
2 Join              {Join-DtcDiagnosticResourceManager, Join-Path}
2 Exit              {Exit-PSHostProcess, Exit-PSSession}
2 Enter             {Enter-PSHostProcess, Enter-PSSession}
2 Copy              {Copy-Item, Copy-ItemProperty}
2 Expand            {Expand-WindowsCustomDataImage, Expand-WindowsImage}
2 Measure           {Measure-Command, Measure-Object}
2 Connect           {Connect-PSSession, Connect-WSMan}
2 Mount             {Mount-AppxVolume, Mount-WindowsImage}
2 Dismount          {Dismount-AppxVolume, Dismount-WindowsImage}
1 Pop               {Pop-Location}
1 Trace             {Trace-Command}
1 Uninstall         {Uninstall-Package}
1 Checkpoint        {Checkpoint-Computer}
1 Tee               {Tee-Object}
1 Unprotect         {Unprotect-CmsMessage}
1 Where             {Where-Object}
1 Switch            {Switch-Certificate}
1 Compare           {Compare-Object}
1 Limit             {Limit-EventLog}
1 Install           {Install-Package}
1 Protect           {Protect-CmsMessage}
1 Optimize          {Optimize-WindowsImage}
1 ForEach           {ForEach-Object}
1 Find              {Find-Package}
1 Initialize        {Initialize-Tpm}
1 Group             {Group-Object}
1 Reset             {Reset-ComputerMachinePassword}
1 Repair            {Repair-WindowsImage}
1 Sort              {Sort-Object}
1 Restore           {Restore-Computer}
1 Push              {Push-Location}
1 Publish           {Publish-DscConfiguration}
1 Confirm           {Confirm-SecureBootUEFI}
1 Read              {Read-Host}
```

A function is not required to accept any parameters. In fact, many functions do not require input to perform their job in the script. Let's use an example to illustrate this point. A common task for network administrators is obtaining the operating system version. Script writers often need to do this to ensure that their script uses the correct interface or exits gracefully. It is also quite common that one set of files would be copied to a desktop running one version of the operating system, and a different set of files would be copied for another version of the operating system. The first step in creating a function is to come up with a name. Because the function is going to retrieve information, in the listing of cmdlet verbs shown earlier, the best verb to use is *Get*. For the noun portion of the name, it is best to use something that describes the information that will be obtained. In this example, a noun of *OperatingSystemVersion* makes sense. An example of such a function is shown in the Get-OperatingSystemVersion.ps1 script. The *Get-OperatingSystemVersion* function uses Windows Management Instrumentation (WMI) to obtain the version of the operating system. In this basic form of the function, you have the function keyword followed by the name of the function, and a script block with code in it, which is delimited by braces. This pattern is shown here.

```
Function Function-Name
{
 #insert code here
}
```

In the Get-OperatingSystemVersion.ps1 script, the *Get-OperatingSystemVersion* function is at the top of the script. It uses the *Function* keyword to define the function, followed by the name, *Get-OperatingSystemVersion*. The script block opens, followed by the code, and then the script block closes. The function uses the *Get-CimInstance* cmdlet to retrieve an instance of the *Win32_Operating-System* WMI class. Because this WMI class only returns a single instance, the properties of the class are directly accessible. The *version* property is the one you'll work with, so use parentheses to force the evaluation of the code inside. The returned management object is used to emit the version value. The braces are used to close the script block. The operating system version is returned to the code that calls the function. In this example, a string that writes *This OS is version* is used. A subexpression is used to force evaluation of the function. The version of the operating system is returned to the place where the function was called. This is shown here.

Get-OperatingSystemVersion.ps1

```
Function Get-OperatingSystemVersion
{
 (Get-CimInstance -Class Win32_OperatingSystem).Version
} #end Get-OperatingSystemVersion

"This OS is version $(Get-OperatingSystemVersion)"
```

Now let's look at choosing the cmdlet verb. In the earlier listing of cmdlet verbs, there is one cmdlet that uses the verb *Read*. It is the *Read-Host* cmdlet, which is used to obtain information from the command line. This would indicate that the verb *Read* is not used to describe reading a file. There is no verb called *Display*, and the *Write* verb is used in cmdlet names such as *Write-Error* and *Write-Debug*, both of which do not really seem to have the concept of displaying information. If you were writing a function that would read the content of a text file and display statistics about that file, you might call the function *Get-TextStatistics*. This is in keeping with cmdlet names such as *Get-Process* and *Get-Service*, which include the concept of emitting their retrieved content within their essential functionality. The *Get-TextStatistics* function accepts a single parameter called *path*. The interesting thing about parameters for functions is that when you pass a value to the parameter, you use a hyphen. When you refer to the value inside the function, it is a variable such as *$path*. To call the *Get-TextStatistics* function, you have a couple of options. The first is to use the name of the function and put the value inside parentheses. This is shown here.

```
Get-TextStatistics("C:\fso\mytext.txt")
```

This is a natural way to call the function, and it works when there is a single parameter. It does not work when there are two or more parameters. Another way to pass a value to the function is to use the hyphen and the parameter name. This is shown here.

```
Get-TextStatistics -path "C:\fso\mytext.txt"
```

Note from the previous example that no parentheses are required. You can also use positional arguments when passing a value. In this usage, you omit the name of the parameter entirely and simply place the value for the parameter following the call to the function. This is illustrated here.

```
Get-TextStatistics "C:\fso\mytext.txt"
```

Note The use of positional parameters works well when you are working from the command line and want to speed things along by reducing the typing load. However, it can be a bit confusing to rely on positional parameters, and in general I tend to avoid them—even when working at the command line. This is because I often copy my working code from the console directly into a script, and as a result, I would need to retype the command a second time to get rid of aliases and unnamed parameters. With the improvements in tab expansion, I feel that the time saved by using positional parameters or partial parameters does not sufficiently warrant the time involved in retyping commands when they need to be transferred to scripts. The other reason for always using named parameters is that it helps you to be aware of the exact command syntax.

One additional way to pass a value to a function is to use partial parameter names. All that is required is enough of the parameter name to disambiguate it from other parameters. This is illustrated here.

```
Get-TextStatistics -p "C:\fso\mytext.txt"
```

The complete text of the *Get-TextStatistics* function is shown here.

Get-TextStatistics Function

```
Function Get-TextStatistics($path)
{
 Get-Content -path $path |
 Measure-Object -line -character -word
}
```

Between Windows PowerShell 1.0 and Windows PowerShell 2.0, the number of verbs grew from 40 to 60. In Windows PowerShell 5.0, the number of verbs remained consistent at 98. The list of approved verbs is shown here.

Add	Clear	Close	Copy	Enter	Exit	Find
Format	Get	Hide	Join	Lock	Move	New
Open	Optimize	Pop	Push	Redo	Remove	Rename
Reset	Resize	Search	Select	Set	Show	Skip
Split	Step	Switch	Undo	Unlock	Watch	Backup
Checkpoint	Compare	Compress	Convert	ConvertFrom	ConvertTo	Dismount
Edit	Expand	Export	Group	Import	Initialize	Limit
Merge	Mount	Out	Publish	Restore	Save	Sync
Unpublish	Update	Approve	Assert	Complete	Confirm	Deny
Disable	Enable	Install	Invoke	Register	Request	Restart
Resume	Start	Stop	Submit	Suspend	Uninstall	Unregister
Wait	Debug	Measure	Ping	Repair	Resolve	Test
Trace	Connect	Disconnect	Read	Receive	Send	Write
Block	Grant	Protect	Revoke	Unblock	Unprotect	Use

After the function has been named, you should specify any parameters the function might require. The parameters are contained within parentheses. In the *Get-TextStatistics* function, the function accepts a single parameter: *-path*. When you have a function that accepts a single parameter, you can pass the value to the function by placing the value for the parameter inside parentheses. This is known as calling a function like a method, and is disallowed when you use *Set-StrictMode* with the *Latest* value for the *-Version* parameter. The following command generates an error when the latest strict mode is in effect—otherwise, it is a permissible way to call a function.

```
Get-TextLength("C:\fso\test.txt")
```

The path C:\fso\test.txt is passed to the *Get-TextStatistics* function via the *-path* parameter. Inside the function, the string C:\fso\text.txt is contained in the *$path* variable. The *$path* variable lives only within the confines of the *Get-TextStatistics* function. It is not available outside the scope of the function. It is available from within child scopes of the *Get-TextStatistics* function. A *child scope* of *Get-TextStatistics* is one that is created from within the *Get-TextStatistics* function. In the Get-TextStatisticsCallChildFunction. ps1 script, the *Write-Path* function is called from within the *Get-TextStatistics* function. This means the *Write-Path* function will have access to variables that are created within the *Get-TextStatistics* function. This is the concept of *variable scope*, which is extremely important when working with functions. As you use functions to separate the creation of objects, you must always be aware of where the objects get created, and where you intend to use them. In the *Get-TextStatisticsCallChildFunction*, the *$path* variable does not obtain its value until it is passed to the function. It therefore lives within the *Get-TextStatistics* function. But because the *Write-Path* function is called from within the *Get-TextStatistics* function, it inherits the variables from that scope. When you call a function from within another function, variables created within the parent function are available to the child function. This is shown in the Get-TextStatisticsCallChildFunction.ps1 script, which follows.

Get-TextStatisticsCallChildFunction.ps1

```
Function Get-TextStatistics($path)
{
 Get-Content -path $path |
```

```
 Measure-Object -line -character -word
 Write-Path
}

Function Write-Path()
{
 "Inside Write-Path the `$path variable is equal to $path"
}

Get-TextStatistics("C:\fso\test.txt")
"Outside the Get-TextStatistics function `$path is equal to $path"
```

Inside the *Get-TextStatistics* function, the *$path* variable is used to provide the path to the *Get-Content* cmdlet. When the *Write-Path* function is called, nothing is passed to it. But inside the *Write-Path* function, the value of *$path* is maintained. Outside both of the functions, however, *$path* does not have any value. The output from running the script is shown here.

```
       Lines            Words          Characters Property
       -----            -----          ---------- --------
         3               41              210
Inside Write-Path the $path variable is equal to C:\fso\test.txt
Outside the Get-TextStatistics function $path is equal to
```

You will then need to open and close a script block. A pair of opening and closing braces is used to delimit the script block on a function. As a best practice, when writing a function, I will always use the *Function* keyword, and type in the name, the input parameters, and the braces for the script block at the same time. This is shown here.

```
Function My-Function
{
 #insert code here
}
```

In this manner, I make sure I do not forget to close the braces. Trying to identify a missing brace within a long script can be somewhat problematic, because the error that is presented does not always correspond to the line that is missing the brace. For example, suppose the closing brace is left off the *Get-TextStatistics* function, as shown in the Get-TextStatisticsCallChildFunction-DoesNOTWork-MissingClosingBrace.ps1 script. An error will be generated, as shown here.

```
Missing closing '}' in statement block.
At C:\Scripts\Get-TextStatisticsCallChildFunction-DoesNOTWork-MissingClosingBracket.ps1:28
char:1
```

The problem is that the position indicator of the error message points to the first character on line 28. Line 28 happens to be the first blank line after the end of the script. This means that Windows PowerShell scanned the entire script looking for the closing brace. Because it did not find it, it states that the error is at the end of the script. If you were to place a closing brace on line 28, the error in this example would go away, but the script would not work. The Get-TextStatisticsCallChildFunction-DoesNOTWork-MissingClosingBracket.ps1 script is shown here, with a comment that indicates where the missing closing brace should be placed.

Get-TextStatisticsCallChildFunction-DoesNOTWork-MissingClosingBrace.ps1

```
Function Get-TextStatistics($path)
{
 Get-Content -path $path |
 Measure-Object -line -character -word
 Write-Path
# Here is where the missing brace goes

Function Write-Path()
{
 "Inside Write-Path the `$path variable is equal to $path"
}
Get-TextStatistics("C:\fso\test.txt")
Write-Host "Outside the Get-TextStatistics function `$path is equal to $path"
```

One other technique to guard against the problem of the missing brace is to add a comment to the closing brace of each function.

Using functions to provide ease of code reuse

When scripts are written using well-designed functions, it makes it easier to reuse them in other scripts, and to provide access to these functions from within the Windows PowerShell console. To get access to these functions, you will need to *dot-source* the containing script by placing a dot in front of the path to the script when you call it, and put the functions in a module or load them via the profile. An issue with dot-sourcing scripts to bring in functions is that often the scripts might contain global variables or other items you do not want to bring into your current environment.

An example of a useful function is the ConvertToMeters.ps1 script because it converts feet to meters. There are no variables defined outside the function, and the function itself does not use the *Write-Host* cmdlet to break up the pipeline. The results of the conversion will be returned directly to the calling code. The only problem with the ConvertToMeters.ps1 script is that when it is dot-sourced into the Windows PowerShell console, it runs and returns the data because all executable code in the script is executed. The ConvertToMeters.ps1 script is shown here.

ConvertToMeters.ps1

```
Function Script:ConvertToMeters($feet)
{
  "$feet feet equals $($feet*.31) meters"
} #end ConvertToMeters
$feet = 5
ConvertToMeters -Feet $feet
```

With well-written functions, it is trivial to collect them into a single script—you just cut and paste. When you are done, you have created a function library.

When pasting your functions into the function library script, pay attention to the comments at the end of the function. The comments at the closing brace for each function not only point to the end of the script block, they also provide a nice visual indicator for the end of each function. This can be helpful when you need to troubleshoot a script. An example of such a function library is the ConversionFunctions.ps1 script, which is shown here.

ConversionFunctions.ps1

```
Function Script:ConvertToMeters($feet)
{
  "$feet feet equals $($feet*.31) meters"
} #end ConvertToMeters

Function Script:ConvertToFeet($meters)
{
  "$meters meters equals $($meters * 3.28) feet"
} #end ConvertToFeet

Function Script:ConvertToFahrenheit($celsius)
{
  "$celsius celsius equals $((1.8 * $celsius) + 32 ) fahrenheit"
} #end ConvertToFahrenheit

Function Script:ConvertTocelsius($fahrenheit)
{
  "$fahrenheit fahrenheit equals $( (($fahrenheit - 32)/9)*5 ) celsius"
} #end ConvertTocelsius

Function Script:ConvertToMiles($kilometer)
{
  "$kilometer kilometers equals $( ($kilometer *.6211) ) miles"
} #end convertToMiles

Function Script:ConvertToKilometers($miles)
{
  "$miles miles equals $( ($miles * 1.61) ) kilometers"
} #end convertToKilometers
```

One way to use the functions from the ConversionFunctions.ps1 script is to use the dot-sourcing operator to run the script so that the functions from the script are part of the calling scope. To dot-source the script, you use the dot-source operator (the period, or dot symbol), followed by a space, followed by the path to the script containing the functions you want to include in your current scope. (Dot-sourcing is covered in more depth in the following section.) After you do this, you can call the function directly, as shown here.

```
PS C:\> . C:\scripts\ConversionFunctions.ps1
PS C:\> convertToMiles 6
6 kilometers equals 3.7266 miles
```

All of the functions from the dot-sourced script are available to the current session. This can be demonstrated by creating a listing of the function drive, as shown here.

```
PS C:\> dir function: | Where { $_.name -like 'conv*'} |
Format-Table -Property name, definition -AutoSize

Name               Definition
----               ----------
ConvertToMeters    param($feet) "$feet feet equals $($feet*.31) meters"...
```

```
ConvertToFeet        param($meters) "$meters meters equals $($meters * 3.28) feet"...
ConvertToFahrenheit param($celsius) "$celsius celsius equals $((1.8 * $celsius) + 32 )
fahrenheit"...
ConvertTocelsius     param($fahrenheit) "$fahrenheit fahrenheit equals $( (($fahrenheit -
32)/9)*5 ) celsius...
ConvertToMiles       param($kilometer) "$kilometer kilometers equals $( ($kilometer *.6211) )
miles"...
ConvertToKilometers param($miles) "$miles miles equals $( ($miles * 1.61) ) kilometers"...
```

Including functions in the Windows PowerShell environment

In Windows PowerShell 1.0, you could include functions from previously written scripts by dot-sourcing the script. The use of a module, which was introduced in Windows PowerShell 2.0, offers greater flexibility than dot-sourcing because you can create a *module manifest*, which specifies exactly which functions and programming elements will be imported into the current session.

Using dot-sourcing

This technique of dot-sourcing still works in Windows PowerShell 5.0, and it offers the advantage of simplicity and familiarity. In the TextFunctions.ps1 script shown following, two functions are created. The first function is called *New-Line*, and the second is called *Get-TextStats*. The TextFunctions.ps1 script is shown here.

TextFunctions.ps1

```
Function New-Line([string]$stringIn)
{
 "-" * $stringIn.length
} #end New-Line

Function Get-TextStats([string[]]$textIn)
{
 $textIn | Measure-Object -Line -word -char
} #end Get-TextStats
```

The *New-Line* function creates a string of hyphen characters as long as the length of the input text. This is helpful when you want an underline that is sized to the text, for text separation purposes. An example of using the *New-Line* text function in this manner is shown here.

CallNew-LineTextFunction.ps1

```
Function New-Line([string]$stringIn)
{
 "-" * $stringIn.length
} #end New-Line

Function Get-TextStats([string[]]$textIn)
{
 $textIn | Measure-Object -Line -word -char
} #end Get-TextStats

# *** Entry Point to script ***
"This is a string" | ForEach-Object  {$_ ; New-Line $_}
```

When the script runs, it returns the following output.

```
This is a string
----------------
```

Of course, this is a bit inefficient and limits your ability to use the functions. If you have to copy the entire text of a function into each new script you want to produce, or edit a script each time you want to use a function in a different manner, you dramatically increase your workload. If the functions were available all the time, you might be inclined to use them more often. To make the text functions available in your current Windows PowerShell console, you need to dot-source the script containing the functions into your console, put it in a module, or load it via your profile. You will need to use the entire path to the script unless the folder that contains the script is in your search path. The syntax to dot-source a script is so easy that it actually becomes a stumbling block for some people who are expecting some complex formula or cmdlet with obscure parameters. It is none of that—just a period (dot), followed by a space, followed by the path to the script that contains the function. This is why it is called dot-sourcing: you have a dot and the source (path) to the functions you want to include. This is shown here.

```
PS C:\> . C:\fso\TextFunctions.ps1
```

After you have included the functions in your current console, all the functions in the source script are added to the Function drive. This is shown in Figure 6-1.

FIGURE 6-1 Functions from a dot-sourced script are available via the Function drive.

Using dot-sourced functions

After the functions have been introduced to the current console, you can incorporate them into your normal commands. This flexibility should also influence the way you write the function. If the functions are written so they will accept pipelined input and do not change the system environment—by adding global variables, for example—you will be much more likely to use the functions, and they will be less likely to conflict with either functions or cmdlets that are present in the current console.

As an example of using the *New-Line* function, consider the fact that the *Get-CimInstance* cmdlet allows the use of an array of computer names for the *-ComputerName* parameter. In this example, BIOS information is obtained from two separate workstations. This is shown here.

```
PS C:\> Get-CimInstance win32_bios -ComputerName dc1, c10
```

```
SMBIOSBIOSVersion : 090006
Manufacturer      : American Megatrends Inc.
Name              : BIOS Date: 05/23/12 17:15:53  Ver: 09.00.06
SerialNumber      : 5198-1332-9667-8393-5778-4501-39
Version           : VRTUAL - 5001223
PSComputerName    : c10

SMBIOSBIOSVersion : Hyper-V UEFI Release v1.0
Manufacturer      : Microsoft Corporation
Name              : Hyper-V UEFI Release v1.0
SerialNumber      : 3601-6926-9922-0181-5225-8175-58
Version           : VRTUAL - 1
PSComputerName    : dc1
```

You can improve the display of the information returned by *Get-CimInstance* by pipelining the output to the *New-Line* function so that you can underline each computer name as it comes across the pipeline. You do not need to write a script to produce this kind of display. You can enter the command directly into the Windows PowerShell console. The first thing you need to do is to dot-source the TextFunctions.ps1 script. This makes the functions directly available in the current Windows PowerShell console session. You then use the same *Get-CimInstance* query you used earlier to obtain BIOS information via WMI from two computers. Pipeline the resulting management objects to the *ForEach-Object* cmdlet. Inside the script block section, you use the $_ automatic variable to reference the current object on the pipeline and retrieve the *PSComputerName* property. You send this information to the *New-Line* function so the server name is underlined, and you display the BIOS information that is contained in the $_ variable.

The command to import the *New-Line* function into the current Windows PowerShell session and use it to underline the server names is shown here.

```
PS C:\> . C:\fso\TextFunctions.ps1
PS C:\> Get-CimInstance win32_bios -ComputerName dc1, c10 | ForEach-Object { $_.PSComputerName
; New-Line $_.PSComputerName ; $_}
```

The results of using the *New-Line* function are shown in Figure 6-2.

```
Select powershell                                                    —    □    ×
PS C:\> Get-CimInstance win32_bios -ComputerName dc1, c10 | ForEach-Object { $_.PSCom ^
puterName ; New-Line $_.PSComputerName ; $_}
c10
---


SMBIOSBIOSVersion : 090006
Manufacturer      : American Megatrends Inc.
Name              : BIOS Date: 05/23/12 17:15:53  Ver: 09.00.06
SerialNumber      : 5198-1332-9667-8393-5778-4501-39
Version           : VRTUAL - 5001223
PSComputerName    : c10

dc1
---
SMBIOSBIOSVersion : Hyper-V UEFI Release v1.0
Manufacturer      : Microsoft Corporation
Name              : Hyper-V UEFI Release v1.0
SerialNumber      : 3601-6926-9922-0181-5225-8175-58
Version           : VRTUAL - 1
PSComputerName    : dc1



PS C:\> _
```

FIGURE 6-2 Functions that are written to accept pipelined input find an immediate use in your daily work routine.

The *Get-TextStats* function from the TextFunctions.ps1 script provides statistics based upon an input text file or text string. After the TextFunctions.ps1 script is dot-sourced into the current console, the statistics it returns when the function is called are word count, number of lines in the file, and number of characters. An example of using this function is shown here.

```
Get-TextStats "This is a string"
```

When the *Get-TextStats* function is used, the following output is produced.

```
      Lines               Words         Characters Property
      -----               -----         ---------- --------
          1                   4                 16
```

In this section, the use of functions was discussed. The reuse of functions could be as simple as copying the text of the function from one script into another script. It is easier, however, to dot-source the function than to reuse it. This can be done from within the Windows PowerShell console or from within a script.

Adding help for functions

When you dot-source functions into the current Windows PowerShell console, one problem is introduced. Because you are not required to open the file that contains the function to use it, you might be unaware of everything the file contains within it. In addition to functions, the file could contain variables, aliases, Windows PowerShell drives, or any number of other things. Depending on what you are actually trying to accomplish, this might or might not be an issue. The need sometimes arises, however, to have access to help information about the features provided by the Windows PowerShell script.

Using a *here-string* object for help

In Windows PowerShell 1.0, you could solve this problem by adding a *help* parameter to the function and storing the help text within a *here-string* object. You can also use this approach in Windows PowerShell 5.0, but as shown in Chapter 7, "Creating advanced functions and modules," there is a better approach to providing help for functions. The classic *here-string* approach for help is shown in the GetWmiClassesFunction.ps1 script, which follows. The first step that needs to be done is to define a switch parameter named *$help*. The second step involves creating and displaying the results of a *here-string* object that includes help information. The GetWmiClassesFunction.ps1 script is shown here.

GetWmiClassesFunction.ps1

```
Function Get-WmiClasses(
                $class=($paramMissing=$true),
                $ns="root\cimv2",
                [switch]$help
                )
{
  If($help)
   {
    $helpstring = @"
    NAME
      Get-WmiClasses
    SYNOPSIS
      Displays a list of WMI Classes based upon a search criteria
    SYNTAX
     Get-WmiClasses [[-class] [string]] [[-ns] [string]] [-help]
    EXAMPLE
     Get-WmiClasses -class disk -ns root\cimv2"
     This command finds wmi classes that contain the word disk. The
     classes returned are from the root\cimv2 namespace.
"@
    $helpString
      break #exits the function early
   }
  If($local:paramMissing)
    {
      throw "USAGE: Get-WmiClasses -class <class type> -ns <wmi namespace>"
    } #$local:paramMissing
  "`nClasses in $ns namespace ...."
  Get-WmiObject -namespace $ns -list |
  Where-Object {
                $_.name -match $class -and `
                $_.name -notlike 'cim*'
               }
  #
} #end get-wmiclasses
```

The *here-string* technique works pretty well for providing function help if you follow the cmdlet help pattern. This is shown in Figure 6-3.

```
powershell                                                      —    □    ✕
PS C:\> . C:\fso\GetWmiClassesFunction.ps1
PS C:\> Get-WmiClasses -help
    NAME
      Get-WmiClasses
    SYNOPSIS
      Displays a list of WMI Classes based upon a search criteria
    SYNTAX
    Get-WmiClasses [[-class] [string]] [[-ns] [string]] [-help]
    EXAMPLE
    Get-WmiClasses -class disk -ns root\cimv2"
    This command finds wmi classes that contain the word disk. The
    classes returned are from the root\cimv2 namespace.
PS C:\> _
```

FIGURE 6-3 Manually created help can mimic the look of core cmdlet help.

The drawback with manually creating help for a function is that it is tedious, and as a result, only the most important functions receive help information when you use this methodology. This is unfortunate, because it then requires the user to memorize the details of the function contract. One way to work around this is to use the *Get-Content* cmdlet to retrieve the code that was used to create the function. This is much easier than searching for the script that was used to create the function and opening it up in Notepad. To use the *Get-Content* cmdlet to display the contents of a function, you enter *Get-Content* and supply the path to the function. All functions available to the current Windows PowerShell environment are available via the Function Windows PowerShell drive. You can therefore use the following syntax to obtain the content of a function.

```
PS C:\> Get-Content Function:\Get-WmiClasses
```

The technique of using *Get-Content* to read the text of the function is shown in Figure 6-4.

An easier way to add help, by using comment-based help, is discussed in Chapter 7. Comment-based help, although more complex than the method discussed here, offers a number of advantages—primarily due to the integration with the Windows PowerShell help subsystem. When you add comment-based help, users of your function can access your help in exactly the same manner as for any of the core Windows PowerShell cmdlets.

FIGURE 6-4 The *Get-Content* cmdlet can retrieve the contents of a function.

Using two input parameters

To create a function that uses multiple input parameters, you use the *Function* keyword, specify the name of the function, use a variable for each input parameter, and then define the script block within the braces. The pattern is shown here.

```
Function My-Function($Input1,$Input2)
{
 #Insert Code Here
}
```

An example of a function that takes multiple parameters is the *Get-FreeDiskSpace* function, which is shown in the Get-FreeDiskSpace.ps1 script at the end of this section.

The Get-FreeDiskSpace.ps1 script begins with the *Function* keyword and is followed by the name of the function and the two input parameters. The input parameters are placed inside parentheses, as shown here.

```
Function Get-FreeDiskSpace($drive,$computer)
```

Inside the function's script block, the *Get-FreeDiskSpace* function uses the *Get-WmiObject* cmdlet to query the *Win32_LogicalDisk* WMI class. It connects to the computer specified in the *$computer* parameter, and it filters out only the drive that is specified in the *$drive* parameter. When the function is called, each parameter is specified as *-drive* and *-computer*. In the function definition, the variables *$drive* and *$computer* are used to hold the values supplied to the parameters.

After the data from WMI is retrieved, it is stored in the *$driveData* variable. The data that is stored in the *$driveData* variable is an instance of the *Win32_LogicalDisk* class. This variable contains a complete instance of the class. The members of this class are shown in Table 6-1.

TABLE 6-1 Members of the *Win32_LogicalDisk* class

Name	Member type	Definition
Chkdsk	Method	System.Management.ManagementBaseObject Chkdsk(System. Boolean FixErrors, System.Boolean VigorousIndexCheck, System. Boolean SkipFolderCycle, System.Boolean ForceDismount, System. Boolean RecoverBadSectors, System.Boolean OkToRunAtBootUp)
Reset	Method	System.Management.ManagementBaseObject Reset()
SetPowerState	Method	System.Management.ManagementBaseObject SetPowerState(System.UInt16 PowerState, System.String Time)
Access	Property	System.UInt16 Access {get;set;}
Availability	Property	System.UInt16 Availability {get;set;}
BlockSize	Property	System.UInt64 BlockSize {get;set;}
Caption	Property	System.String Caption {get;set;}
Compressed	Property	System.Boolean Compressed {get;set;}
ConfigManagerErrorCode	Property	System.UInt32 ConfigManagerErrorCode {get;set;}
ConfigManagerUserConfig	Property	System.Boolean ConfigManagerUserConfig {get;set;}
CreationClassName	Property	System.String CreationClassName {get;set;}
Description	Property	System.String Description {get;set;}
DeviceID	Property	System.String DeviceID {get;set;}
DriveType	Property	System.UInt32 DriveType {get;set;}
ErrorCleared	Property	System.Boolean ErrorCleared {get;set;}
ErrorDescription	Property	System.String ErrorDescription {get;set;}
ErrorMethodology	Property	System.String ErrorMethodology {get;set;}
FileSystem	Property	System.String FileSystem {get;set;}
FreeSpace	Property	System.UInt64 FreeSpace {get;set;}
InstallDate	Property	System.String InstallDate {get;set;}
LastErrorCode	Property	System.UInt32 LastErrorCode {get;set;}
MaximumComponentLength	Property	System.UInt32 MaximumComponentLength {get;set;}
MediaType	Property	System.UInt32 MediaType {get;set;}
Name	Property	System.String Name {get;set;}
NumberOfBlocks	Property	System.UInt64 NumberOfBlocks {get;set;}
PNPDeviceID	Property	System.String PNPDeviceID {get;set;}

Name	Member type	Definition
PowerManagementCapabilities	Property	System.UInt16[] PowerManagementCapabilities {get;set;}
PowerManagementSupported	Property	System.Boolean PowerManagementSupported {get;set;}
ProviderName	Property	System.String ProviderName {get;set;}
Purpose	Property	System.String Purpose {get;set;}
QuotasDisabled	Property	System.Boolean QuotasDisabled {get;set;}
QuotasIncomplete	Property	System.Boolean QuotasIncomplete {get;set;}
QuotasRebuilding	Property	System.Boolean QuotasRebuilding {get;set;}
Size	Property	System.UInt64 Size {get;set;}
Status	Property	System.String Status {get;set;}
StatusInfo	Property	System.UInt16 StatusInfo {get;set;}
SupportsDiskQuotas	Property	System.Boolean SupportsDiskQuotas {get;set;}
SupportsFileBasedCompression	Property	System.Boolean SupportsFileBasedCompression {get;set;}
SystemCreationClassName	Property	System.String SystemCreationClassName {get;set;}
SystemName	Property	System.String SystemName {get;set;}
VolumeDirty	Property	System.Boolean VolumeDirty {get;set;}
VolumeName	Property	System.String VolumeName {get;set;}
VolumeSerialNumber	Property	System.String VolumeSerialNumber {get;set;}
__CLASS	Property	System.String __CLASS {get;set;}
__DERIVATION	Property	System.String[] __DERIVATION {get;set;}
__DYNASTY	Property	System.String __DYNASTY {get;set;}
__GENUS	Property	System.Int32 __GENUS {get;set;}
__NAMESPACE	Property	System.String __NAMESPACE {get;set;}
__PATH	Property	System.String __PATH {get;set;}
__PROPERTY_COUNT	Property	System.Int32 __PROPERTY_COUNT {get;set;}
__RELPATH	Property	System.String __RELPATH {get;set;}
__SERVER	Property	System.String __SERVER {get;set;}
__SUPERCLASS	Property	System.String __SUPERCLASS {get;set;}
PSStatus	Property set	PSStatus {Status, Availability, DeviceID, StatusInfo}
ConvertFromDateTime	Script method	System.Object ConvertFromDateTime();
ConvertToDateTime	Script method	System.Object ConvertToDateTime();

When you have the data stored in the *$driveData* variable, you will want to print some information to the user of the script. The first thing to do is print the name of the computer and the name of the drive. To do this, you can place the variables inside double quotation marks. Double quotation marks denote expanding strings, and variables placed inside double quotation marks emit their value, not their name. This is shown here.

```
"$computer free disk space on drive $drive"
```

The next thing you will want to do is format the data that is returned. To do this, use the Microsoft .NET Framework format strings to specify two decimal places. You will need to use a subexpression to prevent the unraveling of the WMI object inside the expanding-string double quotation marks. The subexpression uses the dollar sign and a pair of parentheses to force the evaluation of the expression before returning the data to the string. This is shown here.

Get-FreeDiskSpace.ps1

```
Function Get-FreeDiskSpace($drive,$computer)
{
 $driveData = Get-WmiObject -class win32_LogicalDisk `
 -computername $computer -filter "Name = '$drive'"
"
 $computer free disk space on drive $drive
    $("{0:n2}" -f ($driveData.FreeSpace/1MB)) MegaBytes
"
}

Get-FreeDiskSpace -drive "C:" -computer "C10"
```

Obtaining specific WMI data

Though storing the complete instance of the object in the *$driveData* variable is a bit inefficient due to the amount of data it contains, in reality the class is rather small, and the ease of using the *Get-WmiObject* cmdlet is usually worth the wasteful methodology. If performance is a primary consideration, the use of the *[wmi]* type accelerator would be a better solution. To obtain the free disk space by using this method, you would use the following syntax.

```
([wmi]"Win32_logicalDisk.DeviceID='c:'").FreeSpace
```

To put the preceding command into a usable function, you would need to substitute the hard-coded drive letter for a variable. In addition, you would want to modify the class constructor to receive a path to a remote computer. The newly created function is contained in the Get-DiskSpace.ps1 script, shown here.

Get-DiskSpace.ps1

```
Function Get-DiskSpace($drive,$computer)
{
  ([wmi]"\\$computer\root\cimv2:Win32_logicalDisk.DeviceID='$drive'").FreeSpace
}
Get-DiskSpace -drive "C:" -computer "Office"
```

After you have made the preceding changes, the code only returns the value of the *FreeSpace* property from the specific drive. If you were to send the output to *Get-Member*, you would find that you have an integer. This technique is more efficient than storing an entire instance of the *Win32_LogicalDisk* class and then selecting a single value.

Using a type constraint in a function

When you are accepting parameters for a function, it might be important to use a type constraint to ensure that the function receives the correct type of data. To do this, you place the name of the type you want inside brackets in front of the input parameter. This constrains the data type and prevents the entry of an incorrect type of data. Frequently used type accelerators are shown in Table 6-2.

TABLE 6-2 Data type aliases

Alias	Type
[int]	32-bit signed integer
[long]	64-bit signed integer
[string]	Fixed-length string of Unicode characters
[char]	Unicode 16-bit character
[bool]	True/false value
[byte]	8-bit unsigned integer
[double]	Double-precision 64-bit floating-point number
[decimal]	128-bit decimal value
[single]	Single-precision 32-bit floating-point number
[array]	Array of values
[xml]	XML object
[hashtable]	Hashtable object (similar to a dictionary object)

In the *Resolve-ZipCode* function, which is shown in the following Resolve-ZipCode.ps1 script, the *$zip* input parameter is constrained to allow only a 32-bit signed integer for input. (Obviously, the *[int]* type constraint would eliminate most of the world's postal codes, but the web service the script uses only resolves US-based postal codes, so it is a good addition to the function.)

In the *Resolve-ZipCode* function, the first thing that is done is to use a string that points to the WSDL (Web Services Description Language) for the web service. Next, the *New-WebServiceProxy* cmdlet is used to create a new web service proxy for the ZipCode service. The WSDL for the ZipCode service defines a method called the *GetInfoByZip* method. It will accept a standard US-based postal code. The results are displayed as a table. The Resolve-ZipCode.ps1 script is shown here.

Resolve-ZipCode.ps1

```
#Requires -Version 5.0
Function Resolve-ZipCode([int]$zip)
{
 $URI = "http://www.webservicex.net/uszip.asmx?WSDL"
 $zipProxy = New-WebServiceProxy -uri $URI -namespace WebServiceProxy -class ZipClass
 $zipProxy.getinfobyzip($zip).table
} #end Get-ZipCode

Resolve-ZipCode 28273
```

When you use a type constraint on an input parameter, any deviation from the expected data type will generate an error similar to the one shown here.

```
Resolve-ZipCode : Cannot process argument transformation on parameter 'zip'. Cannot convert
value "COW" to type "System
.Int32". Error: "Input string was not in a correct format."
At C:\Users\ed\AppData\Local\Temp\tmp3351.tmp.ps1:22 char:16
+ Resolve-ZipCode <<<<  "COW"
    + CategoryInfo          : InvalidData: (:) [Resolve-ZipCode],
ParameterBindin...mationException
    + FullyQualifiedErrorId : ParameterArgumentTransformationError,Resolve-ZipCode
```

Needless to say, such an error could be distracting to the users of the function. One way to handle the problem of confusing error messages is to use the *Trap* keyword. In the DemoTrapSystemException.ps1 script, the *My-Test* function uses *[int]* to constrain the *$myinput* variable to accept only a 32-bit unsigned integer for input. If such an integer is received by the function when it is called, the function will return the string *It worked*. If the function receives a string for input, an error will be raised, similar to the one shown previously.

Rather than display a raw error message, which most users and many IT professionals find confusing, it is a best practice to suppress the display of the error message, and perhaps inform the user that an error condition has occurred and provide more meaningful and direct information that the user can then relay to the help desk. Many times, IT departments will display such an error message, complete with either a local telephone number for the appropriate help desk, or even a link to an internal webpage that provides detailed troubleshooting and corrective steps the user can perform. You could even provide a webpage that hosted a script that the user could run to fix the problem. This is similar to the "Fix it for me" webpages Microsoft introduced.

When an instance of a *System.SystemException* class occurs (when a system exception occurs), the *Trap* statement will trap the error, rather than allowing it to display the error information on the screen. If you were to query the *$error* variable, you would find that the error had in fact occurred and was actually received by the error record. You would also have access to the *ErrorRecord* class via the *$_* automatic variable, which means that the error record has been passed along the pipeline. This gives you the ability to build a rich error-handling solution. In this example, the string *error trapped* is displayed, and the *Continue* statement is used to continue the script execution on the next line of code. In this example, the next line of code that is executed is the *After the error* string. When the DemoTrapSystemException.ps1 script is run, the following output is shown.

```
error trapped
After the error
```

The complete DemoTrapSystemException.ps1 script is shown here.

DemoTrapSystemException.ps1

```
Function My-Test([int]$myinput)
{

 "It worked"
} #End my-test function
# *** Entry Point to Script ***

Trap [SystemException] { "error trapped" ; continue }
My-Test -myinput "string"
"After the error"
```

Using more than two input parameters

When using more than two input parameters, I consider it a best practice to modify the way the function is structured. This not only makes the function easier to read, it also permits cmdlet binding. In the basic function pattern shown here, the function accepts three input parameters. When you consider the default values and the type constraints, you can tell that the parameters begin to become long. Moving them to the inside of the function body highlights the fact that they are input parameters, and it makes them easier to read, understand, and maintain. It also allows for decorating the parameters with attributes.

```
Function Function-Name
{
  Param(
        [int]$Parameter1,
        [String]$Parameter2 = "DefaultValue",
        $Parameter3
        )
#Function code goes here
} #end Function-Name
```

An example of a function that uses three input parameters is the *Get-DirectoryListing* function. With the type constraints, default values, and parameter names, the function signature would be rather cumbersome to include on a single line. This is shown here.

```
Function Get-DirectoryListing ([String]$Path,[String]$Extension = "txt",[Switch]$Today)
```

If the number of parameters were increased to four, or if a default value for the *-Path* parameter was wanted, the signature would easily scroll to two lines. The use of the *Param* statement inside the function body also provides the ability to specify input parameters to a function.

> **Note** The use of the *Param* statement inside the function body is often regarded as a
> personal preference. It requires additional work, and often leaves the reader of the script
> wondering why this was done. When there are more than two parameters, visually the
> *Param* statement stands out, and it is obvious why it was done in this particular manner.
> But, as will be shown in Chapter 7, using the *Param* statement is the only way to gain
> access to advanced function features such as cmdlet binding, parameter attributes, and
> other powerful features of Windows PowerShell.

Following the *Function* keyword, the name of the function, and the opening script block, the
Param keyword is used to identify the parameters for the function. Each parameter must be separated
from the others by a comma. All the parameters must be surrounded with a set of parentheses. If you
want to assign a default value for a parameter, such as the extension *.txt* for the *Extension* parameter
in the *Get-DirectoryListing* function, you perform a straight value assignment followed by a comma.

In the *Get-DirectoryListing* function, the *Today* parameter is a switch parameter. When it is supplied
to the function, only files written to since midnight on the day the script is run will be displayed. If it is
not supplied, all files matching the extension in the folder will be displayed. The Get-DirectoryListing-
Today.ps1 script is shown here.

Get-DirectoryListingToday.ps1

```
Function Get-DirectoryListing
{
 Param(
       [String]$Path,
       [String]$Extension = "txt",
       [Switch]$Today
      )
 If($Today)
   {
    Get-ChildItem -Path $path\* -include *.$Extension |
    Where-Object { $_.LastWriteTime -ge (Get-Date).Date }
   }
 ELSE
   {
    Get-ChildItem -Path $path\* -include *.$Extension
   }
} #end Get-DirectoryListing

# *** Entry to script ***
Get-DirectoryListing -p c:\fso -t
```

Note As a best practice, you should avoid creating functions that have a large number of input parameters. It is very confusing. When you find yourself creating a large number of input parameters, you should ask if there is a better way to do things. It might be an indicator that you do not have a single-purpose function. In the *Get-DirectoryListing* function, I have a switch parameter that will filter the files returned by the ones written to today. If I were writing the script for production use, instead of just to demonstrate multiple function parameters, I would have created another function called something like *Get-FilesByDate*. In that function, I would have a *Today* switch, and a *Date* parameter to allow a selectable date for the filter. This separates the data-gathering function from the filter/presentation function. See the "Using functions to provide ease of modification" section later in this chapter for more discussion of this technique.

Using functions to encapsulate business logic

There are two kinds of logic with which script writers need to be concerned. The first is program logic, and the second is business logic. *Program logic* includes the way the script works, the order in which things need to be done, and the requirements of code used in the script. An example of program logic is the requirement to open a connection to a database before querying the database.

Business logic is something that is a requirement of the business, but not necessarily a requirement of the program or script. The script can often operate just fine regardless of the particulars of the business rule. If the script is designed properly, it should operate perfectly fine no matter what gets supplied for the business rules.

In the BusinessLogicDemo.ps1 script, a function called *Get-Discount* is used to calculate the discount to be granted to the total amount. One good thing about encapsulating the business rules for the discount into a function is that as long as the contract between the function and the calling code does not change, you can drop any kind of convoluted discount schedule that the business decides to come up with into the script block of the *Get-Discount* function—including database calls to determine on-hand inventory, time of day, day of week, total sales volume for the month, the buyer's loyalty level, and the square root of some random number that is used to determine an instant discount rate.

So, what is the contract with the function? The contract with the *Get-Discount* function says, "If you give me a rate number as a type of *system.double* and a total as an integer, I will return to you a number that represents the total discount to be applied to the sale." As long as you adhere to that contract, you never need to modify the code.

The *Get-Discount* function begins with the *Function* keyword and is followed by the name of the function and the definition for two input parameters. The first input parameter is the *$rate* parameter, which is constrained to be of type *system.double* (which will permit you to supply decimal numbers). The second input parameter is the *$total* parameter, which is constrained to be of type *system.integer*, and therefore will not allow decimal numbers. In the script block, the value of the *-total* parameter is multiplied by the value of the *-rate* parameter. The result of this calculation is returned to the pipeline.

The *Get-Discount* function is shown here.

```
Function Get-Discount([double]$rate,[int]$total)
{
  $rate * $total
} #end Get-Discount
```

The entry point to the script assigns values to both the *$total* and *$rate* variables, as shown here.

```
$rate = .05
$total = 100
```

The variable *$discount* is used to hold the result of the calculation from the *Get-Discount* function. When calling the function, it is a best practice to use the full parameter names. It makes the code easier to read and will help make it immune to unintended problems if the function signature ever changes.

```
$discount = Get-Discount -rate $rate -total $total
```

> **Note** The signature of a function consists of the order and names of the input parameters. If you typically supply values to the signature via positional parameters, and the order of the input parameters changes, the code will fail, or worse yet, produce inconsistent results. If you typically call functions via partial parameter names, and an additional parameter is added, the script will fail due to difficulty with the disambiguation process. Obviously, you take this into account when first writing the script and the function, but months or years later, when you are making modifications to the script or calling the function via another script, the problem can arise.

The remainder of the script produces output for the screen. The results of running the script are shown here.

```
Total: 100
Discount: 5
Your Total: 95
```

The complete text of the BusinessLogicDemo.ps1 script is shown here.

BusinessLogicDemo.ps1

```
Function Get-Discount([double]$rate,[int]$total)
{
  $rate * $total
} #end Get-Discount


$rate = .05
$total = 100
```

```
$discount = Get-Discount -rate $rate -total $total
"Total: $total"
"Discount: $discount"
"Your Total: $($total-$discount)"
```

Business logic does not have to be related to business purposes. Business logic is anything that is arbitrary that does not affect the running of the code. In the FindLargeDocs.ps1 script, there are two functions. The first function, *Get-Doc*, is used to find document files (files with an extension of *.doc*, *.docx*, or *.dot*) in a folder that is passed to the function when it is called. The *-Recurse* switch parameter, when used with the *Get-ChildItem* cmdlet, causes the function to look in the present folder, and within child folders. This function is a stand-alone function and has no dependency on any other functions.

The *LargeFiles* piece of code is a filter. A filter is a kind of special-purpose function that uses the *Filter* keyword rather than the *Function* keyword when it is created. (For more information on filters, see the "Understanding filters" section later in this chapter.) The FindLargeDocs.ps1 script is shown here.

FindLargeDocs.ps1

```
Function Get-Doc($path)
{
 Get-ChildItem -Path $path -include *.doc,*.docx,*.dot -recurse
} #end Get-Doc

Filter LargeFiles($size)
{
  $_ |
  Where-Object { $_.length -ge $size }
} #end LargeFiles

Get-Doc("C:\FSO") | LargeFiles 1000
```

Using functions to provide ease of modification

It is a truism that a script is never completed. There is always something else to add to a script—a change that will improve it, or additional functionality that someone requests. When a script is written as one long piece of inline code, without recourse to functions, it can be rather tedious and error-prone to modify.

An example of an inline script is the InLineGetIPDemo.ps1 script. The first line of code uses the *Get-WmiObject* cmdlet to retrieve the instances of the *Win32_NetworkAdapterConfiguration* WMI class that IP enabled. The results of this WMI query are stored in the *$IP* variable. This line of code is shown here.

```
$IP = Get-WmiObject -class Win32_NetworkAdapterConfiguration -Filter "IPEnabled = $true"
```

When the WMI information has been obtained and stored, the remainder of the script prints information to the screen. The *IPAddress*, *IPSubNet*, and *DNSServerSearchOrder* properties are all stored in an array. For this example, you are only interested in the first IP address, and you therefore print element 0, which will always exist if the network adapter has an IP address. This section of the script is shown here.

```
"IP Address: " + $IP.IPAddress[0]
"Subnet: " + $IP.IPSubNet[0]
"GateWay: " + $IP.DefaultIPGateway
"DNS Server: " + $IP.DNSServerSearchOrder[0]
"FQDN: " + $IP.DNSHostName + "." + $IP.DNSDomain
```

When the script is run, it produces output similar to the following.

```
IP Address: 192.168.2.5
Subnet: 255.255.255.0
GateWay: 192.168.2.1
DNS Server: 192.168.2.1
FQDN: w8client1.nwtraders.com
```

The complete InLineGetIPDemo.ps1 script is shown here.

InLineGetIPDemo.ps1

```
$IP = Get-WmiObject -class Win32_NetworkAdapterConfiguration -Filter "IPEnabled = $true"
"IP Address: " + $IP.IPAddress[0]
"Subnet: " + $IP.IPSubNet[0]
"GateWay: " + $IP.DefaultIPGateway
"DNS Server: " + $IP.DNSServerSearchOrder[0]
"FQDN: " + $IP.DNSHostName + "." + $IP.DNSDomain
```

With just a few modifications to the script, a great deal of flexibility can be obtained. The modifications, of course, involve moving the inline code into functions. As a best practice, a function should be narrowly defined and should encapsulate a single thought. Though it would be possible to move the entire previous script into a function, you would not have as much flexibility. There are two thoughts or ideas that are expressed in the script. The first is obtaining the IP information from WMI, and the second is formatting and displaying the IP information. It would be best to separate the gathering and the displaying processes from one another, because they are logically two different activities.

To convert the InLineGetIPDemo.ps1 script into a script that uses a function, you only need to add the *Function* keyword, give the function a name, and surround the original code with a pair of braces. The transformed script is now named GetIPDemoSingleFunction.ps1 and is shown here.

GetIPDemoSingleFunction.ps1

```
Function Get-IPDemo
{
 $IP = Get-WmiObject -class Win32_NetworkAdapterConfiguration -Filter "IPEnabled = $true"
 "IP Address: " + $IP.IPAddress[0]
 "Subnet: " + $IP.IPSubNet[0]
 "GateWay: " + $IP.DefaultIPGateway
 "DNS Server: " + $IP.DNSServerSearchOrder[0]
 "FQDN: " + $IP.DNSHostName + "." + $IP.DNSDomain
} #end Get-IPDemo

# *** Entry Point To Script ***

Get-IPDemo
```

If you go to all the trouble to transform the inline code into a function, what benefit do you derive? By making this single change, your code will become

- Easier to read

- Easier to understand

- Easier to reuse

- Easier to troubleshoot

The script is easier to read because you do not really need to read each line of code to understand what it does. You can tell that there is a function that obtains the IP address, and it is called from outside the function. That is all the script does.

The script is easier to understand because you can tell there is a function that obtains the IP address. If you want to know the details of that operation, you read that function. If you are not interested in the details, you can skip that portion of the code.

The script is easier to reuse because you can dot-source the script, as shown here. When the script is dot-sourced, all the executable code in the script is run.

As a result, because each of the scripts prints information, the following is displayed.

```
IP Address: 192.168.2.5
Subnet: 255.255.255.0
GateWay: 192.168.2.1
DNS Server: 192.168.2.1
FQDN: C10.nwtraders.com


 C10 free disk space on drive C:
    48,767.16 MegaBytes


This OS is version 10.0
```

The DotSourceScripts.ps1 script is shown following. As you can tell, it provides you with a certain level of flexibility to choose the information required, and it also makes it easy to mix and match the required information. If each of the scripts had been written in a more standard fashion, and the output had been more standardized, the results would have been more impressive. As it is, three lines of code produce an exceptional amount of useful output that could be acceptable in a variety of situations.

DotSourceScripts.ps1

```
. C:\Scripts\GetIPDemoSingleFunction.ps1
. C:\Scripts\Get-FreeDiskSpace.ps1
. C:\Scripts\Get-OperatingSystemVersion.ps1
```

A better way to work with the function is to think about the things the function is actually doing. In the FunctionGetIPDemo.ps1 script, there are two functions. The first connects to WMI, which returns a management object. The second function formats the output. These are two completely unrelated tasks. The first task is data gathering, and the second task is the presentation of the information. The FunctionGetIPDemo.ps1 script is shown here.

FunctionGetIPDemo.ps1

```
Function Get-IPObject
{
 Get-WmiObject -class Win32_NetworkAdapterConfiguration -Filter "IPEnabled = $true"
} #end Get-IPObject

Function Format-IPOutput($IP)
{
 "IP Address: " + $IP.IPAddress[0]
 "Subnet: " + $IP.IPSubNet[0]
 "GateWay: " + $IP.DefaultIPGateway
 "DNS Server: " + $IP.DNSServerSearchOrder[0]
 "FQDN: " + $IP.DNSHostName + "." + $IP.DNSDomain
} #end Format-IPOutput

# *** Entry Point To Script

$ip = Get-IPObject
Format-IPOutput -ip $ip
```

By separating the data-gathering and the presentation activities into different functions, you gain additional flexibility. You could easily modify the *Get-IPObject* function to look for network adapters that were not IP enabled. To do this, you would need to modify the *-Filter* parameter of the *Get-WmiObject* cmdlet. Because most of the time you would actually be interested only in network adapters that are IP enabled, it would make sense to set the default value of the input parameter to *$true*. By default, the behavior of the revised function is exactly as it was prior to modification. The advantage is that you can now use the function and modify the objects returned by it. To do this, you supply *$false* when calling the function. This is illustrated in the Get-IPObjectDefaultEnabled.ps1 script.

Get-IPObjectDefaultEnabled.ps1

```
Function Get-IPObject([bool]$IPEnabled = $true)
{
 Get-WmiObject -class Win32_NetworkAdapterConfiguration -Filter "IPEnabled = $IPEnabled"
} #end Get-IPObject

Get-IPObject -IPEnabled $False
```

By separating the gathering of the information from the presentation of the information, you gain flexibility not only in the type of information that is garnered, but also in the way the information is displayed. When you are gathering network adapter configuration information from a network adapter that is not enabled for IP, the results are not as impressive as for one that is enabled for IP. You might therefore decide to create a different display to list only the pertinent information. Because the function that displays the information is different from the one that gathers the information, a change can easily be made to customize the information that is most germane. The *Begin* section of the function is run once during the execution of the function. This is the perfect place to create a header for the output data. The *Process* section executes once for each item on the pipeline, which in this example will be each of the non-IP-enabled network adapters. The *Write-Host* cmdlet is used to easily write the data out to the Windows PowerShell console. The backtick-*t* character combination (`` `t ``) is used to produce a tab.

Note The `` `t `` character is a string character, and as such it works with cmdlets that accept string input.

The Get-IPObjectDefaultEnabledFormatNonIPOutput.ps1 script is shown here.

Get-IPObjectDefaultEnabledFormatNonIPOutput.ps1

```
Function Get-IPObject([bool]$IPEnabled = $true)
{
 Get-WmiObject -class Win32_NetworkAdapterConfiguration -Filter "IPEnabled = $IPEnabled"
} #end Get-IPObject

Function Format-NonIPOutput($IP)
{
  Begin { "Index #  Description" }
 Process {
  ForEach ($i in $ip)
  {
   Write-Host $i.Index `t $i.Description
  } #end ForEach
 } #end Process
} #end Format-NonIPOutPut

$ip = Get-IPObject -IPEnabled $False
Format-NonIPOutput($ip)
```

You can use the *Get-IPObject* function to retrieve the network adapter configuration, and you can use the *Format-NonIPOutput* and *Format-IPOutput* functions in a script to display the IP information as specifically formatted output, as shown in the CombinationFormatGetIPDemo.ps1 script shown here.

CombinationFormatGetIPDemo.ps1

```
Function Get-IPObject([bool]$IPEnabled = $true)
{
 Get-WmiObject -class Win32_NetworkAdapterConfiguration -Filter "IPEnabled = $IPEnabled"
} #end Get-IPObject

Function Format-IPOutput($IP)
{
 "IP Address: " + $IP.IPAddress[0]
 "Subnet: " + $IP.IPSubNet[0]
 "GateWay: " + $IP.DefaultIPGateway
 "DNS Server: " + $IP.DNSServerSearchOrder[0]
 "FQDN: " + $IP.DNSHostName + "." + $IP.DNSDomain
} #end Format-IPOutput

Function Format-NonIPOutput($IP)
{
  Begin { "Index #  Description" }
```

```
 Process {
  ForEach ($i in $ip)
  {
   Write-Host $i.Index `t $i.Description
  } #end ForEach
 } #end Process
} #end Format-NonIPOutPut

# *** Entry Point ***
$IPEnabled = $false
$ip = Get-IPObject -IPEnabled $IPEnabled
If($IPEnabled) { Format-IPOutput($ip) }
ELSE { Format-NonIPOutput($ip) }
```

Understanding filters

A filter is a special-purpose function. It is used to operate on each object in a pipeline and is often used to reduce the number of objects that are passed along the pipeline. Typically, a filter does not use the *Begin* or the *End* parameters that a function might need to use. So a filter is often thought of as a function that only has a *Process* block. Many functions are written without using the *Begin* or *End* parameters, but filters are never written in such a way that they use the *Begin* or the *End* parameters. The biggest difference between a function and a filter is a bit subtler, however. When a function is used inside a pipeline, it actually halts the processing of the pipeline until the first element in the pipeline has run to completion. The function then accepts the input from the first element in the pipeline and begins its processing. When the processing in the function is completed, it then passes the results along to the next element in the script block. A function runs once for the pipelined data. A filter, on the other hand, runs once for each piece of data passed over the pipeline. In short, a filter will stream the data when in a pipeline, and a function will not. This can make a big difference in the performance. To illustrate this point, let's examine a function and a filter that accomplish the same things.

In the MeasureAddOneFilter.ps1 script, which follows, an array of 50,000 elements is created by using the *1..50000* syntax. (In Windows PowerShell 1.0, 50,000 was the maximum size of an array created in this manner. In Windows PowerShell 5.0, this ceiling has a maximum size of an *[Int32]* (2,146,483,647). The use of this size is dependent upon memory. This is shown here.

```
PS C:\> 1..[Int32]::MaxValue
Array dimensions exceeded supported range.
At line:1 char:1
+ 1..[Int32]::MaxValue
+ ~~~~~~~~~~~~~~~~~~~~~
    + CategoryInfo          : OperationStopped: (:) [], OutOfMemoryException
    + FullyQualifiedErrorId : System.OutOfMemoryException
```

The array is then pipelined into the *AddOne* filter. The filter prints out the string *add one filter* and then adds the number 1 to the current number on the pipeline. The length of time it takes to run the command is then displayed. On my computer, it takes about 2.6 seconds to run the MeasureAddOne-Filter.ps1 script.

```
Filter AddOne
{
 "add one filter"
  $_ + 1
}
```

```
Measure-Command { 1..50000 | addOne }
```

The function version is shown following. In a similar fashion to the MeasureAddOneFilter.ps1 script, it creates an array of 50,000 numbers and pipelines the results to the *AddOne* function. The string *Add One Function* is displayed. An automatic variable is created when pipelining input to a function. It is called *$input*. The *$input* variable is an enumerator, not just a plain array. It has a *moveNext* method, which can be used to move to the next item in the collection. Because *$input* is not a plain array, you cannot index directly into it—*$input[0]* would fail. To retrieve a specific element, you use the *$input.current* property. When I run the following script, it takes 4.3 seconds on my computer (that is almost twice as long as the filter).

MeasureAddOneFunction.ps1

```
Function AddOne
{
   "Add One Function"
   While ($input.moveNext())
    {
      $input.current + 1
    }
}
```

```
Measure-Command { 1..50000 | addOne }
```

What was happening that made the filter so much faster than the function in this example? The filter runs once for each item on the pipeline. This is shown here.

```
add one filter
2
add one filter
3
add one filter
4
add one filter
5
add one filter
6
```

The DemoAddOneFilter.ps1 script is shown here.

DemoAddOneFilter.ps1

```
Filter AddOne
{
 "add one filter"
  $_ + 1
}
```

```
1..5 | addOne
```

The *AddOne* function runs to completion once for all the items in the pipeline. This effectively stops the processing in the middle of the pipeline until all the elements of the array are created. Then all the data is passed to the function via the *$input* variable at one time. This type of approach does not take advantage of the streaming nature of the pipeline, which in many instances is more memory-efficient.

```
Add One Function
2
3
4
5
6
```

The DemoAddOneFunction.ps1 script is shown here.

DemoAddOneFunction.ps1

```
Function AddOne
{
  "Add One Function"
  While ($input.moveNext())
    {
      $input.current + 1
    }
}

1..5 | addOne
```

To close this performance issue between functions and filters when used in a pipeline, you can write your function so that it behaves like a filter. To do this, you must explicitly call out the *Process* block. When you use the *Process* block, you are also able to use the *$_* automatic variable instead of being restricted to using *$input*. When you do this, the script will look like DemoAddOneR2Function.ps1, the results of which are shown here.

```
add one function r2
2
add one function r2
3
add one function r2
4
add one function r2
5
add one function r2
6
```

The complete DemoAddOneR2Function.ps1 script is shown here.

DemoAddOneR2Function.ps1

```
Function AddOneR2
{
   Process {
   "add one function r2"
   $_ + 1
   }
} #end AddOneR2

1..5 | addOneR2
```

What does using an explicit *Process* block do to the performance? When run on my computer, the function takes about 2.6 seconds, which is virtually the same amount of time taken by the filter. The MeasureAddOneR2Function.ps1 script is shown here.

MeasureAddOneR2Function.ps1

```
Function AddOneR2
{
    Process {
    "add one function r2"
    $_ + 1
    }
} #end AddOneR2

Measure-Command {1..50000 | addOneR2 }
```

Another reason for using filters is that they visually stand out, and therefore improve readability of the script. The typical pattern for a filter is shown here.

```
Filter FilterName
{
 #insert code here
}
```

The *HasMessage* filter, found in the FilterHasMessage.ps1 script, begins with the *Filter* keyword, and is followed by the name of the filter, which is *HasMessage*. Inside the script block (the braces), the $_ automatic variable is used to provide access to the pipeline. It is sent to the *Where-Object* cmdlet, which performs the filter. In the calling script, the results of the *HasMessage* filter are sent to the *Measure-Object* cmdlet, which tells the user how many events in the application log have a message attached to them. The FilterHasMessage.ps1 script is shown here.

FilterHasMessage.ps1

```
Filter HasMessage
{
 $_ |
 Where-Object { $_.message }
} #end HasMessage

Get-WinEvent -LogName Application | HasMessage | Measure-Object
```

Although the filter has an implicit *Process* block, this does not prevent you from using the *Begin*, *Process*, and *End* script blocks explicitly. In the FilterToday.ps1 script, a filter named *IsToday* is created. To make the filter a stand-alone entity with no external dependencies required (such as the passing of a *DateTime* object to it), you need the filter to obtain the current date. However, if the call to the *Get-Date* cmdlet was done inside the *Process* block, the filter would continue to work, but the call to *Get-Date* would be made once for each object found in the input folder. So, if there were 25 items in the folder, the *Get-Date* cmdlet would be called 25 times. When you have something that you want to occur only once in the processing of the filter, you can place it in a *Begin* block. The *Begin* block is called only once, whereas the *Process* block is called once for each item in the pipeline. If you wanted any post-processing to take place (such as printing a message stating how many files were found today), you would place the relevant code in the *End* block of the filter.

The FilterToday.ps1 script is shown here.

FilterToday.ps1

```
Filter IsToday
{
 Begin {$dte = (Get-Date).Date}
  Process { $_ |
         Where-Object { $_.LastWriteTime -ge $dte }
        }
}

Get-ChildItem -Path C:\fso | IsToday
```

Creating a function: Step-by-step exercises

In this exercise, you'll explore the use of the *Get-Verb* cmdlet to find permissible Windows PowerShell verbs. You will also use *Function* keyword and create a function. After you have created the basic function, you'll add additional functionality to the function in the next exercise.

Creating a basic function

1. Start the Windows PowerShell ISE.

2. Use the *Get-Verb* cmdlet to obtain a listing of approved verbs.

3. Select a verb that would be appropriate for a function that obtains a listing of files by date last modified. In this case, the appropriate verb is *Get*.

4. Create a new function named *Get-FilesByDate*. The code to do this is shown here.

    ```
    Function Get-FilesByDate
    {

    }
    ```

5. Add four command-line parameters to the function. The first parameter is an array of file types, the second is for the month, the third parameter is for the year, and the last parameter is an array of file paths. This portion of the function is shown here.

    ```
    Param(
       [string[]]$fileTypes,
       [int]$month,
       [int]$year,
       [string[]]$path)
    ```

6. Following the *Param* portion of the function, add the code to perform a recursive search of paths supplied via the *$path* variable. Limit the search to include only file types supplied via the *$filetypes* variable. This portion of the code is shown here.

    ```
    Get-ChildItem -Path $path -Include $filetypes -Recurse |
    ```

7. Add a *Where-Object* clause to limit the files returned to the month of the *lastwritetime* property that equals the month supplied via the command line, and the year supplied via the command line. This portion of the function is shown here.

```
Where-Object {
    $_.lastwritetime.month -eq $month -AND $_.lastwritetime.year -eq $year }
```

8. Save the function in a .ps1 file named Get-FilesByDate.ps1.

9. Run the script containing the function inside the Windows PowerShell ISE.

10. In the command pane, call the function and supply appropriate parameters for the function. One such example of a command line is shown here.

```
Get-FilesByDate -fileTypes *.docx -month 5 -year 2012 -path c:\data
```

The completed function is shown here.

```
Function Get-FilesByDate
{
 Param(
   [string[]]$fileTypes,
   [int]$month,
   [int]$year,
   [string[]]$path)
   Get-ChildItem -Path $path -Include $filetypes -Recurse |
   Where-Object {
   $_.lastwritetime.month -eq $month -AND $_.lastwritetime.year -eq $year }
 } #end function Get-FilesByDate
```

This concludes this step-by-step exercise.

In the following exercise, you will add additional functionality to your Windows PowerShell function. In this additional functionality you will include a default value for the file types and make the *$month*, *$year*, and *$path* parameters mandatory.

Adding additional functionality to an existing function

1. Start the Windows PowerShell ISE.

2. Open the Get-FilesByDate.ps1 script (created in the previous exercise) and use the Save As feature of the Windows PowerShell ISE to save the file with a new name of Get-FilesByDateV2.ps1.

3. Create an array of default file types for the *$filetypes* input variable. Assign the array of file types to the *$filetypes* input variable. Use array notation when creating the array of file types. For this exercise, use *.doc* and *.docx*. The command to do this is shown here.

```
[string[]]$fileTypes = @(".doc","*.docx"),
```

4. Use the *[Parameter(Mandatory=$true)]* parameter tag to make the *$month* parameter mandatory. The tag appears just above the input parameter in the *param* portion of the script. Do
   the same thing for the *$year* and *$path* parameters. The revised portion of the *param* section
   of the script is shown here.

```
[Parameter(Mandatory=$true)]
   [int]$month,
   [Parameter(Mandatory=$true)]
   [int]$year,
   [Parameter(Mandatory=$true)]
   [string[]]$path)
```

5. Save and run the function. Call the function without assigning a value for the path. An input
   box should appear prompting you to enter a path. Enter a single path residing on your system,
   and press Enter. A second prompt appears (because the *$path* parameter accepts an array).
   Simply press Enter a second time. An appropriate command line is shown here.

```
Get-FilesByDate -month 10 -year 2011
```

6. Now run the function and assign a path value. An appropriate command line is shown here.

```
Get-FilesByDate -month 10 -year 2011 -path c:\data
```

7. Now run the function and look for a different file type. In the example shown here, I look for
   Microsoft Excel documents.

```
Get-FilesByDate -month 10 -year 2011 -path c:\data -fileTypes *.xlsx,*.xls
```

The revised function is shown here.

```
Function Get-FilesByDate
{
 Param(
  [string[]]$fileTypes = @(".DOC","*.DOCX"),
  [Parameter(Mandatory=$true)]
  [int]$month,
  [Parameter(Mandatory=$true)]
  [int]$year,
  [Parameter(Mandatory=$true)]
  [string[]]$path)
  Get-ChildItem -Path $path -Include $filetypes -Recurse |
  Where-Object {
  $_.lastwritetime.month -eq $month -AND $_.lastwritetime.year -eq $year }
 } #end function Get-FilesByDate
```

This concludes the exercise.

Chapter 6 quick reference

To	Do this
Create a function	Use the *Function* keyword, and provide a name and a script block.
Reuse a Windows PowerShell function	Dot-source the file containing the function.
Constrain a data type	Use a type constraint in brackets and place it in front of the variable or data to be constrained.
Provide input to a function	Use the *Param* keyword and supply variables to hold the input.
To use a function	Load the function into memory.
To store a function	Place the function in a script file.
To name a function	Use *Get-Verb* to identify an appropriate verb, and use the verb-noun naming convention.

Creating advanced functions and modules

After completing this chapter, you will be able to

- Understand the use of the *[cmdletbinding]* attribute.

- Configure *Write-Verbose* to provide additional information.

- Use parameter validation attributes to prevent errors.

- Configure *SupportsShouldProcess* to permit the use of *-WhatIf*.

- Create a module.

- Install a module.

Advanced functions incorporate advanced Windows PowerShell features and can therefore behave like cmdlets. They do not have to be complicated. In fact, advanced functions do not even have to be difficult to write or to use. What makes a function advanced is the capabilities it possesses that enable it to behave in a similar manner to a cmdlet. Back during the beta of Windows PowerShell 2.0, the name for the advanced function was *script cmdlet*, and although the name change is perhaps understandable because script cmdlets really are just advanced functions, in reality, the name was very descriptive. This is because an advanced function mimics the behavior of a regular Windows PowerShell cmdlet. In fact, the best advanced functions behave exactly like a Windows PowerShell cmdlet and implement the same capabilities.

The *[cmdletbinding]* attribute

The first step in creating an advanced function is to add the *[cmdletbinding]* attribute to modify the way the function works. This single addition adds several capabilities, such as additional parameter checking and the ability to easily use the *Write-Verbose* cmdlet. To use the *[cmdletbinding]* attribute, you place the attribute in a bracketed attribute tag and include it in the first noncommented line in the function. In addition, the *[cmdletbinding]* attribute requires the use of the *Param* keyword. If your advanced function requires no parameters, you can use the *Param* keyword without specifying any parameters.

This technique is shown here.

```
function my-function
{
 [cmdletbinding()]
 Param()


}
```

After you have the basic outline of the advanced function, you can begin to fill in the blanks. For example, to use the *Write-Verbose* cmdlet you only need to add the command. Without the use of the *[cmdletbinding]* attribute, you would need to manually change the value of the *$VerbosePreference* automatic variable from *silentlycontinue* to *continue* (and presumably later change it back to the default value). The use of the *[cmdletbinding]* attribute and *Write-Verbose* is shown here.

```
function my-function
{
 [cmdletbinding()]
 Param()
 Write-Verbose "verbose stream"
}
```

Enabling cmdlet binding for a function

1. Begin a function by using the *Function* keyword and supplying the name of the function.

2. Open a script block.

3. Enter the *[cmdletbinding()]* attribute.

4. Add the *Param* statement.

5. Close the script block.

Easy verbose messages

When loaded, the function permits the use of the *-Verbose* switch parameter. Use of this parameter causes each *Write-Verbose* statement to write to the Windows PowerShell console output. When the function runs without the *-Verbose* switch parameter, no output displays from the verbose stream. Use of this technique is shown in Figure 7-1.

The great thing about using the *-Verbose* switch parameter is that detailed information (such as the progress in making remote connections, loading modules, and other operations that could cause a script to fail) is output as events happen. This provides a built-in diagnostic mode for the advanced function—with virtually no additional programming required.

FIGURE 7-1 When specified, the *[cmdletbinding]* attribute enables easy access to the verbose stream.

Providing verbose output

1. Inside a function, add the *[cmdletbinding()]* attribute.

2. Add a *Param* statement.

3. Use the *Write-Verbose* cmdlet for each status message to display.

4. When calling the function, use the *-Verbose* switch parameter.

Automatic parameter checks

The default behavior for a Windows PowerShell function is that any additional values beyond the defined number of arguments are supplied to an unnamed argument and are therefore available in the automatic *$args* variable. This behavior, though potentially useful, easily becomes a source of errors for a script. The following function illustrates this behavior.

```
function my-function
{
 #[cmdletbinding()]
 Param($a)
 $a
 #$args
}
```

When the preceding function runs, any value supplied to the *-a* parameter appears in the output. This is shown here.

```
PS C:\Users\ed.NWTRADERS> my-function -a 1,2,3,4
1
2
3
4
```

If, however, when you are calling the function you omit the first comma, no error is generated—but the output displayed does not meet expectations. This is shown here.

```
PS C:\Users\ed.NWTRADERS> my-function -a 1 2,3,4
1
```

The remaining parameters appear in the automatic *$args* variable. Placing the *$args* variable in the function illustrates this. First add the *$args* automatic variable, as shown here.

```
function my-function
{
 #[cmdletbinding()]
 Param($a)
 $a
 $args
}
```

Now, when calling the function, if you omit the first comma, the following output appears.

```
PS C:\Users\ed.NWTRADERS> my-function -a 1 2,3,4
1
2
3
4
```

Though this is interesting, you might not want this supplying-of-additional-values-to-an-unnamed-argument behavior. One way to correct it is to check the number of arguments supplied to the function. You can do this by monitoring the *count* property of the *$args* variable. This is shown here.

```
function my-function
{
 #[cmdletbinding()]
 Param($a)
 $a
 $args.count
}
```

When you are passing multiple arguments to the function, the value of *count* increments. In the output shown here, the first number, 1, returns from the *-a* position. The number 3 is the count of extra arguments (those not supplied for the named argument).

```
PS C:\Users\ed.NWTRADERS> my-function 1 2 3 4
1
3
```

By using this feature and checking the *count* property of *$args*, you can detect extra arguments coming to the function with one line of code. This change is shown here.

```
function my-function
{
 #[cmdletbinding()]
 Param($a,$b)
 $a
 $b
 if($args.count -gt 0) {Write-Error "unhandled arguments supplied"}
}
```

When the code is run, as shown following, the first two parameters supplied are accepted for the *-a* and the *-b* parameters. The two remaining parameters go into the *$args* automatic variable. This increases the *count* property of *$args* to a value greater than 0, and therefore an error occurs.

```
PS C:\> my-function 1 2 3 4
1
2
my-function : unhandled arguments supplied
At line:1 char:1
+ my-function 1 2 3 4
+ ~~~~~~~~~~~~~~~~~~~
    + CategoryInfo          : NotSpecified: (:) [Write-Error], WriteErrorException
    + FullyQualifiedErrorId : Microsoft.PowerShell.Commands.WriteErrorException,my-function
```

The easiest way to identify unhandled parameters supplied to a Windows PowerShell function is to use the *[cmdletbinding]* attribute. One of the features of the *[cmdletbinding]* attribute is that it generates an error when unhandled parameter values appear on the command line. The following function illustrates the *[cmdletbinding]* attribute.

```
function my-function
{
 [cmdletbinding()]
 Param($a,$b)
 $a
 $b
}
```

When you call the preceding function with too many arguments, the following error appears.

```
PS C:\> my-function 1 2 3 4
my-function : A positional parameter cannot be found that accepts argument '3'.
At line:1 char:1
+ my-function 1 2 3 4
+ ~~~~~~~~~~~~~~~~~~~
    + CategoryInfo          : InvalidArgument: (:) [my-function], ParameterBindingException
    + FullyQualifiedErrorId : PositionalParameterNotFound,my-function
```

Adding support for the -*WhatIf* switch parameter

One of the great features of Windows PowerShell is the use of the -*WhatIf* switch parameter on cmdlets that change system state, such as the *Stop-Service* and *Stop-Process* cmdlets. If you consistently use the -*WhatIf* switch parameter, you can avoid many inadvertent system outages or potential data loss. As a Windows PowerShell best practice, you should also implement the -*WhatIf* switch parameter in advanced functions that potentially change system state. In the past, this meant creating special parameters and adding a lot of extra code to handle the output. Now it requires a single line of code.

> **Note** *[cmdletbinding()]* appears with empty parentheses because there are other things, such as *SupportsShouldProcess*, that can appear between the parentheses.

Inside the parentheses of the *[cmdletbinding]* attribute, set *SupportsShouldProcess* to *true*. The following function illustrates this technique.

```
function my-function
{
 [cmdletbinding(SupportsShouldProcess=$True)]
 Param($path)
 md $path
}
```

Now when you call the function by using the -*WhatIf* switch parameter, a message appears in the output detailing the exact behavior the cmdlet takes when run without the -*WhatIf* switch parameter. This is shown in Figure 7-2.

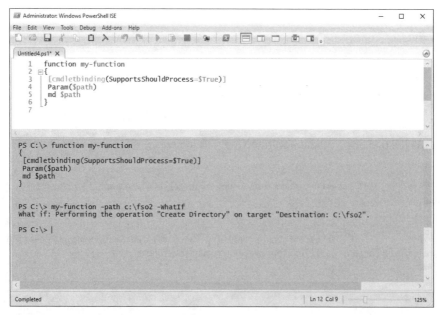

FIGURE 7-2 Using -*WhatIf* when running a function that includes *SupportsShouldProcess* informs you what the function will do when run.

1. Inside a function, add the *[cmdletbinding()]* attribute.

2. Inside the parentheses of the *[cmdletbinding]* attribute, add *SupportsShouldProcess = $true*.

3. Add a *Param* statement.

4. When calling the function, use the -*WhatIf* switch parameter.

Adding support for the -*Confirm* switch parameter

If all you want to do is to enable users of your function to use the -*Confirm* switch parameter when calling the function, the command is exactly the same as the one to enable -*WhatIf*. The *SupportsShould-Process* attribute turns on both -*WhatIf* and -*Confirm*. Therefore, when you run the function that follows with the -*Confirm* switch parameter, it prompts you prior to executing the specific action.

```
function my-function
{
 [cmdletbinding(SupportsShouldProcess=$True)]
 Param($path)
 md $path
}
```

The following command illustrates calling the function with the -*Confirm* switch parameter.

```
my-function -path c:\mytest -confirm
```

The dialog box shown in Figure 7-3 is displayed as a result of the previous command line when the code runs from within the Windows PowerShell ISE.

FIGURE 7-3 Use of *SupportsShouldProcess* also enables the -*Confirm* switch.

Most of the time when you do something in Windows PowerShell, it executes the command instead of prompting. For example, the following command stops all processes on the computer.

```
Get-Process | Stop-Process
```

Note On Windows 8 and later, the preceding command prompts prior to stopping the CRSS process that will cause the computer to shut down. On operating systems prior to Windows 8, the command executes without prompting.

If you do not want a cmdlet to execute by default—that is, if you want it to prompt by default—you add an additional property to the *[cmdletbinding]* attribute: the *ConfirmImpact* property. This technique is shown here.

```
[cmdletbinding(SupportsShouldProcess=$True, confirmimpact="high")]
```

The values for the *ConfirmImpact* property are *High*, *Medium*, *Low*, and *None*. They correspond to the values for the automatic *$ConfirmPreference* variable.

Specifying the default parameter set

Properties specified for the *[cmdletbinding]* attribute affect the entire function. Therefore, when an advanced function contains multiple parameter sets (or different groupings of parameters for the same cmdlet), the function needs to know which one of several potential possibilities is the default. The following command illustrates finding the default Windows PowerShell parameter set for a cmdlet.

```
PS C:\> (Get-Command Stop-Process).parametersets | Format-Table name, isdefault -AutoSize

Name         IsDefault
----         ---------
Id               True
Name            False
InputObject     False
```

To specify a default parameter set for an advanced function, use the *DefaultParameterSetName* property of the *[cmdletbinding]* attribute. When doing this, you tell Windows PowerShell that if a particular parameter set is not specified and not resolved by its data type, the parameter set with the *DefaultParameterSetName* attribute is to be used. Here is the code to specify the *DefaultParameterSetName* property of the *[cmdletbinding]* attribute.

```
[cmdletbinding(DefaultParameterSetName="name")]
```

The following section provides more information about creating parameter sets.

The *Parameter* attribute

The *parameter* attribute accepts several properties that add power and flexibility to your advanced Windows PowerShell functions. The *parameter* attribute properties are shown in Table 7-1.

TABLE 7-1 Advanced function parameter attribute properties and their meanings

Parameter attribute property	Example	Meaning
Mandatory	*Mandatory=$true*	The parameter must be specified.
Position	*Position=0*	The parameter occupies the first position when the function is called.

Parameter attribute property	Example	Meaning
ParameterSetName	ParameterSetName="name"	The parameter belongs to the specified parameter set.
ValueFromPipeline	ValueFromPipeline=$true	The parameter accepts pipe-lined input.
ValueFromPipelineByPropertyName	ValueFromPipelineByPropertyName=$true	The parameter uses a property of the object instead of the entire object.
ValueFromRemainingArguments	ValueFromRemainingArguments=$true	The parameter collects un-assigned arguments.
HelpMessage	HelpMessage="parameter help info"	A short help message for the parameter is displayed.

The *Mandatory* parameter property

The *Mandatory* parameter attribute property turns a function's parameter from optional to mandatory. By default, all parameters to an advanced function are optional; by using the *Mandatory* property, you can change that behavior on a parameter-by-parameter basis. When a function runs with missing mandatory parameters, Windows PowerShell prompts for the missing parameter.

Use of the *Mandatory* parameter is shown here.

```
Function Test-Mandatory
{
 Param(
 [Parameter(mandatory=$true)]
 $name)
 "hello $name"
}
```

When you run the *Test-Mandatory* function without supplying a value for the *name* parameter, Windows PowerShell prompts for the missing value. This is shown in the output that follows.

```
PS C:\> Test-Mandatory
cmdlet Test-Mandatory at command pipeline position 1
Supply values for the following parameters:
name: Ed Wilson
hello Ed Wilson
```

If the user does not supply a value for the missing parameter but instead skips past the prompt, no error occurs, and the function continues to run, because the user is really assigning something (*$null*) to the parameter.

Note If the code itself generates errors when run with no parameter values, these errors are displayed. In this way, the *mandatory* parameter property causes a prompt to appear, but it is not an error-handling technique.

The output is shown in Figure 7-4.

FIGURE 7-4 No error appears when a mandatory parameter is skipped.

The *Position* parameter property

The *Position* parameter property tells Windows PowerShell that the specific parameter receives values when it occupies a specific position. Position numbers are zero based, and therefore the first position is parameter position 0. By default, Windows PowerShell parameters are positional—that is, you can supply values for them in the order in which they appear in the parameter set. However, when you use the *Position* parameter property for any single parameter, the remaining parameters without a *Position* value will default to being nonpositional—that is, you will now need to use the parameter names to supply values.

> **Note** When supplying values for named parameters, you need to type only enough of the parameter name to distinguish it from other parameter names (including the default parameters).

The code shown here illustrates using the *Position* parameter property.

```
Function Test-Positional
{
 Param(
 [Parameter(Position=0)]
 $greeting,
 $name)
 "$greeting $name"
}
```

The *ParameterSetName* parameter property

The *ParameterSetName* property identifies groups of parameters that, taken together, create a specific command set. It is quite common for cmdlets and advanced functions to expose multiple ways of calling the code. One thing to keep in mind when creating different parameter sets is that the same parameter cannot appear in more than one parameter set. Therefore, only the parameters that are unique to each parameter set appear.

> **Note** When creating a parameter set, it is a best practice always to include one mandatory parameter in each set.

If your parameter set uses more than a single parameter, use the *ParameterSetName* property from the automatic *$PSCmdlet* variable in a *switch* statement to evaluate actions to take place. This technique is shown in the *Test-ParameterSet* function that follows.

```
Function Test-ParameterSet
{
 Param(
  [Parameter(ParameterSetName="City",Mandatory=$true)]
  $city,
  [Parameter(ParameterSetName="City")]
  $state,
  [Parameter(ParameterSetName="phone",Mandatory=$true)]
  $phone,
  [Parameter(ParameterSetName="phone")]
  $ext,
  [Parameter(Mandatory=$true)]
  $name)
  Switch ($PSCmdlet.ParameterSetName)
  {
   "city" {"$name from $city in $state"}
   "phone" {"$name phone is $Phone extension $ext"}
  }
}
```

The *ValueFromPipeline* property

The *ValueFromPipeline* property causes Windows PowerShell to accept objects from the pipeline. The entire object passes into the function's *Process* block when you use the *ValueFromPipeline* parameter property. Because the entire object passes to the function, you can access specific properties from the pipeline with dotted notation. An example of this technique is shown here.

```
Function Test-PipedValue
{
 Param(
    [Parameter(ValueFromPipeline=$true)]
    $process)
    Process {Write-Host $process.name  $process.id}
}
```

Instead of receiving an entire object from the pipeline, you can use the *ValueFromPipelineByProperty-Name* property, which can often simplify code by allowing your function to pick properties from the input object directly from the pipeline. The *Test-PipedValueByPropertyName* function illustrates this technique.

```
Function Test-PipedValueByPropertyName
{
 Param(
    [Parameter(ValueFromPipelineByPropertyName=$true)]
    $processname,
    [Parameter(ValueFromPipelineByPropertyName=$true)]
    $id)
    Process {Write-Host $processname  $id}
}
```

When you need to accept arbitrary information that might or might not align with specific parameters, the *ValueFromRemainingArguments* parameter property provides the answer. Such a technique permits flexibility in the use of the parameters, and the remaining items in the arguments make up an array and are therefore accessible via standard array notation. The *Test-ValueFromRemainingArguments* function illustrates using the *ValueFromRemainingArguments* parameter property in a function.

```
Function Test-ValueFromRemainingArguments
{
 Param(
    $Name,
    [Parameter(ValueFromRemainingArguments=$true)]
    $otherInfo)
    Process { "Name: $name `r`nOther info: $otherinfo" }
}
```

Figure 7-5 illustrates calling the *Test-ValueFromRemainingArguments* function and providing additional arguments to the function.

FIGURE 7-5 The *ValueFromRemainingArguments* parameter property permits access to extra arguments.

The *HelpMessage* property

The *HelpMessage* property provides a small amount of help related to a specific parameter. This information becomes accessible when Windows PowerShell prompts for a missing parameter. This means that it only makes sense to use the *HelpMessage* parameter property when it is coupled with the *Mandatory* parameter property.

> **Note** It is a Windows PowerShell best practice to use the *HelpMessage* parameter property when using the *Mandatory* parameter property.

When Windows PowerShell prompts for a missing parameter, and when the *HelpMessage* parameter property exists, an additional line appears in the output. This line is shown here.

```
(Type !? for Help.)
```

To view the help, enter **!?** and press Enter. The string value for the *HelpMessage* parameter property will be displayed.

```
Function Test-HelpMessage
{
 Param(
    [Parameter(Mandatory=$true, HelpMessage="Enter your name please")]
    $name)
    "Good to meet you $name"
}
```

Understanding modules

Windows PowerShell 2.0 introduced the concept of modules. A module is a package that can contain Windows PowerShell cmdlets, aliases, functions, variables, type/format XML, help files, other scripts, and even providers. In short, a Windows PowerShell module can contain the kinds of things that you might put into your profile, but it can also contain things that Windows PowerShell 1.0 required a developer to incorporate into a Windows PowerShell snap-in. There are several advantages of modules over snap-ins:

- Anyone who can write a Windows PowerShell script can create a module.

- To install a module, you do not need to write a Windows Installer package.

- To install a module, you do not have to have administrator rights.

These advantages should be of great interest to the IT professional.

Locating and loading modules

There are three default locations for Windows PowerShell modules. The first location is the user's home directory, the second is the Windows PowerShell Program Files directory, and the third is the Windows PowerShell home directory. These locations are defined in *$env:PSModulePath*, a default environmental variable. You can add additional default module path locations by editing this variable. The modules directory in the Windows PowerShell home directory always exists. However, the modules directory in the user's home directory is not present by default. The modules directory only exists in the user's home directory if it has been created. The creation of the modules directory in the user's home directory does not usually happen until someone has decided to create and store modules there. A nice feature of the modules directory is that when it exists, it is the first place Windows PowerShell uses when it searches for a module. If the user's module directory does not exist, the modules directory within the Windows PowerShell home directory is used.

Listing available modules

Windows PowerShell modules exist in two states: loaded and unloaded. To display a list of all loaded modules, use the *Get-Module* cmdlet without any parameters. This is shown here.

```
PS C:\> Get-Module

ModuleType Version   Name                            ExportedCommands
---------- -------   ----                            ----------------
Script     1.0.0.0   ISE                             {Get-IseSnippet, Import-IseSnippet,...
Manifest   3.1.0.0   Microsoft.PowerShell.Management  {Add-Computer, Add-Content, Checkpo...
Manifest   3.1.0.0   Microsoft.PowerShell.Utility     {Add-Member, Add-Type, Clear-Variab...
```

If there are multiple modules loaded when the *Get-Module* cmdlet runs, each module will appear on its own individual line along with its accompanying exported commands.

This is shown here.

```
PS C:\> Get-Module

ModuleType Version    Name                            ExportedCommands
---------- -------    ----                            ----------------
Manifest   3.1.0.0    Microsoft.PowerShell.Management  {Add-Computer, Add-Cont...
Manifest   3.1.0.0    Microsoft.PowerShell.Utility     {Add-Member, Add-Type, ...
```

If no modules are loaded, nothing displays to the Windows PowerShell console. No errors appear, nor is there any confirmation that the command has actually run. This situation never occurs on Windows 10 because Windows PowerShell core cmdlets reside in two basic modules, which are the *Microsoft.PowerShell.Management* and *Microsoft.PowerShell.Utility* modules.

To obtain a listing of all modules that are available on the system, you use the *Get-Module* cmdlet with the *-ListAvailable* switch parameter. The *Get-Module* cmdlet with the *-ListAvailable* switch parameter lists all modules that are available, whether or not the modules are loaded into the Windows PowerShell console. The output shown here illustrates the default installation of a Windows 10 client system.

```
PS C:\> Get-Module -ListAvailable


    Directory: C:\Program Files\WindowsPowerShell\Modules


ModuleType Version    Name                 ExportedCommands
---------- -------    ----                 ----------------
Binary     1.0.0.0    PackageManagement    {Find-Package, Get-Pack...
Script     3.3.5      Pester               {Describe, Context, It,...
Script     1.0        PowerShellGet        {Install-Module, Find-M...
Script     1.1        PSReadline           {Get-PSReadlineKeyHandl...


    Directory: C:\Windows\system32\WindowsPowerShell\v1.0\Modules


ModuleType Version    Name                        ExportedCommands
---------- -------    ----                        ----------------
Manifest   1.0.0.0    AppBackgroundTask           {Disable-AppBackgroundT...
Manifest   2.0.0.0    AppLocker                   {Get-AppLockerFileInfor...
Manifest   2.0.0.0    Appx                        {Add-AppxPackage, Get-A...
Script     1.0.0.0    AssignedAccess              {Clear-AssignedAccess, ...
Manifest   1.0.0.0    BitLocker                   {Unlock-BitLocker, Susp...
Manifest   2.0.0.0    BitsTransfer                {Add-BitsFile, Complete...
Manifest   1.0.0.0    BranchCache                 {Add-BCDataCacheExtensi...
Manifest   1.0.0.0    CimCmdlets                  {Get-CimAssociatedInsta...
Manifest   1.0        Defender                    {Get-MpPreference, Set-...
Manifest   1.0.0.0    DirectAccessClientComponents {Disable-DAManualEntryP...
Script     3.0        Dism                        {Add-AppxProvisionedPac...
Manifest   1.0.0.0    DnsClient                   {Resolve-DnsName, Clear...
Manifest   1.0.0.0    EventTracingManagement      {New-EtwTraceSession, G...
Manifest   2.0.0.0    International                {Get-WinDefaultInputMet...
Manifest   1.0.0.0    iSCSI                       {Get-IscsiTargetPortal,...
```

```
Script      1.0.0.0   ISE                                 {New-IseSnippet, Import...
Manifest    1.0.0.0   Kds                                 {Add-KdsRootKey, Get-Kd...
Manifest    1.0.0.0   Microsoft.PowerShell.Archive        {Compress-Archive, Expa...
Manifest    3.0.0.0   Microsoft.PowerShell.Diagnostics    {Get-WinEvent, Get-Coun...
Manifest    3.0.0.0   Microsoft.PowerShell.Host           {Start-Transcript, Stop...
Manifest    3.1.0.0   Microsoft.PowerShell.Management      {Add-Content, Clear-Con...
Script      1.0       Microsoft.PowerShell.ODataUtils     Export-ODataEndpointProxy
Manifest    3.0.0.0   Microsoft.PowerShell.Security       {Get-Acl, Set-Acl, Get-...
Manifest    3.1.0.0   Microsoft.PowerShell.Utility        {Format-List, Format-Cu...
Manifest    3.0.0.0   Microsoft.WSMan.Management           {Disable-WSManCredSSP, ...
Manifest    1.0       MMAgent                             {Disable-MMAgent, Enabl...
Manifest    1.0.0.0   MsDtc                               {New-DtcDiagnosticTrans...
Manifest    2.0.0.0   NetAdapter                          {Disable-NetAdapter, Di...
Manifest    1.0.0.0   NetConnection                       {Get-NetConnectionProfi...
Manifest    1.0.0.0   NetEventPacketCapture               {New-NetEventSession, R...
Manifest    2.0.0.0   NetLbfo                             {Add-NetLbfoTeamMember,...
Manifest    1.0.0.0   NetNat                              {Get-NetNat, Get-NetNat...
Manifest    2.0.0.0   NetQos                              {Get-NetQosPolicy, Set-...
Manifest    2.0.0.0   NetSecurity                         {Get-DAPolicyChange, Ne...
Manifest    1.0.0.0   NetSwitchTeam                       {New-NetSwitchTeam, Rem...
Manifest    1.0.0.0   NetTCPIP                            {Get-NetIPAddress, Get-...
Manifest    1.0.0.0   NetworkConnectivityStatus           {Get-DAConnectionStatus...
Manifest    1.0.0.0   NetworkSwitchManager                {Disable-NetworkSwitchE...
Manifest    1.0.0.0   NetworkTransition                   {Add-NetIPHttpsCertBind...
Manifest    1.0.0.0   PcsvDevice                          {Get-PcsvDevice, Start-...
Manifest·   1.0.0.0   PKI                                 {Add-CertificateEnrollm...
Manifest    1.0.0.0   PnpDevice                           {Get-PnpDevice, Get-Pnp...
Manifest    1.1       PrintManagement                     {Add-Printer, Add-Print...
Manifest·   1.1       PSDesiredStateConfiguration         {Set-DscLocalConfigurat...
Script      1.0.0.0   PSDiagnostics                       {Disable-PSTrace, Disab...
Binary      1.1.0.0   PSScheduledJob                      {New-JobTrigger, Add-Jo...
Manifest    2.0.0.0   PSWorkflow                          {New-PSWorkflowExecutio...
Manifest    1.0.0.0   PSWorkflowUtility                   Invoke-AsWorkflow
Manifest    1.0.0.0   ScheduledTasks                      {Get-ScheduledTask, Set...
Manifest.   2.0.0.0   SecureBoot                          {Confirm-SecureBootUEFI...
Manifest    2.0.0.0   SmbShare                            {Get-SmbShare, Remove-S...
Manifest    2.0.0.0   SmbWitness                          {Get-SmbWitnessClient, ...
Manifest    1.0.0.0   StartLayout                         {Export-StartLayout, Im...
Manifest    2.0.0.0   Storage                             {Add-InitiatorIdToMaski...
Manifest    2.0.0.0   TLS                                 {New-TlsSessionTicketKe...
Manifest    1.0.0.0   TroubleshootingPack                 {Get-TroubleshootingPac...
Manifest    2.0.0.0   TrustedPlatformModule               {Get-Tpm, Initialize-Tp...
Manifest    2.0.0.0   VpnClient                           {Add-VpnConnection, Set...
Manifest    1.0.0.0   Wdac                                {Get-OdbcDriver, Set-Od...
Manifest    1.0.0.0   WindowsDeveloperLicense             {Get-WindowsDeveloperLi...
Script      1.0       WindowsErrorReporting               {Enable-WindowsErrorRep...
Manifest    1.0.0.0   WindowsSearch                       {Get-WindowsSearchSetti...
Manifest·   1.0.0.0   WindowsUpdate                       Get-WindowsUpdateLog
```

Note Windows PowerShell 5.0 still installs into the $env:SystemRoot\system32\ WindowsPowerShell\v1.0 directory (even on Windows 10). The reason for adherence to this location is for compatibility with applications that expect this location. I often receive questions via the Hey Scripting Guy! blog (*www.scriptingguys.com/blog*) related to this folder name. To determine the version of Windows PowerShell you are running, use the *$PSVersionTable* automatic variable.

Loading modules

When you have identified a module you want to load, you use the *Import-Module* cmdlet to load the module into the current Windows PowerShell session. This is shown here.

```
PS C:\> Import-Module -Name NetConnection
PS C:\>
```

If the module exists, the *Import-Module* cmdlet completes without displaying any information. If the module is already loaded, no error message displays. This behavior is shown in the following code, where the Up Arrow key is pressed to retrieve the previous command and Enter is pressed to execute the command. The *Import-Module* command runs three times, but no errors appear.

```
PS C:\> Import-Module -Name NetConnection
PS C:\> Import-Module -Name NetConnection
PS C:\> Import-Module -Name NetConnection
PS C:\>
```

After you import the module, you might want to use the *Get-Module* cmdlet to quickly view the functions exposed by the module. (You can also use the *Get-Command -Module <modulename>* command.) It is not necessary to enter the complete module name. You can use wildcards, and you can even use tab expansion to expand the module name. The wildcard technique is shown here.

```
PS C:\> Get-Module net*

ModuleType Version    Name                     ExportedCommands
---------- -------    ----                     ----------------
Manifest   1.0.0.0    netconnection            {Get-NetConnectionProfi...
```

As shown previously, the *netconnection* module exports two commands: the *Get-NetConnectionProfile* function, and some other command that is probably *Set-NetConnectionProfile.* (The guess is due to the fact that the *Get* and *Set* Windows PowerShell verbs often go together. I am assuming the command name.) The one problem with using the *Get-Module* cmdlet is that it truncates the *ExportedCommands* property (the truncate behavior is controlled by the value assigned to the *$FormatEnumerationLimit* automatic variable). The easy solution to this problem is to pipeline the resulting *PSModuleInfo* object to the *Select-Object* cmdlet and expand the *ExportedCommands* property.

This technique is shown here.

```
PS C:\> Get-Module net* | select -expand *comm*

Key                                     Value
---                                     -----
Get-NetConnectionProfile                Get-NetConnectionProfile
Set-NetConnectionProfile                Set-NetConnectionProfile
```

When loading modules that have long names, you are not limited to entering the entire module name. You can use wildcards or tab expansion to complete the module name. When using wildcards to load modules, it is a best practice to enter a significant portion of the module name so that you only match a single module from the list of modules that are available. If you do not match a single module, an error is generated. The following error appears because *net** matches multiple modules.

```
PS C:\> ipmo net*
ipmo : The specified module 'net*' was not loaded because no valid module file was
found in any module directory.
At line:1 char:1
+ ipmo net*
+ ~~~~~~~~~
    + CategoryInfo          : ResourceUnavailable: (net*:String) [Import-Module], F
   ileNotFoundException
    + FullyQualifiedErrorId : Modules_ModuleNotFound,Microsoft.PowerShell.Commands.
   ImportModuleCommand
```

> **Important** In previous versions of Windows PowerShell, if a wildcard pattern matched more than one module name, the first matched module loaded and the remaining matches were ignored. This led to inconsistent and unpredictable results. Therefore, in Windows PowerShell 5.0, an error generates when a wildcard pattern matches more than one module name.

If you want to load all of the modules that are available on your system, you can use the *Get-Module* cmdlet with the *-ListAvailable* parameter and pipeline the resulting *PSModuleInfo* objects to the *Import-Module* cmdlet. This is shown here.

```
PS C:\> Get-Module -ListAvailable | Import-Module
PS C:\>
```

If you have a module that contains a function, cmdlet, or workflow that uses a verb that is not on the allowed verb list, a warning message displays when you import the module. The functions in the module still work, and the module will work, but the warning displays to remind you to check the authorized verb list. This behavior is shown here.

```
PS C:\> Import-Module HelloUser
WARNING: The names of some imported commands from the module 'HelloUser' include
unapproved verbs that might make them less discoverable. To find the commands with
unapproved verbs, run the Import-Module command again with the Verbose parameter.
For a list of approved verbs, type Get-Verb.
PS C:\> hello-user
hello administrator
```

To obtain more information about which unapproved verbs are being used, you use the -*Verbose* parameter of *Import-Module*. This command is shown here.

```
PS C:\> Import-Module HelloUser -Verbose
```

The results of the *Import-Module -Verbose* command are shown in Figure 7-6.

```
powershell                                                    —   □   ×
PS C:\> Import-Module Hello-User -Verbose
VERBOSE: Loading module from path 'C:\Program
Files\WindowsPowerShell\Modules\Hello-User\Hello-User.psm1'.
VERBOSE: Exporting function 'hello-user'.
WARNING: The names of some imported commands from the module 'Hello-User' include
unapproved verbs that might make them less discoverable. To find the commands with
unapproved verbs, run the Import-Module command again with the Verbose parameter.
For a list of approved verbs, type Get-Verb.
VERBOSE: The 'hello-user' command in the Hello-User' module was imported, but
because its name does not include an approved verb, it might be difficult to find.
For a list of approved verbs, type Get-Verb.
VERBOSE: Importing function 'hello-user'.
PS C:\>
```

FIGURE 7-6 The -*Verbose* parameter of *Import-Module* displays information about each function exported, in addition to unapproved verb names. The *hello* verb used in *Hello-User* is not an approved verb.

In this section, the concept of locating and loading modules was discussed. You can list modules by using the -*ListAvailable* switch parameter with the *Get-Module* cmdlet. Modules are loaded via the *Import-Module* cmdlet.

Installing modules

One of the features of modules is that they can be installed without elevated rights. Because each user has a modules folder in the %userprofile% directory that the user has rights to use, the installation of a module does not require administrator rights to install into the personal module store. An additional feature of modules is that they do not require a specialized installer (of course, some complex modules do use specialized installers to make it easier for users to deploy). The files associated with a module can be copied by using the Xcopy utility, or they can be copied by using Windows PowerShell cmdlets.

Creating a per-user modules folder

The user's modules folder does not exist by default. To avoid confusion, you might decide to create the modules directory in the user's profile prior to deploying modules, or you might simply create a module-installer script (or even a logon script) that checks for the existence of the user's modules folder, creates the folder if it does not exist, and then copies the modules. One thing to remember when directly accessing the user's modules directory is that the modules folder is in a different location depending on the version of the operating system. On Windows XP and Windows Server 2003, the user's modules folder is in the My Documents folder, and on Windows Vista and later, the user's modules folder is in the Documents folder.

Note Windows PowerShell 5.0 does not install on Windows versions prior to Windows 7 or Windows 2008 R2. So, in a pure Windows PowerShell 5.0 environment, you can skip the operating system check and simply create the folder in the Documents folder. Or better yet, use PowerShellGet to do the installation (for more information, see Chapter 22, "Using the PowerShell Gallery").

In the Copy-Modules.ps1, you solve the problem of different modules folder locations by using the *Get-OperatingSystemVersion* function, which retrieves the major version number of the operating system. The *Get-OperatingSystemVersion* function is shown here.

```
Function Get-OperatingSystemVersion
{
 (Get-WmiObject -Class Win32_OperatingSystem).Version
} #end Get-OperatingSystemVersion
```

The *Test-ModulePath* function uses the major version number of the operating system. If the major version number of the operating system is greater than 6, the operating system is at least Windows Vista, and the function will therefore use the Documents folder in the path to the modules. If the major version number of the operating system is not greater than 6, the script will use the *My Documents* folder for the module location. When the version of the operating system is determined and the path to the module location is ascertained, it is time to determine whether the modules folders exist. The best tool for the job of checking for the existence of folders is the *Test-Path* cmdlet. The *Test-Path* cmdlet returns a Boolean value. Because you are only interested in the absence of the folder, you can use the *-not* operator in the completed *Test-ModulePath* function, as shown here.

```
Function Test-ModulePath
{
 $VistaPath = "$env:userProfile\documents\WindowsPowerShell\Modules"
 $XPPath =  "$env:Userprofile\my documents\WindowsPowerShell\Modules"
 if ([int](Get-OperatingSystemVersion).substring(0,1) -ge 6)
   {
     if(-not(Test-Path -path $VistaPath))
       {
         New-Item -Path $VistaPath -itemtype directory | Out-Null
       } #end if
   } #end if
Else
   {
     if(-not(Test-Path -path $XPPath))
       {
         New-Item -path $XPPath -itemtype directory | Out-Null
       } #end if
   } #end else
} #end Test-ModulePath
```

After the user's Modules folder has been created, it is time to create a child folder to hold the new module. A module installs into a folder that has the same name as the module itself. The name of the module is the name of the folder. For the module to be valid, it needs a file of the same name with either a .psm1 or .psd1 extension.

The location is shown in Figure 7-7.

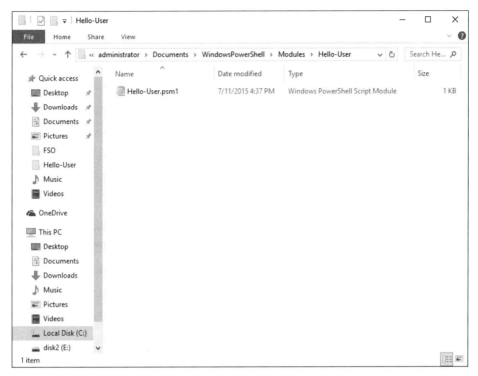

FIGURE 7-7 Modules are placed in the user's Modules directory.

In the *Copy-Module* function from the Copy-Modules.ps1 script, the first action retrieves the value of the *PSModulePath* environmental variable. Because there are two default locations in which modules can be stored, the *PSModulePath* environmental variable contains the path to both locations. *PSModulePath* is not stored as an array; it is stored as a string. The value contained in *PSModulePath* is shown here.

```
PS C:\> $env:PSModulePath
C:\Users\administrator\Documents\WindowsPowerShell\Modules;C:\Windows\system32\WindowsPowerShell
\v1.0\Modules\
```

If you attempt to index into the data stored in the *PSModulePath* environmental variable, you will retrieve one letter at a time. This is shown here.

```
PS C:\> $env:psmodulePath[0]
C
PS C:\> $env:psmodulePath[1]
:
PS C:\> $env:psmodulePath[2]
\
PS C:\> $env:psmodulePath[3]
U
```

Attempting to retrieve the path to the user's module location one letter at a time would be problematic at best and error prone at worst. Because the data is a string, you can use string methods to manipulate the two paths. To break a string into a usable array, you use the *Split* method from the *System.String* class. You only need to pass a single value to the *Split* method: the character upon which to split. Because the value stored in the *PSModulePath* environment variable is a set of strings separated by semicolons, you can access the *Split* method directly. This technique is shown here.

```
PS C:\> $env:PSModulePath.Split(";")
C:\Users\administrator\Documents\WindowsPowerShell\Modules
C:\Windows\system32\WindowsPowerShell\v1.0\Modules\
```

You can tell from the preceding output that the first string displayed is the path to the user's modules folder, and the second string is the path to the system modules folder. Because the *Split* method turns a string into an array, you can now index into the array and retrieve the path to the user's modules folder by using the *[0]* syntax. You do not need to use an intermediate variable to store the returned array of paths if you do not want to. You can index into the returned array directly. If you were to use the intermediate variable to hold the returned array, and then index into the array, the code would resemble the following.

```
PS C:\> $aryPaths = $env:PSModulePath.Split(";")
PS C:\> $aryPaths[0]
C:\Users\administrator\Documents\WindowsPowerShell\Modules
```

Because the array is immediately available after the *split* method has been called, you directly retrieve the user's modules path. This is shown here.

```
PS C:\> $env:PSModulePath.Split(";")[0]
C:\Users\administrator\Documents\WindowsPowerShell\Modules
```

Working with the *$modulePath* variable

The path that will be used to store the module is stored in the *$modulepath* variable. This path includes the path to the user's modules folder plus a child folder that has the same name as the module itself. To create the new path, it is a best practice to use the *Join-Path* cmdlet instead of doing string concatenation and attempting to manually build the path to the new folder. The *Join-Path* cmdlet will put together a parent path and a child path to create a new path. This is shown here.

```
$ModulePath = Join-Path -path $userPath `
            -childpath (Get-Item -path $name).basename
```

Windows PowerShell adds a script property called *basename* to the *System.Io.FileInfo* class. This makes it easy to retrieve the name of a file without the file extension. Prior to Windows PowerShell 2.0, it was common to use the *Split* method or some other string-manipulation technique to remove the extension from the file name. Use of the *BaseName* property is shown here.

```
PS C:\> (Get-Item -Path C:\fso\HelloWorld.psm1).basename
HelloWorld
```

Finally, you need to create the subdirectory that will hold the module, and copy the module files into the directory. To avoid cluttering the display with the returned information from the *New-Item* and *Copy-Item* cmdlets, the results are pipelined to the *Out-Null* cmdlet. This is shown here.

```
New-Item -path $modulePath -itemtype directory | Out-Null
Copy-Item -path $name -destination $ModulePath | Out-Null
```

The entry point to the Copy-Modules.ps1 script calls the *Test-ModulePath* function to determine whether the user's modules folder exists. It then uses the *Get-ChildItem* cmdlet to retrieve a listing of all the module files in a particular folder. The *-Recurse* switch parameter is used to retrieve all the module files in the path. The resulting *FileInfo* objects are pipelined to the *ForEach-Object* cmdlet. The *FullName* property of each *FileInfo* object is passed to the *Copy-Module* function. This is shown here.

```
Test-ModulePath
Get-ChildItem -Path C:\fso -Include *.psm1,*.psd1 -Recurse |
ForEach-Object { Copy-Module -name $_.fullname }
```

The complete Copy-Modules.ps1 script is shown here.

Copy-Modules.ps1
```
Function Get-OperatingSystemVersion
{
 (Get-WmiObject -Class Win32_OperatingSystem).Version
} #end Get-OperatingSystemVersion

Function Test-ModulePath
{
 $VistaPath = "$env:userProfile\documents\WindowsPowerShell\Modules"
 $XPPath =  "$env:Userprofile\my documents\WindowsPowerShell\Modules"
 if ([int](Get-OperatingSystemVersion).substring(0,1) -ge 6)
   {
     if(-not(Test-Path -path $VistaPath))
       {
          New-Item -Path $VistaPath -itemtype directory | Out-Null
       } #end if
   } #end if
 Else
   {
     if(-not(Test-Path -path $XPPath))
       {
          New-Item -path $XPPath -itemtype directory | Out-Null
       } #end if
   } #end else
} #end Test-ModulePath

Function Copy-Module([string]$name)
{
 $UserPath = $env:PSModulePath.split(";")[0]
 $ModulePath = Join-Path -path $userPath `
              -childpath (Get-Item -path $name).basename
 New-Item -path $modulePath -itemtype directory | Out-Null
 Copy-Item -path $name -destination $ModulePath | Out-Null
}
```

```
# *** Entry Point to Script ***
Test-ModulePath
Get-ChildItem -Path C:\fso -Include *.psm1,*.psd1 -Recurse |
ForEach-Object { Copy-Module -name $_.fullname }
```

> **Note** To use user-created script modules, you must set the script execution policy to permit
> the running of scripts. Script support does not need to be enabled in Windows PowerShell
> for you to be able to use the system modules. However, to run Copy-Modules.ps1 to install
> modules to the user's profile, you need scripting support. To enable scripting support in
> Windows PowerShell, you use the *Set-ExecutionPolicy* cmdlet.

Creating a module drive

An easy way to work with modules is to create a couple of Windows PowerShell drives by using the
filesystem provider. Because the modules live in a location that is not easily navigated to from the
command line, and because *$env:PSModulePath* returns a string that contains the path to both the
user's and system modules folders, it makes sense to provide an easier way to work with the modules'
locations. To create a Windows PowerShell drive for the user module location, you use the *New-PSDrive*
cmdlet, specify a name, such as mymods, use the filesystem provider, and obtain the root location
from the *$env:PSModulePath* environmental variable by using the *Split* method from the Microsoft
.NET Framework *String* class. For the user's modules folder, you use the first element from the returned
array. This is shown here.

```
PS C:\> New-PSDrive -Name mymods -PSProvider filesystem -Root ($env:PSModulePath.Split(";")[0])

Name          Used (GB)    Free (GB) Provider     Root
----          ---------    --------- --------     ----
mymods                        116.50 FileSystem   C:\Users\administrator\Docum...
```

The command to create a Windows PowerShell drive for the system module location is similar to the
one used to create a Windows PowerShell drive for the user module location. The differences are that
you would specify a different name, such as sysmods, and choose the second element from the array
obtained via the *Split* method call on the *$env:PSModulePath* variable. This command is shown here.

```
PS C:\> New-PSDrive -Name sysmods -PSProvider filesystem -Root ($env:PSModulePath.Split(";")[1])

Name          Used (GB)    Free (GB) Provider     Root
----          ---------    --------- --------     ----
sysmods                       116.50 FileSystem   C:\Windows\system32\WindowsP...
```

You can also write a script that creates Windows PowerShell drives for each of the two module
locations. To do this, you first create an array of names for the Windows PowerShell drives. You then
use a *For* statement to walk through the array of Windows PowerShell drive names and call the *New-
PSDrive* cmdlet. Because you are running the commands inside a script, the new Windows PowerShell
drives by default will live within the script scope. When the script ends, the script scope goes away.
This means that the Windows PowerShell drives will not be available when the script ends—which

would defeat your purposes in creating them in the first place. To combat this scoping issue, you need to create the Windows PowerShell drives within the global scope, which means that they will be available in the Windows PowerShell console after the script has completed running. To avoid displaying confirmation messages when creating the Windows PowerShell drives, you pipeline the results to the *Out-Null* cmdlet.

In the New-ModulesDrive.ps1 script, which is shown here, you create another function. This function displays global file system Windows PowerShell drives. When the script runs, call the *New-ModuleDrive* function. Then call the *Get-FileSystemDrives* function. The complete *New-ModuleDrive* function appears here.

```
New-ModuleDrive function
Function New-ModuleDrive
{
<#
    .SYNOPSIS
    Creates two PS drives: myMods and sysMods
    .EXAMPLE
    New-ModuleDrive
    Creates two PS drives: myMods and sysMods. These correspond
    to the users' modules folder and the system modules folder respectively.
#>
 $driveNames = "myMods","sysMods"

 For($i = 0 ; $i -le 1 ; $i++)
 {
  New-PSDrive -name $driveNames[$i] -PSProvider filesystem `
  -Root ($env:PSModulePath.split(";")[$i]) -scope Global |
  Out-Null
 } #end For
} #end New-ModuleDrive

Function Get-FileSystemDrives
{
<#
    .SYNOPSIS
    Displays global PS drives that use the filesystem provider
    .EXAMPLE
    Get-FileSystemDrives
    Displays global PS drives that use the filesystem provider
#>
 Get-PSDrive -PSProvider FileSystem -scope Global
} #end Get-FileSystemDrives

# *** EntryPoint to Script ***
New-ModuleDrive
Get-FileSystemDrives
```

This section covered the concept of installing modules. Before you install modules, create a special modules folder in the user's profile. In this section, a script was developed that will perform this action. The use of a *$modulepath* variable was examined. The section concluded with a script that creates a Windows PowerShell drive to provide easy access to installed modules.

Checking for module dependencies

One problem with using modules is that you now have a dependency to external code, and this means that a script that uses the module must have the module installed, or the script will fail. If you control the environment, an external dependency is not a bad thing; if you do not control the environment, an external dependency can be a disaster.

Because of the potential for problems, Windows PowerShell 5.0 contains the *#requires* statement. The *#requires* statement can check for Windows PowerShell version, modules, snap-ins, and even module and snap-in version numbers. Unfortunately, use of *#requires* only works in a script, not in a function, cmdlet, or snap-in. In addition, tab expansion does not work for the *#requires* statement. So you pretty much have to know what you want to require the script to do. Figure 7-8 illustrates the use of the *#requires* statement to ensure the presence of a specific module prior to script execution. The script requires a module named *bogus*, which does not exist. Because the *bogus* module does not exist, an error occurs.

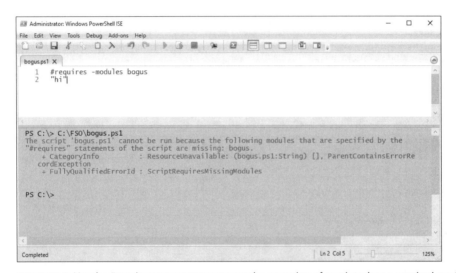

FIGURE 7-8 Use the *#requires* statement to prevent the execution of a script when a required module does not exist.

Because you cannot use the *#requires* statement inside a function, you might want to use the *Get-MyModule* function to determine whether a module exists or is already loaded (the other way to do this is to use a manifest). The complete *Get-MyModule* function is shown here.

Get-MyModule.ps1

```
Function Get-MyModule
{
 Param([string]$name)
 if(-not(Get-Module -name $name))
   {
     if(Get-Module -ListAvailable |
         Where-Object { $_.name -eq $name })
       {
         Import-Module -Name $name
         $true
```

```
        } #end if module available then import
     else { $false } #module not available
     } # end if not module
   else { $true } #module already loaded

} #end function get-MyModule

get-mymodule -name "bitsTransfer"
```

The *Get-MyModule* function accepts a single string: the name of the module to check. The *if* statement is used to determine whether the module is currently loaded. If it is not loaded, the *Get-Module* cmdlet is used to determine whether the module exists on the system. If it does exist, the module is loaded.

If the module is already loaded into the current Windows PowerShell session, the *Get-MyModule* function returns *$true* to the calling code. Let's dig into the function a bit further to look at how it works.

The first thing you do is use the *if* statement to determine whether the module is not loaded into the current session. To do this, use the *-not* operator to determine whether the module is not loaded. Use the *Get-Module* cmdlet to search for the required module by name. This section of the script is shown here.

```
Function Get-MyModule
{
 Param([string]$name)
 if(-not(Get-Module -name $name))
   {
```

To obtain a list of modules that are installed on a system, use the *Get-Module* cmdlet with the *-ListAvailable* switch. If the module exists on the system, the function uses the *Import-Module* cmdlet to import the module, and it returns *$true* to the calling code. This section of the script is shown here.

```
if(Get-Module -ListAvailable |
       Where-Object { $_.name -eq $name })
       {
        Import-Module -Name $name
        $true
       } #end if module available then import
```

Finally, you need to handle the two other cases. If the module is not available, the *Where-Object* cmdlet will not find anything. This triggers the first *else* clause, where *$false* is returned to the calling code. If the module is already loaded, the second *else* clause returns *$true* to the script. This section of the script is shown here.

```
     else { $false } #module not available
     } # end if not module
   else { $true } #module already loaded

} #end function get-MyModule
```

A simple use of the *Get-MyModule* function is to call the function and pass the name of a module to it. This example is actually shown in the last line of the Get-MyModule.ps1 script, as shown here.

```
get-mymodule -name "bitsTransfer"
```

When called in this manner, the *Get-MyModule* function will load the BitsTransfer module if it exists on your system and if it is not already loaded. If the module is already loaded, or if it is loaded by the function, *$true* is returned to the script. If the module does not exist, *$false* is returned. The use of the *Get-MyModule* function is shown in Figure 7-9.

FIGURE 7-9 Use the *Get-MyModule* function to ensure that a module exists prior to attempting to load it.

A better use of the *Get-MyModule* function is as a prerequisite check for a function that uses a particular module. Your syntax might look something like this.

```
If(Get-MyModule -name "bitsTransfer") { call your bits code here }
ELSE { "Bits module is not installed on this system. " ; exit }
```

Using a module from a share

Using a module from a central file share is no different from using a module from one of the three default locations. When a module is placed in the %windir%\System32\WindowsPowerShell\v1.0\Modules folder or the %SystemDrive%\Program Files\WindowsPowerShell\Modules folder, it is available to all users. If a module is placed in the %UserProfile%\My documents\WindowsPowerShell\Modules folder, it is only available to the specific user. The advantage of placing modules in the %UserProfile% location is that the user automatically has permission to perform the installation; modules in the system locations, however, require administrator rights.

On the subject of the installation of Windows PowerShell modules, in many cases the installation of a Windows PowerShell module is no more complicated than placing the *.psm1 file in a folder in the default user location. The key point is that the folder created under the \Modules folder must have the same name as the module itself. When you install a module on a local computer, use the Copy-Modules.ps1 script to simplify the process of creating and naming the folders.

When copying a Windows PowerShell module to a network-shared location, follow the same rules: make sure that the folder that contains the module has the same name as the module. In the following procedure, you'll copy the ConversionModuleV6 module to a network share.

Using a network-shared module

1. Create a share on a networked server and assign appropriate permissions.

2. Use the *Get-ChildItem* cmdlet (for which *dir* is the alias) to view the share and the associated modules. Here's an example.

```
PS C:\> dir '\\DC1\shared'


    Directory: \\DC1\shared


Mode                LastWriteTime     Length Name
----                -------------     ------ ----
d----         6/30/2015   1:00 PM            ConversionModuleV6
```

3. Import the module by using the *Import-Module* cmdlet and the Universal Naming Convention (UNC) path to the folder containing the module. The following command imports the module from the DC1 server.

```
PS C:\> Import-Module \\DC1\shared\Conv*
```

4. Verify that the module has loaded properly by using the *Get-Module* cmdlet. This command is shown here.

```
PS C:\> Get-Module

ModuleType Name                               ExportedCommands
---------- ----                               ----------------
Script     ConversionModuleV6                 {ConvertTo-celsius, ConvertTo-Fahr...
Manifest   Microsoft.PowerShell.Management    {Add-Computer, Add-Content, Checkp...
Manifest   Microsoft.PowerShell.Security      {ConvertFrom-SecureString, Convert...
Manifest   Microsoft.PowerShell.Utility       {Add-Member, Add-Type, Clear-Varia...
```

5. Use the *Get-Command* cmdlet to view the commands exported by the module. This technique is shown here (*gcm* is an alias for the *Get-Command* cmdlet).

```
PS C:\> gcm -Module conv*

CommandType     Name                                ModuleName
-----------     ----                                ----------
Function        ConvertTo-celsius                   ConversionModu...
Function        ConvertTo-Fahrenheit                ConversionModu...
Function        ConvertTo-Feet                      ConversionModu...
```

```
Function          ConvertTo-Kilometers                      ConversionModu...
Function          ConvertTo-Liters                          ConversionModu...
Function          ConvertTo-Meters                          ConversionModu...
Function          ConvertTo-MetersPerSecond                 ConversionModu...
Function          ConvertTo-Miles                           ConversionModu...
Function          ConvertTo-Pounds                          ConversionModu...
```

You need to keep in mind a couple of things. The first is that a Windows PowerShell module is basically a script—in our particular application. If the script execution policy is set to the default level of *Restricted*, an error will be generated—even if the logged-on user is an administrator. Fortunately, the error that is returned informs you of that fact. Even if the execution policy is set to *Restricted* on a particular machine, you can always run a Windows PowerShell script (or module) if you start Windows PowerShell with the *bypass* option. The command to do this is shown here.

```
powershell -executionpolicy bypass
```

One of the really cool uses of a shared module is to permit centralization of Windows PowerShell profiles for networked users. To do this, the profile on the local computer would simply import the shared module. In this way, you only need to modify one module in one location to permit updates for all the users on the network.

Creating a module

The first thing you will probably want to do is to create a module. You can create a module in the Windows PowerShell ISE. The easiest way to create a module is to use functions you have previously written. One of the first things to do is to locate the functions you want to store in the module. You can copy them directly into the Windows PowerShell ISE. This technique is shown in Figure 7-10.

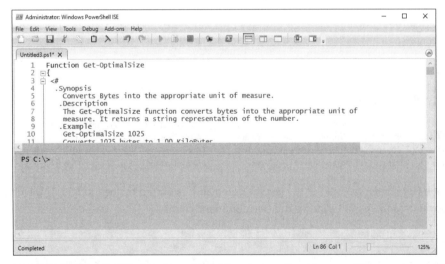

FIGURE 7-10 Using the Windows PowerShell ISE makes creating a new module as easy as copying and pasting existing functions into a new file.

After you have copied your functions into the new module, save it with the .psm1 extension. The basicFunctions.psm1 module is shown here.

BasicFunctions.psm1

```
Function Get-OptimalSize
{
 <#
  .Synopsis
   Converts Bytes into the appropriate unit of measure.
  .Description
   The Get-OptimalSize function converts bytes into the appropriate unit of
   measure. It returns a string representation of the number.
  .Example
   Get-OptimalSize 1025
   Converts 1025 bytes to 1.00 KiloBytes
   .Example
   Get-OptimalSize -sizeInBytes 10099999
   Converts 10099999 bytes to 9.63 MegaBytes
  .Parameter SizeInBytes
   The size in bytes to be converted
  .Inputs
   [int64]
  .OutPuts
   [string]
  .Notes
   NAME:  Get-OptimalSize
   AUTHOR: Ed Wilson
   LASTEDIT: 6/30/2015
   KEYWORDS: Scripting Techniques, Modules
  .Link
    Http://www.ScriptingGuys.com
 #Requires -Version 5.0
 #>
[CmdletBinding()]
param(
      [Parameter(Mandatory = $true,Position = 0,valueFromPipeline=$true)]
      [int64]
      $sizeInBytes
) #end param
 Switch ($sizeInBytes)
  {
   {$sizeInBytes -ge 1TB} {"{0:n2}" -f  ($sizeInBytes/1TB) + " TeraBytes";break}
   {$sizeInBytes -ge 1GB} {"{0:n2}" -f  ($sizeInBytes/1GB) + " GigaBytes";break}
   {$sizeInBytes -ge 1MB} {"{0:n2}" -f  ($sizeInBytes/1MB) + " MegaBytes";break}
   {$sizeInBytes -ge 1KB} {"{0:n2}" -f  ($sizeInBytes/1KB) + " KiloBytes";break}
   Default { "{0:n2}" -f $sizeInBytes + " Bytes" }
  } #end switch
  $sizeInBytes = $null
} #end Function Get-OptimalSize

Function Get-ComputerInfo
{
 <#
  .Synopsis
   Retrieves basic information about a computer.
  .Description
```

```
    The Get-ComputerInfo cmdlet retrieves basic information such as
    computer name, domain name, and currently logged on user from
    a local or remote computer.
   .Example
    Get-ComputerInfo
    Returns computer name, domain name and currently logged on user
    from local computer.
   .Example
    Get-ComputerInfo -computer berlin
    Returns computer name, domain name and currently logged on user
    from remote computer named berlin.
   .Parameter Computer
    Name of remote computer to retrieve information from
   .Inputs
    [string]
   .OutPuts
    [object]
   .Notes
    NAME:  Get-ComputerInfo
    AUTHOR: Ed Wilson
    LASTEDIT: 6/30/2015
    KEYWORDS: Desktop mgmt, basic information
   .Link
     Http://www.ScriptingGuys.com
 #Requires -Version 5.0
 #>
 Param([string]$computer=$env:COMPUTERNAME)
 $wmi = Get-WmiObject -Class win32_computersystem -ComputerName $computer
 $pcinfo = New-Object psobject -Property @{"host" = $wmi.DNSHostname
            "domain" = $wmi.Domain
            "user" = $wmi.Username}
 $pcInfo
} #end function Get-ComputerInfo
```

You can control what is exported from the module by creating a manifest (or you can control what the module exports by using the *Export-ModuleMember* cmdlet). If you place together related functions that you will more than likely want to use in a single session, you can avoid creating a manifest (although you might still want to create a manifest for documentation and for management purposes). In the BasicFunctions.psm1 module, there are two functions: one that converts numbers from bytes to a more easily understood numeric unit, and another function that returns basic computer information.

The *Get-ComputerInfo* function returns a custom object that contains information about the user, computer name, and computer domain. After you have created and saved the module, you will need to install the module by copying it to your module store. You can do this manually by navigating to the module directory, creating a folder for the module, and placing a copy of the module in the folder. I prefer to use the Copy-Modules.ps1 script discussed earlier in this chapter.

When the module has been copied to its own directory (installed), you can use the *Import-Module* cmdlet to import it into the current Windows PowerShell session.

If you are not sure of the name of the module, you can use the *Get-Module* cmdlet with the *-ListAvailable* switch, as shown here.

```
PS C:\> Get-Module -ListAvailable


    Directory: C:\Users\administrator\Documents\WindowsPowerShell\Modules


ModuleType Version    Name                            ExportedCommands
---------- -------    ----                            ----------------
Script     0.0        Basic-Functions                 {Get-OptimalSize, Get-C...
Script     0.0        Hello-User                      hello-user


    Directory: C:\Program Files\WindowsPowerShell\Modules


ModuleType Version    Name                            ExportedCommands
---------- -------    ----                            ----------------
Binary     1.0.0.0    PackageManagement               {Find-Package, Get-Pack...
Script     3.3.5      Pester                          {Describe, Context, It,...
Script     1.0        PowerShellGet                   {Install-Module, Find-M...
Script     1.1        PSReadline                      {Get-PSReadlineKeyHandl...


    Directory: C:\Windows\system32\WindowsPowerShell\v1.0\Modules


ModuleType Version    Name                            ExportedCommands
---------- -------    ----                            ----------------
Manifest   1.0.0.0    AppBackgroundTask               {Disable-AppBackgroundT...
Manifest   2.0.0.0    AppLocker                       {Get-AppLockerFileInfor...
Manifest   2.0.0.0    Appx                            {Add-AppxPackage, Get-A...
Script     1.0.0.0    AssignedAccess                  {Clear-AssignedAccess, ...
Manifest   1.0.0.0    BitLocker                       {Unlock-BitLocker, Susp...
Manifest   2.0.0.0    BitsTransfer                    {Add-BitsFile, Complete...
Manifest   1.0.0.0    BranchCache                     {Add-BCDataCacheExtensi...
Manifest   1.0.0.0    CimCmdlets                      {Get-CimAssociatedInsta...
Manifest   1.0        Defender                        {Get-MpPreference, Set-...
Manifest   1.0.0.0    DirectAccessClientComponents    {Disable-DAManualEntryP...
Script     3.0        Dism                            {Add-AppxProvisionedPac...
Manifest   1.0.0.0    DnsClient                       {Resolve-DnsName, Clear...
Manifest   1.0.0.0    EventTracingManagement          {New-EtwTraceSession, G...
Manifest   2.0.0.0    International                   {Get-WinDefaultInputMet...
Manifest   1.0.0.0    iSCSI                           {Get-IscsiTargetPortal,...
Script     1.0.0.0    ISE                             {New-IseSnippet, Import...
Manifest   1.0.0.0    Kds                             {Add-KdsRootKey, Get-Kd...
Manifest   1.0.0.0    Microsoft.PowerShell.Archive    {Compress-Archive, Expa...
Manifest   3.0.0.0    Microsoft.PowerShell.Diagnostics {Get-WinEvent, Get-Coun...
Manifest   3.0.0.0    Microsoft.PowerShell.Host       {Start-Transcript, Stop...
```

```
Manifest    3.1.0.0    Microsoft.PowerShell.Management     {Add-Content, Clear-Con...
Script      1.0        Microsoft.PowerShell.ODataUtils     Export-ODataEndpointProxy
Manifest    3.0.0.0    Microsoft.PowerShell.Security       {Get-Acl, Set-Acl, Get-...
Manifest    3.1.0.0    Microsoft.PowerShell.Utility        {Format-List, Format-Cu...
Manifest    3.0.0.0    Microsoft.WSMan.Management           {Disable-WSManCredSSP, ...
Manifest    1.0        MMAgent                              {Disable-MMAgent, Enabl...
Manifest    1.0.0.0    MsDtc                                {New-DtcDiagnosticTrans...
Manifest    2.0.0.0    NetAdapter                           {Disable-NetAdapter, Di...
Manifest    1.0.0.0    NetConnection                        {Get-NetConnectionProfi...
Manifest    1.0.0.0    NetEventPacketCapture                {New-NetEventSession, R...
Manifest    2.0.0.0    NetLbfo                              {Add-NetLbfoTeamMember,...
Manifest    1.0.0.0    NetNat                               {Get-NetNat, Get-NetNat...
Manifest    2.0.0.0    NetQos                               {Get-NetQosPolicy, Set-...
Manifest    2.0.0.0    NetSecurity                          {Get-DAPolicyChange, Ne...
Manifest    1.0.0.0    NetSwitchTeam                        {New-NetSwitchTeam, Rem...
Manifest    1.0.0.0    NetTCPIP                             {Get-NetIPAddress, Get-...
Manifest    1.0.0.0    NetworkConnectivityStatus            {Get-DAConnectionStatus...
Manifest    1.0.0.0    NetworkSwitchManager                 {Disable-NetworkSwitchE...
Manifest    1.0.0.0    NetworkTransition                    {Add-NetIPHttpsCertBind...
Manifest    1.0.0.0    PcsvDevice                           {Get-PcsvDevice, Start-...
Manifest    1.0.0.0    PKI                                  {Add-CertificateEnrollm...
Manifest    1.0.0.0    PnpDevice                            {Get-PnpDevice, Get-Pnp...
Manifest    1.1        PrintManagement                      {Add-Printer, Add-Print...
Manifest    1.1        PSDesiredStateConfiguration          {Set-DscLocalConfigurat...
Script      1.0.0.0    PSDiagnostics                        {Disable-PSTrace, Disab...
Binary      1.1.0.0    PSScheduledJob                       {New-JobTrigger, Add-Jo...
Manifest    2.0.0.0    PSWorkflow                           {New-PSWorkflowExecutio...
Manifest    1.0.0.0    PSWorkflowUtility                    Invoke-AsWorkflow
Manifest    1.0.0.0    ScheduledTasks                       {Get-ScheduledTask, Set...
Manifest    2.0.0.0    SecureBoot                           {Confirm-SecureBootUEFI...
Manifest    2.0.0.0    SmbShare                             {Get-SmbShare, Remove-S...
Manifest    2.0.0.0    SmbWitness                           {Get-SmbWitnessClient, ...
Manifest    1.0.0.0    StartLayout                          {Export-StartLayout, Im...
Manifest    2.0.0.0    Storage                              {Add-InitiatorIdToMaski...
Manifest    2.0.0.0    TLS                                  {New-TlsSessionTicketKe...
Manifest    1.0.0.0    TroubleshootingPack                  {Get-TroubleshootingPac...
Manifest    2.0.0.0    TrustedPlatformModule                {Get-Tpm, Initialize-Tp...
Manifest    2.0.0.0    VpnClient                            {Add-VpnConnection, Set...
Manifest    1.0.0.0    Wdac                                 {Get-OdbcDriver, Set-Od...
Manifest    1.0.0.0    WindowsDeveloperLicense              {Get-WindowsDeveloperLi...
Script      1.0        WindowsErrorReporting                {Enable-WindowsErrorRep...
Manifest    1.0.0.0    WindowsSearch                        {Get-WindowsSearchSetti...
Manifest    1.0.0.0    WindowsUpdate                        Get-WindowsUpdateLog
```

After you have imported the module, you can use the *Get-Command* cmdlet with the *-Module* parameter to determine what commands are exported by the module, as shown here.

```
PS C:\> ipmo Basic-Functions
PS C:\> Get-Command -Module basic*

CommandType     Name                            Version    Source
-----------     ----                            -------    ------
Function        Get-ComputerInfo                0.0        Bas...
Function        Get-OptimalSize                 0.0        Bas...
```

When you have added the functions from the module, you can use them directly from the Windows PowerShell prompt. Using the *Get-ComputerInfo* function is illustrated here.

```
PS C:\> Get-ComputerInfo

host                                domain                          user
----                                ------                          ----
mred1                               NWTraders.Com                   NWTRADERS\ed


PS C:\> (Get-ComputerInfo).user
NWTRADERS\ed
PS C:\> (Get-ComputerInfo).host
mred1
PS C:\> Get-ComputerInfo -computer C10 | Format-Table -AutoSize

host    domain          user
----    ------          ----
C10 NWTraders.Com NWTRADERS\Administrator


PS C:\>
```

Because the help tags were used when creating the functions, you can use the *Get-Help* cmdlet to obtain information about using the function. In this manner, the function that was created in the module behaves exactly like a regular Windows PowerShell cmdlet. This includes tab expansion. In the following output, the *Get-Help* cmdlet displays comment-based help from a function named *Get-ComputerInfo*.

```
PS C:\> Get-Help Get-ComputerInfo

NAME
    Get-ComputerInfo

SYNOPSIS
    Retrieves basic information about a computer.


SYNTAX
    Get-ComputerInfo [[-computer] <String>] [<CommonParameters>]


DESCRIPTION
    The Get-ComputerInfo cmdlet retrieves basic information such as
    computer name, domain name, and currently logged on user from
    a local or remote computer.


RELATED LINKS
    Http://www.ScriptingGuys.com
    #Requires -Version 5.0
```

To see the examples, type: "Get-Help Get-ComputerInfo -examples".
For more information, type: "Get-Help Get-ComputerInfo -detailed".
For technical information, type: "Get-Help Get-ComputerInfo -full".


```
PS C:\> Get-Help Get-ComputerInfo -Examples
```

NAME
    Get-ComputerInfo

SYNOPSIS
    Retrieves basic information about a computer.

    ------------------------ EXAMPLE 1 ------------------------

    C:\PS>Get-ComputerInfo

    Returns computer name, domain name and currently logged on user
    from local computer.

    ------------------------ EXAMPLE 2 ------------------------

    C:\PS>Get-ComputerInfo -computer berlin

    Returns computer name, domain name and currently logged on user
    from remote computer named berlin.


```
PS C:\>
```

The *Get-OptimalSize* function can even receive input from the pipeline, as shown here.

```
PS C:\> (Get-WmiObject win32_volume -Filter "driveletter = 'c:'").freespace
26513960960
PS C:\> (Get-WmiObject win32_volume -Filter "driveletter = 'c:'").freespace | Get-OptimalSize
24.69 GigaBytes
PS C:\>
```

Creating, installing, and importing a module

1. Place functions into a text file and save the file with a .psm1 extension.

2. Copy the newly created module containing the functions to the modules directory. Use the
   Copy-Modules.ps1 script to do this.

3. Obtain a listing of available modules by using the *Get-Modules* cmdlet with the *-ListAvailable* switch parameter.

4. Optionally, import modules into your current Windows PowerShell session by using the *Import-Module* cmdlet.

5. List the commands that are available from the newly created module by using the *Get-Command* cmdlet with the *-Module* parameter.

6. Use *Get-Help* to obtain information about the imported functions.

7. Use the functions as you would use any other cmdlet.

Creating an advanced function and installing a module: Step-by-step exercises

In this exercise, you'll explore creating an advanced function. You will use a template from the Windows PowerShell ISE to create the basic framework. Next, you will add help and functionality to the advanced function. Following this exercise, you will add the advanced function to a module and install the module on your system.

Creating an advanced function

1. Start the Windows PowerShell ISE.

2. Use the *cmdlet (advanced function)* snippet from the Windows PowerShell ISE to create the basic framework for an advanced function.

3. Move the comment-based help from outside the function body to inside the function body. The moved comment-based help is shown here.

```
function Verb-Noun
{
 <#
.Synopsis
   Short description
.DESCRIPTION
   Long description
.EXAMPLE
   Example of how to use this cmdlet
.EXAMPLE
   Another example of how to use this cmdlet
#>
```

4. Change the name of the function from *Verb-Noun* to Get-MyBios. This change is shown here.

```
function Get-MyBios
```

5. Modify the comment-based help. Fill in the synopsis, description, and example parameters. Add a comment for *parameter*. This revised comment-based help is shown here.

```
<#
.Synopsis
   Gets bios information from local or remote computer
.DESCRIPTION
   This function gets bios information from local or remote computer
.Parameter computername
 The name of the remote computer
.EXAMPLE
   Get-MyBios
   Gets bios information from local computer
.EXAMPLE
   Get-MyBios -cn remoteComputer
   Gets bios information from remote computer named remotecomputer
#>
```

6. Add the *#requires* statement and require Windows PowerShell version 5.0. This command is shown here.

```
#requires -version 5.0
```

7. Modify the parameter name to computername. Add an *alias* attribute with a value of *cn*. Configure parameter properties for *ValueFromPipeline* and *ParameterSetName*. Constrain the *computername* parameter to be a string. The code to do this is shown here.

```
Param
    (
        # name of remote computer
        [Alias("cn")]
        [Parameter(ValueFromPipeline=$true,
                   Position=0,
                   ParametersetName="remote")]
        [string]
        $ComputerName)
```

8. Remove the *begin* and *end* statements from the snippet.

9. Add a *Switch* statement within the Process script block that evaluates *$PSCmdlet.Parameter-SetName*. If *ParameterSetName* equals *remote*, use the *-ClassName* and *-ComputerName* parameters from the *Get-CimInstance* cmdlet. Default to querying the *Get-CimInstance* cmdlet without using the *-ComputerName* parameter. The *Switch* statement is shown here.

```
Switch ($PSCmdlet.ParameterSetName)
    {
      "remote" { Get-CimInstance -ClassName win32_bios -cn $ComputerName }
       DEFAULT { Get-CimInstance -ClassName Win32_BIOS }
     } #end switch
```

10. Save the advanced function as Get-MyBios.ps1 in an easily accessible folder, because you'll turn this into a module in the next exercise.

11. Inside the Windows PowerShell ISE, run the function.

12. In the command pane, call the *Get-MyBios* function with no parameters. You should receive back BIOS information from your local computer.

13. Now call the *Get-MyBios* function with the *-cn* alias and the name of a remote computer. You should receive BIOS information from the remote computer.

14. Use *help* and view the full help from the advanced function. Sample output is shown here.

```
PS C:\> help Get-MyBios -Full

NAME
    Get-MyBios

SYNOPSIS
    Gets bios information from local or remote computer

SYNTAX
    Get-MyBios [[-ComputerName] <String>] [<CommonParameters>]

DESCRIPTION
    This function gets bios information from local or remote computer

PARAMETERS
    -ComputerName <String>
        The name of the remote computer

        Required?                 false
        Position?                 1
        Default value
        Accept pipeline input?    true (ByValue)
        Accept wildcard characters?  false

    <CommonParameters>
        This cmdlet supports the common parameters: Verbose, Debug,
        ErrorAction, ErrorVariable, WarningAction, WarningVariable,
        OutBuffer and OutVariable. For more information, see
        about_CommonParameters (http://go.microsoft.com/fwlink/?LinkID=113216).

INPUTS

OUTPUTS

    ------------------------- EXAMPLE 1 -------------------------

    C:\PS>Get-MyBios


    Gets bios information from local computer


    ------------------------- EXAMPLE 2 -------------------------

    C:\PS>Get-MyBios -cn remoteComputer
```

```
Gets bios information from remote computer named remotecomputer

requires -version 5.0
```

RELATED LINKS

This concludes this step-by-step exercise.

In the following exercise, you'll explore creating a module.

Creating and installing a module

1. Start the Windows PowerShell ISE.

2. Open the Get-MyBios.ps1 file you created in the previous exercise and copy the contents into an empty Windows PowerShell ISE script pane.

3. Save the newly copied code as a module by specifying the .psm1 file extension. Name your file mybios.psm1. Choose the Save As option from the File menu, and save the file in a convenient location.

4. In your mybios.psm1 file, just after the end of the script block for the *Get-MyBios* function, use the *New-Alias* cmdlet to create a new alias named gmb. Set the value of this alias to *Get-MyBios*. This command is shown here.

   ```
   New-Alias -Name gmb -Value Get-MyBios
   ```

5. Add the *Export-ModuleMember* cmdlet to the script to export all aliases and functions from the mybios module. This command is shown here.

   ```
   Export-ModuleMember -Function * -Alias *
   ```

6. Save your changes and close the module file.

7. Use the *Copy-Modules* script to create a modules folder named mybios in your current user's directory and copy the module to that location.

8. Open the Windows PowerShell console and use the *Import-Module* cmdlet to import the mybios module. This command is shown here.

   ```
   Import-Module mybios
   ```

9. Use the *Get-MyBios* advanced function to return the BIOS information from the current computer.

10. Use the *Help* function to retrieve complete help information from the advanced function. This command is shown here.

    ```
    help Get-MyBios -full
    ```

11. Pipeline the name of a remote computer to the *Get-MyBios* advanced function. This command is shown here.

```
"w8s504" | Get-MyBios
```

This concludes the exercise.

Chapter 7 quick reference

To	Do this
Display help for a command that is missing a parameter	Use the *HelpMessage* parameter property.
Make a parameter mandatory	Use the *Mandatory* parameter property in the *param* section of the function.
Implement -*Verbose* in a function	Use the *[cmdletbinding()]* attribute and write the messages via the *Write-Verbose* cmdlet.
Implement the -*WhatIf* switch parameter in a function	Use the *[cmdletbinding()]* attribute with the *SupportsShouldProcess* property.
Ensure that only defined parameters pass values to the function	Use the *[cmdletbinding()]* attribute.
Group sets of parameters for ease of use and checking	Create a parameter set via the *ParameterSetName* parameter property.
Assign a specific position to a parameter	Use the *Position* parameter property and assign a specific zero-based numeric position.

Using the Windows PowerShell ISE

After completing this chapter, you will be able to

- Understand the use of tab completion to complete cmdlet names, types, and paths.

- Use code snippets to simplify programming.

- Use the Commands add-on to run or insert commands.

- Run script commands without saving the script.

- Write, save, and load a Windows PowerShell script.

Running the Windows PowerShell ISE

On a Windows 10 computer, the Windows PowerShell ISE seems to be hidden. In fact, on a Windows Server 2012 R2 computer, it also is a bit hidden. However, on a Windows Server 2012 R2 computer, a Windows PowerShell shortcut automatically appears on the desktop taskbar. Likewise, pinning Windows PowerShell to the Windows 10 desktop taskbar is a Windows PowerShell best practice. To start the Windows PowerShell ISE, you have a couple of choices. On the Start page of Windows Server 2012, you can enter **PowerShell**, and both Windows PowerShell and the Windows PowerShell ISE appear as search results. However, in Windows 10, this is not the case. You must enter **PowerShell_ISE** to find the Windows PowerShell ISE. You can also launch the Windows PowerShell ISE by right-clicking the Windows PowerShell icon and choosing either Open or Run As Administrator from the Tasks menu that appears. This Tasks menu (produced from a pinned icon on the taskbar) is shown in Figure 8-1.

Inside the Windows PowerShell console, you only need to enter **ise** to launch the Windows PowerShell ISE. This shortcut gives you quick access to the Windows PowerShell ISE when you need to enter more than a few interactive commands.

Open
Open file location
Run as administrator
Run as different user
Pin to Start
Unpin from taskbar

Copy as path
Restore previous versions

Send to   >

Cut
Copy

Create shortcut
Delete
Rename

Properties

FIGURE 8-1 Holding down the Shift key and right-clicking the Windows PowerShell icon on the desktop taskbar brings up the Tasks menu, from which you can launch the Windows PowerShell ISE.

Navigating the Windows PowerShell ISE

When the Windows PowerShell ISE launches, two panes appear. On the left side of the screen is an interactive Windows PowerShell console. On the right side of the screen is the Commands add-on. The Commands add-on is really a Windows PowerShell command explorer window. When you are using the Windows PowerShell ISE in an interactive fashion, the Commands add-on provides you with the ability to build a command by using the mouse. After you have built the command, click the Run button to copy the command to the console window and execute the command. This view of the Windows PowerShell ISE is shown in Figure 8-2.

Entering something into the Name box causes the Commands add-on to search through all Windows PowerShell modules to retrieve a matching command. This is a great way to discover and locate commands. By default, the Commands add-on uses a wildcard search pattern. Therefore, entering **wmi** returns five cmdlets that include that letter pattern. This is shown in Figure 8-3.

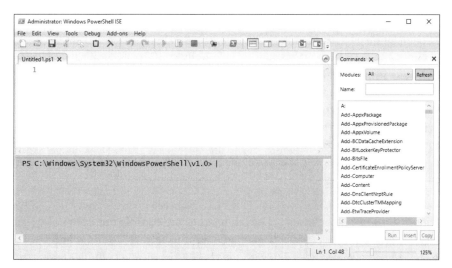

FIGURE 8-2 The Windows PowerShell ISE presents a Windows PowerShell console on the left and a Commands add-on on the right side of the screen.

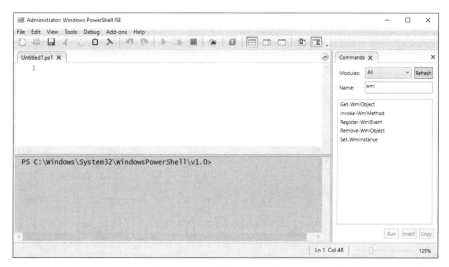

FIGURE 8-3 The Commands add-on uses a wildcard search pattern to find matching cmdlets.

When you find the cmdlet that interests you, select it from the filtered list of cmdlet names. Upon selection, the Commands pane changes to display the parameters for the selected cmdlet. Each parameter set appears on a different tab. Screen resolution really affects the usability of this feature. The greater the screen resolution, the more usable this feature becomes. With a small resolution, you have to scroll back and forth to see the parameter sets, and you have to scroll up and down to see the available parameters for a particular parameter set. In this view, it is easy to miss important parameters. In Figure 8-4, the *Get-WmiObject* cmdlet queries the *Win32_Bios* Windows Management Instrumentation (WMI) class. After entering the WMI class name in the Class box, click the Run button to execute the command. The console pane displays first the command, and then the output from running the command.

> **Note** Clicking the Insert button inserts the command to the console but does not execute the command. This is great for occasions when you want to review the command prior to actually executing it. It also provides you with the chance to edit the command prior to execution.

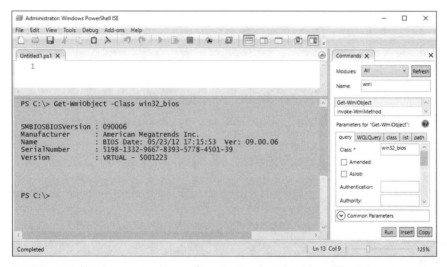

FIGURE 8-4 Select the command to run from the Commands add-on, fill out the required parameters, and click Run to execute Windows PowerShell cmdlets inside the Windows PowerShell ISE.

Finding and running commands via the Commands add-on

1. In the Name box of the Commands add-on, enter the command you are interested in running.

2. Select the command from the filtered list.

3. Enter the parameters in the *Parameters For* box.

4. Click the Run button when finished.

Working with the script pane

Clicking the arrow beside the word *script* in the upper-right corner of the console pane reveals a new script pane into which you can start entering a script. This only appears if you have the console pane (the bottom pane) maximized. You can also obtain a new script pane by selecting New from the File menu or clicking the small white piece-of-paper icon in the upper-left corner of the Windows PowerShell ISE. You can also use the keyboard shortcut Ctrl+N.

Although it is called the *script pane*, you don't have to enable script support to use it. As long as the file is not saved, you can enter commands that are as complex as you want into the script pane, with script support restricted, and the code will run when you execute it. When the file is saved, however, it becomes a script, and you will need to deal with the script execution policy at that point.

You can still use the Commands add-on with the script pane, but doing so requires an extra step. Use the Commands add-on as described in the previous section, but instead of using the Run or the Insert button, use the Copy button. Navigate to the appropriate section in the script pane, and then use the Paste command (which you can access from the shortcut menu, from the Edit menu, by clicking the Paste icon on the toolbar, or by pressing Ctrl+V).

> **Note** If you click the Insert button while the script pane is maximized, the command is inserted into the hidden console pane. Clicking Insert a second time inserts the command a second time on the same command line in the hidden console pane. You will receive no notification that this has occurred.

To run commands present in the script pane, click the Run Script button (the green triangle in the middle of the toolbar), press F5, or choose Run from the File menu. The commands from the script pane are transferred to the console pane and then executed. Any output associated with the commands appears under the transferred commands. When saved as a script, the commands no longer are transferred to the command pane. Rather, the path to the script appears in the console pane along with any associated output.

You can continue to use the Commands add-on to build your commands as you pipeline the output from one cmdlet to another one. In Figure 8-5, the output from the *Get-WmiObject* cmdlet is pipelined to the *Format-Table* cmdlet. The properties chosen in the *Format-Table* cmdlet and the implementation of the -*Wrap* switch are configured via the Commands add-on.

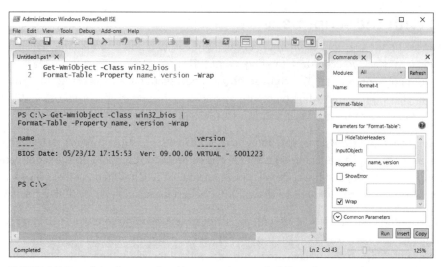

FIGURE 8-5 Use of the Commands add-on permits easy building of commands.

Using tab expansion and IntelliSense

Novice scripters will find the Commands add-on very useful, but it does consume valuable screen real estate, and it requires the use of the mouse to find and create commands. For advanced scripters, tab expansion and IntelliSense are the keys to productivity. To turn off the Commands add-on, either click the X in the upper-right corner of the Commands add-on or cancel the selection of the Show Commands Add-On option on the View menu. After you've done this, the Windows PowerShell ISE remembers your preference and will not display the Commands add-on again until you reselect the option.

IntelliSense provides pop-up help and options while you type, permitting rapid command development without requiring complete syntax knowledge. As you are entering a cmdlet name, IntelliSense supplies possible matches. When you select the cmdlet, IntelliSense displays the complete syntax of the cmdlet. This is shown in Figure 8-6.

After selecting a cmdlet, if you enter parameter names, IntelliSense displays the applicable parameters in a list. When IntelliSense appears, use the Up Arrow and Down Arrow keys to navigate within the list. Press Enter to accept the highlighted option. You can then fill in required values for parameters and go to the next parameter. Again, as you approach a parameter position, IntelliSense displays the appropriate options in a list. This process continues until you complete the command. IntelliSense even provides enum expansion, displaying valid enum values for specific parameters. Figure 8-7 illustrates the selection of the *Recurse* parameter from the IntelliSense list of optional parameters.

FIGURE 8-6 When you select a particular cmdlet from the list, IntelliSense displays the complete syntax.

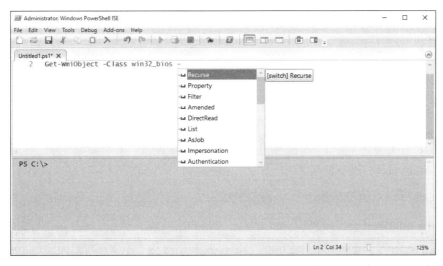

FIGURE 8-7 IntelliSense displays parameters in a drop-down list. When you select a particular parameter, the data type of the property appears.

Working with Windows PowerShell ISE snippets

Snippets are pieces of code, or code fragments. They are designed to simplify routine coding tasks by permitting the insertion of boilerplate code directly into the script. Even experienced scripters love to use the Windows PowerShell ISE snippets because they are great time savers. It takes just a little bit of familiarity with the snippets themselves, along with a bit of experience with the Windows PowerShell syntax. When you have met these requirements, you will be able to use the Windows PowerShell ISE snippets and create code faster than you previously believed was possible. The great thing is that you can create your own snippets, and even share them with others via the TechNet wiki.

Using Windows PowerShell ISE snippets to create code

To start the Windows PowerShell ISE snippets, use the Ctrl+J key combination (you can also use the mouse to choose Start Snippets from the Edit menu). When the snippets appear, enter the first letter of the snippet name to quickly jump to the appropriate portion of the snippets (you can also use the mouse to navigate up and down the snippet list). When you have identified the snippet you want to use, press Enter to place the snippet at the current insertion point in your Windows PowerShell script pane.

The following two exercises go into greater depth about working with snippets.

Creating a new function by using Windows PowerShell ISE snippets

1. Press Ctrl+J to start the Windows PowerShell ISE snippets.

2. Enter **f** to move to the "F" section of the Windows PowerShell ISE snippets.

3. Press the Down Arrow key until you arrive at the simple *function* snippet.

4. Press Enter to enter the simple *function* snippet into your code.

Using Windows PowerShell ISE snippets to complete a simple function

1. Start the Windows PowerShell ISE.

2. Add a new script pane. To do this, press Ctrl+N.

3. Start the Windows PowerShell ISE snippets by pressing Ctrl+J.

4. Select the simple *function* snippet and add it to your script pane. Use the Down Arrow key to select the snippet, and press Enter to insert it into your script.

5. Move the cursor to inside the script block for the function.

6. Start the Windows PowerShell ISE snippets again by pressing Ctrl+J.

7. Select the *switch* statement by entering **s** to move to the "Switch" section of the snippet list. Press Enter to insert the snippet into your script block.

8. Double-click *$param1*, and press Ctrl+C to copy the parameter name. Double-click *value1* and press Ctrl+V to paste *$param1*.

9. Double-click *$param2* to select it, and press Ctrl+C to copy the parameter name. Double-click *value3* to select it, and press Ctrl+V to paste *param2*.

10. Check your work. At this point, your code should appear as shown here.

```
function MyFunction ($param1, $param2)
{
    switch ($x)
    {
        'param1' {}
        {$_ -in 'A','B','C'} {}
        'param2' {}
        Default {}
    }
}
```

11. Delete the following line, because it will not be used.

```
{$_ -in 'A','B','C'} {}
```

12. Delete the line for the default parameter, shown here.

```
Default {}
```

13. Replace the *$x* condition with the code to display the keys of the bound parameters collection. This line of code is shown here.

```
$MyInvocation.BoundParameters.Keys
```

14. In the script block for *param1*, add a line of code that describes the parameter and displays the value. The code is shown here.

```
"param1" { "param1 is $param1" }
```

15. In the script block for *param2*, add a line of code that describes the parameter and displays the value. The code is shown here.

```
"param2" { "param2 is $param2" }
```

The completed function is shown here.

```
function MyFunction ($param1, $param2)
{
    switch ($MyInvocation.BoundParameters.Keys)
    {
     "param1" { "param1 is $param1" }
     "param2" { "param2 is $param2" }
     }
}
```

This concludes the procedure.

Creating new Windows PowerShell ISE snippets

After you spend a bit of time using Windows PowerShell ISE snippets, you will wonder how you ever existed previously. In that same instant, you will also begin to think in terms of new snippets. Luckily, it is very easy to create a new Windows PowerShell ISE snippet. In fact, there is even a cmdlet to do this: the *New-IseSnippet* cmdlet.

> **Note** To create or use a user-defined Windows PowerShell ISE snippet, you must change the script execution policy to permit the execution of scripts. This is because user-defined snippets load from XML files. Reading and loading files (of any type) requires the script execution policy to permit running scripts. To verify your script execution policy, use the *Get-ExecutionPolicy* cmdlet. To set the script execution policy, use the *Set-ExecutionPolicy* cmdlet.

You can use the *New-IseSnippet* cmdlet to create a new Windows PowerShell ISE snippet. After you create the snippet, it becomes immediately available in the Windows PowerShell ISE when you start the Windows PowerShell ISE snippets. The command syntax is simple, but the command takes a fairly large amount of space to complete. Only three parameters are required: *Description*, *Text*, and *Title*. The name of the snippet is specified via the *Title* parameter. The snippet itself is entered into the *Text* parameter. A great way to simplify snippet creation is to place the snippet into a *here-string* object, and then pass that value to the *New-IseSnippet* cmdlet. When you want your code to appear on multiple lines, use the `r special character. Of course, doing this means that your *Text* parameter must appear inside double quotation marks, not single quotation marks. The following code creates a new Windows PowerShell ISE snippet that has a simplified *switch* syntax. It is a single logical line of code.

```
New-IseSnippet -Title SimpleSwitch -Description "A simple switch statement"
-Author "ed wilson" -Text "Switch () `r{'param1' {  }`r}" -CaretOffset 9
```

When you execute the *New-IseSnippet* command, it creates a new snippets.xml file in the Snippets directory within your WindowsPowerShell folder in your Documents folder. The simple *switch* snippet XML file is shown in Figure 8-8.

User-defined snippets are permanent—that is, they survive closing and reopening the Windows PowerShell ISE. They also survive restarts because they reside as XML files in your WindowsPowerShell folder.

FIGURE 8-8 Windows PowerShell snippets are stored in a **.snippets.xml* file in your WindowsPowerShell folder.

Removing user-defined Windows PowerShell ISE snippets

Although there is a *New-IseSnippet* cmdlet and there is a *Get-IseSnippet* cmdlet, there is no *Remove-IseSnippet* cmdlet. There is no need for one, really, because you can use *Remove-Item* instead. To delete all of your custom Windows PowerShell ISE snippets, use the *Get-IseSnippet* cmdlet to retrieve the snippets and the *Remove-Item* cmdlet to delete them. The command is shown here.

```
Get-IseSnippet | Remove-Item
```

If you do not want to delete all of your custom Windows PowerShell ISE snippets, use the *Where-Object* cmdlet to filter only the ones you do want to delete. The following uses the *Get-IseSnippet* cmdlet to list all the user-defined Windows PowerShell ISE snippets on the system.

```
PS C:\> Get-IseSnippet


    Directory: C:\Users\administrator\Documents\WindowsPowerShell\Snippets


Mode                LastWriteTime         Length Name
----                -------------         ------ ----
-a----         7/11/2015     5:45 PM          702 AnotherSnippet.snippets.ps1xml
-a----         7/11/2015     5:45 PM          707 BogusSnippet.snippets.ps1xml
-a----         7/11/2015     5:39 PM          708 SimpleSwitch.snippets.ps1xml
```

Next, use the *Where-Object* cmdlet (*?* is an alias for *Where-Object*) to return all of the user-defined Windows PowerShell ISE snippets except the ones that contain the word *switch* within the name. The snippets that make it through the filter are pipelined to the *Remove-Item* cmdlet. In the code that follows, the *-WhatIf* switch parameter shows which snippets would be removed by the command.

```
PS C:\> Get-IseSnippet | ? name -NotMatch 'switch' | Remove-Item -WhatIf
What if: Performing the operation "Remove File" on target
"C:\Users\administrator\Documents\Windo
wsPowerShell\Snippets\AnotherSnippet.snippets.ps1xml".
What if: Performing the operation "Remove File" on target
"C:\Users\administrator\Documents\Windo
wsPowerShell\Snippets\BogusSnippet.snippets.ps1xml".
```

When you have confirmed that only the snippets you do not want to keep will be deleted, remove the *-WhatIf* switch parameter from the *Remove-Item* cmdlet and run the command a second time. To confirm which snippets remain, use the *Get-IseSnippet* cmdlet to find out which Windows PowerShell ISE snippets are left on the system, as shown here.

```
PS C:\> Get-IseSnippet | ? name -NotMatch 'switch' | Remove-Item

PS C:\> Get-IseSnippet


    Directory: C:\Users\administrator\Documents\WindowsPowerShell\Snippets


Mode                LastWriteTime         Length Name
----                -------------         ------ ----
-a----        7/11/2015     5:39 PM          708 SimpleSwitch.snippets.ps1xml
```

Using the Commands add-on and snippets: Step-by-step exercises

In this exercise, you will explore using the Commands add-on by looking for cmdlets related to WMI. You will then select the *Invoke-WmiMethod* cmdlet from the list and create new processes. Following this exercise, you will use Windows PowerShell ISE snippets to create a WMI script.

Using the Commands add-on to call WMI methods

1.   Start the Windows PowerShell ISE.

2.   Use the Commands add-on to search for cmdlets related to WMI.

3.   Select the *Invoke-WmiMethod* cmdlet from the list.

4. In the *class* block, add the WMI class name **Win32_Process**.

5. In the *name* block, enter the method name **create**.

6. In the argument list, enter **notepad**.

7. Click the Run button. In the output console, you should get the following command, and on the next line the output from the command. The command and sample output are shown here.

Note Your *processID* will more than likely be different than mine.

```
PS C:\Windows\system32> Invoke-WmiMethod -Class win32_process -Name create -ArgumentList
notepad
```

```
__GENUS          : 2
__CLASS          : __PARAMETERS
__SUPERCLASS     :
__DYNASTY        : __PARAMETERS
__RELPATH        :
__PROPERTY_COUNT : 2
__DERIVATION     : {}
__SERVER         :
__NAMESPACE      :
__PATH           :
ProcessId        : 2960
ReturnValue      : 0
PSComputerName   :
```

8. Modify the *ArgumentList* block by adding *calc* to the argument list. Use a semicolon to separate the arguments, as shown here.

```
Notepad; calc
```

9. Click the Run button a second time to execute the revised command.

10. In the Commands add-on, look for cmdlets with the word *process* in the name. Select the *Stop-Process* cmdlet from the list of cmdlets.

11. Choose the *name* parameter set in the *parameters for Stop-Process* block.

Note On Windows 10, *calc* launches calculator.exe. You will need to substitute *calculator* for *calc* on Windows 10.

12. In the Name box, enter **notepad** and **calc**. The command is shown here.

```
notepad, calc
```

13. Click the Run button to execute the command.

14. Under the *name* block showing the process-related cmdlets, choose the *Get-Process* cmdlet.

15. In the *name* parameter set, enter **calc, notepad**.

16. Click the Run button to execute the command.

Two errors should appear, stating that the *calc* and *notepad* processes aren't running. The errors are shown here.

```
PS C:\Windows\system32> Get-Process -Name calc, notepad
Get-Process : Cannot find a process with the name "calc". Verify the process
name and call the cmdlet again.
At line:1 char:1
+ Get-Process -Name calc, notepad
+ ~~~~~~~~~~~~~~~~~~~~~~~~~~~~~~~~
    + CategoryInfo          : ObjectNotFound: (calc:String) [Get-Process],
    ProcessCommandException
    + FullyQualifiedErrorId : NoProcessFoundForGivenName,Microsoft.PowerShell.
    Commands.GetProcessCommand

Get-Process : Cannot find a process with the name "notepad". Verify the
process name and call the cmdlet again.
At line:1 char:1
+ Get-Process -Name calc, notepad
+ ~~~~~~~~~~~~~~~~~~~~~~~~~~~~~~~~
    + CategoryInfo          : ObjectNotFound: (notepad:String) [Get-Process],
    ProcessCommandException
    + FullyQualifiedErrorId : NoProcessFoundForGivenName,Microsoft.PowerShell.
    Commands.GetProcessCommand
```

This concludes the exercise. Leave the Windows PowerShell ISE console open for the next exercise.

In the following exercise, you will explore using Windows PowerShell ISE snippets to simplify script creation.

Using Windows PowerShell ISE snippets

1. Start the Windows PowerShell ISE.

2. Close the Commands add-on.

3. Display the script pane.

4. Use the *Get-WmiObject* cmdlet to retrieve a listing of process objects from the local host. Store the returned process objects in a variable named *$process*. As you enter the command, ensure that you use IntelliSense to reduce typing. You should be able to enter **Get-Wm** and press Enter to select the *Get-WmiObject* cmdlet from the IntelliSense list. You should also be able to enter **-c** and then press Enter to choose the -*Class* parameter from the IntelliSense list. The complete command is shown here.

```
$process = Get-WmiObject -Class win32_process
```

5. Use the *foreach* code snippet to walk through the collection of process objects stored in the *$process* variable. To do this, press Ctrl+J to start the code snippets. When the snippet list appears, enter **f** to quickly move to the "F" section of the snippets. To choose the *foreach* snippet, you can continue to enter **fore** and then press Enter to add the *foreach* snippet to your code. It is easier, however, to use the Down Arrow key when you are in the "F" section of the snippets. The complete *foreach* snippet is shown here.

```
foreach ($item in $collection)
{

}
```

6. Change the *$collection* variable in the *foreach* snippet to *$process* because that variable holds your collection of process objects. The easiest way to do this is to double-click the *$process* variable on line 1 of your code. Doing this only selects the noun portion of variable name, not the dollar sign. So the technique is to double-click *$process*, press Ctrl+C, double-click *$collection*, and press Ctrl+V. The *foreach* snippet now appears as shown here.

```
foreach ($item in $process)
{

}
```

7. Inside the script block portion of the *foreach* snippet, use the *$item* variable to display the name of each process object. The code to do this is shown here.

```
$item.name
```

8. Run the code by either clicking the green triangle on the toolbar or pressing F5. The output should list the name of each process on your system. The completed code is shown here.

```
$process = Get-WmiObject -Class win32_process
foreach ($item in $process)
{
    $item.name
}
```

This concludes the exercise.

Chapter 8 quick reference

To	Do this
Create a Windows PowerShell command without typing	Use the Commands add-on.
Find a specific Windows PowerShell command	Use the Commands add-on and enter a search term in the *Name* box.
Quickly enter a command in either the script pane or the console pane	Use IntelliSense and press Enter to use the selected command or parameter.
Run a script from the Windows PowerShell ISE	Press F5 to run the entire script.
Create a user-defined Windows PowerShell ISE snippet	Use the *New-IseSnippet* cmdlet and enter the *Title*, *Description*, and *Text* parameters.
Remove all user-defined Windows PowerShell ISE snippets	Use the *Get-IseSnippet* cmdlet and pipeline the results to the *Remove-Item* cmdlet.

Working with Windows PowerShell profiles

After completing this chapter, you will be able to

- Understand the different Windows PowerShell profiles.

- Use *New-Item* to create a new Windows PowerShell profile.

- Use the *$profile* automatic variable.

- Describe the best profile to provide specific functionality.

Six different Windows PowerShell profiles

A Windows PowerShell profile creates a standardized environment by creating custom functions, aliases, PS drives, and variables upon startup. Windows PowerShell profiles are a bit confusing—there are, in fact, six different ones. Both the Windows PowerShell console and the Windows PowerShell ISE have their own profiles. In addition, there are profiles for the current user, and profiles for all users. Table 9-1 lists the six different profiles and their associated locations. In the table, the automatic variable *$home* points to the users\username directory on the system. The *$pshome* automatic variable points to the Windows PowerShell installation folder. This location typically is C:\Windows\System32 \WindowsPowerShell\v1.0. (For compatibility reasons, the Windows PowerShell installation folder is in the v1.0 folder—even on Windows PowerShell 5.0.)

TABLE 9-1 The six Windows PowerShell profiles and their paths

Description	Path
Current User, Current Host (console)	$Home\[My]Documents\WindowsPowerShell\Profile.ps1
Current User, All Hosts	$Home\[My]Documents\Profile.ps1
All Users, Current Host (console)	$PsHome\Microsoft.PowerShell_profile.ps1
All Users, All Hosts	$PsHome\Profile.ps1
Current User, Current Host (ISE)	$Home\[My]Documents\WindowsPowerShell \Microsoft.PowerShellISE_profile.ps1
All Users, Current Host (ISE)	$PsHome\Microsoft.PowerShellISE_profile.ps1

Understanding the six Windows PowerShell profiles

The first thing to do in understanding the six Windows PowerShell profiles is to keep in mind that the value of *$profile* changes depending on which Windows PowerShell host you use. As long as you realize that it is a moving target, you will be fine. In most cases, when talking about the Windows PowerShell profile, people are referring to the Current User, Current Host profile. In fact, if there is no qualifier for the Windows PowerShell profile with its associated scope or description, it is safe to assume that the reference is to the Current User, Current Host profile.

> **Note** The Windows PowerShell profile (any one of the six) is simply a Windows PowerShell script. It has a special name, and it resides in a special place, but it is simply a script. In this regard, it is sort of like the old-fashioned autoexec.bat batch file. Because the Windows PowerShell profile is a Windows PowerShell script, you must enable the script execution policy prior to configuring and using a Windows PowerShell profile.

Examining the *$profile* variable

In Windows PowerShell, the *$profile* automatic variable contains the path to the Current User, Current Host profile. This makes sense and is a great way to easily access the path to the profile. The following illustrates this technique from within the Windows PowerShell console.

```
PS C:\> $profile
C:\Users\ed.NWTRADERS\Documents\WindowsPowerShell\Microsoft.PowerShell_profile.ps1
```

Inside the Windows PowerShell ISE, when I query the *$profile* automatic variable, I receive the output shown here.

```
PS C:\Users\ed.NWTRADERS> $profile
C:\Users\ed.NWTRADERS\Documents\WindowsPowerShell\Microsoft.PowerShellISE_profile.ps1
```

To save you a bit of analyzing, the difference between the Windows PowerShell console Current User, Current Host profile path and the Windows PowerShell ISE Current User, Current Host profile path is three letters: *ISE*.

> **Note** These three letters, *ISE*, often cause problems. When modifying your profile, you might be setting something in your Windows PowerShell console profile, and it is not available inside the Windows PowerShell ISE.

Unraveling the different profiles

You can pipeline the *$profile* variable to the *Get-Member* cmdlet and view additional properties that exist on the *$profile* variable.

This technique is shown here.

```
PS C:\> $PROFILE | Get-Member -MemberType NoteProperty | select Name
Name
----
AllUsersAllHosts
AllUsersCurrentHost
CurrentUserAllHosts
CurrentUserCurrentHost
```

If you are accessing the *$profile* variable from within the Windows PowerShell console, the *AllUsersCurrentHost* and *CurrentUserCurrentHost* note properties refer to the Windows PowerShell console. If you access the *$profile* variable from within the Windows PowerShell ISE, the *AllUsersCurrentHost* and *CurrentUserCurrentHost* note properties refer to the Windows PowerShell ISE profiles.

Using the *$profile* variable to refer to more than the current host

When you reference the *$profile* variable, by default it refers to the Current User, Current Host profile. If you pipeline the variable to the *Format-List* cmdlet, it still refers to the Current User, Current Host profile. This technique is shown here.

```
PS C:\> $PROFILE | Format-List *
C:\Users\ed.NWTRADERS\Documents\WindowsPowerShell\Microsoft.PowerShell_profile.ps1
```

This can lead to a bit of confusion, especially because the *Get-Member* cmdlet reveals the existence of multiple profiles and multiple note properties. The way to view all of the profiles for the current host is to use the *-force* parameter—it reveals the hidden properties. The command illustrating this technique is shown here.

```
$PROFILE | Format-List * -Force
```

The command to display the various profiles and the associated output from the command are shown in Figure 9-1.

FIGURE 9-1 The *$profile* variable contains the path to several Windows PowerShell profiles.

It is possible to directly access each of these specific properties—just as you would access any other property—via dotted notation. This technique is shown here.

```
$PROFILE.CurrentUserAllHosts
```

The paths to each of the four profiles for the Windows PowerShell console are shown in Figure 9-2.

```
powershell                                                    —    □    ×
PS C:\> $PROFILE.CurrentUserAllHosts
C:\Users\administrator\Documents\WindowsPowerShell\profile.ps1
PS C:\> $PROFILE.CurrentUserCurrentHost
C:\Users\administrator\Documents\WindowsPowerShell\Microsoft.PowerShell_profile.ps1
PS C:\> $PROFILE.AllUsersAllHosts
C:\Windows\System32\WindowsPowerShell\v1.0\profile.ps1
PS C:\> $PROFILE.AllUsersCurrentHost
C:\Windows\System32\WindowsPowerShell\v1.0\Microsoft.PowerShell_profile.ps1
PS C:\> _
```

FIGURE 9-2 Use dotted notation to access the various properties of the *$profile* variable.

Determining whether a specific profile exists

To determine whether a specific profile exists, use the *Test-Path* cmdlet and the appropriate note property of the *$profile* variable. For example, to determine whether a Current User, Current Host profile exists, you can use the *$profile* variable with no modifier, or you can use the *CurrentUser-CurrentHost* note property. The following example illustrates both of these.

```
PS C:\> test-path $PROFILE
True
PS C:\> test-path $PROFILE.CurrentUserCurrentHost
True
PS C:\>
```

In the same manner, the other three profiles that apply to the current host (in this example, I am using the Windows PowerShell console) are found not to exist. This is shown in the code that follows.

```
PS C:\> test-path $PROFILE.AllUsersAllHosts
False
PS C:\> test-path $PROFILE.AllUsersCurrentHost
False
PS C:\> test-path $PROFILE.CurrentUserAllHosts
False
PS C:\>
```

Creating a new profile

To create a new profile for the Current User, All Hosts profile, use the *CurrentUserAllHosts* property of the *$profile* automatic variable and the *New-Item* cmdlet. This technique is shown here.

```
PS C:\> new-item $PROFILE.CurrentUserAllHosts -ItemType file -Force


    Directory: C:\Users\ed.NWTRADERS\Documents\WindowsPowerShell


Mode                LastWriteTime     Length Name
----                -------------     ------ ----
-a---          6/17/2015   2:59 PM         0 profile.ps1
```

To open the profile for editing, use the *ise* alias, as shown here.

```
ise $PROFILE.CurrentUserAllHosts
```

When you are finished editing the profile, save it, close the Windows PowerShell console, reopen the Windows PowerShell console, and test to confirm that your changes work properly.

Design considerations for profiles

The first thing to do when deciding how to implement your Windows PowerShell profile is to analyze the way in which you use Windows PowerShell. For example, if you confine yourself to running a few Windows PowerShell scripts from within the Windows PowerShell ISE, there is little reason to worry about a Windows PowerShell console profile. If you use a different Windows PowerShell scripting environment than the Windows PowerShell ISE, but you also work interactively from the Windows PowerShell console, you might need to add commands to the other scripting environment's profile (assuming it has one), and the Windows PowerShell console profile, to maintain a consistent environment. If you work extensively in both the scripting environment and the Windows PowerShell console, and you find yourself wanting certain modifications to both environments, that leads to a different scenario.

There are three different names used for the Windows PowerShell profiles. The names are shown in Table 9-2, along with the profile usage.

TABLE 9-2 Windows PowerShell profile names and name usage

Profile name	Name usage
Microsoft.PowerShell_profile.ps1	Refers to profiles (either current user or all users) for the Windows PowerShell console
profile.ps1	Refers to profiles (either current user or all users) for all Windows PowerShell hosts
Microsoft.PowerShellISE_profile.ps1	Refers to profiles (either current user or all users) for the Windows PowerShell ISE

The distinction between the Windows PowerShell ISE profiles and the Windows PowerShell console profiles is the *ISE* in the name of the Windows PowerShell ISE profiles. The location of the Windows PowerShell profile determines the scoping (whether the profile applies to either the current user or to all users). All user profiles (any one of the three profiles detailed in Table 9-2) exist in the Windows \system32\WindowsPowerShell\v1.0 directory, a location referenced by the *$pshome* variable. The following illustrates using the *$pshome* variable to obtain this folder.

```
PS C:\Users\ed.NWTRADERS> $PSHOME
C:\Windows\System32\WindowsPowerShell\v1.0
```

The folder containing the three different Current User Windows PowerShell profiles is the WindowsPowerShell folder in the user's mydocuments special folder. The location of the user's mydocuments special folder is obtained by using the *GetFolderPath* method from the *System.Environment* class of the Microsoft .NET Framework. This technique is shown here.

```
PS C:\> [environment]::getfolderpath("mydocuments")
C:\Users\ed.NWTRADERS\Documents
```

Table 9-3 details a variety of use-case scenarios and points to the profile to use for specific purposes.

TABLE 9-3 Windows PowerShell usage patterns, profile names, and locations

Windows PowerShell use	Location and profile name
Near-exclusive Windows PowerShell console work as a non-administrative user	MyDocuments Microsoft.PowerShell_profile.ps1
Near-exclusive Windows PowerShell console work as an administrative user	$PSHome Microsoft.PowerShell_profile.ps1
Near-exclusive Windows PowerShell ISE work as a non-administrative user	MyDocuments Microsoft.PowerShellISE_profile.ps1
Near-exclusive Windows PowerShell ISE work as an administrative user	$PSHome Microsoft.PowerShellISE_profile.ps1
Balanced Windows PowerShell work as a non-administrative user	MyDocuments profile.ps1
Balanced Windows PowerShell work as an administrative user	$psHome profile.ps1

Note Depending on how you perform administrative work, you might decide that you want to use a Current User type of profile. This would be because you log on with a specific account to perform administrative work. If your work requires that you log on with several different user accounts, it makes sense to use an All Users type of profile.

Using one or more profiles

Many Windows PowerShell users end up using more than one Windows PowerShell profile—it might not be intentional, but that is how it works out. What happens is that the user begins by creating a Current User, Current Host profile via the Windows PowerShell *$profile* variable. After adding some items in the Windows PowerShell profile, the user decides that he would like the same features in the Windows PowerShell console or the Windows PowerShell ISE—whichever one he did not use in the beginning. Then, after creating an additional profile, he soon realizes that he is duplicating his work. In addition, various packages, such as the Script Explorer, add commands to the Windows PowerShell profile.

Depending on how much you add to your Windows PowerShell profile, you might be perfectly fine with having multiple Windows PowerShell profiles. If your profile does not have very many items in it, using one Windows PowerShell profile for the Windows PowerShell console and another profile for the Windows PowerShell ISE might be a perfectly acceptable solution. Simplicity makes this approach work. For example, certain commands, such as the *Start-Transcript* cmdlet, do not work in the Windows PowerShell ISE. In addition, other commands, such as those requiring Single-Threaded Apartment model (STA), do not work by default in the Windows PowerShell console. By creating multiple *$profile* profiles (Current User, Current Host) and only editing them from the appropriate environment, you can greatly reduce the complexity of the profile-creation process.

However, it will not be long before duplication leads to inconsistency, which leads to frustration, and finally a need for correction and solution. A better approach is to plan for multiple environments from the beginning. The following list describes the advantages and disadvantages to using more than one profile, along with the scenarios in which you'd most likely do this:

- Advantages of using more than one profile:

  - It's simple and hassle-free.

  - *$profile* always refers to the correct profile.

  - It removes concern about incompatible commands.

- Disadvantages:

  - It often means you're duplicating effort.

  - It can cause inconsistencies between profiles (for variables, functions, PS drives, and aliases).

  - Maintenance might increase due to the number of potential profiles.

- Uses:

  - Use with a simple profile.

  - Use when you do not have administrator or non-elevated user requirements.

Using modules in profiles

If you need to customize both the Windows PowerShell console and the Windows PowerShell ISE (or other Windows PowerShell host), and you need to log on with multiple credentials, your need for Windows PowerShell profiles increases exponentially. Attempting to keep several different Windows PowerShell profiles in sync quickly becomes a maintenance nightmare. This is especially true if you are prone to making quick additions to your Windows PowerShell profile as you find a particular need.

In addition to having a large number of profiles, it is also possible for a Windows PowerShell profile to grow to inordinate proportions—especially when you begin to add very many nicely crafted Windows PowerShell functions and helper functions. One solution to the problem (in fact, the best solution) is to use modules; my Windows PowerShell ISE profile uses four different modules—the profile itself consists of the lines loading the modules. (For more information about modules, see Chapter 7, "Creating advanced functions and modules.")

The following list discusses the advantages, disadvantages, and uses of the one-profile approach:

- Advantages of using one profile:
  - It requires less work.
  - It's easy to keep different profiles in sync.
  - It allows you to achieve consistency between different Windows PowerShell environments.
  - It's portable; the profile can more easily travel to different machines.
- Disadvantages:
  - It's complex to set up.
  - It requires more planning.
  - *$profile* does not point to the correct location.
- Uses:
  - Use with more complex profiles.
  - Use when your work requires multiple user accounts or multiple Windows PowerShell hosts.
  - Use if your work takes you to different computers or virtual machines.

 Note The approach of containing functionality for a profile inside modules and then loading the modules from the profile file is detailed in the "Create a Really Cool PowerShell ISE Profile" article on the Hey Scripting Guy! blog, at *www.scriptingguys.com/blog*.

Using the All Users, All Hosts profile

One way to use a single Windows PowerShell profile is to put everything into the All Users, All Hosts profile. I know some companies that create a standard Windows PowerShell profile for everyone in the company, and they use the All Users, All Hosts profile as a means of standardizing their Windows PowerShell environment. The changes go in during the image-build process, and therefore the profiles are available to machines built from that image.

- Advantages of using the All Users, All Hosts profile:

  - It's simple; you can use one location for everything, especially when it is added during the build process.

  - One file affects all Windows PowerShell users and hosts.

  - It avoids conflict between admin users and non-admin users, since both types of users use the same profile.

  - *$profile.AllUsersAllHosts* always points to the correct file.

  - It's great for central management—one file is used for all users of a machine.

- Disadvantages:

  - You must have admin rights on the current machine to make changes to the file.

  - It provides no distinction between different hosts—some commands will not work in the Windows PowerShell ISE and others will not work in the Windows PowerShell console.

  - It makes no distinction between admin users and non-admin users. Non-admin users will not be able to run certain commands.

  - The files are distributed among potentially thousands of different machines. To make one change to a profile, you must copy a file to all machines that are using that profile (although you can use Group Policy to assist in this endeavor). This can be a major problem for computers such as laptops that connect only occasionally to the network. It is also a problem when attempting to use a shutdown script on a Windows 8-based device. (Because Windows 8 and later devices do not perform a true shutdown, the shutdown script does not always run.)

- Uses:

  - Use for your personal profile when duties require both elevation and non-elevation of permissions across multiple Windows PowerShell hosts.

  - Use as part of a standard image build to deploy static functionality to numerous machines and users.

Using your own file

Because the Windows PowerShell profile is a Windows PowerShell script (with the added benefit of having a special name and residing in a special location), it means that anything that can be accomplished in a Windows PowerShell script can be accomplished in a Windows PowerShell profile. A much better approach to dealing with Windows PowerShell profiles is to keep the profile itself as simple as possible, but bring in the functionality you require via other means. One way to do this is to add the profile information you require to a file. Store that file in a central location, and then dot-source it to the profile.

Using a central profile script

1. Create a Windows PowerShell script containing the profile information you require. Include aliases, variables, functions, Windows PowerShell drives, and commands to execute on Windows PowerShell startup.

2. In the Windows PowerShell profile script to host the central profile, dot-source the central profile file. The following command, placed in the *$profile* script, brings in functionality stored in a Windows PowerShell script named myprofile.ps1 that resides in a shared folder named C:\fso.

   ```
   . c:\fso\myprofile.ps1
   ```

One of the advantages of using a central Windows PowerShell script to store your profile information is that only one location requires updating when you add additional functionality to your profile. In addition, if folder permissions permit, the central Windows PowerShell script becomes available to any user for any host on the local machine. If you store this central Windows PowerShell script on a network file share, you only need to update one file for the entire network.

- Advantages of using a central script for a Windows PowerShell profile:
  - It provides one place to modify the profile, for all users and all hosts having access to the file.
  - It's easy to keep functionality synchronized among all Windows PowerShell hosts and users.
  - It makes it possible to have one profile for the entire network.

- Disadvantages:
  - It's more complicated due to multiple files.
  - It provides no access to the central file, which means you won't have a profile for machines without network access.
  - It is possible that non–role-specific commands will become available to users.
  - Filtering out specific commands for specific hosts becomes more complex.
  - One central script becomes very complicated to maintain when it grows to hundreds of lines.

- Uses:
  - Use to provide basic functionality among multiple hosts and multiple users.
  - Use for a single user who wants to duplicate capabilities between Windows PowerShell hosts.
  - Use to provide a single profile for networked computers via a file share.

Grouping similar functionality into a module

One of the main ways to clean up your Windows PowerShell profile is to group related items into modules. For example, suppose your Windows PowerShell profile contains a few utility functions such as the following:

- A function to determine admin rights
- A function to determine whether the computer is a laptop or a desktop
- A function to determine whether the host is the Windows PowerShell ISE or the Windows PowerShell console
- A function to determine whether the computer is a 32-bit or a 64-bit machine
- A function to write to a temporary file

All of the preceding functions are utility types of functions. They are not specific to one technology and are, in fact, helper functions, useful in a wide variety of scripts and applications. It is also true that as useful as these utilities are, you might not need to use them everywhere, at all times. This is the advantage of moving the functionality into a module—you can easily load and unload them as required.

Where to store the profile module

If you run your system as a non-elevated user, do not use the user module location for modules that require elevation of privileges. This will be an exercise in futility, because after you elevate the user account to include admin rights, your profile shifts to another location, and then you do not have access to the module you were attempting to access.

Therefore, it makes sense to store modules requiring admin rights in the system32 directory hierarchy. Keep in mind that updates to admin modules will also require elevation and therefore could add a bit of complication. Store modules that do not require admin rights in the user profile module location. When modules reside in one of the two default locations, Windows PowerShell automatically picks up on them and displays them when you use the *ListAvailable* command, as shown here.

```
Get-Module -ListAvailable
```

However, this does not mean you are limited to modules from only the default locations. If you are centralizing your Windows PowerShell profile and storing it on a shared network drive, it makes sense to likewise store the module (and module manifest) in the shared network location.

> **Note** Keep in mind that the Windows PowerShell profile is a script, as is a Windows PowerShell module. Therefore, your script execution policy affects the ability to run scripts (and to load modules) from a shared network location. Even if you have a script execution policy of *Unrestricted*, if you have not added the network share to the Internet Explorer trusted sites, you will be prompted each time you open Windows PowerShell. You can use Group Policy to set the Internet Explorer trusted sites for your domain, or you can add them manually. You might also want to examine code signing for your scripts.

Creating and adding functionality to a profile: Step-by-step exercises

In this exercise, you'll use the *New-Item* cmdlet to create a new Windows PowerShell profile. You'll also use the *Get-ExecutionPolicy* cmdlet to ensure that script execution is enabled on your local system. You'll also create a function to edit your Windows PowerShell profile. In the next exercise, you'll add additional functionality to the profile.

Creating a basic Windows PowerShell profile

1. Start the Windows PowerShell console.

2. Use the *Test-Path* cmdlet to determine whether a Windows PowerShell console profile exists. This command is shown here.

    ```
    Test-Path $PROFILE
    ```

3. If a profile exists, make a backup copy of the profile by using the *Copy-Item* cmdlet. The command shown here copies the profile to the profileBackup.ps1 file in the C:\fso folder.

    ```
    Copy-Item $profile c:\fso\profileBackUp.ps1
    ```

4. Delete the existing *$profile* file by using the *Remove-Item* cmdlet. The command to do this is shown here.

    ```
    Remove-Item $PROFILE
    ```

5. Use the *Test-Path* cmdlet to ensure that the *$profile* file is properly removed. The command to do this is shown here.

    ```
    Test-Path $PROFILE
    ```

6. Use the *New-Item* cmdlet to create a new Windows PowerShell console profile. Use the *$profile* automatic variable to refer to the Windows PowerShell console profile for the current user. Use the *-Force* switch parameter to avoid any prompting. Specify an *ItemType* of *file* to ensure that a Windows PowerShell file is properly created. The command to accomplish these tasks is shown here.

```
New-Item $PROFILE -ItemType file -Force
```

Sample output from the command to create a Windows PowerShell profile for the Windows PowerShell console host and the current user is shown here.

```
    Directory: C:\Users\administrator.NWTRADERS\Documents\WindowsPowerShell


Mode                LastWriteTime     Length Name
----                -------------     ------ ----
-a---         5/27/2012   3:51 PM          0 Microsoft.PowerShell_profile.ps1
```

7. Open the Windows PowerShell console profile in the Windows PowerShell ISE. To do this, enter the command shown here.

```
Ise $profile
```

8. Create a function named *Set-Profile* that opens the Windows PowerShell Current User, Current Host profile for editing in the Windows PowerShell ISE. To do this, begin by using the *function* keyword, and then assign the name *Set-Profile* to the function. These commands are shown here.

```
Function Set-Profile
{

} #end function set-profile
```

9. Add the Windows PowerShell code to the *Set-Profile* function to open the profile for editing in the Windows PowerShell ISE. The command to do this is shown here.

```
ISE $profile
```

10. Save the newly modified profile and close the Windows PowerShell ISE.

11. Close the Windows PowerShell console.

12. Open the Windows PowerShell console and look for errors.

13. Test the *Set-Profile* function by entering the command shown here into the Windows PowerShell console.

```
Set-Profile
```

The Windows PowerShell console profile for the current user should open in the Windows PowerShell ISE. The *Set-Profile* function should be the only thing in the profile file.

This concludes the exercise.

In the following exercise, you will add a variable, an alias, and a Windows PowerShell drive to your Windows PowerShell profile.

Adding profile functionality

1. Start the Windows PowerShell console.

2. Call the *Set-Profile* function (you added this function to your Windows PowerShell console profile during the previous exercise). The command to do this is shown here.

   ```
   Set-Profile
   ```

3. Add comment sections at the top of the Windows PowerShell profile for the following four sections: *Variables*, *Aliases*, *PS Drives*, and *Functions*. The code to do this is shown here.

   ```
   #Variables

   #Aliases

   #PS drives

   #Functions
   ```

4. Create three new variables. The first variable is *MyDocuments*, the second variable is *Console-Profile*, and the third variable is *ISEProfile*. Use the code shown here to assign the proper values to these variables.

   ```
   New-Variable -Name MyDocuments -Value ([environment]::GetFolderPath("mydocuments"))
   New-Variable -Name ConsoleProfile -Value (Join-Path -Path $mydocuments -ChildPath
   WindowsPowerShell\Microsoft.PowerShell_profile.ps1)
   New-Variable -Name ISEProfile -Value (Join-Path -Path $mydocuments -ChildPath
   WindowsPowerShell\Microsoft.PowerShellISE_profile.ps1)
   ```

5. Create two new aliases. One alias is named *gh* and refers to the *Get-Help* cmdlet. The second alias is named *I* and refers to the *Invoke-History* cmdlet. The code to do this is shown here.

   ```
   New-Alias -Name gh -Value get-help
   New-Alias -Name i -Value Invoke-History
   ```

6. Create two new PS drives. The first PS drive refers to the HKEY_CLASSES_ROOT location of the registry. The second PS drive refers to the current user's *my* location. The code to create these two PS drives is shown here.

   ```
   New-PSDrive -Name HKCR -PSProvider Registry -Root hkey_classes_root
   New-PSDrive -Name mycerts -PSProvider Certificate -Root Cert:\CurrentUser\My
   ```

7. Following the *Set-Profile* function, add another comment for commands. This code is shown here.

   ```
   #commands
   ```

8. Add three commands. The first command starts the transcript functionality, the second sets the working location to the root of drive C, and the last clears the Windows PowerShell console.

    These three commands are shown here.

    ```
    Start-Transcript
    Set-Location -Path c:\
    Clear-Host
    ```

9. Save the Windows PowerShell profile and close the Windows PowerShell ISE. Also close the Windows PowerShell console. Open the Windows PowerShell console and look for errors. Test each of the newly created features to ensure that they work. The commands to test the profile are shown here.

    ```
    gh
    $MyDocuments
    $ConsoleProfile
    $ISEProfile
    sl hkcr:
    sl mycerts:
    sl c:\
    Stop-Transcript
    set-profile
    ```

    This concludes the exercise.

Chapter 9 quick reference

To	Do this
Determine the existence of a Windows PowerShell profile	Use the *Test-Path* cmdlet and supply the *$profile* automatic variable.
Create a Windows PowerShell profile	Use the *New-Item* cmdlet and supply a value of *file* for the item type. Use the *-force* switch to avoid prompting.
Add items to a Windows PowerShell profile that all users will use	Use the All Users, All Hosts profile.
Obtain the path to the All Users, All Hosts profile	Use the *$profile* automatic variable and specify the *AllUsersAllHosts* property.
Add items to a Windows PowerShell profile that the current user will use	Use the Current User, All Hosts profile.
Obtain the path to the Current User, All Hosts profile	Use the *$profile* automatic variable and specify the *CurrentUserAllHosts* property.
Edit a specific Windows PowerShell profile	From the Windows PowerShell console, enter ISE and specify the path to the required Windows PowerShell profile by using the *$profile* automatic variable and the appropriate property.

Using WMI

After completing this chapter, you will be able to

- Understand the concept of WMI namespaces.

- Use the WMI namespaces.

- Navigate the WMI namespaces.

- Understand the use of WMI providers.

- Discover classes supplied by WMI providers.

- Use the *Get-WmiObject* cmdlet to perform simple WMI queries.

- Use the *Get-CimInstance* cmdlet to perform simple WMI queries.

- Use the *Get-CimClass* cmdlet to find WMI classes.

- Produce a listing of all WMI classes.

- Perform searches to find WMI classes.

The inclusion of Windows Management Instrumentation (WMI) in virtually every operating system released by Microsoft since Windows NT 4.0 should give you an idea of the importance of this underlying technology. From a network management perspective, many useful tasks can be accomplished by using just Windows PowerShell, but to begin to truly unleash the power of scripting, you need to bring in additional tools. This is where WMI comes into play. WMI provides access to many powerful ways of managing Windows-based systems. This chapter will dive into a discussion of the pieces that make up WMI. It will cover several concepts—namespaces, providers, and classes—and show how these concepts can help you take advantage of WMI in your Windows PowerShell scripts. All the scripts mentioned in this chapter are available via the book's website.

Each new version of Windows introduces improvements to WMI, including new WMI classes, in addition to new capabilities for existing WMI classes. In products such as Microsoft Exchange Server, SQL Server, and Internet Information Services (to mention a few), support for WMI continues to grow and expand. The following lists some of the tasks you can perform with WMI:

- Report on drive configuration for locally attached drives and for mapped drives.

- Report on available memory, both physical and virtual.

- Back up the event log.

- Modify the registry.

- Schedule tasks.

- Share folders.

- Switch from a static to a dynamic IP address.

- Enable or disable a network adapter.

- Defragment a hard disk drive.

Understanding the WMI model

WMI is a *hierarchical namespace*, in which the layers build on one another, like the Lightweight Directory Access Protocol (LDAP) directory used in Active Directory Domain Services (AD DS) or the file system structure on your hard drive. Although it is true that WMI is a hierarchical namespace, the term by itself does not really convey the richness of WMI. The WMI model has three sections—resources, infrastructure, and consumers—with the following uses:

- **WMI resources** Resources include anything that can be accessed by using WMI, such as the file system, networked components, event logs, files, folders, disks, and AD DS.

- **WMI infrastructure** The infrastructure is made up of three parts: the WMI service, the WMI repository, and the WMI providers. Of these parts, WMI providers are the most important because they provide the means for WMI to gather needed information.

- **WMI consumers** A consumer provides a prepackaged way to process data from WMI. A consumer can be a Windows PowerShell cmdlet, a Microsoft Visual Basic Scripting Edition (VBScript) script, an enterprise management software package, or some other tool or utility that executes WMI queries.

Working with objects and namespaces

You can think of a *namespace* as a way to organize or collect data related to similar items. Visualize an old-fashioned filing cabinet. Each drawer can represent a particular namespace. Inside each drawer are hanging folders that collect information related to a subset of what the drawer actually holds. For example, at home in my filing cabinet, I have a drawer reserved for information related to my woodworking tools. Inside this particular drawer are hanging folders for my table saw, my planer, my joiner, my dust collector, and other tools. In the folder for the table saw is information about the motor, the blades, and the various accessories I purchased for the saw (such as an overarm blade guard).

WMI organizes the namespaces in a similar fashion. The filing cabinet analogy can extend to include the three elements of WMI with which you will work. The three elements are namespaces, providers, and classes. The namespaces are the file cabinets. The providers are the drawers in the file cabinets. Finally, the WMI classes are the folders in the drawers of the file cabinets. These namespaces are shown in Figure 10-1.

FIGURE 10-1 WMI namespaces displayed in the WMI Control Properties dialog box.

Namespaces can contain other namespaces, in addition to other objects, and these objects contain properties you can manipulate. I'll use a WMI command to illustrate the organization of the WMI namespaces. In the command that follows, the *Get-CimInstance* cmdlet is used to make the connection into WMI. The *-ClassName* parameter specifies the name of the class. In this example, the class name is *__NAMESPACE* (the WMI class from which all WMI namespaces derive). Yes, you read that class name correctly—it is the word *NAMESPACE* preceded by two underscore characters (a double underscore is used for all WMI system classes because it makes them easy to find in sorted lists; the double underscore, when sorted, rises to the top of the list). The *-Namespace* parameter is *root* because it specifies the root level (the top namespace) in the WMI namespace hierarchy. The *Get-CimInstance* line of code appears here.

```
Get-CimInstance -ClassName __NAMESPACE -Namespace root
```

The command and the associated output are shown in Figure 10-2.

FIGURE 10-2 Namespace output obtained via the *Get-CimInstance* cmdlet.

When the *Get-CimInstance* cmdlet runs, it returns a collection of management objects, which contains the *name* property of those namespaces. Because of nesting (one namespace existing inside another namespace), the command returns a portion of the total namespaces on the computer. If you want to return all the namespaces available on a computer, you must use a recursive command. To do this, you will need the __*Path* system property, which is exposed with a different cmdlet. Normally, *Get-CimInstance* returns all the WMI information needed, but for this type of situation, where you need to access system properties, you must use *Get-WmiObject*. To perform the recursive listing, you must use a custom function. Stepping through the *Get-WmiNameSpace* function I created, you first create a couple of input parameters: *namespace* and *computer*. The default values of these parameters are *root*, for the root of the WMI namespace, and *localhost*, which refers to the local computer. This portion of the function is shown here.

```
Param(
  $nameSpace = "root",
  $computer = "localhost"
 )
```

It is possible to change the behavior of the *Get-WmiNameSpace* function by passing new values when calling the function.

> **Note** When you are performing a WMI query against a remote computer, the user account performing the query must be a member of the local administrators group on the remote machine. One way to accomplish this is to hold down Shift and right-click the Windows PowerShell icon, select *Run As Different User* from the menu that appears, and specify an account that has administrative rights to the remote computer.

An example of calling the *Get-WmiNameSpace* function with alternate parameter values is shown here.

```
Get-WmiNameSpace -nameSpace root\cimv2 -computer dc1
```

The *Get-WmiObject* cmdlet command looks for instances of the *__NAMESPACE* class on the computer and in the namespace specified when calling the function. One thing that is interesting is the use of a *custom error action*—a requirement due to a possible lack of rights on some of the namespaces. If you set the value of *ErrorAction* to *SilentlyContinue*, any error generated, including the Access Denied error, does not appear, and the script ignores the error and continues to run. Without this change, the function would halt at the first Access Denied error; otherwise, by default, lots of Access Denied errors would clutter the output window and make the results difficult to read. This portion of the *Get-WmiNameSpace* function is shown here.

```
Get-WmiObject -Class __NAMESPACE -computer $computer '
 -namespace $namespace -ErrorAction "SilentlyContinue"
```

The results from the first *Get-WmiObject* command pass down the pipeline to a *Foreach-Object* cmdlet. Inside the associated *process* script block, the *Join-Path* cmdlet builds up a new namespace string using the *namespace* and *name* properties. The function skips any namespaces that contain the word *directory* to make the script run faster and to ignore any LDAP-type classes contained in the Root\Directory\LDAP WMI namespace. After the namespace has been created, the new namespace name passes to the *Get-WmiObject* cmdlet, where a new query runs. This portion of the function is shown here.

```
Foreach-Object '
 -Process '
   {
     $subns = Join-Path -Path $_.__NAMESPACE -ChildPath $_.name
     if($subns -notmatch 'directory') {$subns}
     $namespaces += $subns + "'r'n"
     Get-WmiNameSpace -namespace $subNS -computer $computer
   }
} #end Get-WmiNameSpace
```

The complete *Get-WmiNameSpace* function is shown here.

Get-WmiNameSpace
```
Function Get-WmiNameSpace
{
 Param(
  $nameSpace = "root",
  $computer = "localhost"
 )
 Get-WmiObject -class __NAMESPACE -computer $computer '
 -namespace $namespace -ErrorAction "SilentlyContinue" |
 Foreach-Object '
 -Process '
```

```
    {
      $subns = Join-Path -Path $_.__NAMESPACE -ChildPath $_.name
      if($subns -notmatch 'directory') {$subns}
      $namespaces += $subns + "'r'n"
      Get-WmiNameSpace -namespace $subNS -computer $computer
    }
} #end Get-WmiNameSpace
```

An example of calling the *Get-WmiNameSpace* function, along with a sample of the output, is shown in Figure 10-3.

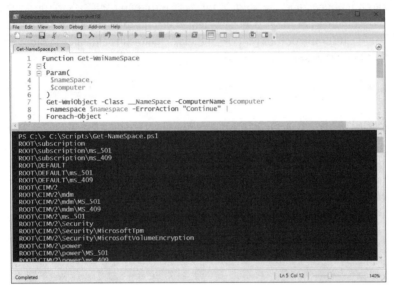

FIGURE 10-3 WMI namespaces revealed by the *Get-WmiNameSpace* function.

So what does all this mean? It means that there are more than a dozen different WMI namespaces. Each of those WMI namespaces provides information about your computers. Understanding that the different namespaces exist is the first step to being able to navigate WMI to find the information you need. Often, students and others new to Windows PowerShell or VBScript work on a WMI script to make the script perform a certain action, which is a great way to learn scripting. However, what they often do not know is which namespace they need to connect to so that they can accomplish their task. When I tell them which namespace to work with, they sometimes reply, "That's fine for you, but how can I find out that a certain namespace even exists?" By using the *Get-WmiNameSpace* function, you can easily generate a list of namespaces installed on a particular machine; armed with that information, you can search the Microsoft Developer Network (MSDN) website (*http://msdn.microsoft.com/library/default.asp*) to discover what information the namespace is able to provide.

Listing WMI providers

Understanding the namespace assists the network administrator with judiciously applying WMI scripting to his or her network duties. However, as mentioned earlier, to access information through WMI, you must have access to a WMI provider. After implementing the provider, you can gain access to the information the provider makes available.

> **Note** Keep in mind that in nearly every case, installation of providers happens in the background via operating system configuration or management application installation. For example, addition of new roles and features to server stock keeping units (SKUs) often installs new WMI providers and their attendant WMI classes.

WMI bases providers on a system template class called *__Provider*. Armed with this information, if you look for instances of the *__Provider* class, you will get a list of all the providers that reside in your WMI namespace. This is exactly what the *Get-WmiProvider* function does.

The *Get-WmiProvider* function begins by assigning the string *Root\cimv2* to the *$namespace* variable. This value will be used with the *Get-CimInstance* cmdlet to specify where the WMI query will take place.

The *Get-CimInstance* cmdlet queries WMI. The *ClassName* parameter limits the WMI query to the *__Provider* class. The *-Namespace* parameter tells the *Get-CimInstance* cmdlet to look only in the *Root\cimv2* WMI namespace. The array of objects returned from the *Get-CimInstance* cmdlet pipelines to the *Sort-Object* cmdlet, where the listing of objects is alphabetized based on the *name* property. After this process is completed, the reorganized objects pipeline to the *Select-Object* cmdlet, where the name of each provider is displayed. The complete *Get-WmiProvider* function is shown here.

Get-WmiProvider

```
Function Get-WmiProvider
{
 Param(
  [string]$nameSpace,
  [string]$computer)
  Get-CimInstance -ClassName __Provider -Namespace $namespace |
  Sort-Object -property Name |
  Select-Object name
} #end function Get-WmiProvider
Get-WmiProvider -namespace root\cimv2 -computer $env:COMPUTERNAME
```

Working with WMI classes

In addition to working with namespaces, the inquisitive network administrator might want to explore the concept of classes. In WMI parlance, you have core classes, common classes, and dynamic classes. *Core classes* represent managed objects that apply to all areas of management. These classes provide a basic vocabulary for analyzing and describing managed systems. Two examples of core classes are parameters and the *SystemSecurity* class. *Common classes* are extensions to the core classes and represent managed objects that apply to specific management areas. However, common classes are independent of a particular implementation or technology. The *CIM_UnitaryComputerSystem* class is an example of a common class. Network administrators do not use core and common classes, because these types of classes serve as templates from which other classes derive, and as such they are mainly of interest to developers of management applications. The reason IT pros need to know about the core and common classes is to avoid confusion when the time comes to find usable WMI classes.

Many of the classes stored in *Root\cimv2*, therefore, are abstract classes and are of use as templates to create other WMI classes. However, a few classes in *Root\cimv2* are dynamic classes used to hold actual information. The important aspect to remember about *dynamic classes* is that providers generate instances of a dynamic class; therefore, dynamic WMI classes are more likely to retrieve live data from the system.

To produce a simple listing of WMI 0, you can use the *Get-WmiObject* cmdlet and specify the *-list* argument. This code is shown here.

```
Get-WmiObject -list
```

Partial output from the previous command is shown here.

```
Win32_TSGeneralSetting              Win32_TSPermissionsSetting
Win32_TSClientSetting               Win32_TSEnvironmentSetting
Win32_TSNetworkAdapterListSetting   Win32_TSLogonSetting
Win32_TSSessionSetting              Win32_DisplayConfiguration
Win32_COMSetting                    Win32_ClassicCOMClassSetting
Win32_DCOMApplicationSetting        Win32_MSIResource
Win32_ServiceControl                Win32_Property
```

One of the big difficulties with WMI is finding the WMI class needed to solve a particular problem. With literally thousands of WMI classes installed on even a basic Windows installation, searching through all the classes is difficult at best. Though it is possible to search MSDN, a faster solution is to use Windows PowerShell itself. As just shown, using the *-list* switch parameter produces a listing of all the WMI classes in a particular namespace. It would be possible to combine this feature with the *Get-WmiNameSpace* function examined earlier to produce a listing of every WMI class on a computer—but that would only compound an already complicated situation.

A better solution is to stay focused on a single WMI namespace, and to use wildcard characters to assist in finding appropriate WMI classes. The Windows PowerShell cmdlet *Get-CimClass* was invented specifically to assist in searching for WMI classes. You can provide wildcard patterns to it to help limit the amount of classes returned. For example, you can use the wildcard pattern *bios* to find all WMI classes that contain the letters *bios* in the class name. Because the cmdlet expects a string pattern, you do not have to enclose the pattern in quotation marks. The code that follows accomplishes this task.

```
Get-CimClass *bios*
```

The command and associated output appear in Figure 10-4.

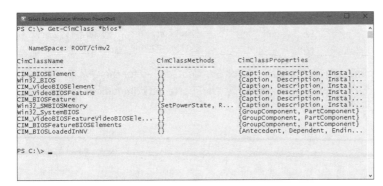

FIGURE 10-4 Listing of WMI classes containing the pattern *bios* in the class name.

In the output shown in Figure 10-4, not all of the WMI classes return data. In fact, you should not use all of the classes for direct querying, because querying abstract classes is not supported. Nevertheless, some of the classes are useful; some of them solve a specific problem. "Which ones should I use?" you may ask. A simple answer—not completely accurate, but something to get you started—is to use only the WMI classes that begin with *win32*. You can easily modify the previous *Get-CimClass* query to return only WMI classes that begin with *win32*. But what you really need to know are which WMI classes are dynamic and will return actual information, as opposed to abstract template types of WMI classes. This is where the *Get-CimClass* cmdlet really shines, because you can easily specify that you want to find abstract or dynamic WMI classes. To do this, use the *-QualifierName* parameter, and specify either *dynamic* or *abstract*. This technique is shown here.

```
PS C:\> Get-CimClass *bios* -QualifierName abstract

   NameSpace: ROOT/cimv2

CimClassName                        CimClassMethods      CimClassProperties
------------                        ---------------      ------------------
CIM_BIOSElement                     {}                   {Caption, Description, I...
CIM_VideoBIOSElement                {}                   {Caption, Description, I...
CIM_VideoBIOSFeature                {}                   {Caption, Description, I...
CIM_BIOSFeature                     {}                   {Caption, Description, I...
Win32_SMBIOSMemory                  {SetPowerState, R... {Caption, Description, I...
CIM_VideoBIOSFeatureVideoBIOSEle... {}                   {GroupComponent, PartCom...
CIM_BIOSFeatureBIOSElements         {}                   {GroupComponent, PartCom...
CIM_BIOSLoadedInNV                  {}                   {Antecedent, Dependent, ...
```

You can use the same technique to return only the dynamic WMI classes that contain the word *bios*. This technique is shown here.

```
PS C:\> Get-CimClass *bios* -QualifierName dynamic


   NameSpace: ROOT/cimv2

CimClassName                        CimClassMethods        CimClassProperties
------------                        ---------------        ------------------
Win32_BIOS                          {}                     {Caption, Description, I...
Win32_SystemBIOS                    {}                     {GroupComponent, PartCom...
```

The short form of the command uses the alias *gcls* for *Get-CimClass*, *-q* for the *QualifierName* parameter, and a wildcard character for the qualifier *dynamic*. The shortened command is shown here.

```
gcls *bios -q dyn*
```

Exploring WMI objects

1. Open the Windows PowerShell console.

2. Use the *Get-CimClass* cmdlet to find WMI classes that contain the string *bios* in their name. Use the alias *gcls* for the *Get-CimClass* cmdlet. The command is shown here.

    ```
    gcls *bios*
    ```

3. Use the *Get-CimInstance* cmdlet to query the *Win32_Bios* WMI class. Use the *gcim* alias. This command is shown here.

    ```
    gcim win32_bios
    ```

4. Store the results of the previous query in a variable named *a*. Press the Up Arrow key to retrieve the previous command instead of retyping everything. This command is shown here.

    ```
    $a = gcim win32_bios
    ```

5. View the contents of the *$a* variable. This command is shown here.

    ```
    $a
    ```

6. Pipeline the results stored in the *$a* variable to the *Get-Member* cmdlet. To do this, press the Up Arrow key to retrieve the previous command. Use the alias *gm* instead of typing the complete *Get-Member* cmdlet name. The command is shown here.

    ```
    $a | gm
    ```

7. Pipeline the results of the *Get-CimInstance* command to the *Get-Member* cmdlet. To do this, press the Up Arrow key four times to retrieve the previous command. Use the alias *gm* instead of typing the complete *Get-Member* cmdlet name. The command is shown here.

```
gcim win32_bios | gm
```

8. Compare the results of the two *Get-Member* commands; the output should be the same.

9. Use the *Select-Object* cmdlet to view all of the information available from the *Win32_Bios* WMI class; choose all of the properties by using the * wildcard character. Use the alias *select* for the *Select-Object* cmdlet. The command is shown here.

```
gcim win32_bios | select *
```

This completes the procedure.

Querying WMI

In most situations, when you use WMI, you are performing some sort of query. Even when you are going to set a particular property, you still need to execute a query to return a data set with which you will perform the configuration. (A *data set* includes the data that comes back to you as the result of a query—that is, it is a set of data.) In this section, you will examine the use of the *Get-CimInstance* cmdlet to query WMI.

Using the *Get-CimInstance* cmdlet to query a specific WMI class

1. Connect to WMI by using the *Get-CimInstance* cmdlet.

2. Specify a valid WMI class name to query.

3. Specify a value for the namespace; omit the *-Namespace* parameter to use the default *root\cimv2* namespace.

4. Specify a value for the *-ComputerName* parameter; omit the *-ComputerName* parameter to use the default value of *localhost*.

Windows PowerShell makes it easy to query WMI. In fact, at the command's most basic level, the only thing required is *gcim* (the alias for the *Get-CimInstance* cmdlet) and the WMI class name, and possibly the name of the WMI namespace if you are using a non-default namespace. An example of this simple syntax appears here, along with the associated output.

```
PS C:\> gcim win32_bios
SMBIOSBIOSVersion : 090006
Manufacturer      : American Megatrends Inc.
Name              : BIOS Date: 05/23/12 17:15:53  Ver: 09.00.06
SerialNumber      : 8570-3709-4791-5943-3863-4381-72
Version           : VRTUAL - 5001223
```

As shown in the "Exploring WMI objects" procedure in the preceding section, however, there are more properties available in the *Win32_Bios* WMI class than the five displayed in the output just shown. The command displays this limited output because a custom view of the *Win32_Bios* class defined in the *Types.ps1xml* file resides in the Windows PowerShell home directory on your system. The following command uses the *Select-String* cmdlet to search the *Types.ps1xml* file to find out whether there is any reference to the WMI class *Win32_Bios*.

```
Select-String -Path $pshome\*.ps1xml -SimpleMatch "Win32_Bios"
```

In Figure 10-5, the results of several *Select-String* commands are displayed when a special format exists for a particular WMI class. The last query, for the *Win32_CurrentTime* WMI class, does not return any results, indicating that no special formatting exists for this class.

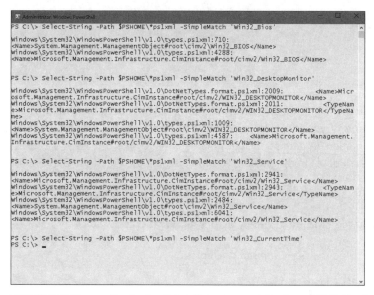

FIGURE 10-5 The results of using *Select-String* to search the format XML files for special formatting instructions.

The *Select-String* queries shown in Figure 10-5 indicate that there is special formatting for the *Win32_Bios*, *Win32_DesktopMonitor,* and *Win32_Service* WMI classes. The *Types.ps1xml* file contains information that tells Windows PowerShell how to display a particular WMI class. When an instance of the *Win32_Bios* WMI class appears, Windows PowerShell uses the *DefaultDisplayPropertySet* configuration to display only five properties (if a *<view>* configuration is defined, it trumps the default property that is set). The portion of the *Types.ps1xml* file that details these five properties is shown here.

```
<PropertySet>
    <Name>DefaultDisplayPropertySet</Name>
    <ReferencedProperties>
        <Name>SMBIOSBIOSVersion</Name>
        <Name>Manufacturer</Name>
        <Name>Name</Name>
        <Name>SerialNumber</Name>
        <Name>Version</Name>
    </ReferencedProperties>
</PropertySet>
```

The complete type definition for the *Win32_Bios* WMI class is shown in Figure 10-6.

FIGURE 10-6 The *Types.ps1xml* file controls which properties are displayed by default for specific WMI classes.

Special formatting instructions for the *Win32_Bios* WMI class indicate that there is an alternate property set available—a property set that is in addition to the *DefaultDisplayPropertySet*. This additional property set, named *PSStatus*, contains four properties. The four properties appear in the *PropertySet* description shown here.

```
<PropertySet>
    <Name>PSStatus</Name>
    <ReferencedProperties>
        <Name>Status</Name>
        <Name>Name</Name>
        <Name>Caption</Name>
        <Name>SMBIOSPresent</Name>
    </ReferencedProperties>
</PropertySet>
```

Finding the *psstatus* property set is more than a simple academic exercise, because the *psstatus* property set can be used directly with Windows PowerShell cmdlets such as *Select-Object* (*select* is an alias), *Format-List* (*fl* is an alias), and *Format-Table* (*ft* is an alias). The following commands illustrate the technique of using the *psstatus* property set to control data output.

```
gcim win32_bios | select psstatus
gcim win32_bios | fl psstatus
gcim win32_bios | ft psstatus
```

Unfortunately, you cannot use the alternate property set *psstatus* to select the properties via the *property* parameter. Therefore, the command that appears here fails.

```
gwmi win32_bios -Property psstatus
```

Figure 10-7 shows the previous commands using the *psstatus* property set, along with the associated output.

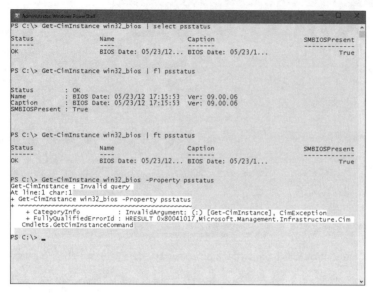

FIGURE 10-7 Use of the *psstatus* property set, illustrated by various commands.

Querying the *Win32_Desktop* class

1. Open the Windows PowerShell console.

2. Use the *Get-CimInstance* cmdlet to query for information about desktop profiles stored on your local computer. To do this, use the *Win32_Desktop* WMI class, and use the alias *gcim* instead of typing *Get-CimInstance*. Select only the *name* property by using the *Select-Object* cmdlet. Use the alias *select* instead of typing the *Select-Object* cmdlet name. The command is shown here.

    ```
    gcim win32_desktop | select name
    ```

3. Execute the command. Your output will contain only the name of each profile stored on your machine that you have access to. It will be similar to output that is shown here.

    ```
    name
    ----
    NT AUTHORITY\SYSTEM
    IAMMRED\ed
    .DEFAULT
    ```

4. To retrieve the name of the screen saver, add the property *ScreenSaverExecutable* to the *Select-Object* command. This is shown here.

    ```
    gcim win32_desktop | select name, ScreenSaverExecutable
    ```

5. Run the command. Your output will be similar to the following.

```
name                                   ScreenSaverExecutable
----                                   ---------------------
NT AUTHORITY\SYSTEM
IAMMRED\ed                             C:\Windows\WLXPGSS.SCR
```

6. To identify whether the screen saver is secure, you need to query the *ScreenSaverSecure* property. This modified line of code is shown here.

```
gcim win32_desktop | select name, ScreenSaverExecutable, ScreenSaverSecure
```

7. Run the command. Your output will be similar to the following.

```
name                   ScreenSaverExecutable    ScreenSaverSecure
----                   ---------------------    -----------------
NT AUTHORITY\SYSTEM
IAMMRED\ed             C:\Windows\WLXPGSS.SCR    True
.DEFAULT
```

8. To identify the screen saver timeout values, you need to query the *ScreenSaverTimeout* property. The modified command is shown here.

```
gcim win32_desktop | select name, ScreenSaverExecutable, ScreenSaverSecure,
ScreenSaverTimeout
```

9. Run the command. The output will be similar to the following.

```
name                  ScreenSaverExecutable   ScreenSaverSecure   ScreenSaverTimeout
----                  ---------------------   -----------------   ------------------
NT AUTHORITY\SYSTEM
IAMMRED\ed            C:\Windows\WLXPGS...    True                600
.DEFAULT
```

10. If you want to retrieve all the properties related to screen savers, you can use a wildcard-character asterisk screen-filter pattern. Delete the three screen saver properties and replace them with the *Screen** wildcard pattern. The revised command is shown here.

```
gcim win32_desktop | select name, Screen*
```

11. Run the command. The output will appear similar to that shown here.

```
name                  : NT AUTHORITY\SYSTEM
ScreenSaverActive     : False
ScreenSaverExecutable :
ScreenSaverSecure     :
ScreenSaverTimeout    :

name                  : IAMMRED\ed
ScreenSaverActive     : True
ScreenSaverExecutable : C:\Windows\WLXPGSS.SCR
ScreenSaverSecure     : True
ScreenSaverTimeout    : 600
```

```
name                   : .DEFAULT
ScreenSaverActive      : False
ScreenSaverExecutable  :
ScreenSaverSecure      :
ScreenSaverTimeout     :
```

This concludes the procedure.

Obtaining service information: Step-by-step exercises

In this exercise, you will explore the use of the *Get-Service* cmdlet as you retrieve service information from your computer. You will sort and filter the output from the *Get-Service* cmdlet. In the second exercise, you will use WMI to retrieve similar information. You should compare the two techniques for ease of use and completeness of data.

Obtaining Windows service information by using the *Get-Service* cmdlet

1. Start the Windows PowerShell console.

2. From the Windows PowerShell prompt, use the *Get-Service* cmdlet to obtain a listing of all the services and their associated status. This is shown here.

    ```
    Get-Service
    ```

    A partial listing of the output from this command is shown here.

    ```
    Status   Name          DisplayName
    ------   ----          -----------
    Running  ALG           Application Layer Gateway Service
    Stopped  AppMgmt       Application Management
    Stopped  aspnet_state  ASP.NET State Service
    Running  AudioSrv      Windows Audio
    Running  BITS          Background Intelligent Transfer Ser...
    ```

3. Use the *Sort-Object* cmdlet to sort the listing of services. Specify the *status* property for *Sort-Object*. To sort the data based upon status, pipeline the results of the *Get-Service* cmdlet into the *Sort-Object* cmdlet. Use the *sort* alias for the *Sort-Object* cmdlet to reduce the amount of typing. The results are shown here.

    ```
    Get-Service | sort -Property status
    ```

    Partial output from this command is shown here.

    ```
    Status   Name          DisplayName
    ------   ----          -----------
    Stopped  RasAuto       Remote Access Auto Connection Manager
    Stopped  RDSessMgr     Remote Desktop Help Session Manager
    Stopped  odserv        Microsoft Office Diagnostics Service
    Stopped  ose           Office Source Engine
    ```

4. Use the *Get-Service* cmdlet to produce a listing of services. Sort the resulting list of services alphabetically by name. To do this, use the *Sort-Object* cmdlet to sort the listing of services by the *name* property. Pipeline the object returned by the *Get-Service* cmdlet into the *Sort-Object* cmdlet. The command to do this, using the *sort* alias for *Sort-Object*, is shown here.

```
Get-Service | sort -Property name
```

Partial output of this command is shown here.

```
Status   Name          DisplayName
------   ----          -----------
Running  ALG           Application Layer Gateway Service
Stopped  AppMgmt       Application Management
Stopped  aspnet_state  ASP.NET State Service
Running  AudioSrv      Windows Audio
Running  BITS          Background Intelligent Transfer Ser...
```

5. Use the *Get-Service* cmdlet to produce a listing of services. Sort the objects returned by both the name and the status of the service. The command to do this is shown here.

```
Get-Service | sort status, name
```

Partial output of this command is shown here.

```
Status   Name          DisplayName
------   ----          -----------
Stopped  AppMgmt       Application Management
Stopped  aspnet_state  ASP.NET State Service
Stopped  Browser       Computer Browser
Stopped  CcmExec       SMS Agent Host
Stopped  CiSvc         Indexing Service
```

6. Use the *Get-Service* cmdlet to return objects containing service information, using the *DisplayName* parameter and specifying **server** to retrieve all service objects that contain the word *server* in the display name.

```
Get-Service -DisplayName *server*
```

The resulting listing is shown here.

```
Status   Name              DisplayName
------   ----              -----------
Running  DcomLaunch        DCOM Server Process Launcher
Stopped  lanmanserver      Server
Stopped  MSSQL$SQLEXPRESS  SQL Server (SQLEXPRESS)
Stopped  MSSQLServerADHe...SQL Server Active Directory Helper
Stopped  SQLBrowser        SQL Server Browser
Stopped  SQLWriter         SQL Server VSS Writer
```

7. Use the *Get-Service* cmdlet with the *Name* parameter to retrieve an object that represents the BITS service. The code that does this is shown here.

```
Get-Service -Name BITS
```

8. Press the Up Arrow key to retrieve the previous command that retrieves the BITS service. Store the resulting object in a variable called *$a*. This code is shown here.

```
$a=Get-Service -Name BITS
```

9. Pipeline the object contained in the *$a* variable into the *Get-Member* cmdlet. You can use the *gm* alias to simplify typing. This code is shown here.

```
$a | gm
```

10. By using the object contained in the *$a* variable, obtain the status of the Bits service. The code that does this is shown here.

```
$a.status
```

11. If the Bits service is running, stop it. To do so, use the *Stop-Service* cmdlet. Instead of pipe-lining the object in the *$a* variable, you use the *-InputObject* argument from the *Stop-Service* cmdlet. The code to do this is shown here.

```
Stop-Service -InputObject $a
```

12. If the Bits service stops, use the *Start-Service* cmdlet instead of the *Stop-Service* cmdlet. Use the *-inputobject* argument to supply the object contained in the *$a* variable to the cmdlet. This is shown here.

```
Start-Service -InputObject $a
```

13. Query the *status* property of the object contained in the *$a* variable to confirm that the Bits service's status has changed. This is shown here.

```
$a.status
```

This concludes this step-by-step exercise.

 Note If you are working with a service that has its startup type set to Disabled, Windows PowerShell will not be able to start it and will return an error. If you do not have adminis-trator rights, Windows PowerShell will be unable to stop the service.

In the following exercise, you will explore the use of the *Win32_Service* WMI class by using the *Get-WmiObject* cmdlet as you retrieve service information from your computer.

Using WMI for service information

1. Start the Windows PowerShell console.

2. From the Windows PowerShell prompt, use the *Get-CimInstance* cmdlet to obtain a listing of all the services and their associated statuses. Use the *gcim* alias instead of typing *Get-CimInstance*. The command to do this is shown here.

```
gcim win32_service
```

A partial listing of the output from this command is shown here.

```
ProcessId    Name            StartMode    State      Status    ExitCode
---------    ----            ---------    -----      ------    --------
0            AJRouter        Manual       Stopped    OK        1077
0            ALG             Manual       Stopped    OK        1077
0            AppIDSvc        Manual       Stopped    OK        1077
940          Appinfo         Manual       Running    OK        0
0            AppMgmt         Manual       Stopped    OK        1077
0            AppReadiness    Manual       Stopped    OK        1077
```

3. Use the *Sort-Object* cmdlet to sort the listing of services. Specify the *state* property for the *Sort-Object* cmdlet. To sort the service information based upon the *state* of the service, pipeline the results of the *Get-CimInstance* cmdlet into the *Sort-Object* cmdlet. Use the *sort* alias for the *Sort-Object* cmdlet to reduce the amount of typing. The results are shown here.

```
gcim win32_service | sort state
```

Partial output from this command is shown here.

```
ProcessId    Name              StartMode    State      Status    ExitCode
---------    ----              ---------    -----      ------    --------
1448         MpsSvc            Auto         Running    OK        0
992          vmickvpexchange   Manual       Running    OK        0
972          vmicrdv           Manual       Running    OK        0
324          lmhosts           Manual       Running    OK        0
656          LSM               Auto         Running    OK        0
```

4. Use the *Get-CimInstance* cmdlet to produce a listing of services. Sort the resulting list of services alphabetically by *DisplayName*. To do this, use the *Sort-Object* cmdlet to sort the listing of services by the *name* property. Pipeline the object returned by the *Get-CimInstance* cmdlet into the *Sort-Object* cmdlet. The command to do this, using the *sort* alias for *Sort-Object*, is shown here.

```
gcim win32_service | sort DisplayName
```

Notice that the output does not appear to actually be sorted by the *DisplayName* property. There are two problems at work. The first is that there is a difference between the *name* property and the *DisplayName* property. The second problem is that the *DisplayName* property is not displayed by default. Partial output of this command appears here.

```
1448       BFE           Auto      Running    OK    0
0          BDESVC        Manual    Stopped    OK    1077
0          wbengine      Manual    Stopped    OK    1077
0          bthserv       Manual    Stopped    OK    1077
0          PeerDistSvc   Manual    Stopped    OK    1077
940        CertPropSvc   Manual    Running    OK    0
0          ClipSVC       Manual    Stopped    OK    0
```

5. Produce a service listing that is sorted by *DisplayName*. This time, use the *Select-Object* cmdlet to display both the *state* and the *DisplayName* properties. Use the *gcim*, *sort*, and *select* aliases to reduce typing. The command appears here.

```
gcim win32_service | sort DisplayName | select state, DisplayName
```

A sample of the output from the previous command appears here.

```
state                          DisplayName
-----                          -----------
Stopped                        ActiveX Installer (AxInstSV)
Stopped                        AllJoyn Router Service
Stopped                        App Readiness
Stopped                        Application Identity
Running                        Application Information
Stopped                        Application Layer Gateway Service
Stopped                        Application Management
```

6. Use the *Get-CimInstance* cmdlet to return an object containing service information. Pipeline the resulting object into a *Where-Object* cmdlet. Look for the word *server* in the display name. The resulting command is shown here.

```
gcim win32_service | ? displayname -match 'server'
```

The resulting listing is shown here.

```
ProcessId   Name           StartMode   State     Status   ExitCode
---------   ----           ---------   -----     ------   --------
656         DcomLaunch     Auto        Running   OK       0
940         LanmanServer   Auto        Running   OK       0
```

7. Use the *Get-CimInstance* cmdlet to retrieve a listing of service objects. Pipeline the resulting object to *Where-Object*. Use the *-equals* argument to return an object that represents the Bits service. The code that does this is shown here.

```
gcim win32_service | ? name -eq 'bits'
```

8. Press the Up Arrow key to retrieve the command that retrieves the Bits service. Store the resulting object in a variable called *$a*. This code is shown here.

```
$a= gcim win32_service | ? name -eq 'bits'
```

9. Pipeline the object contained in the *$a* variable into the *Get-Member* cmdlet. You can use the *gm* alias to simplify typing. This code is shown here.

```
$a | gm
```

10. By using the object contained in the *$a* variable, obtain the status of the Bits service. The code that does this is shown here.

```
$a.state
```

11. If the Bits service is running, stop it. To do so, use the *StopService* method. To call a WMI method, use the *Invoke-CimMethod* cmdlet. Pass the object contained in the *$a* variable as the *Input-Object* and specify the *StopService* method to the *MethodName* parameter. Tab completion works for the method name parameter, so you can type *s* and press the Tab key a couple of times until the *StopService* method appears. The code to do this is shown here.

```
Invoke-CimMethod -InputObject $a -MethodName StopService
```

12. If the Bits service stops, you will get a *ReturnValue* of 0. If you get a *ReturnValue* of 2, it means that access is denied, and you will need to start the Windows PowerShell console with administrator rights to stop the service. Query the *state* property of the object contained in the *$a* variable to confirm that the Bits service's status has changed. This is shown here.

```
$a.state
```

13. If you do not refresh the object stored in the *$a* variable, the original state is reported—regardless of whether the command has completed or not. To refresh the data stored in the *$a* variable, run the WMI query again. The code to do this is shown here.

```
$a = gcim Win32_Service | ? name -eq 'bits'
$a.state
```

14. If the Bits service is stopped, go ahead and start it back up by using the *StartService* method. The code to do this is shown here.

```
Invoke-CimMethod -InputObject $a -MethodName StartService
```

This concludes this step-by-step exercise.

Chapter 10 quick reference

To	Do this
Find the default WMI namespace on a computer	Use the Advanced tab in the WMI Control Properties dialog box.
Browse WMI classes on a computer	Use the *Get-CimClass* cmdlet. Use a wildcard character for the WMI class name.
Make a connection into WMI	Use the *Get-CimInstance* cmdlet in your script.
Use a shortcut name for the local computer	Use a dot (.) and assign it to the variable holding the computer name in the script.
Find detailed information about all WMI classes on a computer	Use the Platform SDK information found in the MSDN library (*http://msdn2.microsoft.com/en-us/library/aa394582.aspx*)
List the namespaces on a computer	Query for a class named *__NAMESPACE*.
List all providers installed in a particular namespace	Query for a class named *__Win32Provider*.
List all the classes in a particular namespace on a computer	Use the * wildcard character for the *Get-CimClass* cmdlet.
Quickly retrieve similarly named properties from a class	Use the *Select-Object* cmdlet and supply a wildcard-character asterisk (*) for the *-Property* parameter.

# CHAPTER 11

Querying WMI

After completing this chapter, you will be able to

- Understand the different methods for querying WMI.

- Use the *Select-Object* cmdlet to create a custom object from a WMI query.

- Configure the *-filter* argument to limit information returned by WMI.

- Configure the WMI query to return selected properties.

After network administrators and consultants get their hands on a couple of Windows Management Instrumentation (WMI) scripts, they begin to arrange all kinds of scenarios for use. This is both a good thing and a bad thing. The good thing is that WMI is powerful technology that can quickly solve many real problems. The bad thing is that a poorly written WMI script can adversely affect the performance of everything it touches—from client machines logging on to the network for the first time to huge infrastructure servers that provide the basis for mission-critical networked applications. This chapter examines the fundamentals of querying WMI in an effective manner. Along the way, it examines some of the more useful WMI classes and adds to your Windows PowerShell skills.

Alternate ways to connect to WMI

Chapter 10, "Using WMI," examined the basics of the *Get-WmiObject* and *Get-CimInstance* cmdlets to obtain specific information. When you make a connection to WMI, it is important to realize that there are default values used for the WMI connection.

The default values are stored in the following registry location: HKEY_LOCAL_MACHINE\SOFTWARE\ Microsoft\WBEM\Scripting. There are two keys: DEFAULT IMPERSONATION LEVEL and DEFAULT NAMESPACE. DEFAULT IMPERSONATION LEVEL is set to a value of 3, which means that WMI impersonates the logged-on user and therefore uses the logged-on user name, credentials, and rights. The default namespace is *Root\cimv2*, which means that for many of the tasks you will need to perform, the classes are immediately available. Use the *Get-ItemProperty* cmdlet to verify the default WMI configuration on a local computer. This command is shown here.

```
Get-ItemProperty HKLM:\SOFTWARE\Microsoft\WBEM\Scripting
```

In Figure 11-1, the *Get-ItemProperty* cmdlet retrieves the default WMI settings on a local computer. Next, the *ICM* alias for the *Invoke-Command* cmdlet retrieves the same information from a remote computer named DC1. Because the account that launched the Windows PowerShell ISE has rights on the remote computer, additional credentials are not required to run the command on the remote computer. Both the commands and the output from the commands are shown in the figure.

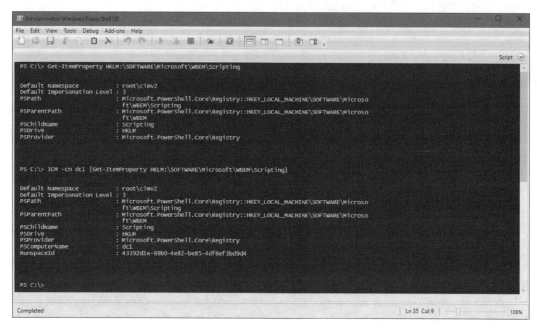

FIGURE 11-1 Use of the *Get-ItemProperty* cmdlet to verify default WMI settings from local and from remote computers.

In reality, a default namespace of *root/cimv2* and a default impersonation level of *impersonate* are good defaults. The default computer is the local machine, so you do not need to specify the computer name when you are simply running against the local machine.

 Tip Use default WMI values to simplify your WMI scripts. If you only want to return information from the local machine, the WMI class resides in the default namespace, and you intend to impersonate the logged-on user, the defaults are perfect. The defaults are fine when you are logged on to a machine with an account that has permission to access the information you need. The following command illustrates obtaining BIOS information from the local computer.

```
Get-CimInstance win32_bios
```

When you use the *Get-CimInstance* cmdlet and only supply the name of the WMI class, you are relying on the default values: default computer, default WMI namespace, and default impersonation level. The output from the previous command produces the information shown here, which is the main information you would want to know about the BIOS: the version, name, serial number, and maker.

```
SMBIOSBIOSVersion : 090006
Manufacturer      : American Megatrends Inc.
Name              : BIOS Date: 05/23/12 17:15:53  Ver: 09.00.06
SerialNumber      : 8570-3709-4791-5943-3863-4381-72
Version           : VRTUAL - 5001223
```

The amazing thing is that you can obtain such useful information by typing about 15 characters on the keyboard (using tab completion). Doing this in Microsoft Visual Basic Scripting Edition (VBScript) would require much more typing. However, if you want to retrieve different information from the *Win32_Bios* WMI class, or if you would like to get a different kind of output, you will need to work with the *Format* cmdlets, *Select-Object*, or *Out-GridView*. This technique appears in the procedure.

Retrieving properties

1. Open the Windows PowerShell console.

2. Use the *Get-CimInstance* cmdlet to retrieve the default properties of the *Win32_ComputerSystem* WMI class.

   ```
   Get-CimInstance Win32_ComputerSystem
   ```

   The results, with the default properties, are shown here.

   ```
   Name PrimaryOwnerName        Domain        TotalPhysicalMemory  Model           Manufa
                                                                                   cturer

   ---- ----------------        ------        -------------------  -----           ------
   C10  mredwilson@NWTraders.com NWTraders.com 4294496256           Virtual Machine Micros
                                                                                   oft Co
                                                                                   rporat
                                                                                   ion
   ```

3. If you are only interested in the name and the make and model of the computer, you will need to pipeline the results into a *Format-List* cmdlet and choose only the properties you want. This revised command is shown here.

   ```
   Get-CimInstance Win32_ComputerSystem | Format-List name, model, manufacturer
   ```

   The results are shown here.

   ```
   name         : C10
   model        : Virtual Machine
   manufacturer : Microsoft Corporation
   ```

4. If you are interested in all the properties from the *Win32_ComputerSystem* class, you have several options. The first is to use the Up Arrow key and modify the *Format-List* cmdlet. Instead of choosing three properties, use an asterisk (*). This revised command is shown here.

   ```
   Get-CimInstance Win32_ComputerSystem | Format-List *
   ```

   The results from this command are shown following this paragraph. Notice, however, that although the results seem impressive at first, interpreting the information will require a bit of work because many of the properties return coded values—that is, what exactly is an Admin-PasswordStatus of 3? Although useful to WMI gurus, these results are less exciting to typical network administrators unless they take the time to translate the coded values by looking up the *Win32_ComputerSystem* class in the WMI reference documentation.

```
AdminPasswordStatus            : 3
BootupState                    : Normal boot
ChassisBootupState             : 3
KeyboardPasswordStatus         : 3
PowerOnPasswordStatus          : 3
PowerSupplyState               : 3
PowerState                     : 0
FrontPanelResetStatus          : 3
ThermalState                   : 1
Status                         : OK
Name                           : C10
PowerManagementCapabilities    :
PowerManagementSupported       :
Caption                        : C10
Description                    : AT/AT COMPATIBLE
InstallDate                    :
CreationClassName              : Win32_ComputerSystem
NameFormat                     :
PrimaryOwnerContact            :
PrimaryOwnerName               : mredwilson@NWTraders.com
Roles                          : {LM_Workstation, LM_Server, NT}
InitialLoadInfo                :
LastLoadInfo                   :
ResetCapability                : 1
AutomaticManagedPagefile       : True
AutomaticResetBootOption       : True
AutomaticResetCapability       : True
BootOptionOnLimit              : 0
BootOptionOnWatchDog           : 0
BootROMSupported               : True
BootStatus                     : {0, 0, 0, 0...}
ChassisSKUNumber               :
CurrentTimeZone                : -480
DaylightInEffect               : False
DNSHostName                    : C10
Domain                         : NWTraders.com
DomainRole                     : 1
EnableDaylightSavingsTime      : True
HypervisorPresent              : True
InfraredSupported              : False
Manufacturer                   : Microsoft Corporation
Model                          : Virtual Machine
NetworkServerModeEnabled       : True
NumberOfLogicalProcessors      : 1
NumberOfProcessors             : 1
OEMLogoBitmap                  :
OEMStringArray                 : {[MS_VM_CERT/SHA1/9b80ca0d5dd061ec9da4e494f4c3fd119627
                                 0c22], 00000000000000000000000000000000, To be filed
                                 by MSFT}
```

```
PartOfDomain                : True
PauseAfterReset             : 3932100000
PCSystemType                : 1
PCSystemTypeEx              : 1
ResetCount                  : -1
ResetLimit                  : -1
SupportContactDescription   :
SystemFamily                :
SystemSKUNumber             :
SystemStartupDelay          :
SystemStartupOptions        :
SystemStartupSetting        :
SystemType                  : x64-based PC
TotalPhysicalMemory         : 4294496256
UserName                    :
WakeUpType                  : 6
Workgroup                   :
PSComputerName              :
CimClass                    : root/cimv2:Win32_ComputerSystem
CimInstanceProperties       : {Caption, Description, InstallDate, Name...}
CimSystemProperties         : Microsoft.Management.Infrastructure.CimSystemProperties
```

5. To get only the properties from the list that are added by the *CIM* cmdlets, use the Up Arrow key to retrieve the *Get-CimInstance Win32_ComputerSystem | Format-List ** command. Delete the asterisk in the *Format-List* command and replace it with an expression that limits the results to property names that begin with the letters *Cim*. This command is shown here.

```
Get-CimInstance Win32_ComputerSystem | Format-List Cim*
```

6. To get a listing of properties that begin with the letter *d*, use the Up Arrow key to retrieve the *Get-CimInstance Win32_ComputerSystem | Format-List Cim** command and change the *Format-List* cmdlet to retrieve only properties that begin with the letter *d*. To do this, substitute *d** for *Cim**. The revised command is shown here.

```
Get-CimInstance Win32_ComputerSystem | Format-List d*
```

7. Retrieve a listing of all the properties and their values that begin with either the letter *d* or the letter *t* from the *Win32_ComputerSystem* WMI class. Use the Up Arrow key to retrieve the previous *Get-CimInstance Win32_ComputerSystem | Format-List d** command. Use a comma to separate the *t** from the previous command. The revised command is shown here.

```
Get-CimInstance Win32_ComputerSystem | Format-List d*,t*
```

This concludes the procedure.

Tip After you use the *Get-CimInstance* cmdlet for a while, you might get tired of using tab completion and having to type **Get-CimI<tab>**. It might be easier to use the default alias of *gcim*. This alias can be discovered by using the following command.

```
Get-Alias -Definition Get-CimInstance
```

Working with disk drives

1. Open the Windows PowerShell console.

2. Use the *gcim* alias to retrieve the default properties for each drive defined on your system. To do this, use the *Win32_LogicalDisk* WMI class. This command is shown here.

```
gcim Win32_LogicalDisk
```

The results of the *gcim Win32_LogicalDisk* command are shown here.

```
DeviceID    DriveType    ProviderName    VolumeName    Size            FreeSpace
--------    ---------    ------------    ----------    ----            ---------
A:          2
C:          3                                          135996108800 12473370...
D:          5
```

3. To limit the drives returned by the WMI query to only local disk drives, you can supply a value of 3 for the *DriveType* property. Use the Up Arrow key to retrieve the previous command. Add the *DriveType* property to the *-Filter* parameter of the *Get-CimInstance* cmdlet with a value of 3. This revised command is shown here.

```
gcim Win32_LogicalDisk -Filter 'drivetype = 3'
```

The resulting output from the *gcim Win32_LogicalDisk -filter 'drivetype = 3'* command is shown here.

```
DeviceID    DriveType    ProviderName    VolumeName    Size            FreeSpace
--------    ---------    ------------    ----------    ----            ---------
C:          3                                          135996108800 12473370...
```

4. Open the Windows PowerShell ISE or some other script editor, and save the file as *<yourname>Logical Disk.ps1*.

5. Use the Up Arrow key in the Windows PowerShell console to retrieve the *gcim Win32_LogicalDisk -filter 'drivetype = 3'* command. Select the command, and then press Enter.

6. Paste the command into the *<yourname>LogicalDisk.ps1* script.

7. Declare a variable called *$Disk* at the top of your script. This command is shown here.

```
$Disk
```

8. Use the *$Disk* variable to hold the object returned by the command you copied from your Windows PowerShell console. Because you are planning to save the script, replace the *gcim* alias with the actual name of the cmdlet. The resulting command is shown here.

```
$Disk = Get-CimInstance Win32_LogicalDisk -Filter 'drivetype = 3'
```

9. Use the *Measure-Object* cmdlet to retrieve the minimum and maximum values for the *freespace* property. To do this, pipeline the previous object into the *Measure-Object* cmdlet. Specify *freespace* for the *-Property* parameter, and use the *-Minimum* and *-Maximum* switch parameters. Use the pipe character (|) to break your code into two lines. This command is shown here.

```
$Disk=Get-CimInstance Win32_LogicalDisk -Filter 'drivetype = 3' |
    Measure-Object -Property freespace -Minimum -Maximum
```

10. Print the resulting object that is contained in the *$Disk* variable. This command is shown here.

```
$Disk
```

The resulting printout on my computer is shown here.

```
Count    : 2
Average  :
Sum      :
Maximum  : 11944701952
Minimum  : 6163550208
Property : freespace
```

11. To remove the empty properties from the output, pipeline the previous command into a *Select-Object* cmdlet and select the *Property*, *Minimum*, and *Maximum* properties. Use the pipe character to break your code into multiple lines. The revised command is shown here.

```
$Disk=Get-CimInstance Win32_LogicalDisk -Filter 'drivetype = 3' |
    Measure-Object -Property freespace  -Minimum -Maximum |
    Select-Object -Property property, maximum, minimum
```

12. Save and run the script. Notice how the output is spread over the console. To tighten up the display, pipeline the resulting object into the *Format-Table* cmdlet. Use the *-AutoSize* switch parameter. The revised command is shown here.

```
$Disk=Get-CimInstance Win32_LogicalDisk -Filter 'drivetype = 3' |
    Measure-Object -Property freespace  -Minimum -Maximum |
    Select-Object -Property property, maximum, minimum |
    Format-Table -AutoSize
```

13. Save and run the script. The output on my computer is shown here.

```
Property    Maximum     Minimum
--------    -------     -------
freespace 11944685568 6164058112
```

> **Note** The *Win32_LogicalDisk* WMI class property *DriveType* can have a value of 0 through 6 (inclusive). The most useful of these values are as follows: 3 (local disk), 4 (network drive), 5 (compact disk), and 6 (RAM disk).

Tell me everything about everything!

When novices first write WMI scripts, they nearly all begin by asking for every property from every instance of a class. That is, the queries will essentially say, "Tell me everything about every process." (This is also referred to as the infamous *select* * query.) This approach can often return an overwhelming amount of data, particularly when you are querying a class such as installed software or processes and threads. Rarely would you need to have so much data. Typically, when looking for installed software, you're looking for information about a *particular* software package.

There are, however, several occasions when you might want to use the "Tell me everything about all instances of a particular class" query, including the following:

- During development of a script to get representative data

- When troubleshooting a more directed query—for example, when you're possibly trying to filter on a field that does not exist

- When the returned items are so few that being more precise doesn't make sense

To return all information from all instances, perform the following steps:

1. Make a connection to WMI by using the *Get-CimInstance* cmdlet.

2. Use the *-Query* parameter to supply the WMI Query Language (WQL) query to the *Get-CimInstance* cmdlet.

3. In the query, use the *Select* statement to choose everything.

   ```
   Select *
   ```

4. In the query, use the *From* statement to indicate the class from which you want to retrieve data—for example, *From Win32_Share*.

In the next script, you'll make a connection to the default namespace in WMI and return all the information about all the shares on a local machine. Reviewing the shares on your system is actually good practice, because in the past, numerous worms have propagated through unsecured shares, and you might have unused shares around. For example, a user might create a share for a friend and then forget to delete it. In the script that follows, called *ListShares.ps1*, all the information about shares present on the machine is reported. The information returned by *ListShares.ps1* will include the properties for the *Win32_Share* class that appear in Table 11-1.

ListShares.Ps1

```
$Query = "Select * from Win32_Share"
Get-CimInstance -query $Query
```

TABLE 11-1 *Win32_Share* properties

Data type	Property	Meaning
Boolean	*AllowMaximum*	Allow maximum number of connections? (*true* or *false*)
String	*Caption*	Short one-line description
String	*Description*	Description
Datetime	*InstallDate*	When the share was created (optional)
Uint32	*MaximumAllowed*	Number of concurrent connections allowed (only valid when *AllowMaximum* is set to *false*)
String	*Name*	Share name
String	*Path*	Physical path to the share
String	*Status*	Current status of the share (degraded, OK, or failed)
Uint32	*Type*	Type of resource shared (such as disk, file, or printer)

Quick check

Q. What is the syntax for a query that returns all properties of a specified WMI object?

A. *Select * from <WMI class name>* returns all properties of a specified object.

Q. What is one reason for using *Select * * instead of a more directed query?

A. In troubleshooting, *Select * * is useful because it returns any available data. In addition, *Select * * is useful for trying to characterize the data that might be returned from a query.

Returning selective data from all instances

The next level of sophistication (from using *Select * *) is to return only the properties you are interested in. This is a more efficient strategy than returning everything from a class. For instance, in the previous example, you entered *Select * *, which returned a lot of data you might not necessarily have been interested in. Suppose you want to know only what shares are on each machine.

To select specific data, perform the following steps:

1. Make a connection to WMI by using the *Get-CimInstance* cmdlet.

2. Use the *-Query* parameter to supply the WMI query to the *Get-CimInstance* cmdlet.

3. In the query, use the *Select* statement to choose the specific property you are interested in—for example, *Select name*.

4. In the query, use the *From* statement to indicate the class from which you want to retrieve data—for example, *From Win32_Share*.

You only need to make two small changes in the *ListShares.ps1* script to garner specific data through the WMI script. In place of the asterisk in the *Select* statement assigned at the beginning of the script, substitute the property you want. In this case, only the name of the shares is required.

The second change is to eliminate all unwanted properties from the *Output* section. The strange thing here is the way that Windows PowerShell works. In the *Select* statement, you selected only the *name* property. However, if you were to print out the results without further refinement, you would also retrieve unwanted additional properties. By using the *Select-Object* cmdlet and selecting only the property name, you eliminate the unwanted excess. To make the output more readable, the *Sort-Object* cmdlet is used to sort the listing alphabetically. Here is the modified *ListNameOnlyShares.ps1* script.

ListNameOnlyShares.Ps1

```
$Query = "Select Name from Win32_Share"
Get-CimInstance -Query $Query |
Sort-Object name |
Select-Object name
```

Selecting multiple properties

If you're interested in only certain properties, you can use *Select* to specify that. All you have to do is separate the properties by a comma. Suppose you run the preceding script and find a number of undocumented shares on one of the servers—you might want a little bit more information, such as the path to the share and how many people are allowed to connect to it. By default, when a share is created, the "maximum allowed" bit is set, which basically says anyone who has rights to the share can connect. This can be a problem, because if too many people connect to a share, they can degrade the performance of the server. To preclude such an eventuality, I always specify a maximum number of connections to the server. The commands to list these properties are in the *ListNamePathShare.ps1* script, which follows.

> **Note** Occasionally, people ask whether spaces or capitalization in the property list matter. In fact, when I first started writing scripts and they failed, I often modified spacing and capitalization in feeble attempts to make the script work. Spacing and capitalization *do not matter* for WMI properties.

ListNamePathShare.ps1

```
$Query = "Select Name, Path, AllowMaximum from Win32_Share"
Get-CimInstance -Query $Query |
Sort-Object name |
Select-Object name, Path, AllowMaximum
```

Working with running processes

1.   Open the Windows PowerShell console.

2.   Use the *Get-Process* cmdlet to obtain a listing of processes on your machine.

A portion of the results from the command is shown here.

```
Handles  NPM(K)    PM(K)      WS(K) VM(M)     CPU(s)      Id ProcessName
-------  ------    -----      ----- -----     ------      -- -----------
    101       5     1132       3436    32       0.03     660 alg
    439       7     1764       2856    60       6.05    1000 csrss
    121       5      912       3532    37       0.22    1256 ctfmon
    629      19    23772      23868   135     134.13     788 explorer
    268       7    12072      18344   109       1.66    1420 hh
```

3. To return information about a process named *explorer*, use the *-Name* parameter. This command is shown here.

```
Get-Process -Name explorer
```

The results of this command are shown here.

```
Handles  NPM(K)    PM(K)      WS(K) VM(M)     CPU(s)      Id ProcessName
-------  ------    -----      ----- -----     ------      -- -----------
    619      18    21948      22800   115     134.28     788 explorer
```

4. Use the *Get-CimInstance* cmdlet to retrieve information about processes on the machine. Pipeline the results into the *more* function, as shown here.

```
Get-CimInstance Win32_Process | more
```

Notice that the results go on for a page or two. The last few lines of the first page are shown here.

```
2524            csrss.exe      260          1544192          2199114883072
2648            winlogon.exe   165           970752          2199075414016
2572            dwm.exe        295         22958080          2199164170240
2928            taskhostex.exe 273          4722688          2199290822656
-- More   --
```

5. To retrieve information only about the Explorer.exe process, use the *-filter* argument and specify that the *name* property is equal to *explorer.exe*. The revised command is shown here.

```
Get-CimInstance Win32_Process -Filter "name = 'explorer.exe'"
```

6. To display a table that is similar to the one produced by *Get-Process,* use the Up Arrow key to retrieve the previous *Get-CimInstance* command. Copy it to the Clipboard by selecting it and then pasting it into Notepad or some other script editor. Pipeline the results into the *Format-Table* cmdlet and choose the appropriate properties, as shown in the following code. Saving this command into a script makes it easier to work with later. It also makes it easier to write the script by breaking the lines instead of requiring you to type one long command. I called the script *ExplorerProcess.ps1,* and it is shown here.

```
Get-CimInstance Win32_Process -Filter "name='explorer.exe'" |
Format-Table handlecount,quotaNonPagedPoolUsage, PeakVirtualSize,
WorkingSetSize, VirtualSize, UserModeTime,KernelModeTime,
ProcessID, Name
```

Note The preceding code is a single-line Windows PowerShell command. If pasted directly into either the Windows PowerShell ISE or the Windows PowerShell console, it will run properly. However, if you are entering it into the Windows PowerShell console, remember that the end of each line does not terminate the command and that it should continue to flow to the next line as it wraps.

This concludes the working with running processes procedure.

 Caution When using the *-Filter* parameter of the *Get-CimInstance* cmdlet, pay attention to the use of quotation marks. The *-Filter* parameter is surrounded by double quotation marks. The value being supplied for the property is surrounded by single quotation marks—for example, *-Filter "name = 'explorer.exe'"*. This can cause a lot of frustration if not followed exactly.

Adding logging

1. Open the Windows PowerShell console.

2. Use the alias for the *Get-CimInstance* cmdlet and supply the *Win32_LogicalDisk* class as the argument to it. Use the redirection arrow (>) to redirect output to a file called *Diskinfo.txt*. Place this file in the C:\MyOutput folder. This command is shown here.

   ```
   gcim Win32_LogicalDisk >c:\MyOutput\DiskInfo.txt
   ```

3. Use the Up Arrow key to retrieve the previous command. This time, change the class name to *Win32_OperatingSystem* and call the text file *OSinfo.txt*. This command is shown here.

   ```
   gcim Win32_OperatingSystem >c:\MyOutput\OSinfo.txt
   ```

4. Use the Up Arrow key to retrieve the previous *gcim Win32_OperatingSystem* command. Change the WMI class to *Win32_ComputerSystem* and use two redirection arrows (>>) to cause the output to append to the file. Use Notepad to open the file, but include the *Get-CimInstance* (*gcim*) command, separated by a semicolon. This is illustrated next. (I've continued the command to the next line by using the grave accent character [`] for readability.)

   ```
   gcim Win32_ComputerSystem >>c:\MyOutput\OSinfo.txt; `
   notepad c:\MyOutput\OSinfo.txt
   ```

   This concludes the procedure.

Quick check

Q. To select specific properties from an object, what do you need to do on the *Select* line?

A. You need to separate the specific properties of an object with a comma on the *Select* line.

Q. To avoid error messages, what must be done when you select individual properties on the *Select* line?

A. Errors can be avoided if you make sure each property used is specified on the *Select* line. For example, the WMI query is just like a paper bag that gets filled with items that are picked up by using the *Select* statement. If you do not put something in the paper bag, you cannot pull anything out of it. In the same manner, if you do not select a property, you cannot later print or sort on that property. This is exactly the way that an SQL *Select* statement works.

Q. What can you check for in your script if it fails with an "object does not support this method or property" error?

A. If you are getting this type of error message, you might want to ensure that you have referenced the property in your *Select* statement before trying to work with it in an *Output* section. In addition, you might want to check to ensure that the property actually exists.

Choosing specific instances

In many situations, you will want to limit the data you return to a specific instance of a particular WMI class in the data set. If you go back to your query and add a *Where* clause to the *Select* statement, you'll be able to greatly reduce the amount of information returned by the query. Notice that in the value associated with the WMI query, you added a dependency that indicated you wanted only information with share name *C$* (in the *ListShares.ps1* script associated with the book). This value is not case sensitive, but it must be surrounded with single quotation marks, as you can tell in the *WMI Query* string in the *ListSpecificShares.ps1* script associated with the files for the book. These single quotation marks are important because they tell WMI that the value is a string value and not some other programmatic item. Because the addition of the *Where* statement was the only thing you really added to the *ListShares.ps1* script, I won't provide a long discussion of the *ListSpecificShares.ps1* script. The *ListSpecificShares.ps1* script is shown here.

```
$Query = "Select Name from Win32_Share where name = 'C$'"
Get-CimInstance -query $Query |
Sort-Object name |
Select-Object name
```

To limit specific data, do the following:

1. Make a connection to WMI by using the *Get-CimInstance* cmdlet.

2. Use the *Select* statement in the *WMI Query* argument to choose the specific property you are interested in—for example, *Select name*.

3. Use the *From* statement in the *WMI Query* argument to indicate the class from which you want to retrieve data—for example, *From Win32_Share*.

4. Add a *Where* clause in the *WMI Query* argument to further limit the data set that is returned. Make sure the properties specified in the *Where* clause are first mentioned in the *Select* statement—for example, *Where name*.

5. Add an evaluation operator. You can use the equal sign (=) or the less-than (<) or greater-than (>) signs—for example, *Where name = 'C$'*.

Eliminating the *WMI Query* argument

1. Open the Windows PowerShell ISE or the Windows PowerShell script editor.

2. Declare a variable and call it *$Filter*. This variable will be used to hold the string that will contain the WMI filter to be used with the *Get-CimInstance* command. The variable and the associated string value are shown here.

```
$Filter = "name='c$'"
```

3. Use the *Get-CimInstance* cmdlet to perform the query. Specify the class name as *Win32_Share*. Add the filter contained in the *$Filter* variable to the *–Filter* parameter. This line of code is shown here.

```
Get-CimInstance –ClassName Win32_Share –Filter $Filter
```

4. At the end of the line, add the pipe character and press Enter. At the beginning of the third line, add the *Format-List* cmdlet. Use the asterisk to tell the *Format-List* cmdlet you want to retrieve all properties. This line of code is shown here.

```
Format-List *
```

The completed script is shown here.

```
$Filter = "name='c$'"
Get-CimInstance –ClassName Win32_Share –filter $Filter |
Format-List *
```

Sample output is shown here.

```
Status              : OK
Type                : 2147483648
Name                : C$
Caption             : Default share
Description         : Default share
InstallDate         :
AccessMask          :
AllowMaximum        : True
MaximumAllowed      :
Path                : C:\
PSComputerName      :
```

```
CimClass              : root/cimv2:Win32_Share
CimInstanceProperties : {Caption, Description, InstallDate, Name...}
CimSystemProperties   : Microsoft.Management.Infrastructure.CimSystemProperties
```

5. If your results are not similar, compare your script with the *ShareNoQuery.ps1* script.

This completes the procedure.

Using an operator

One of the nice things you can do is use greater-than and less-than operators in your evaluation clause. What is so great about greater-than? It makes working with some alphabetic and numeric characters easy. If you work on a server that hosts home directories for users (which are often named after their user names), you can easily produce a list of all home directories from the letters *D* through *Z* by using the *> D* operation. Keep in mind that *D$* is greater than *D*, and if you really want shares that begin with the letter *E*, you can specify "greater than or equal to E." This command would look like *>='E'*.

ListGreaterThanShares.ps1

```
$Query = "Select name from win32_Share where name > 'd'"

Get-CimInstance -query $Query |
Sort-Object -property name |
Format-List -property name
```

Identifying service accounts

1. Open the Windows PowerShell ISE or some other script editor.

2. On the first line, declare a variable called *$Query*. You will select only the *startname* property and the *name* property from the *Win32_Service* WMI class. This line of code is shown here.

    ```
    $Query = "Select startName, name from Win32_Service"
    ```

3. On the next line, use the *Get-CimInstance* cmdlet. Use the *-Query* parameter of the *Get-CimInstance* cmdlet to use the query you specified earlier. Because you will pipeline the results of the command to the next cmdlet, use the pipe character at the end of the line. The code that does this is shown here.

    ```
    Get-CimInstance -Query $Query |
    ```

4. Use the object that comes back from the *Get-CimInstance* cmdlet and pipeline it into the *Sort-Object* cmdlet. Use the *Sort-Object* cmdlet to sort the list first by the *startName* property and second by the *name* property. Place the pipe character at the end of the line because you will pipeline this object into another cmdlet. The code that does this is shown here.

    ```
    Sort-Object startName, name |
    ```

5. Finally, you will receive the pipelined object into the *Format-List* cmdlet. You first format the list by the *name* property from *Win32_Service* and then print out the *startName*. This code is shown here.

```
Format-List name, startName
```

The completed script is shown here.

```
$Query = "Select startName, name from win32_service"
Get-CimInstance -Query $Query |
Sort-Object startName, name |
Format-List name, startName
```

6. Save the script as *<yourname>IdentifyServiceAccounts.ps1*. Run the script. You should get output similar that shown here. If not, compare your script to the *IdentifyServiceAccounts.ps1* script.

```
name      : Appinfo
startName : LocalSystem

name      : AppMgmt
startName : LocalSystem

name      : AppReadiness
startName : LocalSystem

name      : AppXSvc
startName : LocalSystem
```

This completes the procedure.

Logging service accounts

1. Open the *IdentifyServiceAccounts.ps1* script in Notepad or your favorite script editor. Save the script as *<yourname>IdentifyServiceAccountsLogged.ps1*.

2. Declare a new variable called *$Query*. This variable will contain the WMI query to select services information from the Win32_Service WMI class. Select the StartName and name from Win32_Service. This code is shown here.

```
$Query = "Select StartName, Name from Win32_Service"
```

3. On the next line, declare a new variable called *$File*. This variable will be used for the *-FilePath* parameter of the *Out-File* cmdlet. Assign the string *C:\MyOutPut\ServiceAccounts.txt* to the *$File* variable. This code is shown here.

```
$File = "c:\MyOutPut\ServiceAccounts.txt"
```

4. Under the line of code where you declared the *$File* variable, use the *New-Variable* cmdlet to create a constant called *ASCII*. When you assign the *ASCII* value to the *-Name* parameter of the *New-Variable* cmdlet, remember to leave off the dollar sign. Use the *-Value* parameter of the *New-Variable* cmdlet to assign a value of *ASCII* to the *ASCII* constant. Use the *-Option* parameter and supply *constant* as the value for the parameter. The completed command is shown here.

```
New-Variable -Name ASCII -Value "ASCII" -Option constant
```

5. On the next line, use the *Get-CimInstance* cmdlet and the *-Query* parameter with the *$Query* variable declared previously to query the Win32_Service WMI class. At the end of the line, add a pipe character. The code is shown here.

```
Get-CimInstance -Query $Query |
```

6. By pipelining the results of the previous cmdlet into the *Sort-Object* cmdlet, you ensure that the data returned will be sorted by StartName followed by Name. At the end of the line, add a pipe character. The code is shown here.

```
Sort-Object StartName, Name |
```

7. On the next line, use the *Format-List* cmdlet to display only the *Name* and *StartName* properties. At the end of the *Format-List* line, place the pipe character. This is shown here.

```
Format-List name, startName |
```

8. On the next line, use the *Out-File* cmdlet to produce an output file containing the results of the previous command. Use the *-FilePath* argument to specify the path and file name to create. Use the value contained in the *$File* variable. To ensure that the output file is easily read, use ASCII encoding. To do this, use the *-Encoding* parameter of the *Out-File* cmdlet and supply the value contained in the *$ASCII* variable. To make sure you add information to the file, use the *-Append* switch parameter and the *-NoClobber* switch parameter to keep from overwriting the file. The resulting code is shown here.

```
Out-File -FilePath $File -Encoding $ASCII -Append -NoClobber
```

9. Save and run your script. You should find a file called *ServiceAccounts.txt* in your MyOutPut directory on drive C. The contents of the file will be similar to the output shown here.

```
name      : AppMgmt
startName : LocalSystem

name      : AudioSrv
startName : LocalSystem

name      : BITS
startName : LocalSystem
```

This concludes the procedure.

Quick check

Q. To limit the specific data returned by a query, what WQL technique can you use?

A. The *Where* clause of the *Query* argument is very powerful in limiting the specific data returned by a query.

Q. What are three possible operators that can be employed in creating powerful *Where* clauses for WMI queries?

A. The equal sign (=) and the greater-than (>) and less-than (<) signs can be used to evaluate the data before returning the data set.

Shortening the syntax

Windows PowerShell is a great tool to use interactively from the command line. The short syntax, cmdlet and function parameters, and shortcut aliases to common cmdlets all work together to create a powerful command-line environment. WMI also benefits from this optimization. Rather than typing complete WQL *select* statements and *where* clauses and storing them into a variable, and then using the *-Query* parameter from the *Get-CimInstance* cmdlet, you can use the *-Property* and *-Filter* parameters from the cmdlet. Use the *-Property* parameter to replace the property names normally supplied as part of the *select* clause, and the *-Filter* parameter to replace the portion of code usually contained in the *where* clause of the WQL statement.

Using the *-Property* parameter

In the code that follows, the traditional WQL *select* statement retrieves the *name* and *handle* properties from the *Win32_Process* WMI class. The $query variable stores the WQL query, and the *Get-CimInstance* cmdlet uses this query to retrieve the requested information from the WMI class. When this code is executed, notice that the *handle* property is not displayed in the console. This is due to the default formatting for the Type *Microsoft.Management.Infrastructure.CimInstance#root/cimv2/Win32_Process*, which does not include this property; however, using the *Format-List* cmdlet as noted later addresses this issue.

```
$query = "Select name, handle from Win32_Process"
Get-CimInstance -Query $query
```

You can obtain the same information in a single line by using the *-ClassName* parameter to specify the WMI class name. The *-Property* parameter is used to select the two properties from the *Win32_Process* WMI class. The revised code appears here.

```
Get-CimInstance -ClassName Win32_Process -Property name, handle
```

The difference between the two commands—the one that uses the WQL syntax and the one that supplies values directly for parameters—is not in the information returned, aside from the formatting noted above, but rather in the approach to using the *Get-CimInstance* cmdlet. For some people, the WQL syntax might be more natural, and for others, the use of direct parameters might be easier. WMI treats both types of commands in the same manner.

It is possible to shorten the length of the WQL type of command by supplying the WQL query directly to the *query* parameter. This technique appears here.

```
Get-CimInstance -Query "Select name, handle from Win32_Process"
```

For short WQL queries, this technique is perfectly valid; however, for longer WQL queries that extend to multiple lines of code, it is more readable to store the query in a variable and supply the variable to the *query* parameter instead of using the query directly.

Using the *-Filter* parameter

The *-Filter* parameter of the *Get-CimInstance* cmdlet replaces the *where* clause of a WQL query. For example, in the code that follows, the WQL query chooses the *name* and *handle* properties from the *Win32_Process* WMI class, where the name of the process begins with a letter greater than *t* in the alphabet. The WQL query stored in the *$query* variable executes via the *Get-CimInstance* cmdlet, and the results pipeline to the *Format-Table* cmdlet, where the column's name and handle are automatically sized to fit the Windows PowerShell console. The commands appear here.

```
$query = "Select name, handle from Win32_Process where name > 't'"
Get-CimInstance -Query $query | Format-Table name, handle -autosize
```

To perform the same WMI query by using the parameters of the *Get-CimInstance* cmdlet instead of composing a WQL query, you simply use the property names that follow the *select* statement in the original WQL query, in addition to the filter that follows the *where* clause. The resulting command appears here.

```
Get-CimInstance -Class Win32_Process -Filter "name > 't'"
```

To display succinct output from the previous command, pipeline the results to the *Format-Table* cmdlet and select the two properties named in the *properties* parameter, and use the *-autosize* switch to tighten up the output in the Windows PowerShell console. The revised commands, along with the associated output, are shown in Figure 11-2.

```
PS C:\> $query = "Select name, handle from Win32_Process where name > 't'"
PS C:\> Get-CimInstance -Query $query | Format-Table name, handle -AutoSize

name           handle
----           ------
wininit.exe    472
winlogon.exe   520
VSSVC.exe      1672
winlogon.exe   2648
taskhostex.exe 2928
TscHelp.exe    3736
taskhostw.exe  3880
wmpnetwk.exe   1204
WmiPrvSE.exe   352


PS C:\> Get-CimInstance -ClassName Win32_Process -Filter "Name > 't'" | ft name, hand
le -AutoSize

name           handle
----           ------
wininit.exe    472
winlogon.exe   520
VSSVC.exe      1672
winlogon.exe   2648
taskhostex.exe 2928
TscHelp.exe    3736
taskhostw.exe  3880
wmpnetwk.exe   1204
WmiPrvSE.exe   352


PS C:\> _
```

FIGURE 11-2 WMI output derived from a WQL query and use of the *Get-CimInstance* parameters.

Working with software: Step-by-step exercises

In the first exercise, you will explore the use of *Win32_Product* and classes provided by the WMI Microsoft Installer (MSI) provider. In the second exercise, you will work with the environment provider.

> **Note** The first exercise, which takes advantage of the *Win32_Product* class, is for illustrative purposes, to demonstrate the power of WMI and Windows PowerShell. The *Win32_Product* class, when queried, will initiate an MSI consistency check, which can have undesirable effects. When working with this class, use caution.

Using WMI to find installed software

1. Open the Windows PowerShell ISE or your favorite script editor.

2. On the first line, you will use the variable *$Query* to hold your WMI query. This query will select everything from the *Win32_Product* WMI class. This code is shown here.

   ```
   $Query = "Select * from Win32_Product"
   ```

3. Because this query can take a rather long time to complete (depending on the speed of your machine, CPU load, and number of installed applications), use the *Write-Host* cmdlet to inform the user that the script could take a while to run. As long as you're using *Write-Host*, let's have

a little fun and specify the -*ForegroundColor* parameter of the *Write-Host* cmdlet, which will change the color of your font. I chose blue, but you can choose any color you want. Use the `n escape sequence to specify a new line at the end of your command. I used the grave accent character to break the line of code for readability, but this certainly is not necessary for you. The completed code is shown here.

```
Write-Host "Counting Installed Products. This" `
   "may take a little while. " -ForegroundColor blue `n
```

4. On the next line, use the *Get-CimInstance* cmdlet. Supply the -*Query* parameter with the value contained in the *$Query* variable. This code is shown here.

```
Get-CimInstance -Query $Query
```

5. Save and run your script. Call it *<yourname>MSI_InstalledApplications.ps1*. You should get output similar to that shown here. If you do not, compare it with *MSI_InstalledApplications.ps1*.

```
Counting Installed Products. This may take a little while.


Name    Caption   Vendor            Version   IdentifyingNumber
----    -------   ------            -------   -----------------
NWT 11  NWT 11    NWTraders Corporation  11.4.0    {5EAF3FAA-C4B6-5741-81B4-64CD...
```

6. Now you'll add a timer to your script to find out how long it takes to execute. On the first line of your script, above the *$Query* line, declare a variable called *$dteStart* and assign the date object that is returned by the *Get-Date* cmdlet to it. This line of code is shown here.

```
$dteStart = Get-Date
```

7. At the end of your script, under the last *Get-CimInstance* command, declare a variable called *$dteEnd* and assign the date object that is returned by the *Get-Date* cmdlet to it. This line of code is shown here.

```
$dteEnd = Get-Date
```

8. On the next line, declare a variable called *$dteDiff* and assign the date object that is returned by the *New-TimeSpan* cmdlet to it. Use the *New-TimeSpan* cmdlet to subtract the two date objects contained in the *$dteStart* and *$dteEnd* variables. The *$dteStart* variable will go first. This command is shown here.

```
$dteDiff = New-TimeSpan $dteStart $dteEnd
```

9. Use the *Write-Host* cmdlet to print the total number of seconds it took for the script to run. This value is contained in the *totalSeconds* property of the date object held in the *$dteDiff* variable. This command is shown here.

```
Write-Host "It took " $dteDiff.totalSeconds " Seconds" `
   " for this script to complete"
```

10. Save your script as *\<yourname>MSI_InstalledApplications_Timed.ps1*. Run your script and compare your output with that shown here. If your results are not similar, compare your script with the *MSI_InstalledApplications_Timed.ps1* script.

```
Counting Installed Products. This may take a little while.

Name      Caption    Vendor                  Version    IdentifyingNumber
----      -------    ------                  -------    -----------------
NWT 11    NWT 11     NWTraders Corporation   11.4.0     {5EAF9FAA-C4B6-4741-81B4-74CD...

It took  28.1859347  Seconds  for this script to complete
```

This concludes the exercise.

In the following exercise, you'll explore Windows environment variables.

Working with Windows environment variables

1. Open the Windows PowerShell console.

2. Use the *Get-CimInstance* cmdlet to view the common properties of the *Win32_Environment* WMI class. Use the *gcim* alias to make it easier to type. This command is shown here.

```
gcim Win32_Environment
```

Partial output from this command is shown here.

```
Name          UserName                     VariableValue
----          --------                     -------------
USERNAME      <SYSTEM>                     SYSTEM
Path          <SYSTEM>                     %SystemRoot%\system32;%SystemR...
ComSpec       <SYSTEM>                     %SystemRoot%\system32\cmd.exe
TMP           <SYSTEM>                     %SystemRoot%\TEMP
OS            <SYSTEM>                     Windows_NT
```

3. To view all the properties of the *Win32_Environment* class, pipeline the object returned by the *Get-CimInstance* cmdlet to the *Format-List* cmdlet while specifying the asterisk. Use the Up Arrow key to retrieve the previous *gcim* command. This command is shown here.

```
gcim Win32_Environment | Format-List *
```

The output from the previous command will be similar to that shown here.

```
Status           : OK
Name             : USERNAME
SystemVariable   : True
Caption          : <SYSTEM>\USERNAME
Description      : <SYSTEM>\USERNAME
InstallDate      :
UserName         : <SYSTEM>
VariableValue    : SYSTEM
PSComputerName   :
CimClass         : root/cimv2:Win32_Environment
```

```
CimInstanceProperties : {Caption, Description, InstallDate, Name...}
CimSystemProperties   : Microsoft.Management.Infrastructure.CimSystemProperties
```

4. Scroll through the results returned by the previous command, and examine the properties and their associated values. *Name*, *UserName*, and *VariableValue* are the most important properties from the class. Use the Up Arrow key to retrieve the previous *gcim* command and change *Format-List* to *Format-Table*. After the *Format-Table* cmdlet, type the three properties you want to retrieve: *Name*, *VariableValue*, and *Username*. This command is shown here.

```
gcim Win32_Environment | Format-Table name, variableValue, userName
```

5. The results from this command will be similar to the partial results shown here.

```
name                variableValue                userName
----                -------------                --------
USERNAME            SYSTEM                       <SYSTEM>
Path                %SystemRoot%\system32;%S...  <SYSTEM>
ComSpec             %SystemRoot%\system32\cm...  <SYSTEM>
TMP                 %SystemRoot%\TEMP            <SYSTEM>
OS                  Windows_NT                   <SYSTEM>
```

6. Use the Up Arrow key to retrieve the previous *gcim* command, and delete the *userName* property and the trailing comma. This command is shown here.

```
gcim Win32_Environment | Format-Table name, variableValue
```

The results from this command will be similar to those shown here.

```
name                variableValue
----                -------------
USERNAME            SYSTEM
Path                %SystemRoot%\system32;%SystemRoot%;%Sy...
ComSpec             %SystemRoot%\system32\cmd.exe
TMP                 %SystemRoot%\TEMP
OS                  Windows_NT
```

7. Notice that the spacing is a little strange. To correct this, use the Up Arrow key to retrieve the previous command. Add the *-AutoSize* argument to the *Format-Table* command. You can use tab completion to finish the command by typing **-a** and pressing the Tab key. The completed command is shown here.

```
gcim Win32_Environment | Format-Table name, variableValue -AutoSize
```

8. Now that you have a nicely formatted list, you'll compare the results with those produced by the environment provider. To do this, you'll use the Environment (Env:) PowerShell drive. Use the *Set-Location* cmdlet to set your location to the Env: drive. The command to do this is shown here. (You can, of course, use the *sl* alias if you prefer.)

```
Set-Location env:
```

9. Use the *Get-ChildItem* cmdlet to produce a listing of all the environment variables on the computer. The command to do this is shown here.

```
Get-ChildItem
```

Partial output from the *Get-ChildItem* cmdlet is shown here.

```
Name                        Value
----                        -----
ALLUSERSPROFILE             C:\ProgramData
APPDATA                     C:\Users\administrator\AppData\Roaming
CLIENTNAME                  EDLT
CommonProgramFiles          C:\Program Files\Common Files
CommonProgramFiles(x86)     C:\Program Files (x86)\Common Files
CommonProgramW6432          C:\Program Files\Common Files
COMPUTERNAME                C10
ComSpec                     C:\Windows\system32\cmd.exe
```

10. Set your location back to drive C. The command to do this is shown here.

```
Set-Location c:\
```

11. Retrieve the alias for the *Get-History* cmdlet. To do this, use the *Get-Alias* cmdlet with *Get-History* as the value for the *-Definition* parameter. The command to do this is shown here.

```
Get-Alias -Definition Get-History
```

The resulting output, shown here, tells you there are three aliases defined for *Get-History*.

```
CommandType     Name                              Version    Source
-----------     ----                              -------    ------
Alias           ghy -> Get-History
Alias           h -> Get-History
Alias           history -> Get-History
```

12. Use the Up Arrow key and retrieve the previous *Get-Alias* command. Change the definition from *Get-History* to *Invoke-History*. This command is shown here.

```
Get-Alias -Definition Invoke-History
```

13. The resulting output, shown here, tells you there are two aliases defined for *Invoke-History*.

```
CommandType     Name                              Version    Source
-----------     ----                              -------    ------
Alias           ihy -> Invoke-History
Alias           r -> Invoke-History
```

14. Use the *Get-History* cmdlet to retrieve a listing of all the commands you have typed into Windows PowerShell. I prefer to use *ghy* for *Get-History* because of similarity with *ihy* (for *Invoke-History*). The *Get-History* command using *ghy* is shown here.

```
ghy
```

15. Examine the output from the *Get-History* cmdlet. You will get a list similar to the one shown here.

```
1 gcim win32_environment
```

```
 2 gcim win32_environment | Format-List *
 3 gcim win32_environment | Format-Table name, variableValue, userName
 4 gcim win32_environment | Format-Table name, variableValue
 5 gcim win32_environment | Format-Table name, variableValue -AutoSize
 6 sl env:
 7 gci
 8 sl c:\
 9 Get-Alias -Definition Get-History
10 Get-Alias -Definition Invoke-History
```

16. Produce the listing of environment variables by using the Env: drive. This time, you will do it in a single command. Use *Set-Location* to set the location to the Env: drive. Then continue the command by using a semicolon and then *Get-ChildItem* to produce the list. Use the *sl* alias and the *gci* alias to type this command. The command is shown here.

```
sl env:;gci
```

17. Note that your PS drive is still set to the Env: drive. Use the *Set-Location* cmdlet to change back to the C PS drive. This command is shown here.

```
sl c:\
```

18. Use the Up Arrow key to bring up the *sl env:;gci* command, and this time, add another semicolon and another *sl* command to change back to the C PS drive. The revised command is shown here.

```
sl env:;gci;sl c:\
```

You should now have output similar to that shown here, and you should also be back at the C PS drive.

```
Name                            Value
----                            -----
ALLUSERSPROFILE                 C:\ProgramData
APPDATA                         C:\Users\administrator\AppData\Roaming
CLIENTNAME                      EDLT
CommonProgramFiles              C:\Program Files\Common Files
CommonProgramFiles(x86)         C:\Program Files (x86)\Common Files
CommonProgramW6432              C:\Program Files\Common Files
COMPUTERNAME                    C10
ComSpec                         C:\Windows\system32\cmd.exe
HOMEDRIVE                       C:
HOMEPATH                        \Users\administrator
LOCALAPPDATA                    C:\Users\administrator\AppData\Local
LOGONSERVER                     \\DC1
NUMBER_OF_PROCESSORS            1
OS                              Windows_NT
Path                            C:\Windows\system32;C:\Windows;C:\Windows\System32...
PATHEXT                         .COM;.EXE;.BAT;.CMD;.VBS;.VBE;.JS;.JSE;.WSF;.WSH;....
PROCESSOR_ARCHITECTURE          AMD64
PROCESSOR_IDENTIFIER            Intel64 Family 6 Model 58 Stepping 9, GenuineIntel
PROCESSOR_LEVEL                 6
PROCESSOR_REVISION              3a09
ProgramData                     C:\ProgramData
```

```
ProgramFiles                          C:\Program Files
ProgramFiles(x86)                     C:\Program Files (x86)
ProgramW6432                          C:\Program Files
PSModulePath                          C:\Users\administrator\Documents\WindowsPowerShell...
PUBLIC                                C:\Users\Public
SESSIONNAME                           31C5CE94259D4006A9E4#0
SystemDrive                           C:
SystemRoot                            C:\Windows
TEMP                                  C:\Users\ADMINI~1\AppData\Local\Temp
TMP                                   C:\Users\ADMINI~1\AppData\Local\Temp
USERDNSDOMAIN                         NWTRADERS.COM
USERDOMAIN                            NWTRADERS
USERDOMAIN_ROAMINGPROFILE             NWTRADERS
USERNAME                              administrator
USERPROFILE                           C:\Users\administrator
windir                                C:\Windows
```

19. Now use the *ghy* alias to retrieve a history of your commands. Identify the line that contains your previous *gcim* command that uses *Format-Table* with the *-AutoSize* parameter. This command and abbreviated results are shown here.

```
ghy

Id CommandLine
-- -----------
.. ...
17 gcim Win32_Environment | Format-Table name, variableValue -AutoSize
.. ...
```

20. Use the *ihy* alias to invoke the history command that corresponds to the command identified in step 19. For me (yours might differ), the command is *ihy 17*, as shown here.

```
ihy 17
```

21. When the command runs, it prints the value of the command you are running on the first line. After this, you obtain the results normally associated with the command. Partial output is shown here.

```
gcim Win32_Environment | Format-Table name, variableValue -AutoSize

name                    variableValue
----                    -------------
USERNAME                SYSTEM
Path                    %SystemRoot%\system32;%SystemRoot%;%SystemRoot%\System32\W...
ComSpec                 %SystemRoot%\system32\cmd.exe
TMP                     %SystemRoot%\TEMP
OS                      Windows_NT
windir                  %SystemRoot%
PROCESSOR_ARCHITECTURE  AMD64
TEMP                    %SystemRoot%\TEMP
PSModulePath            %SystemRoot%\system32\WindowsPowerShell\v1.0\Modules\
PATHEXT                 .COM;.EXE;.BAT;.CMD;.VBS;.VBE;.JS;.JSE;.WSF;.WSH;.MSC
NUMBER_OF_PROCESSORS    1
PROCESSOR_LEVEL         6
PROCESSOR_IDENTIFIER    Intel64 Family 6 Model 58 Stepping 9, GenuineIntel
```

```
PROCESSOR_REVISION      3a09
TMP                     %USERPROFILE%\AppData\Local\Temp
TEMP                    %USERPROFILE%\AppData\Local\Temp
TMP                     %USERPROFILE%\AppData\Local\Temp
TEMP                    %USERPROFILE%\AppData\Local\Temp
TMP                     %USERPROFILE%\AppData\Local\Temp
TEMP                    %USERPROFILE%\AppData\Local\Temp
TMP                     %USERPROFILE%\AppData\Local\Temp
TEMP                    %USERPROFILE%\AppData\Local\Temp
TMP                     %USERPROFILE%\AppData\Local\Temp
TEMP                    %USERPROFILE%\AppData\Local\Temp
```

22. Scroll up in the Windows PowerShell console, and compare the output from the *gcim* command you just ran with the output from the *sl env:;gci* command.

This concludes this exercise.

Chapter 11 quick reference

To	Do this
Simplify connecting to WMI while using default security permissions	Use the *Get-CimInstance* cmdlet.
Control security when making a remote connection	Specify the impersonation levels in your script.
Allow a script to use the credentials of the person launching the script	Use the *impersonate* impersonation level.
Get rid of system properties when printing all properties of a WMI class	Use the *Format-List* cmdlet and specify that the -*Property* argument must be in the range of *[a-z]**.
Get the current date and time	Use the *Get-Date* cmdlet.
Subtract two dates	Use the *New-TimeSpan* cmdlet. Supply two date objects as arguments.
Retrieve a listing of all commands typed during a Windows PowerShell session	Use the *Get-History* cmdlet.
Run a command from the Windows PowerShell session history	Use the *Invoke-History* cmdlet.
Retrieve the minimum and maximum values from an object	Use the *Measure-Object* cmdlet while specifying the -*Property*, -*Minimum*, and -*Maximum* parameters.
Produce paged output from a long-scrolling command	Pipeline the resulting object from the command into the *more* function.

Remoting WMI

After completing this chapter, you will be able to

- Use native WMI remoting to connect to a remote system.

- Use Windows PowerShell remoting to run WMI commands on a remote system.

- Use the CIM cmdlets to query WMI classes on a remote system.

- Receive the results of remote WMI commands.

- Run WMI remote commands as a job.

Using WMI against remote systems

Windows Management Instrumentation (WMI) remoting is an essential part of Windows PowerShell. In fact, way back in Windows PowerShell 1.0, WMI remoting was one of the primary ways of making configuration changes on remote systems. Each server operating system beginning with Windows Server 2012 permits remote WMI by default; however, client operating systems, such as Windows 10, do not. The best way to manage client operating systems such as Windows 10 is to use Group Policy to permit the use of WMI inbound. Keep in mind that the issue here is the Windows firewall, not WMI itself. The steps to use Group Policy to configure WMI are as follows:

1. Open the Group Policy Management Console.

2. Expand Computer Configuration | Policies | Windows Settings | Security Settings | Windows Firewall with Advanced Security | Windows Firewall with Advanced Security.

3. Right-click the Inbound Rules node and click New Rule.

4. Choose Predefined, and select Windows Management Instrumentation (WMI) from the list.

5. There are a number of options here, but you should start with one: the (WMI-In) option with the Domain profile value. If you aren't sure what you need, just remember that you can come back and add the others later. Click Next.

6. Leave Allow The Connection selected. Click Finish.

Until the Windows firewall permits WMI connection, attempts to connect result in a remote procedure call (RPC) error. This error appears here, where an attempt to connect to a computer named C10 fails because the firewall does not permit WMI traffic to pass.

```
PS C:\> gwmi win32_bios -cn C10
gwmi : The RPC server is unavailable. (Exception from HRESULT: 0x800706BA)
At line:1 char:1
+ gwmi win32_bios -cn C10
+ ~~~~~~~~~~~~~~~~~~~~~~~~
    + CategoryInfo          : InvalidOperation: (:) [Get-WmiObject], COMException
    + FullyQualifiedErrorId : GetWMICOMException,Microsoft.PowerShell.Commands.
GetWmiObjectCommand
```

Additionally, the remote caller must be a member of the local administrators group on the target machine. By default, members of the Domain Admin group are placed into the local administrators group when the system joins the domain. If you attempt to make a remote WMI connection without membership in the local admin group on the target system, an Access Denied error is raised. This error appears as follows when a user attempts to connect to a remote system without permission.

```
PS C:\Users\ed.NWTRADERS> gwmi win32_bios -cn C10
gwmi : Access is denied. (Exception from HRESULT: 0x80070005 (E_ACCESSDENIED))
At line:1 char:1
+ gwmi win32_bios -cn C10
+ ~~~~~~~~~~~~~~~~~~~~~~~~
    + CategoryInfo          : NotSpecified: (:) [Get-WmiObject],
UnauthorizedAccessException
    + FullyQualifiedErrorId : System.UnauthorizedAccessException,Microsoft.PowerShell.
Commands.GetWmiObjectCommand
```

Important Pay close attention to the specific errors returned by WMI when you are attempting to make a remote connection. The error tells you whether the problem is related to the firewall or security access. This information is vital in making remote WMI work.

Supplying alternate credentials for the remote connection

A non-privileged user can make a remote WMI connection by supplying credentials that have local admin rights on the target system. The *Get-WMIObject* Windows PowerShell cmdlet accepts a credential object. There are two common ways of supplying the credential object for the remote connection. The first way is to type the domain and the user name values directly into the *credential* parameter. When the *Get-WmiObject* cmdlet runs, it prompts for the password. The syntax of this command appears here.

```
PS C:\Users\ed.NWTRADERS> gwmi win32_bios -cn C10 -Credential NWTraders\administrator
```

When you run the command, a dialog box appears, prompting for the password to use for the connection. When the password is supplied, the command continues. The dialog box appears in Figure 12-1.

FIGURE 12-1 When run with the *Credential* parameter, the *Get-WmiObject* cmdlet prompts for the account password.

Storing the credentials for a remote connection

There is only one problem with supplying the credential directly to the *Credential* parameter for the *Get-WmiObject* cmdlet—it requires you to supply the credential each time you run the command. This requirement is enforced when you use the Up Arrow key to retrieve the command, and for any subsequent connections to the same remote system.

When opening a Windows PowerShell console session that might involve a connection to numerous remote systems, or even multiple connections to the same system, it makes sense to store the credential object in a variable for the duration of the Windows PowerShell session. To store your credentials for later consumption, use the *Get-Credential* Windows PowerShell cmdlet to retrieve your credentials and store the resulting credential object in a variable. If you work with multiple systems with different passwords, it makes sense to create variables that will facilitate remembering which credentials go to which system. Remember that the Windows PowerShell console has tab expansion; therefore, it is not necessary to use short cryptic variable names just to reduce typing. The following command obtains a credential object and stores the resulting object in the *$credential* variable.

```
$credential = Get-Credential -Credential NWTraders\administrator
```

The use of the credential object to make a remote WMI connection is shown here.

```
PS C:\> $credential = Get-Credential -Credential NWTraders\administrator
PS C:\> gwmi win32_bios -cn DC1 -Credential $credential


SMBIOSBIOSVersion : Hyper-V UEFI Release v1.0
Manufacturer      : Microsoft Corporation
Name              : Hyper-V UEFI Release v1.0
SerialNumber      : 3601-6926-9922-0181-5225-8175-58
Version           : VRTUAL - 1
```

When the same query must be executed against remote systems that use the same credential, the *Get-WmiObject* cmdlet makes it easy to execute the command. The following code runs the same query with the same credentials against three different systems. The remote computers are a combination of three Windows Server 2012 and Windows 2008 R2 servers. The commands and the related output are shown here.

```
PS C:\> $credential = Get-Credential -Credential NWTraders\administrator
PS C:\> $cn = "DC1", "SGW"
PS C:\> gwmi win32_bios -cn $CN -Credential $credential


SMBIOSBIOSVersion : Hyper-V UEFI Release v1.0
Manufacturer      : Microsoft Corporation
Name              : Hyper-V UEFI Release v1.0
SerialNumber      : 3601-6926-9922-0181-5225-8175-58
Version           : VRTUAL - 1

SMBIOSBIOSVersion : 090006
Manufacturer      : American Megatrends Inc.
Name              : BIOS Date: 05/23/12 17:15:53  Ver: 09.00.06
SerialNumber      : 0455-8008-7191-5868-7444-8309-07
Version           : VRTUAL - 5001223
```

One problem with the preceding output is that it does not contain the name of the remote system. The returned WMI object contains the name of the system in the __*Server* property, but the default display does not include this information. Therefore, a *Select-Object* cmdlet (which has an alias of *select*) is required to pick up the __*Server* property. The revised command and associated output are shown here.

```
PS C:\> gwmi win32_bios -cn $CN -Credential $credential | select smbiosbiosversion, m
anufacturer, name, serialnumber, __server


smbiosbiosversion : Hyper-V UEFI Release v1.0
manufacturer      : Microsoft Corporation
name              : Hyper-V UEFI Release v1.0
serialnumber      : 3601-6926-9922-0181-5225-8175-58
__SERVER          : DC1

smbiosbiosversion : 090006
manufacturer      : American Megatrends Inc.
name              : BIOS Date: 05/23/12 17:15:53  Ver: 09.00.06
serialnumber      : 0455-8008-7191-5868-7444-8309-07
__SERVER          : SGW
```

In addition to WMI remoting, Windows PowerShell also permits using Windows PowerShell remoting. The advantage to using Windows PowerShell remoting is that in addition to permitting WMI to connect to remote systems with elevated permissions, Windows PowerShell remoting also permits running WMI commands with alternate credentials from within the same Windows PowerShell session against the local computer. WMI does not support alternate credentials for a local connection, but Windows PowerShell remoting does. In the code that follows, the *Get-WmiObject* cmdlet queries the *Win32_LoggedOnUser* WMI class. It returns only the antecedent property from this association class. The results show that the logged-on user is NWTraders\ed.

```
PS C:\> (gwmi win32_loggedonuser).antecedent
\\.\root\cimv2:Win32_Account.Domain="C10",Name="ed"
```

Next, the credentials of the administrator account are retrieved via the *Get-Credential* Windows PowerShell cmdlet and stored in the *$credential* variable. The *Invoke-Command* cmdlet (*icm* is the alias) runs the *Get-WmiObject* cmdlet and queries the *Win32_LoggedOnUser* WMI class against the local machine by using the administrator credentials. The results reveal all of the logged-on users, not merely the non-admin user, illustrating the different user context that was used for the query.

```
PS C:\> $credential = Get-Credential NWTraders\administrator
PS C:\> icm {(gwmi win32_loggedonuser).antecedent} -cn localhost -Credential $credential
\\.\root\cimv2:Win32_Account.Domain="C10",Name="SYSTEM"
\\.\root\cimv2:Win32_Account.Domain="C10",Name="LOCAL SERVICE"
\\.\root\cimv2:Win32_Account.Domain="C10",Name="NETWORK SERVICE"
\\.\root\cimv2:Win32_Account.Domain="NWTRADERS",Name="administrator"
\\.\root\cimv2:Win32_Account.Domain="C10",Name="ANONYMOUS LOGON"
\\.\root\cimv2:Win32_Account.Domain="C10",Name="DWM-1"
\\.\root\cimv2:Win32_Account.Domain="C10",Name="DWM-1"
\\.\root\cimv2:Win32_Account.Domain="C10",Name="DWM-2"
\\.\root\cimv2:Win32_Account.Domain="C10",Name="DWM-2"
```

Using Windows PowerShell remoting to run WMI

Use of the *Get-WMIObject* cmdlet is a requirement for using WMI to talk to down-level systems—systems that will not even run Windows PowerShell. There are several disadvantages to using native WMI remoting:

- WMI remoting requires special firewall rules to permit access to client systems.

- WMI remoting requires opening multiple holes in the firewall.

- WMI remoting requires local administrator rights.

- WMI remoting provides no support for alternate credentials on a local connection.

- WMI remoting output does not return the name of the target system by default.

Beginning with Windows PowerShell 2.0, you can use Windows PowerShell remoting to run your WMI commands. By using Windows PowerShell remoting, you can configure different access rights for the remote endpoint that do not require admin rights on the remote system. In addition, use of *Enable-PSRemoting* simplifies configuration of the firewall and the services. Also, Windows PowerShell remoting requires that only a single port be open, not the wide range of ports required by the WMI protocols (RPC and DCOM). Finally, Windows PowerShell remoting supports alternate credentials for a local connection. (For more information about Windows PowerShell remoting, see Chapter 4, "Using Windows PowerShell remoting and jobs.")

In the code shown here, the *Get-Credential* cmdlet stores a credential object in the *$credential* variable. Next, this credential is used with the *Invoke-Command* cmdlet to run a script block containing a WMI command. The results return to the Windows PowerShell console.

```
PS C:\Users\ed.NWTRADERS> $credential = Get-Credential NWTraders\administrator
PS C:\Users\ed.NWTRADERS> Invoke-Command -cn C10
   -ScriptBlock {gwmi win32_bios} -Credential $credential

SMBIOSBIOSVersion : 090004
Manufacturer      : American Megatrends Inc.
Name              : BIOS Date: 03/19/09 22:51:32  Ver: 09.00.04
SerialNumber      : 0385-4074-3362-4641-2411-8229-09
Version           : VRTUAL - 3000919
PSComputerName    : C10
```

Use Windows PowerShell remoting to communicate to any system that runs Windows PowerShell 2.0 or later. As shown here, you can run WMI commands against remote systems with a single command, and engage multiple operating systems. The nice thing is the inclusion of the *PSComputerName* property. Because the *Invoke-Command* cmdlet accepts an array of computer names, the command is very simple.

```
PS C:\> $credential = Get-Credential -Credential NWTraders\administrator
PS C:\> $cn = "DC1", "SGW"
PS C:\> Invoke-Command -cn $cn -cred $credential -ScriptBlock {Gwmi win32_operatingsy
stem}


SystemDirectory : C:\Windows\system32
Organization    :
BuildNumber     : 9600
RegisteredUser  : Windows User
SerialNumber    : 00252-00050-01533-AA892
Version         : 6.3.9600
PSComputerName  : DC1

SystemDirectory : C:\Windows\system32
Organization    :
BuildNumber     : 9600
RegisteredUser  : Windows User
SerialNumber    : 00252-00106-34541-AA026
Version         : 6.3.9600
PSComputerName  : SGW
```

Using CIM classes to query WMI classes

There are several ways of using the Common Information Model (CIM) classes to perform remote WMI queries. The most basic way is to use the *Get-CimInstance* cmdlet. In fact, this generic method is required if no specific CIM implementation class exists. The following steps are required to use the *Get-CimInstance* cmdlet to query a remote system.

Using CIM to query remote WMI data

1. If you want to use an alternate credential, you must use the *New-CimSession* cmdlet to create a new CIM session by using the *Credential* parameter. Store the returned session in a variable.

2. Supply the stored CIM session from the variable to the *-CimSession* parameter when querying with the *Get-CimInstance* cmdlet.

    In the code shown here, the *New-CimSession* cmdlet creates a new CIM session with a target computer of C10 and a user name of NWTraders\administrator. The cmdlet returns a CIM session that it stores in the *$C10* variable. Next, the *Get-CimInstance* cmdlet uses the CIM session to connect to the remote C10 system and to return the data from the *Win32_BIOS* WMI class. The output is displayed in the Windows PowerShell console.

    ```
    PS C:\> $C10 = New-CimSession -ComputerName C10 -Credential nwtraders\administrator
    PS C:\> Get-CimInstance -CimSession $C10 -ClassName Win32_Bios

    SMBIOSBIOSVersion : 090006
    Manufacturer      : American Megatrends Inc.
    Name              : BIOS Date: 05/23/12 17:15:53  Ver: 09.00.06
    SerialNumber      : 8570-3709-4791-5943-3863-4381-72
    Version           : VRTUAL - 5001223
    PSComputerName    : C10
    ```

3. Besides automatically returning the target computer name, *Get-CimInstance* automatically converts the date from a UTC string to a *datetime* type. However, if *Get-WmiObject* is used, as shown here, an extra step is required to convert the WMI UTC string to a *datetime* type.

    ```
    PS C:\> $bios = gwmi Win32_Bios
    PS C:\> $bios.ReleaseDate
    20120523000000.000000+000
    PS C:\> $bios.ConvertToDateTime($bios.ReleaseDate)

    Tuesday, May 22, 2012 5:00:00 PM
    ```

4. Notice how *Get-CimInstance* does not require this conversion. The code is shown here.

    ```
    PS C:\> $bios = Get-CimInstance -CimSession $C10 -ClassName Win32_Bios
    PS C:\> $bios.ReleaseDate

    Tuesday, May 22, 2012 5:00:00 PM


    PS C:\> $bios.ReleaseDate.GetType()

    IsPublic IsSerial Name                                     BaseType
    -------- -------- ----                                     --------
    True     True     DateTime                                 System.ValueType
    ```

As long as the credentials work, you can create a new CIM session connection for multiple computers, and even for multiple operating systems. This works because the *-ComputerName* parameter of the *New-CimSession* cmdlet accepts an array of computer names. In the code shown here, the

New-CimSession cmdlet creates a new CIM session with two target computers and the same credentials. It then stores the returned CIM session in the *$cn* variable. Next, the *Get-CimInstance* cmdlet queries the *Win32_OperatingSystem* WMI class from the CIM session stored in the *$cn* variable. The code and the results from the code appear here.

```
PS C:\> $cn = New-CimSession -ComputerName DC1, SGW -Credential Nwtraders\administrat
or
PS C:\> Get-CimInstance -CimSession $cn -ClassName Win32_OperatingSystem

SystemDirect Organizatio BuildNumber RegisteredU SerialNumbe Version   PSComputerN
ory          n                       ser         r                     ame
------------ ----------- ----------- ----------- ----------- -------   -----------
C:\Window...             9600        Windows ... 00252-00... 6.3.9600  SGW
C:\Window...             9600        Windows ... 00252-00... 6.3.9600  DC1
```

Working with remote results

When you are working with remote systems, it might be important to consider the network bandwidth and the cost of repeatedly retrieving unfiltered data. There are basically two choices—the first choice involves gathering the information and storing it in a local variable. By using this technique, you incur the bandwidth cost once, and you can use the same data in multiple ways without incurring the bandwidth hit again. But if your data changes rapidly, this technique does not help much.

> **Important** In potentially bandwidth-constrained situations, it is a best practice to store data retrieved locally to facilitate reuse of the information at a later time. The easiest place to store the data is in a variable, but do not forget about storing the data in XML for a more persisted storage. The *Export-Clixml* cmdlet is extremely easy to use and preserves the data relationships well.

In the command shown here, the *Get-CimInstance* cmdlet retrieves all of the process information from the remote computer session stored in the *$session* variable. The process information is stored in the *$process* variable. Next, the data is explored and the name and process IDs are returned.

```
PS C:\> $process = Get-CimInstance -ClassName Win32_Process -CimSession $session
PS C:\> $process | ft name, processid -AutoSize

name                               processid
----                               ---------
System Idle Process                        0
System                                     4
smss.exe                                 252
csrss.exe                                348
csrss.exe                                412
wininit.exe                              420
winlogon.exe                             448
services.exe                             508
lsass.exe                                516
```

svchost.exe	572
svchost.exe	612
LogonUI.exe	704
dwm.exe	720
svchost.exe	728
svchost.exe	760
svchost.exe	832
svchost.exe	948
svchost.exe	500
spoolsv.exe	1108
svchost.exe	1132
svchost.exe	1188
svchost.exe	1204
svchost.exe	1696
svchost.exe	1732
VSSVC.exe	1900
msdtc.exe	2396
sqlwriter.exe	2464
sqlservr.exe	2516
svchost.exe	2676
alg.exe	2796
iashost.exe	2852
WmiPrvSE.exe	608
System Idle Process	0
System	4
smss.exe	224
csrss.exe	320
csrss.exe	384
wininit.exe	392
winlogon.exe	420
services.exe	484
lsass.exe	492
svchost.exe	620
svchost.exe	660
LogonUI.exe	756
dwm.exe	776
svchost.exe	800
svchost.exe	848
svchost.exe	892
svchost.exe	968
svchost.exe	388
rundll32.exe	296
spoolsv.exe	1232
Microsoft.ActiveDirectory...	1260
dfsrs.exe	1300
dns.exe	1336
ismserv.exe	1356
dfssvc.exe	1460
vds.exe	1844
svchost.exe	1876
svchost.exe	1904
svchost.exe	1924
VSSVC.exe	1084
msdtc.exe	2900
WmiPrvSE.exe	3916

Upon examining the data, the next command returns only processes with the name svchost.exe. Again, the data is displayed in a table.

```
PS C:\> $process.Where({$psitem.name -eq 'svchost.exe'}) | ft name, processID -auto

name          processID
----          ---------
svchost.exe         572
svchost.exe         612
svchost.exe         728
svchost.exe         760
svchost.exe         832
svchost.exe         948
svchost.exe         500
svchost.exe        1132
svchost.exe        1188
svchost.exe        1204
svchost.exe        1696
svchost.exe        1732
svchost.exe        2676
svchost.exe         620
svchost.exe         660
svchost.exe         800
svchost.exe         848
svchost.exe         892
svchost.exe         968
svchost.exe         388
svchost.exe        1876
svchost.exe        1904
svchost.exe        1924
```

Now a different property needs to be added to the data—the *commandline* property, which is used to launch the process. This information provides clues as to what process runs in the particular svchost.exe process. Because some of the command lines are rather long, I add the -*Wrap* switch parameter to the command. This causes lines that are too long to appear in the console on a single line to wrap to the next line, before continuing the subsequent lines in the table. This makes it possible to display additional information in the output. The command is shown here.

```
PS C:\> $process.Where({$psitem.name -eq 'svchost.exe'}) | ft name, processID, commandline -auto
-Wrap

name          processID commandline
----          --------- -----------
svchost.exe         572 C:\Windows\system32\svchost.exe -k DcomLaunch
svchost.exe         612 C:\Windows\system32\svchost.exe -k RPCSS
svchost.exe         728 C:\Windows\System32\svchost.exe -k
                        LocalServiceNetworkRestricted
svchost.exe         760 C:\Windows\system32\svchost.exe -k netsvcs
svchost.exe         832 C:\Windows\system32\svchost.exe -k LocalService
svchost.exe         948 C:\Windows\system32\svchost.exe -k NetworkService
svchost.exe         500 C:\Windows\system32\svchost.exe -k LocalServiceNoNetwork
svchost.exe        1132 C:\Windows\system32\svchost.exe -k apphost
svchost.exe        1188 C:\Windows\System32\svchost.exe -k
                        LocalSystemNetworkRestricted
```

```
svchost.exe         1204 C:\Windows\system32\svchost.exe -k iissvcs
svchost.exe         1696 C:\Windows\System32\svchost.exe -k termsvcs
svchost.exe         1732 C:\Windows\system32\svchost.exe -k ICService
svchost.exe         2676 C:\Windows\System32\svchost.exe -k
                         NetworkServiceAndNoImpersonation
svchost.exe          620 C:\Windows\system32\svchost.exe -k DcomLaunch
svchost.exe          660 C:\Windows\system32\svchost.exe -k RPCSS
svchost.exe          800 C:\Windows\System32\svchost.exe -k
                         LocalServiceNetworkRestricted
svchost.exe          848 C:\Windows\system32\svchost.exe -k netsvcs
svchost.exe          892 C:\Windows\system32\svchost.exe -k LocalService
svchost.exe          968 C:\Windows\system32\svchost.exe -k NetworkService
svchost.exe          388 C:\Windows\system32\svchost.exe -k LocalServiceNoNetwork
svchost.exe         1876 C:\Windows\System32\svchost.exe -k termsvcs
svchost.exe         1904 C:\Windows\system32\svchost.exe -k ICService
svchost.exe         1924 C:\Windows\system32\svchost.exe -k
                         LocalSystemNetworkRestricted
```

Now, home in on the data a bit more to find out which of the svchost.exe processes requires the largest working set size of memory and is using the most kernel mode time. The answer to the question of which instance uses the most resources appears in the code shown here.

```
PS C:\> $process.Where({$psitem.name -eq 'svchost.exe'}) | ft ProcessID, WorkingSetSi
ze, Kernel* -auto

ProcessID WorkingSetSize KernelModeTime
--------- -------------- --------------
      572        4726784         468750
      612        3969024        1093750
      728        8613888        4062500
      760       23834624       12031250
      832       10293248        1406250
      948       16977920        2031250
      500       11595776        7031250
     1132        6602752              0
     1188       11935744         937500
     1204        7364608         312500
     1696        7143424         468750
     1732        7348224        4687500
     2676       10637312        3125000
      620        4964352         312500
      660        4177920        3437500
      800        7962624        4687500
      848       21065728       20781250
      892        5632000         937500
      968       12828672        1093750
      388        9195520         156250
     1876        2842624         468750
     1904        3026944        7968750
     1924        9854976        3281250
```

The second approach involves filtering the data at the source and only returning the needed information to the local client machine. There are two ways of doing this: the first is to use the Windows PowerShell -*Property* and -*Filter* parameters to reduce the data returned; the second is to use a native WMI Query Language (WQL) query to reduce the data.

Reducing data via Windows PowerShell parameters

The first method to reduce data and filter it at the source involves using two Windows PowerShell parameters. The first parameter, the *-Property* parameter, reduces properties returned, but it does not reduce instances. The second parameter, the *-Filter* parameter, reduces the instances returned but does not reduce the number of properties. For example, the code that follows retrieves only the name and the start mode of services on a remote server named C10. The command executes as the administrator from the domain.

```
PS C:\> $session = New-CimSession -ComputerName C10 -Credential NWTraders\administrator
PS C:\> Get-CimInstance -ClassName win32_service -CimSession $session -Property name, startmode
```

The command that follows uses the previously created session on the remote computer named C10, and this time it also introduces the *-Filter* parameter. Now the command returns the name and start mode of only the running services on the remote system. The services are sorted by start mode, and a table displays the results. The command and the associated output are shown here.

```
PS C:\> Get-CimInstance -ClassName win32_service -CimSession $session -Property name,
 startmode -Filter "state = 'running'" | sort startmode | ft name, startmode -AutoSize
```

name	startmode
WSearch	Auto
RpcEptMapper	Auto
ProfSvc	Auto
SENS	Auto
Schedule	Auto
SamSs	Auto
NlaSvc	Auto
Netlogon	Auto
MpsSvc	Auto
Power	Auto
PcaSvc	Auto
nsi	Auto
ShellHWDetection	Auto
Winmgmt	Auto
WinDefend	Auto
Wcmsvc	Auto
wscsvc	Auto
WMPNetworkSvc	Auto
WinRM	Auto
SystemEventsBroker	Auto
SysMain	Auto
Spooler	Auto
UserManager	Auto
TrkWks	Auto
Themes	Auto
dmwappushservice	Auto
BITS	Auto
DiagTrack	Auto
BFE	Auto
DPS	Auto
Dnscache	Auto
DcomLaunch	Auto

```
CryptSvc                    Auto
CoreUIRegistrar             Auto
Dhcp                        Auto
BrokerInfrastructure        Auto
DeviceAssociationService    Auto
LanmanWorkstation           Auto
LanmanServer                Auto
iphlpsvc                    Auto
LSM                         Auto
RpcSs                       Auto
AudioEndpointBuilder        Auto
EventSystem                 Auto
FontCache                   Auto
EventLog                    Auto
Audiosrv                    Auto
vmicvss                     Manual
vmictimesync                Manual
vmickvpexchange             Manual
vmicrdv                     Manual
vmicshutdown                Manual
WinHttpAutoProxySvc         Manual
WdiServiceHost              Manual
wlidsvc                     Manual
VSS                         Manual
Appinfo                     Manual
W32Time                     Manual
DsmSvc                      Manual
PolicyAgent                 Manual
SessionEnv                  Manual
ScDeviceEnum                Manual
lmhosts                     Manual
NcbService                  Manual
PlugPlay                    Manual
netprofm                    Manual
SSDPSRV                     Manual
upnphost                    Manual
UmRdpService                Manual
vmicheartbeat               Manual
CertPropSvc                 Manual
TermService                 Manual
swprv                       Manual
TimeBroker                  Manual
tiledatamodelsvc            Manual
```

Reducing data via WQL query

You can obtain the same results by using a WQL query. The easiest way to do this is to create a new variable named $query to hold the WQL query. In the WQL query, choose the WMI properties and the WMI class name, and limit the instances to only those that are running. Next, supply the WMI query stored in the $query variable to the -Query parameter of the Get-CimInstance cmdlet. The Query parameter sets do not permit use of the -Query parameter at the same time as the use of the -ClassName, -Property or -Filter parameters. After the change is made, the sorting and formatting of the output is the same. The results, as expected, are the same. The code and the output associated with the code are shown here.

```
PS C:\> $query = "Select name, startmode from win32_Service where state ='running'"
PS C:\> Get-CimInstance -Query $query -CimSession $session  | sort startmode | ft nam
e, startmode -AutoSize


name                       startmode
----                       ---------
RpcSs                      Auto
WSearch                    Auto
ProfSvc                    Auto
SENS                       Auto
Schedule                   Auto
SamSs                      Auto
NlaSvc                     Auto
Netlogon                   Auto
MpsSvc                     Auto
Power                      Auto
PcaSvc                     Auto
nsi                        Auto
ShellHWDetection           Auto
Winmgmt                    Auto
WinDefend                  Auto
Wcmsvc                     Auto
wscsvc                     Auto
WMPNetworkSvc              Auto
WinRM                      Auto
SystemEventsBroker         Auto
SysMain                    Auto
Spooler                    Auto
UserManager                Auto
TrkWks                     Auto
Themes                     Auto
LSM                        Auto
BITS                       Auto
DiagTrack                  Auto
Dnscache                   Auto
BFE                        Auto
DPS                        Auto
Dhcp                       Auto
CoreUIRegistrar            Auto
CryptSvc                   Auto
DcomLaunch                 Auto
BrokerInfrastructure       Auto
DeviceAssociationService   Auto
EventLog                   Auto
AudioEndpointBuilder       Auto
LanmanServer               Auto
iphlpsvc                   Auto
dmwappushservice           Auto
RpcEptMapper               Auto
LanmanWorkstation          Auto
gpsvc                      Auto
EventSystem                Auto
FontCache                  Auto
Audiosrv                   Auto
vmicvss                    Manual
vmicrdv                    Manual
vmictimesync               Manual
```

```
vmicshutdown            Manual
vmickvpexchange         Manual
Appinfo                 Manual
WinHttpAutoProxySvc     Manual
wlidsvc                 Manual
VSS                     Manual
W32Time                 Manual
WdiServiceHost          Manual
DsmSvc                  Manual
PolicyAgent             Manual
SessionEnv              Manual
ScDeviceEnum            Manual
NcbService              Manual
lmhosts                 Manual
PlugPlay                Manual
netprofm                Manual
SSDPSRV                 Manual
upnphost                Manual
UmRdpService            Manual
vmicheartbeat           Manual
CertPropSvc             Manual
TermService             Manual
swprv                   Manual
TimeBroker              Manual
tiledatamodelsvc        Manual
```

Running WMI jobs

If DCOM is not an issue and you are using the *Get-WmiObject* cmdlet to work with remote systems, it is easy to run a remote WMI job. To do so, use the *Get-WmiObject* cmdlet and specify the *-AsJob* switch parameter. After you do that, use the *Get-Job* cmdlet to check on the status of the job, and use *Receive-Job* to receive the job results. (For more information about Windows PowerShell remoting and jobs, see Chapter 4.) In the following code, the *Get-WmiObject* cmdlet retrieves information from the *Win32_BIOS* WMI class from a machine named dc3. The *-AsJob* switch parameter is used to ensure that the command runs as a job. The output is a *PSWmiJob* object. This output is shown here.

```
PS C:\> gwmi Win32_Bios -CN DC1 -AsJob

Id   Name       PSJobTypeName    State      HasMoreData    Location
--   ----       -------------    -----      -----------    --------
3    Job3       WmiJob           Running    True           DC1
```

The *Get-Job* cmdlet is used to retrieve the status of the WMI job. From the output appearing here, it is apparent that the job with an ID of 2 has completed, and that the job has more data to deliver.

```
PS C:\Users\administrator.NWTRADERS> Get-Job -id 2

Id   Name       PSJobTypeName    State        HasMoreData    Location
--   ----       -------------    -----        -----------    --------
2    Job2       WmiJob           Completed    True           dc3
```

As with any other job in Windows PowerShell, to receive the results of the WMI job, use the *Receive-Job* cmdlet. This is shown here.

```
PS C:\Users\administrator.NWTRADERS> Receive-Job -id 2

SMBIOSBIOSVersion : 090004
Manufacturer      : American Megatrends Inc.
Name              : BIOS Date: 03/19/09 22:51:32  Ver: 09.00.04
SerialNumber      : 8994-9999-0865-2542-2186-8044-69
Version           : VRTUAL - 3000919
```

If you do not have DCOM and RPC access to the remote system, you can use the *Invoke-Command* cmdlet to run the WMI command on the remote system as a job. To do this, use the *-AsJob* parameter on the *Invoke-Command* cmdlet. This technique appears here, where first the *Get-Credential* cmdlet creates a new credential object for the remote system. The *Invoke-Command* cmdlet uses Windows PowerShell remoting to connect to the remote system and query WMI by using the *Get-WmiObject* cmdlet to ask for information from the *Win32_Service* class. The *-AsJob* parameter causes the query to occur as a job.

```
PS C:\> $credential = Get-Credential nwtraders\administrator
PS C:\> Invoke-Command -ComputerName dc1 -Credential $credential -ScriptBlock {GWMI W
in32_Bios} -AsJob

Id   Name         PSJobTypeName   State     HasMoreData   Location
--   ----         -------------   -----     -----------   --------
9    Job9         RemoteJob       Running   True          dc1
```

The *Get-Job* cmdlet queries for the status of job 4, and as shown in the following code, the job has completed and has more data. Notice this time that the job is of type *remotejob*, not *wmijob*, as was created earlier. Next, the *Receive-Job* cmdlet is used to receive the results of the WMI query. The *-Keep* switch parameter tells Windows PowerShell to retain the results for further analysis.

```
PS C:\> Get-Job -Id 9

Id   Name         PSJobTypeName   State       HasMoreData   Location
--   ----         -------------   -----       -----------   --------
9    Job9         RemoteJob       Completed   True          dc1


PS C:\> Receive-Job -Id 9 -Keep


SMBIOSBIOSVersion : Hyper-V UEFI Release v1.0
Manufacturer      : Microsoft Corporation
Name              : Hyper-V UEFI Release v1.0
SerialNumber      : 3601-6926-9922-0181-5225-8175-58
Version           : VRTUAL - 1
PSComputerName    : dc1
```

You can also use the CIM cmdlets as jobs by using the *Invoke-Command* cmdlet. The following example uses *Get-Credential* to retrieve a credential object. Next, the *Invoke-Command* cmdlet runs the *Get-CimInstance* cmdlet on a remote computer named C10. The command runs as a job. The *Get-Job* cmdlet checks on the status of the job, and the *Receive-Job* cmdlet retrieves the results. The code and output are shown here.

```
PS C:\> $credential = Get-Credential nwtraders\administrator
PS C:\> Invoke-Command -ComputerName C10 -ScriptBlock {Get-CimInstance Win32_BIOS} -C
redential $credential -AsJob

Id     Name         PSJobTypeName    State     HasMoreData    Location
--     ----         -------------    -----     -----------    --------
11     Job11        RemoteJob        Running   True           C10


PS C:\> Get-Job -Id 11

Id     Name         PSJobTypeName    State     HasMoreData    Location
--     ----         -------------    -----     -----------    --------
11     Job11        RemoteJob        Completed True           C10


PS C:\> Receive-Job -Id 11


SMBIOSBIOSVersion : 090006
Manufacturer      : American Megatrends Inc.
Name              : BIOS Date: 05/23/12 17:15:53  Ver: 09.00.06
SerialNumber      : 8570-3709-4791-5943-3863-4381-72
Version           : VRTUAL - 5001223
PSComputerName    : C10
```

Using Windows PowerShell remoting and WMI: Step-by-step exercises

In this exercise, you will practice using Windows PowerShell remoting to run remote commands. For the purpose of this exercise, you can use your local computer, but commands designed to fail (in the exercise) will more than likely succeed instead of creating the errors that appear here.

Using Windows PowerShell remoting to retrieve remote information

1. Log on to your computer with a user account that does not have administrator rights.

2. Open the Windows PowerShell console.

3. Use the *Get-CimInstance* cmdlet to retrieve process information from a remote system that has WMI remoting enabled on it. Do not supply alternate credentials. The command is shown here.

   ```
   Get-CimInstance -CimSession C10 -ClassName win32_process
   ```

4. The command fails due to an Access Denied error. Now create a new CIM session to the remote system and connect with alternate credentials. Store the CIM session in a variable named *$session*. This command is shown here. (Use a remote system accessible to you and credentials appropriate to that system.)

```
$session = New-CimSession -Credential NWTraders\administrator -ComputerName C10
```

5. Use the stored CIM session from the *$session* variable to retrieve process information from the remote system. The command is shown here.

```
Get-CimInstance -CimSession $session -ClassName win32_process
```

6. Use the stored CIM session from the *$session* variable to retrieve the name and the status of all services on the remote system. Sort the output by state, and format a table with the name and the state. The command is shown here.

```
Get-CimInstance -CimSession $session -ClassName win32_service -Property name, state |
sort state | ft name, state -AutoSize
```

7. Use the *Get-WmiObject* cmdlet to run a WMI command on a remote system. Use the *Win32_BIOS* WMI class and target the same remote system you used earlier. Specify appropriate credentials for the connection. Here is an example.

```
$credential = Get-Credential NWTraders\administrator
Get-WmiObject -Class win32_bios -ComputerName C10 -Credential $credential
```

8. Use Windows PowerShell remoting by using the *Invoke-Command* cmdlet to run a WMI command against a remote system. Use the credentials you stored earlier. Use the *Get-CimInstance* cmdlet to retrieve BIOS information from WMI. The command is shown here.

```
Invoke-Command -ComputerName C10 -ScriptBlock {Get-CimInstance win32_bios} -Credential
$credential
```

This concludes the exercise. Leave the Windows PowerShell console open for the next exercise.

In the following exercise, you will create and receive WMI jobs.

Creating and receiving WMI jobs

1. Open the Windows PowerShell console (if it is not already open) as a non-elevated user.

2. Use the *Get-WmiObject* cmdlet to retrieve BIOS information from a remote system. Use the *-AsJob* switch parameter to run the command as a job. Use the credentials you stored in the *$credential* variable in the previous exercise.

```
Get-WmiObject win32_bios -ComputerName C10 -Credential $credential -AsJob
```

3. Check on the success or failure of the job by using the *Get-Job* cmdlet. Make sure you use the job ID from the previous command. A sample is shown here.

```
Get-Job -Id 10
```

4. If the job was successful, receive the results of the job by using the *Receive-Job* cmdlet. Do not bother with storing the results in a variable or keeping the results, because you will not need them.

5. Create a new Windows PowerShell session object by using the *New-PSSession* cmdlet. Store the results in a variable named *$psSession*. The command is shown here. (Use appropriate computer names and credentials for your network.)

```
$PSSession = New-PSSession -Credential NWTraders\administrator -ComputerName C10
```

6. Use the *Invoke-Command* cmdlet to make the *Get-WmiObject* cmdlet retrieve BIOS information from the remote system. Use the session information stored in the *$psSession* variable. Make sure you use the *-AsJob* switch parameter with the command. The command is shown here.

```
Invoke-Command -Session $PSSession -ScriptBlock {gwmi win32_bios} -AsJob
```

7. Use the *Get-Job* cmdlet with the job ID returned by the previous command to check on the status of the job. The command will be similar to the one shown here.

```
Get-Job -id 12
```

8. Use the *Receive-Job* cmdlet to retrieve the results of the WMI command. Store the returned information in a variable named *$bios*. The command is shown here (make sure that you use the job ID number from your system).

```
$bios = Receive-Job -id 12
```

9. Now query the BIOS version by accessing the *version* property from the *$bios* variable. This is shown here.

```
$bios.Version
```

This concludes the exercise.

Chapter 12 quick reference

To	Do this
Retrieve WMI information from a remote down-level system	Use the *Get-WmiObject* cmdlet and specify credentials as needed, and the target system.
Retrieve WMI information from a system running Windows 8 and later or Windows Server 2012 and later	Use the *Get-CimInstance* cmdlet and specify the target computer and WMI class.
Run a WMI command on multiple computers running Windows 8 and later or Windows Server 2012 and later	Use the *New-CimSession* cmdlet to create a CIM session for the multiple systems. Then specify that session for *Get-CimInstance*.
Filter returning WMI data	Use the *-Filter* parameter with either *Get-WmiObject* or *Get-CimInstance*.
Reduce the number of returned properties	Use the *-Property* parameter with either *Get-WmiObject* or *Get-CimInstance*.
Use a WQL type of query	Use the *-Query* parameter with either *Get-WmiObject* or *Get-CimInstance*.
Retrieve the WMI results with a job	Use the *Start-Job* and *Receive-Job* cmdlets with *Get-CimInstance* or the *-AsJob* switch parameter with *Get-WmiObject*.

Calling WMI methods on WMI classes

After completing this chapter, you will be able to

■ Use WMI cmdlets to execute instance methods.

■ Use WMI cmdlets to execute static methods.

Using WMI cmdlets to execute instance methods

There are actually several ways to call Windows Management Instrumentation (WMI) methods in Windows PowerShell. One reason for this is that some WMI methods are *instance methods*, which means they only work on an instance of a class. Other methods are *static methods*, which means they do not operate on an instance of the class. For example, the *Terminate* method from the *Win32_Process* class is an instance method—it will only operate against a specific instance of the *Win32_Process* class. If you do not have a reference to a process, you cannot terminate the process—which makes sense. On the other hand, if you want to *create* a new instance of a *Win32_Process* class, you do not grab a reference to an instance of the class. For example, you do not grab an instance of a running Calculator process to create a new instance of a Notepad process. Therefore, you need a static method that is always available.

Let's examine the first of these two approaches—using instance methods—with a short example. First, create an instance of notepad.exe. Then use the *Get-WmiObject* cmdlet to view the process. (As you might recall from earlier chapters, *gwmi* is an alias for *Get-WmiObject*). This appears here.

```
PS C:\> Start-Process notepad
PS C:\> gwmi Win32_Process -Filter "name = 'notepad.exe'"


__GENUS             : 2
__CLASS             : Win32_Process
__SUPERCLASS        : CIM_Process
__DYNASTY           : CIM_ManagedSystemElement
__RELPATH           : Win32_Process.Handle="3192"
__PROPERTY_COUNT    : 45
__DERIVATION        : {CIM_Process, CIM_LogicalElement,
                      CIM_ManagedSystemElement}
```

```
__SERVER                    : C10
__NAMESPACE                 : root\cimv2
__PATH                      : \\C10\root\cimv2:Win32_Process.Handle="3192"
Caption                     : notepad.exe
CommandLine                 : "C:\Windows\system32\notepad.exe"
CreationClassName           : Win32_Process
CreationDate                : 20150317180423.369317-420
CSCreationClassName         : Win32_ComputerSystem
CSName                      : C10
Description                 : notepad.exe
ExecutablePath              : C:\Windows\system32\notepad.exe
ExecutionState              :
Handle                      : 3192
HandleCount                 : 92
InstallDate                 :
KernelModeTime              : 156250
MaximumWorkingSetSize       : 1380
MinimumWorkingSetSize       : 200
Name                        : notepad.exe
OSCreationClassName         : Win32_OperatingSystem
OSName                      : Microsoft Windows 10 Pro Technical
                              Preview|C:\Windows|\Device\Harddisk0\Partition2
OtherOperationCount         : 65
OtherTransferCount          : 110
PageFaults                  : 2420
PageFileUsage               : 1464
ParentProcessId             : 2900
PeakPageFileUsage           : 1464
PeakVirtualSize             : 2199123750912
PeakWorkingSetSize          : 9208
Priority                    : 8
PrivatePageCount            : 1499136
ProcessId                   : 3192
QuotaNonPagedPoolUsage      : 9
QuotaPagedPoolUsage         : 192
QuotaPeakNonPagedPoolUsage  : 9
QuotaPeakPagedPoolUsage     : 193
ReadOperationCount          : 1
ReadTransferCount           : 60
SessionId                   : 2
Status                      :
TerminationDate             :
ThreadCount                 : 2
UserModeTime                : 0
VirtualSize                 : 2199123746816
WindowsVersion              : 10.0.10002
WorkingSetSize              : 9428992
WriteOperationCount         : 0
WriteTransferCount          : 0
PSComputerName              : C10
ProcessName                 : notepad.exe
Handles                     : 92
VM                          : 2199123746816
WS                          : 9428992
Path                        : C:\Windows\system32\notepad.exe
```

When you have the instance of the Notepad process you want to terminate, there are at least five choices to stop the process:

- You can call the method directly by using dotted notation (because there is only one instance of Notepad), as long as there was not an instance of Notepad running prior to issuing the "Start-Process notepad" step.

- You can store the reference in a variable and then terminate it directly.

- You can use the *Invoke-WmiMethod* cmdlet.

- You can use the *[wmi]* type accelerator.

- You can use Common Information Model (CIM) cmdlets to terminate the process. CIM cmdlets are covered in Chapter 14, "Using the CIM cmdlets."

The first four techniques are described in the following sections.

Using the *Terminate* method directly

Notice that most of the time when a WMI method is called, a *ReturnValue* property is returned from the method call. This value is used to determine whether the method completed successfully. Return codes are documented for the *Terminate* method on the Microsoft Developer Network (MSDN). (Most methods have their return codes detailed on MSDN.)

> **Note** Not all WMI methods behave the same; at times, a bit of experimentation is required to figure out how to call them and how to evaluate return codes. A return code of 0 often means that the method call succeeded, but at times even this is not assured. For example, the 0 might simply mean that the method call did not generate any errors, but that is not the same thing as meaning that it succeeded in accomplishing what one thought it might do. As in all things, it is important to test your code in a sandboxed environment prior to running it in a production environment.

Because there is only one instance of the notepad.exe process running on the system, it is possible to use the group-and-dot procedure. *Grouping characters* (that is, opening and closing parentheses) placed around the expression return an instance of the object. From there, you can directly call the *Terminate* method by using dotted notation. An example of this syntax appears next. (This technique works in the same manner when there is more than one instance of the object.)

```
PS C:\Users\ed.IAMMRED> (gwmi win32_process –Filter "name = 'notepad.exe'").terminate()


__GENUS          : 2
__CLASS          : __PARAMETERS
__SUPERCLASS     :
__DYNASTY        : __PARAMETERS
__RELPATH        :
__PROPERTY_COUNT : 1
```

```
__DERIVATION      : {}
__SERVER          :
__NAMESPACE       :
__PATH            :
ReturnValue       : 0
PSComputerName    :
```

The second way of calling the *Terminate* method directly is to use WMI to return an instance of the object, store the returned object in a variable, and then call the method via dotted notation.

To directly call an instance method, use the *Get-WmiObject* cmdlet to return an object containing an instance method, and store the returned object in a variable. After they are stored, instance methods are directly available to you.

The example that follows uses group-and-dot dotted notation to call the method. In this example, two instances of the notepad.exe process start. The *Get-WmiObject* cmdlet returns both instances of the process and stores them in a variable. Next, dotted notation calls the *Terminate* method. This technique of calling the method was introduced in Windows PowerShell 3.0. In Windows PowerShell 2.0, a direct call to the *Terminate* method fails because the object contained in the variable is an array.

 Note Tab expansion does not enumerate the *Terminate* method when the underlying object is an array; therefore, this is one instance where you must type out the entire method name.

```
PS C:\> notepad
PS C:\> notepad
PS C:\> $a = gwmi win32_process -Filter "name = 'notepad.exe'"
PS C:\> $a.terminate()


__GENUS           : 2
__CLASS           : __PARAMETERS
__SUPERCLASS      :
__DYNASTY         : __PARAMETERS
__RELPATH         :
__PROPERTY_COUNT  : 1
__DERIVATION      : {}
__SERVER          :
__NAMESPACE       :
__PATH            :
ReturnValue       : 0
PSComputerName    :

__GENUS           : 2
__CLASS           : __PARAMETERS
__SUPERCLASS      :
__DYNASTY         : __PARAMETERS
```

```
__RELPATH         :
__PROPERTY_COUNT  : 1
__DERIVATION      : {}
__SERVER          :
__NAMESPACE       :
__PATH            :
ReturnValue       : 0
PSComputerName    :
```

Using the *Invoke-WmiMethod* cmdlet

If you want to use the *Invoke-WmiMethod* Windows PowerShell cmdlet to call an instance method, you must pass a path to the instance to be operated upon. The easiest way to obtain the path to the instance is to first perform a WMI query, and then use the *__RelPath* system property. The *__RelPath* system property contains the relative path to the instance of the class. In the example shown here, an instance of the notepad.exe process starts. Next, the *Get-WmiObject* cmdlet retrieves an instance of the process. Next, the *__RELPATH* system property is retrieved from the object stored in the *$a* variable.

```
PS C:\> notepad
PS C:\> $a = gwmi win32_process -Filter "name = 'notepad.exe'"
PS C:\> $a.__RELPATH
Win32_Process.Handle="1872"
```

If you are working against a remote machine, you must use the complete path to the instance. The complete path includes the machine name and the WMI namespace, in addition to the class and the key to the class. The complete path appears in the *__Path* system property, as shown in the following code. (Do not get confused; the *Win32_Process* WMI class also contains a *path* property.) The complete path to the current notepad.exe process stored in the *$a* variable is shown here.

```
PS C:\> $a.__PATH
\\C10\root\WMIv2:Win32_Process.Handle="1872"
```

If you have multiple instances of the notepad.exe process stored in the *$a* variable, you can still access the *__path* and *__relpath* properties, as shown here.

```
PS C:\> notepad
PS C:\> notepad
PS C:\> notepad
PS C:\> $a = gwmi win32_process -Filter "name = 'notepad.exe'"
PS C:\> $a.__RELPATH
Win32_Process.Handle="1644"
Win32_Process.Handle="2940"
Win32_Process.Handle="828"
PS C:\> $a.__PATH
\\C10\root\WMIv2:Win32_Process.Handle="1644"
\\C10\root\WMIv2:Win32_Process.Handle="2940"
\\C10\root\WMIv2:Win32_Process.Handle="828"
```

As shown in the following code, first create an instance of the Notepad process, use the *Get-WmiObject* cmdlet to retrieve that instance of the process, display the value of the *__RELPATH* property, and then call the *Invoke-WmiMethod* cmdlet. When calling the *Invoke-WmiMethod* cmdlet, pass the path to the instance and the name of the method to use. This appears in the following commands.

```
PS C:\> notepad
PS C:\> $a = gwmi win32_process -Filter "name = 'notepad.exe'"
PS C:\> $a.__RELPATH
Win32_Process.Handle="1264"
PS C:\> Invoke-WmiMethod -Path $a.__RELPATH -Name terminate


__GENUS          : 2
__CLASS          : __PARAMETERS
__SUPERCLASS     :
__DYNASTY        : __PARAMETERS
__RELPATH        :
__PROPERTY_COUNT : 1
__DERIVATION     : {}
__SERVER         :
__NAMESPACE      :
__PATH           :
ReturnValue      : 0
PSComputerName   :
```

Using the *[wmi]* type accelerator

Another way to call an instance method is to use the *[wmi]* type accelerator. The *[wmi]* type accelerator works with WMI instances. Therefore, if you pass a path to the *[wmi]* type accelerator, you can call instance methods directly. For this example, start an instance of the Notepad process. Next, use the *Get-WmiObject* cmdlet to retrieve all instances of Notepad (there is only one instance). Next, pass the value of the *__RELPATH* system property to the *[wmi]* type accelerator. This command returns the entire instance of the *Win32_Process* class. That is, it returns all properties and methods that are available. All of the properties associated with the *Win32_Process* WMI class (the same properties shown earlier) for the specific instance of *Win32_Process* are available via the *__RelPath* system property (keep in mind that *__RelPath* is preceded with two underscores—a double underscore—not one). To observe this object in action, select only the *name* property from the object and display it on the screen. At this point, you can retrieve a specific instance of a *Win32_Process* WMI class via the *[wmi]* type accelerator. Therefore, it is time to call the *Terminate* method. This technique appears here, along with the associated output.

```
PS C:\> notepad
PS C:\> $a = gwmi win32_process -Filter "name = 'notepad.exe'"
PS C:\> [wmi]$a.__RELPATH | select name
```

```
name
----
notepad.exe
PS C:\> ([wmi]$a.__RELPATH).terminate()


__GENUS          : 2
__CLASS          : __PARAMETERS
__SUPERCLASS     :
__DYNASTY        : __PARAMETERS
__RELPATH        :
__PROPERTY_COUNT : 1
__DERIVATION     : {}
__SERVER         :
__NAMESPACE      :
__PATH           :
ReturnValue      : 0
PSComputerName   :
```

Using WMI cmdlets to work with static methods

When you are working with WMI and Windows PowerShell, it is common to think about using the *Get-WmiObject* cmdlet. Unfortunately, when you use the *Get-WmiObject* cmdlet with the *Win32_SecurityDescriptorHelper* class, nothing happens. When you attempt to pipeline the results to *Get-Member*, an error is produced. The two commands appear here (note that *gwmi* is an alias for *Get-WmiObject* and *gm* is an alias for *Get-Member*).

```
PS C:\> gwmi win32_SecurityDescriptorHelper
PS C:\> gwmi win32_SecurityDescriptorHelper | gm
gm : No object has been specified to the Get-Member cmdlet.
At line:1 char:39
+ gwmi win32_SecurityDescriptorHelper | gm
+                                        ~~
    + CategoryInfo          : CloseError: (:) [Get-Member], InvalidOperationException
    + FullyQualifiedErrorId : NoObjectInGetMember,Microsoft.PowerShell.Commands.
   GetMemberCommand
```

Look up the class in the Windows Management Instrumentation Tester (WbemTest). The WbemTest tool always exists with WMI. To find it, you can type **WbemTest** from within Windows PowerShell. From WbemTest, click Connect. Click Connect again to connect to the default namespace. Next, click Open Class and enter **Win32_SecurityDescriptorHelper**, and then click OK. In the Object editor window, you can tell that *Win32_SecurityDescriptorHelper* is a dynamic class, and that there are many methods available from the class. This appears in Figure 13-1.

FIGURE 13-1 The WbemTest tool shows that the *Win32_SecurityDescriptorHelper* WMI class is dynamic and contains many methods.

When you click the Instances button (the sixth button from the top on the right), you will discover that there are no instances available. Next, click the Show MOF button (the third button from the top on the right), and you'll find that all methods are implemented. A method will only work if it is marked as "implemented." For example, the *Win32_Processor* WMI class has two methods listed—*Reset* and *SetPowerState*—but unfortunately, neither method is implemented, and therefore neither method works (in the case of *Win32_Processor*, the methods are defined on the abstract class *WMI_LogicalDevice* and are inherited). The Managed Object Format (MOF) description for the *Win32_SecurityDescriptorHelper* WMI class appears in Figure 13-2.

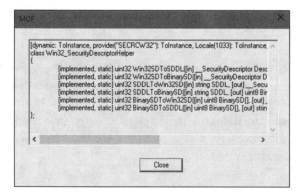

FIGURE 13-2 The *Win32_SecurityDescriptorHelper* methods are implemented. They are also static.

Notice that each method is static. Static methods do not use an instance of the WMI class—the *Get-WmiObject* command does not work with *Win32_SecurityDescriptorHelper* because *Get-WmiObject* returns instances of the class. With this WMI class, there are no instances.

Perhaps the easiest way to work with a static WMI method is to use the *[wmiclass]* type accelerator. The *SDDLToBinarySD* method will translate a Security Descriptor Definition Language (SDDL) string into binary byte array security descriptor (binary SD) format. The best way to talk about this technique is to walk through an example of converting an SDDL string to binary SD format. First, you need to obtain an SDDL string—you can do that by using the *Get-Acl* cmdlet. The next thing to do is give the *Get-Acl* cmdlet (ACL stands for access control list) the path to a file on your computer. Then store the resulting object in the *$acl* variable, and examine the SDDL string associated with the file by querying the *SDDL* property. These two lines of code appear here.

```
$acl = Get-Acl C:\bootmgr
$acl.Sddl
```

The two commands and associated output are shown in Figure 13-3.

FIGURE 13-3 Use the *Get-Acl* cmdlet to retrieve the ACL from a directory. Next, obtain the SDDL via the *sddl* property.

To convert the SDDL string to binary SD format, use the *[wmiclass]* type accelerator and call the method directly while supplying an SDDL string to the *SDDLToBinarySD* method. The syntax for the command is shown here.

```
([wmiclass]"Win32_SecurityDescriptorHelper").SDDLToBinarySD($acl.Sddl)
```

One thing that is a bit confusing is that in Windows PowerShell, double colons are required to call a static method. For example, to obtain the sine of a 45-degree angle, use the *SIN* static method from the *system.math* class. This is shown here.

```
[math]::sin(45)
```

But here, in WMI, there appears to be no difference between calling a static method or calling an instance method.

All the methods return both the *returnvalue* property, which provides the status of the command, and the specific output for the converted security descriptor. To retrieve only the binary SD output, you can add that to the end of the method call. The syntax of this command is shown here.

```
([wmiclass]"Win32_SecurityDescriptorHelper").SDDLToBinarySD($acl.Sddl).BinarySD
```

One of the cool things that you can do with the static methods from the *Win32_SecurityDescriptorHelper* class is convert an SDDL security descriptor into an instance of the *Win32_SecurityDescriptor* WMI class. The *Win32_SecurityDescriptor* WMI class is often used to provide security for various resources. For example, if you create a new share and want to assign security to the share, you will need to provide an instance of *Win32_SecurityDescriptor*. By using the *SDDLToWin32SD* method, you can use an SDDL string to get the *Win32_SecurityDescriptor* you need. To practice using the *SDDLToWin32SD* method, use the *Invoke-WmiMethod* cmdlet to perform the conversion. The following one-line command illustrates using the *Invoke-WmiMethod* cmdlet to call the *SDDLToWin32SD* method.

```
PS C:\> Invoke-WmiMethod -Class Win32_SecurityDescriptorHelper -Name SDDLToWin32SD
-ArgumentList $acl.Sddl
```

```
__GENUS           : 2
__CLASS           : __PARAMETERS
__SUPERCLASS      :
__DYNASTY         : __PARAMETERS
__RELPATH         :
__PROPERTY_COUNT  : 2
__DERIVATION      : {}
__SERVER          :
__NAMESPACE       :
__PATH            :
Descriptor        : System.Management.ManagementBaseObject
ReturnValue       : 0
PSComputerName    :
```

The other WMI methods from this class behave in a similar fashion, and therefore will not be explored.

Executing instance methods: Step-by-step exercises

In this exercise, you will use the *Terminate* instance method from the *Win32_Process* WMI class. This provides practice calling WMI instance methods. In the next exercise, you will practice calling static class methods.

Stopping several instances of a process by using WMI

1. Log on to your computer with a user account that does not have administrator rights.

2. Open the Windows PowerShell console.

3. Start five copies of Notepad. The command is shown here.

    ```
    1..5 | % {notepad}
    ```

4. Use the *Get-WmiObject* cmdlet to retrieve all instances of the notepad.exe process. The command is shown here.

    ```
    gwmi win32_process -Filter "name = 'notepad.exe'"
    ```

5. Now pipeline the resulting objects to the *Remove-WmiObject* cmdlet.

    ```
    gwmi win32_process -Filter "name = 'notepad.exe'" | Remove-WmiObject
    ```

6. Start five instances of Notepad. The command is shown here.

```
1..5 | % {notepad}
```

7. Use the Up Arrow key to retrieve the *Get-WmiObject* command that retrieves all instances of notepad.exe. The command is shown here.

```
gwmi win32_process -Filter "name = 'notepad.exe'"
```

8. Store the returned WMI objects in a variable named *$process*. This command is shown here.

```
$process = gwmi win32_process -Filter "name = 'notepad.exe'"
```

9. Call the *Terminate* method from the *$process* variable. The command is shown here.

```
$process.terminate()
```

10. Start five copies of Notepad back up. The command appears here.

```
1..5 | % {notepad}
```

11. Use the Up Arrow key to retrieve the *Get-WmiObject* command that retrieves all instances of notepad.exe. The command appears here.

```
gwmi win32_process -Filter "name = 'notepad.exe'"
```

12. Call the *Terminate* method from the previous expression. Put parentheses around the expression, and use dotted notation to call the method. The command is shown here.

```
(gwmi win32_process -Filter "name = 'notepad.exe'").terminate()
```

This concludes the exercise.

In the following exercise, you will use the static *Create* method from the *Win32_Share* WMI class to create a new share.

Executing static WMI methods

1. Open the Windows PowerShell console as a user who has admin rights on the local computer. To do this, you can right-click the Windows PowerShell console shortcut and click Run As Administrator on the menu.

2. Create a test folder off the root named testshare. Here is the command, which uses the *MD* alias for the *mkdir* function.

```
MD c:\testshare
```

3. Create the *Win32_Share* ManagementClass object and store it in a variable named *$share*. Use the *[wmiclass]* type accelerator. The code is shown here.

```
$share = [wmiclass]"win32_share"
```

4. Call the static *create* method from the *Win32_Share* object stored in the *$share* variable. The arguments are *path*, *name*, *type*, *maximumallowed*, *description*, *password*, and *access*. However, you need to supply only the first three. The value of the *type* argument is 0, which is a disk drive share. The syntax of the command is shown here.

```
$share.Create("C:\testshare","testshare",0)
```

5. Use the *Get-WmiObject* cmdlet and the *Win32_Share* class to verify that the share was properly created. The syntax of the command is shown here.

```
gwmi win32_share
```

6. Now add a filter so that the *Get-WmiObject* cmdlet returns only the newly created share. The syntax is shown here.

```
gwmi win32_share -Filter "name = 'testshare'"
```

7. Remove the newly created share by pipelining the results of the previous command to the *Remove-WmiObject* cmdlet. The syntax of the command is shown here.

```
gwmi win32_share -Filter "name = 'testshare'" | Remove-WmiObject
```

8. Use the *Get-WmiObject* cmdlet and the *Win32_Share* WMI class to verify that the share was properly removed. The command is shown here.

```
gwmi win32_share
```

This concludes the exercise.

Chapter 13 quick reference

To	Do this
Use the *Terminate* method directly	Group the returning WMI object and use dotted notation to call the *Terminate* method.
Use the *Terminate* method from a variable containing the WMI object	Use dotted notation to call the *Terminate* method.
Call a static method via the *Invoke-WmiMethod* cmdlet	Use the *-Class* parameter to specify the WMI class name, and specify the name of the method via the *-Name* parameter.
Call a static WMI method without using the *Invoke-WmiMethod* cmdlet	Use the *[wmi]* type accelerator to retrieve the WMI class, store the resulting object in a variable, and use dotted notation to call the method.
Stop processes via WMI and not call the *Terminate* method	Use the *Get-WmiObject* cmdlet to return the process objects, and pipeline the results to the *Remove-WMIObject* cmdlet.
Find static WMI methods	Use the *[wmiclass]* type accelerator to create the WMI object, and pipeline the resulting object to the *Get-Member* cmdlet.
Find the relative path to a particular WMI instance	Use the *Get-WmiObject* cmdlet to retrieve instances, and choose the __RELPATH system property.

Using the CIM cmdlets

After completing this chapter, you will be able to

- Use the CIM cmdlets to explore WMI classes.

- Use CIM classes to obtain WMI data classes.

- Use the CIM cmdlets to run remote commands.

Using the CIM cmdlets to explore WMI classes

In Windows PowerShell 5.0, the Common Information Model (CIM) exposes an application programming interface (API) for working with Windows Management Instrumentation (WMI) information. The CIM cmdlets support multiple ways of exploring WMI. They work well when you are working in an interactive fashion. For example, tab expansion expands the namespace when you use the CIM cmdlets, so you can explore namespaces easily. These namespaces might not otherwise be very discoverable. You can even drill down into namespaces by using this technique of tab expansion. All CIM cmdlets support tab expansion of the *namespace* parameter, in addition to the -*ClassName* parameter. But to explore WMI classes, you will want to use the cmdlet specifically designed for class exploration, the *Get-CimClass* cmdlet.

 Note The default WMI namespace on all operating systems after Windows NT 4.0 is *Root/Cimv2*. Therefore, all of the CIM cmdlets default to *Root/Cimv2*. The only time you need to change the default WMI namespace (via the *Namespace* parameter) is when you need to use a WMI class from a nondefault WMI namespace.

Using the *Get-CimClass* cmdlet and the -*ClassName* parameter

By using the *Get-CimClass* cmdlet, you can use wildcards for the -*ClassName* parameter to quickly identify potential WMI classes for perusal. In the example here, the *Get-CimClass* cmdlet looks for WMI classes related to computers. To do this, the code uses the asterisk twice: once at the beginning of the word *computer* and once at the end. This pattern includes any WMI class where the word *computer* appears in the class name.

```
PS C:\> Get-CimClass -ClassName *computer*


   NameSpace: ROOT/CIMV2

CimClassName                       CimClassMethods        CimClassProperties
------------                       ---------------        ------------------
Win32_ComputerSystemEvent          {}                     {SECURITY_DESCRIPTOR, TI...
Win32_ComputerShutdownEvent        {}                     {SECURITY_DESCRIPTOR, TI...
CIM_ComputerSystem                 {}                     {Caption, Description, I...
CIM_UnitaryComputerSystem          {SetPowerState}        {Caption, Description, I...
Win32_ComputerSystem               {SetPowerState, R...   {Caption, Description, I...
CIM_ComputerSystemPackage          {}                     {Antecedent, Dependent}
Win32_ComputerSystemProcessor      {}                     {GroupComponent, PartCom...
CIM_ComputerSystemResource         {}                     {GroupComponent, PartCom...
CIM_ComputerSystemMappedIO         {}                     {GroupComponent, PartCom...
CIM_ComputerSystemDMA              {}                     {GroupComponent, PartCom...
CIM_ComputerSystemIRQ              {}                     {GroupComponent, PartCom...
Win32_ComputerSystemProduct        {}                     {Caption, Description, I...
Win32_NTLogEventComputer           {}                     {Computer, Record}
```

Note If you try to use a wildcard for the *-ClassName* parameter of the *Get-CimInstance* cmdlet, an error returns because the parameter design does not permit wildcard characters.

Providing a more useful WMI class search requires becoming more selective with the wildcard characters. The first thing to do is to remove the trailing asterisk. The revised command and output are shown here.

```
PS C:\> Get-CimClass -ClassName *computer


   NameSpace: ROOT/cimv2

CimClassName                       CimClassMethods        CimClassProperties
------------                       ---------------        ------------------
Win32_NTLogEventComputer           {}                     {Computer, Record}
```

That reduced the output too much, perhaps. From the previous output, the word *computer* seemed to always be followed by the word *system* in the most interesting WMI classes. So a quick revision is shown here.

```
PS C:\> Get-CimClass -ClassName *computerSystem*


   NameSpace: ROOT/CIMV2

CimClassName                       CimClassMethods        CimClassProperties
------------                       ---------------        ------------------
Win32_ComputerSystemEvent          {}                     {SECURITY_DESCRIPTOR, TI...
CIM_ComputerSystem                 {}                     {Caption, Description, I...
CIM_UnitaryComputerSystem          {SetPowerState}        {Caption, Description, I...
Win32_ComputerSystem               {SetPowerState, R...   {Caption, Description, I...
```

```
CIM_ComputerSystemPackage            {}                    {Antecedent, Dependent}
Win32_ComputerSystemProcessor        {}                    {GroupComponent, PartCom...
CIM_ComputerSystemResource           {}                    {GroupComponent, PartCom...
CIM_ComputerSystemMappedIO           {}                    {GroupComponent, PartCom...
CIM_ComputerSystemDMA                {}                    {GroupComponent, PartCom...
CIM_ComputerSystemIRQ                {}                    {GroupComponent, PartCom...
Win32_ComputerSystemProduct          {}                    {Caption, Description, I...
```

That output appears to be more selective, but it includes WMI classes that begin with the letters *CIM*. From previous experience, you know that those WMI classes generally do not provide useful information. So removing the initial asterisk produces a more select output. The revised command and output are shown here.

```
PS C:\> Get-CimClass -ClassName Win32_computerSystem*


   NameSpace: ROOT/CIMV2

CimClassName                    CimClassMethods        CimClassProperties
------------                    ---------------        ------------------
Win32_ComputerSystemEvent       {}                     {SECURITY_DESCRIPTOR, TI...
Win32_ComputerSystem            {SetPowerState, R...   {Caption, Description, I...
Win32_ComputerSystemProcessor   {}                     {GroupComponent, PartCom...
Win32_ComputerSystemProduct     {}                     {Caption, Description, I...
```

But you are not limited to using the asterisk. You can also use the question mark wildcard character. Whereas the asterisk represents any number of characters, the question mark represents a single character. To find a particular WMI class, you might find the question mark helpful. Notice that the revised query produces a single WMI class.

```
PS C:\> Get-CimClass -ClassName Win32_computerSystem?????


   NameSpace: ROOT/CIMV2

CimClassName                    CimClassMethods        CimClassProperties
------------                    ---------------        ------------------
Win32_ComputerSystemEvent       {}                     {SECURITY_DESCRIPTOR, TI...
```

Finding WMI class methods

The simple definition of a method is that a method does something. A property describes something. Therefore, making changes to a system requires the identification and use of methods. If you want to find WMI classes related to processes that contain methods, you use a command similar to the one here.

```
PS C:\> Get-CimClass -ClassName *process -MethodName *


   NameSpace: ROOT/cimv2
```

```
CimClassName                      CimClassMethods        CimClassProperties
------------                      ---------------        ------------------
Win32_Process                     {Create, Terminat...   {Caption, Description, I...
```

To find any class that contains the word *process* in the WMI class name and that exposes a method that begins with the word *term*, you use a command similar to the one shown here.

```
PS C:\> Get-CimClass -ClassName *process* -MethodName term*


    NameSpace: ROOT/cimv2

CimClassName                      CimClassMethods        CimClassProperties
------------                      ---------------        ------------------
Win32_Process                     {Create, Terminat...   {Caption, Description, Instal...
```

To find all WMI classes related to processes that expose any methods, you would use the command shown here.

```
PS C:\> Get-CimClass -ClassName *process* -MethodName *


    NameSpace: ROOT/cimv2

CimClassName                      CimClassMethods        CimClassProperties
------------                      ---------------        ------------------
Win32_Process                     {Create, Terminat...   {Caption, Description, Instal...
CIM_Processor                     {SetPowerState, R...   {Caption, Description, Instal...
Win32_Processor                   {SetPowerState, R...   {Caption, Description, Instal...
```

To bore into the methods exposed by a particular WMI class, choose all of the methods and pipeline the output to the *Select-Object* cmdlet. Choose the *CimClassName* property, and expand the *CimClassMethods* property. The resulting command and associated output are shown here.

```
PS C:\> Get-CimClass -ClassName *process -MethodName * | select-object -Property cimc
lassname -expandproperty cimclassmethods


CimClassName : Win32_Process
Name         : Create
ReturnType   : UInt32
Parameters   : {CommandLine, CurrentDirectory, ProcessStartupInformation, ProcessId}
Qualifiers   : {Constructor, Implemented, MappingStrings, Privileges...}

CimClassName : Win32_Process
Name         : Terminate
ReturnType   : UInt32
Parameters   : {Reason}
Qualifiers   : {Destructor, Implemented, MappingStrings, Privileges...}

CimClassName : Win32_Process
Name         : GetOwner
ReturnType   : UInt32
Parameters   : {Domain, User}
```

```
Qualifiers    : {Implemented, MappingStrings, ValueMap}

CimClassName : Win32_Process
Name          : GetOwnerSid
ReturnType    : UInt32
Parameters    : {Sid}
Qualifiers    : {Implemented, MappingStrings, ValueMap}

CimClassName : Win32_Process
Name          : SetPriority
ReturnType    : UInt32
Parameters    : {Priority}
Qualifiers    : {Implemented, MappingStrings, ValueMap}

CimClassName : Win32_Process
Name          : AttachDebugger
ReturnType    : UInt32
Parameters    : {}
Qualifiers    : {Implemented, ValueMap}

CimClassName : Win32_Process
Name          : GetAvailableVirtualSize
ReturnType    : UInt32
Parameters    : {AvailableVirtualSize}
Qualifiers    : {Implemented, ValueMap}
```

To find any WMI class in the *Root/Cimv2* WMI namespace that exposes a method called *create*, use the command shown here.

```
PS C:\> Get-CimClass -ClassName * -MethodName create


   NameSpace: ROOT/cimv2

CimClassName                   CimClassMethods      CimClassProperties
------------                   ---------------      ------------------
Win32_Process                  {Create, Terminat... {Caption, Description, Instal...
Win32_ScheduledJob             {Create, Delete}     {Caption, Description, Instal...
Win32_DfsNode                  {Create}             {Caption, Description, Instal...
Win32_BaseService              {StartService, St... {Caption, Description, Instal...
Win32_SystemDriver             {StartService, St... {Caption, Description, Instal...
Win32_Service                  {StartService, St... {Caption, Description, Instal...
Win32_TerminalService          {StartService, St... {Caption, Description, Instal...
Win32_Share                    {Create, SetShare... {Caption, Description, Instal...
Win32_ClusterShare             {Create, SetShare... {Caption, Description, Instal...
Win32_ShadowCopy               {Create, Revert}     {Caption, Description, Instal...
Win32_ShadowStorage            {Create}             {AllocatedSpace, DiffVolume, ...
```

Filtering classes by qualifier

To find WMI classes that possess a particular WMI qualifier, use the *-QualifierName* parameter. You can also use wildcards for the *-QualifierName* parameter. For example, the following command finds WMI classes that relate to computers and have the *supportsupdate* WMI qualifier.

```
PS C:\> Get-CimClass -ClassName *computer* -QualifierName *update


    NameSpace: ROOT/cimv2

CimClassName                        CimClassMethods        CimClassProperties
------------                        ---------------        ------------------
Win32_ComputerSystem                {SetPowerState, R...   {Caption, Description, Instal...
```

To find the available WMI qualifiers, use the *Get-CimClass* cmdlet, choose all WMI classes and all qualifiers, and then pipeline the results to the *Select-Object* cmdlet. Expand the *CimClassQualifiers* property, select the unique names of the qualifiers, and sort them. The command and its associated output are shown in the following code block.

> **Note** WMI, like other management interfaces, is not case sensitive. Therefore, some CIM Class Qualifiers appear twice in the output, once in all lowercase and once with an initial capital.

```
PS C:\> Get-CimClass -ClassName * -QualifierName * | Select-Object -ExpandProperty Ci
mClassQualifiers | Select-Object Name -Unique | Sort-Object Name

Name
----
Abstract
abstract
Aggregation
Association
AutoCook
AutoCook_RawClass
ClassContext
Cooked
Costly
CreateBy
DeleteBy
DEPRECATED
Description
description
DetailLevel
DisplayName
DisplayName009
dynamic
Embed
EnumPrivileges
EventId
EventType
Exception
GenericPerfCtr
HelpIndex
HiPerf
ImplementationSource
Indication
inpartition
InsertionStringTemplates
```

```
Locale
locale
MappingStrings
PerfDefault
PerfIndex
Privileges
provider
RegistryKey
Singleton
singleton
SupportsCreate
SupportsDelete
SupportsUpdate
UMLPackagePath
UUID
Version
```

Combining the parameters produces powerful searches that would require rather complicated scripting if it were not for the CIM cmdlets. For example, the following command finds all WMI classes in the *Root/Cimv2* namespace that have the *singleton* qualifier and that expose a method. I can shorten the command by leaving out the *-ClassName* parameter because the command automatically searches all classes in the default namespace.

```
PS C:\> Get-CimClass  -QualifierName singleton -MethodName *


   NameSpace: ROOT/cimv2

CimClassName                     CimClassMethods         CimClassProperties
------------                     ---------------         ------------------
__SystemSecurity                 {GetSD, GetSecuri... {}
Win32_OperatingSystem            {Reboot, Shutdown... {Caption, Description, Instal...
Win32_OfflineFilesCache          {Enable, RenameIt... {Active, Enabled, Location}
```

One qualifier that is important to review is the *deprecated* qualifier. Deprecated WMI classes are not recommended for use because they are being phased out. You can use the *Get-CimClass* cmdlet to make it easy to spot these WMI classes. This technique is shown here.

```
PS C:\> Get-CimClass -QualifierName deprecated


   NameSpace: ROOT/cimv2

CimClassName                     CimClassMethods         CimClassProperties
------------                     ---------------         ------------------
Win32_PageFile                   {TakeOwnerShip, C... {Caption, Description, Instal...
Win32_DisplayConfiguration       {}                      {Caption, Description, Settin...
Win32_DisplayControllerConfigura... {}                   {Caption, Description, Settin...
Win32_VideoConfiguration         {}                      {Caption, Description, Settin...
Win32_AllocatedResource          {}                      {Antecedent, Dependent}
```

By using this technique, it is easy to find association classes. *Association classes* relate two or more WMI classes. For example, the *Win32_DisplayConfiguration* WMI class relates displays and the associated configuration. The code that follows finds all of the WMI classes in the *Root/Cimv2* WMI namespace that relate to sessions. In addition, it looks for the *association* qualifier. Luckily, you can use wildcards for the qualifier names; in keeping with this, the following code uses *assoc** instead of the typed-out *association*.

> **Tip** Using wildcard characters with qualifier queries is extremely useful because tab expansion does not work for qualifier names.

```
PS C:\> Get-CimClass -ClassName *session* -QualifierName assoc*


   NameSpace: ROOT/cimv2

CimClassName                    CimClassMethods      CimClassProperties
------------                    ---------------      ------------------
Win32_SubSession                {}                   {Antecedent, Dependent}
Win32_SessionConnection         {}                   {Antecedent, Dependent}
Win32_LogonSessionMappedDisk    {}                   {Antecedent, Dependent}
Win32_SessionResource           {}                   {Antecedent, Dependent}
Win32_SessionProcess            {}                   {Antecedent, Dependent}
```

One qualifier you should definitely look for is the *dynamic* qualifier. This is because querying abstract WMI classes is unsupported. An abstract WMI class is basically a template class that is used by WMI when creating new WMI classes. Therefore, all *dynamic* WMI classes derive from an abstract class. Therefore, when looking for WMI classes, you will want to ensure that at some point you run your list through the *dynamic* filter. In the code that follows, three WMI classes related to time are returned.

```
PS C:\> Get-CimClass -ClassName *time


   NameSpace: ROOT/cimv2

CimClassName                    CimClassMethods      CimClassProperties
------------                    ---------------      ------------------
Win32_CurrentTime               {}                   {Day, DayOfWeek, Hour, Millis...
Win32_LocalTime                 {}                   {Day, DayOfWeek, Hour, Millis...
Win32_UTCTime                   {}                   {Day, DayOfWeek, Hour, Millis...
```

By adding the query for the qualifier, you identify the appropriate WMI classes. One class is abstract, and the other two are dynamic classes that could prove to be useful. In the following code, the *dynamic* qualifier is first used, and the *abstract* qualifier appears second.

```
PS C:\> Get-CimClass -ClassName *time -QualifierName dynamic


   NameSpace: ROOT/cimv2

CimClassName                    CimClassMethods      CimClassProperties
------------                    ---------------      ------------------
Win32_LocalTime                 {}                   {Day, DayOfWeek, Hour, Millis...
Win32_UTCTime                   {}                   {Day, DayOfWeek, Hour, Millis...
```

```
PS C:\> Get-CimClass -ClassName *time -QualifierName abstract


   NameSpace: ROOT/cimv2

CimClassName                    CimClassMethods     CimClassProperties
------------                    ---------------     ------------------
Win32_CurrentTime               {}                  {Day, DayOfWeek, Hour, Millis...
```

Retrieving WMI instances

To query for WMI data, use the *Get-CimInstance* cmdlet. The easiest way to use the *Get-CimInstance* cmdlet is to query for all properties and all instances of a particular WMI class on the local machine. This is extremely easy to do. The following command illustrates returning BIOS information from the local computer.

```
PS C:\> Get-CimInstance Win32_BIOS

SMBIOSBIOSVersion : 090006
Manufacturer      : American Megatrends Inc.
Name              : BIOS Date: 05/23/12 17:15:53  Ver: 09.00.06
SerialNumber      : 8570-3709-4791-5943-3863-4381-72
Version           : VRTUAL - 5001223
```

The *Get-CimInstance* cmdlet returns the entire WMI object, but it honors the *.format.ps1xml* files that Windows PowerShell uses to determine which properties are displayed by default for a particular WMI class. The following command shows the properties available from the *Win32_BIOS* WMI class.

```
PS C:\> $b = Get-CimInstance Win32_BIOS
PS C:\> $b.CimClass.CimClassProperties | fw name -Column 3
```

Caption	Description	InstallDate
Name	Status	BuildNumber
CodeSet	IdentificationCode	LanguageEdition
Manufacturer	OtherTargetOS	SerialNumber
SoftwareElementID	SoftwareElementState	TargetOperatingSystem
Version	PrimaryBIOS	BiosCharacteristics
BIOSVersion	CurrentLanguage	InstallableLanguages
ListOfLanguages	ReleaseDate	SMBIOSBIOSVersion
SMBIOSMajorVersion	SMBIOSMinorVersion	SMBIOSPresent

Reducing returned properties and instances

To limit the amount of data returned from a remote connection, you can reduce the number of properties returned, in addition to the number of instances. To reduce properties, use the *-Property* parameter. To reduce the number of returned instances, use the *-Filter* parameter. The following command uses *gcim*, which is an alias for the *Get-CimInstance* cmdlet. The command also abbreviates the *-ClassName* parameter and the *-Filter* parameter. As shown here, the command returns only the name and the state of the *bits* service. The default output, however, shows all of the property names in addition to the system properties. As shown here, however, only the two selected properties contain data.

```
PS C:\> gcim -clas win32_service -Property name, state -Fil "name = 'bits'"
```

```
Name                      : BITS
Status                    :
ExitCode                  :
DesktopInteract           :
ErrorControl              :
PathName                  :
ServiceType               :
StartMode                 :
Caption                   :
Description               :
InstallDate               :
CreationClassName         :
Started                   :
SystemCreationClassName   :
SystemName                :
AcceptPause               :
AcceptStop                :
DisplayName               :
ServiceSpecificExitCode   :
StartName                 :
State                     : Running
TagId                     :
CheckPoint                :
ProcessId                 :
WaitHint                  :
PSComputerName            :
CimClass                  : root/cimv2:Win32_Service
CimInstanceProperties     : {Caption, Description, InstallDate, Name...}
CimSystemProperties       : Microsoft.Management.Infrastructure.CimSystemProperties
```

Cleaning up output from the command

To produce cleaner output, send the selected data to the *Format-Table* cmdlet (you can use the *ft* alias for the *Format-Table* cmdlet, to reduce typing).

```
PS C:\> gcim -clas win32_service -Property name, state -Fil "name = 'bits'" | ft name, state
```

```
name                                     state
----                                     -----
BITS                                     Running
```

Make sure you choose properties you have already selected in the *-Property* parameter, otherwise they will not display. In the command shown here, the *status* property is selected in the *Format-Table* cmdlet. There is a *status* property on the *Win32_Service* WMI class, but it was not chosen when the properties were selected.

```
PS C:\> gcim -clas win32_service -Property name, state -Fil "name = 'bits'" |
ft name, state, status

name                           state                          status
----                           -----                          ------
BITS                           Running
```

The *Get-CimInstance* cmdlet does not accept a wildcard parameter for property names (neither does the *Get-WmiObject* cmdlet, for that matter). One thing that can simplify some of your coding is to put your property selection into a variable. That way, you can use the same property names in both the *Get-CimInstance* cmdlet and the *Format-Table* cmdlet (or *Format-List* or *Select-Object*, or whatever you are using after you get your WMI data) without having to type things twice. This technique is shown here.

```
PS C:\> $property = "name","state","startmode","startname"
PS C:\> gcim -clas win32_service -Pro $property -fil "name = 'bits'" | ft $property -A

name state   startmode startname
---- -----   --------- ---------
BITS Running Manual    LocalSystem
```

Working with associations

In the old-fashioned days of VBScript (Microsoft Visual Basic Scripting Edition), working with association classes was extremely complicated. This is unfortunate, because WMI association classes are extremely powerful and useful. Earlier versions of Windows PowerShell simplified working with association classes, primarily because it simplified working with WMI data in general. However, figuring out how to use the Windows PowerShell advantage was still pretty much an advanced technique. Luckily, the CIM cmdlets provide the *Get-CimAssociatedInstance* cmdlet.

The first thing to do when attempting to find a WMI association class is to retrieve a CIM instance and store it in a variable. In the example that follows, instances of the *Win32_LogonSession* WMI class are retrieved and stored in the *$logon* variable. The entire WMI class is not required—only the key properties from the class. Next, the *Get-CimAssociatedInstance* cmdlet is used to retrieve instances associated with this class. Because the cmdlet associates two WMI classes, a specific instance of the *Win32_LogonSession* is required. The easy way to obtain this is to index into the array. To find out what type of objects will return from the command, pipeline the results to the *Get-Member* cmdlet. As shown here, three things are returned: the *Win32_SystemAccount* and *Win32_UserAccount* classes, and all processes that are related to the corresponding user account in the form of instances of the *Win32_Process* class.

```
PS C:\> $logon = Get-CimInstance Win32_LogonSession -KeyOnly
PS C:\> Get-CimAssociatedInstance $logon[1] | Get-Member


   TypeName:
Microsoft.Management.Infrastructure.CimInstance#root/cimv2/Win32_SystemAccount
```

Name	MemberType	Definition
Clone	Method	System.Object ICloneable.Clone()
Dispose	Method	void Dispose(), void IDisposable.Dispose()
Equals	Method	bool Equals(System.Object obj)
GetCimSessionComputerName	Method	string GetCimSessionComputerName()
GetCimSessionInstanceId	Method	guid GetCimSessionInstanceId()
GetHashCode	Method	int GetHashCode()
GetObjectData	Method	void GetObjectData(System.Runtime.Serializa...
GetType	Method	type GetType()
ToString	Method	string ToString()
Caption	Property	string Caption {get;}
Description	Property	string Description {get;}
Domain	Property	string Domain {get;}
InstallDate	Property	CimInstance#DateTime InstallDate {get;}
LocalAccount	Property	bool LocalAccount {get;set;}
Name	Property	string Name {get;}
PSComputerName	Property	string PSComputerName {get;}
SID	Property	string SID {get;}
SIDType	Property	byte SIDType {get;}
Status	Property	string Status {get;}
PSStatus	PropertySet	PSStatus {Status, SIDType, Name, Domain}

```
    TypeName:
Microsoft.Management.Infrastructure.CimInstance#root/cimv2/Win32_Process
```

Name	MemberType	Definition
Handles	AliasProperty	Handles = Handlecount
ProcessName	AliasProperty	ProcessName = Name
VM	AliasProperty	VM = VirtualSize
WS	AliasProperty	WS = WorkingSetSize
Clone	Method	System.Object ICloneable.Clone()
Dispose	Method	void Dispose(), void IDisposable.Dispose()
Equals	Method	bool Equals(System.Object obj)
GetCimSessionComputerName	Method	string GetCimSessionComputerName()
GetCimSessionInstanceId	Method	guid GetCimSessionInstanceId()
GetHashCode	Method	int GetHashCode()
GetObjectData	Method	void GetObjectData(System.Runtime.Seria...
GetType	Method	type GetType()
ToString	Method	string ToString()
Caption	Property	string Caption {get;}
CommandLine	Property	string CommandLine {get;}
CreationClassName	Property	string CreationClassName {get;}
CreationDate	Property	CimInstance#DateTime CreationDate {get;}
CSCreationClassName	Property	string CSCreationClassName {get;}
CSName	Property	string CSName {get;}
Description	Property	string Description {get;}
ExecutablePath	Property	string ExecutablePath {get;}
ExecutionState	Property	uint16 ExecutionState {get;}
Handle	Property	string Handle {get;}
HandleCount	Property	uint32 HandleCount {get;}
InstallDate	Property	CimInstance#DateTime InstallDate {get;}
KernelModeTime	Property	uint64 KernelModeTime {get;}
MaximumWorkingSetSize	Property	uint32 MaximumWorkingSetSize {get;}
MinimumWorkingSetSize	Property	uint32 MinimumWorkingSetSize {get;}

```
Name                        Property        string Name {get;}
OSCreationClassName         Property        string OSCreationClassName {get;}
OSName                      Property        string OSName {get;}
OtherOperationCount         Property        uint64 OtherOperationCount {get;}
OtherTransferCount          Property        uint64 OtherTransferCount {get;}
PageFaults                  Property        uint32 PageFaults {get;}
PageFileUsage               Property        uint32 PageFileUsage {get;}
ParentProcessId             Property        uint32 ParentProcessId {get;}
PeakPageFileUsage           Property        uint32 PeakPageFileUsage {get;}
PeakVirtualSize             Property        uint64 PeakVirtualSize {get;}
PeakWorkingSetSize          Property        uint32 PeakWorkingSetSize {get;}
Priority                    Property        uint32 Priority {get;}
PrivatePageCount            Property        uint64 PrivatePageCount {get;}
ProcessId                   Property        uint32 ProcessId {get;}
PSComputerName              Property        string PSComputerName {get;}
QuotaNonPagedPoolUsage      Property        uint32 QuotaNonPagedPoolUsage {get;}
QuotaPagedPoolUsage         Property        uint32 QuotaPagedPoolUsage {get;}
QuotaPeakNonPagedPoolUsage  Property        uint32 QuotaPeakNonPagedPoolUsage {get;}
QuotaPeakPagedPoolUsage     Property        uint32 QuotaPeakPagedPoolUsage {get;}
ReadOperationCount          Property        uint64 ReadOperationCount {get;}
ReadTransferCount           Property        uint64 ReadTransferCount {get;}
SessionId                   Property        uint32 SessionId {get;}
Status                      Property        string Status {get;}
TerminationDate             Property        CimInstance#DateTime TerminationDate {g...
ThreadCount                 Property        uint32 ThreadCount {get;}
UserModeTime                Property        uint64 UserModeTime {get;}
VirtualSize                 Property        uint64 VirtualSize {get;}
WindowsVersion              Property        string WindowsVersion {get;}
WorkingSetSize              Property        uint64 WorkingSetSize {get;}
WriteOperationCount         Property        uint64 WriteOperationCount {get;}
WriteTransferCount          Property        uint64 WriteTransferCount {get;}
Path                        ScriptProperty  System.Object Path {get=$this.Executabl...
```

When the command runs without piping to the *Get-Member* object, the instance of the *Win32_UserAccount* and/or *Win32_SystemAccount* WMI classes are returned. The output shows the user name, account type, security identifier (SID), domain, and caption of the user account. As shown in the output from *Get-Member*, a lot more information is available, but this is the default display. Following the user account information, the default process information displays the process ID, name, and a bit of performance information related to the processes associated with the user account.

```
PS C:\> $logon = Get-CimInstance Win32_LogonSession -KeyOnly
PS C:\> Get-CimAssociatedInstance $logon[1]

ProcessId      Name            HandleCount      WorkingSetSize    VirtualSize
---------      ----            -----------      --------------    -----------
404            svchost.exe     589              7921664           2199130411008
388            svchost.exe     686              19054592          2199123230720
812            svchost.exe     275              3391488           2199080689664
1204           svchost.exe     468              14712832          2199128973312
1660           dasHost.exe     90               778240            2199043690496
1864           taskhostw.exe   2681             36458496          2200347521024


Caption : C10\LOCAL SERVICE
Domain  : C10
Name    : LOCAL SERVICE
SID     : S-1-5-19
```

If you do not want to retrieve a specific class from the association query, you can specify the resulting class by name. To do this, use the -*ResultClassName* parameter from the *Get-CimAssociatedInstance* cmdlet. In the code that follows, only the *Win32_UserAccount* WMI class is returned from the query. In my example here, I used the value 3 to index into the fourth item in the array. Your results may vary.

```
PS C:\> $logon = Get-CimInstance Win32_LogonSession -KeyOnly
PS C:\> Get-CimAssociatedInstance $logon[3] -ResultClassName Win32_UserAccount
```

Name	Caption	AccountType	SID	Domain
----	-------	-----------	---	------
administrator	NWTRADERS\adm...	512	S-1-5-21-1893...	NWTRADERS

When you are working with the *Get-CimAssociatedInstance* cmdlet, the *inputobject* you supply must be a single instance. If you supply an object that contains more than one instance of the class, an error is raised. This error is shown in the following code, where more than one disk is provided to the *inputobject* parameter.

```
PS C:\> $logon = Get-CimInstance Win32_LogonSession -KeyOnly
PS C:\> Get-CimAssociatedInstance $logon
Get-CimAssociatedInstance : Cannot convert 'System.Object[]' to the type
'Microsoft.Management.Infrastructure.CimInstance' required by parameter
'InputObject'. Specified method is not supported.
At line:1 char:27
+ Get-CimAssociatedInstance $logon
+                           ~~~~~~
    + CategoryInfo          : InvalidArgument: (:) [Get-CimAssociatedInstance], Par
    ameterBindingException
    + FullyQualifiedErrorId : CannotConvertArgument,Microsoft.Management.Infrastruc
    ture.CimCmdlets.GetCimAssociatedInstanceCommand
```

There are two ways to correct this particular error. The first, and the easiest, is to use *array indexing*. This technique places square brackets beside the variable holding the collection and retrieves a specific instance from the collection. This is the technique used earlier with the *Win32_LogonSession* query. This technique appears here, in working with where the first disk returns associated instances.

```
PS C:\> $disk = Get-CimInstance Win32_LogicalDisk -KeyOnly
PS C:\> Get-CimAssociatedInstance $disk[0]
```

Name	PrimaryOwnerN ame	Domain	TotalPhysical Memory	Model	Manufacturer
----	-------------	------	-------------	-----	------------
C10	mredwilson...	NWTraders.com	4294496256	Virtual M...	Microsoft...

```
PS C:\> Get-CimAssociatedInstance $disk[1]
```

Name	Hidden	Archive	Writeable	LastModified
----	------	-------	---------	------------
c:\				

```
NumberOfBlocks    : 265617408
BootPartition     : False
```

```
Name             : Disk #0, Partition #1
PrimaryPartition : True
Size             : 135996112896
Index            : 1


Domain              : NWTraders.com
Manufacturer        : Microsoft Corporation
Model               : Virtual Machine
Name                : C10
PrimaryOwnerName    : mredwilson@outlook.com
TotalPhysicalMemory : 4294496256


Caption             : C:
DefaultLimit        : -1
SettingID           :
State               : 0
VolumePath          : C:\
DefaultWarningLimit : -1


Caption : C10\Administrators
Domain  : C10
Name    : Administrators
SID     : S-1-5-32-544
```

The use of array indexing is fine when you are working with an object that contains an array. However, the results might be a bit inconsistent. For example, the C10 computer explored in the previous WMI query actually has four logical disks attached. This is shown here.

```
PS C:\> Get-CimInstance Win32_LogicalDisk

DeviceID   DriveType   ProviderName   VolumeName   Size          FreeSpace
--------   ---------   ------------   ----------   ----          ---------
A:         2
C:         3                                       135996108800  12471651...
D:         5
H:         4           \\dc1\Share                 135810510848  12553025...
```

> **Tip** As is often the case when you are working with Windows PowerShell, it is important to know and understand what typical data might look like. This makes it possible to ensure that you are using the best approach to achieve the solution you want.

A better approach is to ensure that you do not have an array in the first place. To do this, use the *-Filter* parameter to reduce the number of instances of your WMI class returned by the query. In the code that follows, the filter reduces the number of possible WMI instances to only drives with a name of *C:*.

```
PS C:\> $disk = Get-CimInstance Win32_LogicalDisk -Filter "Name = 'C:'" -KeyOnly
PS C:\> Get-CimAssociatedInstance $disk
```

```
Name            Hidden          Archive         Writeable       LastModified
----            ------          -------         ---------       ------------
c:\
```

```
NumberOfBlocks   : 265617408
BootPartition    : False
Name             : Disk #0, Partition #1
PrimaryPartition : True
Size             : 135996112896
Index            : 1
```

```
Domain              : NWTraders.com
Manufacturer        : Microsoft Corporation
Model               : Virtual Machine
Name                : C10
PrimaryOwnerName    : mredwilson@outlook.com
TotalPhysicalMemory : 4294496256
```

```
Caption            : C:
DefaultLimit       : -1
SettingID          :
State              : 0
VolumePath         : C:\
DefaultWarningLimit : -1
```

```
Caption : C10\Administrators
Domain  : C10
Name    : Administrators
SID     : S-1-5-32-544
```

An easy way to view the objects returned by the *Get-CimAssociatedInstance* cmdlet is to pipeline the returned objects to the *Get-Member* cmdlet and then select the *typename* property. Because more than one instance of the object might return and clutter the output, it is important to choose unique type names. This command is shown here.

```
PS C:\> Get-CimAssociatedInstance $disk | gm | select typename -Unique
```

```
TypeName
--------
Microsoft.Management.Infrastructure.CimInstance#root/cimv2/Win32_Directory
Microsoft.Management.Infrastructure.CimInstance#root/cimv2/Win32_DiskPartition
Microsoft.Management.Infrastructure.CimInstance#root/cimv2/Win32_ComputerSystem
Microsoft.Management.Infrastructure.CimInstance#root/cimv2/Win32_QuotaSetting
Microsoft.Management.Infrastructure.CimInstance#root/cimv2/Win32_Group
```

When you are armed with this information, it is easy to explore the returned associations. This technique is shown here.

```
PS C:\> Get-CimAssociatedInstance $disk -ResultClassName win32_directory

Name              Hidden          Archive          Writeable       LastModified
----              ------          -------          ---------       ------------
c:\


PS C:\> Get-CimAssociatedInstance $disk -ResultClassName win32_diskpartition

Name              NumberOfBlock BootPartition PrimaryPartit Size        Index
                  s                           ion
----              ------------- ------------- ------------- ----        -----
Disk #0, Part... 265617408      False         True          135996112896 1


PS C:\> Get-CimAssociatedInstance $disk -ResultClassName win32_Computersystem

Name              PrimaryOwnerN Domain        TotalPhysical Model     Manufacturer
                  ame                         Memory
----              ------------- ------        ------------- -----     ------------
C10               mredwilson... NWTraders.com 4294496256    Virtual M... Microsoft...


PS C:\> Get-CimAssociatedInstance $disk -ResultClassName Win32_QuotaSetting

SettingID         Caption         State          VolumePath      DefaultLimit DefaultWarnin
                                                                              gLimit
---------         -------         -----          ----------      ------------ -------------
                  C:              0              C:\             -1           -1


PS C:\> Get-CimAssociatedInstance $disk -ResultClassName Win32_Group

SID                      Name             Caption              Domain
---                      ----             -------              ------
S-1-5-32-544             Administrators   C10\Administrators   C10
```

Keep in mind that the entire WMI class is returned from the previous command, and that it is therefore ripe for further exploration by IT professionals who are interested in the disk subsystems of their computers. The easy way to do this exploring is to store the results into a variable, and then walk through the data. After you have what interests you, you might decide to display a nicely organized table. This is shown here.

```
PS C:\> $dp = Get-CimAssociatedInstance $disk -ResultClassName win32_diskpartition
PS C:\> $dp | FT deviceID, BlockSize, NumberOfBLocks, Size, StartingOffSet -AutoSize

deviceID             BlockSize NumberOfBLocks  Size         StartingOffSet
--------             --------- --------------  ----         --------------
Disk #0, Partition #1 512      265617408       135996112896 368050176
```

Retrieving WMI instances: Step-by-step exercises

In these exercises, you will practice using the CIM cmdlets to find and retrieve WMI instances. The first exercise uses the CIM cmdlets to explore WMI classes related to video. In the second exercise, you will examine WMI association classes.

Exploring WMI video classes

1. Log on to your computer with a user account that does not have administrator rights.

2. Open the Windows PowerShell console.

3. Use the *Get-CimClass* cmdlet to identify WMI classes related to video. The command and associated output are shown here.

```
PS C:\> Get-CimClass *video*


   NameSpace: ROOT/cimv2

CimClassName                       CimClassMethods        CimClassProperties
------------                       ---------------        ------------------
CIM_VideoBIOSElement               {}                     {Caption, Description, Instal...
CIM_VideoController                {SetPowerState, R...   {Caption, Description, Instal...
CIM_PCVideoController              {SetPowerState, R...   {Caption, Description, Instal...
Win32_VideoController              {SetPowerState, R...   {Caption, Description, Instal...
CIM_VideoBIOSFeature               {}                     {Caption, Description, Instal...
CIM_VideoControllerResolution      {}                     {Caption, Description, Settin...
Win32_VideoConfiguration           {}                     {Caption, Description, Settin...
CIM_VideoSetting                   {}                     {Element, Setting}
Win32_VideoSettings                {}                     {Element, Setting}
CIM_VideoBIOSFeatureVideoBIOSEle... {}                    {GroupComponent, PartComponent}
```

4. Filter the output to return only dynamic WMI classes related to video. The command and associated output are shown here.

```
PS C:\> Get-CimClass *video* -QualifierName dynamic


   NameSpace: ROOT/cimv2

CimClassName                       CimClassMethods        CimClassProperties
------------                       ---------------        ------------------
Win32_VideoController              {SetPowerState, R...   {Caption, Description, Instal...
CIM_VideoControllerResolution      {}                     {Caption, Description, Settin...
Win32_VideoSettings                {}                     {Element, Setting}
```

5. Display the *cimclassname* and the *cimclassqualifiers* properties of each found WMI class. To do this, use the *Format-Table* cmdlet. The command and associated output are shown here.

```
PS C:\> Get-CimClass *video* -QualifierName dynamic | ft cimclassname, cimclassqualifiers

CimClassName                          CimClassQualifiers
------------                          ------------------
Win32_VideoController                 {Locale, UUID, dynamic, provider}
CIM_VideoControllerResolution         {Locale, UUID, dynamic, provider}
Win32_VideoSettings                   {Association, Locale, UUID, dynamic...}
```

6. Change the *$FormatEnumerationLimit* value from the original value of 4 to 8 to so that you can view the truncated output. Remember that you can use tab expansion to avoid having to type the entire variable name. The command is shown here.

```
$FormatEnumerationLimit = 8
```

7. Now use the Up Arrow key to retrieve the previous *Get-CimClass* command. Add the *-AutoSize* parameter to the table. The command and associated output are shown here.

```
PS C:\> Get-CimClass *video* -QualifierName dynamic | ft cimclassname, cimclassqualifiers
-autosize

CimClassName                  CimClassQualifiers
------------                  ------------------
Win32_VideoController         {Locale, UUID, dynamic, provider}
CIM_VideoControllerResolution {Locale, UUID, dynamic, provider}
Win32_VideoSettings          {Association, Locale, UUID, dynamic, provider}
```

8. Query each of the three WMI classes. To do this, pipeline the result of the *Get-CimClass* command to the *ForEach-Object* command. Inside the script block, call *Get-CimInstance* and pass the *cimclassname* property. The command is shown here.

```
PS C:\> Get-CimClass *video* -QualifierName dynamic | % {Get-CimInstance $_.cimclassname}
```

This concludes the exercise. Leave your Windows PowerShell console open for the next exercise.

In the next exercise, you will receive information from WMI association classes.

Retrieving WMI association classes

1. Open the Windows PowerShell console as a non-elevated user (if it is not open from the previous exercise).

2. Use the *Get-CimInstance* cmdlet to retrieve the *Win32_VideoController* WMI class. To simplify typing, use the *gcim* alias. The command is as follows. Store the returned WMI object in the *$v* variable.

```
PS C:\> $v = gcim Win32_VideoController -KeyOnly
```

3. Use the *Get-CimAssociatedInstance* cmdlet and supply *$v* to the *inputobject* parameter. The command is shown here.

```
PS C:\> Get-CimAssociatedInstance -InputObject $v
```

4. Use the Up Arrow key to retrieve the previous command. Pipeline the returned WMI objects to the *Get-Member* cmdlet. Pipeline the results from the *Get-Member* cmdlet to the *Select-Object* cmdlet and use the *-Unique* switched parameter to limit the amount of information returned. The command is shown here.

```
PS C:\> Get-CimAssociatedInstance -InputObject $v | Get-Member | select typename -Unique
```

5. Use the Up Arrow key to retrieve the previous command and change it so that it returns only instances of *Win32_PNPEntity* WMI classes. The command is shown here.

```
PS C:\> Get-CimAssociatedInstance -InputObject $v -ResultClassName win32_PNPEntity
```

6. Display the complete information from each of the associated classes. To do this, pipeline the result from the *Get-CimAssociatedInstance* cmdlet to a *ForEach-Object* cmdlet, and inside the loop, pipeline the current object on the pipeline to the *Format-List* cmdlet. The command is shown here.

```
PS C:\> Get-CimAssociatedInstance -InputObject $v | ForEach-Object {$input | Format-List *}
```

This concludes the exercise.

Chapter 14 quick reference

To	Do this
Find WMI classes related to disks	Use the *Get-CimClass* cmdlet and use a wildcard pattern such as **disk**.
Find WMI classes that have a method named *create*	Use the *Get-CimClass* cmdlet and a wildcard for the *-ClassName* parameter. Use the *-MethodName* parameter to specify that you want classes that have the *create* method.
Find dynamic WMI classes	Use the *Get-CimClass* cmdlet and specify that you want the qualifier named *dynamic*.
Reduce the number of instances returned by the *Get-CimInstance* cmdlet	Use the *-Filter* parameter and supply a filter that reduces the instances.
Reduce the number of properties returned by the *Get-CimInstance* cmdlet	Use the *-Property* parameter and enumerate the required properties to return.
Find the types of WMI classes returned by the *Get-CimAssociatedInstance* cmdlet	Pipeline the resulting objects to the *Get-Member* cmdlet and select the *typename* property.
Only return a particular associated WMI class from the *Get-CimAssociatedInstance* cmdlet	Use the *-ResultClassName* parameter and specify the name of one of the returned objects.

Working with Active Directory

After completing this chapter, you will be able to

- Make a connection to Active Directory.

- Create organizational units in Active Directory.

- Understand the use of ADSI providers.

- Understand how to work with Active Directory namespaces.

- Create users in Active Directory.

- Create groups in Active Directory.

- Modify both users and groups in Active Directory.

Creating objects in Active Directory

Network management in the Windows world begins and ends with Active Directory. This chapter covers the user life cycle from a scripting and Active Directory perspective. You will learn how to create organizational units (OUs), users, groups, and computer accounts. The chapter then describes how to modify the users and groups, and finally how to delete a user account. Along the way, you will pick up some more Windows PowerShell techniques.

The most fundamental object in Active Directory is the OU. One of the most frustrating problems for new network administrators is that, by default, when Active Directory is installed, all users are put in the *users* container, and all computers are put in the *computers* container—and of course you cannot apply Group Policy to a container.

Creating an OU

The process of creating an OU in Active Directory provides the basis for creating other objects in Active Directory, because the technique is basically the same. The key to effectively using Windows PowerShell to create objects in Active Directory is to use the Active Directory Service Interfaces (ADSI) accelerator.

To create an object by using ADSI, perform the following steps:

1. Use the *[ADSI]* accelerator.

2. Use the appropriate ADSI provider.

3. Specify the path to the appropriate object in Active Directory.

4. Use the *SetInfo()* method to write the changes.

The CreateOU.ps1 script shown following illustrates each of the steps required to create an object by using ADSI. The variable *$strClass* is used to hold the class of object to create in Active Directory. For this script, you will be creating an OU. You could just as easily create a user or a computer—as you will discover shortly. You use the variable *$strOUName* to hold the name of the OU you are going to create. For the CreateOU.ps1 script, you are going to create an OU called MyTestOU. Because you will pass this variable directly to the *Create* method, it is important that you use the distinguished-name form, shown here.

```
$strOUName = "OU=MyTestOU"
```

The attribute that is used with the *Create* method to create an object in Active Directory is called the *relative distinguished name (RDN)*. Standard attribute types are expected by ADSI—such as *ou* for *organizational unit*. The next line of code in the CreateOU.ps1 script makes the actual connection into Active Directory. To do this, it uses the *[ADSI]* accelerator. The *[ADSI]* accelerator expects to be given the exact path to your connection point in Active Directory (or some other directory, as you will discover shortly) and the name of the ADSI provider. The target of the ADSI operation is called the AdsPath.

In the CreateOU.ps1 script, you are connecting to the root of the NwTraders.msft domain, and you are using the LDAP provider. The other providers you can use with ADSI are shown in Table 15-1. After you make your connection into Active Directory, you hold the *system.DirectoryServices.DirectoryEntry* object in the *$objADSI* variable.

Armed with the connection into Active Directory, you can now use the *create* method to create your new object. The *system.DirectoryServices.DirectoryEntry* object that is returned is held in the *$objOU* variable. You use this object on the last line of the script to call the *SetInfo()* method to write the new object into the Active Directory database. The entire CreateOU.ps1 script is shown here.

CreateOU.ps1

```
$strClass = "organizationalUnit"
$StrOUName = "OU=MyTestOU"
$objADSI = [ADSI]"LDAP://DC=nwtraders,DC=msft"
$objOU = $objADSI.Create($strCLass, $StrOUName)
$objOU.SetInfo()
```

ADSI providers

Table 15-1 lists four providers available to users of ADSI. Connecting to a Windows local user account database requires using the special *WinNT* provider.

TABLE 15-1 ADSI-supported providers

Provider	Purpose
WinNT	To communicate with Windows local account databases for workstations and servers
LDAP	To communicate with LDAP servers, including servers running Active Directory Domain Services
NDS	To communicate with Novell Directory Services servers
NWCOMPAT	To communicate with Novell NetWare 3.x servers

The first time I tried to use ADSI to connect to a machine running Windows NT, I had a very frustrating experience because of the way the provider was implemented. Enter the *WinNT* provider name *exactly* as shown in Table 15-1. It cannot be entered by using all lowercase letters or all upper-case letters. All other provider names must be all uppercase letters, but the *WinNT* name is Pascal-cased—that is, it is partially uppercase and partially lowercase. Remembering this will save a lot of grief later. In addition, you don't get an error message telling you that your provider name is spelled or capitalized incorrectly—rather, the bind operation simply fails to connect.

> **Tip** The ADSI provider names are case sensitive. *LDAP* is all caps; *WinNT* is Pascal-cased. Keep this in mind to save a lot of time in troubleshooting.

After the ADSI provider is specified, you need to identify the path to the directory target. A little knowledge of Active Directory comes in handy here, because of the way the hierarchical naming space is structured. When connecting to an LDAP service provider, you must specify where in the LDAP database hierarchy to make the connection, because the hierarchy is a structure of the database itself—not the protocol or the provider. For instance, in the CreateOU.ps1 script, you create an OU that resides off the root of the domain, which is called MyTestOU. This can get confusing, until you realize that the MyTestOU OU is contained in a domain that is called NWTRADERS.MSFT. It is vital, therefore, that you understand the hierarchy with which you are working. One tool you can use to make sure you understand the hierarchy of your domain is ADSI Edit.

ADSI Edit is included with the feature called *AD DS and AD LDS Tools*. To install these tools on computers running Windows Server beginning with Windows Server 2008, use the *Add-WindowsFeature* cmdlet from the *ServerManager* module. To determine installation status of the Active Directory Domain Services (AD DS) tools, use the *Get-WindowsFeature* cmdlet, as shown here.

```
Get-WindowsFeature RSAT-AD-Tools
```

To determine everything that comes with AD DS and AD LDS Tools, pipeline the result of the previous command to the *Format-List* cmdlet. This technique, along with the associated output from the command, is shown here.

```
PS C:\> Get-WindowsFeature RSAT-AD-Tools| Format-List *


Name                       : RSAT-AD-Tools
DisplayName                : AD DS and AD LDS Tools
Description                : <a href="features.chm::/html/529acbe5-8749-4fb4-9a2a-300
                             6e9250329.htm">Active Directory Domain Services (AD DS)
                             and Active Directory Lightweight Directory Services (AD
                             LDS) Tools</a> includes snap-ins and command-line tools
                             for remotely managing AD DS and AD LDS.
Installed                  : False
InstallState               : Available
FeatureType                : Feature
Path                       : Remote Server Administration Tools\Role Administration
                             Tools\AD DS and AD LDS Tools
Depth                      : 3
DependsOn                  : {}
Parent                     : RSAT-Role-Tools
ServerComponentDescriptor  : ServerComponent_RSAT_AD_Tools
SubFeatures                : {RSAT-AD-PowerShell, RSAT-ADDS, RSAT-ADLDS}
SystemService              : {}
Notification               : {}
BestPracticesModelId       :
EventQuery                 :
PostConfigurationNeeded     : False
AdditionalInfo             : {MajorVersion, MinorVersion, NumericId, InstallName}
```

To install the tools, pipeline the results from the *Get-WindowsFeature* cmdlet to *Add-WindowsFeature*. This is as easy as using the Up Arrow key to retrieve the previous command that displayed the components of the AD DS tools and replacing *Format-List* with *Add-WindowsFeature*. If automatic updates are not enabled, a warning message is displayed. The command and associated warning are shown here.

```
PS C:\> Get-WindowsFeature rsat-ad-tools | Add-WindowsFeature

Success Restart Needed Exit Code     Feature Result
------- -------------- ---------     --------------
True    No             Success       {Remote Server Administration Tools, Activ...
WARNING: Windows automatic updating is not enabled. To ensure that your
newly-installed role or feature is automatically updated, turn on Windows Update.
```

After installing the tools (the output from the *Add-WindowsFeature* cmdlet states that no reboot is needed following this task), open a blank Microsoft Management Console (MMC) and add the ADSI Edit snap-in.

Note If you already have Windows PowerShell open because you were adding the Active Directory tools, you can start the MMC by entering **MMC** at the Windows PowerShell prompt. You can also add additional Active Directory tools, such as Active Directory Users And Computers, Active Directory Domains And Trusts, and Active Directory Sites And Services. Save this custom MMC to your profile for quick ease of reuse.

After you install the snap-in, right-click the ADSI Edit icon, select Connect To, and specify your domain, you will get a result similar to the one shown in Figure 15-1.

FIGURE 15-1 Explore the hierarchy of a forest to ensure the correct path for ADSI.

LDAP names

When specifying the OU and the domain name, you have to use the LDAP naming convention, in which the namespace is described as a series of naming parts called RDNs (mentioned previously). The RDN will always be a name part that assigns a value by using the equal sign. When you put together all the RDNs, along with the RDNs of each of the ancestors all the way back to the root, you end up with a single globally unique distinguished name.

The RDNs are usually made up of an attribute type, an equal sign, and a string value. Table 15-2 lists some of the attribute types you will use when working with Active Directory. An example of a distinguished name is shown in Figure 15-2.

TABLE 15-2 Common relative distinguished name (RDN) attribute types

Attribute	Description
DC	Domain component
CN	Common name
OU	Organizational unit
O	Organization name
Street	Street address
C	Country/region name
UID	User ID

FIGURE 15-2 Use the String Attribute Editor in ADSI Edit to quickly verify the distinguished name of a potential target for ADSI scripting.

Binding

Whenever you want to do anything with ADSI, you must connect to an object in Active Directory—a process also known as *binding*. Think of binding as similar to tying a rope around an object so that you can work with it. Before you can do any work with an object in Active Directory, you must supply binding information. When you use a *binding string* you can use various ADSI elements, including methods and properties. The target of the proposed action is specified as a computer, a domain controller, a user, or another element that resides within the directory structure. A binding string consists of four parts. These parts are described in Table 15-3, which shows a binding string from a sample script.

TABLE 15-3 Sample binding string

Accelerator	Variable	Provider	ADsPath
[ADSI]	$objDomain	LDAP://	OU=hr, dc=a, dc=com

> **Note** Avoid a mistake I made early on: make sure that when you finish connecting and creating, you actually commit your changes to Active Directory. Changes to Active Directory are transactional in nature, so your change will roll back if you don't commit it. Committing the change requires you to use the *SetInfo()* method, as illustrated in the following line from the CreateOU.ps1 script.
>
> ```
> $objOU.SetInfo()
> ```
>
> Also keep in mind when calling a method such as *SetInfo()* that you must append empty parentheses to the method call.

Working with errors

1. Open the Windows PowerShell ISE or some other Windows PowerShell script editor.

2. On the first line of your script, enter a line that will generate an error by trying to create an object called *test*. Use the variable *$a* to hold this object. The code to do this is shown here.

   ```
   $a = New-Object test #creates an error
   ```

3. Print the value of *$Error.Count*. The *count* property should contain a single error when the script is run. This line of code is shown here.

   ```
   $Error.Count
   ```

4. Save your script as *<yourname>*WorkWithErrors.ps1. Run your script; it should print the number 1 to let you know there is an error on the *Error* object.

5. The most recent error will be contained on the variable *$Error[0]*. Use this to return the *CategoryInfo* property of the error. This code is shown here.

   ```
   $Error[0].CategoryInfo
   ```

6. Print the details of the most recent error. The code to do this is shown here.

   ```
   $Error[0].ErrorDetails
   ```

7. Print the exception information. To do this, print the value of the *Exception* property of the *$Error* variable. This is shown here.

   ```
   $Error[0].Exception
   ```

8. Print the fully qualified error ID information. This is contained in the *FullyQualifiedErrorId* property of the *$Error* variable. The code to do this is shown here.

```
$Error[0].FullyQualifiedErrorId
```

9. Print the invocation information about the error. To do this, use the *InvocationInfo* property of the *$Error* variable. The code to do this is shown here.

```
$Error[0].InvocationInfo
```

10. The last property to query from *$Error* is the *TargetObject* property. This is shown here.

```
$Error[0].TargetObject
```

11. Save and run your script. Notice that you will not obtain information from all the properties.

12. The *$Error* variable contains information about all errors that occur during the particular Windows PowerShell session, so it is quite likely to contain more than a single error. To introduce an additional error into your script, try to create a new object called *testB*. Assign the object that comes back to the variable *$b*. This code is shown here.

```
$b = New-Object testB
```

13. Because you now have more than a single error on the *Error* object, you need to walk through the collection of errors. To do this, you can use the *for* statement. Use a variable called *$i* as the counter variable, and proceed until you reach the value of *$Error.Count*. Make sure you enclose the statement in parentheses and increment the value of *$i* at the end of the statement. The first line of this code is shown here.

```
for ($i = 0 ; $Error.Count ; $i++)
```

14. Now change each of the *$Error[0]* statements that print the various properties of the *Error* object to use the counter variable *$i*. Because this will be the code block for the *for* statement, place an opening brace at the beginning of the first statement and a closing one at the end of the last statement. The revised code block is shown here.

```
{$Error[$i].CategoryInfo
    $Error[$i].ErrorDetails
    $Error[$i].Exception
    $Error[$i].FullyQualifiedErrorId
    $Error[$i].InvocationInfo
    $Error[$i].TargetObject}
```

15. Save and run your script. You will get output similar to that shown here.

```
New-Object : Cannot find type [test]: make sure the assembly containing this
 type is loaded.
At D:\BookDocs\WindowsPowerShell\scripts\ch15\WorkWithErrors.PS1:14 char:16
 + $a = New-Object  <<<< test #creates an error
New-Object : Cannot find type [testB]: make sure the assembly containing this
 type is loaded.
At D:\BookDocs\WindowsPowerShell\scripts\ch15\WorkWithErrors.PS1:15 char:16
```

```
+ $b = New-Object  <<<< testB #creates another error

Category   : InvalidType
Activity   : New-Object
Reason     : PSArgumentException
```

16. The first error shown is a result of the Windows PowerShell command interpreter. The last error shown—with the category, activity, and reason—is a result of your error handling. To remove the first run-time error, use the *$ErrorActionPreference* variable and assign a value of *SilentlyContinue* to it. This code is shown here.

```
$ErrorActionPreference = "SilentlyContinue"
```

17. Save and run your script. Notice that the run-time error disappears from the top of your screen.

18. To find out how many errors are on the *Error* object, you can print the value of *$Error.Count*. However, just having a single number at the top of the screen would be a little confusing. To take care of that, add a descriptive string, such as *"There are currently " + $Error.Count + "errors"*. The code to do this is shown here.

```
"There are currently " + $Error.Count + "errors"
```

19. Save and run your script. Notice that the string is printed at the top of your script, as shown here.

```
There are currently 2 errors
```

20. In your Windows PowerShell window, use the *$Error.Clear()* method to clear the errors from the *Error* object, because it continues to count errors until a new Windows PowerShell window is opened. This command is shown here.

```
$Error.Clear()
```

21. Now comment out the line that creates the *testB* object. This revised line of code is shown here.

```
#$b = New-Object testB
```

22. Now save and run your script. Notice that the string at the top of your Windows PowerShell window looks a little strange because of the grammatical error. This is shown here.

```
There is currently 1 errors
```

23. To fix this problem, you need to add some logic to detect whether there is one error or more than one error. To do this, you will use an *If...Else* statement. The first line will evaluate whether *$Error.Count* is equal to 1. If it is, you will print *There is currently 1 error*. This code is shown here.

```
if ($Error.Count -eq 1)
    {"There is currently 1 error"}
```

24. You can just use an *else* clause and add braces around your previous error statement. This revised code is shown here.

```
else
    {"There are currently " + $Error.Count + "errors"}
```

25. Save and run the script. It should correctly detect that there is only one error.

26. Now remove the comment from the beginning of the line of code that creates the *testB* object and run the script. It should detect two errors.

This concludes the procedure.

Adding error handling

1. Use the CreateOU.ps1 script (from earlier in this chapter) and save it as *<yourname>*CreateOU withErrorHandler.ps1.

2. On the first line of the script, use the *$ErrorActionPreference* variable to assign the *Silently-Continue* value. This will tell the script to suppress error messages and continue running the script if possible. This line of code is shown here.

```
$ErrorActionPreference = "SilentlyContinue"
```

3. To ensure there are no current errors on the *Error* object, use the *clear* method. To do this, use the *$Error* variable. This line of code is shown here.

```
$Error.Clear()
```

4. At the end of the script, use an *if* statement to evaluate the error count. If an error has occurred, the count will not be equal to 0. This line of code is shown here.

```
if ($Error.Count -ne 0)
```

5. If the condition occurs, the code block to run should return a message stating that an error has occurred. It should also print the *CategoryInfo* and *InvocationInfo* properties from the current *$Error* variable. The code to do this is shown here.

```
{"An error occurred during the operation. Details follow:"
    $Error[0].CategoryInfo
    $Error[0].InvocationInfo
    $Error[0].ToString()}
```

6. Save and run your script. An error should be generated (due to a duplicate attempt to create MyTestOU).

7. Change the OU name to MyTestOU1 and run the script. An error should not be generated. The revised line of code is shown here.

```
$StrOUName = "ou=MyTestOU1"
```

This concludes the procedure. If you do not get the results you were expecting, compare your script with the CreateOUWithErrorHandler.ps1 script.

> **Quick check**
>
> **Q.** What is the process of connecting to Active Directory called?
>
> **A.** The process of connecting to Active Directory is called binding.
>
> **Q.** When specifying the target of an ADSI operation, what is the target called?
>
> **A.** The target of the ADSI operation is called the AdsPath.
>
> **Q.** An LDAP name is made up of several parts, separated by commas. What do you call each part?
>
> **A.** An LDAP name is made up of multiple parts that are called relative distinguished names (RDNs).

Creating users

One fundamental technique you can use with ADSI makes it very easy to create users. Although using the GUI to create a single user is easy, using it to create a dozen or more users would certainly not be. In addition, as you'll discover, because there is a lot of similarity among ADSI scripts, deleting a dozen or more users is just as simple as creating them. And because you can use the same input text file for all the scripts, ADSI makes creating temporary accounts for use in a lab or school quite simple indeed.

To create users, do the following:

1. Use the appropriate provider for your network.

2. Specify the *User* class and user name of the object.

3. Specify the container and domain.

4. Bind to Active Directory.

5. Use the *Create* method to create the user.

6. Use the *Put* method to at least specify the *sAMAccountName* attribute.

7. Use *SetInfo()* to commit the user to Active Directory.

The CreateUser.ps1 script, which follows, is very similar to the CreateOU.ps1 script. In fact, CreateUser.ps1 was created from CreateOU.ps1, so a detailed analysis of the script is unnecessary. The only difference is that *$strClass* is equal to the *User* class instead of an *organizationalUnit* class.

Tip These scripts use a Windows PowerShell trick. When using Microsoft Visual Basic Scripting Edition (VBScript) to create a user or a group, you must supply a value for the *sAMAccountName* attribute. When you are using Windows PowerShell on a computer running Windows 2000, this is also the case. When you are using Windows PowerShell on a computer running Windows Server 2008 (or later), however, the *sAMAccountName* attribute will be automatically created for you. In the CreateUser.ps1 script, I have included the *$objUser.Put* command, which would be required for Windows 2000, but it is not required for Windows Server 2003 (or later). Keep in mind that the *sAMAccountName* property, when autogenerated, is not very user friendly. Here is an example of such an autogenerated name: $441000-1A0UVA0MRB0T. Any earlier application requiring the *sAMAccount-Name* value would therefore require users to enter a value that is difficult to use at best.

CreateUser.ps1

```
$strClass = "User"
$strName = "CN=MyNewUser"
$objADSI = [ADSI]"LDAP://ou=myTestOU,dc=nwtraders,dc=msft"
$objUser = $objADSI.Create($strClass, $strName)
$objUser.Put("sAMAccountName", "MyNewUser")
$objUser.SetInfo()
```

Quick check

Q. To create a user, which class must be specified?

A. You need to specify the *User* class to create a user.

Q. What is the *Put* method used for?

A. The *Put* method is used to write additional property data to the object that it is bound to.

Creating groups

1. Open the CreateUser.ps1 script in Notepad and save it as *<yourname>*CreateGroup.ps1.

2. Declare a variable called *$intGroupType*. This variable will be used to control the type of group to create. Assign the number 2 to the variable. When used as the group type, a type 2 group will be a distribution group. This line of code is shown here.

   ```
   $intGroupType = 2
   ```

3. Change the value of *$strClass* from *User* to *Group*. This variable will be used to control the type of object that gets created in Active Directory. This is shown here.

   ```
   $strClass = "Group"
   ```

4. Change the value of *$strName* from *CN=MyNewUser* to *CN=MyNewGroup*. This variable contains the name of the new group.

    ```
    $strName = "CN=MyNewGroup"
    ```

5. Change the name of the *$objUser* variable to *$objGroup* (it's less confusing that way). This will need to be done in two places, as shown here.

    ```
    $objGroup = $objADSI.Create($strClass, $strName)
    $objGroup.SetInfo()
    ```

6. Above the *$objGroup.SetInfo()* line, use the *Put* method to create a distribution group. The distribution group has a group type of 2, and you can use the value held in the *$intGroupType* variable. This line of code is shown here.

    ```
    $ObjGroup.Put("GroupType",$intGroupType)
    ```

7. Save and run the script. It should create a group called *MyNewGroup* in the *MyTestOU* in Active Directory. If the script does not perform as expected, compare your script with the CreateGroup.ps1 script.

    This concludes the procedure.

Creating a computer account

1. Open the CreateUser.ps1 script in Notepad and save it as *<yourname>*CreateComputer.ps1.

2. Change the *$strClass* value from *User* to *Computer*. The revised command is shown here.

    ```
    $strClass = "Computer"
    ```

3. Change the *$strName* value from *CN=MyNewUser* to *CN=MyComputer*. This command is shown here.

    ```
    $strName = "CN=MyComputer"
    ```

    The *[ADSI]* accelerator connection string is already connecting to *ou=myTestOU* and should not need modification.

4. Change the name of the *$objUser* variable used to hold the object that is returned from the *Create* method to *$objComputer*. This revised line of code is shown here.

    ```
    $objComputer = $objADSI.Create($strClass, $strName)
    ```

5. Use the *Put* method from the *DirectoryEntry* object created in the previous line to put the value *MyComputer* in the *sAMAccountName* attribute. This line of code is shown here.

    ```
    $objComputer.Put("sAMAccountName", "MyComputer")
    ```

6. Use the *SetInfo()* method to write the changes to Active Directory. This line of code is shown here.

```
$objComputer.SetInfo()
```

7. After the *MyComputer* Computer object has been created in Active Directory, you can modify the *UserAccountControl* attribute. The value 4128 in *UserAccountControl* means the workstation is a trusted account and does not require a password. This line of code is shown here.

```
$objComputer.Put("UserAccountControl",4128)
```

8. Use the *SetInfo()* method to write the change back to Active Directory. This line of code is shown here.

```
$objComputer.SetInfo()
```

9. Save and run the script. A computer account should appear in the Active Directory Users And Computers tool. If your script does not produce the expected results, compare it with Create-Computer.ps1.

This concludes the procedure.

What is user account control?

UserAccountControl is an attribute in Active Directory that can be used to enable or disable a user account, computer account, or other objects defined in Active Directory. It is not a single string attribute; rather, it is a series of bit flags that get computed from the values listed in Table 15-4. Because of the way the *UserAccountControl* attribute is created, simply examining the numeric value is of little help, unless you can decipher the individual numbers that make up the large number. These flags, when added together, control the behavior, for example, of a user or computer account. In the CreateComputer.ps1 script, you set two user account control flags: the *ADS_UF_PASSWD_NOTREQD* flag and the *ADS_UF_WORKSTATION_TRUST_ACCOUNT* flag. The password-not-required flag has a hexadecimal value of 0x20, and the trusted-workstation flag has a hexadecimal value of 0x1000. When added together and turned into a decimal value, they equal 4128, which is the value actually shown in ADSI Edit.

TABLE 15-4 User account control values

ADS constant	Value in hexadecimal
ADS_UF_SCRIPT	0X0001
ADS_UF_ACCOUNTDISABLE	0X0002
ADS_UF_HOMEDIR_REQUIRED	0X0008
ADS_UF_LOCKOUT	0X0010
ADS_UF_PASSWD_NOTREQD	0X0020
ADS_UF_PASSWD_CANT_CHANGE	0X0040

ADS constant	Value in hexadecimal
ADS_UF_ENCRYPTED_TEXT_PASSWORD_ALLOWED	0X0080
ADS_UF_TEMP_DUPLICATE_ACCOUNT	0X0100
ADS_UF_NORMAL_ACCOUNT	0X0200
ADS_UF_INTERDOMAIN_TRUST_ACCOUNT	0X0800
ADS_UF_WORKSTATION_TRUST_ACCOUNT	0X1000
ADS_UF_SERVER_TRUST_ACCOUNT	0X2000
ADS_UF_DONT_EXPIRE_PASSWD	0X10000
ADS_UF_MNS_LOGON_ACCOUNT	0X20000
ADS_UF_SMARTCARD_REQUIRED	0X40000
ADS_UF_TRUSTED_FOR_DELEGATION	0X80000
ADS_UF_NOT_DELEGATED	0X100000
ADS_UF_USE_DES_KEY_ONLY	0x200000
ADS_UF_DONT_REQUIRE_PREAUTH	0x400000
ADS_UF_PASSWORD_EXPIRED	0x800000
ADS_UF_TRUSTED_TO_AUTHENTICATE_FOR_DELEGATION	0x1000000

Working with users

In this section, you will use ADSI to modify user properties stored in Active Directory. The following list summarizes a few of the items you can change or configure:

- Office and telephone contact information

- Mailing address information

- Department, title, manager, and direct reports (people who report to the user inside the chain of command)

User information that is stored in Active Directory can easily replace data that used to be contained in separate, disparate places. For instance, you might have an internal website that contains a telephone directory; you can put phone numbers into Active Directory as attributes of the *User* object. You might also have a website containing a social roster that includes employees and their hobbies; you can put hobby information in Active Directory as a custom attribute. You can also add to Active Directory information such as an organizational chart. The problem, of course, is that during a migration, information such as a user's title is the last thing the harried mind of the network administrator thinks about. To make the most of the investment in Active Directory, you need to enter this type of information because it quickly becomes instrumental in the daily lives of users. This is where ADSI and Windows PowerShell really begin to shine. You can update hundreds or even thousands of records easily and efficiently by using scripting. Such a task would be unthinkable using conventional point-and-click methods.

To modify user properties in Active Directory, do the following:

1. Implement the appropriate protocol provider.

2. Perform binding to Active Directory.

3. Specify the appropriate AdsPath.

4. Use the *Put* method to write selected properties to users.

5. Use the *SetInfo()* method to commit changes to Active Directory.

General user information

One of the more confusing issues about using Windows PowerShell to modify information in Active Directory is that the names displayed on the property page do not correspond with the ADSI nomenclature. This was not done to make your life difficult; rather, the names you find in ADSI are derived from LDAP standard naming convention. Although this naming convention makes traditional LDAP programmers happy, it does nothing for the network administrator who is a casual scripter. This is where the following script, ModifyUserProperties.ps1, comes in handy. The LDAP properties corresponding to each field in Figure 15-3 are used in this script.

Some of the names make sense, but others appear to be rather obscure. Notice the series of *objUser.Put* statements. Each lines up with the corresponding field in Figure 15-3. Use the values to determine which display name maps to which LDAP attribute name. Two of the attributes accept an array: *OtherTelephone* and *url*. The *url* attribute is particularly misleading—first because it is singular, and second because the *othertelephone* value uses the style *otherTelephone*. In addition, the primary webpage uses the name *wwwHomePage*. When supplying values for the *OtherTelephone* and *url* attributes, ensure that the input value is accepted as an array by using the @() characters to cast the string into an array. The use of all these values is illustrated in ModifyUserProperties.ps1, shown here.

ModifyUserProperties.ps1

```
$objUser = [ADSI]"LDAP://cn=MyNewUser,ou=myTestOU,dc=iammred,dc=net"
$objUser.Put("SamaccountName", "myNewUser")
$objUser.Put("givenName", "My")
$objUser.Put("initials", "N.")
$objUser.Put("sn", "User")
$objUser.Put("DisplayName", "My New User")
$objUser.Put("description" , "simple new user")
$objUser.Put("physicalDeliveryOfficeName", "RQ2")
$objUser.Put("telephoneNumber", "555-555-0111")
$objUser.Put("OtherTelephone",@("555-555-0112","555-555-0113"))
$objUser.Put("mail", "myuser@nwtraders.com")
$objUser.Put("wwwHomePage", "http://www.ScriptingGuys.com")
$objUser.Put("url",@("http://www.ScriptingGuys.Com/blog","http://www.ScriptingGuys.com/LearnPowe
rShell"))
$objUser.SetInfo()
```

FIGURE 15-3 ADSI attribute names correspond to the field names on the General tab of Active Directory Users And Computers.

Quick check

Q. What is the field name for the user's first name?

A. The field for the user's first name is *GivenName*. You can find field-mapping information on MSDN.

Q. Why do you need to use the *SetInfo()* command?

A. If you don't use the *SetInfo()* command, all changes introduced during the script will be lost, because the changes are made to a cached set of attribute values for the object being modified. Nothing is committed to Active Directory until you call *SetInfo()*.

Creating the address page

One of the more useful tasks you can perform with Active Directory is exposing address information. This ability is particularly important when a company has more than one location and more than a few hundred employees. I remember one of my first intranet projects, which was to host a centralized list of employees. Such a project quickly paid for itself because the customer no longer needed an administrative assistant to modify, copy, collate, and distribute hundreds of copies of the up-to-date employee directory—potentially a full-time job for one person. After the intranet site was in place, personnel at each location were given rights to modify the list. This was the beginning of a company-wide directory. With Active Directory, you avoid this duplication of work by keeping all information in a centralized location. The second tab in Active Directory Users And Computers is the Address tab, shown in Figure 15-4 with the appropriate Active Directory attribute names filled in.

FIGURE 15-4 Every item on the Address tab in Active Directory Users And Computers can be filled in via ADSI and Windows PowerShell.

In the ModifySecondPage.ps1 script, you use ADSI to set the *Street*, *P.O. Box*, *City*, *State/province*, *Zip/Postal Code*, and *Country/region* values, using their respective Active Directory attribute names, for the *User* object. Table 15-5 lists the Active Directory attribute names and their mappings to the Active Directory Users And Computers "friendly" display names.

TABLE 15-5 Address page mappings

Active Directory Users And Computers label	Active Directory attribute name
Street	*streetAddress*
P.O. Box	*postOfficeBox*
City	*l* (Note that this is lowercase L.)
State/province	*st*
Zip/Postal Code	*postalCode*
Country/region	*c, co, countryCode*

When working with address-type information in Windows PowerShell, the hard thing is keeping track of the country/region codes. These values must be properly supplied. Table 15-6 lists some typical country/region codes. At times, the country/region codes seem to make sense; at others times, they do not. Rather than guess, you can simply make the changes in Active Directory Users And Computers and use ADSI Edit to examine the modified values, or you can look up the codes in ISO 3166-1.

ModifySecondPage.ps1

```
$objUser = [ADSI]"LDAP://cn=MyNewUser,ou=myTestOU,dc=iammred,dc=net"
$objUser.Put("streetAddress", "123 main st")
$objUser.Put("postOfficeBox", "po box 12")
$objUser.Put("l", "Charlotte")
$objUser.Put("st", "SC")
$objUser.Put("postalCode" , "12345")
$objUser.Put("c", "US")
$objUser.Put("co", "United States")
$objUser.Put("countryCode", "840")
$objUser.SetInfo()
```

TABLE 15-6 ISO 3166-1 country/region codes

Country/region code	Country/region name
AF	Afghanistan
AU	Australia
EG	Egypt
LV	Latvia
ES	Spain
US	United States

Caution The three country/region fields are not linked in Active Directory. You could easily have a *c* code value of US, a *co* code value of Zimbabwe, and a *countryCode* value of 470 (Malta). This could occur if someone uses the Active Directory Users And Computers tool to make a change to the *country* property. When this occurs, it updates all three fields. If someone later runs a script to only update the *countryCode* value or the *co* code value, Active Directory Users And Computers will still reflect the translated value of the *c* code. This could create havoc if your enterprise resource planning (ERP) application uses the *co* or *countryCode* value and not the *c* attribute. Best practice is to update all three fields through your script.

Quick check

Q. To set the country/region name on the address page for Active Directory Users And Computers, what is required?

A. To update the country/region name on the address page for Active Directory Users And Computers, you must specify the *c* field and feed it a two-letter code that is found in ISO publication 3166.

Q. What field name in ADSI is used to specify the city information?

A. You set the city information by assigning a value to the *l* (lowercase L) field after making the appropriate connection to Active Directory.

Q. If you put an inappropriate letter code in the c field, what error message is displayed?

A. None.

Modifying the user profile settings

1. Open the ModifySecondPage.ps1 script you created earlier and save it as *<yourname>*ModifyUserProfile.ps1.

2. The user profile page in Active Directory is composed of four attributes. Delete all but four of the *$objUser.Put* commands. The actual profile attributes are shown in Figure 15-5.

3. The first attribute you need to supply a value for is *profilePath*. This controls where the user's profile will be stored. On my server, the location is \\London\Profiles in a folder named after the user, which in this case is MyNewUser. Edit the first of the *$objUser.Put* commands you left in your script to match your environment. The modified *$objUser.Put* command is shown here.

```
$objUser.Put("profilePath", "\\London\Profiles\MyNewUser")
```

FIGURE 15-5 ADSI attributes are used to fill out the Profile tab in Active Directory.

4. The next attribute you need to supply a value for is *ScriptPath*. This controls which logon script will be run when the user logs on. Even though this attribute is called *scriptPath*, it does not expect an actual path statement (it assumes the script is in the *sysvol* share); rather, it simply needs the name of the logon script. On my server, I use a logon script called logon.ps1. Modify the second *$objUser.Put* statement in your script to point to a logon script. The modified command is shown here.

```
$objUser.Put("scriptPath", "logon.ps1")
```

5. The third attribute that needs to be set for the user profile is called *homeDirectory*, and it is used to control where the user's home directory will be stored. This attribute needs a Universal Naming Convention (UNC)–formatted path to a shared directory. On my server, each user has a home directory named after his or her logon user name. The folders are stored in a shared directory called Users. Modify the third *$objUser.Put* statement in your script to point

to the appropriate home directory location for your environment. The completed command is shown here.

```
$objUser.Put("homeDirectory", "\\London\Users\MyNewUser")
```

6. The last user profile attribute that needs to be modified is *homeDrive*. The *homeDrive* attribute in Active Directory is used to control the mapping of a drive letter to the user's home directory. On my server, all users' home drives are mapped to drive H (for *home*). Note that Active Directory does not expect a trailing backslash for the *homeDrive* attribute. Modify the last *$objUser.Put* command to map the user's home drive to the appropriate drive letter for your environment. The modified command is shown here.

```
$objUser.Put("homeDrive", "H:")
```

7. Save and run your script. If it does not modify the user's profile page as expected, compare your script with the ModifyUserProfile.ps1 script shown here.

```
$objUser = [ADSI]"LDAP://cn=MyNewUser,ou=myTestOU,dc=iammred,dc=net"
$objUser.Put("profilePath", "\\London\Profiles\MyNewUser")
$objUser.Put("scriptPath", "logon.vbs")
$objUser.Put("homeDirectory", "\\London\Users\MyNewUser")
$objUser.Put("homeDrive", "H:")
$objUser.SetInfo()
```

This concludes the procedure.

Modifying the user telephone settings

1. Open the ModifySecondPage.ps1 script you created earlier and save the file as *<yourname>*ModifyTelephoneAttributes.ps1.

2. The Telephones tab in Active Directory Users And Computers for a user account is composed of six attributes. These attribute names are shown in Figure 15-6, which also illustrates the field names, as shown in Active Directory Users And Computers on the Telephones tab for the *User* object. Delete all but six of the *$objUser.Put* commands from your script.

3. The first attribute you modify is the *homePhone* attribute for the MyNewUser user account. To do this, change the value of the first *$objUser.Put* command so that it is now writing to the *homePhone* attribute in Active Directory. The phone number for the MyNewUser account is (555) 555-0199 For this example, you are leaving off the international dialing code and enclosing the area code in parentheses. This is not required, however, for Active Directory. The modified line of code is shown here.

```
$objUser.Put("homePhone", "(555)555-0199")
```

FIGURE 15-6 Attributes on the Telephones tab in Active Directory.

4. The next telephone attribute in Active Directory is the *pager* attribute. Your user account has a pager number that is (555) 555-0199. Modify the second *$objUser.Put* line of your script to put this value into the *pager* attribute. The revised line of code is shown here.

```
$objUser.Put("pager", "(555)555-0199")
```

5. The third telephone attribute you need to modify on your user account is the mobile telephone attribute. The name of this attribute in Active Directory is *mobile*. The mobile telephone number for your user is (555) 555-0199. Edit the third *$objUser.Put* command in your script so that you are writing this value into the *mobile* attribute. The revised line of code is shown here.

```
$objUser.Put("mobile", "(555)555-0199")
```

6. The fourth telephone attribute that needs to be assigned a value is for the fax machine. The attribute in Active Directory that is used to hold the fax machine telephone number is *facsimileTelephoneNumber*. This user has a fax number that is (555) 555-0199. Edit the fourth

$objUser.Put command in your script to write the appropriate fax number into the *facsimile-TelephoneNumber* attribute in Active Directory. The revised code is shown here.

```
$objUser.Put("facsimileTelephoneNumber", "(555)555-0199")
```

7. The fifth telephone attribute that needs to be assigned a value for your user is for the IP address of the user's IP telephone. In Active Directory, this attribute is called *ipPhone*. The MyNewUser account has an IP telephone with the IP address of 192.168.6.112. Modify the fifth *$objUser.Put* command so that it will supply this information to Active Directory when the script is run. The revised command is shown here.

```
$objUser.Put("ipPhone", "192.168.6.112")
```

8. Copy the previous telephone attributes and modify them for the *other*-type attributes. These consist of the following: *otherFacsimileTelephoneNumber, otherHomePhone, otherPager, other-Mobile,* and *otherIpPhone.*

9. Finally, the last telephone attribute is the notes. In Active Directory, this field is called the *info* attribute. Use the *Put* method to add the following information to the *info* attribute.

```
$objUser.Put("info", "All contact information is confidential")
```

10. Save and run your script. All the properties on the Telephones tab should be filled in for the MyNewUser account. If this is not the case, you might want to compare your script with the ModifyTelephoneAttributes.ps1 script shown here.

```
$objUser = [ADSI]"LDAP://cn=MyNewUser,ou=myTestOU,dc=iammred,dc=net"
$objUser.Put("homePhone", "555-555-0199")
$objUser.Put("pager", "555-555-0199")
$objUser.Put("mobile", "555-555-0199")
$objUser.Put("facsimileTelephoneNumber", "555-555-0199")
$objUser.Put("ipPhone", "192.168.6.112")
$objUser.Put("otherfacsimileTelephoneNumber", "555-555-0199")
$objUser.Put("otherhomePhone", "555-555-0199")
$objUser.Put("otherpager", "555-555-0199")
$objUser.Put("othermobile", @("555-555-0199","555-555-0199"))
$objUser.Put("otherIpPhone", @("192.168.6.113","192.168.6.114"))
$objUser.Put("info", "All contact information is confidential")
$objUser.SetInfo()
```

This concludes the procedure.

Creating multiple users

1. Open the CreateUser.ps1 script you created earlier and save it as *<yourname>*CreateMultipleUsers.ps1.

2. On the second line of your script, change the name of the variable *$strName* to *$aryNames*, because the variable will be used to hold an array of user names. On the same line, change the *CN=MyNewUser* user name to *CN=MyBoss*. Leave the quotation marks in place. At the end of

the line, add a comma and enter the next user name—**CN=MyDirect1**—ensuring you encase the name in quotation marks. The third user name is going to be *CN=MyDirect2*. The completed line of code is shown here.

```
$aryNames = "CN=MyBoss","CN=MyDirect1","CN=MyDirect2"
```

3. Under the *$objADSI* line that uses the *[ADSI]* accelerator to connect into Active Directory, and above the *$objUser* line that creates the user account, place a *foreach* statement. Inside the parentheses, use the variable *$strName* as the single object and *$aryNames* as the name of the array. This line of code is shown here.

```
foreach($StrName in $aryNames)
```

4. Below the *foreach* line, place an opening brace to mark the beginning of the code block. On the line after *$objUser.setinfo()*, close the code block with a closing brace. The entire code block is shown here.

```
{
  $objUser = $objADSI.Create($strClass, $strName)

  $objUser.setInfo()
}
```

5. Save and run your script. Three user accounts—MyBoss, MyDirect1, and MyDirect2—should magically appear in the MyTestOU OU. If this does not happen, compare your script with the CreateMultipleUsers.ps1 script shown here.

```
$strCLass = "User"
$aryNames = "CN=MyBoss","CN=MyDirect1","CN=MyDirect2"
$objADSI = [ADSI]"LDAP://ou=myTestOU,dc=iammred,dc=net"
foreach($StrName in $aryNames)

{
  $objUser = $objADSI.Create($strCLass, $StrName)
  $objUser.setInfo() }
```

This concludes the procedure.

Note One interesting thing about Windows PowerShell is that it can read inside a string, find a variable, and substitute the value of the variable, instead of just interpreting the variable as a string literal. This makes it easy to build up compound strings from information stored in multiple variables. Here's an example:

```
$objUser = [ADSI]"LDAP://$strUser,$strOU,$strDomain"
```

Modifying the organizational settings

1. Open the ModifySecondPage.ps1 script and save it as
   *<yourname>*ModifyOrganizationalPage.ps1.

2. In this script, you are going to modify four attributes in Active Directory, so you can delete all
   but four of the *$objUser.Put* commands from your script. The Organization tab from Active
   Directory Users And Computers is shown in Figure 15-7, along with the appropriate attribute
   names.

FIGURE 15-7 Organization attributes in Active Directory.

3. To make your script more flexible, you are going to abstract much of the connection string
   information into variables. The first variable you will use is one to hold the domain name. Call
   this variable *$strDomain* and assign it a value of *dc=nwtraders,dc=msft* (assuming this is the
   name of your domain). This code is shown here.

```
$strDomain = "dc=nwtraders,dc=msft"
```

4. The second variable you'll declare is the one that will hold the name of the OU. In this procedure, your users reside in an OU called ou=MyTestOU, so you should assign this value to the variable *$strOU*. This line of code is shown here.

```
$strOU = "ou=MyTestOU"
```

5. The user name you are going to be working with is MyNewUser. Users are not domain components (referred to with *DC*), nor are they OUs; rather, they are containers (referred to with *CN*). Assign the string *cn=MyNewUser* to the variable *$strUser*. This line of code is shown here.

```
$strUser = "cn=MyNewUser"
```

6. The last variable you need to declare and assign a value to is the one that will hold MyNewUser's manager. His name is MyBoss. The line of code that holds this information in the *$strManager* variable is shown here.

```
$strManager = "cn=MyBoss"
```

7. So far, you have hardly used any information from the ModifySecondPage.ps1 script. Edit the *$objUser* line that holds the connection into Active Directory by using the *[ADSI]* accelerator so that it uses the variables you created for the user, OU, and domain. Windows PowerShell will read the value of the variables instead of interpreting them as strings. This makes it really easy to modify the connection string. The revised line of code is shown here.

```
$objUser = [ADSI]"LDAP://$strUser,$strOU,$strDomain"
```

8. Modify the first *$objUser.Put* command so that it assigns the value *Mid-Level Manager* to the *title* attribute in Active Directory. This command is shown here.

```
$objUser.Put("title", "Mid-Level Manager")
```

9. Modify the second *$objUser.Put* command so that it assigns a value of *sales* to the *department* attribute in Active Directory. This command is shown here.

```
$objUser.Put("department", "sales")
```

10. Modify the third *$objUser.Put* command and assign the string *Northwind Traders* to the *company* attribute. This revised line of code is shown here.

```
$objUser.Put("company", "Northwind Traders")
```

11. The last attribute you need to modify is the *manager* attribute. To do this, you will use the last *$objUser.Put* command. The *manager* attribute needs the complete path to the object, so you will use the name stored in *$strManager*, the OU stored in *$strOU*, and the domain stored in *$strDomain*. This revised line of code is illustrated here.

```
$objUser.Put("manager", "$strManager,$strOU,$strDomain")
```

12. Save and run your script. The Organization tab should be filled out in Active Directory Users And Computers. The only attribute that has not been filled out is the attribute for the MyNewUser user's direct reports. However, if you open the MyBoss user, you will find MyNewUser listed as a direct report for the MyBoss user. If your script does not perform as expected, compare your script with the ModifyOrganizationalPage.ps1 script shown here.

```
$strDomain = "dc=nwtraders,dc=msft"
$strOU = "ou=MyTestOU"
$strUser = "cn=MyNewUser"
$strManager = "cn=MyBoss"

$objUser = [ADSI]"LDAP://$strUser,$strOU,$strDomain"
$objUser.Put("title", "Mid-Level Manager")
$objUser.Put("department", "sales")
$objUser.Put("company", "Northwind Traders")
$objUser.Put("manager", "$strManager,$strOU,$strDomain")

$objUser.setInfo()
```

This concludes the procedure.

Deleting users

There are times when you'll need to delete user accounts, and with ADSI, you can very easily delete large numbers of users with the single click of a mouse button. Some reasons for deleting user accounts follow:

- To clean up a computer lab environment—that is, to return machines to a known state.

- To clean up accounts at the end of a school year. Many schools delete all student-related accounts and files at the end of each year. Scripting makes it easy to both create and delete the accounts.

- To clean up temporary accounts created for special projects. If the creation of accounts is scripted, their deletion can also be easily scripted, ensuring that no temporary accounts are left lingering in the directory.

To delete users, take the following steps:

1. Specify *User* for the *object* class.

2. Define the *CN* of the *User* object.

3. Specify the appropriate provider and AdsPath to the OU.

4. Use *[ADSI]* to make a connection.

5. Call the *Delete* method by using the *object* class and *CN* of the object as arguments.

To delete a user, call the *Delete* method after binding to the appropriate level in the Active Directory namespace. Then specify both the *object* class, which in this case is *User*, and the *CN* attribute value of the user to be deleted. This can actually be accomplished in only a few lines of code, as illustrated in the following procedure.

If you modify the CreateUser.ps1 script, you can easily transform it into the DeleteUser.ps1 script, which follows. The main change is in the worker section of the script. The binding string, shown here, is the same as earlier.

```
$objADSI = [ADSI]"LDAP://ou=MyTestOU,dc=nwtraders,dc=msft"
```

However, in this case, you use the connection that was made in the binding string and call the *Delete* method. You specify the class of the object in the *$strClass* variable in the reference section of the script. You also list the *$strName*. The syntax is *Delete(Class, Target)*. The deletion takes effect immediately. The *SetInfo()* method is not required. This command is shown here.

```
$objUser = $objADSI.Delete($strCLass, $strName)
```

The DeleteUser.ps1 script entailed only two real changes from the CreateUser.ps1 script. This makes user management very easy. If you need to create a large number of temporary users, you can save the script and then use it to get rid of them when they have completed their projects. The complete DeleteUser.ps1 script is shown here.

```
# DeleteUser.ps1
$strClass = "User"
$strName = "CN=MyNewUser"
$objADSI = [ADSI]"LDAP://ou=MyTestOU,dc=nwtraders,dc=msft"
$objUser = $objADSI.Delete($strClass, $strName)
```

Creating multiple OUs: Step-by-step exercises

In these exercises, you will explore the use of a text file to hold the names of multiple OUs you want to create in Active Directory. After you create the organizational units in the first exercise, you will add users to an OU, as an example, in the second exercise.

> **Note** To complete these exercises, you will need access to a computer running Windows Server and Active Directory Domain Services. Modify the domain names listed in the exercises to match the name of your domain.

Creating OUs from a text file

1. Open the Windows PowerShell ISE or some other script editor.

2. Create a text file called stepbystep.txt. The contents of the text file are shown here.

   ```
   ou=NorthAmerica
   ou=SouthAmerica
   ou=Europe
   ou=Asia
   ou=Africa
   ```

3. Make sure you have the exact path to this file. On the first line of your script, create a variable called *$aryText*. Use this variable to hold the object that is returned by the *Get-Content* cmdlet. Specify the path to the stepbystep.txt file as the value of the *-Path* parameter. The line of code that does this is shown here.

   ```
   $aryText = Get-Content -Path "c:\labs\ch15\stepbystep.txt"
   ```

4. When the *Get-Content* cmdlet is used, it creates an array from a text file. To walk through each element of the array, you will use the *foreach* statement. Use a variable called *$aryElement* to hold the line from the *$aryText* array. This line of code is shown here.

   ```
   foreach ($aryElement in $aryText)
   ```

5. Begin your script block with an opening brace. This is shown here.

   ```
   {
   ```

6. Use the variable *$strClass* to hold the string *organizationalUnit*, because this is the kind of object you will be creating in Active Directory. The line of code to do this is shown here.

   ```
   $strClass = "organizationalUnit"
   ```

7. The name of each OU you are going to create comes from each line of the stepbystep.txt file. In your text file, to simplify the coding task, you included *ou=* as part of each OU name. The *$strOUName* variable that will be used in the *Create* command has a straight value assignment of one variable to another. This line of code is shown here.

   ```
   $strOUName = $aryElement
   ```

8. The next line of code in your code block is the one that connects into Active Directory by using the *[ADSI]* accelerator. You are going to use the LDAP provider and connect to the NwTraders.msft domain. You assign the object that is created to the *$objADSI* variable. This line of code is shown here.

   ```
   $objADSI = [ADSI]"LDAP://dc=nwtraders,dc=msft"
   ```

9. Now you are ready to actually create the OUs in Active Directory. To do this, you will use the *Create* method. You specify two arguments for the *Create* method: the name of the class to create and the name of the object to create. Here, the name of the class is stored in the variable *$strClass*. The name of the object to create is stored in the *$strOUName* variable. The object that is returned is stored in the *$objOU* variable. This line of code is shown here.

```
$objOU = $objADSI.Create($strClass, $strOUName)
```

10. To write changes back to Active Directory, you use the *SetInfo()* method. This is shown here.

```
$objOU.setInfo()
```

11. Now you must close the code block. To do this, close it with a brace, as shown here.

```
}
```

12. Save your script as *<yourname>*StepByStep.ps1. Run your script. You should get five OUs created off the root of your domain. If this is not the case, compare your script with the StepByStep.ps1 script that appears here.

```
$aryText = Get-Content -Path "c:\labs\ch15\stepbystep.txt"

foreach ($aryElement in $aryText)
{
    $strClass = "organizationalUnit"
    $strOUName = $aryElement
    $objADSI = [ADSI]"LDAP://dc=nwtraders,dc=msft"
    $objOU = $objADSI.Create($strCLass, $strOUName)
    $objOU.SetInfo()
}
```

This concludes the exercise.

In the following exercise, you will create nine temporary user accounts by using concatenation. You'll specify values for the users from a text file and populate attributes on both the Address tab and the Telephones tab.

Creating multivalued users

1. Open the Windows PowerShell ISE or your favorite Windows PowerShell script editor.

2. Create a text file called OneStepFurther.txt. The contents of this file are shown here.

```
123 Main Street
Box 123
Atlanta
```

```
Georgia
123456
US
united states
840
1-555-345-0199
All information is confidential and is for official use only
```

3. Use the *Get-Content* cmdlet to open the OneStepFurther.txt file. Use the *-Path* parameter to point to the exact path to the file. Hold the array that is created in a variable called *$aryText*. This line of code is shown here.

```
$aryText = Get-Content -Path "c:\labs\ch15\OneStepFurther.txt"
```

4. Create a variable called *$strClass*. This will be used to determine the class of object to create in Active Directory. Assign the string *User* to this variable. This line of code is shown here.

```
$strClass = "User"
```

5. Create a variable called *$intUsers*. This variable will be used to determine how many users to create. For this exercise, you will create nine users, so assign the integer 9 to the value of the variable. This code is shown here.

```
$intUsers = 9
```

6. Create a variable called *$strName*. This variable will be used to create the prefix for each user that is created. Because these will be temporary users, use the prefix *cn=tempuser*. This code is shown here.

```
$strName = "cn=tempUser"
```

7. Create a variable called *$objADSI*. This variable will be used to hold the object that is returned by using the *[ADSI]* accelerator that is used to make the connection into Active Directory. Specify the LDAP provider and connect to the NorthAmerica OU that resides in the NwTraders.msft domain. This line of code is shown here.

```
$objADSI = [ADSI]"LDAP://ou=NorthAmerica,dc=nwtraders,dc=msft"
```

8. Use a *for* loop to count from 1 to 9. Use the *$i* variable as the counter variable. When the value of *$i* is less than or equal to the integer stored in the *$intUsers* variable, exit the loop. Use the *$i++* operator to increment the value of *$i*. This code is shown here.

```
for ($i=1; $i -le $intUsers; $i++)
```

9. Open and close your code block by using braces. This is shown here.

```
{

}
```

10. Between the braces, use the object contained in the *$objADSI* variable to create the class of object stored in the variable *$strClass*. The name of each object will be created by concatenating the *$strName* prefix with the number current in *$i*. Store the object returned by the *Create* method in the variable *$objUser*.

This line of code is shown here.

```
$objUser = $objADSI.Create($strClass, $strName+$i)
```

11. On the next line in the code block, write the new *User* object to Active Directory by using the *SetInfo()* method. This line of code is shown here.

```
$objUser.SetInfo()
```

12. Open the OneStepFurther.txt file and examine the contents. Note that each line corresponds to a property in Active Directory. The trick is to ensure that each line in the text file matches each position in the array. Beginning at *element*, use the array contained in the variable *$aryText* to write the *streetAddress, postOfficeBox, l, st, postalCode, c, co, countryCode, facsimileTelephoneNumber*, and *info* attributes for each *User* object that is created. This section of code, shown here, is placed after the *User* object is created, and *SetInfo()* writes it to Active Directory.

```
$objUser.Put("streetAddress", $aryText[0])
$objUser.Put("postOfficeBox", $aryText[1])
$objUser.Put("l", $aryText[2])
$objUser.Put("st", $aryText[3])
$objUser.Put("postalCode" , $aryText[4])
$objUser.Put("c", $aryText[5])
$objUser.Put("co", $aryText[6])
$objUser.Put("countryCode", $aryText[7])
$objUser.Put("facsimileTelephoneNumber", $aryText[8])
$objUser.Put("info", $aryText[9])
```

13. Commit the changes to Active Directory by calling the *SetInfo()* method. This line of code is shown here.

```
$objUser.SetInfo()
```

14. Save your script as *<yourname>*OneStepFurtherPt1.ps1. Run your script and examine Active Directory Users And Computers. You should find the nine users with attributes on both the Address tab and the Telephones tab. If this is not the case, compare your script with the OneStepFurtherPt1.ps1 script shown here.

```
$aryText = Get-Content -Path "c:\labs\ch15\OneStepFurther.txt"
$strClass = "User"
$intUsers = 9
$strName = "cn=tempUser"

$objADSI = [ADSI]"LDAP://ou=myTestOU,dc=nwtraders,dc=msft"
for ($i=1; $i -le $intUsers; $i++)
{
```

```
$objUser = $objADSI.Create($strCLass, $StrName+$i)
$objUser.setInfo()
$objUser.Put("streetAddress", $aryText[0])
$objUser.Put("postOfficeBox", $aryText[1])
$objUser.Put("l", $aryText[2])
$objUser.Put("st", $aryText[3])
$objUser.Put("postalCode" , $aryText[4])
$objUser.Put("c", $aryText[5])
$objUser.Put("co", $aryText[6])
$objUser.Put("countryCode", $aryText[7])
$objUser.Put("facsimileTelephoneNumber", $aryText[8])
$objUser.Put("info", $aryText[9])
$objUser.SetInfo()
```

15. After the users are created, proceed to the second part of the exercise, described in the following steps.

16. Save OneStepFurtherPt1.ps1 as *<yourname>*OneStepFurtherPt2.ps1.

17. Delete the line *$aryText = Get-Content -Path "c:\labs\ch15\OneStepFurther.txt"* from the script.

18. Delete everything from inside the code block except for the line of code that creates the *User* object. This line of code is *$objUser = $objADSI.Create($strClass, $strName+$i)*. The code to delete is shown here.

```
$objUser.SetInfo()
$objUser.Put("streetAddress", $aryText[0])
$objUser.Put("postOfficeBox", $aryText[1])
$objUser.Put("l", $aryText[2])
$objUser.Put("st", $aryText[3])
$objUser.Put("postalCode" , $aryText[4])
$objUser.Put("c", $aryText[5])
$objUser.Put("co", $aryText[6])
$objUser.Put("countryCode", $aryText[7])
$objUser.Put("facsimileTelephoneNumber", $aryText[8])
$objUser.Put("info", $aryText[9])
$objUser.SetInfo()
```

19. Inside the code block, change the *Create* method in the *$objADSI Create* command to *Delete*, as shown here.

```
$objUser = $objADSI.Delete($strCLass, $StrName+$i)
```

20. Save and run your script. The nine users, created earlier, should disappear. If this does not happen, compare your script with the OneStepFurtherPt2.ps1 script shown here.

```
$strCLass = "User"
$intUsers = 9
$strName = "cn=tempUser"
$objADSI = [ADSI]"LDAP://ou=NorthAmerica,dc=nwtraders,dc=msft"
for ($i=1; $i -le $intUsers; $i++)

{
  $objUser = $objADSI.Delete($strClass, $strName+$i)

}
```

This concludes the exercise.

Chapter 15 quick reference

To	Do this
Delete users easily	Modify the script you used to create the user and change the *Create* method to *Delete*.
Commit changes to Active Directory when deleting a user	Do nothing—changes take place automatically when users are deleted.
Find country/region codes used in Active Directory Users And Computers	Use ISO 3166.
Modify a user's first name via ADSI	Add a value to the *givenName* attribute. Use the *SetInfo()* method to write the change to Active Directory. Use the *Put* method to at least specify the *sAMAccountName* attribute if you are using a Windows 2000 Active Directory environment.
Overwrite a field that is already populated in Active Directory	Use the *Put* method.
Read a text file and turn it into an array	Use the *Get-Content* cmdlet and specify the path to the file by using the *-Path* parameter.

Working with the AD DS module

After completing this chapter, you will be able to

■ Use the AD DS cmdlets to manage users.

■ Use the AD DS cmdlets to manage organizational units.

■ Use the AD DS cmdlets to manage computer objects.

■ Use the AD DS cmdlets to manage groups.

Understanding the Active Directory module

Microsoft first made the Active Directory Domain Services (AD DS) Windows PowerShell cmdlets available with Windows Server 2008 R2. You can also download and install the Active Directory Management Gateway Service (ADMGS). ADMGS provides a web service interface to Active Directory domains and to Active Directory Lightweight Directory Services. ADMGS runs on the domain controller. ADMGS can run on Windows Server 2008. On Windows Server 2008 R2 and later, ADMGS installs as a role and does not require an additional download. When you have one domain controller running Windows Server 2008 R2 (or later) in your domain, you can use the new cmdlets to manage your AD DS installation. Installing ADMGS on Windows Server 2008 does not make it possible to load the Active Directory module on those machines, but it does permit you to use the Active Directory module from another machine to manage those servers.

Installing the Active Directory module

The Active Directory module is available beginning with Windows 7 on the client side and with Windows 2008 R2 on servers. To make the cmdlets available on the desktop operating system, you need to download and install the Remote Server Administration Tools (RSAT). The Active Directory cmdlets ship in a Windows PowerShell module, so you might be interested in the *Get-MyModule* function from the Microsoft Script Center Script Repository. The *Get-MyModule* function is useful because it verifies the presence of an optional module prior to its use in a Windows PowerShell script. When you are using optional modules, scripts commonly fail because a particular module might not be available on all systems. The *Get-MyModule* function helps to detect this condition prior to actual script failure.

To install the Active Directory module on a computer running Windows Server 2008 R2 or later, you can use the *Add-WindowsFeature* cmdlet. This is because the Active Directory module is directly available to the operating system as an optional Windows feature. Therefore, installation on a server operating system does not require downloading RSAT.

 Note The *Get-WindowsFeature* and *Add-WindowsFeature* cmdlets exist only on server editions of the operating system. To install RSAT for Active Directory on a client version of the operating system, you must download it from the Microsoft Download Center at *http://www.microsoft.com/en-us/download/default.aspx*.

To install RSAT for Active Directory, use the procedure that follows.

Installing the Active Directory module

1. Use the *Get-WindowsFeature* cmdlet to verify that the *rsat-ad-tools* feature is available to install. The command is shown here.

   ```
   Get-WindowsFeature rsat-ad-tools
   ```

2. Use the Up Arrow key to retrieve the *Get-WindowsFeature* command and pipeline the results to the *Add-WindowsFeature* cmdlet. The command is shown here.

   ```
   Get-WindowsFeature rsat-ad-tools | Add-WindowsFeature
   ```

3. Use the Up Arrow key twice to retrieve the first *Get-WindowsFeature* command. The command is shown here.

   ```
   Get-WindowsFeature rsat-ad-tools
   ```

The use of the procedure and the associated output are shown in Figure 16-1.

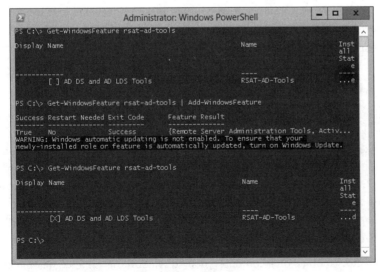

FIGURE 16-1 Installing RSAT provides access to the Active Directory module.

Getting started with the Active Directory module

After you have installed RSAT, you will want to verify that the Active Directory module is present and that it loads properly. To do this, follow the next procedure.

Verifying the Active Directory module

1. Use the *Get-Module* cmdlet with the *-ListAvailable* switch to verify that the Active Directory module is present. The command to do this is shown here.

   ```
   Get-Module -ListAvailable ActiveDirectory
   ```

2. Use the *Import-Module* cmdlet to import the Active Directory module. The command to do this is shown next. (In Windows PowerShell 3.0, you don't have to explicitly import the Active Directory module. However, if you know you are going to use the module, it makes sense to go ahead and explicitly import it, because it is faster.)

   ```
   Import-Module ActiveDirectory
   ```

3. Use the *Get-Module* cmdlet to verify that the Active Directory module loaded properly. The command to do this is shown here.

   ```
   Get-Module ActiveDirectory
   ```

4. After the Active Directory module loads, you can obtain a listing of the Active Directory cmdlets by using the *Get-Command* cmdlet and specifying the *-Module* parameter. This command is shown here.

   ```
   Get-Command -Module ActiveDirectory
   ```

Using the Active Directory module

It is not necessary to always load the Active Directory module (or for that matter, any module), because Windows PowerShell 3.0 or later automatically loads the module containing a referenced cmdlet. The location searched by Windows PowerShell for modules comes from the environment variable *PSModulePath*. To view the value of this environment variable, prefix the variable name with the environment drive. The following command retrieves the default module locations and displays the associated paths.

```
PS C:\> $env:PSModulePath
C:\Users\mredw\Documents\WindowsPowerShell\Modules;C:\Program
Files\WindowsPowerShell\Modules;C:\Windows\system32\WindowsPowerShell\v1.0\Modules\
```

If you do not want to install the Active Directory module on your client operating systems, all you need to do is to add the *rsat-ad-tools* feature to at least one server. After it's installed on the server, use Windows PowerShell remoting to connect to the server hosting the *rsat-ad-tools* feature from your client workstation. When you are in the remote session, if the remote server is running Windows PowerShell 3 or later, all you need to do is call one of the Active Directory cmdlets. The Active Directory module automatically loads, and the information returns. The following commands illustrate this technique.

```
$credential = Get-Credential nwtraders\administrator
Enter-PSSession -cn dc1 -Credential $credential
Get-ADDomain
```

Figure 16-2 illustrates the techniques for using Windows PowerShell remoting to connect to a server that contains the Active Directory module and for automatically loading that module while using a cmdlet from it.

Note Many network administrators who spend the majority of their time working with Active Directory import the Active Directory module via their Windows PowerShell profile. In this way, they never need to worry about the initial performance hit that occurs due to autoloading the Active Directory module.

FIGURE 16-2 Use Windows PowerShell remoting to obtain Active Directory information without first loading the module.

Finding the FSMO role holders

To find information about domain controllers and Flexible Single Master Operation (FSMO) roles, you do not have to write a Windows PowerShell script; you can do it directly from the Windows PowerShell console or ISE by using the Active Directory cmdlets. The first thing you'll need to do, more than likely, is load the Active Directory module into the current Windows PowerShell session. Though it is possible to add the *Import-Module* command to your Windows PowerShell profile, in general it is not a good idea to load a bunch of modules that you might or might not use on a regular basis. In fact, you can load all the modules at once by pipelining the results of the *Get-Module -ListAvailable* command to the *Import-Module* cmdlet.

Note Your output might vary, depending on what options you have enabled and what modules are actually installed on your machine.

A sample output is shown here.

```
PS C:\> Get-Module -ListAvailable | Import-Module
PS C:\> Get-Module

ModuleType Name                     ExportedCommands
---------- ----                     ----------------
Script     BasicFunctions           {Get-ComputerInfo, Get-OptimalSize}
Script     ConversionModuleV6       {ConvertTo-Feet, ConvertTo-Miles, ConvertTo-...
Script     PowerShellPack           {New-ByteAnimationUsingKeyFrames, New-TiffBi...
Script     PSCodeGen                {New-Enum, New-ScriptCmdlet, New-PInvoke}
Script     PSImageTools             {Add-CropFilter, Add-RotateFlipFilter, Add-O...
Script     PSRss                    {Read-Article, New-Feed, Remove-Article, Rem...
Script     PSSystemTools            {Test-32Bit, Get-USB, Get-OSVersion, Get-Mul...
Script     PSUserTools              {Start-ProcessAsAdministrator, Get-CurrentUs...
Script     TaskScheduler            {Remove-Task, Get-ScheduledTask, Stop-Task, ...
Script     WPK                      {Get-DependencyProperty, New-ModelVisual3D, ...
Manifest   ActiveDirectory          {Set-ADOrganizationalUnit, Get-ADDomainContr...
Manifest   AppLocker                {Get-AppLockerPolicy, Get-AppLockerFileInfor...
Manifest   BitsTransfer             {Start-BitsTransfer, Remove-BitsTransfer, Re...
Manifest   FailoverClusters         {Set-ClusterParameter, Get-ClusterParameter,...
Manifest   GroupPolicy              {Get-GPStarterGPO, Get-GPOReport, Set-GPInhe...
Manifest   NetworkLoadBalancingCl... {Stop-NlbClusterNode, Remove-NlbClusterVip, ...
Script     PSDiagnostics            {Enable-PSTrace, Enable-WSManTrace, Start-Tr...
Manifest   TroubleshootingPack      {Get-TroubleshootingPack, Invoke-Troubleshoo...
```

After you have loaded the Active Directory module, you will want to use the *Get-Command* cmdlet to view the cmdlets that are exported by the module. This is shown here.

```
PS C:\> Get-Command -Module ActiveDirectory

CommandType Name                              Definition
----------- ----                              ----------
Cmdlet      Add-ADComputerServiceAccount      Add-ADComputerServiceAccount [...
Cmdlet      Add-ADDomainControllerPasswordR... Add-ADDomainControllerPassword...
Cmdlet      Add-ADFineGrainedPasswordPolicy... Add-ADFineGrainedPasswordPolic...
Cmdlet      Add-ADGroupMember                 Add-ADGroupMember [-Identity] ...
```

```
Cmdlet       Add-ADPrincipalGroupMembership   Add-ADPrincipalGroupMembership...
Cmdlet       Clear-ADAccountExpiration        Clear-ADAccountExpiration [-Id...
Cmdlet       Disable-ADAccount                Disable-ADAccount [-Identity] ...
Cmdlet       Disable-ADOptionalFeature        Disable-ADOptionalFeature [-Id...
Cmdlet       Enable-ADAccount                 Enable-ADAccount [-Identity] <...
Cmdlet       Enable-ADOptionalFeature         Enable-ADOptionalFeature [-Ide...
Cmdlet       Get-ADAccountAuthorizationGroup  Get-ADAccountAuthorizationGrou...
Cmdlet       Get-ADAccountResultantPasswordR... Get-ADAccountResultantPassword...
Cmdlet       Get-ADComputer                   Get-ADComputer -Filter <String...
<output truncated>
```

To find a single domain controller, if you are not sure that you have one in your site, you can use the *-Discover* switch on the *Get-ADDomainController* cmdlet. One thing to keep in mind is that the *-Discover* parameter could return information from the cache. If you want to ensure that a fresh discover command is sent, use the *-ForceDiscover* switch in addition to the *-Discover* switch. These techniques are shown here.

```
PS C:\> Get-ADDomainController -Discover -ForceDiscover

Domain      : NWTraders.com
Forest      : NWTraders.com
HostName    : {DC1.NWTraders.com}
IPv4Address : 192.168.10.1
IPv6Address :
Name        : DC1
Site        : Default-First-Site-Name
```

When you use the *Get-ADDomainController* cmdlet, a minimal amount of information is returned. If you want to view additional information from the domain controller you discovered, you would need to connect to it by using the *-Identity* parameter. The value of the *Identity* parameter can be an IP address, a GUID, a host name, or even a NetBIOS type of name. This technique is shown here.

```
PS C:\> Get-ADDomainController -Identity DC1


ComputerObjectDN          : CN=DC1,OU=Domain Controllers,DC=NWTraders,DC=com
DefaultPartition          : DC=NWTraders,DC=com
Domain                    : NWTraders.com
Enabled                   : True
Forest                    : NWTraders.com
HostName                  : DC1.NWTraders.com
InvocationId              : 4bb144a4-a8eb-46a0-aab4-e9dad6de0d34
IPv4Address               : 192.168.10.1
IPv6Address               :
IsGlobalCatalog           : True
IsReadOnly                : False
LdapPort                  : 389
Name                      : DC1
NTDSSettingsObjectDN      : CN=NTDS Settings,CN=DC1,CN=Servers,CN=Default-First-Sit
                            e-Name,CN=Sites,CN=Configuration,DC=NWTraders,DC=com
OperatingSystem           : Windows Server 2012 R2 Standard
OperatingSystemHotfix     :
OperatingSystemServicePack :
OperatingSystemVersion    : 6.3 (9600)
```

```
OperationMasterRoles        : {SchemaMaster, DomainNamingMaster, PDCEmulator,
                              RIDMaster...}
Partitions                  : {DC=ForestDnsZones,DC=NWTraders,DC=com,
                              DC=DomainDnsZones,DC=NWTraders,DC=com,
                              CN=Schema,CN=Configuration,DC=NWTraders,DC=com,
                              CN=Configuration,DC=NWTraders,DC=com...}
ServerObjectDN              : CN=DC1,CN=Servers,CN=Default-First-Site-Name,CN=Sites,C
                              N=Configuration,DC=NWTraders,DC=com
ServerObjectGuid            : 3242a3ce-83b6-4cbe-803e-b45409f02e22
Site                        : Default-First-Site-Name
SslPort                     : 636
```

As shown in the preceding output, the server named DC1 is a global catalog server (the *IsGlobal-Catalog* property is *True*). It also holds all the FSMO roles. The output shown previously is truncated, hence the ellipse at the end of RIDMaster, which means there is another property value present but not shown. The server is running Windows Server 2012 R2 Standard Edition. The *Get-ADDomain-Controller* cmdlet accepts a *-Filter* parameter that can be used to perform a search-and-retrieve operation. It uses a special search syntax that is discussed in the online help files. Unfortunately, it does not accept Lightweight Directory Access Protocol (LDAP) syntax.

Luckily, you do not have to learn the special filter syntax, because the *Get-ADObject* cmdlet will accept an LDAP dialect filter. You can simply pipeline the results of *the Get-ADObject* cmdlet to the *Get-ADDomainController* cmdlet. This technique is shown here.

```
PS C:\> Get-ADObject -LDAPFilter "(objectclass=computer)" -searchbase "ou=domain cont
rollers,dc=nwtraders,dc=com" | Get-ADDomainController
```

```
ComputerObjectDN          : CN=DC1,OU=Domain Controllers,DC=NWTraders,DC=com
DefaultPartition          : DC=NWTraders,DC=com
Domain                    : NWTraders.com
Enabled                   : True
Forest                    : NWTraders.com
HostName                  : DC1.NWTraders.com
InvocationId              : 4bb144a4-a8eb-46a0-aab4-e9dad6de0d34
IPv4Address               : 192.168.10.1
IPv6Address               :
IsGlobalCatalog           : True
IsReadOnly                : False
LdapPort                  : 389
Name                      : DC1
NTDSSettingsObjectDN      : CN=NTDS Settings,CN=DC1,CN=Servers,CN=Default-First-Sit
                            e-Name,CN=Sites,CN=Configuration,DC=NWTraders,DC=com
OperatingSystem           : Windows Server 2012 R2 Standard
OperatingSystemHotfix     :
OperatingSystemServicePack :
OperatingSystemVersion    : 6.3 (9600)
OperationMasterRoles      : {SchemaMaster, DomainNamingMaster, PDCEmulator,
                            RIDMaster...}
Partitions                : {DC=ForestDnsZones,DC=NWTraders,DC=com,
                            DC=DomainDnsZones,DC=NWTraders,DC=com,
                            CN=Schema,CN=Configuration,DC=NWTraders,DC=com,
                            CN=Configuration,DC=NWTraders,DC=com...}
ServerObjectDN            : CN=DC1,CN=Servers,CN=Default-First-Site-Name,CN=Sites,C
```

```
                               N=Configuration,DC=NWTraders,DC=com
ServerObjectGuid          : 3242a3ce-83b6-4cbe-803e-b45409f02e22
Site                      : Default-First-Site-Name
SslPort                   : 636
```

If this returns too much information, note that the Active Directory cmdlets work just like any other Windows PowerShell cmdlets and therefore permit the use of the pipe character to choose the information you want to display. To obtain only the FSMO information, you really only need to use two commands. (If you want to include importing the Active Directory module in your count, you'll need three commands, and if you need to make a remote connection to a domain controller to run the commands, you'll need four.) One useful thing about using Windows PowerShell remoting is that you specify the credentials you need to run the command. If your normal account is a standard user account, you only use an elevated account when you need to do things with elevated rights. If you have already started the Windows PowerShell console with elevated credentials, you can skip typing in credentials when you enter the remote Windows PowerShell session (assuming that the elevated account also has rights on the remote server). The command shown here creates a remote session on a remote domain controller.

```
Enter-PSSession dc1
```

After the Active Directory module loads, you type a one-line command to get the forest FSMO roles, and another one-line command to get the domain FSMO roles. These two commands are shown here.

```
Get-ADForest NWTraders.Com | Format-Table SchemaMaster,DomainNamingMaster
Get-ADDomain NWTraders.Com | Format-Table PDCEmulator,RIDMaster,InfrastructureMaster
```

That is it—two or three one-line commands, depending on how you want to count. Even in the worst case, this is much easier to type than the 33 lines of code that would be required if you did not have access to the Active Directory module. In addition, the Windows PowerShell code is much easier to read and understand. The commands and the associated output are shown in Figure 16-3.

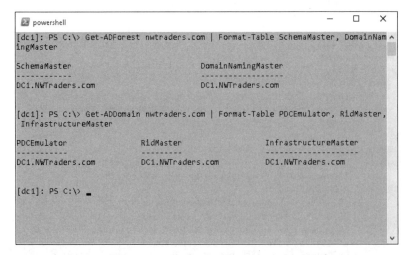

FIGURE 16-3 Use Windows PowerShell remoting to obtain FSMO information.

Discovering Active Directory

By using the Active Directory Windows PowerShell cmdlets and remoting, you can easily discover information about the forest and the domain. The first thing you need to do is to enter a PS session on the remote computer. To do this, you use the *Enter-PSSession* cmdlet. Next, you import the Active Directory module and set the working location to the root of drive C. The reason for setting the working location to the root of drive C is to regain valuable command-line space. These commands are shown here.

```
PS C:\Users\Administrator.NWTRADERS> Enter-PSSession dc1
[dc1]: PS C:\Users\Administrator\Documents> Import-Module activedirectory
[dc1]: PS C:\Users\Administrator\Documents> Set-Location c:\
```

After you have connected to the remote domain controller, you can use the *Get-CimInstance* cmdlet to verify your operating system on that computer. This command and the associated output are shown here.

```
[dc1]: PS C:\> Get-CimInstance Win32_OperatingSystem

SystemDirecto Organization  BuildNumber  RegisteredUs SerialNumber Version
ry                                        er
------------- ------------  -----------  ------------ ------------ -------
C:\Windows...               9600         Windows User 00252-000... 6.3.9600
```

Now you want to get information about the forest. To do this, you use the *Get-ADForest* cmdlet. The output from *Get-ADForest* includes lots of great information such as the domain-naming master, forest mode, schema master, and domain controllers. The command and associated output are shown here.

```
[dc1]: PS C:\> Get-ADForest


ApplicationPartitions : {DC=DomainDnsZones,DC=NWTraders,DC=com,
                        DC=ForestDnsZones,DC=NWTraders,DC=com}
CrossForestReferences : {}
DomainNamingMaster    : DC1.NWTraders.com
Domains               : {NWTraders.com}
ForestMode            : Windows2012R2Forest
GlobalCatalogs        : {DC1.NWTraders.com}
Name                  : NWTraders.com
PartitionsContainer   : CN=Partitions,CN=Configuration,DC=NWTraders,DC=com
RootDomain            : NWTraders.com
SchemaMaster          : DC1.NWTraders.com
Sites                 : {Default-First-Site-Name}
SPNSuffixes           : {}
UPNSuffixes           : {}
```

Next, you'll use the *Get-ADDomain* cmdlet to obtain information about the domain. The command returns important information, such as the location of the default domain controller OU, the PDC Emulator, and the RID Master.

The command and associated output are shown here.

```
[dc1]: PS C:\> Get-ADDomain
AllowedDNSSuffixes                 : {}
ChildDomains                       : {}
ComputersContainer                 : CN=Computers,DC=nwtraders,DC=com
DeletedObjectsContainer            : CN=Deleted Objects,DC=nwtraders,DC=com
DistinguishedName                  : DC=nwtraders,DC=com
DNSRoot                            : nwtraders.com
DomainControllersContainer         : OU=Domain Controllers,DC=nwtraders,DC=com
DomainMode                         : Windows2008Domain
DomainSID                          : S-1-5-21-909705514-2746778377-2082649206
ForeignSecurityPrincipalsContainer : CN=ForeignSecurityPrincipals,DC=nwtraders,DC=com
Forest                             : nwtraders.com
InfrastructureMaster               : DC1.nwtraders.com
LastLogonReplicationInterval       :
LinkedGroupPolicyObjects           : {CN={31B2F340-016D-11D2-945F-00C04FB984F9},CN=Policies,CN=
                                     System,DC=nwtraders,DC=com}
LostAndFoundContainer              : CN=LostAndFound,DC=nwtraders,DC=com
ManagedBy                          :
Name                               : nwtraders
NetBIOSName                        : NWTRADERS
ObjectClass                        : domainDNS
ObjectGUID                         : 0026d1fc-2e4d-4c35-96ce-b900e9d67e7c
ParentDomain                       :
PDCEmulator                        : DC1.nwtraders.com
QuotasContainer                    : CN=NTDS Quotas,DC=nwtraders,DC=com
ReadOnlyReplicaDirectoryServers    : {}
ReplicaDirectoryServers            : {DC1.nwtraders.com}
RIDMaster                          : DC1.nwtraders.com
SubordinateReferences              : {DC=ForestDnsZones,DC=nwtraders,DC=com, DC=DomainDnsZones,
                                     DC=nwtraders,DC=com, CN=Configuration,DC=nwtraders,DC=com}
SystemsContainer                   : CN=System,DC=nwtraders,DC=com
UsersContainer                     : CN=Users,DC=nwtraders,DC=com
```

From a security perspective, you should always check the domain password policy. To do this, use the *Get-ADDefaultDomainPasswordPolicy* cmdlet. Things you'll want to pay attention to are the use of complex passwords, minimum password length, password age, and password retention. Of course, you also need to check the account lockout policy. It is especially important to review this policy closely when inheriting a new network. Here is the command and associated output to do this.

```
[dc1]: PS C:\> Get-ADDefaultDomainPasswordPolicy

ComplexityEnabled          : True
DistinguishedName          : DC=nwtraders,DC=com
LockoutDuration            : 00:30:00
LockoutObservationWindow   : 00:30:00
LockoutThreshold           : 0
MaxPasswordAge             : 42.00:00:00
MinPasswordAge             : 1.00:00:00
MinPasswordLength          : 7
objectClass                : {domainDNS}
objectGuid                 : 0026d1fc-2e4d-4c35-96ce-b900e9d67e7c
PasswordHistoryCount       : 24
ReversibleEncryptionEnabled : False
```

Finally, you need to check the domain controllers themselves. To do this, use the *Get-ADDomain-Controller* cmdlet. This command returns important information about domain controllers, such as whether the domain controller is read-only, is a global catalog server, or owns one of the operations master roles; it also returns operating system information. Here is the command and associated output.

```
[dc1]: PS C:\> Get-ADDomainController -Identity dc1
```

```
ComputerObjectDN            : CN=DC1,OU=Domain Controllers,DC=NWTraders,DC=com
DefaultPartition            : DC=NWTraders,DC=com
Domain                      : NWTraders.com
Enabled                     : True
Forest                      : NWTraders.com
HostName                    : DC1.NWTraders.com
InvocationId                : 4bb144a4-a8eb-46a0-aab4-e9dad6de0d34
IPv4Address                 : 192.168.10.1
IPv6Address                 :
IsGlobalCatalog             : True
IsReadOnly                  : False
LdapPort                    : 389
Name                        : DC1
NTDSSettingsObjectDN        : CN=NTDS Settings,CN=DC1,CN=Servers,CN=Default-Firs
                              t-Site-Name,CN=Sites,CN=Configuration,DC=NWTraders
                              ,DC=com
OperatingSystem             : Windows Server 2012 R2 Standard
OperatingSystemHotfix       :
OperatingSystemServicePack  :
OperatingSystemVersion      : 6.3 (9600)
OperationMasterRoles        : {SchemaMaster, DomainNamingMaster, PDCEmulator,
                              RIDMaster...}
Partitions                  : {DC=ForestDnsZones,DC=NWTraders,DC=com,
                              DC=DomainDnsZones,DC=NWTraders,DC=com,
                              CN=Schema,CN=Configuration,DC=NWTraders,DC=com,
                              CN=Configuration,DC=NWTraders,DC=com...}
ServerObjectDN              : CN=DC1,CN=Servers,CN=Default-First-Site-Name,CN=Si
                              tes,CN=Configuration,DC=NWTraders,DC=com
ServerObjectGuid            : 3242a3ce-83b6-4cbe-803e-b45409f02e22
Site                        : Default-First-Site-Name
SslPort                     : 636
```

Producing a report is as easy as redirecting the output to a text file. The following commands gather the information discussed earlier in this section and store the retrieved information in a file named *AD_Doc.txt*. The commands also illustrate that it is possible to redirect the information to a file stored in a network share.

```
Get-ADForest >> \\dc1\shared\AD_Doc.txt
Get-ADDomain >> \\dc1\shared\AD_Doc.txt
Get-ADDefaultDomainPasswordPolicy >> \\dc1\shared\AD_Doc.txt
Get-ADDomainController -Identity dc1 >>\\dc1\shared\AD_Doc.txt
```

The file, as viewed in Notepad, appears in Figure 16-4.

FIGURE 16-4 Active Directory documentation can be displayed in Notepad.

Renaming Active Directory sites

It is easy to rename a site. All you need to do is to right-click the site and select Rename from the action menu in the Microsoft Management Console (MMC). By default, the first site is called Default-First-Site-Name, which is not very illuminating. To work with Active Directory sites, it is necessary to understand that they are a bit strange. First, they reside in the configuration-naming context. Connecting to this context by using the Active Directory module is rather simple. All you need to do is use the *Get-ADRootDSE* cmdlet and then select the *ConfigurationNamingContext* property. First, you have to make a connection to the domain controller and import the Active Directory module (assuming that you do not have RSAT installed on your client computer). This is shown here.

```
Enter-PSSession -ComputerName dc3 -Credential nwtraders\administrator
Import-Module activedirectory
```

Here is the code that will retrieve all of the sites. It uses the *Get-ADObject* cmdlet to search the configuration-naming context for objects that are of class *site*.

```
Get-ADObject -SearchBase (Get-ADRootDSE).ConfigurationNamingContext -filter "objectclass -eq
'site'"
```

When you have the site you want to work with, you first change the *DisplayName* attribute. To do this, you pipeline the *site* object to the *Set-ADObject* cmdlet. You can use the *Set-ADObject* cmdlet to set a variety of attributes on an object.

This command appears following. (This is a single command that is broken into two pieces at the pipe character.)

```
Get-ADObject -SearchBase (Get-ADRootDSE).ConfigurationNamingContext -filter "objectclass -eq
'site'" | Set-ADObject -DisplayName CharlotteSite
```

Because you have set the *displayName* attribute, you can also rename the object itself. To do this, you use a cmdlet called *Rename-ADObject*. Again, to simplify things, you pipeline the *site* object to the cmdlet and assign a new name for the site. This command appears following. (This is also a one-line command broken at the pipe.)

```
Get-ADObject -SearchBase (Get-ADRootDSE).ConfigurationNamingContext -filter "objectclass -eq
'site'" | Rename-ADObject -NewName CharlotteSite
```

Managing users

To create a new organizational unit (OU), you use the *New-ADOrganizationalUnit* cmdlet, as shown here.

```
New-ADOrganizationalUnit -Name TestOU -Path "dc=nwtraders,dc=com"
```

If you want to create a child OU, you use the *New-ADOrganizationalUnit* cmdlet, but in the path, you list the location that will serve as the parent. This is illustrated here.

```
New-ADOrganizationalUnit -Name TestOU1 -Path "ou=TestOU,dc=nwtraders,dc=com"
```

If you want to create several child OUs in the same location, use the Up Arrow key to retrieve the previous command and edit the name of the child. You can use the Home key to move to the beginning of the line, the End key to move to the end of the line, and the Left Arrow and Right Arrow keys to find your place on the line so you can edit it. A second child OU is created here.

```
New-ADOrganizationalUnit -Name TestOU2 -Path "ou=TestOU,dc=nwtraders,dc=com"
```

To create a computer account in one of the newly created child OUs, you must type the complete path to the OU that will house the new computer account. The *New-ADComputer* cmdlet is used to create new computer accounts in AD DS. In this example, the TestOU1 OU is a child of the TestOU OU, and therefore both OUs must appear in the *-Path* parameter. Keep in mind that the path that is supplied to the *-Path* parameter must be contained inside quotation marks, as shown here.

```
New-ADComputer -Name Test -Path "ou=TestOU1,ou=TestOU,dc=nwtraders,dc=com"
```

To create a user account, you use the *New-ADUser* cmdlet, as shown here.

```
New-ADUser -Name TestChild -Path "ou=TestOU1,ou=TestOU,dc=nwtraders,dc=com"
```

Because there could be a bit of typing involved that tends to become redundant, you might want to write a script to create the OUs at the same time that the computer and user accounts are created. A sample script that creates OUs, users, and computers is the UseADCmdletsToCreateOuComputerAndUser.ps1 script shown here.

UseADCmdletsToCreateOuComputerAndUser.ps1

```
Import-Module -Name ActiveDirectory
$Name = "ScriptTest"
$DomainName = "dc=nwtraders,dc=com"
$OUPath = "ou={0},{1}" -f $Name, $DomainName

New-ADOrganizationalUnit -Name $Name -Path $DomainName -ProtectedFromAccidentalDeletion $false

For($you = 0; $you -le 5; $you++)
{
 New-ADOrganizationalUnit -Name $Name$you -Path $OUPath -ProtectedFromAccidentalDeletion $false
}

For($you = 0 ; $you -le 5; $you++)
{
 New-ADComputer -Name  "TestComputer$you" -Path $OUPath
 New-ADUser -Name "TestUser$you" -Path $OUPath
}
```

The UseADCmdletsToCreateOuComputerAndUser.ps1 script begins by importing the Active Directory module. It then creates the first OU. When you are testing a script, it is important to disable the deletion protection by using the *-ProtectedFromAccidentalDeletion* parameter. When you do this, you can easily delete the OU and avoid having to change the protected status on each OU in the Advanced view in Active Directory Users And Computers.

After the ScriptTest OU is created, the other OUs and user and computer accounts can be created inside the new location. It might seem obvious that you cannot create a child OU inside the parent OU if the parent has not yet been created, but it is easy to make a logic error like this.

To create a new global security group, use the *New-ADGroup* Windows PowerShell AD DS cmdlet. The *New-ADGroup* cmdlet requires three parameters: *-Name*, for the name of the group; *-Path*, for a path inside the directory to the location where the group will be stored; and *-GroupScope*, which can be *global*, *universal*, or *domainlocal*. Before running the command shown here, remember that you must import the Active Directory module into your current Windows PowerShell session.

```
New-ADGroup -Name TestGroup -Path "ou=TestOU,dc=nwtraders,dc=com" -GroupScope global
```

To create a new universal group, you only need to change the *-GroupScope* parameter value, as shown here.

```
New-ADGroup -Name TestGroup1 -Path "ou=TestOU,dc=nwtraders,dc=com" -GroupScope universal
```

To add a user to a group by using the *New-ADGroup* cmdlet, you must supply values for the *-Identity* parameter and the *-Members* parameter. The value you use for the *-Identity* parameter is the name of the group. You do not need to use the LDAP syntax of *cn=groupname*; you only need to supply the name. Use ADSI Edit to examine the requisite LDAP attributes needed for a group in ADSI Edit.

It is a bit unusual that the *-Members* parameter is named *-Members* and not *-Member*, because most Windows PowerShell cmdlet parameter names are singular, not plural. The parameter names are singular even when they accept an array of values (such as the *-ComputerName* parameter). The command to add a new group named *TestGroup1* to the *UserGroupTest* group is shown here.

```
Add-ADGroupMember -Identity TestGroup1 -Members UserGroupTest
```

To remove a user from a group, use the *Remove-ADGroupMember* cmdlet with the name of the user and group. The *-Identity* and the *-Members* parameters are required, but the command will not execute without confirmation, as shown here.

```
PS C:\> Remove-ADGroupMember -Identity TestGroup1 -Members UserGroupTest

Confirm
Are you sure you want to perform this action?
Performing operation "Set" on Target "CN=TestGroup1,OU=TestOU,DC=NWTraders,DC=Com".
[Y] Yes  [A] Yes to All  [N] No  [L] No to All  [S] Suspend  [?] Help (default is "Y"): y
PS C:\>
```

If you are sure you want to remove the user from the group and you want to suppress the query, you use the *-Confirm* parameter and assign the value *$false* to it. Note that you will need to supply a colon between the parameter and the *$false* value.

Note The use of the colon after the *-Confirm* parameter is not documented, but the technique works on several different cmdlets. Unfortunately, you cannot use the *-Force* switched parameter to suppress the query.

The command is shown here.

```
Remove-ADGroupMember -Identity TestGroup1 -Members UserGroupTest -Confirm:$false
```

You need the ability to suppress the confirmation prompt to be able to use the *Remove-ADGroup-Member* cmdlet in a script. The first thing the RemoveUserFromGroup.ps1 script does is load the Active Directory module. After the module is loaded, the *Remove-ADGroupMember* cmdlet is used to remove the user from the group. To suppress the confirmation prompt, the *-Confirm:$false* command is used. The RemoveUserFromGroup.ps1 script is shown here.

RemoveUserFromGroup.ps1

```
import-module activedirectory
Remove-ADGroupMember -Identity TestGroup1 -Members UserGroupTest -Confirm:$false
```

Creating a user

In this section, you'll create a new user in Active Directory with the name Ed. The command to create a new user is simple: it is *New-ADUser* and the user name. The command to create a disabled user account in the *Users* container in the default domain is shown here.

```
New-ADUser -Name Ed
```

When the command that creates a new user completes, nothing is returned to the Windows PowerShell console. To check to ensure that the user has been created, use the *Get-ADUser* cmdlet to retrieve the *User* object. This command is shown here.

```
Get-ADUser Ed
```

When you are certain that your new user has been created, you can create an OU to store the user account. The command to create a new OU off the root of the domain is shown here.

```
New-ADOrganizationalUnit Scripting
```

As with the previously used *New-ADUser* cmdlet, nothing returns to the Windows PowerShell console. If you use the *Get-ADOrganizationalUnit* cmdlet, you must use a different methodology. When using the *Get-ADOrganizationalUnit* cmdlet, ensure that you specify either the -Filter parameter or the -LDAPFilter parameter to find the OU, as follows.

```
Get-ADOrganizationalUnit -LDAPFilter "(name=scripting)"
```

Now that you have a new user and a new OU, you need to move the user from the *Users* container to the newly created Scripting OU. To do that, you use the *Move-ADObject* cmdlet. You first get the *distinguishedname* attribute for the Scripting OU and store it in a variable called *$oupath*. Next, you use the *Move-ADObject* cmdlet to move the Ed user to the new OU. The trick here is that whereas the *Get-ADUser* cmdlet is able to find a user with the name of Ed, the *Move-ADObject* cmdlet must have the distinguished name of the *Ed USER* object in order to move it. You could use the *Get-ADUser* cmdlet to retrieve the distinguished name in a similar manner as you did with the Scripting OU.

The next thing you need to do is enable the user account. To do this, you need to assign a password to the user account prior to enabling the account. The password must be a secure string. To ensure that it is a secure string, you can use the *ConvertTo-SecureString* cmdlet. By default, warnings about converting text to a secure string are displayed, but you can suppress these prompts by using the *-Force* parameter. Here is the command you use to create a secure string for a password.

```
$pwd = ConvertTo-SecureString -String "P@ssword1" -AsPlainText -Force
```

Now that you have created a secure string to use for a password for your user account, you call the *Set-ADAccountPassword* cmdlet to set the password. Because this is a new password, you need to use the *-NewPassword* parameter. In addition, because you do not have a previous password, you use the *-Reset* parameter. This command is shown here.

```
Set-ADAccountPassword -Identity ed -NewPassword $pwd -Reset
```

When the account has an assigned password, it is time to enable the user account. This command is shown here.

```
Enable-ADAccount -Identity ed
```

As with the previous cmdlets, none of these cmdlets returns any information. To ensure that you have actually enabled the Ed user account, you use the *Get-ADUser* cmdlet. In the output, you are looking for the value of the *enabled* property. The *enabled* property is a Boolean, so therefore expect the value to be *true*.

Finding and unlocking Active Directory user accounts

When you are using the Active Directory cmdlets, locating locked-out users is very easy. The *Search-ADAccount* cmdlet even has a *-LockedOut* switch. Use the *Search-ADAccount* cmdlet with the *-LockedOut* parameter to find all user accounts in the domain that are locked out. This command is shown here.

```
Search-ADAccount -LockedOut
```

The *Search-ADAccount* command and the associated output are shown here.

```
[dc1]: PS C:\> Search-ADAccount -LockedOut


AccountExpirationDate :
DistinguishedName     : CN=Bob,CN=Users,DC=NWTraders,DC=com
Enabled               : True
LastLogonDate         : 4/20/2015 9:25:58 AM
LockedOut             : True
Name                  : Bob
ObjectClass           : user
ObjectGUID            : fbaf1c57-e97d-4fa1-b507-4d319c443152
PasswordExpired       : False
PasswordNeverExpires  : True
SamAccountName        : Bob
SID                   : S-1-5-21-1893272736-1364514926-820579994-19781
UserPrincipalName     : Bob@NWTraders.com
```

You can also unlock the locked-out user account—assuming you have permission. Figure 16-5 shows an attempt to unlock the user account with an account that is for a normal user.

Note People are often worried about Windows PowerShell from a security perspective. Windows PowerShell is only an application, and therefore users are not able to do anything that they do not have rights or permission to accomplish. The example described here is a case in point.

If your user account does not have admin rights, you need to start Windows PowerShell with an account that has the ability to unlock a user account. To do this, you right-click the Windows PowerShell icon while holding down the Shift key; this allows you to select Run As Different User from the Tasks menu.

When you start Windows PowerShell back up with an account that has rights to unlock users, the Active Directory module needs to load again. You then check to ensure that you can still locate the locked-out user accounts. When you can do that, you pipeline the results of the *Search-ADAccount* cmdlet to *Unlock-ADAccount*. A quick check ensures you have unlocked all the locked-out accounts. The series of commands is shown here.

```
Search-ADAccount -LockedOut
Search-ADAccount -LockedOut | Unlock-ADAccount
Search-ADAccount -LockedOut
```

The commands and associated output are shown in Figure 16-5.

```
powershell                                                    —  □  ×

[dc1]: PS C:\> Search-ADAccount -LockedOut


AccountExpirationDate :
DistinguishedName     : CN=Bob,CN=Users,DC=NWTraders,DC=com
Enabled               : True
LastLogonDate         : 4/20/2015 9:25:58 AM
LockedOut             : True
Name                  : Bob
ObjectClass           : user
ObjectGUID            : fbaf1c57-e97d-4fa1-b507-4d319c443152
PasswordExpired       : False
PasswordNeverExpires  : True
SamAccountName        : Bob
SID                   : S-1-5-21-1893272736-1364514926-820579994-19781
UserPrincipalName     : Bob@NWTraders.com



[dc1]: PS C:\> Search-ADAccount -LockedOut | Unlock-ADAccount
[dc1]: PS C:\> Search-ADAccount -LockedOut
[dc1]: PS C:\> _
```

FIGURE 16-5 Use the Active Directory module to find and to unlock user accounts.

Note Keep in mind that the command *Search-ADAccount -LockedOut | Unlock-ADAccount* will unlock every account that you have permission to unlock. In most cases, you will want to investigate prior to unlocking all locked-out accounts. If you do not want to unlock all locked-out accounts, use the *-Confirm* parameter to be prompted prior to unlocking an account.

Finding disabled users

Luckily, by using Windows PowerShell and the Active Directory cmdlets, you can retrieve the disabled users from your domain with a single line of code. The command appears following. (Keep in mind that running this command automatically imports the Active Directory module into the current Windows PowerShell host.)

```
Get-ADUser -Filter 'enabled -eq $false' -Server dc1
```

Not only is the command a single line of code, it is also a single line of *readable* code. You get users from AD DS; you use a filter that looks for the *enabled* property set to *false*. You also specify that you want to query a server named dc1 (the name of one of the domain controllers on my network). In addition, if you want to find out what type of information would be returned by the command, you can specify a particular number of records to return by using the *ResultSetSize* parameter. I like to do this before I go to the trouble of running a command that might take a long time to return. The command and the associated output are shown in Figure 16-6.

FIGURE 16-6 You can use *Get-ADUser* to find disabled user accounts.

If you want to work with a specific user, you can use the *-Identity* parameter. The *-Identity* parameter accepts several things: *distinguishedName, objectSid (SID), objectGUID (GUID),* and *sAMAccountName.* Probably the easiest one to use is the *sAMAccountName.* This command and associated output are shown here.

```
PS C:\> Get-ADUser -Server dc3 -Identity teresa
DistinguishedName : CN=Teresa Wilson,OU=Charlotte,Dc=Nwtraders,dc=Com
Enabled           : True
GivenName         : Teresa
Name              : Teresa Wilson
ObjectClass       : user
ObjectGUID        : 75f12010-b952-4d16-9b22-3ada7d26eed8
SamAccountName    : Teresa
SID               : S-1-5-21-1457956834-3844189528-3541350385-1104
Surname           : Wilson
UserPrincipalName : Teresa@NWTraders.Com
```

To use the *distinguishedName* value for the *-Identity* parameter, you need to supply it inside a pair of quotation marks—either single or double. This command and associated output are shown here.

```
PS C:\> Get-ADUser -Server dc3 -Identity 'CN=Teresa Wilson,OU=Charlotte,
Dc=Nwtraders,dc=Com'

DistinguishedName : CN=Teresa Wilson,OU=Charlotte,Dc=Nwtraders,dc=Com
Enabled           : True
GivenName         : Teresa
Name              : Teresa Wilson
ObjectClass       : user
ObjectGUID        : 75f12010-b952-4d16-9b22-3ada7d26eed8
SamAccountName    : Teresa
SID               : S-1-5-21-1457956834-3844189528-3541350385-1104
Surname           : Wilson
UserPrincipalName : Teresa@NWTraders.Com
```

It is not necessary to use quotation marks when using the SID for the value of the *-Identity* parameter. This command and associated output are shown here.

```
PS C:\> Get-ADUser -Server dc3 -Identity S-1-5-21-1457956834-3844189528-
3541350385-1104

DistinguishedName : CN=Teresa Wilson,OU=Charlotte,Dc=Nwtraders,dc=Com
Enabled           : True
GivenName         : Teresa
Name              : Teresa Wilson
ObjectClass       : user
ObjectGUID        : 75f12010-b952-4d16-9b22-3ada7d26eed8
SamAccountName    : Teresa
SID               : S-1-5-21-1457956834-3844189528-3541350385-1104
Surname           : Wilson
UserPrincipalName : Teresa@NWTraders.Com
```

Again, you can also use the *ObjectGUID* for the *-Identity* parameter value. This does not require quotation marks either. This command and associated output are shown here.

```
PS C:\> Get-ADUser -Server dc3 -Identity 75f12010-b952-4d16-9b22-
3ada7d26eed8

DistinguishedName : CN=Teresa Wilson,OU=Charlotte,Dc=Nwtraders,dc=Com
Enabled           : True
GivenName         : Teresa
Name              : Teresa Wilson
ObjectClass       : user
ObjectGUID        : 75f12010-b952-4d16-9b22-3ada7d26eed8
SamAccountName    : Teresa
SID               : S-1-5-21-1457956834-3844189528-3541350385-1104
Surname           : Wilson
UserPrincipalName : Teresa@NWTraders.Com
```

Finding unused user accounts

To obtain a listing of all the users in Active Directory, supply a wildcard to the *-Filter* parameter of the *Get-ADUser* cmdlet. This technique is shown here.

```
Get-ADUser -Filter *
```

If you want to change the base of the search operations, use the *-SearchBase* parameter. The *-SearchBase* parameter accepts an LDAP style of naming. The following command changes the search base to the TestOU OU.

```
Get-ADUser -Filter * -SearchBase "ou=TestOU,dc=nwtraders,dc=com"
```

When you use the *Get-ADUser* cmdlet, only a certain subset of user properties are displayed (10 properties, to be exact). These properties will be displayed when you pipeline the results to *Format-List* and use a wildcard and the *-Force* parameter, as shown here.

```
PS C:\> Get-ADUser -Identity bob | format-list -Property * -Force

DistinguishedName : CN=bob,OU=TestOU,DC=NWTraders,DC=Com
Enabled           : True
GivenName         : bob
Name              : bob
ObjectClass       : user
ObjectGUID        : 5cae3acf-f194-4e07-a466-789f9ad5c84a
SamAccountName    : bob
SID               : S-1-5-21-3746122405-834892460-3960030898-3601
Surname           :
UserPrincipalName : bob@NWTraders.Com
PropertyNames     : {DistinguishedName, Enabled, GivenName, Name...}
PropertyCount     : 10
```

Anyone who knows very much about AD DS knows that there are certainly more than 10 properties associated with a *User* object. If you try to display a known property, such as the *whenCreated* property, it is not returned by default when using the *Get-ADUser* cmdlet. This is shown here.

```
PS C:\> Get-ADUser -Identity bob | Format-List -Property name, whenCreated

name        : bob
whencreated :
```

The *whenCreated* property for the *User* object has a value—it just is not displayed. However, suppose you were looking for users who had never logged on to the system. Suppose you used a query such as the one shown here, and you were going to base a delete operation upon the results—the consequences could be disastrous.

```
PS C:\> Get-ADUser -Filter * | Format-Table -Property name, LastLogonDate

name                                LastLogonDate
----                                -------------
Administrator
Guest
krbtgt
testuser2
ed
SystemMailbox{1f05a927-a261-4eb4-8360-8...
SystemMailbox{e0dc1c29-89c3-4034-b678-e...
FederatedEmail.4c1f4d8b-8179-4148-93bf-...
Test
TestChild
<results truncated>
```

To retrieve a property that is not a member of the default 10 properties, you must select it by using the *-Property* parameter. The reason that *Get-ADUser* does not automatically return all properties and their associated values is because of performance issues on large networks—there is no reason to return a large data set when a small data set will suffice. To display the *name* and the *whenCreated* date for the user named bob, you can use the following command.

```
PS C:\> Get-ADUser -Identity bob -Properties whencreated | Format-List -Property name
, whencreated

name        : bob
whencreated : 6/11/2010 8:19:52 AM
```

To retrieve all of the properties associated with a *User* object, use the wildcard * for the *-Properties* parameter value. You would use a command similar to the one shown here.

```
Get-ADUser -Identity kimakers -Properties *
```

Both the command and the results associated with the command to return all user properties appear in Figure 16-7.

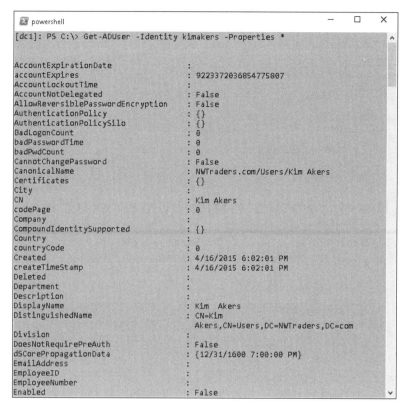

FIGURE 16-7 Use the *Get-ADUser* cmdlet to display all user properties.

To produce a listing of all the users and their last logon date, you can use a command similar to the one shown here. This is a single command that might wrap onto additional lines depending on your screen resolution.

```
Get-ADUser -Filter * -Properties "LastLogonDate" |
sort-object -property lastlogondate -descending |
Format-Table -property name, lastlogondate -AutoSize
```

The output produces a nice table. Both the command and the output associated with the command to obtain the time a user last logged on appear in Figure 16-8.

```
powershell                                            —   □   ✕
[dc1]: PS C:\> Get-ADUser -Filter * -Properties "LastLogonDate" | Sort-Object -P
roperty LastLogonDate -Descending | Format-Table -Property name, lastlogondate -
AutoSize

name                  lastlogondate
----                  -------------
Administrator         6/23/2015 1:23:18 PM
Bob                   4/20/2015 9:25:58 AM
Sc Oveson
Ro Owens
Jo Orton
Jó Óskarsson
In Ozhogina
Wi Pais
Ja Pak
```

FIGURE 16-8 Use the *Get-ADUser* cmdlet to identify the last logon times for users.

Updating Active Directory objects: Step-by-step exercises

In these exercises, you will search for users in a specific OU that do not have a *description* attribute populated. You will create a script that updates this value. In addition, you will change the password for users in Active Directory.

> **Note** To complete these exercises, you will need access to a Windows-based server running AD DS. Modify the domain names listed in the exercises to match the name of your domain.

Using the Active Directory module to update Active Directory objects

1. Open the Windows PowerShell ISE or some other script editor.

2. Use the *Import-Module* cmdlet to import the Active Directory module.

   ```
   Import-Module ActiveDirectory
   ```

3. Set the *$users* and *$you* variables to *$null*.

   ```
   $users = $you = $null
   ```

4. Use the *Get-ADUser* cmdlet to retrieve users from the TestOU OU in the nwtraders.com domain. The *Filter* parameter is required, so you give it a wildcard * to tell it you want everything returned. In addition, you specify that you want the *description* property returned in the search results.

   ```
   $users = Get-ADUser -SearchBase "ou=testou,dc=nwtraders,dc=com" -filter * '
       -property description
   ```

5. Use the *ForEach* statement to walk through the collection. Inside the collection, use the static *isNullOrEmpty* method from the *system.string* Microsoft .NET Framework class to check the *description* property on the *User* object. If the property is empty or null, display a string that states that the script will modify the *User* object. The code to do this is shown here.

```
ForEach($user in $users)
  {
   if([string]::isNullOrEmpty($user.description))
     {
       "modifying $($user.name)"
```

6. Use the *Set-ADUser* cmdlet to modify the user. Pass the *-Identity* parameter a distinguished name. Use the *-Description* parameter to hold the value to add to the *description* attribute on the object. This command is shown here.

```
Set-ADUser -Identity $user.distinguishedName -Description "added via script"
```

7. Increment the *$you* counter variable and display a summary string. This portion of the script is shown here.

```
$you++
    }
 }
 "modified $you users"
```

8. Compare your script with the one that is shown here.

```
SetADPropertyADCmdlets.ps1
Import-Module ActiveDirectory
 $users = $you = $null
 $users = Get-ADUser -SearchBase "ou=testou,dc=nwtraders,dc=com" -filter * '
  -property description
 ForEach($user in $users)
   {
    if([string]::isNullOrEmpty($user.description))
      {
        "modifying $($user.name)"
        Set-ADUser -Identity $user.distinguishedName -Description "added via script"
        $you++
      }
 }
 "modified $you users"
```

In the following exercise, you will change a user's password.

Changing user passwords

1. Open the Windows PowerShell console with administrator rights.

2. Use the *Get-Credential* cmdlet to retrieve and store credentials that have permission on a remote domain controller. Store the credentials in a variable named *$credential*.

   ```
   $credential = Get-Credential
   ```

3. Use the *Enter-PSSession* cmdlet to enter a remote Windows PowerShell session on a domain controller that contains the Active Directory module.

   ```
   Enter-PSSession -ComputerName DC1 -Credential $credential
   ```

4. Use the *Get-ADUser* cmdlet to identify a user whose password you want to reset.

   ```
   Get-ADUser ed
   ```

5. Use the *Set-ADAccountPassword* cmdlet to reset the password.

   ```
   Set-ADAccountPassword -Identity ed -Reset
   ```

6. A warning appears stating that the remote computer is requesting to read a line securely. Enter the new password for the user.

   ```
   Password
   ```

7. A second warning appears with a prompt to repeat the password. The warning itself is the same as the previous warning about reading a secure line. Enter the same password you previously entered.

8. Enter **Get-History** to review the commands you entered during the remote session.

9. Enter **Exit** to exit the remote session.

10. Enter **Get-History** to review the commands you entered prior to entering the remote session.

    This concludes the exercise.

> **Note** If you need to work with local user accounts, download the Local User Management module from the Microsoft Script Center Script Repository. This module provides the ability to create, modify, and delete both local users and groups. It also permits you to change local user account passwords.

Chapter 16 quick reference

To	Do this
Find domain FSMO role holders	Use the *Get-ADDomain* cmdlet and select *PDCEmulator, RIDMaster,* and *InfrastructureMaster.*
Find forest FSMO role holders	Use the *Get-ADForest* cmdlet and select *SchemaMaster* and *DomainNamingMaster.*
Rename a site in AD DS	Use the *Get-ADObject* cmdlet to retrieve the site and the *Rename-ADObject* cmdlet to set a new name.
Create a new user in AD DS	Use the *New-ADUser* cmdlet.
Find locked-out user accounts in AD DS	Use the *Search-ADAccount* cmdlet with the *-LockedOut* parameter.
Unlock a user account in AD DS	Use the *Unlock-ADAccount* cmdlet.
Set a user's password in AD DS	Use the *Set-ADAccountPassword* cmdlet.

Deploying Active Directory by using Windows PowerShell

After completing this chapter, you will be able to

- Use the Active Directory module to deploy a new forest and a new domain controller.

- Use the Active Directory module to add a new domain controller to an existing domain.

- Use the Active Directory module to deploy a read-only domain controller.

Using the Active Directory module to deploy a new forest

Deploying Microsoft Active Directory Domain Services (AD DS) is not a simple matter. There are prerequisites that must be met and multiple items that need to be configured. One of the first things that you might need to do is set the script execution policy. Although the easiest way to do this is via Group Policy, if you are configuring the first domain controller in the first domain in a new forest, you do not have that luxury. To set the script execution policy, use the *Set-ExecutionPolicy* cmdlet and set it to something like *remotesigned*. The command is shown following. (The command must execute with admin rights, but more than likely you will be logged on as an administrator anyway, if you are just beginning your configuration.)

```
Set-ExecutionPolicy remotesigned -force
```

Some of the infrastructure prerequisites are listed here:

- Ensure that the server has the correct name.

- Set a static IP address configuration.

- Ensure that the DNS Server Windows feature is deployed and configured.

In addition to infrastructure prerequisites, the following role-based prerequisites need to be deployed:

- The Active Directory module for Windows PowerShell

- The Active Directory Administrative Center tools

- AD DS snap-ins and command-line tools

Luckily, all of these tools are installable via the *ServerManager* module and the *Add-Windows-Feature* cmdlet. In fact, from a Windows feature standpoint, the *rsat-ad-tools* feature group gives you everything you need here. The AddADPrereqs.ps1 script sets a static IP address by using the *New-NetIPAddress* cmdlet. To determine the interface index, the *Get-NetAdapter* cmdlet is used. This portion of the script is shown here.

```
# set static IP address
$ipaddress = "192.168.0.225"
$ipprefix = "24"
$ipgw = "192.168.0.1"
$ipdns = "192.168.0.225"
$ipif = (Get-NetAdapter).ifIndex
New-NetIPAddress -IPAddress $ipaddress -PrefixLength $ipprefix `
    -InterfaceIndex $ipif -DefaultGateway $ipgw
```

When the new IP address is assigned, the *Rename-Computer* cmdlet assigns a new name to the computer. The *Rename-Computer* cmdlet has a *-restart* parameter, but the AddADPrereqs.ps1 script delays restarting the script until the end, and therefore the *restart* parameter is not used. This portion of the script is shown here.

```
# rename the computer
$newname = "dc10"
Rename-Computer -NewName $newname -force
```

Now that the computer has received a new IP address and has been renamed, it is time to add the features. The first thing the script does is create a log file in a directory named poshlog. This log will hold details resulting from adding the features. In addition, when the configuration completes, a *Get-WindowsFeature* command runs to gather the installed features. The result is written to a log file in the poshlog directory. The *Add-WindowsFeature* cmdlet appears to accept an array for the features to be installed, but when you attempt to add multiple features with a single call to the *Add-Windows-Feature* cmdlet, the secondary features get lost in the call. Therefore, it is best to add tools one at a time. This portion of the script installs the AD DS tools that include the Active Directory Windows PowerShell module. The command is shown here.

```
# install features
$featureLogPath = "c:\poshlog\featurelog.txt"
New-Item $featureLogPath -ItemType file -Force
$addsTools = "RSAT-AD-Tools"

Add-WindowsFeature $addsTools
Get-WindowsFeature | Where installed >> $featureLogPath
```

The last thing to accomplish here is restarting the computer. This is performed via a simple call to the *Restart-Computer* cmdlet. This command is shown here.

```
# restart the computer
Restart-Computer
```

The complete AddAdPrereqs.ps1 script is shown here.

AddAdPrereqs.ps1

```
# set static IP address
$ipaddress = "192.168.0.225"
$ipprefix = "24"
$ipgw = "192.168.0.1"
$ipdns = "192.168.0.225"
$ipif = (Get-NetAdapter).ifIndex
New-NetIPAddress -IPAddress $ipaddress -PrefixLength $ipprefix `
    -InterfaceIndex $ipif -DefaultGateway $ipgw

# rename the computer
$newname = "dc10"
Rename-Computer -NewName $newname -force

# install features
$featureLogPath = "c:\poshlog\featurelog.txt"
New-Item $featureLogPath -ItemType file -Force
$addsTools = "RSAT-AD-Tools"

Add-WindowsFeature $addsTools
Get-WindowsFeature | Where installed >>$featureLogPath

# restart the computer
Restart-Computer
```

After the computer restarts, log on and check things. The Server Manager utility immediately launches and provides feedback that the name change and the IP address change completed successfully. Server Manager is shown in Figure 17-1.

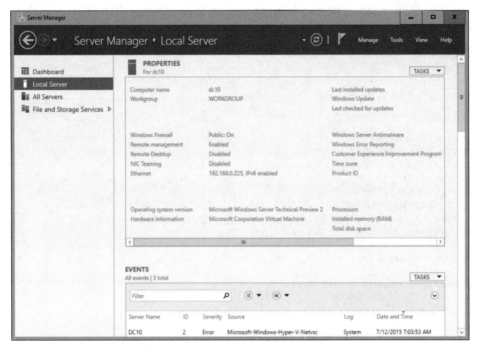

FIGURE 17-1 After the AddAdPrereqs.ps1 script is run, Server Manager appears and confirms that the name change and the IP address assignment completed successfully.

Next, you'll verify that the roles and features have been added properly. To do this, use the FeatureLog.txt log file that was created prior to the restart. Figure 17-2 shows what will be displayed if the features and roles have been added properly.

FIGURE 17-2 The FeatureLog.txt file confirms that the roles and features have been added successfully to the computer.

When you have your computer renamed, with a static IP address and RSAT installed, it is time to add the AD DS role, the DNS Server role, and the Group Policy management feature. The first thing to do is add the log path for the report at the end of the script. When this is done, the script starts a job named *addfeature*. The use of a job allows the script to wait until the job completes prior to executing the next step of the script. Because the script adds the features in the background, no progress tests appear in the foreground. Each of the *Add-WindowsFeature* commands includes all of the subfeatures and the management tools. This is a great way to ensure that you obtain the bits your specific feature needs. You can always fine-tune it at a later time. When the job executes, the *Wait-Job* cmdlet pauses the script until the *addfeature* job completes. Then it returns the completed job object. At this time, the final command is a *Get-WindowsFeature* cmdlet call that writes all installed features to the log file. The complete Add-ADFeatures.ps1 script is shown here.

Add-ADFeatures.ps1

```
#Install AD DS, DNS and GPMC
$featureLogPath = "c:\poshlog\featurelog.txt"
start-job -Name addFeature -ScriptBlock {
  Add-WindowsFeature -Name "ad-domain-services" -IncludeAllSubFeature -IncludeManagementTools
  Add-WindowsFeature -Name "dns" -IncludeAllSubFeature -IncludeManagementTools
  Add-WindowsFeature -Name "gpmc" -IncludeAllSubFeature -IncludeManagementTools    }
Wait-Job -Name addFeature
Get-WindowsFeature | Where installed >> $featureLogPath
```

When the script finishes running, the featurelog text file can be examined. The log is shown in Figure 17-3.

FIGURE 17-3 The feature log details all installed features and roles on the system.

Now it is time to create the new forest, and add the server as the first domain controller in the newly created forest. The tool required is contained in the *ADDSDeployment* module. The Install-NewForest.ps1 script is essentially one cmdlet: *Install-ADDSForest*. The domain name and the Net-BIOS domain name appear as variables. When the script first runs, it prompts for an Active Directory password. This password becomes the administrator password for the new domain. Following the installation, the function automatically restarts the computer to complete configuration. The complete InstallNewForest.ps1 script is shown here.

InstallNewForest.ps1

```
# Create New Forest, add Domain Controller
$domainname = "nwtraders.msft"
$netbiosName = "NWTRADERS"

 Import-Module ADDSDeployment
 Install-ADDSForest -CreateDnsDelegation:$false `
  -DatabasePath "C:\Windows\NTDS" `
  -DomainMode "Win2012" `
  -DomainName $domainname `
  -DomainNetbiosName $netbiosName `
  -ForestMode "Win2012" `
  -InstallDns:$true `
  -LogPath "C:\Windows\NTDS" `
  -NoRebootOnCompletion:$false `
  -SysvolPath "C:\Windows\SYSVOL" `
  -Force:$true
```

While the script is running, a progress bar appears. This is shown in Figure 17-4.

FIGURE 17-4 A progress bar is displayed while the script runs. This lets you know the progress of the operations.

When the script finishes running, a quick check of the DNS Manager tool should reveal that Domain Name System (DNS) is set up properly. The nwtraders.msft forward-lookup zone should be configured properly, and an A record, NS record, and SOA record should be configured. This is shown in Figure 17-5.

FIGURE 17-5 Following the running of the InstallNewForest.ps1 script, DNS Manager reveals a properly set up forward-lookup zone.

Adding a new domain controller to an existing domain

After you install the first domain controller into your forest root, it is time to add a second domain controller to the domain. The process is similar to the steps required for configuring and installing the first domain controller. There are the usual system configuration steps that must take place, such as setting a static IP address, renaming the computer, and adding the AD DS role and tools. Because this is a second domain controller, it is not necessary to add the DNS server role if you do not want to do so. But the server must have the ability to resolve names, so you must assign a DNS server to the DNS client. To add a DNS server to the IP configuration, use the *Set-DNSClientServerAddress* cmdlet. Specify the same interface index that the *New-NetIPAddress* cmdlet uses. Finally, specify the DNS server IP address to the *-ServerAddresses* parameter. This portion of the script is shown here.

```
#set static IP address
$ipaddress = "192.168.0.226"
$ipprefix = "24"
$ipgw = "192.168.0.1"
$ipdns = "192.168.0.225"
$ipif = (Get-NetAdapter).ifIndex
New-NetIPAddress -IPAddress $ipaddress -PrefixLength $ipprefix -InterfaceIndex $ipif -
DefaultGateway $ipgw
Set-DnsClientServerAddress -InterfaceIndex $ipif -ServerAddresses $ipdns
```

Following the IP address configuration, it is time to rename the server. This portion of the script is exactly the same as in the AddAdPrereqs.ps1 script and will not be discussed here. Note that because only the AD DS pieces are required, the script goes ahead and adds the role-based portion of the installation. This reduces the need for an additional script. The portion of the script that installs the AD DS role is shown here.

```
#install roles and features
$featureLogPath = "c:\poshlog\featurelog.txt"
New-Item $featureLogPath -ItemType file -Force

Add-WindowsFeature -Name "ad-domain-services" -IncludeAllSubFeature -IncludeManagementTools
Get-WindowsFeature | Where installed >>$featureLogPath
```

Finally, it is time to restart the server. To do that, use the *Restart-Computer* cmdlet. The complete Add-DNDSPrereqsDC2.ps1 script is shown here.

Add-DNDSPrereqsDC2.ps1

```
#set static IP address
$ipaddress = "192.168.0.226"
$ipprefix = "24"
$ipgw = "192.168.0.1"
$ipdns = "192.168.0.225"
$ipif = (Get-NetAdapter).ifIndex
New-NetIPAddress -IPAddress $ipaddress -PrefixLength $ipprefix -InterfaceIndex $ipif -
DefaultGateway $ipgw
Set-DnsClientServerAddress -InterfaceIndex $ipif -ServerAddresses $ipdns

#rename the computer
$newname = "dc28508"
Rename-Computer -NewName $newname -force

#install roles and features
$featureLogPath = "c:\poshlog\featurelog.txt"
New-Item $featureLogPath -ItemType file -Force

Add-WindowsFeature -Name "ad-domain-services" -IncludeAllSubFeature -IncludeManagementTools
Get-WindowsFeature | Where installed >>$featureLogPath

#restart the computer
Restart-Computer
```

After the computer restarts, it is time to add the server to the domain as a domain controller. The first step is to import the *ADDSDeployment* module. Next, the *Install-ADDSDomainController* cmdlet is used to add the server as a domain controller to an existing domain. Because you did not want to install DNS, the *-InstallDns* parameter receives *$false*. In addition, the *-ReplicationSourceDC* parameter is set to the first domain controller that was built.

The complete CreateAdditionalDC.ps1 script is shown here.

CreateAdditionalDC.ps1

```
Import-Module ADDSDeployment
Install-ADDSDomainController `
-NoGlobalCatalog:$false `
-CreateDnsDelegation:$False `
-Credential (Get-Credential) `
-CriticalReplicationOnly:$false `
-DatabasePath "C:\Windows\NTDS" `
-DomainName "nwtraders.msft" `
-InstallDns:$False `
-LogPath "C:\Windows\NTDS" `
-NoRebootOnCompletion:$false `
-ReplicationSourceDC "dc8508.nwtraders.msft" `
-SiteName "Default-First-Site-Name" `
-SysvolPath "C:\Windows\SYSVOL" `
-Force:$true
```

When the server is finished restarting, it is time to log on to the server by using domain credentials. The server needs a little time to complete configuration. Back on the first domain controller, Active Directory Users And Computers shows domain controllers in the Domain Controllers organizational unit (OU). This is shown in Figure 17-6.

FIGURE 17-6 Active Directory Users And Computers shows domain controllers in the Domain Controllers OU.

Adding a read-only domain controller

Adding a read-only domain controller to an existing domain is only slightly different from adding a full domain controller to an existing domain. The process is a two-step procedure. First, the prerequisites must be installed, and then, following the restart, the server is configured as a read-only domain controller. The prerequisite installation script can be simplified a bit from the prerequisite script developed in the previous section. The first portion of the script creates the static IP address and sets the DNS client to point to the DNS server running on the first domain controller that was installed. This portion of the script is the same as the Add-DNDSPrereqsDC2.ps1 script in the previous section. Next, the server is renamed via the *Rename-Computer* cmdlet. This simple command is the same one that was used in the previous scripts.

The big change involves using the *Add-WindowsFeature* cmdlet to add the AD DS role and all associated features and management tools. This is a great shortcut that simplifies your task. The change is shown here.

```
#install AD DS Role and tools
Add-WindowsFeature -Name "ad-domain-services" -IncludeAllSubFeature -IncludeManagementTools
```

The last step is to use the *Restart-Computer* cmdlet to restart the server. The complete CreateDC3-Prereqs.ps1 script is shown here.

CreateDC3Prereqs.ps1

```
#set static IP address
$ipaddress = "192.168.0.227"
$ipprefix = "24"
$ipgw = "192.168.0.1"
$ipdns = "192.168.0.225"
$ipif = (Get-NetAdapter).ifIndex
New-NetIPAddress -IPAddress $ipaddress -PrefixLength $ipprefix -InterfaceIndex $ipif -
DefaultGateway $ipgw
Set-DnsClientServerAddress -InterfaceIndex $ipif -ServerAddresses $ipdns

#rename the computer
$newname = "dc38508"
Rename-Computer -NewName $newname -force

#install AD DS Role and tools
Add-WindowsFeature -Name "ad-domain-services" -IncludeAllSubFeature -IncludeManagementTools

#restart the computer
Restart-Computer
```

When the server has been given IP configuration and you've loaded the prerequisites, it is time to add a read-only domain controller to the domain. The script for this first imports the *ADDSDeployment* module, and then it calls the *Install-ADDomainController* cmdlet. Because the domain controller is read-only, the *AllowPasswordReplicationAccountName* parameter must be used to specify whose passwords will be replicated. This value is an array. The credentials for contacting the domain must be supplied. To do this, you use the *Get-Credential* cmdlet and enter the domain admin credentials. Next, the Directory Restore Password prompt appears. In addition to specifying who can replicate the passwords, you must also specify who cannot replicate passwords. This array is entered on multiple lines to make it easier to read. This scenario did not call for installing and configuring DNS on this particular machine, and therefore that role is not added. The complete CreateReadOnlyDomainController. ps1 script is shown here.

CreateReadOnlyDomainController.ps1

```
Import-Module ADDSDeployment
Install-ADDSDomainController `
-AllowPasswordReplicationAccountName @("NWTRADERS\Allowed RODC Password Replication Group") `
-NoGlobalCatalog:$false `
-Credential (Get-Credential -Credential nwtraders\administrator) `
-CriticalReplicationOnly:$false `
-DatabasePath "C:\Windows\NTDS" `
-DenyPasswordReplicationAccountName @("BUILTIN\Administrators",
  "BUILTIN\Server Operators", "BUILTIN\Backup Operators",
  "BUILTIN\Account Operators",
  "NWTRADERS\Denied RODC Password Replication Group") `
-DomainName "nwtraders.msft" `
-InstallDns:$false `
-LogPath "C:\Windows\NTDS" `
-NoRebootOnCompletion:$false `
-ReadOnlyReplica:$true `
-SiteName "Default-First-Site-Name" `
-SysvolPath "C:\Windows\SYSVOL" `
-Force:$true
```

When the script runs, Active Directory Users And Computers on the first domain controller refreshes to include the new read-only domain controller. This is shown in Figure 17-7.

FIGURE 17-7 Active Directory Users And Computers shows the newly added read-only domain controller.

Installing domain controller prerequisites and adding to a forest: Step-by-step exercises

In the first exercise, you will install the base requirements for a domain controller on a fresh installation of Windows Server. This exercise will assign a static IP address, rename the server, and install the AD DS admin tools. In the subsequent exercise, you will add a new domain controller to a new forest.

Installing domain controller prerequisites

1. Log on to your server by using the administrator account.

2. Open the Windows PowerShell ISE.

3. Set the script execution policy to *remotesigned*. The command is shown here.

   ```
   Set-ExecutionPolicy remotesigned -force
   ```

4. Use the *Get-NetAdapter* cmdlet to determine the interface index number of the active network adapter. The command is shown here.

   ```
   $ipif = (Get-NetAdapter).ifIndex
   ```

5. Use the *New-NetIPAddress* cmdlet to assign a static IP address to the active network adapter. Specify the *ipaddress, prefixlength, interfaceindex, and defaultgateway* values that are appropriate for your network. Sample values are shown here.

   ```
   $ipaddress = "192.168.0.225"
   $ipprefix = "24"
   $ipgw = "192.168.0.1"
   $ipdns = "192.168.0.225"
   $ipif = (Get-NetAdapter).ifIndex
   New-NetIPAddress -ipaddress $ipaddress -prefixlength $ipprefix `
       -interfaceindex $ipif -defaultgateway $ipgw
   ```

6. Use the *Rename-Computer* cmdlet to rename the computer. Specify a new name that follows your naming convention. The command is shown here with a sample name.

   ```
   $newname = "dc8508"
   Rename-Computer -NewName $newname -force
   ```

7. Add the AD DS, DNS, and Group Policy Management Console (GPMC) features and roles, including all subfeatures and tools, by using the *Add-WindowsFeature* cmdlet. The command is shown here.

```
Add-WindowsFeature -Name "ad-domain-services" -IncludeAllSubFeature
-IncludeManagementTools
Add-WindowsFeature -Name "dns" -IncludeAllSubFeature -IncludeManagementTools
Add-WindowsFeature -Name "gpmc" -IncludeAllSubFeature -IncludeManagementTools
```

8. Restart the computer by using the *Restart-Computer* cmdlet. This command is shown here.

```
Restart-Computer -force
```

This concludes the exercise.

In the following exercise, you will add the server configured in the preceding exercise to a new forest.

Adding a domain controller to a new forest

1. Log on to the freshly restarted server as the administrator.

2. Open the Windows PowerShell ISE.

3. Create a variable for your fully qualified domain name. An example is shown here.

```
$domainname = "nwtraders.msft"
```

4. Create a variable to hold your NetBIOS name. Normally, the NetBIOS name is the same as your domain name without the extension. An example is shown here.

```
$netbiosName = "NWTRADERS"
```

5. Import the *ADDSDeployment* module. The command is shown here.

```
Import-Module ADDSDeployment
```

6. Add the *Install-ADDSForest* cmdlet to your script. Use tab expansion to simplify entry. Add the *-CreateDnsDelegation* parameter and set it to *false*. Add the line-continuation character at the end of the line. This is shown here.

```
Install-ADDSForest -CreateDnsDelegation:$false `
```

7. Specify the *-DatabasePath*, *-DomainMode*, *-DomainName*, and *-DomainNetbiosName* parameters. Use the domain name and NetBIOS name stored in the variables created earlier. Make sure you have line continuation at the end of each line. This portion of the command is shown here.

```
-DatabasePath "C:\Windows\NTDS" `
-DomainMode "Win2012" `
-DomainName $domainname `
-DomainNetbiosName $netbiosName
```

8. Specify the *-ForestMode*, *-LogPath*, and *-SysVolpath* parameters. In addition, you will need to supply options for the *-InstallDns* and *-NoRebootonCompletion* parameters. Use the *-Force* parameter. This portion of the script is shown here.

```
-ForestMode "Win2012" `
-InstallDns:$true `
-LogPath "C:\Windows\NTDS" `
-NoRebootOnCompletion:$false `
-SysvolPath "C:\Windows\SYSVOL" `
-Force:$true
```

9. Run the script. You will be prompted for a directory-restore password, and you'll have to enter it twice. Your server will also restart when the configuration is completed. To log on to the server, use your directory-restore password.

This concludes the exercise.

Chapter 17 quick reference

To	Do this
Assign a static IP address	Use the *New-NetIPAddress* cmdlet.
Install a new Windows feature or role	Use the *Add-WindowsFeature* cmdlet from the *ServerManager* module.
Restart a computer	Use the *Restart-Computer* cmdlet.
Find the index number of the active network adapter	Use *Get-NetAdapter* cmdlet and select the *IfIndex* property.
View what features or roles are installed on a server	Use the *Get-WindowsFeature* cmdlet, pipeline the results to the *Where-Object* cmdlet, and filter on the installed property.
Add a Windows role and the associated management tools	Use the *Add-WindowsFeature* cmdlet and specify the *-includemanagementtools* parameter.
Create a new forest	Use the *Install-ADDSForest* cmdlet from the *ADDSDeployment* module.

Debugging scripts

After completing this chapter, you will be able to

- Use the *Write-Debug* cmdlet to provide detailed information from a script.

- Use the *Set-StrictMode* cmdlet to prevent errors during development.

- Understand how to work with the Windows PowerShell debugger.

Understanding debugging in Windows PowerShell

No one enjoys debugging scripts. In fact, the best debugging is no debugging. It is also true that well-written, well-formatted, well-documented, and clearly constructed Windows PowerShell code requires less effort to debug than poorly formatted, undocumented spaghetti code. It is fair to say that debugging begins when you first open the Windows PowerShell ISE. Therefore, you might want to review Chapter 5, "Using Windows PowerShell scripts," Chapter 6, "Working with functions," and Chapter 7, "Creating advanced functions and modules," before you dive too deeply into this chapter.

If you can read and understand your Windows PowerShell code, chances are you will need to do very little debugging. But what if you do need to do some debugging? Well, just as excellent golfers spend many hours practicing chipping out of the sand trap in hopes that they will never need to use the skill, so too must competent Windows PowerShell scripters practice debugging skills in hopes that they will never need to apply the knowledge. Understanding the color coding of the Windows PowerShell ISE, detecting when closing quotation marks are missing, and knowing which pair of braces corresponds to which command can greatly reduce the debugging that might be needed later.

Understanding the three different types of errors

Debugging is a skill used to track down and eliminate errors from a Windows PowerShell script. There are three different types of errors that coders make: syntax errors, run-time errors, and logic errors.

Working with syntax errors

Syntax errors are the easiest to spot, and you usually correct them at design time—that is, while you have the Windows PowerShell ISE open and you are writing your script. Syntax errors generally get corrected at design time because the language parser runs in the background of the Windows PowerShell ISE, and when it detects a syntax error, it marks it with a squiggly line (thus indicating that the command requires additional parameters, decoration, or other attention). Seasoned scripters don't usually view this process as error correction, but as simply completing commands so that scripts run properly. (Learning to use IntelliSense inside the Windows PowerShell ISE is a good way to reduce these errors.) The most seasoned scripters learn to pay attention to the syntax parser and fix errors indicated by the red squiggly lines prior to actually running the code. When syntax errors aren't corrected, the error messages generated often provide good guidance toward correcting the offending command. Figure 18-1 illustrates a syntax error.

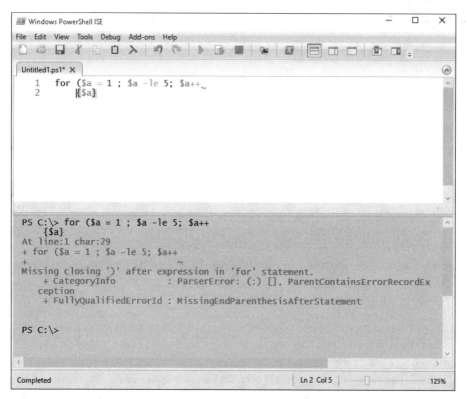

FIGURE 18-1 The Windows PowerShell ISE highlights potential errors with a red squiggly line. The error message states the offending command and often provides clarification for required changes.

Working with run-time errors

The syntax parser often does not detect run-time errors. Rather, run-time errors are problems that manifest themselves only when a script runs. Examples of these types of errors include an unavailable resource (such as a drive or a file), permission problems (such as a non-elevated user not having the rights to perform an operation), misspelled words, and code dependencies that are not met (such as access to a required module). The good thing is that many of these run-time errors are detectible from within the Windows PowerShell ISE due to the robust tab expansion mechanism in Windows PowerShell 3.0 and later. For example, it is possible to eliminate the Resource Not Available run-time error if you use tab expansion. This is possible because tab expansion works even to enumerate files in folders. Figure 18-2 shows an example of employing this feature when attempting to use the *Get-Content* cmdlet to read the contents of a file from a folder named *fso* on drive C.

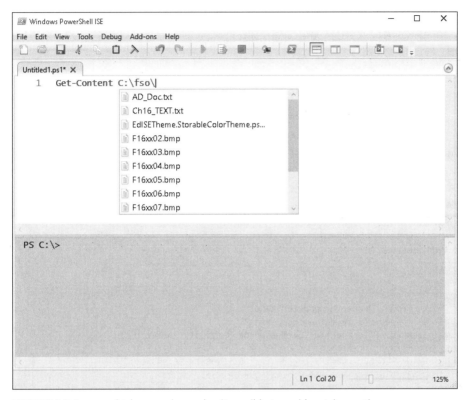

FIGURE 18-2 Improved tab expansion makes it possible to avoid certain run-time errors.

Unfortunately, tab expansion does not help when it comes to dealing with permission issues. Paying attention to the returned error message, however, helps to identify that you are dealing with a permission issue. In these cases, you usually receive an Access Is Denied error message. Such an error message appears here when bogususer attempts to access the DC1 server to perform a Windows Management Instrumentation (WMI) query.

```
PS C:\> Get-WmiObject win32_bios -cn dc1 -Credential iammred\bogususer
Get-WmiObject : Access is denied. (Exception from HRESULT: 0x80070005
(E_ACCESSDENIED))
At line:1 char:1
+ Get-WmiObject win32_bios -cn dc1 -Credential iammred\bogususer
+ ~~~~~~~~~~~~~~~~~~~~~~~~~~~~~~~~~~~~~~~~~~~~~~~~~~~~~~~~~~~~~~~~
    + CategoryInfo          : NotSpecified: (:) [Get-WmiObject],
  Unauthorized AccessException
    + FullyQualifiedErrorId : System.UnauthorizedAccessException,
  Microsoft.PowerShell.Commands.GetWmiObjectCommand
```

One way to detect run-time errors is to use the *Write-Debug* cmdlet to display the contents of variables that are most likely to contain erroneous data. By moving from a one-line command to a simple script containing variables and a variety of *Write-Debug* commands, you are automatically set up to perform the most common troubleshooting techniques on your script. For example, in the script that appears here, there are two main sources of run-time errors: the availability of the target computer and the credentials used to perform the connection.

RemoteWMISessionNoDebug.ps1

```
$credential = Get-Credential
$cn = Read-Host -Prompt "enter a computer name"
Get-WmiObject win32_bios -cn $cn -Credential $credential
```

By using the immediate window in the Windows PowerShell ISE, you can interrogate the value of the *$cn* and *$credential* variables. You can also use the *Test-Connection* cmdlet to check the status of the *$cn* computer. By performing these typical debugging steps in advance, you can get the script to display the pertinent information and therefore shortcut any debugging required to make the script work properly. The DebugRemoteWMISession.ps1 script shown here illustrates using the *Write-Debug* cmdlet to provide debugging information.

DebugRemoteWMISession.ps1

```
$oldDebugPreference = $DebugPreference
$DebugPreference = "continue"
$credential = Get-Credential
$cn = Read-Host -Prompt "enter a computer name"
Write-Debug "user name: $($credential.UserName)"
Write-Debug "password: $($credential.GetNetworkCredential().Password)"
Write-Debug "$cn is up:
  $(Test-Connection -Computername $cn -Count 1 -BufferSize 16 -quiet)"
Get-WmiObject win32_bios -cn $cn -Credential $credential
$DebugPreference = $oldDebugPreference
```

Figure 18-3 illustrates running the DebugRemoteWMISession.ps1 script inside the Windows PowerShell ISE to determine why the script fails. According to the output, the remote server, DC1, is available, but the user Bogus User with the password of BogusPassowrd is receiving an Access Is Denied error. It might be that the user does not have an account or access rights, or that the password is not really BogusPassowrd. The detailed debugging information should help to clarify the situation.

A better way to use the *Write-Debug* cmdlet is to combine it with the *[CmdletBinding()]* attribute at the beginning of the script (or function). Getting the *[CmdletBinding()]* attribute to work requires a couple of things. First, the *param* keyword must be present in the script. Second, the *[CmdletBinding()]* attribute must appear prior to the *param* keyword. After it is implemented, this change permits use of the common *-Debug* parameter. When calling the script or function, use of the *-Debug* switch parameter causes the debug stream from the *Write-Debug* cmdlet in the code to appear in the output. This simple change also means that your code no longer needs to change the value of the *$DebugPreference* variable. It also means that you do not need to create your own switch *-Debug* parameter and include code such as the following at the beginning of your script.

```
Param([switch]$debug)
If($debug) {$DebugPreference = "continue"}
```

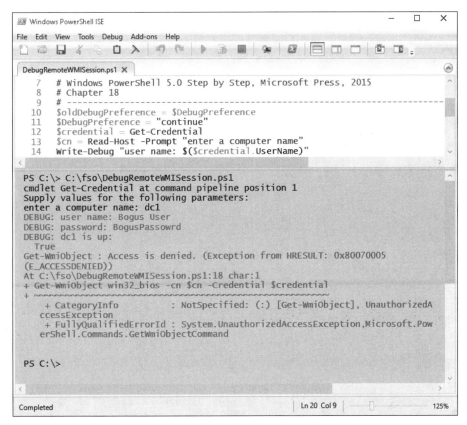

FIGURE 18-3 Detailed debugging makes solving run-time errors more manageable.

The revised and simplified DebugRemoteWMISession.ps1 script appears following, as Switch_DebugRemoteWMISession.ps1. The changes to the script include the addition of the *[CmdletBinding()]* attribute, the creation of a parameter named *cn*, and the setting of the default value to the name of the local computer. The other changes involve removing the toggling of the *$DebugPreference* variable. The complete script is shown here.

Switch_DebugRemoteWMISession.ps1

```
[CmdletBinding()]
Param($cn = $env:computername)
$credential = Get-Credential
Write-Debug "user name: $($credential.UserName)"
Write-Debug "password: $($credential.GetNetworkCredential().Password)"
Write-Debug "$cn is up:
  $(Test-Connection -Computername $cn -Count 1 -BufferSize 16 -quiet)"
Get-WmiObject win32_bios -cn $cn -Credential $credential
```

When the Switch_DebugRemoteWMISession.ps1 script runs with the *-Debug* switch from the Windows PowerShell console, in addition to displaying the debug stream, it also prompts to continue the script. This permits execution to be halted when an unexpected value is reached. Figure 18-4 illustrates this technique, in which a user named Bogus User, who wants to connect to a remote server named DC1, unexpectedly discovers that he is connecting to a workstation named C10.

FIGURE 18-4 Use the *-Debug* switch parameter to step through potential problems in a script.

Working with logic errors

Logic errors can be very difficult to detect because they might be present even when your script appears to be working correctly. But when things go wrong, they can be difficult to fix. Most of the time, just examining the values of variables does not solve the problem, because the code itself works fine. The problem often lies in what are called the *business rules* of the script. These are decisions the code makes that have nothing to do with the correct operation of, for example, a *switch* statement. At times, it might appear that the *switch* statement is not working correctly, because the wrong value is displayed at the end of the code, but quite often, the business rules themselves are causing the problem.

For a simple example of a logic error, consider the function called *my-function* that is shown here.

My-Function.ps1

```
Function my-function
{
 Param(
  [int]$a,
  [int]$b)
  "$a plus $b equals four"
}
```

The *my-function* function accepts two command-line parameters: *a* and *b*. It then combines the two values and outputs a string stating that the value is *four*. The tester performs four different tests, and each time the function performs as expected. These tests and the associated output are shown here.

```
PS C:\> C:\fso\my-function.ps1

PS C:\> my-function -a 2 -b 2
2 plus 2 equals four

PS C:\> my-function -a 1 -b 3
1 plus 3 equals four

PS C:\> my-function -a 0 -b 4
0 plus 4 equals four

PS C:\> my-function -a 3 -b 1
3 plus 1 equals four
```

When the function goes into production, however, users begin to complain. Most of the time, the function displays incorrect output. However, the users also report that no errors are generated when the function runs. What is the best way to solve the logic problem? Simply adding a couple of *Write-Debug* commands to display the values of the variables *a* and *b* will probably not lead to the correct solution. A better way is to step through the code one line at a time and examine the associated output. The easy way to do this is to use the *Set-PSDebug* cmdlet—the topic of the next section in this chapter.

Using the *Set-PSDebug* cmdlet

The *Set-PSDebug* cmdlet has been around since Windows PowerShell 1.0. This does not mean that it is a neglected feature, but rather that it does what it needs to do. For performing basic debugging quickly and easily, you cannot beat the combination of features that are available. There are three things you can do with the *Set-PSDebug* cmdlet: you can trace script execution in an automated fashion, you can step through the script interactively, and you can enable *strict mode* to force good Windows PowerShell coding practices. Each of these features will be examined in this section. The *Set-PSDebug* cmdlet is not designed to do heavy debugging; it is a lightweight tool that is useful when you want to produce a quick trace or rapidly step through a script.

Tracing the script

One of the simplest ways to debug a script is to turn on script-level tracing. When you turn on script-level tracing, each command that is executed is displayed to the Windows PowerShell console. By watching the commands as they are displayed to the Windows PowerShell console, you can determine whether a line of code in your script executes or whether it is being skipped. To enable script tracing, you use the *Set-PSDebug* cmdlet and specify one of three levels for the *-Trace* parameter. The three levels of tracing are shown in Table 18-1.

TABLE 18-1 *Set-PSDebug* trace levels

Trace level	Meaning
0	Turns script tracing off.
1	Traces each line of the script as it is executed. Lines in the script that are not executed are not traced. Does not display variable assignments, function calls, or external scripts.
2	Traces each line of the script as it is executed. Displays variable assignments, function calls, and external scripts. Lines in the script that are not executed are not traced.

To understand the process of tracing a script and the differences between the different trace levels, examine the CreateRegistryKey.ps1 script. It contains a single function called *Add-RegistryValue*. In the *Add-RegistryValue* function, the *Test-Path* cmdlet is used to determine whether the registry key exists. If the registry key exists, a property value is set. If the registry key does not exist, the registry key is created and a property value is set. The *Add-RegistryValue* function is called when the script executes. The complete CreateRegistryKey.ps1 script is shown here.

CreateRegistryKey.ps1

```
Function Add-RegistryValue
{
 Param ($key,$value)
 $scriptRoot = "HKCU:\software\ForScripting"
 if(-not (Test-Path -path $scriptRoot))
   {
    New-Item -Path HKCU:\Software\ForScripting | Out-Null
    New-ItemProperty -Path $scriptRoot -Name $key -Value $value `
    -PropertyType String | Out-Null
   }
 Else
   {
    Set-ItemProperty -Path $scriptRoot -Name $key -Value $value | `
    Out-Null
   }

} #end function Add-RegistryValue

# *** Entry Point to Script ***
Add-RegistryValue -key forscripting -value test
```

Working with trace level 1

When the trace level is set to 1, each line in the script that executes is displayed to the Windows PowerShell console. To set the trace level to 1, you use the *Set-PSDebug* cmdlet and assign a value of 1 to the *-Trace* parameter.

When the trace level has been set, it applies to everything that is entered in the Windows PowerShell console. If you run an interactive command, run a cmdlet, or execute a script, it will be traced. When the CreateRegistryKey.ps1 script is run and there is no registry key present, the first command-debug line displays the path to the script that is being executed. Because Windows PowerShell parses from the top down, the next line that is executed is the line that creates the *Add-RegistryValue* function. The function starts on line 12, with the opening brace of the script, because the actual script that executed contains

9 lines that are commented out. When you add the status bar to Notepad (via View | Status Bar), the status bar in the lower-right corner of Notepad will display the line number. By default, Notepad does not display line and column numbers. This is shown in Figure 18-5.

```
CreateRegistryKey.ps1 - Notepad                                    —    □    ✕

File  Edit  Format  View  Help
# ----------------------------------------------------------------------
# Script: CreateRegistryKey.ps1
# Author: ed wilson, msft
# Date: 7/8/2015
# Keywords: Debugging
# comments: Errors
# Windows PowerShell 5.0 Step by Step, Microsoft Press, 2015
# Chapter 18
# ----------------------------------------------------------------------

Function Add-RegistryValue
{
 Param ($key,$value)
 $scriptRoot = "HKCU:\software\ForScripting"
 if(-not (Test-Path -path $scriptRoot))
    {
     New-Item -Path HKCU:\Software\ForScripting | Out-Null
     New-ItemProperty -Path $scriptRoot -Name $key -Value $value `
     -PropertyType String | Out-Null
    }
  Else
    {
     Set-ItemProperty -Path $scriptRoot -Name $key -Value $value | `
     Out-Null
    }

} #end function Add-RegistryValue

# *** Entry Point to Script ***
Add-RegistryValue -key forscripting -value test
```

FIGURE 18-5 By default, Notepad does not display line numbers.

After the function is created, the next line of the script that executes is line 30. Line 30 of the CreateRegistryKey.ps1 script follows the comment that points to the entry point to the script (this last line is shown in Figure 18-5) and calls the *Add-RegistryValue* function by passing two values for the *-key* and *-value* parameters. This is shown here.

```
PS C:\> Set-PSDebug -Trace 1
PS C:\> C:\fso\CreateRegistryKey.ps1
DEBUG:    1+ >>>> C:\fso\CreateRegistryKey.ps1
DEBUG:   30+ >>>> Add-RegistryValue -key forscripting -value test
```

When control of script execution is inside the *Add-RegistryValue* function, the *HKCU:\software\ForScripting* string is assigned to the *$scriptRoot* variable. This is shown here.

```
DEBUG:   12+ >>>> {
DEBUG:   14+ >>>> $scriptRoot = "HKCU:\software\ForScripting"
```

The *if* statement is now evaluated. If the *Test-Path* cmdlet is unable to find the *$scriptRoot* location in the registry, the *if* statement is entered and the commands inside the associated script block will be executed. In this example, *$scriptRoot* is located and the commands inside the script block are not executed. This is shown here.

```
DEBUG:   15+  if( >>>> -not (Test-Path -path $scriptRoot))
```

The *Set-ItemProperty* cmdlet is called on line 23 of the CreateRegistryKey.ps1 script. This is shown here.

```
DEBUG:   23+     >>>> Set-ItemProperty -Path $scriptRoot -Name $key –Value
$value | `
```

When the *Set-ItemProperty* cmdlet has executed, the script ends. The Windows PowerShell console parser now enters, with the same feedback shown when the tracing was first enabled. This is shown here.

```
DEBUG:   27+  >>>> } #end function Add-RegistryValue
PS C:\>
```

When you set the debug trace level to 1, a basic outline of the execution plan of the script is produced. This technique is good for quickly determining the outcome of branching statements (such as the *if* statement) to find out if a script block is being entered. This is shown in Figure 18-6.

FIGURE 18-6 Script-level 1 tracing displays each executing line of the script.

Working with trace level 2

When the trace level is set to 2, each line in the script that executes is displayed to the Windows PowerShell console. In addition, each variable assignment, function call, and outside script call is displayed. These additional tracing details are all prefixed with an exclamation mark to make them easier to spot. When the *Set-PSDebug -Trace* parameter is set to 2, an extra line is displayed, indicating a variable assignment.

When the CreateRegistryKey.ps1 script is run, the function trace points first to the script, stating that it is calling a function called CreateRegistryKey.ps1. Calls to functions are prefixed with *! CALL*, making them easy to spot. Windows PowerShell treats scripts as functions. The next function that is called is the *Add-RegistryValue* function. The trace also states where the function is defined by indicating the path to the file. This is shown here.

```
PS C:\> Set-PSDebug -Trace 2
PS C:\> C:\fso\CreateRegistryKey.ps1
DEBUG:    1+  >>>> C:\fso\CreateRegistryKey.ps1
DEBUG:      ! CALL function '<ScriptBlock>'
DEBUG:   30+  >>>> Add-RegistryValue -key forscripting -value test
DEBUG:      ! CALL function '<ScriptBlock>'  (defined in file
'C:\fso\CreateRegistryKey.ps1')
DEBUG:   12+  >>>> {
DEBUG:      ! CALL function 'Add-RegistryValue'  (defined in file
'C:\fso\CreateRegistryKey.ps1')
```

The *! SET* keyword is used to preface variable assignments. The first variable that is assigned is the *$scriptRoot* variable. This is shown here.

```
DEBUG:      ! SET $scriptRoot = 'HKCU:\software\ForScripting'.
DEBUG:   15+  if( >>>> -not (Test-Path -path $scriptRoot))
DEBUG:   23+     >>>> Set-ItemProperty -Path $scriptRoot -Name $key -Value
$value |  `
DEBUG:   27+  >>>> } #end function Add-RegistryValue
PS C:\>
```

When the CreateRegistryKey.ps1 script is run with trace level 2, the detailed tracing shown in Figure 18-7 is displayed.

FIGURE 18-7 Script-level 2 tracing adds variable assignments, function calls, and external script calls.

Stepping through the script

Watching the script trace the execution of the lines of code in the script can often provide useful insight that can lead to a solution for a misbehaving script. If a script is complicated and is composed of several functions, a simple trace might not be a workable solution. For the occasions when your script is complex and is made up of multiple functions, you will want the ability to step through the script. When you step through a script, you are prompted before each line of the script runs.

An example of a script that you might want to step through is the BadScript.ps1 script shown here.

BadScript.ps1

```
Function AddOne([int]$num)
{
 $num+1
} #end function AddOne

Function AddTwo([int]$num)
{
 $num+2
} #end function AddTwo

Function SubOne([int]$num)
{
 $num-1
} #end function SubOne

Function TimesOne([int]$num)
{
   $num*2
} #end function TimesOne

Function TimesTwo([int]$num)
{
 $num*2
} #end function TimesTwo

Function DivideNum([int]$num)
{
 12/$num
} #end function DivideNum

# *** Entry Point to Script ***

$num = 0
SubOne($num) | DivideNum($num)
AddOne($num) | AddTwo($num)
```

The BadScript.ps1 script contains several functions that are used to add numbers, subtract numbers, multiply numbers, and divide numbers. There are some problems with the way the script runs, because it contains several errors. It would be possible for you to set the trace level to 2 and examine the trace of the script. But with the large number of functions and the types of errors contained in the script, it might be difficult to spot the problems with the script. By default, the trace level is set to level 1 when stepping is enabled, and in nearly all cases this is the best trace level for this type of solution.

> **Note** When you are debugging a script, the exact line number displayed will depend on things such as comments, code breaks, and other things as you format the script. The important thing is not the line number, but that you look very carefully at the feedback provided by the debugger.

You might prefer to be able to step through the script as each line executes. There are two benefits to using the -*Step* parameter from the *Set-PSDebug* cmdlet. The first benefit is that you are able to watch what happens when each line of the script executes. This allows you to very carefully walk through the script. With the trace feature of *Set-PSDebug*, it is possible to miss important clues that would help solve problems because everything is displayed on the Windows PowerShell console. With the prompt feature, you are asked to choose a response before each line in the script executes. The default choice is *Y* for yes (continue the operation), but you have other choices. When you respond with *Y*, the debug line is displayed to the Windows PowerShell console. This is the same debug statement shown in the trace output, and it is governed by your debug-trace–level settings. The step prompting is shown here.

```
PS C:\> Set-PSDebug -Step
PS C:\> C:\fso\BadScript.ps1

Continue with this operation?
   1+ >>>> C:\fso\BadScript.ps1
[Y] Yes  [A] Yes to All  [N] No  [L] No to All  [S] Suspend  [?] Help
(default is "Y"):y
DEBUG:    1+ >>>> C:\fso\BadScript.ps1

Continue with this operation?
  43+ >>>> $num = 0
[Y] Yes  [A] Yes to All  [N] No  [L] No to All  [S] Suspend  [?] Help
(default is "Y"):y
DEBUG:    43+ >>>> $num = 0

Continue with this operation?
  44+ >>>> SubOne($num) | DivideNum($num)
[Y] Yes  [A] Yes to All  [N] No  [L] No to All  [S] Suspend  [?] Help
(default is "Y"):y
DEBUG:    44+ >>>> SubOne($num) | DivideNum($num)

Continue with this operation?
  22+ >>>> {
[Y] Yes  [A] Yes to All  [N] No  [L] No to All  [S] Suspend  [?] Help
(default is "Y"):y
DEBUG:    22+ >>>> {

Continue with this operation?
  23+   >>>> $num-1
[Y] Yes  [A] Yes to All  [N] No  [L] No to All  [S] Suspend  [?] Help
(default is "Y"):y
DEBUG:    23+   >>>> $num-1

Continue with this operation?
  24+ >>>> } #end function SubOne
[Y] Yes  [A] Yes to All  [N] No  [L] No to All  [S] Suspend  [?] Help
(default is "Y"):
```

The second benefit to using the -*Step* parameter with the *Set-PSDebug* cmdlet is the ability to suspend script execution, run additional Windows PowerShell commands, and then return to the script execution. The ability to return the value of a variable from within the Windows PowerShell console can offer important clues to the problem of what the script is doing. If you choose *S* (for suspend) at the prompt, you are dropped into a nested Windows PowerShell prompt. From there, you retrieve the variable value the same way you do when working at a regular Windows PowerShell console—by entering the name of the variable (tab expansion even works). When you are finished retrieving the value of the variable, you enter **exit** to return to the stepping trace. This is shown here.

```
Continue with this operation?
  24+  >>>> } #end function SubOne
[Y] Yes  [A] Yes to All  [N] No  [L] No to All  [S] Suspend  [?] Help
(default is "Y"):s
PS C:\>> $num
0
PS C:\>> exit
```

If you decide that you would like to find out what happens if you run continuously from the point you just inspected, you can choose *A* (for "yes to all"), and the script will run to completion without further prompting. If this is the case, you have found the problem. It is also possible that you might get an error such as the one shown here, where the script attempts to divide by zero.

```
Continue with this operation?
  24+  >>>> } #end function SubOne
[Y] Yes  [A] Yes to All  [N] No  [L] No to All  [S] Suspend  [?] Help
(default is "Y"):a
DEBUG:   24+  >>>> } #end function SubOne
Attempted to divide by zero.
At C:\fso\BadScript.ps1:38 char:2
+   12/$num
+   ~~~~~~~
    + CategoryInfo          : NotSpecified: (:) [], RuntimeException
    + FullyQualifiedErrorId : RuntimeException

2
PS C:\>
```

When you have found a specific error, you might want to change the value of a variable from within the suspended Windows PowerShell console to determine whether it corrects the remaining logic. To do this, you run the script again and choose *S* (for suspend) at the line that caused the error. This is where some careful reading of the error messages comes into play. When you chose *A* ("yes to all") in the previous example, the script ran until it came to line 38. The line number indicator follows a colon after the script name. The plus sign (+) indicates the command, which is *12/ $num*. The four left-pointing arrows indicate that it is the value of the *$num* variable that is causing the problem. This is shown here.

```
Attempted to divide by zero.
At C:\FSO\BadScript.ps1:43 char:5
+   >>>> 12/$num
```

You will need to step through the code until you come to the prompt for line 43. This will be shown as *43+ >>>> 12/$num*, which means you are at line 43, and the operation will be to divide 12 by the value of the number contained in the *$num* variable. At this point, you will want to enter **S** (for suspend) to drop into a nested Windows PowerShell prompt. Inside there, you can query the value contained in the *$num* variable and change it to a number such as 2. You exit the nested Windows PowerShell prompt and are returned to the stepping. At this point, you should continue to step through the code to find out if any other problems arise. If they do not, you know you have located the source of the problem. This is shown here.

```
Continue with this operation?
   28+  $num- >>>> 1
[Y] Yes  [A] Yes to All  [N] No  [L] No to All  [S] Suspend  [?] Help
(default is "Y"):y
DEBUG:    28+  $num- >>>> 1

Continue with this operation?
   43+  12/ >>>> $num
[Y] Yes  [A] Yes to All  [N] No  [L] No to All  [S] Suspend  [?] Help
(default is "Y"):s
PS C:\>>> $num
0
PS C:\>>> $num = 2
PS C:\>>> exit

Continue with this operation?
   43+  12/ >>>> $num
[Y] Yes  [A] Yes to All  [N] No  [L] No to All  [S] Suspend  [?] Help
(default is "Y"):y
DEBUG:    43+  12/ >>>> $num
6

Continue with this operation?
   50+  >>>> AddOne($num) | AddTwo($num)
[Y] Yes  [A] Yes to All  [N] No  [L] No to All  [S] Suspend  [?] Help
(default is "Y"):
```

Of course, locating the source of the problem is not the same as solving the problem, but the previous example points to a problem with the value of *$num*. Your next step would be to look at how *$num* is being assigned its values.

There are a couple of annoyances when working with the *Set-PSDebug* tracing features. The first problem is stepping through the extra lines of output created by the debugging features. The prompts and output will use half of the Windows PowerShell console window. If you use *Clear-Host* to attempt to clear the host window, you will spend several minutes attempting to step through all the commands used by *Clear-Host*. This is also true if you attempt to change the debug tracing level in midstream. By default, the trace level is set to 1 by the *Set-PSDebug -Step* parameter. The second problem with the *Set-PSDebug -Step* parameter occurs when you attempt to bypass a command in the script. You are not allowed to step over a command. Instead, the stepping session ends with an error displayed to the Windows PowerShell console. This is shown in Figure 18-8.

FIGURE 18-8 *Set-PSDebug -Step* does not allow you to step over functions or commands.

To turn off stepping, you use the *-Off* parameter. You will also be prompted to step through this command. This is shown here.

```
PS C:\> Set-PSDebug -Off
Continue with this operation?
   1+ Set-PSDebug -Off
[Y] Yes  [A] Yes to All  [N] No  [L] No to All  [S] Suspend  [?] Help
(default is "Y"):y
DEBUG:    1+ Set-PSDebug -Off
PS C:\>
```

Enabling strict mode

One easily correctable problem that can cause debugging nightmares in a script involves variables. Variables often are used incorrectly, are nonexistent, or are initialized improperly. An easy mistake to make when using variables is a simple typing error. Simple typing errors can also cause problems when they are contained in a large, complex script. Enabling strict mode causes Windows PowerShell to display an error if a variable is not declared. This helps you to avoid the problem of nonexistent or improperly initialized variables.

Using *Set-PSDebug -Strict*

An example of a simple typing error in a script is shown in the SimpleTypingError.ps1 script.

SimpleTypingError.ps1

```
$a = 2
$b = 5
$d = $a + $b
'The value of $c is: ' + $c
```

When the SimpleTypingError.ps1 script is run, the following output is shown.

```
PS C:\> C:\fso\SimpleTypingError.ps1
The value of $c is:
PS C:\>
```

As you can tell, the value of the *$c* variable is not displayed. If you use the *-Strict* parameter from the *Set-PSDebug* cmdlet, an error is generated. The error tells you that the value of *$c* has not been set. This is shown here.

```
PS C:\> Set-PSDebug -Strict
PS C:\> C:\fso\SimpleTypingError.ps1
The variable '$c' cannot be retrieved because it has not been set.
At C:\fso\SimpleTypingError.ps1:13 char:26
+ 'The value of $c is: ' + $c
+                          ~~
    + CategoryInfo          : InvalidOperation: (c:String) [], RuntimeExceptio
   n
    + FullyQualifiedErrorId : VariableIsUndefined
```

When you go back to the SimpleTypingError.ps1 script and examine it, you will find that the sum of *$a* and *$b* was assigned to *$d*, not *$c*. The way to correct the problem is to assign the sum of *$a* and *$b* to *$c* instead of *$d* (which was probably the original intention). It is possible to include the *Set-PSDebug -Strict* command in your scripts to provide a quick check for uninitialized variables while you are actually writing the script, and you can therefore avoid the error completely.

If you routinely use an expanding string to display the value of your variables, you need to be aware that an uninitialized variable is not reported as an error. The SimpleTypingErrorNotReported.ps1 script uses an expanding string to display the value of the *$c* variable. The first instance of the *$c* variable is escaped by the use of the backtick character. This causes the variable name to be displayed and does not expand its value. The second occurrence of the *$c* variable is expanded. The actual line of code that does this is shown here.

```
"The value of `$c is: $c"
```

When the SimpleTypingErrorNotReported.ps1 script is run, the following is displayed.

```
PS C:\> Set-PSDebug -Strict
PS C:\> C:\fso\SimpleTypingErrorNotReported.ps1
The value of $c is:
PS C:\>
```

The complete SimpleTypingErrorNotReported.ps1 script is shown here.

SimpleTypingErrorNotReported.ps1

```
$a = 2
$b = 5
$d = $a + $b
"The value of `$c is: $c"
```

To disable strict mode, you use the *Set-PSDebug -Off* command.

Using the *Set-StrictMode* cmdlet

The *Set-StrictMode* cmdlet can also be used to enable strict mode. It has the advantage of being scope aware. Whereas the *Set-PSDebug* cmdlet applies globally, if the *Set-StrictMode* cmdlet is used inside a function, it enables strict mode for only the function. There are two modes of operation that can be defined when using the *Set-StrictMode* cmdlet. The first is version 1, which behaves the same as the *Set-PSDebug -Strict* command (except that scope awareness is enforced). This is shown here.

```
PS C:\> Set-StrictMode -Version 1
PS C:\> C:\fso\SimpleTypingError.ps1
The variable '$c' cannot be retrieved because it has not been set.
At C:\fso\SimpleTypingError.ps1:4 char:28
+ 'The value of $c is: ' + $c >>>>
    + CategoryInfo          : InvalidOperation: (c:Token) [], RuntimeException
    + FullyQualifiedErrorId : VariableIsUndefined
PS C:\>
```

The *Set-StrictMode* cmdlet is not able to detect the uninitialized variable contained in the expanding string that is shown in the SimpleTypingErrorNotDetected.ps1 script.

When version 2 is enacted, the technique of calling a function like a method is stopped. The AddTwoError.ps1 script, shown below, passes two values to the *add-two* function via method notation. Because method notation is allowed when calling functions, usually no error is generated. But using method notation to pass parameters for functions only works when there is a single value to pass to the function. To pass multiple parameters, you must use function notation, as shown here.

```
add-two 1 2
```

Another way to call the *add-two* function correctly is to use the parameter names when passing the values. This is shown here.

```
add-two -a 1 -b 2
```

Either of the two syntaxes would produce the correct result. The method notation of calling the function displays incorrect information but does not generate an error. An incorrect value being returned from a function with no error being generated can take a significant amount of time to debug. The method notation of calling the *add-two* function is used in the AddTwoError.ps1 script and is shown here.

```
add-two(1,2)
```

When the script is run and the *Set-StrictMode -Version 2* command has not been enabled, no error is generated. The output seems to be confusing because the result of adding the two variables *$a* and *$b* is not displayed. This is shown here.

```
PS C:\> C:\fso\AddTwoError.ps1
1
2
PS C:\>
```

When the *Set-StrictMode -Version 2* command has been entered and the AddTwoError.ps1 script is run, an error is generated. The error that is generated states that the function was called as if it were a method. The error points to the exact line where the error occurred and shows the function call that caused the error. The function call is preceded with a + sign, followed by the name of the function, followed by four arrows that indicate what was passed to the function. The error message is shown here.

```
PS C:\> Set-StrictMode -Version 2
PS C:\> C:\fso\AddTwoError.ps1
The function or command was called as if it were a method. Parameters should be
 separated by spaces. For information about parameters, see the about_Parameters Help topic.
At C:\FSO\AddTwoError.ps1:7 char:8
+ add-two >>>> (1,2)
    + CategoryInfo          : InvalidOperation: (:) [], RuntimeException
    + FullyQualifiedErrorId : StrictModeFunctionCallWithParens
PS C:\>
```

The complete AddTwoError.ps1 script is shown here.

AddTwoError.ps1

```
Function add-two ($a,$b)
{
 $a + $b
}

add-two(1,2)
```

When you specify *Set-StrictMode* for version 2, it checks the following items:

- References to uninitialized variables, both directly and from within expanded strings

- References to nonexistent properties of an object

- Functions that are called like methods

- Variables without a name

If you set strict mode for version 1, it only checks for references to uninitialized variables.

If you are not sure whether you want to use strict mode for Windows PowerShell version 2, 3, 4, or 5.0 (there have been no changes since strict mode version 2), an easy way to solve the problem is to use the value *latest*. By using *latest* for the value of the *-Version* parameter, you always ensure that your script will use the latest strict mode rules. This technique appears here.

```
Set-StrictMode -version latest
```

One issue that can arise with using *latest* is that you do not know what the latest changes might do to your script, and a new set of rules might break your script. Therefore, it is generally safer to use version 1 or version 2 when looking for specific types of protection.

To turn off strict mode, use the *-Off* parameter. This is shown here.

```
Set-StrictMode -Off
```

Debugging the script

The debugging features of Windows PowerShell 5.0 make the use of the *Set-PSDebug* cmdlet seem rudimentary or even cumbersome. When you are more familiar with the debugging features of Windows PowerShell 5.0, you might decide to look no longer at the *Set-PSDebug* cmdlet. Several cmdlets enable debugging from the Windows PowerShell console and from the Windows PowerShell ISE. The debugging cmdlets are listed in Table 18-2.

TABLE 18-2 Windows PowerShell debugging cmdlets

Cmdlet name	Cmdlet function
Set-PSBreakpoint	Sets breakpoints on lines, variables, and commands
Get-PSBreakpoint	Gets breakpoints in the current session
Disable-PSBreakpoint	Turns off breakpoints in the current session
Enable-PSBreakpoint	Re-enables breakpoints in the current session
Remove-PSBreakpoint	Deletes breakpoints from the current session
Get-PSCallStack	Displays the current call stack

Setting breakpoints

The debugging features in Windows PowerShell use breakpoints. A breakpoint is something that is very familiar to developers who have used products such as Microsoft Visual Studio in the past. But for many IT professionals without a programming background, the concept of a breakpoint is somewhat foreign. A breakpoint is a spot in the script where you would like the execution of the script to pause. Because the script pauses, it is like the stepping functionality shown earlier. But because you control where the breakpoint will occur, instead of halting on each line of the script, the stepping experience is much faster. In addition, because many different methods for setting breakpoints are available, you can tailor your breakpoints to reveal precisely the information you are looking for.

Setting a breakpoint on a line number

To set a breakpoint, you use the *Set-PSBreakpoint* cmdlet. The easiest way to set a breakpoint is to set it on line 1 of the script. To set a breakpoint on the first line of the script, you use the *line* and *script* parameters. When you set a breakpoint, an instance of the *System.Management.Automation.LineBreak* .NET Framework class is returned. It lists the *ID*, *Script*, and *Line* properties that were assigned when the breakpoint was created. This is shown here.

```
PS C:\> Set-PSBreakpoint -line 1 -script C:\fso\BadScript.ps1
  ID Script           Line Command       Variable       Action
  -- ------           ---- -------       --------       ------
   0 BadScript.ps1       1
```

After a breakpoint is set, the next time the script runs it will cause the script to break into the code immediately. You can then step through the function in the same way you did by using the *Set-PSDebug* cmdlet with the *-Step* parameter. When you run the script, it stops at the breakpoint that was set on the first line of the script, and Windows PowerShell enters the script debugger, permitting you to use the debugging features of Windows PowerShell. Windows PowerShell enters the debugger every time the BadScript.ps1 script is run from the C:\fso folder. When Windows PowerShell enters the debugger, the Windows PowerShell prompt changes to *[DBG]: PS C:\>>>* to visually alert you that you are inside the Windows PowerShell debugger. To step to the next line in the script, you enter **s**. To quit the debugging session, you enter **q**. (The debugging commands are not case sensitive.) This is shown here.

```
PS C:\> Set-PSBreakpoint -Line 1 -Script C:\fso\BadScript.ps1

  ID Script           Line Command       Variable       Action
  -- ------           ---- -------       --------       ------
   4 BadScript.ps1       1


PS C:\> C:\fso\BadScript.ps1
Hit Line breakpoint on 'C:\fso\BadScript.ps1:1'

At C:\fso\BadScript.ps1:43 char:1
+ $num = 0
+ ~~~~~~~~
[DBG]: PS C:\>> s
At C:\fso\BadScript.ps1:44 char:1
+ SubOne($num) | DivideNum($num)
+ ~~~~~~~~~~~~~~~~~~~~~~~~~~~~~~~
[DBG]: PS C:\>> s
At C:\fso\BadScript.ps1:22 char:1
+ {
+ ~
[DBG]: PS C:\>> s
At C:\fso\BadScript.ps1:23 char:2
+  $num-1
+  ~~~~~~
[DBG]: PS C:\>> s
At C:\fso\BadScript.ps1:24 char:1
+ } #end function SubOne
+ ~
[DBG]: PS C:\>> s
At C:\fso\BadScript.ps1:37 char:1
+ {
+ ~
[DBG]: PS C:\>> s
At C:\fso\BadScript.ps1:38 char:2
+  12/$num
+  ~~~~~~~
[DBG]: PS C:\>> s
Attempted to divide by zero.
```

```
At C:\fso\BadScript.ps1:38 char:2
+   12/$num
+   ~~~~~~~
    + CategoryInfo          : NotSpecified: (:) [], RuntimeException
    + FullyQualifiedErrorId : RuntimeException

At C:\fso\BadScript.ps1:39 char:1
+ } #end function DivideNum
+ ~
[DBG]: PS C:\>> s
At C:\fso\BadScript.ps1:45 char:1
+ AddOne($num) | AddTwo($num)
+ ~~~~~~~~~~~~~~~~~~~~~~~~~~~~
[DBG]: PS C:\>> s
At C:\fso\BadScript.ps1:12 char:1
+ {
+ ~
[DBG]: PS C:\>> s
At C:\fso\BadScript.ps1:13 char:2
+   $num+1
+   ~~~~~~
[DBG]: PS C:\>> s
At C:\fso\BadScript.ps1:14 char:1
+ } #end function AddOne
+ ~
[DBG]: PS C:\>> s
At C:\fso\BadScript.ps1:17 char:1
+ {
+ ~
[DBG]: PS C:\>> s
At C:\fso\BadScript.ps1:18 char:2
+   $num+2
+   ~~~~~~
[DBG]: PS C:\>> s
2
At C:\fso\BadScript.ps1:19 char:1
+ } #end function AddTwo
+ ~
[DBG]: PS C:\>> s
PS C:\>
```

Note Keep in mind that breakpoints are dependent upon the location of the specific script when you specify a breakpoint on a script. When you create a breakpoint for a script, you specify the location of the script on which you want to set a breakpoint. I often have several copies of a script that I keep in different locations (for version control). At times, I get confused in a long debug session, and I might open up the wrong version of the script to debug it. This will not work. If the script is identical to another in all respects except for the path to the script, it will not break. If you want to use a single breakpoint that could apply to a specific script that is stored in multiple locations, you can set the breakpoint for the condition inside the Windows PowerShell console, and not use the *-Script* parameter.

Setting a breakpoint on a variable

Setting a breakpoint on line 1 of the script is useful for easily entering a debug session, but setting a breakpoint on a variable can often make a problem with a script easy to detect. This is, of course, especially true when you have already determined that the problem is with a variable that is either being assigned a value or being ignored. There are three modes that can be used when the breakpoint is specified for a variable. You specify these modes by using the *-Mode* parameter. The three modes of operation are listed in Table 18-3.

TABLE 18-3 Variable breakpoint access modes

Access mode	Meaning
Write	Stops execution immediately before a new value is written to the variable.
Read	Stops execution when the variable is read—that is, when its value is accessed, either to be assigned, displayed, or used. In read mode, execution does not stop when the value of the variable changes.
ReadWrite	Stops execution when the variable is read or written.

To find out when the BadScript.ps1 script writes to the *$num* variable, you would use write mode. When you specify the value for the *-Variable* parameter, do not include the dollar sign in front of the variable name. To set a breakpoint on a variable, you only need to supply the path to the script, the name of the variable, and the access mode. When a variable breakpoint is set, the *System.Management.Automation.LineBreak* .NET Framework class object that is returned does not include the access mode value. This is true even if you use the *Get-PSBreakpoint* cmdlet to directly access the breakpoint. If you pipeline the *System.Management.Automation.LineBreak* .NET Framework class object to the *Format-List* cmdlet, you will be able to tell that the access mode property is available. In this example, you set a breakpoint when the *$num* variable is written to in the C:\fso\BadScript.ps1 script.

```
PS C:\> Set-PSBreakpoint -Variable num -Mode write -Script C:\FSO\BadScript.ps1
  ID Script            Line Command          Variable         Action
  -- ------            ---- -------          --------         ------
   3 BadScript.ps1                           num


PS C:\> Get-PSBreakpoint
  ID Script            Line Command          Variable         Action
  -- ------            ---- -------          --------         ------
   3 BadScript.ps1                           num


PS C:\> Get-PSBreakpoint  | Format-List *
AccessMode : Write
Variable   : num
Action     :
Enabled    : True
HitCount   : 0
Id         : 3
Script     : C:\FSO\BadScript.ps1
```

After setting the breakpoint, when you run the script (if the other breakpoints have been removed or deactivated, which will be discussed later), the script enters the Windows PowerShell debugger when the breakpoint is hit (that is, when the value of the *$num* variable is written to). If you step through the script by using the *s* command, you will be able to follow the sequence of operations. Only one breakpoint is hit when the script is run. This is on line 43 when the value is set to 0 (if you are following along with this chapter, your line numbers might be different than mine). This is shown here.

```
PS C:\> C:\fso\BadScript.ps1
Entering debug mode. Use h or ? for help.

Hit Variable breakpoint on 'C:\fso\BadScript.ps1:$num' (Write access)

At C:\fso\BadScript.ps1:43 char:1
+ $num = 0
+ ~~~~~~~~
[DBG]: PS C:\>> $num
0
[DBG]: PS C:\>> Write-Host $num
0
[DBG]: PS C:\>> s
At C:\fso\BadScript.ps1:44 char:1
+ SubOne($num) | DivideNum($num)
+ ~~~~~~~~~~~~~~~~~~~~~~~~~~~~~~
[DBG]: PS C:\>> $num
0
[DBG]: PS C:\>> q
PS C:\>
```

> **Note** To quickly remove all breakpoints from a Windows PowerShell session, use the *Get-PSBreakpoint* cmdlet and pipeline the output to the *Remove-PSBreakpoint* cmdlet. This command is shown here.
>
> ```
> Get-PSBreakpoint | Remove-PSBreakpoint
> ```

To set a breakpoint on a read operation for the variable, you specify the *-Variable* parameter and name of the variable, the *-Script* parameter with the path to the script, and *read* as the value for the *-Mode* parameter. This is shown here.

```
PS C:\> Set-PSBreakpoint -Variable num -Script C:\FSO\BadScript.ps1 -Mode read
```

ID	Script	Line	Command	Variable	Action
4	BadScript.ps1			num	

When you run the script, a breakpoint will be displayed each time you hit a read operation on the variable. Each breakpoint will be displayed in the Windows PowerShell console as *Hit Variable breakpoint*, followed by the path to the script and the access mode of the variable. In the BadScript.ps1 script, the value of the *$num* variable is read several times. The truncated output is shown here.

```
PS C:\> C:\fso\BadScript.ps1
Hit Variable breakpoint on 'C:\fso\BadScript.ps1:$num' (Read access)

At C:\fso\BadScript.ps1:44 char:1
+ SubOne($num) | DivideNum($num)
+ ~~~~~~~~~~~~~~~~~~~~~~~~~~~~~
[DBG]: PS C:\>> s
Hit Variable breakpoint on 'C:\fso\BadScript.ps1:$num' (Read access)

At C:\fso\BadScript.ps1:44 char:1
+ SubOne($num) | DivideNum($num)
+ ~~~~~~~~~~~~~~~~~~~~~~~~~~~~~
[DBG]: PS C:\>> s
At C:\fso\BadScript.ps1:22 char:1
+ {
+ ~
[DBG]: PS C:\>> s
At C:\fso\BadScript.ps1:23 char:2
+   $num-1
+   ~~~~~~
[DBG]: PS C:\>>
```

If you set the *readwrite* access mode for the *-Mode* parameter for the variable *$num* for the BadScript.ps1 script, you receive the feedback shown here.

```
PS C:\> Set-PSBreakpoint -Variable num -Mode ReadWrite -Script C:\FSO\BadScript.ps1

 ID Script            Line Command        Variable        Action
 -- ------            ---- -------        --------        ------
  6 BadScript.ps1                         num
```

When you run the script (assuming you have disabled the other breakpoints), you will hit a breakpoint each time the *$num* variable is read to or written to. If you get tired of typing *s* and pressing Enter while you are in the debugging session, you can press Enter, and your previous *s* command will be repeated as you continue to step through the breakpoints. When the script has stepped through the code, enter **q** to exit the debugger. This is shown here.

```
PS C:\> C:\fso\BadScript.ps1
Hit Variable breakpoint on 'C:\fso\BadScript.ps1:$num' (ReadWrite access)

At C:\fso\BadScript.ps1:43 char:1
+ $num = 0
+ ~~~~~~~~
[DBG]: PS C:\>> s
At C:\fso\BadScript.ps1:44 char:1
+ SubOne($num) | DivideNum($num)
+ ~~~~~~~~~~~~~~~~~~~~~~~~~~~~~
[DBG]: PS C:\>> s
Hit Variable breakpoint on 'C:\fso\BadScript.ps1:$num' (ReadWrite access)

At C:\fso\BadScript.ps1:44 char:1
+ SubOne($num) | DivideNum($num)
+ ~~~~~~~~~~~~~~~~~~~~~~~~~~~~~
```

```
[DBG]: PS C:\>> s
Hit Variable breakpoint on 'C:\fso\BadScript.ps1:$num' (ReadWrite access)

At C:\fso\BadScript.ps1:44 char:1
+ SubOne($num) | DivideNum($num)
+ ~~~~~~~~~~~~~~~~~~~~~~~~~~~~~
[DBG]: PS C:\>> s
At C:\fso\BadScript.ps1:22 char:1
+ {
+ ~
[DBG]: PS C:\>> q
PS C:\>
```

When you use the readwrite access mode of the *-Mode* parameter for breaking on variables, the breakpoint does not tell you whether the operation is a read operation or a write operation. You have to look at the code that is being executed to determine whether the value of the variable is being written or read.

By specifying a value for the *-Action* parameter, you can include regular Windows PowerShell code that will execute when the breakpoint is hit. If, for example, you are trying to follow the value of a variable within the script and you want to display the value of the variable each time the breakpoint is hit, you might want to specify an action that uses the *Write-Host* cmdlet to display the value of the variable. By using the *Write-Host* cmdlet, you can also include a string that indicates that the value of the variable is being displayed. This is crucial for picking up variables that never initialize, and therefore is easier to spot than a blank line that would be displayed if you attempted to display the value of an empty variable. The technique of using the *Write-Host* cmdlet in an *-Action* parameter is shown here.

```
PS C:\> Set-PSBreakpoint -Variable num -Action { write-host "num = $num" ;
Break } -Mode readwrite -script C:\FSO\BadScript.ps1
```

ID Script	Line Command	Variable	Action
5 BadScript.ps1		num	write-host "...

When you run the C:\FSO\BadScript.ps1 script with the breakpoint set, you receive the following output inside the Windows PowerShell debugger.

```
PS C:\> C:\fso\BadScript.ps1
num = 0
Hit Variable breakpoint on 'C:\FSO\BadScript.ps1:$num' (ReadWrite access)

At C:\fso\BadScript.ps1:43 char:1
+ $num = 0
+ ~~~~~~~~
[DBG]: PS C:\>> s
At C:\fso\BadScript.ps1:44 char:1
+ SubOne($num) | DivideNum($num)
+ ~~~~~~~~~~~~~~~~~~~~~~~~~~~~~
[DBG]: PS C:\>> s
num = 0
Hit Variable breakpoint on 'C:\FSO\BadScript.ps1:$num' (ReadWrite access)
```

```
At C:\fso\BadScript.ps1:44 char:1
+ SubOne($num) | DivideNum($num)
+ ~~~~~~~~~~~~~~~~~~~~~~~~~~~~~
[DBG]: PS C:\>> c
num = 0
Hit Variable breakpoint on 'C:\FSO\BadScript.ps1:$num' (ReadWrite access)

At C:\fso\BadScript.ps1:44 char:1
+ SubOne($num) | DivideNum($num)
+ ~~~~~~~~~~~~~~~~~~~~~~~~~~~~~
[DBG]: PS C:\>> q
PS C:\>
```

Setting a breakpoint on a command

To set the breakpoint on a command, you use the *-Command* parameter. You can break on a call to a Windows PowerShell cmdlet, function, or external script. You can use aliases when setting breakpoints. When you create a breakpoint on an alias for a cmdlet, the debugger will only stop on the use of the alias—not the actual command name. In addition, you do not have to specify a script for the debugger to break. If you do not type a path to a script, the debugger will be active for everything within the Windows PowerShell console session. Every occurrence of the *foreach* command will cause the debugger to break. Because *foreach* is both a language statement and an alias for the *Foreach-Object* cmdlet, you might wonder whether the Windows PowerShell debugger will break on both the language statement and the use of the alias for the cmdlet—and the answer is no. You can set breakpoints on language statements, but the debugger will not break on a language statement. As shown here, the debugger breaks on the use of the *Foreach* alias, but not on the use of the *Foreach-Object* cmdlet or the % alias.

```
PS C:\> 1..3 | ForEach-Object {$_}
1
2
3
PS C:\> 1..3 | % {$_}
1
2
3
PS C:\> 1..3 | foreach {$_}
Hit Command breakpoint on 'foreach'

At line:1 char:1
+ 1..3 | foreach {$_}
+ ~~~~~~~~~~~~~~~~~~
[DBG]: PS C:\>> c
1
2
3
PS C:\>
```

When creating a breakpoint for the *DivideNum* function used by the C:\FSO\BadScript.ps1 script, you can leave off the path to the script, because only this script uses the *DivideNum* function. This makes the command easier to type, but could become confusing if you're looking through a collection of breakpoints. If you are debugging multiple scripts in a single Windows PowerShell console session, it could become confusing if you do not specify the script to which the breakpoint applies—unless, of course, you are specifically debugging the function as it is used in multiple scripts. Creating a command breakpoint for the *DivideNum* function is shown here.

```
PS C:\> Set-PSBreakpoint -Command DivideNum

 ID Script          Line Command          Variable        Action
 -- ------          ---- -------          --------        ------
  7                      DivideNum
```

When you run the script, it hits a breakpoint when the *DivideNum* function is called. When BadScript.ps1 hits the *DivideNum* function, the value of *$num* is 0. As you step through the *DivideNum* function, you assign a value of 2 to the *$num* variable, a result of 6 is displayed, and then the *12/$num* operation is carried out. Next, the *AddOne* function is called, and the value of *$num* again becomes 0. When the *AddTwo* function is called, the value of *$num* also becomes 0. This is shown here.

```
PS C:\> C:\fso\BadScript.ps1
Hit Command breakpoint on 'DivideNum'

At C:\fso\BadScript.ps1:37 char:1
+ {
+ ~
[DBG]: PS C:\>> s
At C:\fso\BadScript.ps1:38 char:2
+   12/$num
+   ~~~~~~~
[DBG]: PS C:\>> $num
0
[DBG]: PS C:\>> $num=2
[DBG]: PS C:\>> s
6
At C:\fso\BadScript.ps1:39 char:1
+ } #end function DivideNum
+ ~
[DBG]: PS C:\>> s
At C:\fso\BadScript.ps1:45 char:1
+ AddOne($num) | AddTwo($num)
+ ~~~~~~~~~~~~~~~~~~~~~~~~~~~~
```

```
[DBG]: PS C:\>> $num
0
[DBG]: PS C:\>> s
At C:\fso\BadScript.ps1:12 char:1
+ {
+ ~
[DBG]: PS C:\>> q
PS C:\>
```

Responding to breakpoints

When the script reaches a breakpoint, control of the Windows PowerShell console is turned over to you. Inside the debugger, you can type any legal Windows PowerShell command, and even run cmdlets such as *Get-Process* or *Get-Service*. In addition, there are several debugging commands that can be entered into the Windows PowerShell console when a breakpoint has been reached. The available debug commands are shown in Table 18-4.

TABLE 18-4 Windows PowerShell debugging commands

Keyboard shortcut	Command name	Command meaning
S	*Step-Into*	Executes the next statement and then stops.
V	*Step-Over*	Executes the next statement, but skips functions and invocations. The skipped statements are executed, but not stepped through.
O	*Step-Out*	Steps out of the current function up one level if nested. If the current function is in the main body, execution continues to the end or to the next breakpoint. The skipped statements are executed, but not stepped through.
C	*Continue*	Continues to run until the script is complete or until the next breakpoint is reached. The skipped statements are executed, but not stepped through.
L	*List*	Displays the part of the script that is executing. By default, this displays the current line, 5 previous lines, and 10 subsequent lines. To continue listing the script, press Enter.
L *<M>*	*List*	Displays 16 lines of the script, beginning with the line number specified by *M*.
L *<M>* *<N>*	*List*	Displays the number of lines of the script specified by *N*, beginning with the line number specified by *M*.
Q	*Stop (Quit)*	Stops executing the script and exits the debugger.
K	*Get-PsCallStack*	Displays the current call stack.
Enter	*Repeat*	Repeats the last command if it was *Step-Into, Step-Over*, or *List*. Otherwise, represents a submit action.
H or ?	*Help*	Displays the debugger command help.

When the BadScript.ps1 script is run using the *DivideNum* function as a breakpoint, the script breaks on line 37 when the *DivideNum* function is called. The *s* debugging command is used to step into the next statement and stop the script before the command is actually executed. The *l* (a lowercase L) debugging command is used to list the 5 previous lines of code from the BadScript.ps1 script and the 10 lines of code that follow the current line in the script. This is shown here.

```
PS C:\> C:\fso\BadScript.ps1
Hit Command breakpoint on 'DivideNum'

At C:\fso\BadScript.ps1:37 char:1
+ {
+ ~
[DBG]: PS C:\>> s
At C:\fso\BadScript.ps1:38 char:2
+   12/$num
+   ~~~~~~~
[DBG]: PS C:\>> l


    33:     $num*2
    34:   } #end function TimesTwo
    35:
    36:   Function DivideNum([int]$num)
    37:   {
    38:*  12/$num
    39:   } #end function DivideNum
    40:
    41:   # *** Entry Point to Script ***
    42:
    43:   $num = 0
    44:   SubOne($num) | DivideNum($num)
    45:   AddOne($num) | AddTwo($num)
    46:


[DBG]: PS C:\>>
```

After the code has been reviewed, the *o* debugging command is used to step out of the *Divide-Num* function. The remaining code in the *DivideNum* function is still executed, and therefore the divide-by-zero error is displayed. There are no more prompts until the next line of executing code is met. The *v* debugging statement is used to step over the remaining functions in the script. The remaining functions are still executed, and the results are displayed at the Windows PowerShell console. This is shown here.

```
[DBG]: PS C:\>> o
Attempted to divide by zero.
At C:\fso\BadScript.ps1:38 char:2
+   12/$num
+   ~~~~~~~
    + CategoryInfo          : NotSpecified: (:) [], RuntimeException
    + FullyQualifiedErrorId : RuntimeException

At C:\fso\BadScript.ps1:45 char:1
+ AddOne($num) | AddTwo($num)
+ ~~~~~~~~~~~~~~~~~~~~~~~~~~~
[DBG]: PS C:\>> v
2
PS C:\>
```

Listing breakpoints

When you have set several breakpoints, you might want to know where they were created. One thing to keep in mind is that the breakpoints are stored in the Windows PowerShell environment, not in the individual script. Using the debugging features does not involve editing the script or modifying your source code. This enables you to debug any script without worry of corrupting the code. But because you might have set several breakpoints in the Windows PowerShell environment during a typical debugging session, you might want to know what breakpoints have been defined. To do this, you use the *Get-PSBreakpoint* cmdlet. This is shown here.

```
PS C:\> Get-PSBreakpoint
  ID Script            Line Command       Variable      Action
  -- ------            ---- -------       --------      ------
  11 BadScript.ps1          dividenum
  13 BadScript.ps1          if
   3 BadScript.ps1                        num
   5 BadScript.ps1                        num
   6 BadScript.ps1                        num
   7                        DivideNum
   8                        foreach
   9                        gps
  10                        foreach
PS C:\>
```

If you are interested in which breakpoints are currently enabled, you need to use the *Where-Object* cmdlet and pipeline the results from the *Get-PSBreakpoint* cmdlet. This is shown here.

```
PS C:\> Get-PSBreakpoint | ? enabled

  ID Script            Line Command       Variable      Action
  -- ------            ---- -------       --------      ------
  11 BadScript.ps1          dividenum


PS C:\>
```

You could also pipeline the results of the *Get-PSBreakpoint* to the *Format-Table* cmdlet, as shown here.

```
PS C:\> Get-PSBreakpoint |
Format-Table -Property id, script, command, variable, enabled -AutoSize

Id Script                Command    variable Enabled
-- ------                -------    -------- -------
11 C:\FSO\BadScript.ps1  dividenum            True
13 C:\FSO\BadScript.ps1  if                   False
 3 C:\FSO\BadScript.ps1             num        False
 5 C:\FSO\BadScript.ps1             num        False
 6 C:\FSO\BadScript.ps1             num        False
 7                       DivideNum            False
 8                       foreach              False
 9                       gps                  False
10                       foreach              False
```

Because the creation of the custom-formatted breakpoint table requires a little bit of typing, and because the display is extremely helpful, you might consider placing the code in a function that could be included in your profile, or in a custom debugging module. The function shown here is stored in the Get-EnabledBreakpointsFunction.ps1 script.

Get-EnabledBreakpointsFunction.ps1

```
Function Get-EnabledBreakpoints
{
  Get-PSBreakpoint |
  Format-Table -Property id, script, command, variable, enabled -AutoSize
}

# *** Entry Point to Script ***

Get-EnabledBreakpoints
```

Enabling and disabling breakpoints

While you are debugging a script, you might need to disable a particular breakpoint to find out how the script runs. To do this, you use the *Disable-PSBreakpoint* cmdlet. This is shown here.

```
Disable-PSBreakpoint -id 0
```

Alternatively, you might also need to enable a breakpoint. To do this, you use the *Enable-PSBreakpoint* cmdlet, as shown here.

```
Enable-PSBreakpoint -id 1
```

As a best practice, while in a debugging session, I selectively enable and disable breakpoints to determine how the script is running in an attempt to troubleshoot the script. To keep track of the status of breakpoints, I use the *Get-PSBreakpoint* cmdlet as illustrated in the previous section.

Deleting breakpoints

When you are finished debugging the script, you will want to remove all of the breakpoints that were created during the Windows PowerShell session. There are two ways to do this. The first is to close the Windows PowerShell console. Although this is a good way to clean up the environment, you might not want to do this if you have remote Windows PowerShell sessions defined, or variables that are populated with the results of certain queries. To delete all of the breakpoints, you can use the *Remove-PSBreakpoint* cmdlet. Unfortunately, there is no *all* switch for the *Remove-PSBreakpoint* cmdlet. When you're deleting a breakpoint, the *Remove-PSBreakpoint* cmdlet requires a breakpoint ID number. To remove a single breakpoint, you specify the ID number for the *-Id* parameter. This is shown here.

```
Remove-PSBreakpoint -id 3
```

If you want to remove all of the breakpoints, pipeline the results from *Get-PSBreakpoint* to *Remove-PSBreakpoint*, as shown here.

```
Get-PSBreakpoint | Remove-PSBreakpoint
```

If you want to remove only the breakpoints from a specific script, you can pipeline the results through the *Where* object, as shown here.

```
(Get-PSBreakpoint | Where ScriptName - eq "C:\Scripts\Test.ps1") |
Remove-PSBreakpoint
```

Debugging a function: Step-by-step exercises

In this exercise, you will explore the use of the debugger in the Windows PowerShell ISE. (Note that if you have defined your own custom Windows PowerShell prompt, you might not get the *[DBG]* prompt portion of the Windows PowerShell prompt.) After you have completed debugging a function, in the subsequent exercise you will debug a script.

Using the Windows PowerShell debugger to debug a function

1. Open the Windows PowerShell ISE.

2. Create a function called *My-Function*. The contents of the function are shown following. Save the function to a file named *my-function.ps1*. (If you do not save the file, you are not running a script, and you will not enter the debugger.)

    ```
    Function my-function
    {
     Param(
       [int]$a,
       [int]$b)
       "$a plus $b equals four"
    }
    ```

3. Select the line of code that states that *$a* plus *$b* equals four. This line of code is shown here.

    ```
    "$a plus $b equals four"
    ```

4. From the Debug menu, choose Toggle Breakpoint. The line of code should change colors, indicating that a breakpoint is now set on that line.

5. Run the My-Function script to load the function into memory.

6. In the bottom pane of the Windows PowerShell ISE (the command pane), enter the function name so that you execute the function. (You can use tab expansion to avoid typing the complete *My-Function* name.) This is shown here.

    ```
    My-Function
    ```

7. In the output pane of the Windows PowerShell ISE, you will find that you have now hit a breakpoint. Examine the output and determine which line the breakpoint is defined upon. The line number in the output pane corresponds with the line number in the script pane (the upper pane). Sample output is shown here.

```
PS C:\> my-function
Hit Line breakpoint on 'C:\fso\My-Function.ps1:6'
[DBG]: PS C:\>>
```

8. Examine the prompt in the Windows PowerShell ISE command pane. It should be prefixed by *[DBG]*. This tells you that you are in a debug prompt. This prompt appears here.

```
[DBG]: PS C:\>>
```

9. At the debug prompt in the Windows PowerShell ISE command pane, examine the value of the *$a* variable.

```
[DBG]: PS C:\>> $a
0
```

10. Now examine the value of the *$b* variable.

```
[DBG]: PS C:\>> $b
0
```

11. Now assign a value of 2 to both *$a* and *$b*.

```
[DBG]: PS C:\>> $a = $b = 2
```

12. Now, from the Debug menu, select Step Out to permit the script to continue execution and to run the line upon which the breakpoint was set. Notice that the function now uses the new value of *$a* and *$b*. The output is shown here.

```
[DBG]: PS C:\>>
2 plus 2 equals four
```

13. From the Debug menu, select Remove All Breakpoints. Examine the script pane. The highlighted line of code should now appear normally.

14. In the command pane of the Windows PowerShell ISE, call *My-Function* again. This time, you will notice that the function still exhibits the problem. The output is shown here.

```
PS C:\> my-function
0 plus 0 equals four
```

15. You should now fix the function. To do this, change the output line so that it does not have the hard-coded word *four* in it. This change is shown following. Save the revised function as *my-function1.ps1*.

```
"$a plus $b equals $($a+$b)"
```

This concludes the exercise.

In the next exercise, you will set breakpoints that will be used when debugging a script.

Debugging a script

1. Open the Windows PowerShell console.

2. Use the *Set-PSBreakPoint* cmdlet to set a breakpoint on the *my-function* function inside the script my-function.ps1. Remember that you will need to use the full path to the script when you do this. The command will look something like the following.

   ```
   Set-PSBreakpoint -Script sbs:\chapter18Scripts\my-function.ps1 -Command my-function
   ```

3. Bring the *My-Function* function into your current Windows PowerShell session. The command will look something like the following. (Notice that the command does not break.)

   ```
   PS C:\> . C:\fso\My-Function.ps1
   PS C:\> my-function
   0 plus 0 equals 0
   PS C:\>
   ```

4. Use the *Get-PSBreakPoint* cmdlet to display the breakpoint. The command and associated output are shown here.

   ```
   PS C:\> Get-PSBreakpoint

    ID Script          Line Command      Variable      Action
    -- ------          ---- -------      --------      ------
     0 my-function.ps1      my-function
   ```

5. Remove the breakpoint for the *my-function* command by using the *Remove-PSBreakPoint* cmdlet. It should have an ID of 0. The command is shown here.

   ```
   Remove-PSBreakpoint -Id 0
   ```

6. Set a breakpoint for the *my-function* command without specifying a script. The command is shown here. (Remember, you can use tab completion to complete the command name.)

   ```
   Set-PSBreakpoint -Command my-function
   ```

7. Call *my-function*. When you do, the Windows PowerShell console will enter debug mode. The command and debug mode are shown here.

   ```
   PS C:\> my-function
   Entering debug mode. Use h or ? for help.

   Hit Command breakpoint on 'my-function'

   At C:\fso\My-Function.ps1:2 char:1
   + {
   + ~
   [DBG]: PS C:\>>
   ```

8. Inside debug mode, display the value of the *$a* variable and the *$b* variable. The command and output are shown here.

```
[DBG]: PS C:\>> $a
0
[DBG]: PS C:\>> $b
0
```

9. Exit debug mode by entering the command **exit**. The Windows PowerShell console exits debug mode and continues running the function, as shown here.

```
[DBG]: PS C:\>> exit
0 plus 0 equals four
```

10. Dot-source the my-function1.ps1 script. The command will be similar to the one shown here.

```
. sbs:\chapter18Scripts\my-function1.ps1
```

11. Run the *my-function* function and supply the value 12 for the *a* parameter and the value 14 for the *b* parameter. The command follows. Note that again the Windows PowerShell console enters debug mode.

```
PS C:\> my-function -a 12 -b 14
Hit Command breakpoint on 'my-function'

At C:\fso\My-Function.ps1:2 char:1
+ {
+ ~
[DBG]: PS C:\>>
```

12. Query for the value of *$a* and *$b*. The command and associated values are shown here.

```
[DBG]: PS C:\>> $a
12
[DBG]: PS C:\>> $b
14
```

13. Change the value of *$b* to be equal to 0, and exit debug mode. The commands are shown here.

```
[DBG]: PS C:\>> $b = 0
[DBG]: PS C:\>> exit
```

When the console exits debug mode, the new value for the *b* parameter is used. The output is shown here.

```
12 plus 0 equals 12
```

14. Use the *Get-PSBreakPoint* cmdlet to retrieve all breakpoints, and pipeline them to the *Remove-PSBreakPoint* cmdlet. This command is shown here.

```
Get-PSBreakpoint | Remove-PSBreakpoint
```

15. Use the *Get-PSBreakPoint* cmdlet to ensure that the breakpoint is removed. This command is shown here.

```
Get-PSBreakpoint
```

This concludes the exercise.

Chapter 18 quick reference

To	Do this
Step through a script or a function	Use the *Set-PSDebug* cmdlet and specify the *-Step* parameter.
Follow code execution into and out of functions in a script	Use the *Set-PSDebug* cmdlet and specify a value of 2 for the *-Trace* parameter.
Set a breakpoint for a particular line number in a script	Use the *Set-PSBreakPoint* cmdlet and specify the line number to the *-Line* parameter. Also, specify the script by using the *-Script* parameter.
Set a breakpoint on a script when a particular variable is written to	Use the *Set-PSBreakPoint* cmdlet, specify the variable name to the *-Variable* parameter (leave off the $ sign when specifying the variable name), and specify the script to the *-Script* parameter.
Set a breakpoint when a particular command is run from any script	Use the *Set-PSBreakPoint* cmdlet and the *-Command* parameter to specify the command to watch, and do not set a script name.
List all breakpoints currently defined in the session	Use the *Get-PSBreakpoint* cmdlet.
Delete all breakpoints currently defined in the session	Use the *Get-PSBreakpoint* cmdlet and pipeline the results to the *Remove-PSBreakpoint* cmdlet.

Handling errors

After completing this chapter, you will be able to

- Handle missing parameters in scripts.

- Limit the choices available to users of your scripts.

- Handle missing rights and permissions in scripts.

- Handle missing WMI providers in scripts.

- Use *Try...Catch...Finally* to catch single and multiple errors in scripts.

When it comes to handling run-time errors in your script, you need to have an understanding of the intended use of the script. For example, just because a script runs once does not mean it will run a second time. Disks fail, networks fail, computers fail, and things are constantly in flux. The way that a script will be used is sometimes called the *use-case scenario*, and it describes how the user will interact with the script. If the use-case scenario is simple, the user might not need to do anything more than enter the name of the script inside the Windows PowerShell console. A script such as Get-Bios.ps1, shown following, could run successfully without much need for error handling. This is because there are no inputs to the script. The script is called, it runs, and it displays information that should always be readily available, because the *Win32_Bios* Windows Management Instrumentation (WMI) class is present in all versions of Windows since Windows 2000 (however, even a simple script like Get-Bios.ps1 could fail if it relies on a WMI service that is broken, or if the COM interface is corrupt).

Get-Bios.ps1
```
Get-WmiObject -class Win32_Bios
```

Handling missing parameters

When you examine the Get-Bios.ps1 script, you can tell that it does not receive any input from the command line. This is a good way to avoid user errors in your script, but it is not always practical. When your script accepts command-line input, you are opening the door for all kinds of potential problems. Depending on how you accept command-line input, you might need to test the input data to ensure that it corresponds to the type of input the script is expecting. The Get-Bios.ps1 script does not accept command-line input; therefore, it avoids most potential sources of errors (of course, the Get-Bios.ps1 script is also extremely limited in scope—so you win some and you lose some).

Creating a default value for a parameter

There are two ways to assign default values for a command-line parameter. You can assign the default value in the *param* declaration statement, or you can assign the value in the script itself. Given a choice between the two, it is a best practice to assign the default value in the *param* statement. This is because it makes the script easier to read, which in turn makes the script easier to modify and troubleshoot. For more information on troubleshooting scripts, see Chapter 18, "Debugging scripts."

Detecting a missing value and assigning it in the script

In the Get-BiosInformation.ps1 script, which follows, a command-line parameter, *computerName*, allows the script to target both local and remote computers. If the script runs without a value for the *computerName* parameter, the *Get-WmiObject* cmdlet fails because it requires a value for the *computername* parameter. To solve the problem of the missing parameter, the Get-BiosInformation.ps1 script checks for the presence of the *$computerName* variable. If this variable is missing, that means it was not created via the command-line parameter, and the script therefore assigns a value to the *$computerName* variable. Here is the line of code that populates the value of the *$computerName* variable.

```
If(-not($computerName)) { $computerName = $env:computerName }
```

The completed Get-BiosInformation.ps1 script is shown here.

Get-BiosInformation.ps1

```
Param(
  [string]$computerName
) #end param

Function Get-BiosInformation($computerName)
{
 Get-WmiObject -class Win32_Bios -computerName $computername
} #end function Get-BiosName

# *** Entry Point To Script ***
If(-not($computerName)) { $computerName = $env:computerName }
Get-BiosInformation -computerName $computername
```

Assigning a value in the *param* statement

To assign a default value in the *param* statement, you use the equality operator following the parameter name and assign the value to the parameter. This technique is shown here.

```
Param(
  [string]$computerName = $env:computername
) #end param
```

An advantage of assigning the default value for the parameter in the *param* statement is that it makes the script easier to read. Because the parameter declaration and the default parameter are in the same place, you can tell immediately which parameters have default values and which do not. The second advantage that arises from assigning a default value in the *param* statement is that the script is easier to write. Notice that there is no *if* statement to check the existence of the *$computerName* variable. The Get-BiosInformationDefaultParam.ps1 script illustrates using the *param* statement to assign a default value for a parameter. The complete script is shown here.

Get-BiosInformationDefaultParam.ps1

```
Param(
  [string]$computerName = $env:computername
) #end param

Function Get-BiosInformation($computerName)
{
 Get-WmiObject -class Win32_Bios -computername $computername
} #end function Get-BiosName

# *** Entry Point To Script ***

Get-BiosInformation -computerName $computername
```

Making the parameter mandatory

The best way to handle an error is to ensure that the error does not occur in the first place. In Windows PowerShell 5.0, you can mark a parameter as mandatory (for the scripts and for functions). The advantage of marking a parameter as mandatory is that it requires the user of the script to supply a value for the parameter. If you do not want the user of the script to be able to run the script without making a particular selection, you will want to make the parameter mandatory. To make a parameter mandatory, you use the *mandatory* parameter attribute. This technique is shown here.

```
Param(
   [Parameter(Mandatory=$true)]
   [string]$drive,
   [string]$computerName = $env:computerName
) #end param
```

The complete MandatoryParameter.ps1 script is shown here.

MandatoryParameter.ps1

```
#Requires -version 5.0
Param(
   [Parameter(Mandatory=$true)]
   [string]$drive,
   [string]$computerName = $env:computerName
) #end param

Function Get-DiskInformation($computerName,$drive)
{
 Get-WmiObject -class Win32_volume -computername $computername `
-filter "DriveLetter = '$drive'"
} #end function Get-BiosName

# *** Entry Point To Script ***

 Get-DiskInformation -computername $computerName -drive $drive
```

When a script with a *mandatory* parameter runs without supplying a value for the parameter, an error is not generated. Instead, Windows PowerShell prompts for the required parameter value. This behavior is shown here.

```
PS C:\> .\MandatoryParameter.ps1

cmdlet MandatoryParameter.ps1 at command pipeline position 1
Supply values for the following parameters:
drive:
```

Limiting choices

Depending on the design of the script, several scripting techniques can ease error-checking requirements. If you have a limited number of choices you want to display to your user, you can use the *PromptForChoice* method. If you want to limit the selection to computers that are currently running, you can use the *Test-Connection* cmdlet prior to attempting to connect to a remote computer. If you would like to limit the choice to a specific subset of computers or properties, you can parse a text file and use the *-contains* operator. In this section, you will examine each of these techniques for limiting the permissible input values from the command line.

Using *PromptForChoice* to limit selections

For example, if you use the *PromptForChoice* method of soliciting input from the user, your user has a limited number of options from which to choose. You eliminate the problem of bad input because the user only has specific options available to supply to your script. The user prompt from the *PromptForChoice* method is shown in Figure 19-1.

FIGURE 19-1 The *PromptForChoice* method presents a selectable menu to the user.

The use of the *PromptForChoice* method appears in the Get-ChoiceFunction.ps1 script, which follows. In the *Get-Choice* function, the *$caption* variable and the *$message* variable hold the caption and the message that is used by the *PromptForChoice* method. The choices are an array of instances of the *ChoiceDescription* Microsoft .NET Framework class. When you create the *ChoiceDescription* class, you also supply an array with the choices that will appear. This is shown here.

```
$choices = [System.Management.Automation.Host.ChoiceDescription[]] `
  @("&loopback", "local&host", "&127.0.0.1")
```

You next need to select a number that will be used to represent which choice will be the default choice. When you begin counting, keep in mind that *ChoiceDescription* is an array, and the first option is numbered 0. Next, you call the *PromptForChoice* method and display the options. This is shown here.

```
[int]$defaultChoice = 0
$choiceRTN = $host.ui.PromptForChoice($caption,$message, $choices,$defaultChoice)
```

Because the *PromptForChoice* method returns an integer, you could use the *if* statement to evaluate the value of the *$choiceRTN* variable. The syntax of the *switch* statement is more compact and is actually a better choice for this application. The *switch* statement from the *Get-Choice* function is shown here.

```
switch($choiceRTN)
 {
  0    { "loopback"  }
  1    { "localhost" }
  2    { "127.0.0.1" }
 }
```

When you call the *Get-Choice* function, it returns the computer that was identified by the *PromptForChoice* method. You place the method call in a set of parentheses to force it to be evaluated before the rest of the command. This is shown here.

```
Get-WmiObject -class win32_bios -computername (Get-Choice)
```

This solution to the problem of bad input works well when you have help desk personnel who will be working with a limited number of computers. One caveat to this approach is that you do not want to have to change the choices on a regular basis, so you would want a stable list of computers to avoid creating a maintenance nightmare for yourself. The complete Get-ChoiceFunction.ps1 script is shown here.

Get-ChoiceFunction.ps1

```
Function Get-Choice
{
 $caption = "Please select the computer to query"
 $message = "Select computer to query"
 $choices = [System.Management.Automation.Host.ChoiceDescription[]] `
 @("&loopback", "local&host", "&127.0.0.1")
 [int]$defaultChoice = 0
 $choiceRTN = $host.ui.PromptForChoice($caption,$message, $choices,$defaultChoice)

 switch($choiceRTN)
 {
  0    { "loopback"  }
  1    { "localhost" }
  2    { "127.0.0.1" }
 }
} #end Get-Choice function

Get-WmiObject -class win32_bios -computername (Get-Choice)
```

Using *Test-Connection* to identify computer connectivity

If you have more than a few computers that need to be accessible, or if you do not have a stable list of computers that you will be working with, one solution to the problem of trying to connect to non-existent computers is to ping a computer prior to attempting to make the WMI connection.

You can use the *Win32_PingStatus* WMI class to send a ping to a computer. This establishes computer connectivity, and it also verifies that name resolution works properly. The best way to use the *Win32_PingStatus* WMI class is to use the *Test-Connection* cmdlet because it wraps the WMI class into an easy-to-use package. An example of using the *Test-Connection* cmdlet with default values is shown here.

```
PS C:\> Test-Connection -ComputerName dc1

Source         Destination    IPV4Address        IPV6Address
------         -----------    -----------        -----------
W10CLIENT6     dc1            192.168.0.101
W10CLIENT6     dc1            192.168.0.101
W10CLIENT6     dc1            192.168.0.101
W10CLIENT6     dc1            192.168.0.101
```

If you are only interested in whether the target computer is responding, use the -*Quiet* switch parameter. The -*Quiet* switch parameter returns a Boolean value (*true* if the computer is up; *false* if the computer is down). This is shown here.

```
PS C:\> Test-Connection -ComputerName dc1 -Quiet
True
```

When you use the *Test-Connection* cmdlet, it has a tendency to be slower than the traditional ping utility. It has a lot more capabilities and even returns an object, but it is slower. A few seconds can make a huge difference when attempting to run a single script to manage thousands of computers. To increase performance in these types of fan-out scenarios, use the -*Count* parameter to reduce the default number of pings from four to one. In addition, reduce the default buffer size from 32 to 16.

Because *Test-Connection -Quiet* returns a Boolean value, there is no need to evaluate a number of possible return values. In fact, the logic is simple: either the command returns a value or it does not. If it does return, add the action to take in the *if* statement. If it does not return, add the action to take in the *else* statement. If you do not want to log failed connections, on the other hand, you would only have the action in the *if* statement with which to contend. The Test-ComputerPath.ps1 script illustrates using the *Test-Connection* cmdlet to determine whether a computer is up prior to attempting a remote connection. The complete Test-ComputerPath.ps1 script is shown here.

Test-ComputerPath.ps1

```
Param([string]$computer = $env:COMPUTERNAME)
if(Test-Connection -computer $computer -BufferSize 16 -Count 1 -Quiet)
  { Get-WmiObject -class Win32_Bios -computer $computer }
Else
  { "Unable to reach $computer computer"}
```

Using the *-contains* operator to examine the contents of an array

To verify input that is received from the command line, you can use the *-contains* operator to examine the contents of an array of possible values. This technique is illustrated here, where an array of three values is created and stored in the variable *$noun*. The *-contains* operator is then used to determine whether the array contains *hairy-nosed wombat*. Because the *$noun* variable does not have an array element that is equal to the string *hairy-nosed wombat*, the *-contains* operator returns *false*.

```
PS C:\> $noun = "cat","dog","rabbit"
PS C:\> $noun -contains "hairy-nosed wombat"
False
PS C:\>
```

If an array contains a match, the *-contains* operator returns *true*. This is shown here.

```
PS C:\> $noun = "cat","dog","rabbit"
PS C:\> $noun -contains "rabbit"
True
PS C:\>
```

The *-contains* operator returns *true* only when there is an exact match. Partial matches return *false*. This is shown here.

```
PS C:\> $noun = "cat","dog","rabbit"
PS C:\> $noun -contains "bit"
False
PS C:\>
```

The *-contains* operator is a case-insensitive operator. (There is also the *-icontains* operator, which is case-insensitive, and there is *–ccontains*, which is case-sensitive.) Therefore, it will return *true* when matched, regardless of case. This is shown here.

```
PS C:\> $noun = "cat","dog","rabbit"
PS C:\> $noun -contains "Rabbit"
True
PS C:\>
```

If you need to perform a case-sensitive match, you can use the case-sensitive version of the *-contains* operator, *-ccontains*. As shown here, the operator returns *true* only if the case of the string matches the value contained in the array.

```
PS C:\> $noun = "cat","dog","rabbit"
PS C:\> $noun -ccontains "Rabbit"
False
PS C:\> $noun -ccontains "rabbit"
True
PS C:\>
```

In the Get-AllowedComputers.ps1 script, shown at the end of this section, a single command-line parameter is created that is used to hold the name of the target computer for the WMI query. The *computer* parameter is a string, and it receives the default value from the environment drive. This is a good technique because it ensures that the script will have the name of the local computer, which could then be used in producing a report of the results. If you set the value of the *computer* parameter to *localhost*, you never know what computer the results belong to. This is shown here.

```
Param([string]$computer = $env:computername)
```

The *Get-AllowedComputer* function is used to create an array of permitted computer names and to check the value of the *$computer* variable to determine whether it is present. If the value of the *$computer* variable is present in the array, the *Get-AllowedComputer* function returns *true*. If the value is missing from the array, the *Get-AllowedComputer* function returns *false*. The array of computer names is created by the use of the *Get-Content* cmdlet to read a text file that contains a listing of computer names. The text file, servers.txt, is a plain ASCII text file that has a list of computer names on individual lines, as shown in Figure 19-2.

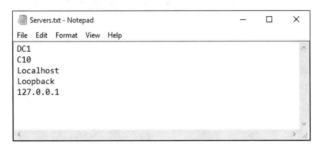

FIGURE 19-2 Using a text file with computer names and addresses is an easy way to work with allowed computers.

A text file of computer names is easier to maintain than a hard-coded array that is embedded into the script. In addition, the text file can be placed on a central share and can be used by many different scripts. The *Get-AllowedComputer* function is shown here.

```
Function Get-AllowedComputer([string]$computer)
{
 $servers = Get-Content -path c:\fso\servers.txt
 $servers -contains $computer
} #end Get-AllowedComputer function
```

Because the *Get-AllowedComputer* function returns a Boolean value (*true* or *false*), it can be used directly in an *if* statement to determine whether the value that is supplied for the *$computer* variable is on the list of permitted computers. If the *Get-AllowedComputer* function returns *true*, the *Get-WmiObject* cmdlet is used to query for BIOS information from the target computer. This is shown here.

```
if(Get-AllowedComputer -computer $computer)
 {
   Get-WmiObject -class Win32_Bios -Computer $computer
 }
```

However, if the value of the *$computer* variable is not found in the *$servers* array, a string that states that the computer is not an allowed computer is displayed. This is shown here.

```
Else
 {
  "$computer is not an allowed computer"
 }
```

The complete Get-AllowedComputer.ps1 script is shown here.

Get-AllowedComputer.ps1

```
Param([string]$computer = $env:computername)

Function Get-AllowedComputer([string]$computer)
{
 $servers = Get-Content -path c:\fso\servers.txt
 $servers -contains $computer
} #end Get-AllowedComputer function

# *** Entry point to Script ***

if(Get-AllowedComputer -computer $computer)
 {
    Get-WmiObject -class Win32_Bios -Computer $computer
 }
Else
 {
  "$computer is not an allowed computer"
 }
```

Using the -*contains* operator to test for properties

You are not limited to only testing for specified computer names in the *Get-AllowedComputer* function. All you need to do is add additional information to the text file in order to check for WMI property names or other information. This is shown in Figure 19-3.

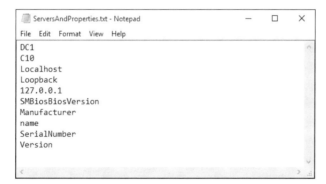

FIGURE 19-3 A text file with server names and properties adds flexibility to the script.

You only need to make a couple of modifications to the Get-AllowedComputer.ps1 script to turn it into the Get-AllowedComputerAndProperty.ps1 script. The first is to add an additional command-line parameter to allow the user to choose which property to display. This is shown here.

```
Param([string]$computer = $env:computername,[string]$property="name")
```

Next, you change the signature to the *Get-AllowedComputer* function to permit the passing of the property name. Instead of directly returning the results of the -*contains* operator, you store the returned values in variables. The *Get-AllowedComputer* function first checks to determine whether the

$servers array contains the computer name. It then checks to determine whether the $servers array contains the property name. Each of the resulting values is stored in variables. The two variables are then anded, and the result is returned to the calling code. When two Boolean values are anded, only the $true -and $true case is equal to *true*; all other combinations return *false*. This is shown here.

```
PS C:\> $true -and $false
False
PS C:\> $true -and $true
True
PS C:\> $false -and $false
False
PS C:\>
```

The revised *Get-AllowedComputer* function is shown here.

```
Function Get-AllowedComputer([string]$computer, [string]$property)
{
 $servers = Get-Content -path c:\fso\serversAndProperties.txt
 $s = $servers -contains $computer
 $p = $servers -contains $property
 Return $s -and $p
} #end Get-AllowedComputer function
```

The *if* statement is used to determine whether both the computer value and the property value are on the list of allowed servers and properties. If the *Get-AllowedComputer* function returns *true*, the *Get-WMIObject* cmdlet is used to display the chosen property value from the selected computer. This is shown here.

```
if(Get-AllowedComputer -computer $computer -property $property)
 {
   Get-WmiObject -class Win32_Bios -Computer $computer |
   Select-Object -property $property
 }
```

If the computer value and the property value are not on the list, the Get-AllowedComputerAnd-Property.ps1 script displays a message stating that there is a nonpermitted value. This is shown here.

```
Else
 {
   "Either $computer is not an allowed computer, `r`nor $property is not an allowed property"
 }
```

The complete Get-AllowedComputerAndProperty.ps1 script is shown here.

Get-AllowedComputerAndProperty.ps1

```
Param([string]$computer = $env:computername,[string]$property="name")

Function Get-AllowedComputer([string]$computer, [string]$property)
{
 $servers = Get-Content -path c:\fso\serversAndProperties.txt
 $s = $servers -contains $computer
 $p = $servers -contains $property
 Return $s -and $p
```

```
} #end Get-AllowedComputer function

# *** Entry point to Script ***

if(Get-AllowedComputer -computer $computer -property $property)
 {
   Get-WmiObject -class Win32_Bios -Computer $computer |
   Select-Object -property $property
 }
Else
 {
  "Either $computer is not an allowed computer, `r`nor $property is not an allowed property"
 }
```

> ## Quick check
>
> **Q.** What is an easy way to handle a missing -*ComputerName* parameter?
>
> **A.** Assign *$env:ComputerName* as the default value.
>
> **Q.** What is a good way to ensure that a script does not run with missing parameters?
>
> **A.** Make the parameters required parameters by using the *[Parameter(Mandatory=$true)]* parameter attribute.
>
> **Q.** What is a good way to limit potential choices for a parameter value?
>
> **A.** Use the *PromptForChoice* method.

Handling missing rights

Another source of potential errors in a script is missing rights. When a script requires elevated permissions to work correctly and those rights or permissions do not exist, an error results. Windows 8 and later make handling these scenarios much easier to implement and allows the user to work without requiring constant access to administrative rights. As a result, more and more users and even network administrators are no longer running their computers with a user account that is a member of the local administrators group. The User Account Control (UAC) feature makes it easy to provide elevated rights for interactive programs, but Windows PowerShell 5.0 and other scripting languages are not UAC-aware and do not therefore prompt when elevated rights are required to perform a specific activity. It is therefore incumbent upon the script writer to take rights into account when writing scripts. The Get-Bios.ps1 script (shown earlier in the chapter), however, does not use a WMI class that requires elevated rights. As the script is currently written, anyone who is a member of the local users group—and that includes everyone who is logged on interactively—has permission to run the Get-Bios.ps1 script. So, testing for rights and permissions prior to making an attempt to obtain information from the WMI class *Win32_Bios* is not required.

Using an attempt-and-fail approach

One way to handle missing rights is to attempt the action, and then fail. This will generate an error. Windows PowerShell has two types of errors: terminating and nonterminating. *Terminating errors*, as the name implies, will stop a script dead in its tracks. *Nonterminating errors* will be displayed to the screen, and the script will continue. Terminating errors are generally more serious than nonterminating errors. Normally, you get a terminating error when you try to use .NET or COM from within Windows PowerShell and you try to use a command that doesn't exist, or when you do not provide all of the required parameters to a command, method, or cmdlet. A good script will handle the errors it expects and will report unexpected errors to the user. Because any good scripting language has to provide decent error handling, Windows PowerShell has a few ways to approach the problem. The old way is to use the *trap* statement, which can sometimes be problematic. The best way (for Windows PowerShell) is to use *Try...Catch...Finally*, which is covered in the "Using *Try...Catch...Finally*" section later in this chapter.

Checking for rights and exiting gracefully

The best way to handle insufficient rights is to check for the rights and, if they are not there, to exit gracefully. What are some of the things that could go wrong with a simple script, such as the Get-Bios.ps1 script examined earlier in the chapter? The Get-Bios.ps1 script will fail, for example, if the Windows PowerShell script execution policy is set to *restricted*. When the script execution policy is set to *restricted*, Windows PowerShell scripts will not run. The problem with a *restricted* execution policy is that because Windows PowerShell scripts do not run, you cannot write code to detect the *restricted* script execution policy. Because the script execution policy is stored in the registry, you could write a Microsoft Visual Basic Scripting Edition (VBScript) script that would query and set the policy prior to launching the Windows PowerShell script, but that would not be the best way to manage the problem. The best way to manage the script execution policy is to use Group Policy to set it to the appropriate level for your network. On a stand-alone computer, you can set the execution policy by opening Windows PowerShell as an administrator and using the *Set-ExecutionPolicy* cmdlet. In most cases, the *remotesigned* setting is appropriate. The command would therefore be the one shown here.

```
PS C:\> Set-ExecutionPolicy remotesigned
PS C:\>
```

The script execution policy is generally dealt with once, after which there are no more problems associated with it. In addition, the error message that is associated with the script execution policy is relatively clear in that it will tell you that script execution is disabled on the system. It also refers you to a help article that explains the various settings.

This is shown here.

```
File C:\Documents and Settings\ed\Local Settings\Temp\tmp2A7.tmp.ps1 cannot be
loaded because the execution of scripts is disabled on this system. Please see
"get-help about_signing" for more details.
At line:1 char:66
+ C:\Documents` and` Settings\ed\Local` Settings\Temp\tmp2A7.tmp.ps1 <<<<
```

Handling missing WMI providers

One of the few things that could actually go wrong with the original Get-Bios.ps1 script intro-duced at the beginning of this chapter is related to WMI itself. If the WMI provider that supplies the *Win32_Bios* WMI class information is corrupted or missing, the script will not work. To check for the existence of the appropriate WMI provider, you will need to know the name of the provider for the WMI class. You can use the WMI Tester (WbemTest), which is included as part of the WMI installation. If a computer has WMI installed on it, it has WbemTest. Because WbemTest resides in the system folders, you can launch it directly from within the Windows PowerShell console by entering the name of the executable file. This is shown here.

```
PS C:\> wbemtest
PS C:\>
```

When WbemTest appears, the first thing you will need to do is connect to the appropriate WMI namespace. To do this, you click the Connect button. In most cases, this namespace will be Root\Cimv2. On Windows Vista and later, Root\Cimv2 is the default WMI namespace for WbemTest. On earlier ver-sions of Windows, the default WbemTest namespace is Root\Default. Change or accept the namespace as appropriate, and click Connect. The display changes to a series of buttons, many of which appear to have cryptic names and functionality. To obtain information about the provider for a WMI class, you will need to open the class. Click the Open Class button and enter the name of the WMI class in the dialog box that appears. You are looking for the provider name for the *Win32_Bios* WMI class, so that is the name that is entered here. Click the OK button when you have entered the class name. The Object Editor for the *Win32_Bios* WMI class now appears. This is shown in Figure 19-4. The first box in the Object Editor lists the qualifiers; *provider* is one of the qualifiers. WbemTest tells you that the provider for *Win32_Bios* is CIMWin32.

FIGURE 19-4 The WMI Tester displays WMI class provider information.

Now that you have the name of the WMI provider, you can use the *Get-WmiObject* cmdlet to determine whether the provider is installed on the computer. To do this, you will query for instances of the *__provider* WMI class. All WMI classes that begin with a double underscore are system classes. The *__provider* WMI class is the class from which all WMI providers are derived. By limiting the query to providers with the name of CIMWin32, you can determine whether the provider is installed on the system. This is shown here.

```
PS C:\> Get-WmiObject -Class __Provider -Filter "name = 'cimwin32'"
```

```
__GENUS                 : 2
__CLASS                 : __Win32Provider
__SUPERCLASS            : __Provider
__DYNASTY               : __SystemClass
__RELPATH               : __Win32Provider.Name="CIMWin32"
__PROPERTY_COUNT        : 24
__DERIVATION            : {__Provider, __SystemClass}
__SERVER                : W8CLIENT6
__NAMESPACE             : ROOT\cimv2
__PATH                  : \\W8CLIENT6\ROOT\cimv2:__Win32Provider.Name="CIMWin32"
ClientLoadableCLSID     :
CLSID                   : {d63a5850-8f16-11cf-9f47-00aa00bf345c}
Concurrency             :
DefaultMachineName      :
Enabled                 :
```

```
HostingModel                      : NetworkServiceHost
ImpersonationLevel                : 1
InitializationReentrancy          : 0
InitializationTimeoutInterval     :
InitializeAsAdminFirst            :
Name                              : CIMWin32
OperationTimeoutInterval          :
PerLocaleInitialization           : False
PerUserInitialization             : False
Pure                              : True
SecurityDescriptor                :
SupportsExplicitShutdown          :
SupportsExtendedStatus            :
SupportsQuotas                    :
SupportsSendStatus                :
SupportsShutdown                  :
SupportsThrottling                :
UnloadTimeout                     :
Version                           :
PSComputerName                    : W8CLIENT6
```

For the purposes of determining whether the provider exists, you do not need all the information to be returned to the script. It is easier to treat the query as if it returned a Boolean value by using the *If* statement. If the provider exists, then you will perform the query. This is shown here.

```
If(Get-WmiObject -Class __provider -filter "name = 'cimwin32'")
 {
  Get-WmiObject -class Win32_bios
 }
```

If the CIMWin32 WMI provider does not exist, you display a message that states that the provider is missing. This is shown here.

```
Else
 {
  "Unable to query Win32_Bios because the provider is missing"
 }
```

The completed CheckProviderThenQuery.ps1 script is shown here.

CheckProviderThenQuery.ps1
```
If(Get-WmiObject -Class __provider -filter "name = 'cimwin32'")
 {
  Get-WmiObject -class Win32_bios
 }
Else
 {
  "Unable to query Win32_Bios because the provider is missing"
 }
```

Another example for finding out whether a WMI class is available is to check for the existence of the provider. In the case of the *Win32_Product* WMI class, the MSIPROV WMI provider supplies that class. In this section, you create a function, the *Get-WmiProvider* function, which can be used to detect the presence of any WMI provider that is installed on the system.

The *Get-WmiProvider* function contains two parameters. The first parameter is the name of the provider, and the second one is a switch parameter named *-verbose*. When the *Get-WmiProvider* function is called with the *-verbose* switch parameter, detailed status information is displayed to the console. The *-verbose* information provides the user of the script with information that could be useful from a troubleshooting perspective.

```
Function Get-WmiProvider([string]$providerName, [switch]$verbose)
```

After the function has been declared, the current value of the *$VerbosePreference* variable is stored. This is because it could be set to one of four potential values. The possible enumeration values are *SilentlyContinue*, *Stop*, *Continue*, and *Inquire*. By default, the value of the *$VerbosePreference* automatic variable is set to *SilentlyContinue*.

When the function finishes running, you will want to set the value of the *$VerbosePreference* variable back to its original value. To enable reverting to the original value of the *$VerbosePreference* variable, store the original value in the *$oldVerbosePreference* variable.

It is time to determine whether the function was called with the *-verbose* switch parameter. If the function was called with the *-verbose* switch parameter, a variable named *$verbose* will be present on the variable drive. If the *$verbose* variable exists, the value of the *$VerbosePreference* automatic variable is set to *Continue*. This is shown here.

```
{
 $oldVerbosePreference = $VerbosePreference
 if($verbose) { $VerbosePreference = "continue" }
```

Next, you need to look for the WMI provider. To do this, you use the *Get-WmiObject* cmdlet to query for all instances of the *__provider* WMI system class. As mentioned previously, all WMI classes that begin with a double underscore are system classes. In most cases, they are not of much interest to IT professionals; however, familiarity with them can often provide powerful tools to the scripter who takes the time to examine them. All WMI providers are derived from the *__provider* WMI class. This is similar to the way that all WMI namespaces are derived from the *__namespace* WMI class. The properties of the *__provider* class are shown in Table 19-1.

TABLE 19-1 Properties of the *__provider* WMI class

Property name	Property type
ClientLoadableCLSID	System.String
CLSID	System.String
Concurrency	System.Int32
DefaultMachineName	System.String
Enabled	System.Boolean
HostingModel	System.String

Property name	Property type
ImpersonationLevel	System.Int32
InitializationReentrancy	System.Int32
InitializationTimeoutInterval	System.String
InitializeAsAdminFirst	System.Boolean
Name	System.String
OperationTimeoutInterval	System.String
PerLocaleInitialization	System.Boolean
PerUserInitialization	System.Boolean
Pure	System.Boolean
SecurityDescriptor	System.String
SupportsExplicitShutdown	System.Boolean
SupportsExtendedStatus	System.Boolean
SupportsQuotas	System.Boolean
SupportsSendStatus	System.Boolean
SupportsShutdown	System.Boolean
SupportsThrottling	System.Boolean
UnloadTimeout	System.String
Version	System.UInt32
__CLASS	System.String
__DERIVATION	System.String[]
__DYNASTY	System.String
__GENUS	System.Int32
__NAMESPACE	System.String
__PATH	System.String
__PROPERTY_COUNT	System.Int32
__RELPATH	System.String
__SERVER	System.String
__SUPERCLASS	System.String

The *-Filter* parameter of the *Get-WmiObject* cmdlet is used to return the provider that is specified in the *$providername* variable. If you do not know the name of the appropriate WMI provider, you will need to search for it by using the WMI Tester. You can start this program by entering the name of the executable file inside your Windows PowerShell console. This is shown here.

```
PS C:\> wbemtest
PS C:\>
```

When the WMI Tester appears, open the *Win32_Product* WMI class. The Object Editor for the *Win32_Product* WMI class is shown in Figure 19-5. The first box of the Object Editor lists the qualifiers; *provider* is one of the qualifiers. WbemTest tells you that the provider for *Win32_Product* is MSIProv.

FIGURE 19-5 The Object Editor for *WIN32_Product* displays qualifiers and methods.

You assign the name of the WMI provider to the *$providername* variable, as shown here.

```
$providerName = "MSIProv"
```

The resulting object is stored in the *$provider* variable. This is shown here.

```
$provider = Get-WmiObject -Class __provider -filter "name = '$providerName'"
```

If the provider was not found, there will be no value in the *$provider* variable. You can therefore tell if the *$provider* variable is *null*. If the *$provider* variable is not equal to *null*, the class ID of the provider is retrieved. The class ID of the WMI provider is stored in the *clsID* property. This is shown here.

```
If($provider -ne $null)
   {
    $clsID = $provider.clsID
```

If the function was run with the *-verbose* switch parameter, the *$VerbosePreference* variable is set to *Continue*. When the value of *$VerbosePreference* is equal to *Continue*, the *Write-Verbose* cmdlet will display information to the console. If, however, the value of the *$VerbosePreference* variable is equal to *SilentlyContinue*, the *Write-Verbose* cmdlet does not emit anything. This makes it easy to implement tracing features in a function without needing to create extensive test conditions. When the function is called with the *-verbose* switch parameter, the class ID of the provider is displayed.

This is shown here.

```
Write-Verbose "$providerName WMI provider found. ClsID is $($clsID)"
}
```

If the WMI provider is not found, the function returns *false* to the calling code. This is shown here.

```
Else
  {
    Return $false
  }
```

The next thing the function does is check the registry to ensure that the WMI provider has been properly registered with DCOM. Again, the *Write-Verbose* cmdlet is used to provide feedback on the status of the provider check. This is shown here.

```
Write-Verbose "Checking for proper registry registration ..."
```

To search the registry for the WMI provider registration, you use the Windows PowerShell registry provider. By default, there is no Windows PowerShell drive for the HKEY_CLASSES_ROOT registry hive. However, you cannot simply assume that someone would not have created such a drive in their Windows PowerShell profile. To avoid a potential error that might arise when creating a Windows PowerShell drive for the HKEY_CLASSES_ROOT hive, you use the *Test-Path* cmdlet to check whether an HKCR drive exists. If the HKCR drive does exist, it will be used, and the *Write-Verbose* cmdlet will be used to print a status message that states that the HKCR drive was found and the search is commencing for the class ID of the WMI provider. This is shown here.

```
If(Test-Path -path HKCR:)
    {
      Write-Verbose "HKCR: drive found. Testing for $clsID"
```

To detect whether the WMI provider is registered with DCOM, you only need to determine whether the class ID of the WMI provider is present in the CLSID section of HKEY_CLASSES_ROOT. The best way to check for the presence of the registry key is to use the *Test-Path* cmdlet. This is shown here.

```
Test-path -path (Join-Path -path HKCR:\CLSID -childpath $clsID)
    }
```

Alternatively, if there is no HKCR drive on the computer, you can go ahead and create one. You can search for the existence of a drive that is rooted in HKEY_CLASSES_ROOT, and if you find it, you can then use the PS drive in your query. To find out whether there are any PS drives rooted in HKEY_CLASSES_ROOT, you can use the *Get-PSDrive* cmdlet, as shown here.

```
Get-PSDrive | Where-Object { $_.root -match "classes" } |
Select-Object name
```

This, however, might be more trouble than it is worth. There is nothing wrong with having multiple PS drives mapped to the same resource. Therefore, if there is no HKCR drive, the *Write-Verbose* cmdlet is used to print a message that the drive does not exist and will be created.

This is shown here.

```
Else
  {
    Write-Verbose "HKCR: drive not found. Creating same."
```

To create a new Windows PowerShell drive, you use the *New-PSDrive* cmdlet to specify the name for the PS drive and the root location of the drive. Because this is going to be a registry drive, you will use the registry provider. When a PS drive is created, it displays feedback back to the Windows PowerShell console. This feedback is shown here.

```
PS C:\> New-PSDrive -Name HKCR -PSProvider registry -Root Hkey_Classes_Root

Name       Provider    Root                            CurrentLocation
----       --------    ----                            ---------------
HKCR       Registry    Hkey_Classes_Root
```

The feedback from creating the registry drive can be distracting. To get rid of the feedback, you can pipeline the results to the *Out-Null* cmdlet. This is shown here.

```
New-PSDrive -Name HKCR -PSProvider registry -Root Hkey_Classes_Root | Out-Null
```

When the Windows PowerShell registry drive has been created, it is time to look for the existence of the WMI provider class ID. Before that is done, the *Write-Verbose* cmdlet is used to provide feedback about this step of the operation. This is shown here.

```
Write-Verbose "Testing for $clsID"
```

The *Test-Path* cmdlet is used to check for the existence of the WMI provider class ID. To build the path to the registry key, you use *Join-Path* cmdlet. The parent path is the HKCR registry drive CLSID hive, and the child path is the WMI provider class ID that is stored in the *$clsID* variable. This is shown here.

```
Test-path -path (Join-Path -path HKCR:\CLSID -childpath $clsID)
```

After the *Test-Path* cmdlet has been used to check for the existence of the WMI provider class ID, the *Write-Verbose* cmdlet is used to display a message stating that the test is complete. This is shown here.

```
Write-Verbose "Test complete."
```

It is a best practice to avoid making permanent modifications to the Windows PowerShell environment in a script. Therefore, you will want to remove the Windows PowerShell drive if it was created in the script. The *Write-Verbose* cmdlet is employed to provide a status update, and the *Remove-PSDrive* cmdlet is used to remove the HKCR registry drive. To avoid cluttering the Windows PowerShell console, you pipeline the result of removing the HKCR registry drive to the *Out-Null* cmdlet.

This is shown here.

```
    Write-Verbose "Removing HKCR: drive."
    Remove-PSDrive -Name HKCR | Out-Null
   }
```

Finally, you need to set $VerbosePreference back to the value that was stored in $oldVerbose-Preference. This line of code is executed even if no change to $VerbosePreference is made. This is shown here.

```
  $VerbosePreference = $oldVerbosePreference
} #end Get-WmiProvider function
```

The entry point to the script assigns a value to the $providername variable. This is shown here.

```
$providername = "msiprov"
```

The Get-WmiProvider function is called, and it passes both the WMI provider name that is stored in the $providername variable and the -verbose switch parameter. The if statement is used because Get-WmiProvider returns a Boolean value: true or false. This is shown here.

```
if(Get-WmiProvider -providerName $providerName  -verbose )
```

If the Get-WmiProvider function returns true, the WMI class supported by the WMI provider is queried via the Get-WMIObject cmdlet. This is shown here.

```
  {

    Get-WmiObject -class win32_product

  }
```

If the WMI provider is not found, a message stating this is displayed to the console. This is shown here.

```
else
  {
    "$providerName provider not found"
  }
```

The complete Get-WmiProviderFunction.ps1 script is shown here.

Get-WmiProviderFunction.ps1

```
Function Get-WmiProvider([string]$providerName, [switch]$verbose)
{
 $oldVerbosePreference = $VerbosePreference
 if($verbose) { $VerbosePreference = "continue" }
 $provider =  Get-WmiObject -Class __provider -filter "name = '$providerName'"
 If($provider -ne $null)
   {
     $clsID = $provider.clsID
     Write-Verbose "$providerName WMI provider found. ClsID is $($clsID)"
   }
 Else
```

```
      {
        Return $false
      }
    Write-Verbose "Checking for proper registry registration ..."
    If(Test-Path -path HKCR:)
        {
           Write-Verbose "HKCR: drive found. Testing for $clsID"
           Test-path -path (Join-Path -path HKCR:\CLSID -childpath $clsID)
        }
    Else
        {
          Write-Verbose "HKCR: drive not found. Creating same."
          New-PSDrive -Name HKCR -PSProvider registry -Root Hkey_Classes_Root | Out-Null
          Write-Verbose "Testing for $clsID"
          Test-path -path (Join-Path -path HKCR:\CLSID -childpath $clsID)
          Write-Verbose "Test complete."
          Write-Verbose "Removing HKCR: drive."
          Remove-PSDrive -Name HKCR | Out-Null
        }
  $VerbosePreference = $oldVerbosePreference
} #end Get-WmiProvider function

# *** Entry Point to Script ***
$providerName = "msiprov"
 if(Get-WmiProvider -providerName $providerName  -verbose )
  {
     Get-WmiObject -class win32_product
  }
else
  {
    "$providerName provider not found"
  }
```

Handling incorrect data types

There are two approaches to ensuring that your users only enter allowed values for the script parameters. The first is to offer only a limited number of values. The second approach allows the user to enter any value for the parameter. The script then determines whether the value is valid before passing it along to the remainder of the script. In the Get-ValidWmiClassFunction.ps1 script, which follows at the end of this section, a function named *Get-ValidWmiClass* is used to determine whether the value that is supplied to the script is a legitimate WMI class name. In particular, the *Get-ValidWmiClass* function is used to determine whether the string that is passed via the *-class* parameter can be cast to a valid instance of the *System.Management.ManagementClass* .NET Framework class. The purpose of using the *[wmiclass]* type accelerator is to convert a string to an instance of the *System.Management.Management Class* class. As shown here, when you assign a string value to a variable, the variable becomes an instance of the *System.String* class. The *GetType* method is used to get the type of a variable. An array variable is an array, yet it can contain integers and other data types. This is a very important concept.

```
PS C:\> $class = "win32_bio"
PS C:\> $class.GetType()

IsPublic IsSerial Name                              BaseType
-------- -------- ----                              --------
True     True     String                            System.Object
```

To convert the string to a WMI class, you can use the *[wmiclass]* type accelerator. The string value must contain the name of a legitimate WMI class. If the WMI class you are trying to create on the computer does not exist, an error is displayed. This is shown here.

```
PS C:\> $class = "win32_bio"
PS C:\> [wmiclass]$class
Cannot convert value "win32_bio" to type "System.Management.ManagementClass".
Error: "Not found "
At line:1 char:16
+ [wmiclass]$class <<<<
```

The Get-ValidWmiClassFunction.ps1 script begins by creating two command-line parameters. The first is the *computer* parameter, which is used to allow the script to run on a local or remote computer. The second parameter is the *-class* parameter, which is used to provide the name of the WMI class that will be queried by the script. A third parameter is used to allow the script to inspect other WMI namespaces. All three parameters are strings. Because the third parameter has a default value assigned, it can be left out when working with the default WMI namespace. This is shown here.

```
Param (
    [string]$computer = $env:computername,
    [string]$class,
    [string]$namespace = "root\cimv2"
) #end param
```

The *Get-ValidWmiClass* function is used to determine whether the value supplied for the *-class* parameter is a valid WMI class on the particular computer. This is important because different versions of operating systems contain unique WMI classes. So checking for the existence of a WMI class on a remote computer is a good practice to ensure that the script will run in an expeditious manner.

The first thing the *Get-ValidWmiClass* function does is retrieve the current value for the *$ErrorActionPreference* variable. There are four possible values for this variable. The possible enumeration values are *SilentlyContinue*, *Stop*, *Continue*, and *Inquire*. The error-handling behavior of Windows PowerShell is governed by these enumeration values. If the value of *$ErrorActionPreference* is set to *SilentlyContinue*, any error that occurs will be skipped, and the script will attempt to execute the next line of code in the script. The behavior is similar to using the VBScript setting *On Error Resume Next*.

Usually you do not want to use this setting because it can make troubleshooting scripts very difficult. It can also make the behavior of a script unpredictable and even lead to devastating consequences. Consider the case in which you write a script that first creates a new directory on a remote server. Next, it copies all of the files from a directory on your local computer to the remote server. Last, it deletes the directory and all the files from the local computer. Now you enable *$ErrorActionPreference = "SilentlyContinue"* and run the script. The first command fails because the remote server is not available. The second command fails because it could not copy the files—but the third command completes successfully, and you have just deleted all the files you wanted to back up, instead of actually backing up the files. Hopefully, in such a case, you have a recent backup of your critical data. If you set *$ErrorActionPreference* to *SilentlyContinue*, you must handle errors that arise during the course of running the script.

In the *Get-ValidWmiClass* function, the old *$ErrorActionPreference* setting is retrieved and stored in the *$oldErrorActionPreference* variable. Next, the *$ErrorActionPreference* variable is set to *SilentlyContinue*. This is done because it is entirely possible that in the process of checking for a valid WMI class name, errors will be generated. Next, the error stack is cleared of errors. Here are the three lines of code that do this.

```
$oldErrorActionPreference = $errorActionPreference
$errorActionPreference = "silentlyContinue"
$Error.Clear()
```

The value stored in the *$class* variable is used with the *[wmiclass]* type accelerator to attempt to create a *System.Management.ManagementClass* object from the string. Because you will need to run this script on a remote computer and on a local computer, the value in the *$computer* variable is used to provide a complete path to the potential management object. When the variables to make the path to the WMI class are concatenated, a trailing colon causes problems with the *$namespace* variable. To work around this, you use a subexpression to force evaluation of the variable before attempting to concatenate the remainder of the string. The subexpression consists of a leading dollar sign and a pair of parentheses. This is shown here.

```
[wmiclass]"\\$computer\$($namespace):$class" | out-null
```

To determine whether the conversion from string to *ManagementClass* was successful, you check the error record. Because the error record was cleared earlier, any error indicates that the command failed. If an error exists, the *Get-ValidWmiClass* function returns *$false* to the calling code. If no error exists, the *Get-ValidWmiClass* function returns *true*. This is shown here.

```
If($error.count) { Return $false } Else { Return $true }
```

The last thing to do in the *Get-ValidWmiClass* function is to clean up. First, the error record is cleared, and then the value of the *$ErrorActionPreference* variable is set back to the original value. This is shown here.

```
$Error.Clear()
$ErrorActionPreference =  $oldErrorActionPreference
```

The next function in the Get-ValidWmiClassFunction.ps1 script is the *Get-WmiInformation* function. This function accepts the values from the *$computer*, *$class*, and *$namespace* variables, and passes them to the *Get-WmiObject* cmdlet. The resulting *ManagementObject* is pipelined to the *Format-List* cmdlet, and all properties that begin with the letters *a* through *z* are displayed. This is shown here.

```
Function Get-WmiInformation ([string]$computer, [string]$class, [string]$namespace)
{
  Get-WmiObject -class $class -computername $computer -namespace $namespace|
  Format-List -property [a-z]*
} # end Get-WmiInformation function
```

The entry point to the script calls the *Get-ValidWmiClass* function, and if it returns *true*, it next calls the *Get-WmiInformation* function. If, however, the *Get-ValidWmiClass* function returns *false*, a message is displayed that details the class name, namespace, and computer name. This information could be used for troubleshooting problems with obtaining the WMI information. This is shown here.

```
If(Get-ValidWmiClass -computer $computer -class $class -namespace $namespace)
  {
    Get-WmiInformation -computer $computer -class $class -namespace $namespace
  }
Else
  {
    "$class is not a valid wmi class in the $namespace namespace on $computer"
  }
```

The complete Get-ValidWmiClassFunction.ps1 script is shown here.

Get-ValidWmiClassFunction.ps1

```
Param (
    [string]$computer = $env:computername,
    [Parameter(Mandatory=$true)]
    [string]$class,
    [string]$namespace = "root\cimv2"
) #end param

Function Get-ValidWmiClass([string]$computer, [string]$class, [string]$namespace)
{
 $oldErrorActionPreference = $errorActionPreference
 $errorActionPreference = "silentlyContinue"
 $Error.Clear()
 [wmiclass]"\\$computer\$($namespace):$class" | out-null
 If($error.count) { Return $false } Else { Return $true }
 $Error.Clear()
 $ErrorActionPreference =  $oldErrorActionPreference
} # end Get-ValidWmiClass function

Function Get-WmiInformation ([string]$computer, [string]$class, [string]$namespace)
{
  Get-WmiObject -class $class -computername $computer -namespace $namespace|
  Format-List -property [a-z]*
} # end Get-WmiInformation function

# *** Entry point to script ***
```

```
If(Get-ValidWmiClass -computer $computer -class $class -namespace $namespace)
  {
    Get-WmiInformation -computer $computer -class $class -namespace $namespace
  }
Else
 {
    "$class is not a valid wmi class in the $namespace namespace on $computer"
 }
```

Handling out-of-bounds errors

When your script receives input from a user, an allowed value for a script parameter is limited to a specified range of values. If the allowable range is small, it might be best to present the user with a prompt that allows selection from a few choices. This was shown earlier in this chapter, in the "Limiting choices" section.

When the allowable range of values is great, however, limiting the choices through a menu-type system is not practical. This is where boundary checking comes into play.

Using a boundary-checking function

One technique is to use a function that will determine whether the supplied value is permissible. One way to create a boundary-checking function is to have the script create a hash table of permissible values. The *Check-AllowedValue* function is used to gather a hash table of volumes that reside on the target computer. This hash table is then used to verify that the volume requested from the *drive* command-line parameter is actually present on the computer. The *Check-AllowedValue* function returns a Boolean *true* or *false* to the calling code in the main body of the script. The complete *Check-Allowed-Value* function is shown here.

```
Function Check-AllowedValue($drive, $computerName)
{
 $drives = $null
 Get-WmiObject -class Win32_Volume -computername $computerName |
 Where-Object { $_.DriveLetter } |
 ForEach-Object { $drives += @{ $_.DriveLetter = $_.DriveLetter } }
 $drives.contains($drive)
} #end function Check-AllowedValue
```

Because the *Check-AllowedValue* function returns a Boolean value, an *if* statement is used to determine whether the value supplied to the *drive* parameter is permissible. If the drive letter is found in the *$drives* hash table that is created in the *Check-AllowedValue* function, the *Get-DiskInformation* function is called. If the *drive* parameter value is not found in the hash table, a warning message is displayed to the Windows PowerShell console, and the script exits. The complete GetDrivesCheck-AllowedValue.ps1 script is shown here.

GetDrivesCheckAllowedValue.ps1

```
Param(
    [Parameter(Mandatory=$true)]
    [string]$drive,
    [string]$computerName = $env:computerName
) #end param

Function Check-AllowedValue($drive, $computerName)
{
 $drives = $null
 Get-WmiObject -class Win32_Volume -computername $computerName |
 Where-Object { $_.DriveLetter } |
 ForEach-Object { $drives += @{ $_.DriveLetter = $_.DriveLetter } }
 $drives.contains($drive)
} #end function Check-AllowedValue

Function Get-DiskInformation($computerName,$drive)
{
 Get-WmiObject -class Win32_volume -computername $computername -filter "DriveLetter = '$drive'"
} #end function Get-BiosName

# *** Entry Point To Script ***

if(Check-AllowedValue -drive $drive -computername $computerName)
  {
    Get-DiskInformation -computername $computerName -drive $drive
  }
else
  {
   Write-Host -foregroundcolor blue "$drive is not an allowed value:"
  }
```

Placing limits on the parameter

In Windows PowerShell 5.0, you can place limits directly on the parameter in the *param* section of the script. This technique works well when you are working with a limited set of allowable values. The *ValidateRange* parameter attribute will create a numeric range of allowable values, but it is also able to create a range of letters. By using this technique, you can greatly simplify the GetDrivesCheckAllowed-Value.ps1 script by creating an allowable range of drive letters. The *param* statement is shown here.

```
Param(
    [Parameter(Mandatory=$true)]
    [ValidateRange("c","f")]
    [string]$drive,
    [string]$computerName = $env:computerName
) #end param
```

Because you are able to control the permissible drive letters from the command line, you increase the simplicity and readability of the script by not having the requirement to create a separate function to validate the allowed values. In the GetDrivesValidRange.ps1 script, which follows, one additional change is required, and that is to concatenate a colon to the end of the drive letter. In the GetDrives-CheckAllowedValue.ps1 script, you were able to include the drive letter and the colon from the command line. But with the *ValidateRange* attribute, this technique will not work. The trick to concatenating the colon to the drive letter is that it needs to be escaped, as shown here.

```
-filter "DriveLetter = '$drive`:'"
```

The complete GetDrivesValidRange.ps1 script is shown here.

GetDrivesValidRange.ps1

```
Param(
    [Parameter(Mandatory=$true)]
    [ValidateRange("c","d")]
    [string]$drive,
    [string]$computerName = $env:computerName
) #end param

Function Get-DiskInformation($computerName,$drive)
{
 Get-WmiObject -class Win32_volume -computername $computername `
 -filter "DriveLetter = '$drive`:'"
} #end function Get-BiosName

# *** Entry Point To Script ***

Get-DiskInformation -computername $computerName -drive $drive
```

Using *Try...Catch...Finally*

When you are using a *Try...Catch...Finally* block, the command you want to execute is placed in the *Try* block. If an error occurs when the command executes, the error will be written to the *$error* variable, and script execution moves to the *Catch* block. The TestTryCatchFinally.ps1 script, which follows later in this section, uses the *Try* command to attempt to create an object. A string states that the script is attempting to create a new object. The object to create is stored in the *$obj1* variable. The *New-Object* cmdlet creates the object. After the object has been created and stored in the *$a* variable, the members of the object are displayed via the *Get-Member* cmdlet. The following code illustrates the technique.

```
Try
  {
   "Attempting to create new object $obj1"
    $a = new-object $obj1
    "Members of the $obj1"
    "New object $obj1 created"
    $a | Get-Member
  }
```

You use the *Catch* block to capture errors that occurred during the *Try* block. You can specify the type of error to catch, in addition to the action you want to perform when the error occurs. The Test-TryCatchFinally.ps1 script monitors for *System.Exception* errors. The *System.Exception* .NET Framework class is the base class from which all other exceptions derive. This means a *System.Exception* error is as generic as you can get—in essence, it will capture all predefined common system run-time exceptions. When you catch the error, you can then specify what code to execute. In this example, a single string states that the script caught a system exception. The *Catch* block is shown here.

```
Catch [system.exception]
  {
   "caught a system exception"
  }
```

The *Finally* block of a *Try...Catch...Finally* sequence always runs—regardless of whether an error is generated. This means that any code cleanup you want to do, such as explicitly releasing COM objects, should be placed in a *Finally* block. In the TestTryCatchFinally.ps1 script, the *Finally* block displays a string that states that the script has ended. This is shown here.

```
Finally
  {
   "end of script"
  }
```

The complete TestTryCatchFinally.ps1 script is shown here.

TestTryCatchFinally.ps1
```
$obj1 = "Bad.Object"
"Begin test"
Try
  {
   "`tAttempting to create new object $obj1"
    $a = new-object $obj1
    "Members of the $obj1"
    "New object $obj1 created"
    $a | Get-Member
  }
Catch [system.exception]
  {
   "`tcaught a system exception"
  }
Finally
  {
   "end of script"
  }
```

When the TestTryCatchFinally.ps1 script runs and the value of *$obj1* is equal to *BadObject*, an error occurs, because there is no object named *BadObject* that can be created via the *New-Object* cmdlet. Figure 19-6 displays the output from the script.

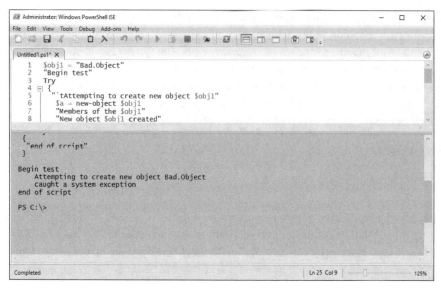

FIGURE 19-6 An attempt to create an invalid object is caught in the *Catch* portion of *Try...Catch...Finally.*

As shown in Figure 19-6, the *Begin test* string is displayed because it is outside the *Try...Catch...Finally* loop. Inside the *Try* block, the string *Attempting to create new object BadObject* is displayed because it comes before the *New-Object* command. This illustrates that the *Try* block is always attempted. The members of the *BadObject* object are not displayed, nor is the string *new object BadObject created*. This indicates that after the error is generated, the script moves to the next block.

The *Catch* block catches and displays the *System.Exception* error. The string *caught a system exception* is also displayed in the ISE. Next, the script moves to the *Finally* block, and the *end of script* string appears.

If the script runs with the value of *$obj1* equal to *system.object* (which is a valid object), the *Try* block completes successfully. As shown in Figure 19-7, the members of *System.Object* are displayed, and the string that states that the object was successfully created also appears in the output. Because no errors are generated in the script, the script execution does not enter the *Catch* block. But the *end of script* string from the *Finally* block is displayed because the *Finally* block always executes regardless of the error condition.

FIGURE 19-7 The *Catch* portion of *Try...Catch...Finally* permits creation of a valid object. The *Finally* portion always runs.

Catching multiple errors

You can have multiple *Catch* blocks in a *Try...Catch...Finally* block. The thing to keep in mind is that when an exception occurs, Windows PowerShell leaves the *Try* block and searches for the *Catch* block. The first *Catch* block that matches the exception that was generated will be used. Therefore, you want to use the most specific exception first, and then move to the more generic exceptions. This is shown in TestTryMultipleCatchFinally.ps1.

TestTryMultipleCatchFinally.ps1

```
$obj1 = "BadObject"
"Begin test ..."
$ErrorActionPreference = "stop"
Try
 {
   "`tAttempting to create new object $obj1 ..."
    $a = new-object $obj1
    "Members of the $obj1"
    "New object $obj1 created"
    $a | Get-Member
 }
```

```
Catch [System.Management.Automation.PSArgumentException]
 {
   "`tObject not found exception. `n`tCannot find the assembly for $obj1"
 }
Catch [system.exception]
 {
   "Did not catch argument exception."
   "Caught a generic system exception instead"
 }
Finally
 {
   "end of script"
 }
```

Figure 19-8 displays the output when the TestTryMultipleCatchFinally.ps1 script is run. In this script, the first *Catch* block catches the specific error that is raised when you are attempting to create an invalid object. To find the specific error, examine the *ErrorRecord* object contained in *$error[0]* after running the command to create the invalid object. The exact category of exception appears in the *Exception* property. The specific error raised is an instance of the *System.Management.Automation. PSArgumentException* object. This is shown here.

```
PS C:\> $Error[0] | fl * -Force


PSMessageDetails        :
Exception               : System.Management.Automation.PSArgumentException:
                          Cannot find type [BadObject]: make sure the assembly
                          containing this type is loaded.
                             at System.Management.Automation.MshCommandRuntime.
                          ThrowTerminatingError(ErrorRecord errorRecord)
TargetObject            :
CategoryInfo            : InvalidType: (:) [New-Object], PSArgumentException
FullyQualifiedErrorId   : TypeNotFound,Microsoft.PowerShell.Commands.
                          NewObjectCommand
ErrorDetails            :
InvocationInfo          : System.Management.Automation.InvocationInfo
ScriptStackTrace        : at <ScriptBlock>, <No file>: line 7
PipelineIterationInfo   : {}
```

If a script has multiple errors, and the error-action preference is set to *Stop*, the first error will cause the script to fail. If you comment out the *$ErrorActionPreference* line, the first error to be generated will be caught by the *System.Exception Catch* block, and the script execution will therefore skip the argument exception. This is shown in Figure 19-9.

FIGURE 19-8 The *Catch* portion of *Try...Catch...Finally* catches specific errors in the order derived.

FIGURE 19-9 The first error raised is the one that will be caught.

Using *PromptForChoice* to limit selections and using *Try...Catch...Finally*: Step-by-step exercises

This exercise explores the use of *PromptForChoice* to limit selections in a script. Following this exercise, you will explore using *Try...Catch...Finally* to detect and to catch errors.

Exploring the *PromptForChoice* construction

1. Open the Windows PowerShell ISE.

2. Create a new script called PromptForChoiceExercise.ps1.

3. Create a variable to be used for the caption. Name the variable *caption* and assign a string value of *This is the caption* to the variable. The code to do this is shown here.

   ```
   $caption = "This is the caption"
   ```

4. Create another variable to be used for the message. Name the variable *message* and assign a string value of *This is the message* to the variable. The code to do this is shown here.

   ```
   $message = "This is the message"
   ```

5. Create a variable named *choices* that will hold the *ChoiceDescription* object. Create an array of three choices—*choice1*, *choice2*, and *choice3*—for the *ChoiceDescription* object. Make the default letter for *choice1* c, the default letter for *choice2* h, and the default letter for *choice3* o. The code to do this is shown here.

   ```
   $choices = [System.Management.Automation.Host.ChoiceDescription[]] `
    @("&choice1", "c&hoice2", "ch&oice3")
   ```

6. Create an integer variable named *defaultChoice* and assign the value *2* to it. The code to do this is shown here.

   ```
   [int]$DefaultChoice = 2
   ```

7. Call the *PromptForChoice* method and assign the return value to the *ChoiceRTN* variable. Provide *PromptForChoice* with the *caption*, *message*, *choices*, and *defaultChoice* variables as arguments to the method. The code to do this is shown here.

   ```
   $choiceRTN = $host.ui.PromptForChoice($caption,$message, $choices,$defaultChoice)
   ```

8. Create a *switch* statement to evaluate the return value contained in the *choiceRTN* variable. The cases are 0, 1, and 2. For case 0, display a string that states *choice1*. For case 1, display a string that states *choice2*, and for case 2, display a string that states *choice3*.

The *switch* statement to do this is shown here.

```
switch($choiceRTN)
  {
   0    { "choice1"  }
   1    { "choice2"  }
   2    { "choice3"  }
  }
```

9. Save and run the script. Test each of the three options to ensure that they work properly. This will require you to run the script three times and select each option in sequence.

   This concludes the exercise.

In the following exercise, you will use *Try...Catch...Finally* in a script to catch specific errors.

Using *Try...Catch...Finally*

1. Open the Windows PowerShell ISE.

2. Create a new script called TryCatchFinallyExercise.ps1.

3. Create a parameter named *object*. Make the variable a mandatory variable, but do not assign a default value to it. The code to do this is shown here.

```
Param(
  [Parameter(Mandatory=$true)]
  $object)
```

4. Display a string that states that the script is beginning the test. This code is shown here.

```
"Beginning test ..."
```

5. Open the *Try* portion of the *Try...Catch...Finally* block. This is shown here.

```
Try
{
```

6. Display a tabbed string that states that the script is attempting to create the object stored in the *object* variable. This code is shown here.

```
"`tAttempting to create object $object"
```

7. Now call the *New-Object* cmdlet and attempt to create the object stored in the *object* variable. This code is shown here.

```
New-Object $object }
```

8. Add the *Catch* statement and have it catch a *[system.exception]* object. This part of the code is shown here.

```
Catch [system.exception]
```

9. Add a script block for the *Catch* statement that moves the insertion point one tab (by using the `t character) and displays a string that says that the script was unable to create the object. This code is shown here.

```
{ "`tUnable to create $object" }
```

10. Add a *Finally* statement that states that the script reached the end. This code is shown here.

```
Finally
  { "Reached the end of the Script" }
```

11. Save the script.

12. Run the script, and at the prompt for an object, enter the letters **sample**. You should get the following output.

```
Beginning sample ...
        Attempting to create object sample
        Unable to create sample
Reached the end of the Script
```

13. Now run the script again. This time, at the object prompt, enter the letters **psobject**. You should get the following output.

```
Beginning test ...
     Attempting to create object psobject

Reached the end of the Script
```

This concludes the exercise.

Chapter 19 quick reference

To	Do this
Handle a potential error arising from a missing value of a *computername* parameter	Use the *param* statement and assign a default value of *$env:computername* to the *ComputerName* parameter.
Make a parameter mandatory	Use the *[Parameter(Mandatory=$true)]* parameter attribute.
Cause the *Test-Connection* cmdlet to return a Boolean value	Use the *-Quiet* switch parameter.
Ensure that a remote computer is on prior to making a remote connection	Use the *Test-Connection* cmdlet.
Ensure that only valid data types are entered	Write a function to test the data prior to executing the remaining portion of the script.
Ensure that code will always run, regardless of whether an error is raised	Place the code in the *Finally* block of a *Try...Catch...Finally* structure.
Gracefully exit a script when a portion of code might cause an error	Use *Try...Catch...Finally* to attempt to execute the code, catch any specific errors, and clean up the environment.

Using the Windows PowerShell workflow

After completing this chapter, you will be able to

- Know when to use a Windows PowerShell workflow.

- Understand workflow activities.

- Know how to checkpoint a Windows PowerShell workflow.

- Know how to add a sequence to a Windows PowerShell workflow.

Why use workflows?

Windows PowerShell workflows are cool because the commands consist of a sequence of related activities. You can use a workflow to run commands that take an extended period of time. When you use a workflow, commands can survive restarts and disconnected sessions, and they can even be suspended and resumed without losing the data. This is because the workflow automatically saves state and data at the beginning and at the end of the workflow. In addition, it can save data at specific points that you specify. These persistence points are like checkpoints or snapshots of the activity. If a failure occurs that is unrecoverable, you can use the persisted data points and resume from the last data point instead of having to begin the entire process anew.

> **Note** Windows PowerShell workflows are Windows Workflow Foundation (WWF), but instead of having to write the workflow in XAML (Extensible Application Markup Language), you can write the workflow by using Windows PowerShell syntax and Windows PowerShell creates the XAMAL for you. You can also package the workflow in a Windows PowerShell module if you want.

The two main reasons for using Windows PowerShell workflows are reliability and performance when performing large-scale or long-running commands. These two reasons break down into the following key points or categories:

- Parallel task execution

- Workflow throttling

- Connection throttling

- Connection pooling

- Integration with disconnection sessions

If your goal for using a Windows PowerShell workflow does not fall into one of these categories, you are probably using the wrong technology, or at the very least adding unnecessary complexity to your Windows PowerShell script. Especially with the introduction of Desired State Configuration (DSC), you might not need to write a workflow at all. DSC is covered in Chapter 21, "Managing Windows Power-Shell DSC." With this caveat in mind, let's now look at the requirements for using Windows PowerShell workflow.

Workflow requirements

You can run a workflow that uses Windows PowerShell cmdlets if the target (the managed node) runs at least Windows PowerShell 2.0. You do not need Windows PowerShell 2.0 if the workflow does not run Windows PowerShell cmdlets. You can use Windows Management Instrumentation (WMI) or Common Information Model (CIM) commands on computers that do not have Windows PowerShell installed—which means that you can use Windows PowerShell workflows in a heterogeneous environment.

The computer that runs the workflow is the host (client) computer. It must be running at least Windows PowerShell 3.0 and have Windows PowerShell remoting enabled. In addition, the target (managed node) computer must have at least Windows PowerShell 2.0 with Windows PowerShell remoting enabled if the workflow includes Windows PowerShell cmdlets.

A simple workflow

Although much of the focus around Windows PowerShell workflows is around the management of large networks, you can use workflows on your local computer. You might want to do this if the task you are working with might take a long time to run. Therefore, from a learning standpoint, it makes sense to begin with a workflow that just works on your local computer. To write a workflow, begin with the *workflow* keyword. Provide a name for the workflow, and inside the braces (that is, within the script block), specify the code you want to use.

The syntax is very much like a Windows PowerShell function. Here is a basic workflow.

HelloUserworkflow.ps1

```
Workflow HelloUser
{ "Hello $env:USERNAME" }
```

Just as with a Windows PowerShell function, you need to run the code and load the workflow prior to using it. In the Windows PowerShell ISE, run the script containing the workflow, and in the immediate window you can use the workflow. This is shown in Figure 20-1.

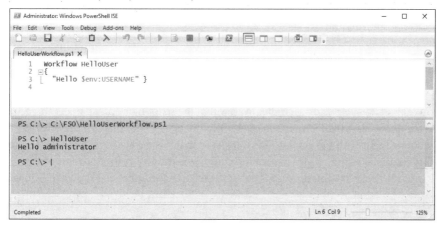

FIGURE 20-1 Run the workflow from the script pane, and execute the workflow in the script pane of the Windows PowerShell ISE.

You can use normal types of Windows PowerShell commands to add logic to the workflow if you want. The following workflow uses the *Get-Date* cmdlet to retrieve the hour in 24-hour format. If the hour is less than 12, it displays *good morning*. If the hour is between 12 and 18, it displays *good afternoon*. Otherwise, it displays *good evening*. Here is the workflow.

HelloUserTimeworkflow.ps1

```
Workflow HelloUserTime
{
 $dateHour = Get-date -UFormat '%H'
 if($dateHour -lt 12) {"good morning"}
 ELSeIF ($dateHour -ge 12 -AND $dateHour -le 18) {"good afternoon"}
 ELSE {"good evening"}
}
```

Parallel PowerShell

One of the reasons for using a Windows PowerShell workflow is to be able to easily execute commands in parallel. This can result in some significant time savings.

Note For an example of the time savings you can achieve by using a Windows PowerShell workflow and executing commands in parallel, see the excellent article, *Use PowerShell Workflow to Ping Computers in Parallel*, written by Windows PowerShell MVP Niklas Goude and available at *http://blogs.technet.com/b/heyscriptingguy/archive /2012/11/20/use-powershell-workflow-to-ping-computers-in-parallel.aspx*.

To perform a parallel activity by using a Windows PowerShell workflow, use the *Foreach* keyword with the *-Parallel* parameter. This is followed by the operation and the associated script block. The following illustrates this technique.

```
Foreach -Parallel ($cn in $computers)
 { Get-CimInstance -PSComputerName $cn -ClassName win32_computersystem }
```

One of the things to keep in mind here—which could be a major source of frustration early on—is that when you call the *Get-CimInstance* cmdlet from within the script block of a parallel *Foreach*, you have to use the automatically added *PSComputerName* parameter, and not the *ComputerName* parameter you would normally use with the cmdlet. This is because that is the way that a Windows PowerShell workflow handles computer names. If you look at the command-line syntax for *Get-CimInstance*, you do not see the *PSComputerName* parameter at all. The syntax for *Get-CimInstance* is shown in Figure 20-2.

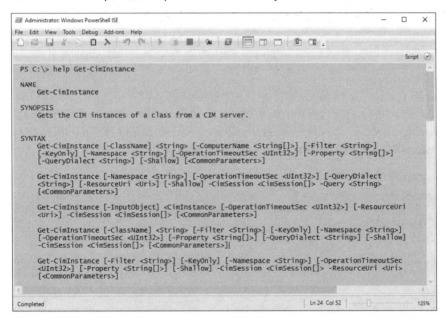

FIGURE 20-2 The *Get-CimInstance* cmdlet does not have a *PSComputerName* parameter.

The nice thing is that if you forget to use -*PSComputerName* and try to run the Windows Power-Shell workflow, an error arises. The error is detailed enough that it actually tells you the problem, and tells you what you need to do to solve the problem. This is shown in Figure 20-3.

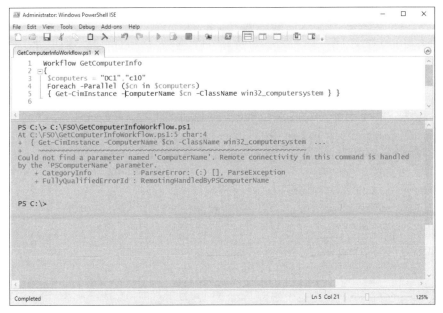

FIGURE 20-3 Omitting the *PSComputerName* parameter results in an informative error message.

After you rename the parameter in *Get-CimInstance*, you can run the workflow, and it does not generate any errors.

The complete GetComputerInfoWorkflow.ps1 script is shown here.

GetComputerInfoWorkFlow.ps1

```
Workflow GetComputerInfo
{
 $computers = "server1","client1"
 Foreach -Parallel ($cn in $computers)
 { Get-CimInstance -PSComputerName $cn -ClassName win32_computersystem } }
```

You call the workflow and are greeted with computer information from each of the servers whose name is stored in the *$computers* variable. The script and the output from the script are shown in Figure 20-4.

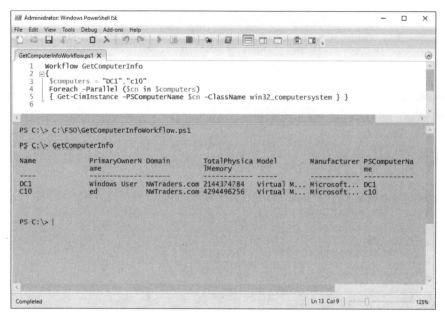

FIGURE 20-4 Running the workflow produces detailed computer information.

Workflow activities

A Windows PowerShell workflow is made up of a series of activities. In fact, the basic unit of work in a Windows PowerShell workflow is called an activity. There are five different types of Windows PowerShell workflow activities that are available for use. Table 20-1 describes the different types of activities.

TABLE 20-1 Workflow activities and associated descriptions

Activity	Description
CheckPoint-Workflow (alias = PSPersist)	Creates a checkpoint. The state and data of a workflow in progress are saved. If the workflow is interrupted or rerun, it can restart from any checkpoint. Use the *Checkpoint-Workflow* activity, along with the *PSPersist* workflow common parameter and the *PSPersistPreference* variable, to make your workflow robust and recoverable.
ForEach -Parallel	Runs the statements in the script block once for each item in a collection. The items are processed in parallel. The statements in the script block run sequentially.
Parallel	Allows all statements in the script block to run at the same time. The order of execution is undefined.

Activity	Description
Sequence	Creates a block of sequential statements within a parallel script block. The sequence script block runs in parallel with other activities in the parallel script block. However, the statements in the sequence script block run in the order in which they appear. This activity is valid only within a parallel script block.
Suspend-Workflow	Stops a workflow temporarily. To resume the workflow, use the *Resume-Job* cmdlet.

Windows PowerShell cmdlets as activities

Windows PowerShell cmdlets from the core modules are automatically implemented as activities for use in a Windows PowerShell workflow. These core modules all begin with the name *Microsoft.PowerShell*. To find these cmdlets, you can use the *Get-Command* cmdlet as shown here.

```
Get-Command -Module microsoft.powershell*
```

The command and the associated output from the *Get-Command* cmdlet are shown in Figure 20-5.

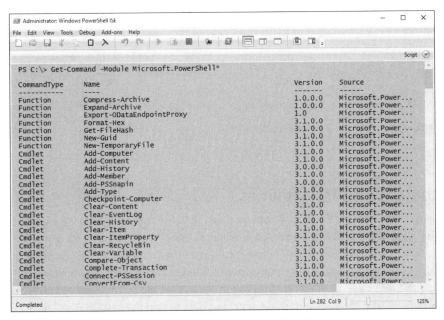

FIGURE 20-5 You can display the core Windows PowerShell cmdlets.

Disallowed core cmdlets

Not all of the cmdlets from the Windows PowerShell core modules are permitted as automatic activities for Windows PowerShell workflows. The reason for this is that some of the core cmdlets do not work well in workflows. A quick look at the disallowed list makes this abundantly clear. The disallowed core cmdlets are shown in the following list.

Disallowed core Windows PowerShell cmdlets

Add-History	Enable-PSBreakpoint	Get-PSBreakpoint
Invoke-History	Set-Alias	Start-Transcript
Add-PSSnapin	Enter-PSSession	Get-PSCallStack
New-Alias	Set-PSBreakpoint	Stop-Transcript
Clear-History	Exit-PSSession	Get-PSSnapin
New-Variable	Set-PSDebug	Trace-Command
Clear-Variable	Export-Alias	Get-Transaction
Out-GridView	Set-StrictMode	Undo-Transaction
Complete-Transaction	Export-Console	Get-Variable
Remove-PSBreakpoint	Set-TraceMode	Use-Transaction
Debug-Process	Get-Alias	Import-Alias
Remove-PSSnapin	Set-Variable	Write-Host
Disable-PSBreakpoint	Get-History	
Remove-Variable	Start-Transaction	

Non-automatic cmdlet activities

If a cmdlet is not in the Windows PowerShell core modules, that does not mean that it is excluded—in fact, it probably is not excluded. When a non-core Windows PowerShell cmdlet is used in a Windows PowerShell workflow, Windows PowerShell automatically runs the cmdlet as an InlineScript activity. An InlineScript activity permits you to run commands in a Windows PowerShell workflow and to share data that would not otherwise be allowed. In the InlineScript script block, you can call any Windows PowerShell command or expression and share state and data within the session. This includes imported modules and variable values. For example, the cmdlets from the table in the previous section that are not permitted in a Windows PowerShell workflow could be included in an InlineScript activity.

Parallel activities

To create a Windows PowerShell workflow that uses a parallel workflow activity, you use the *Parallel* keyword and supply a script block. The following workflow illustrates this technique.

Get-EventLogData.ps1

```
WorkFlow Get-EventLogData
{
 Parallel
 {
    Get-EventLog -LogName application -Newest 1
    Get-EventLog -LogName system -Newest 1
    Get-EventLog -LogName 'Windows PowerShell' -Newest 1 } }
```

After you run the script containing the *Get-EventLogData* workflow, you go to the execution pane of the Windows PowerShell ISE and execute the workflow. What happens is that the three *Get-EventLog* cmdlets execute in parallel. This results in a powerful and quick way to grab event log data. If you call the workflow with no parameters, it executes on your local computer. This is shown in Figure 20-6.

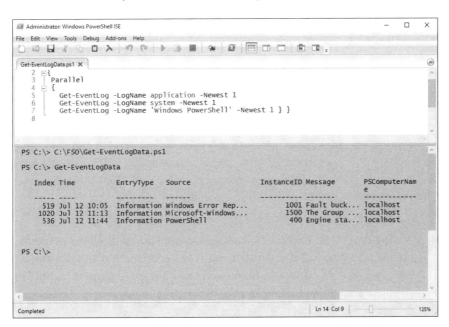

FIGURE 20-6 Running the workflow with no parameters returns event information.

The cool thing is that with a Windows PowerShell workflow, you automatically gain access to several automatic parameters. One of these automatic parameters is *PSComputerName*. Therefore, for example, with no additional work, I can use the automatic *PSComputerName* workflow parameter and run the workflow on two remote servers, even though this workflow does not exist on Server 1 or Server2, it only exists here on my workstation.

Checkpointing Windows PowerShell workflow

If you have a Windows PowerShell workflow and you need to save workflow state or data to disk while the workflow runs, you can configure a checkpoint. In this way, if something interrupts the workflow, it does not need to restart completely. Instead, the workflow resumes from the point of the last checkpoint. Checkpointing of a Windows PowerShell workflow is also sometimes referred to as *persistence* or *persisting a workflow*. Because Windows PowerShell workflows run on large distributed networks or control the execution of long-running tasks, it is vital that the workflow be able to handle interruptions.

Understanding checkpoints

A checkpoint is a snapshot of the workflow's current state. This includes the current values of variables and generated output. Checkpointing persists this data to disk. It is possible to configure multiple checkpoints in a workflow. Windows PowerShell workflows provide multiple methods for implementing checkpointing. Regardless of the method used to generate the checkpoint, Windows PowerShell will use the data in the newest checkpoint for the workflow to recover and to resume the workflow if interrupted. If a workflow runs as a job (for example, by using the *AsJob* workflow common parameter), Windows PowerShell retains the workflow checkpoint until the job is deleted (for example, by using the *Remove-Job* cmdlet).

Placing checkpoints

You can place checkpoints anywhere in a Windows PowerShell workflow. This includes before and after each command or activity. The counterbalance to this sort of a paranoid approach is that each checkpoint uses resources, and therefore it interrupts the processing of the workflow—often with perceptible results. In addition, every time the workflow runs on a target computer, it checkpoints the workflow.

> **Tip** So where are the best places to place a checkpoint? Well, I like to place a checkpoint after a portion of the workflow that is significant—such as something that takes a long time to run. Or I might place one after a section of the workflow that uses a large amount of resources, or even before something that relies on a resource that is not always available.

Adding checkpoints

There are several levels of checkpoint that you can add to a Windows PowerShell workflow. For example, you can add a checkpoint at the workflow level or at the activity level. If you add a checkpoint to the workflow level, it will cause a checkpoint to occur at the beginning and at the end of the workflow.

Workflow checkpoints are free

The absolutely, positively easiest way to add a checkpoint to a Windows PowerShell workflow is to use the -*PSPersist* common parameter when calling the workflow. It requires virtually no extra code, and in fact it is available free after you create a workflow.

The following workflow obtains network adapter, disk, and volume information.

Get-CompInfoWorkflowCheckPointWorkflow.ps1

```
workflow Get-CompInfo
{
  Get-NetAdapter
  Get-Disk
  Get-Volume
}
```

To cause the workflow to checkpoint, call the workflow with the -*PSPersist* parameter and set it to *$true*. The command line is shown here.

```
Get-CompInfo -PSComputerName server1, server2 -PSPersist $true
```

When you run the workflow, a progress bar appears. The progress bar appears for only a few seconds while the checkpoint is created. This progress bar is shown in Figure 20-7.

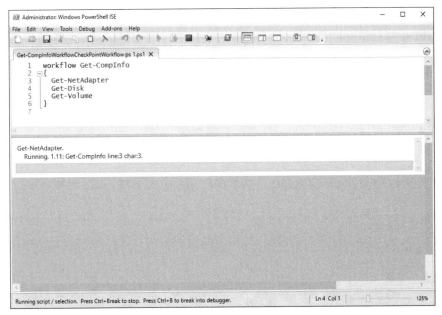

FIGURE 20-7 Checkpoints cause a workflow to take more time to run.

After the checkpoints, the workflow completes quickly and displays the gathered information. Figure 20-8 shows the output and the command line used to call the workflow.

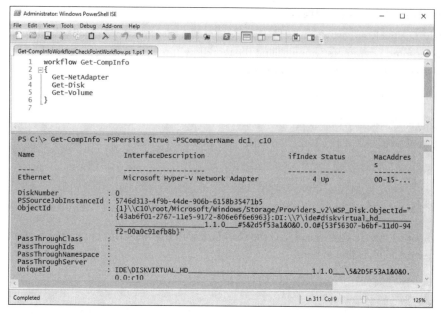

FIGURE 20-8 After running the script to load the workflow, the command line calls the workflow against two computers and checkpoints the workflow.

Checkpointing activities

If you use a core Windows PowerShell cmdlet, it picks up an automatic *PSPersist* parameter. You can then checkpoint the workflow at the activity level. You use the *-PSPersist* parameter at the activity level the same way you do at the workflow level. To add a checkpoint, set the value to *$true*. To disable a checkpoint, set it to *$false*.

In the workflow that follows, a checkpoint is set to occur after the completion of the first and third activities.

Get-CompInfoWorkflowPersist.ps1

```
workflow Get-CompInfo
{
  Get-process -PSPersist $true
  Get-Disk
  Get-service -PSPersist $true
}
```

Therefore, the workflow obtains process information, and then the workflow creates a checkpoint. Next, disk information and service information appear and the final checkpoint occurs.

Using the *CheckPoint-Workflow* activity

The *CheckPoint-Workflow* activity causes a workflow to checkpoint immediately. You can place this activity in any location in the workflow. The big advantage of the *Checkpoint-Workflow* activity is that you can use it to checkpoint a workflow that does not use the core Windows PowerShell cmdlets as activities. This means that, for example, you can use a workflow that includes *Get-NetAdapter*, *Get-Disk*, and *Get-Volume*, and still be able to checkpoint the activity. You need to use *Checkpoint-Workflow* because no *-PSPersist* parameter is added automatically to the non-core Windows PowerShell cmdlets. Get-CompInfoWorkflowCheckPointWorkflow.ps1 contains the revised workflow.

Get-CompInfoWorkflowCheckPointWorkflow.ps1

```
workflow Get-CompInfo
{
  Get-NetAdapter
  Get-Disk
  Get-Volume
  Checkpoint-Workflow
}
```

Adding a sequence activity to a workflow

To add a sequence activity to a Windows PowerShell workflow, all you need to do is use the *Sequence* keyword and specify a script block. When you do this, it causes the commands in the sequence script block to run sequentially and in the specified order. The key concept here is that a sequence activity occurs within a parallel activity. The sequence activity is required when you want commands to execute in a particular order. This is because commands running inside a parallel activity execute in an undetermined order. The commands in the sequence script block run in parallel with all of the commands in the parallel activity. But the commands within the sequence script block run in the order in which they appear in the script block. The Get-WinFeatureServersWorkflow.ps1 script contains the workflow illustrating this technique.

Get-WinFeatureServersWorkflow.ps1

```
workflow get-winfeatures
{
 Parallel {
    InlineScript {Get-WindowsFeature -Name PowerShell*}
    Sequence {
        InlineScript {$env:COMPUTERNAME}
        $PSVersionTable.PSVersion } }
}
```

In this workflow, the order in which *Get-WindowsFeature*, the inline script, and the sequence activities run is not determined. The only thing you know for sure is that the *ComputerName* command runs before you obtain the *PSVersion*—because this is the order specified in the sequence activity script block.

> **Note** In Windows PowerShell 3.0, it was possible to call a Windows PowerShell cmdlet from a system that did not contain the cmdlet directly within the workflow. In Windows PowerShell 5.0, this type of activity must be inside an InlineScript activity.

To run the workflow, first run the PS1 script that contains the workflow. Next, call the workflow and pass two computer names to it via the *PSComputerName* automatic parameter. Here is a sample command line.

```
get-winfeatures -PSComputerName DC1
```

Figure 20-9 shows the Windows PowerShell ISE when calling the workflow. It also illustrates the order in which the commands executed at the time. Note that the commands in the sequence script block executed in the specified order—that is, *ComputerName* executed before *$PsVersionTable.PSVersion* executed—but that they were in the same parallel stream of execution.

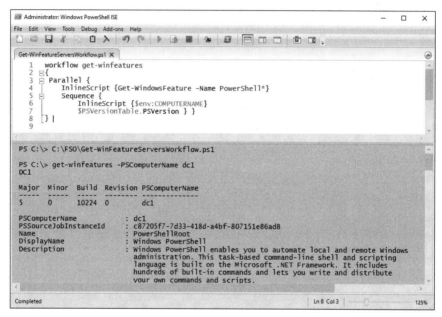

FIGURE 20-9 The order in which the activities run is not guaranteed, except for activities identified in the sequence.

Some workflow coolness

One of the cool things about this workflow is that I executed it from my Windows 8.1 laptop. What is so cool about that? Well the *Get-WindowsFeature* cmdlet does not work on desktop operating systems. Therefore, I ran a command from my laptop that does not exist on my laptop—but it does exist on the target Server1 and Server2 computers. All I have to do is place the cmdlet within an InlineScript activity.

Another cool workflow feature is the InlineScript activity. I am able to access an environmental variable from the remote servers. The InlineScript activity allows me to do things that otherwise would not be permitted in a Windows PowerShell workflow. This adds a lot of flexibility.

Creating a workflow and adding checkpoints: Step-by-step exercises

In this exercise, you'll create a basic workflow in the Windows PowerShell ISE. You will also run the workflow and obtain basic information about your local computer.

Creating a basic Windows PowerShell workflow

1. Start the Windows PowerShell ISE.

2. Use the *Workflow* keyword, specify a workflow name, and open and close the braces. This is shown here.

```
Workflow Basic-Workflow
{

}
```

3. Add the *Get-Disk* cmdlet between the two braces. The command now appears as follows.

```
Workflow Basic-Workflow
{
  Get-Disk
}
```

4. Under the *Get-Disk* cmdlet, add the *Get-Volume* cmdlet. This is shown here.

```
Workflow Basic-Workflow
{
  Get-Disk
  Get-Volume
}
```

5. Under the *Get-Volume* cmdlet, add the *Get-NetAdapter* cmdlet. The complete workflow is shown here.

```
Workflow Basic-Workflow
{
  Get-Disk
  Get-Volume
  Get-NetAdapter
}
```

6. Save the workflow with the name Basic-Workflow.ps1.

7. Run the workflow by pressing the F5 key.

8. In the execution pane (the lower pane) of the Windows PowerShell ISE, enter the workflow name, **Basic-Workflow**, and press the Enter key. This will cause the Basic-Workflow workflow to run. The command is shown here.

```
Basic-Workflow
```

This concludes the exercise.

In the following exercise, you will add a checkpoint and a sequence to the Basic-Workflow. Do not close your Windows PowerShell ISE, nor close the Basic-Workflow.ps1 script.

Adding checkpoints and sequences to a basic workflow

1. If your Windows PowerShell ISE is not already open from the previous exercise, open it and load the Basic-Workflow.ps1 script created in the previous exercise.

2. Save your Basic-Workflow.ps1 script as Basic-WorkflowCheckpoint.ps1.

3. Add a sequence around *Get-Disk*, *Get-Volume*, and *Get-NetAdapter*. This section of the code is shown here.

```
Workflow Basic-WorkflowCheckpoint
{
  Sequence {
    Get-Disk
    Get-Volume
    Get-NetAdapter }
```

4. Add two checkpoints to your workflow inside the sequence. Do this by adding the *-PSPersist $true* command to two core Windows PowerShell cmdlets. The cmdlets are *Get-Process* and *Get-Service*. This portion of the code is shown here.

```
Get-Process -PSPersist $true
Get-Service -PSPersist $true
```

5. Save your modified Basic-WorkflowCheckpoint.ps1 script. The complete code for the workflow is shown here.

```
Workflow Basic-WorkflowCheckpoint
{
  Sequence {
    Get-Disk
    Get-Volume
    Get-NetAdapter }
  Get-Process -PSPersist $true
  Get-Service -PSPersist $true
}
```

6. Run your workflow script by pressing F5 in the Windows PowerShell ISE. This will load the Basic-WorkflowCheckpoint workflow into memory.

7. Execute the workflow against two computers. For practice, you can use *localhost* and *127.0.0.1*. The command line to do this is entered into the output pane of the Windows PowerShell ISE and is shown here.

```
Basic-WorkflowCheckpoint -PSComputerName localhost, "127.0.0.1"
```

8. Scroll through the output. You should be able to discern where the *Get-Disk*, *Get-Volume*, and *Get-NetAdapter* commands ran, and the output should appear in that order.

This concludes the exercise.

Chapter 20 quick reference

To	Do this
Create a Windows PowerShell workflow	Use the *Workflow* keyword, and specify a name and a script block of commands.
Create a checkpoint in a Windows PowerShell workflow	Use the *-PSPersist* parameter and set its value to *$true*, or use the *CheckPoint-Workflow* cmdlet.
Run a workflow against multiple remote computers	Use the *-PSComputerName* automatic parameter when calling the workflow.
Cause Windows PowerShell workflow activities to occur in a specific order	Use the *Sequence* keyword in the workflow, and specify each activity in the order in which it should occur.

CHAPTER 21

Managing Windows PowerShell DSC

After completing this chapter, you will be able to

■ Understand Desired State Configuration.

■ Use Desired State Configuration.

Understanding Desired State Configuration

The marque feature of Windows PowerShell 5.0 is Desired State Configuration (DSC). Although DSC was introduced in Windows PowerShell 4.0, it has been greatly enhanced in Windows PowerShell 5.0. Every presentation at Ignite 2015 in Chicago that discussed DSC received high marks and numerous comments from audience participants. Clearly, this feature resonates soundly with IT pros. So what is Desired State Configuration, how is it used, what are the requirements for implementing it, and how does it help the enterprise administrator?

DSC is a set of extensions to Windows PowerShell with which you can manage systems for both the software and the environment on which software services run. Because DSC is part of the Windows Management Framework (which includes Windows PowerShell 5.0), it is operating-system independent and runs on any computer that is able to run Windows PowerShell 5.0.

The 16 default resource providers included with DSC each support a standard set of configuration properties. The providers and supported properties are shown in Table 21-1.

TABLE 21-1 DSC resource providers and properties

Provider name	Provider properties
File	DestinationPath, Attributes, Checksum, Contents, Credential, DependsOn, Ensure, Force, MatchSource, PsDscRunAsCredential, Recurse, SourcePath, Type
Archive	Destination, Path, Checksum, Credential, DependsOn, Ensure, Force, PsDscRunAsCredential, Validate
Environment	Name, DependsOn, Ensure, Path, PsDscRunAsCredential, Value
Group	GroupName, Credential, DependsOn, Description, Ensure, Members, MembersToExclude, MembersToInclude, PsDscRunAsCredential

Provider name	Provider properties
Log	Message, DependsOn, PsDscRunAsCredential
Package	Name, Path, ProductId, Arguments, Credential, DependsOn, Ensure, LogPath, PsDscRunAsCredential, ReturnCode
Registry	Key, ValueName, DependsOn, Ensure, Force, Hex, PsDscRunAsCredential, ValueData, ValueType
Script	GetScript, SetScript, TestScript, Credential, DependsOn, PsDscRunAsCredential
Service	Name, BuiltInAccount, Credential, Dependencies, DependsOn, Description, DisplayName, Ensure, Path, PsDscRunAsCredential, StartupType, State
User	UserName, DependsOn, Description, Disabled, Ensure, FullName, Password, PasswordChangeNotAllowed, PasswordChangeRequired, PasswordNeverExpires, PsDscRunAsCredential
WaitForAll	NodeName, ResourceName, DependsOn, PsDscRunAsCredential, RetryCount, RetryIntervalSec, ThrottleLimit
WaitForAny	NodeName, ResourceName, DependsOn, PsDscRunAsCredential, RetryCount, RetryIntervalSec, ThrottleLimit
WaitForSome	NodeCount, NodeName, ResourceName, DependsOn, PsDscRunAsCredential, RetryCount, RetryIntervalSec, ThrottleLimit
WindowsFeature	Name, Credential, DependsOn, Ensure, IncludeAllSubFeature, LogPath, PsDscRunAsCredential, Source
WindowsOptionalFeature	Name, DependsOn, Ensure, LogLevel, LogPath, NoWindowsUpdateCheck, PsDscRunAsCredential, RemoveFilesOnDisable, Source
WindowsProcess	Arguments, Path, Credential, DependsOn, Ensure, PsDscRunAsCredential, StandardErrorPath, StandardInputPath, StandardOutputPath, WorkingDirectory

Because it is possible to extend support for additional resources by creating other providers, you are not limited to only configuring these 16 types of resources.

The DSC process

To create a configuration by using DSC, you first need a Managed Object Format (MOF) file. MOF is the syntax used by Windows Management Instrumentation (WMI), and therefore it is a standard text type of format. A sample MOF file for a server named DC1 is shown in Figure 21-1.

You can easily create your own MOF file by creating a DSC configuration script and calling one of the built-in DSC providers or by using a custom provider. To create a configuration script, begin by using the *Configuration* keyword and providing a name for the configuration. Next, open a script block, followed by a *node* and a resource provider. The *node* identifies the target of the configuration. In the ScriptFolderConfig.ps1 script, the configuration creates a directory on a target server named DC1. It uses the *File* resource provider. The source files are copied from a share on the network. The *DestinationPath* parameter defines the folder to be created on DC1. The *type* states that a directory will be created. *Recurse* specifies that all folders beginning at the *SourcePath* and below are copied.

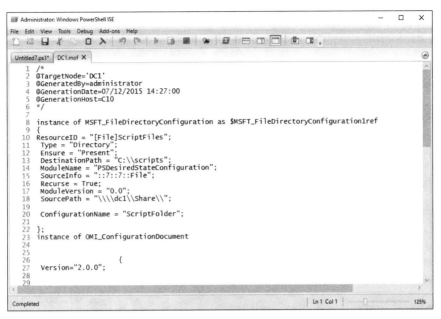

FIGURE 21-1 A DSC MOF file is a stylized text file in the same format that is used by WMI.

The complete ScriptFolderConfig.ps1 script is shown here.

ScriptFolderConfig.ps1

```
#Requires -version 5.0

Configuration ScriptFolder
{
    node 'DC1'
    {
      File ScriptFiles
      {
        SourcePath = "\\dc1\Share\"
        DestinationPath = "C:\scripts"
        Ensure = "Present"
        Type = "Directory"
        Recurse = $true
      }
    }
}
```

After the ScriptFolderConfig.ps1 script runs inside the Windows PowerShell ISE, the *ScriptFolder* configuration loads into memory. The configuration is then called in the same way that a function would be called. When the configuration is called, it creates a MOF file for each node that is identified in the configuration. The path to configuration is used when calling the *Start-DscConfiguration* cmdlet.

There are therefore three distinct phases to this process:

1. Run the script containing the configuration to load the configuration into memory.

2. Call the configuration, and supply any required parameters to create the MOF file for each identified node.

3. Call the *Start-DscConfiguration* cmdlet and supply the path containing the MOF's files created in step 2.

This process is shown in Figure 21-2. The configuration appears in the upper script pane, and the command pane shows the script being run, the configuration being called, and the configuration via the MOF files starting.

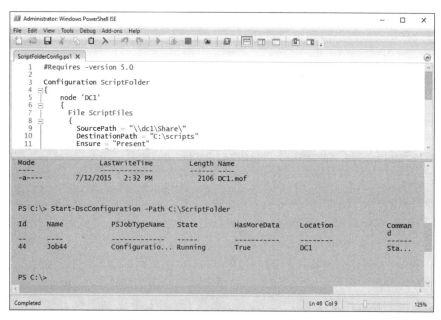

FIGURE 21-2 To run a configuration against a remote server, use the *Start-DscConfiguration* cmdlet and supply the path to a folder containing the appropriate MOF files.

Configuration parameters

To create parameters for a configuration, use the *param* keyword in the same manner as you would for functions. The *param* statement goes just after the opening of the script block for the configuration. As shown in the ScriptFolderVersion.ps1 script, you can even assign default values for the parameters. When a configuration is created, it automatically receives three default parameters: *InstanceName*, *OutputPath*, and *ConfigurationData*. The *InstanceName* parameter holds the instance name of the configuration. The *InstanceName* of a configuration is used to uniquely identify the resource ID used to identify each resource specified in the configuration—usually, the default value for this is sufficient. The *OutputPath* parameter holds the destination for storing the configuration MOF file so that you can redirect the MOF file that is created to a different folder than the one holding the script that is run. The default behavior is to create the MOF files in the same folder that holds the script that creates the configuration. Storing the MOF files in a different location makes it easier to reuse them and update them. The *ConfigurationData* parameter accepts a hash table holding configuration data. In addition, any parameters specified in the *param* statement in the configuration are also available when calling the configuration. By calling the configuration directly from the script that creates the configuration, you are able to simplify the process of creating the MOF. The ScriptFolderVersion.ps1 script adds a second resource provider to the configuration. The *Registry* provider is used to add a registry key, *forscripting*, to the HKLM\Software registry key. The registry value name is *ScriptsVersion* and the data is set to 1.0. The use of the registry provider is shown here.

```
Registry AddScriptVersion
{
   Key = "HKEY_Local_Machine\Software\ForScripting"
   ValueName = "ScriptsVersion"
   ValueData = "1.0"
   Ensure = "Present"
}
```

The additional resource provider call is placed right under the closing brace used to close off the previous call to the *File* resource provider.

The complete ScriptFolderVersion.ps1 script appears here.

ScriptFolderVersion.ps1

```
#Requires -Version 5.0

Configuration ScriptFolderVersion
{
 Param ($server = 'server1')
    node $server
    {
      File ScriptFiles
      {
        SourcePath = "\\dc1\Share\"
        DestinationPath = "C:\scripts"
        Ensure = "present"
        Type = "Directory"
        Recurse = $true
      }
      Registry AddScriptVersion
      {
        Key = "HKEY_Local_Machine\Software\ForScripting"
        ValueName = "ScriptsVersion"
        ValueData = "1.0"
        Ensure = "Present"
      }

    }
}

ScriptFolderVersion
```

Setting dependencies

Everything does not happen at the same time when you call a DSC configuration. Therefore, to ensure that activities occur at the right time, you use the *DependsOn* keyword in the configuration. For example, in the ScriptFolderVersionUnzip.ps1 script, the *Archive* resource provider is used to unzip a compressed file that is copied from a shared folder. The script files are copied from the share by using the *ScriptFiles* activity supported by the *File* resource provider. Because these files must be downloaded from the network share before the zipped folder can be uncompressed, the *DependsOn* keyword is used. Because the *File ScriptFiles* resource activity creates the folder structure containing the compressed folder, the path used by the *Archive* resource provider can be hard-coded. The path is local to the server that actually runs the configuration. The *Archive* activity is shown here.

```
Archive ZippedModule
{
  DependsOn = "[File]ScriptFiles"
  Path = "C:\scripts\PoshModules\PoshModules.zip"
  Destination = $modulePath
  Ensure = "Present"
}
```

The ScriptFolderVersionUnzip.ps1 script parses the *$env:PSModulePath* environment variable to obtain the path to the Windows PowerShell Modules location in the Program Files directory. Following the configuration, it also calls the configuration and redirects the MOF file to the C:\Server1Config folder. It then calls the *Start-DscConfiguration* cmdlet and provides a specific job name for the job. It then uses the *-Verbose* switch parameter to provide more detailed information about the progress. The complete script is shown here.

ScriptFolderVersionUnzip.ps1

```
#Requires -version 5.0

Configuration ScriptFolderVersionUnzip
{
 Param ($modulePath = ($env:PSModulePath -split ';' |
    ?  {$_ -match 'Program Files'}),
    $Server = 'Server1')
    node $Server
    {
      File ScriptFiles
      {
        SourcePath = "\\dc1\Share\"
        DestinationPath = "C:\scripts"
        Ensure = "present"
        Type = "Directory"
        Recurse = $true
      }
      Registry AddScriptVersion
      {
        Key = "HKEY_Local_Machine\Software\ForScripting"
        ValueName = "ScriptsVersion"
        ValueData = "1.0"
        Ensure = "Present"
      }
```

```
      Archive ZippedModule
      {
        DependsOn = "[File]ScriptFiles"
        Path = "C:\scripts\PoshModules\PoshModules.zip"
        Destination = $modulePath
        Ensure = "Present"
      }
    }
}

ScriptFolderVersionUnZip -output C:\server1Config
Start-DscConfiguration -Path C:\server1Config -JobName Server1Config -Verbose
```

Controlling configuration drift

Because Windows PowerShell Desired State Configuration is idempotent, you can run the same configuration script multiple times without fear of creating multiple resources or generating errors. Therefore, if the same configuration runs multiple times, as long as the configuration has not drifted, no changes are made. If the configuration has drifted, you can easily bring the server back into the state you want it to be in. You do not need to worry about modifying the configuration script to correct only detected errors. In fact, you do not even need to worry about configuration drift—when you just run the same configuration, you can be assured that the server will be brought back into state. In the situation where a server must match the desired state, you can use the task scheduler to run *Start-DscConfiguration* at a regular interval that matches the specific urgency of the required checks.

Another way to check for configuration drift is to use the *Test-DscConfiguration* function. The way to do this is to create a CIM session to the remote servers whose configuration needs to be checked. Do this from the same server that was used to create the DSC so that access to the MOF files is assured. After the CIM session is created, pass it to the *Test-DscConfiguration* function. This technique is shown here.

```
PS C:\> $session = New-CimSession -ComputerName server1, server2 -Credential nwtraders\
administrator

PS C:\> Test-DscConfiguration -CimSession $session
True
True
```

The SetServicesConfig.ps1 script creates two configuration MOF files—one for each server specified in the *node* array. This is shown here.

SetServicesConfig.ps1

```
Configuration SetServices
{
 node @('DC1')
 {
  Service Bits
  {
   Name = "Bits"
   StartUpType = "Automatic"
```

```
   State = "Running"
   BuiltinAccount = 'LocalSystem'
  }
  Service Browser
  {
   Name = "Browser"
   StartUpType = "Disabled"
   State = "Stopped"
   BuiltinAccount = 'LocalSystem'
  }
  Service DHCP
  {
   Name = "DHCP"
   StartUpType = "Automatic"
   State = "Running"
   BuiltinAccount = 'LocalService'
  }
 }
}

SetServices -OutputPath C:\ServerConfig
Start-DscConfiguration -Path C:\ServerConfig
```

Figure 21-3 illustrates running the configuration and using CIM to verify that the configuration is still intact.

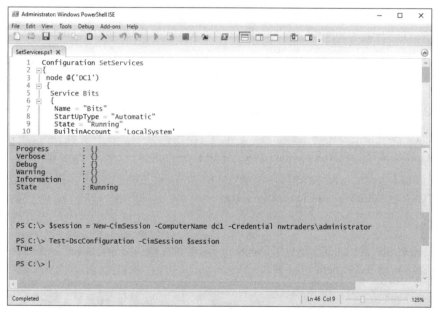

FIGURE 21-3 CIM is used to test the configuration of a DSC-configured target node.

Modifying environment variables

When using built-in Windows PowerShell DSC resources, it is important to import a DSC resource module to avoid warning messages and to ensure that the DSC process runs smoothly. The resource module to import is called the *PSDesiredStateConfiguration* module, which is a default module, just as the built-in DSC resources are default. To import the *PSDesiredStateConfiguration* module, use the *Import-DscResource* cmdlet with the *-ModuleName* parameter. This technique is shown here.

```
Import-DscResource –ModuleName 'PSDesiredStateConfiguration'
```

This command goes just inside the configuration script block that appears under the *Configuration* keyword. I like to place it above the *Node* keyword, as shown here.

```
#Requires -version 5.0

Configuration SetEnvironment
{
 Import-DscResource –ModuleName 'PSDesiredStateConfiguration'
  Node @('C10')
```

To create an environment variable, use the *Environment* built-in DSC resource that comes with Windows PowerShell 5.0 on Windows 10. When using a DSC resource that is unfamiliar, you can use IntelliSense within the Windows PowerShell ISE to show available members and to obtain an idea of acceptable input for the members. To do this, place the cursor just after the DSC resource name and press the spacebar while holding down the Ctrl key. This will start IntelliSense and display the members of the resource. This technique is shown in Figure 21-4.

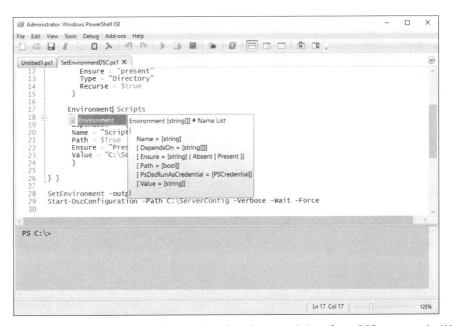

FIGURE 21-4 When you press Ctrl+Spacebar when the cursor is just after a DSC resource, the Windows PowerShell ISE IntelliSense displays members of the resource.

The first thing to do to create an environment variable is to call the *Environment* DSC resource, and then to provide a name for the action. Next, as with all DSC resources, a dependency can be set. Keep in mind, when creating a dependency, that both the resource provider and the name of the action are included inside quotation marks. Next comes the name of the environment variable, whether you want the variable to be present or not, and finally, the value for the variable. In the code shown here, I create an environment variable named *Scripts* and assign it a path to a folder that contains scripts. Because I am assigning a path to a folder, I want to ensure that the folder actually exists, so I set a dependency for a file resource. This is shown here.

```
Environment Scripts
    {
    DependsOn = "[File]ScriptFiles"
    Name = "Scripts"
    Path = $True
    Ensure = "Present"
    Value = "C:\Scripts"
    }
```

When compiling the MOF file (by calling the DSC configuration I just created), I specify a file folder for the output. If the folder does not exist, it will be created when the configuration is compiled. I then start the DSC configuration process by calling the *Start-DscConfiguration* cmdlet, specifying the path to the MOF file, and using the *-Verbose* switch parameter so I can have additional information about the configuration process. I also use the *-Force* switch parameter to force the configuration to take place, and the *-Wait* switch parameter to halt execution until the configuration actually takes place. The complete configuration script is shown here.

SetEnvironmentDSC.ps1

```
#Requires -version 5.0

Configuration SetEnvironment
{
 Import-DscResource –ModuleName 'PSDesiredStateConfiguration'
  Node @('C10')
   {
     File ScriptFiles
      {
        SourcePath = "\\dc1\Share\"
        DestinationPath = "C:\scripts"
        Ensure = "present"
        Type = "Directory"
        Recurse = $true
     }
```

```
    Environment Scripts
    {
    DependsOn = "[File]ScriptFiles"
    Name = "Scripts"
    Path = $True
    Ensure = "Present"
    Value = "C:\Scripts"
    }

} }

SetEnvironment -output C:\ServerConfig
Start-DscConfiguration -Path C:\ServerConfig -Verbose -Wait -Force
```

When I run the configuration script, I get the output shown in Figure 21-5.

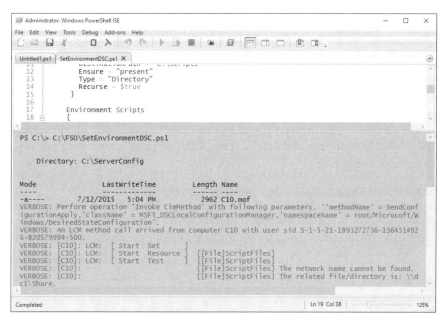

FIGURE 21-5 The *-Verbose* and *-Wait* switch parameters provide useful information when you are first running a DSC configuration script.

One thing to keep in mind when creating environment variables is that they do not take effect until the computer restarts, because that is when the current environment loads. Therefore, a restart is required before you can view the newly created environment variable. After the restart takes place, I use the $env PS drive to view the value of the newly created variable. This technique is shown here.

```
PS C:\> $env:Scripts
C:\Scripts
```

Creating a DSC configuration and adding a dependency: Step-by-step exercises

In this exercise, you'll create a DSC configuration that will run on your local computer. In the DSC configuration, you will use the *File* resource and copy local files to a new directory. In the next exercise, you will add a dependency.

Creating a DSC configuration

1. Start the Windows PowerShell console.

2. Use the *Configuration* keyword to begin your configuration. Use a name like SetFileFolder for the name of the configuration. Begin your script with the *#Requires* directive to use Windows PowerShell 5.0. Open a script block to be used for the remainder of the configuration script. The code is shown here.

   ```
   #Requires -version 5.0

   Configuration SetFileFolder
   {
   ```

3. Use the *Import-DscResource* cmdlet to import the *PSDesiredStateConfiguration* module. The code to do this is shown here.

   ```
   Import-DscResource –ModuleName 'PSDesiredStateConfiguration'
   ```

4. Add a *node* statement to specify the node you want to run the DSC on. In this example, I specify the C10 computer. Open a script block you will use for the resource command. The command to do this is shown here.

   ```
   Node @('C10')
       {
   ```

5. Use the *File* resource, and specify a name such as LogFiles for the resource. Open a script block for the *File* resource. The command to do this is shown here.

   ```
   File LogFiles
       {
   ```

6. Specify the *SourcePath* parameter and use a folder available on your local computer. The command to accomplish these tasks is shown here.

   ```
   SourcePath = "C:\fso"
   ```

7. Specify the *DestinationPath* parameter and specify the folder to create. To do this, enter the command shown here.

```
DestinationPath = "C:\scripts"
```

8. Use the *Ensure* command to ensure that the folder will be present when the DSC configuration runs. This code is shown here.

```
Ensure = "present"
```

9. Specify that you want to create a directory, and that you want to recurse when copying the source files. Close out your script blocks. The command to do this is shown here.

```
Type = "Directory"
      Recurse = $true }
    } }
```

10. Call the configuration, and specify an output folder such as C:\Exercise21. Start your DSC configuration with the *-Verbose*, *-Wait*, and *-Force* switch parameters.

These commands are shown here.

```
SetFileFolder -output C:\Exercise21
Start-DscConfiguration -Path C:\Exercise21 -Verbose -Wait -Force
```

11. Save and run your configuration script. Look for errors and for the creation of the destination folder. If it does not exist, check your work against this sample script.

```
#Requires -version 5.0

Configuration SetFileFolder
{
 Import-DscResource -ModuleName 'PSDesiredStateConfiguration'
  Node @('C10')
   {
     File LogFiles
     {
      SourcePath = "C:\fso"
      DestinationPath = "C:\scripts"
      Ensure = "present"
      Type = "Directory"
      Recurse = $true }
    } }
SetFileFolder -output C:\Exercise21
Start-DscConfiguration -Path C:\Exercise21 -Verbose -Wait -Force
```

This concludes the exercise. Leave your Windows PowerShell ISE open for the next exercise.

In the following exercise, you will add a dependency for your DSC configuration script.

Adding a DSC resource dependency

1. Start the Windows PowerShell ISE if it is not already open. Open the script you created in the previous exercise, and save it with a new name.

2. After the script block for the *File* resource, call the *WindowsProcess* resource, provide it with a name such as Notepad, and open a script block. The command to do this is shown here, added to the correct position in the DSC configuration script.

```
#Requires -version 5.0

Configuration SetFileFolder
{
 Import-DscResource -ModuleName 'PSDesiredStateConfiguration'
  Node @('C10')
   {
     File LogFiles
     {
      SourcePath = "C:\fso"
      DestinationPath = "C:\scripts"
      Ensure = "present"
      Type = "Directory"
      Recurse = $true }

     WindowsProcess notepad
     {


     }
   } }
SetFileFolder -output C:\Exercise21
Start-DscConfiguration -Path C:\Exercise21 -Verbose -Wait -Force
```

3. Under the *WindowsProcess* DSC resource, but inside the script block, add the dependency for the *File* resource. The code to do this is shown here.

```
DependsOn = "[File]LogFiles"
```

4. The *WindowsProcess* DSC resource requires a string argument for the process to create. Use the name of a text file for the argument, such as "text.txt". This command is shown here.

```
Arguments = "text.txt"
```

5. Specify the complete name of the Notepad executable file, which is Notepad.exe. Assign this to the *Path* parameter. As long as an executable file is contained within the search path, you do not need to specify the complete path to the process. The code to do this is shown here.

```
Path = "Notepad.exe"
```

6. To ensure that the process runs, specify that *Ensure* is equal to *present*. The code to do this is shown here.

```
Ensure = "Present"
```

7. Save and run the configuration script. If it generates any errors, compare it with the complete configuration script shown here.

```
#Requires -version 5.0

Configuration SetFileFolder
{
 Import-DscResource -ModuleName 'PSDesiredStateConfiguration'
   Node @('C10')
    {
       File LogFiles
       {
        SourcePath = "C:\fso"
        DestinationPath = "C:\scripts"
        Ensure = "present"
        Type = "Directory"
        Recurse = $true }

       WindowsProcess notepad
       {
        DependsOn = "[File]LogFiles"
        Arguments = "text.txt"
        Path = "Notepad.exe"
        Ensure = "Present"
       }
      } }
SetFileFolder -output C:\Exercise21
Start-DscConfiguration -Path C:\Exercise21 -Verbose -Wait -Force
```

8. Use the *Get-Process* cmdlet to ensure that the Notepad process is running. After you have verified that the Notepad process is running, use the *Stop-Process* cmdlet to stop the process. These two commands are shown here.

```
Get-Process notepad
Stop-Process -Name notepad -Force
```

9. Save the Windows PowerShell script and close out the Windows PowerShell ISE.

This concludes the exercise.

Chapter 21 quick reference

To	Do this
Create a DSC configuration script	Use the *Configuration* keyword.
View existing DSC resources	Use the *Get-DscResource* cmdlet.
Begin DSC configuration	Use the *Start-DscConfiguration* cmdlet and specify a folder containing the MOF file for the configuration.
View progress when a configuration is being applied	Use the -*Verbose* switch parameter of the *Start-DscConfiguration* cmdlet.
Specify where a DSC configuration will apply	Use the *Node* command.

Using the PowerShell Gallery

After completing this chapter, you will be able to

■ Understand the purpose of the PowerShell Gallery.

■ Know how to search the PowerShell Gallery.

■ Know how to download and install Windows PowerShell modules from the PowerShell Gallery.

The decision by the Windows PowerShell team to create a gallery to facilitate deployment of Windows PowerShell modules to client workstations illustrates their commitment to the Windows PowerShell environment. Based upon GitHub, the PowerShell Gallery is made up of both a browsable website and a module for interacting with the gallery.

Exploring the PowerShell Gallery

The PowerShell Gallery is located at *PowerShellGallery.com*. The home page of the Gallery contains a feed about current information. On the Get Started tab, it lists information that tells you how to get started using the PowerShell Gallery. The home page is shown in Figure 22-1.

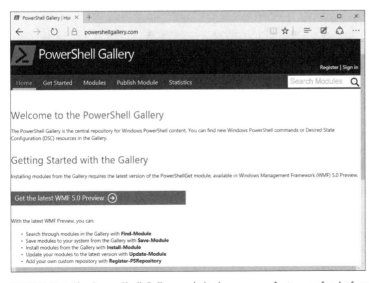

FIGURE 22-1 The PowerShell Gallery website home page features a feed of current PowerShell Gallery news.

From the Modules page, you can search the PowerShell Gallery for modules that you might be interested in. For example, if I want to see what modules are published for DSC, I enter **DSC** in the search box. This is shown in Figure 22-2.

FIGURE 22-2 The Search feature of the PowerShell Gallery is a good way to quickly find modules such as DSC resources.

When you find a module you like, you can click the module in the search pane to go to a specific page with information about that module. Figure 22-3 shows the page for the xRobocopy 1.0.0 module, which is used to install a module that supports copying large files with multithreading and other complex file copy requirements.

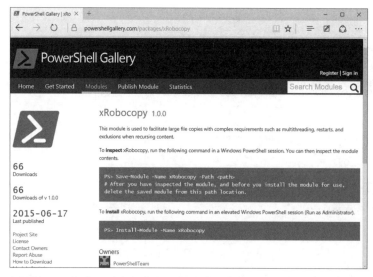

FIGURE 22-3 Each module in the PowerShell Gallery has a page that contains information about its capabilities.

Configuring and using PowerShell Get

The first time you use any cmdlet from the PowerShellGet module, it displays a message that NuGet-anycpu.exe is required to continue. Luckily, it prompts you to install NuGet-anycpu.exe via PowerShellGet from the PowerShell Gallery. Figure 22-4 shows an example in which I use the *Find-Module* cmdlet to look for modules that are available in the PowerShell Gallery. This is the first time I have run any cmdlet from the PowerShellGet module, so a message appears.

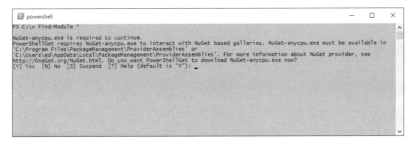

FIGURE 22-4 The first time any cmdlet from the PowerShellGet module runs, it displays a message stating that NuGet-anycpu.exe is required. It prompts to download and to install the required file.

After NuGet-anycpu.exe downloads and is installed, the *Find-Module* cmdlet runs. It does not even require a restart of the Windows PowerShell console or re-entry of the command. Figure 22-5 shows the command, the prompt, and the output from the *Find-Module* cmdlet.

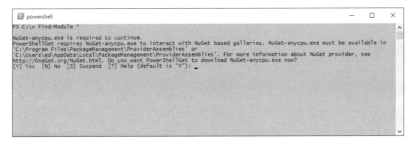

FIGURE 22-5 After the NuGet-anycpu.exe file downloads and is installed from the PowerShell Gallery, the command continues to execute.

The default output from the *Find-Module* cmdlet displays version information, the module name, and a description of the module. It also displays the repository, but because all of the modules come from the PowerShell Gallery, this column is rather useless.

To find which modules have the largest revision numbers, you can use the *Find-Module* cmdlet, sort by version, and then select the first five modules. This command is shown here, along with the output from the command.

```
PS C:\> Find-Module * | sort version -Descending | select version, name -first 5

Version Name
------- ----
6.0     ConversionModule
5.7.4.3 WinSCP
5.1.1   OMSSearch
5.0     Bing
4.8     Reflection
```

To look at the complete package information from a specific module, you can specify the name of the module to the *Find-Module* cmdlet. You can then pipeline the output to the *Format-List* cmdlet. The following command returns detailed module information from the ConversionModule module.

```
PS C:\> Find-Module -Name ConversionModule | Format-List *


Name                         : ConversionModule
Version                      : 6.0
Description                  : a module that performs various unit conversions
Author                       : ed wilson
CompanyName                  :
Copyright                    : 2014
PublishedDate                : 5/6/2014 9:34:14 PM
LicenseUri                   :
ProjectUri                   :
IconUri                      :
Tags                         : {}
Includes                     : {Function, DscResource, Cmdlet, Command}
PowerShellGetFormatVersion   :
ReleaseNotes                 :
Dependencies                 : {}
RepositorySourceLocation     : https://www.powershellgallery.com/api/v2/
Repository                   : PSGallery
PackageManagementProvider    : NuGet
```

Finding all modules from a specific contributor requires pipelining the output from *Find-Module* to *Where-Object*. The command on the following page illustrates searching for modules contributed by Ed Wilson, and the accompanying output from that command.

```
PS C:\> Find-module | ? author -eq 'ed wilson'

Version   Name                  Repository   Description
-------   ----                  ----------   -----------
4.0       PowerShellISEModule   PSGallery    a module that adds capability to the ISE
3.0       LocalUserManagement   PSGallery    a module that performs various local user manage
6.0       ConversionModule      PSGallery    a module that performs various unit conversions
```

You can also search module descriptions. For example, if I want to find modules that contain the word *cookbook* in the description, I can use that in my *Where-Object* command. The following command illustrates searching for *cookbook* in the description and shows the accompanying output from that command.

```
PS C:\> Find-module | ? description -match 'cookbook'

Version   Name                 Repository   Description
-------   ----                 ----------   -----------
1.3.2     PowerShellCookbook   PSGallery    Sample scripts from the Windows PowerShell Cookbook
```

Installing a module from the PowerShell Gallery

To install a module, you need to know the name of the module and the scope of the installation. For example, if I install for the CurrentUser scope, the module will only be available to me as the currently logged-on user. It is best to first use the *Find-Module* cmdlet to identify the module to install. Wildcards are acceptable in the *Name* field, so I can search for **conversion** and find the ConversionModule module. This command and its associated output are shown here.

```
PS C:\> Find-Module *conversion*

Version   Name               Repository   Description
-------   ----               ----------   -----------
6.0       ConversionModule   PSGallery    a module that performs various unit conversions
```

After the module has been identified, the output from the *Find-Module* cmdlet can be pipelined to the *Install-Module* cmdlet. It is a best practice, when doing this, to use the *-WhatIf* parameter to see what the command will actually accomplish. The following command illustrates finding the Conversion-Module, pipelining the output to the *Install-Module* cmdlet, installing in the CurrentUser scope, and using the *-WhatIf* parameter to see what it will actually accomplish.

```
PS C:\> Find-Module *conversion* | Install-Module -Scope CurrentUser -WhatIf
What if: Performing the operation "Install-Module" on target "Version '6.0' of module
'ConversionModule'".
PS C:\>
```

When the action is verified as something that you want to do, you press the Up Arrow key in the Windows PowerShell console, go to the end of the line, and remove the *-WhatIf* parameter from the command.

Configuring trusted installation locations

Install-Module looks for trusted locations. By default, the PSGallery is not a trusted location—in fact, no repositories are trusted. Therefore, the *Install-Module* cmdlet prompts prior to installation. The following command illustrates the installation of the ConversionModule module for the current user and shows the prompt to install that happens by default.

```
PS C:\> Find-Module *conversion* | Install-Module -Scope CurrentUser

You are installing the module(s) from an untrusted repository. If you trust this repository,
change its
InstallationPolicy value by running the Set-PSRepository cmdlet.
Are you sure you want to install software from 'https://www.powershellgallery.com/api/v2/'?
[Y] Yes  [A] Yes to All  [N] No  [L] No to All  [S] Suspend  [?] Help (default is "N"): y
PS C:\>
```

To configure a trusted location, and therefore to suppress the warning prompt, use the *Set-PS-Repository* cmdlet, specify *PSGallery*, and set the *InstallationPolicy* to *Trusted*.

> **Warning** Do not change the installation policy of the PSGallery without considering the consequences that could occur from downloading, installing, and running software from the Internet. First examine the module and test it to ensure that it meets your security policy. You should definitely test the module in an isolated environment prior to installing it on a production machine.

After the installation policy has been configured, a module can be downloaded and installed without any prompts. The following code illustrates this procedure.

```
PS C:\> Set-PSRepository -Name PSGallery -InstallationPolicy Trusted
PS C:\> Find-Module *cookbook* | Install-Module -Scope CurrentUser -WhatIf
What if: Performing the operation "Install-Module" on target "Version '1.3.2' of module
'PowerShellCookbook'".
PS C:\> Find-Module *cookbook* | Install-Module -Scope CurrentUser
PS C:\>
```

Uninstalling a module

To uninstall a module that was installed via the PowerShellGet *Install-Module* cmdlet, you first need to find out what modules have been installed. To do this, use the *Get-InstalledModule* cmdlet. This command, and sample output from the command, are shown here.

```
PS C:\> Get-InstalledModule

Version    Name                 Repository    Description
-------    ----                 ----------    -----------
6.0        ConversionModule     PSGallery     A module that performs various unit conversions
1.3.2      PowerShellCookbook   PSGallery     Sample scripts from the Windows PowerShell Cookbook
```

When the installed modules are displayed, you can use a wildcard pattern to obtain the specific module to uninstall and pipeline the output to the *Uninstall-Module* cmdlet. As a best practice, use the *-WhatIf* parameter to ensure that only the requisite module will be uninstalled. The following code illustrates this procedure and shows sample output from the commands.

```
PS C:\> Get-InstalledModule *conversion* | Uninstall-Module -WhatIf
What if: Performing the operation "Uninstall-Module" on target "Version '6.0' of module
'ConversionModule'".
PS C:\> Get-InstalledModule *conversion* | Uninstall-Module
```

Searching for and installing modules from the PowerShell Gallery: Step-by-step exercises

In this exercise, you'll use the *Find-Module* cmdlet to search for modules available for download via the PowerShell Gallery.

Searching for modules

1. Start the Windows PowerShell console.

2. Use the *Find-Module* cmdlet to search for modules in the PowerShell Gallery. Use a wildcard character for the module names. The code is shown here.

   ```
   Find-Module *
   ```

3. If a prompt appears stating that NuGet-anycpu.exe is required and asking you if you want to download and install the program, press Y to begin the installation. After NuGet-anycpu.exe is installed, a listing of available modules is shown in the Windows PowerShell console. A partial listing is reproduced here.

   ```
   PS C:\> Find-Module *

   Version Name                     Repository Description
   ------- ----                     ---------- -----------
   1.22    ACLReportTools           PSGallery Provides Cmdlets for reporting on Share ACLs.
   1.2     AddCustomAvailabilityDB PSGallery Powershell Module To Add Database(s) to an
   Exist...
   1.0.0.0 AppDomainConfig          PSGallery Manipulate AppDomain configuration for your
   curr...
   0.6.2.8 AppvProvider             PSGallery Powershell OneGet/Package Management Provider
   fo...
   2.6     Authenticode             PSGallery Function wrappers for Authenticode Signing
   cmdlets
   1.0     AutoBrowse               PSGallery AutoBrowse is a module that lets you automate
   br...
   <output truncated>
   ```

4. Look for modules that contain the word *History* in their names. The command to do this is shown here.

```
Find-Module *history*
```

5. Look for modules that have an author that matches the word *powershell*. The command to do this is shown here.

```
Find-Module * | ? author -match 'powershell'
```

6. Look for modules that have the words *resource kit* in their description. The command to accomplish this task is shown here.

```
Find-Module * | ? description -match 'resource kit'
```

This concludes the exercise. Leave your Windows PowerShell console open for the next exercise.

In the following exercise, you will install a Windows PowerShell module from the PowerShell Gallery and then uninstall it.

Installing and uninstalling modules from the PowerShell Gallery

1. Start the Windows PowerShell console, if it is not already open.

2. Find the module from the Windows PowerShell cookbook. To do this, search for the name cookbook, using a wildcard character. The command to do this is shown here.

```
Find-Module *cookbook*
```

3. Press the Up Arrow key in the Windows PowerShell console to retrieve the previous command. Pipeline it to the *Install-Module* cmdlet and set the scope to *currentuser*. Use the *-WhatIf* switch parameter to see what the command will actually do. The code to do this is shown here.

```
Find-Module *cookbook* | Install-Module -Scope CurrentUser -WhatIf
```

4. If the output says that it will install the PowerShellCookbook module, press the Up Arrow key to retrieve the previous command, and then remove the *-WhatIf* switch parameter. This command is shown here.

```
Find-Module *cookbook* | Install-Module -Scope CurrentUser
```

5. If a message about installing from an untrusted location appears, read the message, and then press Y. Make sure you read the warning message first.

6. To see what commands are available from the newly installed module, use the *Get-Command* cmdlet and specify the PowerShellCookbook module. The code to do this is shown here.

```
Get-Command -Module PowerShellCookbook
```

7. Now check to see what modules have been installed via the *Install-Module* cmdlet. To do this, use the *Get-InstalledModule* cmdlet. The command is shown here.

```
Get-InstalledModule
```

8. Now uninstall the PowerShellCookBook module. To do this, first use the Up Arrow key to retrieve the previous *Get-InstalledModule* command. Then pipeline the output to the *Uninstall-Module* cmdlet. Use the *-WhatIf* parameter to see what the command will actually do. If it says it will uninstall the PowerShellCookBook module, remove the *-WhatIf* parameter and run the command a second time. The commands, and their associated output, are shown here.

```
PS C:\> Get-InstalledModule *cookbook* | Uninstall-Module -WhatIf
What if: Performing the operation "Uninstall-Module" on target "Version '1.3.2' of module
'PowerShellCookbook'".
PS C:\> Get-InstalledModule *cookbook* | Uninstall-Module
```

This concludes the exercise.

Chapter 22 quick reference

To	Do this
Find modules that are available in the PowerShell Gallery	Use the *Find-Module* cmdlet.
Install a module from the PowerShell Gallery	Use the *Install-Module* cmdlet.
Configure a trusted installation gallery	Use the *Set-PSRepository* cmdlet and specify the *InstallationPolicy* parameter as *Trusted*.
See what modules have been installed	Use the *Get-InstalledModule* cmdlet.
Uninstall a module	Use the *Uninstall-Module* cmdlet.

Windows PowerShell scripting best practices

One of the great things about Windows PowerShell 5.0 is that it is extremely flexible. This flexibility, however, comes at the cost of readability, complexity, and supportability. The best practices described in this appendix will help you minimize the effects of any of the potential pitfalls. Windows PowerShell is both a command-line environment and a scripting environment, and best practices for scripts are not always the best practices for interactive Windows PowerShell commands. The following best practices apply to the scripting environment.

General script construction

This section looks at some general considerations for the overall construction of scripts. This includes the use of functions, modules, and other considerations.

Include functions in the scripts that use them

Though it is possible to use an include file or dot-source in a function within Windows PowerShell, such an approach can become a support nightmare. If you know which function you want to use, but don't know which script provides it, you have to go looking (unless the function resides in a module stored in a known location). If a script provides the function you want but has other elements that you don't want, it's hard to pick and choose from the script file. Additionally, you must be very careful when it comes to variable-naming conventions because you could end up with conflicting variable names. When you use an include file, you no longer have a portable script. Your script must always travel with the function library.

I use functions in my scripts because it makes them easier to read and maintain. If I were to store these functions in separate files and then dot-source them, neither of my two personal objectives of function use would really be met.

There is one other consideration: when a script references an external script that contains functions, there now exists a relationship that must not be disturbed. If, for instance, you decide you would like to update the function, you might not remember how many external scripts are calling this function and how it will affect their performance and operation. If there is only one script calling the function, the maintenance is easy. However, for only one script, just copy the silly thing into the script file itself and be done with the whole business. The best way to deal with these situations is to store the functions in modules.

Use full cmdlet names and full parameter names

There are several advantages to spelling out cmdlet names and avoiding the use of aliases in scripts. First of all, this makes your scripts nearly self-documenting and therefore much easier to read. Second, it makes the scripts resilient to alias changes by the user and more compatible with future versions of Windows PowerShell. This is easy to do by using the IntelliSense feature of the Windows PowerShell ISE.

Understand the use of aliases

There are three kinds of aliases in Windows PowerShell: compatibility aliases, canonical aliases, and user-defined aliases.

You can identify the compatibility aliases by using this command.

```
Get-childitem alias: |
where-object {$_.options -notmatch "Readonly" }
```

The compatibility aliases are present in Windows PowerShell to provide an easier transition from older command shells. You can remove the compatibility aliases by deleting aliases that are not read-only. To do this every time you start Windows PowerShell, add the following command to your Windows PowerShell profile.

```
Get-childitem alias: |
where-object {$_.options -notmatch "Readonly" } |
remove-item
```

The canonical aliases were created specifically to make the Windows PowerShell cmdlets easier to use from within the Windows PowerShell console. Shortness of length and ease of typing were the primary driving factors in their creation. To find the canonical aliases, use this command.

```
Get-childitem alias: |
where-object {$_.options -match "Readonly" }
```

If you must use an alias, only use canonical aliases in a script

You are reasonably safe in using the canonical aliases in a script; however, they make the script much harder to read. Also, because there are often several aliases for the same cmdlet, different users of Windows PowerShell might have their own personal favorite aliases. Additionally, because the canonical aliases are just read-only, even a canonical alias can be removed. However, worse than deleting an alias is changing its meaning.

Always use the *description* property when creating an alias

When adding aliases to your profile, you might want to specify the *read-only* or *constant* options. You should always include the *description* property for your personal aliases and make the description something that is relatively constant. Here is an example from my personal Windows PowerShell profile.

```
New-Alias -Name gh -Value Get-Help -Description "mred alias"
New-Alias -Name ga -Value get-alias -Description "mred alias"
```

Use *Get-Item* to convert path strings to rich types

This is actually a pretty cool trick. When working with a listing of files, if you use the *Get-Content* cmdlet, you can only read each line and have it as a path to work with. If, however, you use *Get-Item*, you get an object with a corresponding number of both properties and methods to work with. Here's an example that illustrates this.

```
$files = Get-Content "filelist.txt" |
Get-Item $files |
Foreach-object { $_.Fullname }
```

General script readability

The following are points to keep in mind to promote the readability of your script:

- When creating an alias, include the -*Description* parameter, and use it when searching for your personal aliases. An example of this is shown here. (A better approach is to load the aliases from a private module. That way, the *modulepath* parameter also loads.)

```
Get-Alias |
where-object { $_.description -match 'mred' } |
Format-Table -Property "   ",name, definition -autosize `
             -hideTableHeaders
```

- Scripts should provide help. Use comment-based help to do this.

- All procedures should begin with a brief comment describing what they do. This description should not describe the implementation details (how the procedure works), because these often change over time, resulting in unnecessary comment-maintenance work, or worse, erroneous comments. Place comments on individual lines—do not use inline comments.

- Arguments passed to a function should be described when their purpose is not obvious and when the function expects the arguments to be in a specific range.

- Return values for variables that are changed by a function should also be described at the beginning of each function.

- Every important variable declaration should include an inline comment describing the use of the variable, if the name of the variable is not obvious.

- Variables and functions should be named clearly to ensure that inline comments are needed only for complex functions.

- When creating a complex function with multiple code blocks, place an inline comment for each closing brace at the end of the closing brace.

- At the beginning of your script, include an overview that describes the script, significant objects and cmdlets, and any unique requirements for the script.

- When naming functions, use the verb-noun construction used by cmdlet names.

- Scripts should use named parameters if they accept more than one argument. If a script only accepts a single argument, it is okay to use an unnamed (positional) argument.

- Always assume that users will copy your script and modify it to meet their needs. Place comments in the code to facilitate this process.

- Never assume the current path. Always use the full path, either via an environment variable or an explicitly named path.

Format your code

Screen space should be conserved as much as possible while still allowing code formatting to reflect logical structure and nesting. Here are a few suggestions:

- Indent standard nested blocks by at least two spaces.

- Block overview comments for a function by using the Windows PowerShell multiline comment feature.

- Block the highest-level statements, with each nested block indented an additional two spaces.

- Align the begin and end script block brackets. This will make it easier to follow the code flow.

- Avoid single-line statements. In addition to making it easier to follow the flow of the code, this also makes it easier when you end up searching for a missing brace.

- Break each pipelined object at the pipe. Leave all pipes on the right. Do this unless it is a very short, simple pipe statement.

- Avoid line continuation—using the backtick character (`). The exception is when not using line continuation would cause the user to have to scroll to read the code or the output—generally around 90 characters. One way to avoid extremely long command lines for cmdlets with a large number of parameters is to use hash tables and splat parameters to Windows PowerShell cmdlets.

- Scripts should follow Pascal-case guidelines for long variable names—the same as Windows PowerShell parameters.

- Scripts should use the *Write-Progress* cmdlet if they take more than one or two seconds to run.

- Consider supporting the -*WhatIf* and -*Confirm* switch parameters in your functions and in your scripts, especially if they will change system state. Following is an example that uses the -*WhatIf* switch parameter.

```
param(
      [switch]$whatif
     )

function funwhatif()
 {
  "what if: Perform operation xxxx"
 }

if($whatif)
   {
    funwhatif #calls the funwhatif() function
   }
```

- If your script does not accept a variable set of arguments, check the value of *$args.count* and call the *help* function if the number is incorrect. Here is an example.

```
if($args.count -ge 0)
   {
    "wrong number of arguments"
    Funhelp  #calls the funhelp() function
   }
```

- If your script does not accept any arguments, use code such as the following.

```
If($args -ge 0) { funhelp }
```

Work with functions

The following are points to keep in mind when working with your functions. They will make your code easier to read and understand:

- Functions should handle mandatory parameter checking. To make this possible, use parameter property attributes.

- Utility or shared functions should be placed in a module.

- If you are writing a function library script, consider using feature and parameter variable names that incorporate a unique name to minimize the chances of conflict with other variables in the scripts that call them. It is best to store these function libraries in modules to facilitate sharing and use.

- Consider supporting standard parameters when it makes sense for your script. The easiest way to do this is to implement cmdlet binding.

Create template files

The following are points to keep in mind when creating template files. You can create templates that can be used for different types of scripts. Some examples might be WMI scripts, ADSI scripts, and ADO scripts. You can then add these templates to the Windows PowerShell ISE as snippets by using the *New-ISESnippet* cmdlet. When you are creating your templates, consider the following:

- Add in common functions that you would use on a regular basis.

- Do not hard-code specific values that the connection strings might require, such as server names, input file paths, and output file paths. Instead, contain these values in variables.

- Do not hard-code version information into the template.

- Make sure you include comments where the template will require modification to be made functional.

- You might want to turn your templates into code snippets to facilitate their usage.

Format functions

When writing your own functions, you might want to consider the following:

- Create highly specialized functions. Good functions do one thing well.

- Make the function completely self-contained. Good functions should be portable.

- Alphabetize the functions in your script if possible. This promotes readability and maintainability.

- Give your functions descriptive names and follow a verb-noun naming convention. Nouns should be singular. If the function name becomes too long, create an alias for the function and store the alias in the same module as the function.

- Every function should have a single output point (this does not include the error, verbose, or debug streams).

- Every function should have a single entry point.

- Use parameters to avoid problems with local and global variable scopes.

- Implement the common parameters *-Verbose*, *-Debug*, *-WhatIf*, and *-Confirm* where appropriate to promote reusability.

Variables, constants, and naming

When creating variables and constants, and when naming them, there are some things to consider:

- Avoid hard-coded numbers. When calling methods or functions, avoid hard-coding numeric literals. Instead, create a constant that is descriptive enough that someone reading the code would be able to figure out what it is supposed to do. In the ServiceDependencies.ps1 script, a portion of which follows, a number is used to offset the printout. This number is determined by the position of a certain character in the output. Rather than just writing "+14," a constant is created with a descriptive name. Refer to Chapter 12, "Remoting WMI," for more information. The applicable portion of the code is shown here.

```
New-Variable -Name c_padline -value 14 -option constant
Get-WmiObject -Class Win32_DependentService -computername $computer |
Foreach-object `
  {
   "=" * (((([wmi]$_.dependent).pathname).length + $c_padline)
```

- Do not recycle variables. Recycled variables are referred to as *unfocused variables*. Variables should serve a single purpose; those that do are called *focused variables*.

- Give variables descriptive names. Remember that you can use tab completion to simplify typing.

- Minimize variable scope. If you are only going to use a variable in a function, declare it in the function.

- When a constant is needed, use a read-only variable instead. Remember that constants cannot be deleted, nor can their values change.

- Avoid hard-coding values into method calls or in the worker section of the script. Instead, place values into variables.

- When possible, group your variables into a single section of each level of the script.

- Avoid using Hungarian Notation, in which you embed type names into the variable names. Remember that everything in Windows PowerShell is basically an object, so there is no value in naming a variable *$objWMI*.

- There are times when it makes sense to use the following: *bln*, *int*, *dbl*, *err*, *dte*, and *str*. This is due to the fact that Windows PowerShell is a strongly typed language. It just acts like it is not.

- Scripts should avoid populating the global variable space. Instead, consider passing values to a function by reference *[ref]*.

Regular expressions quick reference

One of the really interesting features of Windows PowerShell is its ability to work with regular expressions. Regular expressions are optimized to manipulate text. Windows PowerShell uses regular expressions in many different places. Here is a listing of some of the places where regular expressions might be used:

- Select-String cmdlet

- ConvertFrom-String cmdlet

- Where-Object cmdlet

- Rename-Item cmdlet

- Switch statement

- Split statement

- Match operator

- NotMatch operator

- Replace operator

- Should object

Table B-1 lists the escape sequences you can use with regular expressions.

TABLE B-1 Escape sequences

Character	Description
Ordinary characters	Characters other than . $ ^ { [(	) * + ? \ match themselves.
\a	Matches a bell (alarm) \u0007.
\b	Matches a backspace \u0008 if in a [] character class; in regular expression, it is a word boundary.
\t	Matches a tab \u0009.
\r	Matches a carriage return \u000D.

Character	Description
\v	Matches a vertical tab \u000B.
\f	Matches a form feed \u000C.
\n	Matches a new line \u000A.
\e	Matches an escape \u001B.
\040	Matches an ASCII character as octal (up to three digits); numbers with no leading zero are backreferences if they have only one digit or if they correspond to a capturing group number. For example, the character \040 represents a space.
\x20	Matches an ASCII character using hexadecimal representation (exactly two digits).
\cC	Matches an ASCII control character; for example, \cC is Ctrl+C.
\u0020	Matches a Unicode character using hexadecimal representation (exactly four digits).

The RegExTab.ps1 script illustrates using an escape sequence in a regular expression script. It opens a text file and looks for tab characters. The easiest way to work with regular expressions is to store the pattern in its own variable. This makes it easy to modify and even to experiment without worrying about breaking the script. (You simply use the # sign to comment out the line, and then you create a new line with the same name and a different value.)

In the RegExTab.ps1 script, "\t" is specified as the pattern. According to Table B-1, this means it is looking for tabs. The pattern, contained in *$strPattern*, is fed to the *[regex]* type accelerator, as shown here.

```
$regex = [regex]$strPattern
```

Next the content of the tabline.txt text file is stored into the *$text* variable by using the syntax shown here.

```
$text = ${C:\Chapter02\tabline.txt}
```

The *matches* method is then used to parse the text file and look for matches with the pattern that was specified in *$strPattern*. Notice that the pattern has already been associated with the regular expression object in the *$regex* variable. The script then counts the number of times it finds a match.

RegExTab.ps1

```
$strPattern = "\t"
$regex = [regex]$strPattern

$text = ${C:\Chapter02\tabline.txt}

$mc = $regex.matches($text)
$mc.count
```

Table B-2 lists the character patterns that can be used with regular expressions for performing advanced pattern matching.

TABLE B-2 Character patterns

Character	Description
[character_group]	Matches any character in the specified character group. For example, to specify all vowels, use [aeiou]. To specify all punctuation and decimal digit characters, use [\p{P}\d].
[^character_group]	Matches any character not in the specified character group. For example, to specify all consonants, use [^aeiou]. To specify all characters except punctuation and decimal digit characters, use [^\p{P}\d].
[firstCharacter-lastCharacter]	Matches any character in a range of characters. For example, to specify the range of decimal digits from 0 through 9, the range of lowercase letters from a through f, and the range of uppercase letters from A through F, use [0-9a-fA-F].
.	Matches any character except \n. If modified by the *Singleline* option, a period character matches any character.
\p{name}	Matches any character in the Unicode general category or named block specified by *name* (for example, Ll, Nd, Z, IsGreek, and IsBoxDrawing).
\P{name}	Matches any character not in the Unicode general category or named block specified in *name*.
\w	Matches any word character. Equivalent to the Unicode general categories [\p{Ll}\p{Lu}\p{Lt}\p{Lo}\p{Nd}\p{Pc}\p{Lm}]. If ECMAScript-compliant behavior is specified with the ECMAScript option, \w is equivalent to [a-zA-Z_0-9].
\W	Matches any nonword character. Equivalent to the Unicode general categories [^\p{Ll}\p{Lu}\p{Lt}\p{Lo}\p{Nd}\p{Pc}\p{Lm}]. If ECMAScript-compliant behavior is specified with the ECMAScript option, \W is equivalent to [^a-zA-Z_0-9].
\s	Matches any white-space character. Equivalent to the escape sequences and Unicode general categories [\f\n\r\t\v\x85\p{Z}]. If ECMAScript-compliant behavior is specified with the ECMAScript option, \s is equivalent to [\f\n\r\t\v].
\S	Matches any non–white-space character. Equivalent to the escape sequences and Unicode general categories [^\f\n\r\t\v\x85\p{Z}]. If ECMAScript-compliant behavior is specified with the ECMAScript option, \S is equivalent to [^ \f\n\r\t\v].
\d	Matches any decimal digit. Equivalent to \p{Nd} for Unicode and [0-9] for non-Unicode, ECMAScript behavior.
\D	Matches any nondigit character. Equivalent to \P{Nd} for Unicode and [^0-9] for non-Unicode, ECMAScript behavior.

Suppose you wanted to identify white space in a file. To do this, you could use the match pattern \s, which is listed in Table B-2 as a character pattern. The ability to find white space in a text file is actually quite useful, because for many items, the end-of-line separator is just white space. To illustrate working with white space, the RegWhiteSpace.ps1 script is shown at the end of this section.

On the first line of the script, a line of text to is created for testing against. The pattern comes from Table B-2 and is a simple \s, which tells the regular expression that you want to match on white space. The *$matches* variable is then used to hold the match object returned by the match static method of the *regex* type accelerator.

After the results of the match have been printed, you move to phase two, which is to replace, by using the same pattern. To do this, the pattern is fed to the *replace* method along with the variable containing the unadulterated text message. You then go ahead and print the value of *$strReplace* that now contains the modified object.

RegWhiteSpace.ps1

```
$strText = "a nice line of text. We will search for an expression"
$Pattern = "\s"
$matches = [regex]::match($strText, $pattern)

"Result of using the match method, we get the following:"
$matches

$strReplace = [regex]::replace($strText, $pattern, "_")
"Now we will replace, using the same pattern. We will use
an underscore to replace the space between words:"
```

Index

Symbols

\040 escape sequence 600
$$ variable 148
$^ variable 148
$_ variable 75, 148
$? variable 148
? alias 111
* (asterisk) wildcard character 69
` (backtick) character 144
= (equal sign) operator 168
! (exclamatio-n point) 80
> (greater-than) operator 327
< (less-than) operator 327
. (period) character 601
| (pipe) character 24, 144, 319
? (question mark) character 377

A

\a escape sequence 599
abstract classes, querying 299
abstract WMI class 382
access control list (ACL) 359
AccountsWithNoRequiredPassword.ps1 139
ACL 369
-Action parameter 498
Active Directory
    See also ADSI (Active Directory Service
       Interfaces)
    binding 400
    committing changes 401, 429
    creating objects 395, 396
    installing RSAT 432
    modifying user properties 410
    overwriting fields 429
    user account control values 408, 409

Active Directory Domain Services (AD DS)
    See AD DS (Active Directory Domain Services)
Active Directory Management Gateway Service
    (ADMGS) 431
Active Directory module
    deploying forests 459–465
    importing 433, 434
    installing 431–433
    loading automatically 434
    remote sessions 434
    verifying presence of 433
Active Directory Service Interfaces
    (ADSI) See ADSI (Active Directory Service
    Interfaces)
Active Directory sites, renaming 442, 443, 457
activities, workflow 552
AD DS (Active Directory Domain Services)
    adding features 460, 472
    assigning IP addresses 460, 472
    changing passwords 456
    creating computer accounts 443
    creating users 446, 447
    deploying 459
    deployment tools 460
    installing tools 397, 398
    prerequisites 459
    renaming computers 460
    renaming sites 442, 443, 457
    restarting computers 461, 472
    setting passwords 457
    unlocking accounts 457
    verifying roles and features 462, 472
AD DS and AD LDS Tools 397, 398
Add-ADFeatures.ps1 463

603

D

L

M

N

Q

R

adding checkpoints 558
core cmdlets as 553
definition 552
disallowed core cmdlets 554
InlineScript 554
list of 552
non-automatic cmdlets 554
parallel 555
using CheckPoint-Workflow 558
Windows PowerShell cmdlets as 553
Workflow keyword 548, 563
workflows
adding checkpoints 556, 562
adding logic with cmdlets 549
adding sequence activities 559, 560
adding sequences 562
checkpointing 556–559
creating 561, 563
creating blocks of sequential
statements 553
creating checkpoints 552, 563
errors 551
handling interruptions with checkpoints 556
ordering 563
packaging in modules 547
performing parallel activities 548, 550
persistence points 547
placing checkpoints 556
reasons to use 547, 548
recovering 556
requirements 548
resuming 556

running against remote computers 563
running on remote servers 555
running parallel statements 552
running statements simultaneously 552
syntax 549
throttling 548
writing 547, 548
working with aliases 66
working with directory listings 80
WQL queries 331, 353, 360
-Wrap parameter 350
Write-Debug cmdlet 476
Write-EventLog cmdlet 111
Write-Host cmdlet 332, 554
Write-Verbose cmdlet 257
wscript.shell 50
wshShell object 63
creating a new instance 50, 51
program ID 51
$wshShell variable 51
WS-Management protocol 114
WSMan provider 66

X

\x20 escape sequence 600
[xml] alias 198

Z

$zip variable 198

About the author

ED WILSON is the Microsoft Scripting Guy and a well-known scripting expert. He writes the daily *Hey Scripting Guy!* blog. He has also spoken at TechEd and at the Microsoft internal TechReady conferences. He has written more than a dozen books, including nine on Windows scripting that were published by Microsoft Press. He has also contributed to nearly a dozen other books. His newest book with Microsoft Press is *Windows PowerShell Best Practices*. Ed holds more than 20 industry certifications, including Microsoft Certified Systems Engineer (MCSE) and Certified Information Systems Security Professional (CISSP). Prior to coming to work for Microsoft, he was a senior consultant for a Microsoft Gold Certified Partner, where he specialized in Active Directory design and Microsoft Exchange implementation. In his spare time, he is writing a mystery novel. For more about Ed, you can go to *ewblog.edwilson.com/ewblog/*.

Now that you've read the book...

Tell us what you think!

Was it useful?
Did it teach you what you wanted to learn?
Was there room for improvement?

Let us know at http://aka.ms/tellpress

Your feedback goes directly to the staff at Microsoft Press,
and we read every one of your responses. Thanks in advance!

 Microsoft